An English Baby Boomer:

My Life and Times

by

Neil G M Hall

Bill

All the very best

Neil

The Muncaster Press

AN ENGLISH BABY BOOMER: MY LIFE AND TIMES

The publisher does not have any control over and does not assume any responsibility for author or third-party websites or their content.

Cover art and design by Nicola Thompson

Interior photographs are the property of Neil Hall except Skating at Plön: 1949 a painting by Paul French and Sussex House a painting by John Evans

The photograph of John Godolphin Bennett was taken by Michael Baylis

Published by The Muncaster Press

Digital Design by Telemachus Press, LLC

Visit the author's website:
www.anenglishbabyboomer.co.uk

ISBN: 978-0-9527412-1-3 (ebook)
ISBN: 978-0-9527412-2-0 (paperback)

Version 2014.03.21

Printed in the United States of America

10   9   8   7   6   5   4   3   2   1

Table of Contents

Dedication

To those from whom I have learned and continue to learn

Acknowledgments

This is the tale of a journey, so, I acknowledge with sincere gratitude all those who feature in the story: that is everyone who appears in the anecdotes and those who helped make the events described come to pass. It would also be remiss of me not to honour my parents, Philip and Ann Hall, without whom I would not have had a life at all!

I am also deeply grateful to my sons, Tarquin and Alexander, for the richness they have added to my life and for their encouragement with regard to this book. Perhaps, just being Tarquin and Alexander, has been the greatest contribution they could have made on both accounts. My dear wife, Lucinda, has supported and encouraged me, not only with this project but in all aspects of my life for the past forty five years. How she has put up with me, I sometimes wonder, but I owe her a debt of deep affection, appreciation and thanks that I continually strive to display.

With particular regard to the writing and production of this book I would like to extend sincere thanks to the following for their help and support and, in many cases, invaluable advice. Josceline Dimbleby, Sir Ranulph Fiennes, Irvine Sellar, Alexandra Sellers, Susanna Brigden Lisle, Anne Hacke, Tahir Shah, Bob Gates, Don Elwick, Leon Flamholc, Ken Duxbury, David Spooner, David Chandler, William Sykes, Bill Cornock, Graham Curtis, William Garland, Dr Josef Kees and Barbara Kees, Terry Rogers, David du Croz, John Henry Bowden, Rev John Witheridge, Dr Anthony Bennett, Dr Walter and Margaret Holmstrom, Sarah Thomas, David and Katharine Gaine, Dr Ben and Ann Meisner, Nicholas Kaye of Sussex House, Jane Hammett, Nicola Thompson of Culver Design Ltd, Anne Pennington of Digital Plot, Kate Pool and Lydia Dowdeswell at The Society of Authors,

Philip Banks-Welsh and Lydia Excell at Withy King and Steve Jackson and his team at Telemachus Press.

Many thanks, also, to my friend, Safia Shah, whose book, *'Carnaby Street's Great Uninvited. Around the World in 80 Years'* (2013*)*, alerted me to add the following words to my vocabulary: Blatteroon (a senseless boaster), Ninnyhammer (a fool), Ramfeezled (exhausted), Fratchy (irritable), Begrumpled (sad) and Kedge-belly (a bulging stomach). I wonder if you can find these in my narrative!

I have made every effort to trace copyright owners of excerpts used in this book. In cases where I have been unsuccessful, I offer my apologies for any inadvertent infringement that may have occurred. I have also made tireless efforts to provide factual information accurately, but if I have transgressed with regard to errors or omissions the fault is entirely mine and I apologise. Please inform me if you notice any detail that should be corrected. (neil@anenglishbabyboomer.co.uk)

Various permissions have been obtained as follows:

John Betjeman: Excerpts from *Summoned by Bells, Sunday Afternoon Service in St. Enodoc Church, Cornwall,* and *Middlesex,* Copyright: © John Betjeman by permission of the Estate of John Betjeman.

Dirk Bogarde: Quote. Printed with permission of United Agents on behalf of the Estate of Dirk Bogarde.

Thomas Burn: Extracts from letters, by kind permission of the Archivist at Rugby School.

Richard Burton: Excerpt from *'The Architecture of Ahrends, Burton and Koralek'*, by Kenneth Powell, by kind permission of Richard Burton.

Steven Conner: Excerpt from a lecture at Sussex University (2009), by kind permission of Steven Conner.

The Daily Telegraph: By kind permission to quote from obituaries of PEC Hayman (1997) and TR Garnett (2006).

John Masefield: Excerpts from *'Reynard the Fox'*, by kind permission of The Society of Authors as the literary representatives of the Estate of John Masefield.

Joe McDonald: *'Feel Like I'm Fixing to Die'*. Words and music by Joe McDonald ©1965—renewed by Alcatraz Corner Music Co. BMI.

Richard Pape: Excerpt from *'Boldness Be My Friend'* (1953: Elek), by kind permission of David Higham.

William Rees-Mogg and James Dale-Davidson: Excerpt from *'Blood in the Streets'*, by kind permission of Pan Macmillan: London. Copyright © William Rees Mogg and James Dale Davidson 1988.

Dorothy Reynolds: Excerpt from *'Salad Days'*, by kind permission of Felix de Wolfe Ltd.

The Times: By kind permission to quote from the obituary of Oliver Hall RA (1957).

In addition: I acknowledge with grateful thanks permission to quote several short passages from *The Guardian, The Observer* and *The Evening Standard*.

An English Baby Boomer:

My Life and Times

Introduction

BORN TO A family of diverse provenance and blessed with opportunities for a good education I was, however, Saturday's child. Saturday's child must work hard for its living, and that is part of this tale. Adapting, re-inventing myself, dealing with great success, abject failure, triumphs and disasters, pleasure and misery has been a constant roller-coaster during these Baby Boomer years.

Pick yourself up, dust yourself down and start all over again, could readily have been my watchword.

This is a story set against a time of extraordinary technological, political, and social change, but, when the urge to put two stabbing fingers to work on the PC finally overcame me, I was not thinking in terms of 'biography' or 'memoirs'.

I was more inclined to regard this record of my erratic passage through the second half of the twentieth century as a collection of tales from a journey that began in the twilight years of the British Empire. My efforts would, I hoped, follow the vogue of modern travel-writing by producing a scrapbook of impressions, a kaleidoscopic panorama of places visited and comprehensive minutiae of events that affected me, together with projects undertaken. Above all, it was my intention to document a litany of extraordinary characters that I encountered along the way, many of whom were 'high profile'—a famous writer here, a celebrated actor there or a brave explorer—while others might have been forgotten. All provided lessons, ideas and influence and catalysed experiences far beyond anything that could have been expected in the cosy, sheltered world in which I found myself when it all began.

This is not the first time I have adopted the role of 'scribbler'. On a number of occasions, faced with unusual or interesting experiences—my visit to the wild tribal territories of North West Pakistan, or months spent living in Istanbul, for instance—I have felt compelled to put pen to paper. Indeed, school chums had been astonished to read jottings (dashed off in pencil, by torchlight, under the bedclothes) of what went on behind the scenes at boarding school, and searching for a typist to transcribe my description of railway journeys across Europe in 1968 led directly to meeting my future wife, Lucinda. At several stages in my career, I derived satisfaction from constructing complicated business letters. Dirk Bogarde once wrote, 'It is an astonishing thing ... to find that I am not a bit happy unless I am writing. Even a letter will do.' Slightly exaggerated, in my case, but there is an element of truth there.

Again, with regard to the direct influence of the written word, I consider myself fortunate to have come across a wealth of traditional tales—many of which are hugely entertaining and contain much wisdom. These tend to originate from the Middle East and Central Asia and were published in England during the period recounted. I have referred to various publications, where relevant, and noted the reference details so that others, if so inclined, can enjoy them today. A great deal of this material has contributed to fostering my long term survival.

As my narrative began to unfold, I was spurred on by characteristic enthusiasm and was surprised when my mind unlocked memories that had not surfaced for decades. If I found myself drawn to making any kind of political remark, it would be to state my personal observation that there were fewer restrictions before the current, insidious, 'nanny state' mentality. I was fortunate because much of what befell me was governed to a far lesser degree than it would be today by credit ratings, box-ticking, chip and pin, peer-group fascism, political correctness, regulatory compliance, anaesthetised educational processes, money-laundering procedures, health and safety concerns, police checks, the 'shame and blame' mentality, the outright banning of country and other pursuits and almost every activity where someone else—who may be as far away as Brussels or Washington—is trying to squeeze the individual into a labelled, constricted compartment.

Another surprise, following formative and turbulent years spent at Marlborough College, was how many connections later arose that linked back to that formidable institution, and I have not been able to resist an inclination to record these when they occurred. In such cases I have noted, in brackets, the individual's date of entry to the College and House. Neither have I been able to desist from quoting snatches of poetry or literature that impressed or moved me from time to time—even if it was only because the author just said it so much better than I could!

The names of people or places have been changed where it seemed appropriate to do so and I have only indicated initials in certain cases to preserve anonymity. Sums quoted are the nominal value at the time, and I have made no attempt to calculate the equivalent current values.

One further point that I should clarify is that some of the episodes described in Chapter 11, relating to my visits to many of the great English public schools, occurred after the end of the main corpus of the narrative, but I am not inclined to make any alterations in that respect and hope you, the reader, will agree that this was an appropriate decision.

Not withstanding superficial political slogans, have I developed different modes of thought to those which I inherited? I think so.

Have my children benefited from this development? I think they have.

But, what are these patterns of thinking? If philosophical inspiration is required, I would borrow the words of the intrepid Englishman, Sir Richard Burton, in his poem 'The Kasidah' (which he attributed to one Haji Abdu al-Yazdi). In this poem, written more than a century ago, 'He makes Self-cultivation, with due regard to others, the sole and sufficient object of human life.'

'As long as you breathe, you learn,' someone once remarked, and I would seek to apply this attitude to lessons gleaned from almost everyone I met—at all levels of society.

Chapter 1
In Meiner frühen Kindheit

Life passes. What is Balkh? What is Baghdad?
The cup fills—should we care whether with bitter
Or sweet? Drink on! Know that long after us
The Moon must keep her long determined course.
(1967 translation of *The Rubaiyyat of Omar Khayaam*,
Graves/Ali-Shah)

'PHOTO! PHOTO! YOU want photo?'

My armed guard beckoned.

I slid from the rusty Ford and positioned myself on the edge of the roadside precipice. The khaki hills of Afghanistan's border territory rolled into the distance behind me, peppered by huge black holes—the mouths of redundant railway tunnels that had hosted puffing engines and clattering carriages in better times.

Passing my camera to the ancient, bearded Pakistani, whose black beret clung to his head at a rakish angle, he simultaneously handed me his aged Lee-Enfield .303 calibre rifle. I posed while my guard took a couple of photos and then, together with the driver, we climbed back into the car. Seeking refreshment, we parked close to a *chaikhana* (teahouse) in the centre of Landi Kotal, a dreary potholed, one-horse town. Situated near the head of the Khyber Pass, the only colour was provided by huge, gaudily decorated diesel lorries; the camels of the road, who plied their trade between Kabul and Peshawar, decked out in brightly coloured metallic paint and glistening bells, mirrors and beads. Long past were the days of plumed helmets, red tunics, flashing swords, shiny bayonets and all the paraphernalia of the British army on the move; the attendant cast of the Great Game (the long-standing rivalry between the Russian and British Empires in Central Asia). My grandfather was involved in military action nearby, during the Tirah campaign of 1897.

It was now 1990. A European female aid worker had been murdered in the tribal wastelands earlier that year. What the hell was I doing in that remote and dangerous part of the North West Frontier Province?

Suffice it to say that my twenty-year-old son, Tarquin, had only recently been smuggled into Afghanistan, at night, by the *mujahideen*. He was determined to report for the BBC, one of the youngest to do so. Caught by the Pakistani police, he had already spent an uncomfortable interlude in a grim, border police station before, bravely, continuing on his quest.

Back in the Ford, we set off on our return journey to Peshawar, trailing behind the black fumes emitted by the 'camels' as they wound their way around the hairpin bends of the Khyber. Tired and dusty, I was eventually deposited in the city at the American Club and expressed my thanks to my driver and guard in the traditional way.

There was a huge kerfuffle going on in the reception area when we arrived.

'You Americans; yes, YOU Americans—YOU cause all the trouble!'

These words rang out, loud and clear, across the hall, voiced by a uniformed Pakistani commissionaire. I felt sorry for a group of Yanks who were inexplicably barred from entering their Club, and when they had cleared off, I timidly approached the smartly attired gentleman and whispered:

'Hang on, I'm not American, I'm *British*.'

In a flash, the Pakistani turned to me with outstretched hand.

'British are ALWAYS welcome, ALWAYS welcome—please come this way. Why did you leave us? Things were so much better when you British ran this country.'

He ushered me upstairs and I headed for the terrace bar. The hazy evening sun shimmered over the yardarm.

'A large, long scotch with no ice, and soda to the top,' I requested.

'Shaken but not stirred?' the cheeky Punjabi barman replied with a broad smile.

'No, No!' I beamed. 'I'm not James Bond, you know!'

I stared dreamily across the tennis courts, toward the cantonment where the British had resided while ruling their empire, so many years ago. In fact, I reflected, it was exactly forty-two years since, as a small child, I had departed from another corner of the globe where the sun of the British Empire had now set.

Five weeks out from Durban, *SS Umgeni* eased her way up the Thames and slipped into a reserved berth. *Umgeni* and her sister ship *Umtali* flew the flag of the Natal Line. They were banana carriers, augmenting their income with fares paid by a small contingent of passengers. My parents and I, who occupied a reserved cabin, were among that number, and the entry in my mother's journal for 5th June 1948 reads:

'We landed in England at Tilbury. A long day of great excitement! We woke to see the green fields of Kent from the porthole and the shabby Victorian houses along the banks. It was very moving for us to see these things—there was no mistake, the very smell in the air was English and the misty summer morning was all we had planned and waited for.'

I do not recall my arrival in England. That long month at sea had occupied a significant portion of my young life and had surely exhausted my parents, as my mother recorded:

'He is very active now—strides around the decks—loves to climb up stairs and rails—very chatty and popular with everyone!'

I was born at Claribel Nursing Home in Durban on 15th March 1947—the Ides—by Caesarean section. During the difficult delivery my forehead was badly cut and the scar is still visible.

I was lucky to survive, having arrived in this world a seriously ill rhesus-negative baby with jaundice and pneumonia. How had this state of affairs developed? Presumably, my parents' blood groups were incompatible but at that time very little was known about the condition. It was only the fortunate intervention of one of the first doctors to undertake infant blood transfusions, who happened to be visiting Durban on her way to attend a conference in Australia, that provided my family with any hope. That lady is owed a debt of gratitude. She most certainly saved my life and although I have tried to discover her identity, records are either unavailable or no longer exist.

My first steps had been taken on the lawns and along the corridors of Michaelhouse School in Pietermaritzburg (Natal).

Following his time at Cambridge and a period teaching at Clifton College, my father had taken up an appointment at Michaelhouse—the Eton of Africa—in 1937 but returned to Britain for naval war service.

In 1945, recently married and initially keen to make a life for themselves in Africa, he and my mother emigrated to Natal, however three years later, with the election of the National Government and the implementation of the apartheid regime, they changed their minds and decided to return to England. I wonder if the decision was made easily. They had built a network of good friends, especially with nurses and colleagues who had helped them through my difficult early months. One particular source of strength was Denise Bell, a dedicated nurse who had spent time in a dank South African jail for protesting against the treatment of black Africans. Denise absorbed herself in the scriptures and when my imminent demise was expected she found comfort in the psalmist's words: '… with long life will I satisfy him, and shew him my salvation.'

Coming across this verse in Psalm 91 convinced her that I would pull through.

As far as the long life goes—so far, so good. Does my search for 'the miraculous' in later years bear out this prophesy? Perhaps it does.

To date, I have not returned to South Africa but I have read *Cry the Beloved Country*, Alan Paton's poignant novel set in the troubled land of my birth that opens with the unforgettable words: 'There is a lovely road that runs from Ixopo into the hills. These hills are grass-covered and rolling, and they are lovely beyond any singing of it.'

One day, God willing, I shall retrace my infant footsteps and perhaps even travel the road from Ixopo to Carisbrooke.

My mother's notes record that, as SS *Umgeni* was secured at the dock, other members of the family, who had come up from Sussex to greet us, were spotted on the quayside and soon we were driving through bombed-out suburbs of east London, close to the docks where fine ships from the far-flung empire were moored among a forest of cranes, derricks and masts.

My mother wrote this entry in her journal:

'We drove home away from the docks past St Pauls and thro' London Town. I had forgotten how lovely and gay spring flowers could look in London on the costers' barrows. We bought some cherries to eat and I was shaken by the price of imported bananas!'

Our immediate destination was West Sussex, where most of my extended family could be found, but our stay in England was to be brief.

In September 1948, when I was eighteen months old, we were off on our travels again and took the night boat from Harwich to Hook of Holland, en route to Schleswig-Holstein (Germany), a journey that would become very familiar over the next four years.

Fortunate to find a new job so quickly and attracted by the opportunity, my father had been appointed Housemaster of Churchill House at the newly founded King Alfred School near Plön, a mediaeval market town some forty miles from Lübeck. The school, bearing the postal address BAOR 6 (British Army on the Rhine) was founded to provide co-educational facilities for six hundred children of British personnel stationed in occupied Germany.

We arrived, just after the start of the Berlin Blockade, the hugely dangerous stand-off between the Soviet Bloc and the Western Allies.

I was, naturally, unaware of this period of high political tension and that we were living under direct threat of another European war. Sadly, the shadow of future world conflict would eventually appear on my radar, and would influence the thoughts and actions of the Baby Boomer generation and many others for decades to come.

The blockade had been implemented by the Soviets, by closing the Berlin Corridor, in an attempt to prevent the other allies (Britain, America and France) from supplying fuel, food and general supplies to Berlin and thereby exerting Russian control over the whole city. British and American forces responded by airlifting two million tons of supplies, in 270,000 flights, into the city. The lifting of the blockade, in May 1949, formally marked the founding of two separate states: the Federal Republic of Germany (West Germany) and the German Democratic Republic (East Germany). Berlin would remain a potential Cold War flashpoint for many years.

Less than a hundred miles by road from the East German border, King Alfred occupied a site that was surrounded by woodlands and with a seven-mile shoreline along the beaches of the Grosser Plöner See, a large freshwater lake. During the war it had served as Admiral Doenitz's crack U-boat training base (No. 1 Unterseeboots-Ausbildungs-Abteilung). Doenitz had been visiting the base in April 1945 when it was announced that he had succeeded Adolf Hitler as Reich President.

Constructed with true Teutonic efficiency, it boasted every imaginable resource designed to develop physical and mental prowess and could easily be adapted to an establishment run on English public school lines. Among the assets available were a huge sports stadium with running track, squash and tennis courts, an indoor and outdoor equestrian school, metal and wood workshops and an extensive timber jetty with sailing and swimming facilities on the Plöner See. There was also a home farm, a theatre with full-sized orchestra pit, cinema, chapel, sanatorium and well-equipped classrooms and boarding facilities.

A large central quadrangle, known as the Quarterdeck, was lined with flagpoles and suitable for military parades. I can easily imagine the days before the war, when scarlet banners bearing a forest of sinister black swastikas must have fluttered in the breeze while goose-stepping Germans marched on the tarmac below, and high-ranking Nazis inspected the naval cadets and their officers.

In due course, it proved an excellent venue for a small boy to show off his dark green tricycle, but woe betide me if I stayed out too late. My father could easily resort to using the slipper in the face of filial disobedience.

King Alfred came under the jurisdiction of the British Families Education Service, a division of the Foreign Office whose director was John Trevelyan, former teacher and civil servant who went on to become Secretary of the British Board of Film Censors in 1958. Trevelyan aimed to attract, among others, the children of parents who would have been inclined to send their offspring back to boarding school in England. To achieve this objective he required a 'name' as headmaster; a subject he broached—with, perhaps, a measure of irony—to the German Jew, Kurt Hahn, in 1947.

Who was Kurt Hahn? Hahn, who later converted to Christianity, was born in 1886. Educated at Oxford, Berlin, Heidelberg and Freiberg, he worked as Private Secretary to Prince Max von Baden in the German Department for Foreign Affairs during the Great War. Convinced that the war was largely caused by the rigid European—especially the German—education system, he and von Baden (who had become a close friend) founded, as an experiential and holistic antidote to the system, Schule Schloss Salem in 1920. Hahn remained headmaster during Hitler's rise to power, but was imprisoned in 1933 by the Nazis, after he had publicly condemned the regime, following the brutal murder of a young communist by Hitler's Storm-Troopers. Hahn had a remarkable capacity for what we would now call 'networking', and after five days his release was obtained, following an appeal from British Prime Minister, Ramsay MacDonald. Unable to remain in Germany, Hahn fled to Britain.

In 1934 he established Gordonstoun, the Scottish public school on the Moray Firth, which had a Spartan reputation and was to provide a robust and controversial education for several members of the British Royal Family. In response to Trevelyan's approach, Hahn suggested, as headmaster, Lieutenant Colonel Freddy Spencer-Chapman, explorer, mountaineer and war hero who had been awarded the Distinguished Service Order (DSO) twice. A former housemaster at Gordonstoun, under Kurt Hahn, Spencer-Chapman was in the process of publishing his book, *The Jungle is Neutral.* This grim narrative related his gruesome experiences in the Malayan jungle during the Second World War and Field Marshall Wavell, the former Viceroy of India and author of *Other Men's Flowers*, a remarkable anthology of poetry, contributed the foreword. Wavell, who knew every poem in his anthology by heart, and considered Spencer-Chapman on a par with T.E. Lawrence and Lord Mountbatten, had put his name forward for a Victoria Cross but this was declined.

When Trevelyan approached Freddy, he and his wife Faith jumped at the chance of taking on the challenge because, as he wrote later, 'I was in the very rare position of being able to fulfil the educationalist's dream of starting a new school.'

Indeed, without the baggage of school governors and 'old-boy cliques', Freddy began by naming the barrack-like boarding houses, and his selection reflected the burning idealism with which he wished to infuse King Alfred. He chose 'Churchill' after Winston, the great war leader and defender of parliamentary democracy; 'Roosevelt' to honour the thirty-second American President and instigator of the New Deal; 'Nansen' after the Norwegian champion of injustice, fellow explorer and Nobel prize-winner; 'Temple' in memory of William, the tireless defender of the underdog and ninety-eighth Archbishop of Canterbury; and 'Fleming' to celebrate the work of scientist Sir Alexander, the discoverer of penicillin who was also awarded a Nobel prize. He went on to establish the school motto and, writing at a later date, said:

> ... in the course of this film (*The Winslow Boy*) came
> the invocation "Let right be done" with its echoes of the
> Petition of Right in 1628, and the cry for freedom and jus-
> tice which lies like a gold thread through the tangled skein
> of our national history. At once I thought—that's just what
> I am looking for—that's the motto for King Alfred School.

Spencer-Chapman must have greatly admired Kurt Hahn, who promoted experiential education on a truly international basis. After Gordonstoun, he founded the United World Colleges and schools in Greece, England, Germany and the United States.

He once said: 'It is the sin of the soul to force young people into opin-ions—indoctrination is of the devil—but it is culpable neglect not to impel young people into experiences.' This doctrine led, in part, to the founding of the Duke of Edinburgh's Award Scheme and, in due course, percolated throughout the British education system.

I recently asked a former teacher at Gordonstoun where Hahn's inspi-ration lay.

'Plato certainly,' he replied, 'but he cherry-picked from other sources as well.'

During my research the names Bella Rennie (who was influenced by Montessori), Johann Pestalozzi and John Dewey surfaced.

My father respected the charismatic, handsome and heroic Spencer-Chapman. He was certainly drawn to his idealism and the portrayal of 'Englishness' at its most high-minded that the new headmaster was demon-strably trying to establish at his school. King Alfred School—inspired by Kurt Hahn's philosophy—was to be a beacon in a land ruled by Nazi crimi-nals for twelve long years.

My father's positive response to these influences was not surprising, because he too, was a man who cherished austere moral values, a trait he had inherited from his parents. He was, as I discovered many years later, quite prepared to beat moral values into any boy who transgressed. His fa-ther, the artist Oliver Hall, a true Victorian and son of a successful Scottish silk merchant, was a Royal Academician. Notable examples of his work could be found at the Tate Gallery and Government House in Delhi. He was also a devout follower of the Swedish scientist and philosopher, Emanuel Swedenborg (1688–1772), whose mysticism influenced, amongst others, William Blake, Carl Jung, Arthur Conan Doyle and W.B. Yeats. Assuredly, it left an indelible mark on Oliver and his close family, which raises interesting questions. How far do intense life experiences mark the genes and DNA? Was my own search for 'the miraculous' triggered by a genetic predisposition? Modern research indicates that this could be so. What do I mean by 'the miraculous'? I mean penetration into a higher reality, a consciousness above and beyond the humdrum existence that is the normal lot of man; the development of the Fourth Brain, or higher faculty, of perception.

My paternal grandmother, who died too young, only a few months before my birth, was a loyal member of the Church of England but had a strong Chapel background.

Once we had settled into our new flat in Churchill House, I soon found myself attending kindergarten in the mornings during term-time, but otherwise enjoyed keeping abreast of all the activities that kept the campus and six hundred children in a constant whirl. I watched house matches on the playing fields, swam in the Plöner See, enjoyed games on the sandy beach and took trips on the robust motor launch that buzzed around the sailing boats when they were racing. My parents were experienced equestrians so we had frequent visits to watch dressage events and opportunities for me to take a few early riding lessons under the stern eye of Herr Kauffman, a retired officer from the Prussian cavalry.

In addition, I especially remember a visit from a colourful Scottish regiment who paraded in the athletic stadium with bagpipes, drums and twirling batons. However, I had to be coaxed away from these diversions and from my pet rabbits, whom I loved, despite their proclivity for eating their own young, to go on shopping trips to the NAAFI (*Navy, Army and Air Force Institutes*) where we spent our precious ration coupons. I particularly disliked the powdered milk that came in round blue tins. In February 1949 my mother wrote:

'Here at Plön he misses fresh milk, meat and fish—does not put on weight as he should. Sometimes it is advisable to give him a tin of baby food (Heinz broth, etc.).'

Modern research indicates that a lack of nutrition at this formative age could store up problems in the future. Fingers crossed.

Once a week, we treated ourselves to a trip into Plön. The shopkeepers, whose premises nestled in the cobbled streets, below the mediaeval Schloss that had been a centre for political indoctrination under the Nazis, were anxious to show friendship. A large slice of cold sausage was a frequent and welcome gift from the jolly, red-faced butcher. A piece of gingerbread from the gnarled old crone, who looked like a witch, in the confectioner's next door, was a bonus. My mother would tease me: 'That old Hexa keeps her broomstick and black cat hidden behind the wooden counter at the back of her shop,' she said. 'At the end of the day they will fly off over the rooftops, not stopping until they reach their home, far away, in the Harz Mountains.'

Naturally, I believed her.

A less pleasant event was a regular visit to the German barber, who came up from the town to give all the boys in the boarding houses a haircut. He was an impatient man and I was a hopeless fidget. On one occasion, while attending to my untidy locks he managed to snip a small slice off the top of my right ear and, with blood pouring down the side of my face, soaking my shirt and against a cacophony of 'Mein Gotts!!' I was rushed to the army doctor on the other side of the campus. He was able, with little ado, to return the severed slither to its rightful place and within a week my ear had healed. From then on I kept very still when sitting in the barber's chair.

On the whole our relationship with the local people was cordial, and as I grew older I became aware of furtive black-market trading that occurred between British personnel and the German servants. Chocolate, tobacco and nylons were exchanged for services rendered and local produce.

I made particular friends with Old Hans, the jovial beach-keeper who had a huge handlebar moustache, and still have his photograph. He spent each day combing the sand with a large wooden rake and kept all the bathing huts in good repair. I eventually learned, that he had fought the Russians at Tannenberg, the bloodiest battle on the eastern front in the Kaiser's War.

Another favourite of mine, was a tall slim girl who helped with the cleaning and other domestic duties. She was always kind, and in the afternoons we would wander over to the sturdy wooden bridge, built by Norwegian guest workers in 1949, that crossed over a large pond. Here, she would rummage in her straw bag and produce a few crusts of black bread. We would while away a happy half-hour feeding the ducks and geese. I never knew her real name but we nicknamed her 'Hinker-Klinkers' on account of the pendulous earrings that jangled beneath her long strands of hair. Is 'Hinker-Klinkers' also the name of a game similar to hop-scotch? Possibly.

One day, she suddenly disappeared with no explanation, which left me feeling very sad. It was only many years later, when my mother and I were reminiscing, that it was revealed she had (by the standards of those days) 'disgraced herself' when she became pregnant by her boyfriend.

'And it was the first time they did it!' my mother confided with uncharacteristic vulgarity.

Life at King Alfred exposed me to a continuous torrent of spoken German. Regular chit-chat with German servants, shopkeepers, restaurateurs and many others meant that I picked up much of the basic language and was soon able to take over when my parents needed German spoken.

On 23rd March 1949, just after my second birthday, an entry in my mother's journal reads:

'I heard him this morning saying to a German workman who was passing the garden, "Guten tag—Wir geht est ihr?"'

Many years later, when my wife, Lucinda, and I took a holiday in Thuringia, staying with a German professor and his family, she commented on my rapport with the German people we encountered. Much more, it appeared to her, than I have ever managed to achieve with the French. This surprised her and led us to believe that my four years—impressionable years—spent in Schleswig-Holstein had left a deeper imprint than we had previously supposed. Later studies in psychology would certainly endorse this view, and it also occurs to me that warm friendships with Hans, 'Hinker-Klinkers' and the other Germans served as an antidote to my increasingly formal relationship with my parents—a trend that would continue at boarding school and beyond.

My parents enjoyed their time at King Alfred, especially my father who participated in all the games at which he excelled. He had been a hockey trial-blue at Cambridge and was justly proud of his maroon and gold Hawk's Club tie, for which I shall always remember him, but he also loved cricket and squash. In the evenings, he sometimes wandered off across the Plön marshes, with his shotgun, to bag a few duck that he brought back for the dinner table. I hoped that there were plenty of birds left in the wild.

'Don't shoot all the ducks, Daddy,' I begged. 'Otherwise, Hinker-Klinkers and I will have none to feed.'

When my mother was not looking after me or attending to domestic matters, she spent her spare time at the riding school, or playing tennis, or being involved in the tea and coffee party circuit.

Long holidays presented opportunities to travel. In the summer, we returned to England but at other times we visited places that were closer to our new home. My father particularly enjoyed these trips as he was a geographer by training. We once visited the Harz Mountains, where shimmering waterfalls, plunging hundreds of feet through deeply wooded glades, astounded us at every bend. I kept an eye out for the old Hexa from Plön and her cat, but there was no sign of them; although the souvenir shops were full of witches on broomsticks.

A favourite trip was to Travemünde on the Baltic coast, a much-loved refuge for the Russian writers, Turgenev and Dostoevsky, in the mid-nineteenth century, and where the novelist Thomas Mann spent 'quite definitely the happiest days of [his] life'. During the summer the resort boasted good swimming and boating, but in the bitter winters, as family photographs remind me, frozen ice-caked sea stretched far away, merging with huge, grey, snow-laden skies. What could be more fun than to ride in a horse-drawn sleigh, the sound of bells tinkling, as we skimmed over the iron-hard salt ice? Then, returning to our warm, comfy hotel, I remember being fascinated by the small orchestra that played in the restaurant and, moving away from our table, sitting wide-eyed under the palm trees near the lead virtuoso violinist. As representatives of the occupying power, my parents expected and received, respect and courtesy, while the natives fussed over me whenever an opportunity arose. This was Germany in defeat, but I was not aware of the political implications of the behaviour of the local population that I encountered on a daily basis. The Brits were used to running an empire so occupying their sector may not have felt so very different.

Much of the topography of Schleswig-Holstein is not dissimilar to that of East Friesland, so evocatively described by Erskine Childers in his thrilling spy story, *The Riddle of the Sands*.

On one occasion, after visiting Travemünde we drove further north towards the Danish border. Driving across the flat countryside, with its great tracts of reed-strewn marsh, lakes and wide pastures inhabited by flocks of feathered fowl and where huge numbers of horses grazed, we passed two cyclists.

'Did you see those two?' my father exclaimed.

'Wait!' he continued.

We drove on a bit further and then, after making a sharp, three-point turn, headed back in the direction we had just come.

'Just as I thought!' he chortled with glee as we passed the cyclists again, this time facing them.

'Those two are the King and Queen of Denmark—King Frederick and Queen Ingrid!' he exclaimed.

We returned to Plön late in the evening. Gas lamps flickered across shiny cobblestones, reaching into deep shadows below mediaeval buildings. It would be a long time before I was to enjoy Carol Reed's classic film, *The Third Man* however, when I did, the evocative black and white photography depicting war-torn Vienna, reminded me of evenings spent in Europe's towns and cities when I was a lad.

Our journeys were only possible, after the red letter day when we took a train to Hamburg with the intention of collecting our first car. Hugely excited, we had made our way to the docks and there, twisting and turning in mid-air, a green Hillman Minx, built by Rootes Motors, was being unloaded by crane from the hold of the rusty coaster that had arrived from England. We instantly nicknamed her 'Minky' and drove back to Plön along the autobahn, passing a few VW Beetles on the way. This was the car, the 'Volks-Wagen'('People's Car') that Ferdinand Porsche, with Adolf Hitler's encouragement, had developed in the 1930s. The first factory to produce the 'KdF—Wagen' or 'Strength through joy—Wagen' was opened by the 'little corporal' in 1938. Production, however, came to a halt with the advent of war and after 1945 it fell to the British, in whose zone the first factory lay, to finance, develop and manufacture the People's Car, utilising facilities available in redundant armaments works. The name 'Beetle' had been a nickname from the start, but was only used by Volkswagen in their marketing material from 1967.

As we neared Lübeck, on our journey home, we came across a minor traffic accident. A VW Camper had gone into the ditch after hitting a lorry, whose load of glistening herring, the staple diet of much of the population along the northern seaboard, was scattered across the highway.

We returned to Hamburg on several occasions and stayed at the Hotel Atlantic or the Reichsoff. Here, and especially along the banks of the Alster at Christmas, there were lights and gaiety aplenty, but driving in and out of the city was awesome. We encountered mile after mile of bomb-shattered buildings, deep craters, rubble, burned trees and torn-up roads. The odd thing is, that at the time, my parents did not tell me what had happened. Yes, they admitted that there had been a war, but gave me no details. It was only much later they confessed that they had not wanted to influence me in any way against the Germans. Since they had lost many friends—and in my mother's case, a fiancé—at the hands of our former enemy, I used to think of this self-imposed silence as an act of nobility. However, it has occurred to me that in the face of an innocent child there was an element of guilt, perhaps a sense of shame that human beings—our lot in this instant—could do such horrific things. During those years, my view of the German people was never clouded by the terrible events that preceded our arrival in 1948.

Christmas was the time to be in Schleswig-Holstein. In every home, baubles and tinsel, candles and exquisitely carved wooden angels and replicas of the Holy Family were carefully retrieved from storage cupboards and taken out of their wrapping. Gingerbread, chocolates, crystallised fruits, nuts and marzipan and all sorts of edible fare were piled high on tables and sideboards, as everyone prepared to celebrate the feast of St Nicholas. Outside, thick snow lay over the countryside. Donning our light brown, hooded duffle coats, wooden toggles securely fastened and with my father grasping the handle of a newly sharpened axe, we went in search of a good-sized tree to take home for the festivities. Save for a few deer, the red squirrels and other wildlife were hibernating and a deep silence permeated the dark forest, punctuated only by the thump of snow tumbling from branches as the huge firs stirred in the breeze. Trudging back to Churchill, burdened with our prize evergreen, we glimpsed the view across a frozen lake, dotted with exuberant skaters wearing colourful pom-pom hats like a Brueghel landscape.

The Christmas of 1951, was to be our last in Germany and it was marked with a grand tea party for many of the children of the teaching staff. The venue was the Mill House, a fine property straddling the quick-running stream that flowed from the Plöner See, although during the winter, thick ice covered the millpond.

The inside of the house was warm and comfortable and a colossal tree, decorated with coloured balls, shimmering stars, moons, glass gewgaws and little white candles in silver holders, stood in the hallway. On arrival, all twenty-eight boys and girls, many of whom were in fancy dress, were led into the dining room which was lit by a huge chandelier and where the windowsills and mantelpiece were festooned with thick holly bearing bright red berries. Seated at the long table, covered with a white cloth and piled with sweets and gold, paper-wrapped crackers, we gobbled up jellies, blancmange, cake and other scrumptious grub, pulled noisy crackers and tossed multi-coloured balloons around until they burst.

As our feast came to an end, we were ushered back into the hall.

A mystery guest was about to arrive.

We peered through the long windows and into the frozen darkness. Suddenly, from behind the snow-covered fir trees a horse-drawn sleigh appeared. The horse trotted across the packed ice and soon the driver drew up at the front door, which was lit by guttering gas lamps fixed to each side of the porch.

Almost immediately, a man emerged from the back of the sleigh. He was dressed entirely in red, from his floppy cap to his sturdy boots, and he sported a long white beard. He was carrying a bulging, scarlet sack as he strode towards the door and hammered fiercely on the brass knocker.

In the hall the atmosphere was electric as, with bated breath, we all intoned the words: 'SANTA CLAUS!'

Once inside, Santa, beaming broadly through his white moustache and beard, sat down on a chair, close to the Christmas tree, while one of the matrons, known as 'Bozy-Wozy' invited each child to sit on his knee and tell him what he or she would like for Christmas. Eventually, eying the bulging sack, from which Santa was distributing his little surprise parcels, my turn came and I sat staring saucer-eyed into the face of the kindly old man.

In the early evening, when all the presents had been handed out and before going home, we gathered, in silence, around the tree as the candles were lit with long wax tapers. Lights were extinguished; fifty tiny wicks flickered, silver tinsel and crystal ornaments sparkled and we experienced a few moments of exquisite magic.

> Stille Nacht, heilige Nacht,
> Alles schläft; einsam wacht
> Nur das traute hochheilige Paar.
> Holder Knabe im lockigen Haar,
> Schlaf in himmlischer Ruh!
> Schlaf in himmlischer Ruh!

It was years later that my father confessed to have played the old man's role. He told me that he thought for a moment, as I stared into his hazel eyes, that I had seen through his disguise and wondered if his bristling eyebrows, which were heavily disguised with tufts of white cotton wool, had betrayed him. But I was clearly convinced that I was in the presence of Santa Claus and enjoyed every moment of the charade.

Among the very young children on that afternoon was my brother Richard—a babe in arms—who had been born in Sussex during the summer holidays. This had been an awful time for my parents as Richard was also rhesus-negative and, following a worrying pregnancy, they had to endure further uncertainty. He required a whole series of blood transfusions. Indeed, when he was being dressed for his christening in St George's chapel—a converted Nissan hut—I noticed all the scars on his little body.

Just how Richard became a member of our family was something of a mystery.

'A stork will bring you a brother or sister in the autumn,' my mother informed me.

This seemed clear enough because I had seen storks, with their young, nesting in chimney pots when our travels took us through the Low Countries, and at the age of four, I saw no reason to question the process any further. I do not recall noticing any change in my mother, and the presence of the growing child was certainly not drawn to my attention. That would have been considered very vulgar.

One morning in September, a card arrived on the breakfast table at Lodsworth in West Sussex where I was staying with my grandmother. It announced Richard's presence among us and featured a large stork carrying a baby. Expecting to find a feathered bird, a baby, my mother and presumably a straw nest—echoing scenes of the baby Jesus in a manger—my grandmother and I set off for Zachary Merton Nursing Home in Rustington. However, when we reached my mother's private room all there was to be seen was a tiny infant, sound asleep in his cot, and my poor mother looking decidedly pasty. It was all a great let-down!

In early 1952, two months after the Mill House party and a month before my fifth birthday, we prepared to leave Germany for good, but on 6th February, a gloom descended. Flags on the Quarterdeck flew at half-mast. News of the death of King George VI had reached us:

'The King is dead: God save the Queen.'

Pictures of the young Queen arriving at London Airport from Kenya, where she had received news of her father's death, and being greeted on the tarmac by Prime Minister Winston Churchill, were splashed across the newspapers.

My father and other men donned black ties and black armbands, and my last memory of our time at King Alfred was sitting huddled by our grey Bakelite wireless as we tuned in to the state funeral service that was broadcast from London.

It would be fifty-six years before I returned to Schleswig-Holstein. The school had closed in 1959 when the property was returned to the German naval authorities—now our North Atlantic Treaty Organisation (NATO) partners. During the intervening years a thriving association—the Wyvern Club—had existed, which held reunions and other activities on a regular basis. After my parents died, my wife, Lucinda, and I attended several of these reunions in London, mainly out of curiosity, but when a sixtieth anniversary (1948–2008) 'pilgrimage' was announced we could not resist the temptation to attend.

The event was superbly organised and 143 'pilgrims' turned up at the luxurious Radisson Hotel in Lübeck on 16th May 2008 for a long weekend. We arrived early which gave us time to explore the pretty town and sample the marzipan, for which it is famous. I only retain the dimmest memories of rubble-strewn streets and the bomb-damaged St Michael's church (the 'mother of Gothic brick churches'), but now we admired spotlessly clean cobbled streets and elegant brick buildings, in pristine condition, as we wandered around. The only visible evidence of the devastating attack on the city by British bombers on the night preceding Palm Sunday in 1942 was the semi-melted bells that had crashed from the south tower and still lie, as they fell, in the memorial chapel at the base of the tower.

Entering the gates of what had once been King Alfred School engendered a tinge of emotion, however everything was much as I remembered it. After a brief and remarkably humorous greeting from the German Kommandant we enjoyed a conducted tour. Only the Norwegian bridge seemed much smaller and I was disappointed to find that the beach huts had gone and the beach itself must have slipped under the waters of the Plöner See.

Most of our fellow 'pilgrims' were older than we were and had attended the school as pupils. I felt a bit of an outsider, being the only participant who had arrived at King Alfred at the age of one. The spirit of loyalty, nostalgia and mutual pride the group clearly enjoyed was remarkable, and we put this down to the outstanding education and opportunities for sport that they received, especially when compared to those available in British state schools during the early 1950s.

'It was like going to a top English public school without having to pay,' one of the 'pilgrims' explained.

I have even heard it said that the quality of the facilities exceeded the best public schools at the time. The 'pilgrims' had also enjoyed being at a boarding school, which was not an opportunity available to most children with fathers in the non-commissioned ranks, and their stay at the school was quite often brief, owing to their fathers' short postings in Germany, so they didn't get bored. Many had formed close friendships that had endured for more than fifty years.

Several of the 'pilgrims' remembered my father.

'He inspired my interest in history,' said one.

'He taught me to ride, and I've never looked back,' said another.

'We called him "cobber Hall", and he terrified us,' interjected a third.

'Really?' I replied.

'Oh yes—he was a ferocious whacker with a cane or slipper!'

This was not something I really wanted to hear, although I admit that I had found him pretty scary myself.

'I saw "Cobber" coming down the street in London some years later and I was so frightened of him that I dived into the first shop to avoid him,' one of the men related.

That was enough—I didn't want my afternoon ruined.

On Sunday there was a service in St George's Chapel, where my brother had been christened, and the event ended with a superb dinner at the Schiffergesellschaft Gastatte . This famous restaurant in the heart of Hanseatic Lübeck is housed in a building which was acquired by the 'Brotherhood of Captains' in 1535.

During the meal it was announced that this would be the last 'pilgrimage', which for me meant that a sixty-year cycle had been completed.

To round off our trip. Lucinda and I spent a couple of comfortable nights at the Atlantic Kempinski hotel in Hamburg—for old times' sake. We were astonished to find that the foyer and central lounge areas were dominated by a life-sized ceramic mural of Kaiser Wilhelm II in full military attire.

I have fond memories of Lodsworth, a pleasant village in West Sussex. This is where my maternal grandparents lived, and where we came to stay in the summer of 1952 after leaving Germany. It sprawls across the sandy ridge that runs between the charming market towns of Midhurst and Petworth with fine southerly views to the Downs. To the east, the land drops easily across meadows and into thick woods. Here runs the sleepy River Lod, fed by tiny tributaries that spring from the hillside.

My grandfather, a retired colonel in the 4th (Irish) Dragoon Guards, was referred to as 'Baba', a name that is universally ascribed to a father, grandfather or old man, and my grandmother was nicknamed 'Gawky', a corruption of 'Ugogo', the Zulu for grandmother that I had misappropriated in South Africa. The Mathew-Lannowes, for this was their surname, lived in Holly Cottage, at the centre of the village, on the main road and opposite the Hollist Arms, which was one of two inns in the village. Across the road from Holly Cottage, in front of the Hollist Arms, was a little triangle of grass where children played under the chestnut tree when waiting for the school bus.

The way into the house was through a wooden gate, set in a low stone wall and up a short brick path. There was no real front garden but the path led through an area that was thickly planted with box, pyracantha, cotoneaster and azaleas. In the autumn, it was a sea of colourful berries as well as crimson Virginia creeper that spread up the brickwork, over the porch and across the red Sussex roof tiles. To the south side of Holly Cottage, also facing the Hollist Arms, was a brick and mellow stone extension that housed the ballroom. It was in that spacious room that glamorous balls and dances had been held before the Second World War.

It would be inaccurate to describe Gawky and Baba as rich, but they were comfortably off. What capital they possessed had been inherited from the Mathews' estates in the West Indies and Ireland, from stock market trading, and brewing in Northamptonshire by Gawky's grandfather, Robert Oldrey, during the latter part of the nineteenth century. Their wealth therefore represented an interesting combination of old colonial money and cash that had been generated by an entrepreneur who flourished in the heady days of the late Victorian era. Sadly, by the time I came on the scene the social revolution of the twentieth century had taken its toll and while my grandparents had employed a string of servants before 1939, they were, in 1952, down to one cook, two parlour maids, a part-time cleaner and a gardener. This was the new post-war world—the 'new normal', to utilise a modern term. Did they, I wonder, count their blessings, since many long-established families had suffered far more?

In many cases, with the deaths of so many men in the world wars, estates and businesses had been emaciated and the surviving women often driven into domestic service or worse. Juliet Nicholson's fascinating book, *The Great Silence* (John Murray 2010), deals extensively with this subject, and those who have visited the Lost Gardens of Heligan in Cornwall will be familiar with the concept of gardeners leaving for the war in 1914 and never returning. Those gardens were left like Sleeping Beauty's palace and only restored to their former glory relatively recently.

At the back of the house a beautiful garden ran towards the river valley, commanding magnificent views. Gawky had green fingers and, together with her trusty gardener, Tooth, whose stooped frame and cloth cap could so often be spotted among the flower beds, no effort was spared. A mature herbaceous border lay within well-kept lawns and these led towards a carefully stocked, formal rose garden with gravel paths and a central sundial. On the north side of the garden there were some bushy areas which led to the chicken run.

'Time to feed the chickens', Gawky would announce, and we would collect a large pot of leftovers or porridge from the kitchen. The next job was to search for newly laid eggs, gathering them with great care, in a wicker basket.

Another delightful chore was to harvest grapes in the nearby greenhouses. Although knowledge of viniculture was not as widespread as it is today, there always seemed to be a glut of red and white grapes on the vine in the autumn.

Further away from the house and still on the north side of the garden, a splendid weeping willow and a pretty birch grove flourished. It was here, in summer, under the shimmering branches, that the maids served tea from a silver service. A chunky millstone acted as a table, and hot buttered toast and scones were piled high on the finest china plates, alongside Gawky's homemade jams and honey from her bees. Close by, lounging in rattan or striped deckchairs, family and friends could take a leisurely break from a game of croquet. Surely, these were still the dreamy days of empire.

My favourite part of the garden was beyond the croquet lawn, through a dark arch cut in tall evergreens and past rows of terracotta pots where tiny tips of rhubarb poked up inquisitively from beneath ill-fitting lids. Here, in the vegetable garden, Tooth laboured hard to provide produce for the house.

'Now, Master Neil, let me show you everything I have been growing,' he would say and, taking me by the hand, he would lead me around the garden, pointing out asparagus, lettuce, carrots, spinach, sprouts, cabbage and much else, in due season, carefully laid out in neat lines. In one corner, close to the thatched potting shed that smelt of oil which had dripped on to the earth floor from several mowing machines, Tooth threw all his organic rubbish and fresh grass mowings. Like Mr McGregor's garden, discarded seedlings proliferated and unwanted lettuces that had taken root bolted in profusion.

The autumn was the best time, when the potatoes were raised, releasing that salty-tangy smell, in my mind forever associated with the English kitchen garden. Among the beds were a number of gnarled fruit trees and in September shiny apples, pears, damsons, greengages and plums glistened in the sunlight. There were usually plenty of ripe windfalls that lay where they had tumbled.

'Watch out for wasps!' someone was bound to shout.

Gawky's garden seemed to go on forever. Beyond the fruit cage and the gooseberry bushes there was another path through a gap in a line of leylandii. Passing beyond them one descended, on steps that were cut out of the turf, into a sunken, almost secret, area. Here, surrounded by tall firs, whose sweet scent hung in the enclosed space on soporific, summer days, was the now disused lawn tennis court and, close by, a grassy bank where Gawky kept her busily buzzing bees. My grandparents had bought the property in the late 1920s and it did not require immense imagination to conjure up the sound of the whack of ball on racquet and the ripple of laughter at elegant tennis parties. Certainly my mother remembered happy pre-war days.

Brought up at Holly Cottage, she was educated there by a governess and never attended school.

Did this, I sometimes wonder, adequately prepare her for the tribulations that would attend her children's education?

Her great passion was hunting, and on many dark winter mornings she was off down the lane on Gypsy, her pony, for a day with the Leconfield; the local pack whose kennels were four miles away at Petworth. During the war, she had boyfriends in Bomber Command and swore that they winked their navigation lights when passing over Lodsworth en route to deliver their deadly cargo.

We lived in Lodsworth for about a year, up to the time of my sixth birthday, first at Holly Cottage and then at the Old Bakery, a small house at the top of the village which had recently been converted. Our immediate neighbours, by chance, were the Tooth family, who had a young son called Peter. I could see him, in his grey shorts, playing in the garden on the other side of the hedge that ran between our properties but I was not allowed to talk to him. It was not thought seemly to mix with village children, which was a shame as I would have liked to. I longed to kick a ball around with Peter, but the few scruffy lilac bushes and some ash striplings that ran between our two properties represented more than a demarcation of land. I was learning a harsh lesson in class distinction—an awareness that would follow me for years to come.

I was brought up strictly which, given that my father was a schoolmaster and ex-naval officer and my mother a colonel's daughter, was not surprising. We moved in circles where children were seen but not heard. I was expected to wash my hands and comb my hair before sitting down at the table for meals, and these could be an ordeal if I did not mind my manners, hold my knife and fork in the correct manner and sit bolt upright in my chair. I was not allowed to leave the table at the end of the meal without permission, and could leave only when there was not a morsel left on my plate.

'Sit up straight!' my father would bark.

He often threatened to place a cricket bat between my elbows and across my back, thereby forcing a rigid backbone, although I rarely recall him carrying out the threat. If guests were present, one did not speak unless spoken to and in conversation one never 'contradicted' or 'interrupted' grown-ups and one was never 'disobedient'. One was deferential to one's 'elders and betters' at all times!

A suitable punishment was to be sent to my room or, in very rare cases, to be spanked with a long-handled hairbrush.

By contrast, Gawky spoiled me and of course I adored her.

'Now, when are you coming to have luncheon with me, Neil? I want to hear about everything you have been up to,' she would often enquire; an occasion that would be followed by a spin in her red Morris, when we would pause at Benbow Pond, on the edge of Cowdray Park—famed for its polo grounds—where we admired the water lilies and took Towser, her West Highland terrier for a brisk walk. Then, before returning to Lodsworth, we called in at Maids, the wonderful toyshop in Midhurst, and there she invariably indulged me in 'a little treat', as she would say.

However, I often cried bitterly when it was time to leave her house and return home and my arrival back at the Old Bakery, with tears streaming down my cheeks, would infuriate my parents. Naturally, I loved my parents although they ruled with an iron rod—almost literally—while Gawky indulged me dreadfully!

Beyond the Tooths' house and on a bend in the main street, lived the McNaughtons; kindly, retired army people with small dogs, and across the road were the Gabbatts; old friends of my mother's whose children, Pop and Michael, were the 'right' sort of playmates. Strolling along steep sandy paths, which led off a narrow lane behind the Gabbatts' garden, deep in bracken and keeping an eye out for adders, one reached the home of the Fletchers. Sarah was their daughter and she was very popular because she allowed me to ride her pony.

Further down the main street, towards the Hollist Arms, lived Ronny Lush, the doctor. It was he who sent me off to the Midhurst Cottage Hospital to have my tonsils removed. This was an excruciatingly unpleasant experience and I was glad, after a few days, to return to the nursery at Holly Cottage where I was pampered and treated to lashings of multicoloured ice cream. In the evening, Gawky would mount the short staircase from the hall, draw the curtains, read a story and say a prayer, before turning out the light. On a chair by my bed, there was a cushion whose cover depicted scenes from nursery rhymes. One of these was a scary picture of the big bad wolf blowing down the house where the little pigs lived. I always asked Gawky to hide the wolf by turning the cushion over before she left the room.

A few years later, the doctor was summoned as an emergency when Gawky developed a problem with one of her kidneys. I was shocked to see her carried off in the ambulance to be whisked through the night to the Middlesex Hospital in London. The infected kidney was removed and

Gawky recovered. However, many years later, my cousin, Dr Tim Oldrey, told me that the rogue kidney was still exhibited, suspended in formaldehyde, in the medical school, as it was deemed to be a particularly remarkable specimen. I am sure it was. It had nearly killed Gawky, however she lived for another twenty years without it!

Tim went on to become a brigadier and army doctor. When stationed in Berlin he attended Rudolf Hess at Spandau. What he thought of him I do not know as, sadly, Tim is no longer with us.

Two doors down the hill from Holly Cottage, Mr Talbot—whom I was encouraged to address as 'Talbot'—kept the tiny post office whose shelves were lined with tall glass jars of colourful sweets. This was an excellent place to spend pocket money. Pocket money—a few pennies—was given to me on Saturdays and I could sometimes earn a little extra by weeding the garden or keeping my room especially tidy. Any discussion, beyond the minimum, regarding money, was taboo at home and if, inadvertently, my father had forgotten to give me my allowance on a Saturday, it was absolutely forbidden to raise the topic on Sunday. I would have to wait until Monday.

Would I pay a price for this lack of transparency about money? I think so.

Outside the post office, fixed to the rough stone wall of the building, was a rusty blue petrol pump. Here the good folk of Lodsworth could fill up their tanks, which was fortunate, as the nearest garage was some miles away. I do not recall where the petrol was stored but by today's standards I am sure it was horribly dangerous.

A few yards further down the road was the general store, run by the Clarks, a friendly family whose daughter Petula had been a child star in the 1940s and who went on to record popular hits, arguably the best-known being 'Downtown', 'Colour my World' and 'Don't Sleep in the Subway'.

The only other shop, run by Mr Aubrey the newsagent, was housed above a barn-like building and approached from the main street by a tall flight of roughly-hewn steps. Comics were not allowed at home as my father considered them a bad influence, so I was deprived of the antics of Dennis the Menace, Desperate Dan with his cow pie and a gang of unforgettable characters—until I went to boarding school, when other boys were only too happy to trade back-copies of their *Beano* and *Dandy* in exchange for a handful of Smarties.

However, 'magic' colouring books were allowed and were purchased with a few coins from the piggy bank. It was great fun to cover black and white drawings with a water-logged paintbrush and then, as if by instant magic, bright colours would jump out from the page. Mr Aubrey used to make an early morning delivery of newspapers to houses in the neighbourhood and one day I asked if I could accompany him. He readily agreed and the very next day, at seven o'clock in the morning, I was waiting outside his shop, even before he arrived, ready to hop into his bright green van.

The first call was to take us through noble gates, about half a mile from the centre of the village, and past the huge girths of chestnut trees that were probably planted in Tudor times. Our customers, Mr and Mrs Gordon, lived at Lodsworth House, a château-like building that we approached down a long drive through extensive parkland. When we arrived I hopped out of the van and carefully placed their newspaper on the doormat within the stone porch. I had previously visited Arthur and Marie Gordon for tea with my mother and had found Marie to be an especially kindly lady. She had met her husband in Paris, her home city, during the war, and all sorts of rumours surrounded her background. However, all I can say is that she was very good to us and always sent the most generous presents at Christmas, not only then, but for years to come, long after we had left the village and she had moved to London. When the Gordons had died—and Marie lived to be ninety-eight—two bells were added to the tower in the village church in their memory. The house itself was built in 1840, by Edward Blore, whose name would surface again when I came to research the architecture of the boarding houses at Marlborough College. His client was Hasler Hollist, a local squire and landlord of the fifteenth-century Hollist Arms. Outside what is today an excellent hostelry hangs a sign which features the Hollist coat of arms and family motto that reads:

GARDEZ LE CAPRON
CURRENDO

This appears to be a curious and untranslatable blend of French and Latin.

Soon we were on our way past high, grey aubretia-covered stone walls and the house where Ivy Dennett lived. Ivy, invariably clad in rough tweeds,

jodhpurs and leather boots and with a fag hanging from the corner of her
mouth, had the weather-beaten face of someone who had spent many hours
riding to hounds like Tom Dansey, the 'famous whip' depicted in John
Masefield's 'Reynard the Fox':

> With sunk cheeks weathered to a tan
> Scarred by the spikes of hawthorn sprays
> Dashed thro' head down, on going days.
> In haste to see the line they took.

In all the years I knew Lodsworth, although I often saw her busying
herself as she crossed the main street going to her stables, with riding tackle,
saddles and bales of hay, we never spoke. Perhaps she was more at home with
horses and dogs than humans.

At the end of the high walls, which were something of a feature of the
village, on the corner there was a fine house. Slipping the paper through
the letterbox I jumped back into the van, not foreseeing that one day a blue
plaque would be placed on the front of the house that read, 'Here between
1955 and 1976 lived the artist E.H. Shepard'. He was, as is well known, the
illustrator of *The Wind in the Willows* and *Winnie the Pooh*.

A nearby house was owned by Lady Fiennes. She was abroad at the time
of my early-morning escapade and was the widow of Lieutenant-Colonel Sir
Ranulph Twisleton-Wykeham-Fiennes who had been killed in the Second
World War. Perhaps there will be a plaque there too one day, as this was the
family home of their son, Sir Ranulph, the explorer, whose name first came
to prominence when he blew up a concrete dam in the beautiful Wiltshire
village of Castle Combe. Its presence, as part of the set of the film *Doctor
Doolittle*, had offended him and he paid the price of losing his commission
in the SAS.

He is a little older than I am, but when our paths crossed many years
later and the world had moved on apace we exchanged nostalgic Lodsworth
memories. I think he had taken an adolescent shine to Sarah Fletcher and we
shared the same views on befriending the likes of Peter Tooth.

Handing *The Times*, as we passed, to Admiral Hammick's daughter, we
turned into Church Lane which was familiar to me because we sometimes
walked down the hill, past the church, to Mr Smorridge's farm where large
porkers were usually resting under the oak tree in a field near his house. As

soon as they saw us approaching, they would scramble up from the mud or dust bowl in which they had been basking, and grunting greedily, come over to the fence; eager to guzzle the green acorns that we gathered for them. But on that early morning there was no time for such things and we stopped at Church Cottage, opposite the lych-gate. Here Mr Rodgers was already hard at work. During the day a little counter stretched across the front entrance of the cottage and I could see him within, hammering away and trimming leather, repairing shoes and boots for the local people. As I approached he came over and, taking his paper from me, expressed astonishment at finding 'Colonel Lannowe's grandson' in the role of delivery boy. He walked with a pronounced limp, probably caused by a war wound, which I had noticed at Easter-time when he hobbled up to the church for Sunday service, and when we passed the cottage on our walks I often saw the lame cobbler in his orchard where daffodils and narcissi frolicked in every available space at that time of year.

> 'Ten thousand saw I at a glance
> Tossing their heads in sprightly dance'
> (William Wordsworth: 'Daffodils', 1804).

Our last call, before we were off to the surrounding farms and hamlets, was to a house at the very bottom of the narrow lane. This was near the gate, leading across open fields, to Eel Bridge where we sometimes played pooh-sticks in the sluggish Lod. As we drove, very slowly, down the last section of the track where there was no room for two cars to pass, Harriet Hurst, a short lady with a nice smile and closely curled grey hair, was spotted coming towards us. She was on her way to Holly Cottage, where she worked for my grandparents.

'Bless my soul!' Harriet exclaimed as we drew up beside her and she spotted me in the van's passenger seat. 'If it ain't young Miss Ann's son!'

She greeted us warmly. Harriet lived in a cottage on the edge of the village with her two daughters, Janet and Elizabeth. She had recently lost her husband, who was a builder, not long after a ladder upon which he had been working, slipped and crashed to the ground one cold winter's day. Harriet had joined my grandmother's staff as an under-house parlour maid when she was sixteen, and remained in her service for forty years, although I heard a story that she had once been sacked for laying out the wrong cufflinks for Baba before an important regimental dinner. Loud remonstrations from other members of the family had secured her return to the household. We were all very fond of Harriet, and in later years when she became the cook at Holly Cottage, her tender roast beef with Yorkshire pud and gravy, steak and kidney pies and succulent vegetables were treats that made any journey worthwhile.

Eventually, Harriet moved from Lodsworth when she married the butcher in Petworth, who was thought to be the richest tradesman in the town.

As we left our last customer, we passed St Peter's Holy Well whose water was reputed to provide cures for eye ailments and is said to pre-date the thirteenth-century church. It was a place of pilgrimage in the middle ages and the Bishop of London, who had received the parish from Henry I as a 'Liberty', is said to have received a good income from the pilgrims.

An hour or so later, after delivering more papers to properties in the outlying villages, Mr Aubrey dropped me off at the Old Bakery and, wolfing down my breakfast, I enthusiastically reported every detail of my trip to my parents.

Not long after this adventure, an exciting event was planned.

'We're going to London, tomorrow', I was told.

Gawky, Baba, my parents and I were all going to the capital for the day, by train. It would be my first proper visit to the city and the family had gathered for a very early breakfast in the panelled dining room at Holly Cottage. Cornflakes were served in large bone-china bowls and consumed with heavy silver spoons. Fresh eggs from Gawky's chickens and piping hot bacon, sausage and tomatoes soon arrived and were placed on the sideboard. A further choice was a boiled egg, and a small device to heat them was put on the table. This was a curious glass and chrome apparatus, fuelled by methylated spirit that could be set to boil an egg for the precise time required. Even the faintest whiff of meths still conjures up a scene that is indelibly printed on my mind.

Breakfast complete, and dressed in our best clothes, we piled into the cars before driving to the station at Selham. It was a couple of miles away, past the ambiguously named inn, The Halfway Bridge, and thirteenth-century earthwork known as Lodsworth Castle, in the valley where the rivers Lod and Rother meet.

How ancient are the names of English rivers? I wonder. Most are simple, even monosyllabic. The Arun, Ouse, Brue, Brit, Cam, Don, Ax, Exe, Og, Avon, Piddle, Wye, Stour, Nene, Isis, Test and Severn, to mention just a few. Surely these names have Anglo-Saxon or even Celtic roots.

The branch line from Petersfield and Midhurst, to Pulborough, was still served by steam locomotives, and a fine example was standing at the platform wheezing steam and puffing smoke. We were greeted by the uniformed stationmaster, whose brass buttons shone in the early morning sunshine. He opened a carriage door for us, lending my grandmother a helping hand, and we climbed aboard while coal dust and tumbling specks of soot threatened to blemish our fine attire. With a shrill whistle we were off, white billowing clouds scudding across the water meadows.

We stopped at country stations along the way, on the edge of Petworth and Fittleworth, before joining the main line at Pulborough. Here, my mother pointed to the exact spot where in 1944 she had been struck by Cupid's arrow when she first caught sight of the man who would become her husband—standing on the platform, resplendent in his naval uniform. Their wedding took place in St Giles Cathedral, Edinburgh, the following year and the marriage lasted until their deaths more than fifty years later.

At Fittleworth, peering through the grit-besmirched windowpane I spotted the Grange, my godmother's house, across the river. I had been there for tea on several occasions and could just make out the old conservatory that housed a wonderfully scented lemon verbena and, in the foreground, the little rowing boat moored to the wooden jetty that protruded into the Rother.

Brigadier Hardy Roberts lived in the nearby Mill House, a fine building designed by Edmund Lutyens, and it was there, on 13th July 1962 (the precise anniversary of Hitler's announcement to the Reichstag, of the Rohm Putsch in 1934) that Selwyn Lloyd took refuge from the media after dramatically falling from grace when Harold Macmillan, the British prime minister, had sacked seven members of his cabinet in what became known as the Night of the Long Knives.

Lloyd, who had been Chancellor of the Exchequer, went on to become Speaker of the House of Commons nine years later and Macmillan's ruthless action was famously underscored by Jeremy Thorpe, the future Liberal Party leader who blotted his copy book in the most unpleasant circumstances. At the time, he said: 'greater love hath no man than this: that he lay down his friends for his life.'

My godmother, Mala Bradley-Williams, enjoyed a political association of her own. She had an aged relation, a Miss Disraeli, and was very proud of this connection which linked her, in some way, to the great Victorian Prime Minister. Disraeli, the first Earl of Beaconsfield, was a Jew who was baptised as an Anglican at the age of twelve and was a close friend of Queen Victoria, who hated Gladstone. On one occasion, at one of her little tea parties, Mala introduced the grand old lady with due gravitas. This, however, led, some ten years later when I was a spotty, nervous teenager, to a colossal howler. I had come across Mala, unexpectedly, in the village shop, during the summer holidays and impulsively thinking of something interesting to say and to engage her in convivial conversation, I blurted out:

'Now tell me, how is ... er ... hm ... er ...?'

I was frantically trying to remember her name.

'... Miss ... er ... Gladstone?' I stammered.

Peering over the top of her horn-rimmed spectacles, she responded with arctic precision.

'Is it to Miss Disraeli that you refer?'

I did feel such a ninnyhammer.

As our train approached London, I became more and more excited, constantly asking my parents how much longer the journey would take. But eventually, after passing the great power station with its four huge brick chimneys at Battersea and rattling over the iron railway bridge that crosses the River Thames at Pimlico, we entered Victoria Station. Steam from half a dozen locomotives swirled up towards the glass roof and within seconds a smart porter with a trolley was turning the brass handle of the carriage door. We were only 'in town' for the day so, having no luggage, we quickly headed out into the fresh air. I had implored Gawky and the others to let me ride on a London bus and, as Baba headed off to spend the morning at his club, we were soon clambering up the staircase of a splendid bright red Routemaster. Our ride took us past Green Park.

'That's the Ritz Hotel!' my mother announced. 'You can take us to tea there when you are rich!'

'And there's Fortnum and Mason, the most famous grocer's shop in the world,' chipped in my father.

We continued down Piccadilly and round the Circus, where neon lights flashed on the walls of every building. Eros, the famous statue dedicated in 1893 to the memory of the great Victorian philanthropist Lord Shaftesbury, stood defiantly in the middle of the oval arena, while more red buses, black taxis, cars and lorries circled all around. This was the very heart of the British Empire, my family assured me and, observing the smart gentlemen with their bowler hats, furled umbrellas and gloves, together with elegantly dressed ladies, all exuding an air of quiet confidence as they went about their business, I had no reason to doubt that this was true. I knew something about the Empire from stories retold by H.E. Marshall in her wonderful book, *Our Island Story,* which my father had read to me at bedtime. The names of Captain James Cook, Sir Walter Raleigh, Clive of India and General James Wolfe were already familiar and, of course, I had been born in South Africa, a country that had once been coloured red on the world map, like much of the rest of the globe. No one bothered to tell a very excited five-year-old that the British Empire's days were seriously numbered, if it existed at all by that time.

My father also told me how Baba had served in India and how he had attended the great Durbar in Delhi (1903) when Edward VII and Alexandra were proclaimed Emperor and Empress. My mother believed that he had led the huge parade on horseback, but I have never been able to corroborate the story's accuracy. The Durbar, designed to impress the Indian princes who attended on their magnificent bejewelled elephants, had been organised by the Viceroy, Lord Curzon, and since neither Edward nor Alexandra were present at the ceremonies, the noble lord took centre stage, which is why history records the event as the 'Curzon Durbar'. Half a century later, Britain and the Empire were now ruled, my parents reminded me, by Queen Elizabeth, from Buckingham Palace and we would be going there later in the day.

Our immediate destination was Hamley's toyshop, which had occupied its site in Regent Street since 1881. The original store, in Holborn, had been founded in 1760 by William Hamley, a Cornishman. His aim had been to provide a 'joy emporium' for every kind of toy imaginable, from tin soldiers and wooden hoops to rag dolls and carved rocking-horses.

Today, in the era of Ann Summers, a 'joy emporium' might be assumed to contain more salacious products. Oh dear—the devaluation of the English language.

Hamley certainly succeeded and, as we entered this enchanting toy land, I was wide-eyed with anticipation and particularly drawn to the array of Red Indian outfits and the miniature electric railway that circled around the gallery on the first floor. I had seen pictures of Red Indians and my magic water-colouring books often conjured up vivid images of exotically clad chieftains and their squaws. Gawky, generous to a fault, could see how thrilled I was and insisted on buying me a full-size Red Indian outfit, complete with multi-feathered head-dress. The young assistant, looking me up and down, carefully chose a package from the shelves that she assured us contained clothes that would be just the right size, before transferring them into a cardboard box with a smart Hamley's label and Royal Warrant from old Queen Mary, the present Queen's grandmother. It was a moment that has stayed with me for more than fifty years but little did I know, at the time, that my future wife would be part-Algonquin. I also wonder if my family were aware that Winston Churchill, their wartime hero, also had Red Indian blood running through his veins?

'Just my little treat,' Gawky said as we left Hamley's and climbed into a shiny black taxi with soft roof and squidgy rubber hooter, positioned just outside the cabbie's window. With the box containing our precious purchase on my knee, I could soon see that we were approaching Buckingham Palace, where a huge flag was billowing out against the azure sky from a tall white pole on the roof. Soldiers in their black busbies were marching and military bands played stirring music while crowds gathered by the railings of the splendid building.

It was time for the changing of the guard, a daily ritual.

'The Queen must be at home,' my mother informed me. 'That's why the Royal Standard is flying.'

'Do you think we'll see her?' I asked.

'See the Queen again?' my mother replied, referring to our trip to Cowdray Park, when Baba, who had played polo for England before the Great War, had been refereeing a game a few days earlier. The Queen had arrived in the Royal Enclosure, driving herself, as she often did, accompanied by Charles and Anne.

I asked my mother if she had ever been into the palace and she explained that she had been a debutante and was presented to King George in July 1937.

'What's a debutante?' I asked.

At that moment a regimental brass band passed close by. We could hardly hear ourselves think.

'Never mind, I'll tell you later,' she continued.

We lingered for a while and then, turning away, strolled down the Mall to Trafalgar Square, under the single, watchful eye of Horatio Nelson on the top of his 185-foot column. Here, we purchased birdseed from a street vendor and I was soon engulfed in pigeons that perched on my head, shoulders and arms. Fortunately, they did not mess up the smart blue overcoat I was wearing, because we were due for lunch at 116 Pall Mall, the imposing Regency building designed in the early nineteenth century by John Nash. This fine property had been built for the United Services Club, of which Baba was a member, and we had a splendid lunch in the beautiful dining room, although I was, without doubt, very careful to mind my Ps and Qs. The interior of the whole building—pictures, memorials and artefacts—exuded the power of military might and history of the British Empire. In one corner of the hall a ticker-tape machine was rattling away as it printed news from Reuter's Agency. Thirty years later, when I attended a business presentation in the same building, I recalled my boyhood visit and reflected on how military clout had been replaced by commercial capability. By this time, the Institute of Directors had been granted a sixty-five-year lease by the Crown Estate Commissioners.

My grandfather, Colonel B.H. Mathew-Lannowe, 'Bunny' to his friends, came from a long line of soldiers. His father was a major-general in the Royal Engineers and his brother, Brigadier-General Edmund Byam Buckley Mathew-Lannowe, who was on the General Staff in the Great War, wrote a pamphlet in 1917 entitled 'Armament of the Whippet Tank'. Their grandfather had been a captain in the Coldstream Regiment of Foot Guards, Member of Parliament for Shaftesbury and 'Her Majesty's Envoy Extraordinary and Minister Plenipotentiary to the Emperor of Brasils', sometime Governor of the Bahamas and Companion of the Most Honourable Order of the Bath. In 1836, at St George's, Hanover Square, he married Anne Hoare, the daughter of Henry Hoare of Stourhead in Wiltshire.

Baba was born in 1872 and had seen service on the North West Frontier, notably in the Tirah campaign (1897/98) and in South Africa during the Boer War. He was aide de camp to General Buller at the Siege of Ladysmith. During the Great War he fought on the Western Front where, in 1914, his regiment, the 4th Royal (Irish) Dragoon Guards, was the first cavalry regiment to skirmish with the Germans. This was one of the few successful cavalry charges of the entire war and was the subject of a television documentary ninety years later. Baba subsequently served in Gallipoli when seconded to the Argyll and Sutherland Highlanders. He received the Distinguished Service Order (DSO) and was twice mentioned in despatches.

In the afternoon there was more shopping on the agenda. My father took a taxi to Savile Row to visit Bernard Weatherill, his tailor. He had also served in the 4th Dragoon Guards and in the Indian Army before entering politics. He became Speaker of the House of Commons in June 1983 and died in 2007. My mother had an appointment with her milliner, as she wanted to order a new hat for the Gold Cup match at Cowdray Park and, after a boring hour we managed to fit in a visit to a huge shop in pursuit of Start-rite shoes for me. It was there that I first became acquainted with the shoe-fitting fluoroscope, an ingenious device, invented in America, that enabled a would-be purchaser, together with the attendant sales person, to view an X-ray of the bones in one's feet and thereby determine the suitability of the shoes. The machine was widely used in North America and Great Britain, having been patented in 1919, but concerns regarding radiation exposure led to a total ban in the state of Pennsylvania in 1957, after which its use gradually declined and none were to be seen by the late 1960s.

Before returning to Victoria, we made a hasty visit to Rowe's of Bond Street, the smart children's shop with a beautiful wooden rocking-horse in the window. Rowe's specialised in sailor suits, which were very popular with children from the royal families of Europe. My mother bought me corduroy shorts and a couple of cotton shirts but I would return many times over the years to have bespoke suits and overcoats measured, tailored and fitted.

Where did the money come from for all that? I never asked.

While we waited for the return train to Sussex, I found a Children's Map of London[1] in the newsagent. It showed all the main parks, thoroughfares, famous buildings and of course the great railway stations, of which the Victorians were justly proud. Little ditties and rhymes embellished the map, which is now framed and hangs on a bedroom wall at home.

My favourites are:

> In London once I lost my way,
> In faring to and fro,
> And asked a little ragged boy
> The way that I should go.
> He gave a nod and then a wink,

And told me to get there,
Straight down the crooked lane,
And all around the square.

And, from Alfred Noyes (1880–1958):

Go down to Kew in lilac time
(it isn't far from London!)

The surround of the map is framed with sketches inspired by famous nursery songs and signs pointing the way to the West Country, Dover, Brighton and the Great North Road. Sadly, today one would be more likely to end up in the Great Traffic Jam, and to parody 'Humpty Dumpty', neither the Queen's horses nor the Queen's men seem able to do much about that.

Having left Germany in 1952 and spent the best part of a year in Lodsworth, we moved to the Medway city of Rochester, in Kent. I don't know why we had left King Alfred School and, sadly, it is too late to ask my parents but it seems as though my father then found it difficult to find another job. Teaching was an easy option for many of those who had been demobbed after the Second World War, so there may well have been a shortage of vacancies.

I have given this matter thought, and years later when I became intimately acquainted with some of the grander English public schools, it struck me as a shame that he had not carved himself a niche in one such establishment.

However, in 1953 he was appointed Headmaster of King's Junior School and my parents moved to a Victorian terrace house in Albany Road, a rough unmade cul-de-sac that has not altered to this day. It was a stone's throw from the city centre.

Why my father was attracted to this particular position, I do not know either. Perhaps it was the only headship going at the time. Or he may have relished the school's close association with the cathedral or, perhaps, he was drawn back to Kent, having been head boy at the Free Grammar School of Queen Elizabeth in Cranbrook.

Cranbrook is some twenty miles from Rochester, and my father's contemporaries were Hammond Innes, the novelist, and the broadcaster, Peter

West. In 1932, my father sat and won a scholarship to Emmanuel College, Cambridge.

Our lives changed significantly as we adapted to urban living although, as most small boys would, I welcomed a new adventure. The same could *not* be said for my mother. She missed the comfortable life in Lodsworth, where her father, 'the Colonel', ruled the roost at Holly Cottage and dominated the village pecking order. In fact, she must have come down with a bump as servants that she had relied on in Sussex, Germany and South Africa were no longer available and King's School did not provide the sort of recreational facilities that my parents had enjoyed when they were abroad. Gone was our Alice in Wonderland existence; the pleasant afternoon walks to Mr Smorridge's farm, picking primroses along the way, or a stroll down to the sleepy Lod to play Pooh sticks. To entertain ourselves we now pushed my brother's pram, skirting the allotments and traipsing along hard pavements in search of the more attractive areas of the city.

'Mind those dogs' dirts!' my mother would shriek as we encountered a mound of filth.

Passing through several leafy avenues and past older clapboard houses, we discovered the cathedral close and grounds of the Norman castle. Much of Rochester Castle was a ruin but the noble flint keep still stood majestically in its own small park above the River Medway, guarding the route to London that an invader might once have taken.

To reach this massive fortification with its frowning battlements, we climbed up steps within the ramparts and dallied under the shadow of the huge iron cannon that pointed towards the sea. It was exciting to clamber through gaps in ancient, crumbling walls and along wooden platforms, built for tourists that ran around the keep's interior wall. Far down in the murky interior, grisly dungeons were just visible. Reaching the roof, panoramic views led the eye eastwards over the busy road and railway bridge and down the estuary. To the west, towards the unfortunate village of Borstal where the first prison for bad boys was established in 1902 and whose name has become synonymous with describing houses of correction for delinquent youths, the Medway at low tide, exposed miles of stinking grey mud flats that trapped decayed and rotting barges and military landing craft, abandoned after the Second World War. The only signs of life were the noisy seagulls, swooping over the water and tidal marshes, before perching on the disintegrating hulks.

My father, ever the disciplinarian, would point to Borstal from the castle keep.

'Behave yourselves, boys,' he would say. 'Or you'll end up in there!'

I certainly did not relish that.

Rochester's close proximity to the Royal Naval Dockyards at Chatham ensured that it was always at the centre of military activity during wartime.

In the centre of the river a Sutherland flying boat, built by Shorts who had their main factory on the Medway, was permanently moored. Gawky, at the time of my birth, had flown all the way down the east African coast to Durban, hopping from port to port in a similar craft. Or maybe it was, indeed, the very same plane that now rocked gently on the tidal current.

An alternative route back to Albany Road, might take us along the top of windswept grassland that ran down steeply to the Medway, past St Margaret's church, where we attended matins on Sunday and close to the portals of Fort Clarence. This sinister mass, built to repel would-be conquerors during the Napoleonic wars, also had a history as a lunatic asylum, military hospital and headquarters for the Home Guard—the real 'Dad's Army'—in the Second World War. Now derelict, it was camouflaged by rusty wire netting and scruffy bushes covered in prolific entanglements of white tulip-flowered columbine.

Much of Rochester exuded all the charm of a cathedral city, with its measure of fine Georgian houses and a quiet close. The playing fields at King's, framed by the stark outline of the cathedral and castle, the sound of willow against leather, shambling wooden houses and Dickensian shops, conspired to engender an aura that was as quintessentially English as a fresh breeze over the Thames at Tilbury, daffodils in orchards at Easter or red buses and black cabs in St James's. But scanning the horizon from my attic bedroom, I observed a much harsher world; a city disturbed by the clatter of goods trains in the shunting yards and the crash of metal in the docks. In addition, after dark, great furnaces across the Medway at Stroud belched furious sparks and ferocious flame into the night sky. Staring out into the blackness, I liked to think of these gargantuan steelworks as fierce dragons lurking on a foreign shore.

And the people—foreigners indeed—who lived and worked there, I was informed, were quite different from us. What a shame that I never made friends with Peter Tooth, I would think to myself in my lonely attic.

We settled down to our new life. Every morning I would walk half a mile, past flint-walled almshouses, to the Chestnuts, a pre-prep school run by Miss Snowdon, a fierce elderly lady, with corded spectacles that bounced around on her ample bosom. I detested Miss Snowdon and did not like having my hand slapped with a ruler when I did something that displeased her. I found reading, writing and sums very hard at the age of six and longed for the bell to ring announcing the end of lessons.

When I got home, my mother would have checked my room to assess how tidy I had left it and whether my bed was made properly. She had pinned a day-chart to a board on the bedroom wall, along with a big duo-coloured crayon on a string—one end blue and the other red. I would run up the stairs and approach the noticeboard with apprehension. If the room was shipshape, the space for that day was marked with a neat blue tick; however, if my mother's eagle eyes had found fault it was marked red. Too much red in a week, and there would be big trouble.

'You became a sort of servant, substituting for those your mother missed,' said Lucinda when she read this passage.

Poor Mother; she did not have too good a morning herself one day, when she attempted to light the fire in our sitting room and set the chimney alight. I came home to find three fire engines blocking the road. Fortunately, no great damage was done but the stench of burnt wet soot took ages to disperse.

I think my father enjoyed his new job, but we all secretly pined for the extended family that had been left behind in West Sussex. My mother, above all, must have found living in a small house in the new post-war world with young children and no established friendships very difficult. She was also learning to live on a schoolmaster's salary although her income was augmented by a small trust fund bequeathed to her by Gawky's mother. With the exception of her wartime experiences, when she was billeted in a bedsit in Reading and worked on the factory floor at Miles Aircraft, nothing in life had prepared her for what she once described as a dreary existence in Rochester. There were no horses for her to ride, no tennis parties or sparkling ballroom dances, but we did acquire a canary in a cage and a border terrier named Billy Brock who helped to jolly things along. Years later, my father, who was not an especially social animal, confessed that he used to worry about her and knew that she hankered after a more glamorous life. A spark of excitement was kindled at Christmas when we made an annual pilgrimage to London and after lunching at the Normandy, a rather grand hotel in Knightsbridge that belonged to a bygone age, we attended a matinee at Bertram Mills' Circus in Olympia. I still have a souvenir programme, and flicking through the pages, memories of the masterful clowning of Coco, Beppo, Jimmy Scott, Little Billy and all the others tumble back into my mind. But there was more, much more: trapeze artists that left you breathless, boxing chimpanzees, troops of horses from Switzerland and the Argentine, barking dogs from America who played such hilarious tricks that tears rolled down one's cheeks, elephants, mischievous sea-lions, lions and tigers in huge cages with Alex Kerr, the tamer, who wielded a long whip. They all provided several hours of riveting entertainment and then, after the show, we made a tour of the menagerie to inspect the animals before visiting the fun fair.

Ah! Those were the days.

Today, you can't have that kind of fun because the animal rights people have taken over. They would argue that it was no fun for the animals but, by and large, I'm not so sure.

Every opportunity was taken to drive over to Sussex and one such occasion was the Coronation in June 1953. A great deal has been said about how this unforgettable event raised the spirits of the British people, especially city dwellers who had suffered long, gloomy years of war, deprivation and rationing, and I am sure much of it is true. All the children in Rochester were given Coronation mugs and other mementoes by the mayor of the city, Councillor C.H.R. Skipper. There were street parties and miles of flags and bunting. Hordes flocked to London, not only on 2nd June, but also at other times, just to admire the fantastic decorations festooned across all the main thoroughfares at the centre of the capital and over many buildings too.

However, we spent the great day with my father's elder brother Leslie and his wife Betty and their children. They lived in the pretty cottage where my father had been brought up in Sutton, a small village on the South Downs. From the back of the house there was a magnificent outlook over the Arun valley towards Amberley and Chanctonbury Ring.

A splendid conker tree and a well, which supplied the house with spring water, were special features of the garden, but the tree house that Leslie had built for his youngest daughter, Tessa, attracted the most attention whenever we paid a visit. However, on Coronation Day, the real excitement was that they had a TELEVISION!

It was quite small—black and white, of course—but we had never seen one before and the whole family sat riveted with our eyes glued to the screen as the events in London unfolded. Many consider the crowning of the English monarch to be a mystical ceremony. Well, it may be, and Queen Elizabeth herself forbade the prying eyes of the television cameras from transmitting the sacred moment when the Archbishop of Canterbury placed St Edward's Crown upon her head.

However, after the most significant events, Tessa and I became bored. The long line of ermine-clad peers, kneeling and paying homage to Her Majesty and the subsequent, seemingly endless, columns of troops tramping through London's rain-sodden streets was too much for two six-year-olds.

'Let's go back to the tree house', whispered Tessa and we slipped away.

Tessa was an attractive, lively girl and something of a tomboy. I always enjoyed seeing her. When she was not on her pony she was shinning up trees, and we were soon high up among the branches enjoying a good view down the village high street and into the garden next door. A nearby property, Forge House, belonged to Sir Gerald Barry (B3 1912), the Director General of the Festival of Britain in 1951. His talented son Stephen, coincidentally, was to be my Head of House at Marlborough ten years later but, sadly, died young and his stepson Richard Burton would, in time, become a renowned architect and good friend of mine. Richard's mother, Vera, had worked for the BBC during the Second World War, frequently broadcasting coded messages in French to the resistance in Europe. You know, the kind of tantalising messages one hears in war films:

'Alfred will meet his aunt.'

'Jean has a broken leg.'

'Edward's cat will go to the vet on Friday.'

In fact, Bignor, the next village, had been an important centre supporting the Resistance in France, with Lysanders being launched from the Downs on moonlit nights. The full story of these events based at Bignor Manor is told in the recently published *A House of Spies*—SIS operations into occupied France from a Sussex farmhouse—by old Marlburian Edward Wake-Walker (C2 1966).

A few days after our return to Kent, my father and I went to the grubby cinema in Chatham to watch the full Pathé News colour film of the Coronation. Televisions were rare and, if actually witnessing the scenes in London on 2nd June was not an option, the only way most people could enjoy the historic spectacle, albeit in hindsight, was to visit the cinema. The programme was combined with a documentary about the conquest of Everest by Hillary and Sherpa Tenzing, another significant event that was seen as a timely gift to the new Queen. The expedition had been led by Colonel John Hunt who had been educated at Marlborough College (C2 1924) and there were four other Old Marlburians on his team. The cinema visit is somehow linked in my mind to a viewing of Ealing Studios' first colour comedy *The Titfield Thunderbolt* (1953). My goodness, did we laugh.

What I also recall is that the auditorium was smelly. To be abominably non-PC, the 'great unwashed' come to mind. A high standard of personal hygiene was not endemic among the population at large, as it is today, and domestic plumbing, for the most part, was very basic. Millions of people still relied on an earth-closet in the garden, although the days when some sections of the community stored coal in the bathtub because they could find no other use for it were probably over by the time of the Coronation. Washing machines and tumble dryers were rare. Drip-dry shirts and easy-care clothes had not arrived on the market and most of the population designated Tuesday as 'washing day', when clothes were scrubbed in the back parlour, put through the hand-operated mangle and hung out to dry on the line in the back garden. If there was no washing hanging on the line on Tuesday, the neighbours would want to know why. So ingrained was this custom that a letter, written by Mary Burn from the rectory in Kynnersley to her half-brother, Tom, at Marlborough College in August 1846 is headed 'Tuesday morning: Washing Day'.

Taking excursions into the Kent countryside at all times of the year was enjoyable.

We liked to drive to Tunbridge Wells for tea in the Pantiles and enjoyed strolling under the covered walkways, snooping in the antique shops and soaking up the atmosphere as the brass ensemble played with gusto in the Regency bandstand. In the spring this jaunt meant passing through pink and white blossom-laden orchards, but in September the same boughs were heavy with red and golden apples. The hop groves, upon which the breweries depended, were a special feature of the Kent countryside and remained green and lush in early summer but, in autumn they turned an ochre hue. Each year, hop-picking provided a traditional working holiday for East Enders, who looked forward to travelling down to the Weald for the harvest.

Trainloads of Cockneys invaded the farms. What a splendid crowd they were.

To paraphrase the words of the poet T.S. Eliot, golden October soon declined into sombre November and Kentish winters could be bleak, especially when easterly winds were blowing from Siberia. Much of the land is flat, muddy and desolate in January and February and the horizon is broken only by the gaunt outline of naked trees and lonely oast-houses at deserted farms.

Eliot, an American whom the English hijacked for their own, later catches the ambience in his play *Murder in the Cathedral* (initial chorus, lines 11–13):

> The New Year waits, breathes, waits, whispers in darkness.
> While the labourer kicks off a muddy boot and stretches
> his hand to the fire,
> The New Year waits, destiny waits for the coming.

One winter's day, returning from the country at three o'clock in the afternoon, we descended into pitch-black smog that hung over the Medway valley.

At home, rain or shine, we played in the garden with a wigwam that Gawky had given us and in the homemade sand-pit. I also began to enjoy running, and collected a few prizes at the summer sports day. These were presented by the Dean of Rochester, Dr Thomas Crick, traditionally attired in black gaiters and frock coat. Gaiters were worn by senior clergy and young children in those days, and I am reminded of an episode in Plön, during a visit by the Archbishop of Canterbury, Dr Geoffrey Fisher. When the eminent primate stayed the night with the Spencer-Chapmans and was about to retire to his bedroom at the top of the sweeping staircase, young Nicholas, their son, made sure that Fisher knew the house rules.

'No gaiters upstairs!' he bawled.

In March 1954, at the time of my seventh birthday, I contracted an exceptionally virulent strain of measles and became exceedingly ill. My temperature soared and Gawky arrived from Lodsworth to help look after me. Had she come to say goodbye? I wondered in my semi-delirious state.

'Am I going to die?' I asked my mother between convulsions, and it was then that she told me of the psalmist's words that had provided hope at the time of my birth: 'With long life will I satisfy him, and shew him my salvation.'

'No!' I wasn't going to die, she assured me, and in a few weeks I recovered, in time to be shoved off to boarding school. Another battle for survival was about to commence.

The whole thing had been too much for Gawky, and she crashed her Wolseley on the Common at Tunbridge Wells on the way home to Lodsworth. She was not badly hurt, which was very fortunate.

Chapter 2
Ashfold and Fonthill

Friends of my youth, a last adieu!
Haply some day we meet again;
Yet ne'er the self-same men shall meet
The years shall make us other men.
(Richard Burton, 'The Kasidah' of Haji Abdul El-Yezdi,
1840s)

P-LONK!

I turned. A small package had landed on the front doormat at 6 Albany Road. I picked it up and ran into the kitchen. Mummy opened it. Inside was a coil of white cotton tape, yards and yards of tape, inscribed in blue thread that read: 'Neil Hall 19'—my name and new school number.

A visit to Messrs Kinch and Lack in North Street, Guildford, the outfitters for Ashfold School, was urgently required. After two hours, on the following Saturday, the shop floor was piled high with cotton socks, woollen games socks, white shorts, blue shorts, corduroy shorts, grey shirts, aertex shirts, gym shoes, spiked cricket shoes, handkerchiefs, swimming trunks, underpants, vests and a full-length blue boiler suit, to name but a few listed items that were being packed into a smart brass-cornered trunk. A red blazer and cap were also laid neatly on top of all the other clothes. These final items each featured a badge, colourfully embroidered with a lion, griffin and dragon denoting the 'houses' into which the school was divided.

I was to be a Dragon, and my rugby shirt was bright green.

My mother's job for the next month, was to sew the name-tapes on to every single one of the items purchased. A boring task, indeed.

A few weeks later, on a warm day at the beginning of May, we set off for Ashfold with a new wooden tuck box and overnight bag stowed in the boot of the Hillman Minx. The box bore my initials, NGMH, carefully stencilled in shiny black lettering by my father. The trunk was lashed to the roof rack but my bicycle was to follow by courtesy of the carriers Carter Paterson.

Ashfold was in Sussex, just west of Handcross, a small village where the B2110 crosses the London to Brighton A23.

After the fifty-mile journey from Rochester we arrived at the property. My heart was in the pit of my stomach.

We drove past the red brick lodge and up a long drive that crossed the playing fields (Matcham's Grove), surrounded by fine leafy Spanish chestnut trees whose heavy gnarled boughs leaned down and almost touched the fresh green grass. Near the trees was the pavilion, and newly painted white screens stood ready for the cricket season.

Approaching the fine mansion, originally built as a private residence, a mêlée of parents, staff and boys jostled around the impressive front door. A tall, attractive blonde lady wearing a crisp, blue uniform came forward. My parents and I introduced ourselves.

'I'm Miss Lunn, Head Matron. Welcome,' she responded with a smile.

I liked her immediately.

We entered the school and Matron guided my parents and me up a broad oak staircase and into a large room. The barrack-like space that opened before us was 'Blue', the junior dormitory.

Nothing had prepared me for the sight of twenty blue iron bedsteads, each supporting a horsehair mattress neatly made up with grey blankets, or the stark realisation that this was where I was expected to sleep.

The early summer afternoon had, it seemed, suddenly turned chilly.

'Your bed is over there,' announced Miss Lunn, pointing to the far corner of the room and turning to leave.

The beds were in rows, facing the centre of the room and to each was allocated a wooden locker with a drawer and lower cupboard containing a white china chamber pot.

I found my bed, in the corner, near the window and examined my locker.

'What's this for, Mummy?' I asked.

'Well, you know … if you have to do wee-wee in the night,' she responded a little coyly.

There was a label with my name, clearly printed, resting on the pillow, so I started to unpack my overnight bag. I deposited the one rug we were allowed to bring from home on my bed, tucked striped linen pyjamas under the covers and hung my grey woollen dressing gown with blue piping and face flannel on hooks near the bathroom door. Toothbrush and a new tube of paste went into a plastic mug on the windowsill, also clearly labelled. My Book of Common Prayer, a specified requirement, was placed in the drawer.

The dormitory was filling up with boys and parents. I eyed them with apprehension.

It was time for my people to leave. Making our way slowly back down the staircase to the front door, my throat tightened. Hot tears erupted as my parents climbed back into the Hillman. I managed a couple of sloppy kisses, tugging at my mother's coat, and shook my father's hand.

'Good luck, old boy,' he muttered.

'I'll write in a day or so,' Mother assured me, wiping her eyes with a pretty pink handkerchief as the car started to move.

Then suddenly …

'Oh! The eggs!' she cried.

Rationing had recently ended, but there were still shortages. All parents were required to provide a dozen eggs and some fruit at the beginning of each term. She handed a box through the car window and then, quickly accelerating, they sped off. A sickening sense of something lost tore at me as I turned away and, passing our mandatory culinary contribution to Matron, I was ushered into the noisy refectory in time for high tea. Jostling and chattering boys filled the room. They seemed glad to be back to school. Only the new boys in their starched blazers hung back, homesickness written all over the blotchy red cheeks of young faces. Bedtime followed a plate of Welsh rarebit and an apple, and back in the dorm, I quickly undressed, slipped into my 'pyjams' and buried myself under the scratchy woollen blankets. I hardly heard the call for lights out, and drifted off to the sound of muffled sobbing coming from the next bed.

An earlier property was known to have belonged to Admiral Horatio Nelson's sister, Mrs Matcham. She was the admiral's daughter, Horatia's ward, and Horatia was known to have spent time at Ashfold as a teenager. The ghost of Mrs Matcham was still said to be seen stalking the corridors on stormy nights. At a recent Ashfold reunion, I quizzed my friend Will Sykes, whose father was one of the headmasters.

'Did you ever see the ghost of Mrs Matcham?'

'Definitely,' he responded.

The current mansion—a Victorian reconstruction of an earlier property—was typical of its period with high ceilings and moulded cornices, mullion windows, deep sills and wood panelling. It must have once served as a desirable and elegantly appointed country house. However, when I arrived one would be more likely to trip over a set of carelessly abandoned cricket pads on the polished oak floors in the hallway than encounter Persian rugs or Chippendale furniture. Nor would you find family portraits, porcelain or fine silverware in the dining room, where long oak tables and benches were scrubbed daily with strong soda and where the walls featured team photographs depicting generations of eager young cricket, football and rugby players. In a corner of the hall a large, rather pongy, walk-in cupboard contained piles of mislaid property. This was the 'penny-pound' and to retrieve a linseed oiled cricket bat, pair of dubbined boots or a damp games shirt required a timid knock on the nearby staff common room door (known as Brown's after Headley Brown, one of the teachers) and payment of the appropriate fine. As the thick panelled door of this private refuge opened on the command, 'Enter!' the waft of ale and sweet smell of pipe tobacco filled the nostrils. It was a haven from the ceaseless demands of some ninety boys whose ages ranged from seven to thirteen, and each week a barrel of beer was delivered for the enjoyment of an eclectic group of teachers.

Donning boiler suits on half-days and weekends, we were free to explore extensive grounds, woodland and terraced gardens. Huge rhododendrons clambered up the walls of the squash courts and in the thickets near the main road stood massive concrete blocks. These were tank traps, designed to stop the Germans in 1940, and objects of considerable interest. We played fierce battles, as only small boys can, with sticks and toy cap-guns, imagining that our school had been overrun by 'Jerry' and that we were driving the invader back into the sea.

'Ack! Ack! Ack! Ack! Ack!' The sound of boy soldiers echoed through the woods. But who were these Jerries? I asked myself. Not Hans and Hinker-Klinkers and the jolly butcher and the Hexa—not even Herr Kaufmann. Surely those had been my friends? Inevitably the light was beginning to dawn that the majority of the German people had been our enemies and, that during a terrible war, a lot of people had killed each other.

Sandy paths ran through the wood where there were plenty of opportunities for climbing trees, and of course, bicycling.

When my bright orange bicycle was delivered by the carriers, something of a stir was caused. It had been given to me by my mother's nieces, Tessa and Jill, who had brought it back from Canada, where they were evacuated during the war, but had now outgrown it. I learned to ride the beast in the back yard of the Angel at Midhurst, when we stayed there for Easter. Built for use on rough terrain, which was appropriate on the Ashfold estate; the tyres were chunky and twice as broad as English tyres and a nickname; 'the elephant' was instantly coined.

'Give us a go,' chanted some of the boys, as instant popularity came cheap.

Palladian-style terraces ran the full length of the back of the house and at lunchtime on 30th June, the whole school gathered at the top of the terrace. Each boy and member of staff held a strip of smoked glass through which to view a partial solar eclipse. Observing the moon's passage across the face of the sun was an awesome experience that lasted for several hours—there was a total eclipse in parts of Scandinavia. As we sat, cross-legged, on the ground we were under strict instructions not to view the flaming gaseous mass with the naked eye and not wanting to damage my eyes, I handled the smoked glass with care.

The younger boys were taught to swim a few steps up from where we had been sitting, in an open blue canvas structure, about eight feet in diameter and five feet high, that was kept full of cold water. Wooden steps with a platform were placed with one half on the ground and the other half in the pool like a tripod. On the platform, towering above us, stood Mr Critchley, a veteran of the Great War and distinguished cabinet-maker. His main occupation was to teach us carpentry and was invariably dressed in brown overalls and with half a pencil stuck behind his ear. He was more often than not to be found in his workshop brewing evil-smelling glues made from animal bones like a scene from Hogwarts. It occurs to me that all the modern glues—'Superglue' for instance—now available in DIY shops and supermarkets had not been developed on a commercial scale at that time, so we made do with Mr Critchley's gooey concoctions.

However, Mr Critchley was now poised, arms outstretched, with a harness dangling from a long pole. He instructed each of us, in turn, to slip into this contraption, and while he took our weight we splashed about in the water and attempted to perform the breast-stroke. The exercise worked for some but not for me. It was freezing cold, the harness dug into my chest and armpits and, as I describe it today, various instruments of mediaeval torture come to mind. It probably triggered my intense dislike of swimming in the British Isles that remains with me to this day.

One afternoon a sudden high-pitched shriek startled everyone in the vicinity of the terrace.

'Watch out!' someone else yelled at the top of their voice.

But it was too late.

An unfortunate boy had been leaning against the side of the pool and carelessly pressed a spiked cricket boot against the taut canvas. The wall instantly ruptured, causing hundreds of gallons of water to cascade down the terrace, washing away everything in its path. It was a miracle that no one was harmed or even killed.

Later, under interrogation, the culprit swore that it was an accident, although we all had our doubts.

Facing away from the house and down the valley, towards the South Downs, a gigantic beech tree close to Nelson's walk—an avenue of fine beeches—and nicknamed the 'Signature Tree', dominated the view. It was so named because dozens of boys had carved their initials deep into the bark, a practice that still continued. Beyond the beech, the edge of the estate was determined by a ha-ha, an artificial precipice and clever device first introduced to England by the Normans but developed by eighteenth-century landscape designers to create an uninterrupted vista from country house estates into surrounding parkland while protecting the property from incursion by cattle and other quadrupeds. A less than sober partygoer, tumbling off the edge of the lawn, would be greeted by his peers with raucous jeers of 'Ha! Ha!' On the far side of the ha-ha lush green fields ran down towards more woodland and among the trees was a lake that the school also used for bathing.

As I settled in, bouts of homesickness that I had suffered wore off, by and large, and I became conditioned to my new way of life. I had no choice but to tolerate it and, of course, I was terrified of 'letting the side down'; my parents in particular. It never occurred to me that it was strange to be sent away from home at the age of seven. It was the way people like us did things and I came to accept that one day I would leave Ashfold and go to my 'big school'.

I do remember musing about why we were here at all—on this planet, I mean. Early indications of a search for 'the miraculous'? I wonder.

> And this is all, for this we're born
> To weep a little and to die!
> So sings the shallow bard whose life
> Still labours at the letter I
> (Richard Burton: *The Kasidah* of Haji Abdul El-Yezdi)

I also became familiar with the school hierarchy. Ashfold had been founded in 1927 and was owned by Messrs Harrison, Seccombe and Sykes. Harrison had greying slicked-back hair and a son at Oxford who used to turn up, wearing college cap and cricket togs, in a nippy, open-top sports car, nicknamed 'the thunder bug'. Jim Harrison had been inspired to found the school by a Miss Bella Rennie who was Montessori-trained and had persuaded him to study the Dalton Plan, a revolutionary education system developed in Massachusetts after the Great War. Harrison duly visited the United States and the Dalton Plan was the basis for education at Ashfold. More of the Dalton Plan later.

Meire Seccombe was tall and smoked a pipe and Dick Sykes had a bad limp caused by war wounds. Harrison and Seccombe seemed remote and forbidding and were capable of wielding a slipper or a fierce cane when required, which tended to be their only contact with the smaller boys. Sykes looked after Dragons and encouraged me in all my endeavours during the early days.

They enjoyed entertaining parents to drinks, many of whom were very well-connected and whose names reflected the history of our sceptred isle from Normans to Victorians. Cecil, Cadogan, de Mowbray, Hankey, Rainey, Rufus Isaacs were surnames that featured on the school noticeboards, along with one, Oliver Hoare, whose path I was to cross again years later.

In 1956, during the Suez Crisis, Sir Robert Menzies, the Prime Minister of Australia, visited the school, where his nephews were being educated.

The smallest boys were under the care of Miss Elmes, a teacher and invaluable asset to the school. She taught us the three Rs and general subjects and acted as a quasi-mother figure. Entering her classroom, we knew we were in friendly territory although she would not tolerate any nonsense.

The best time of the week was Saturday mornings. Sinbad, her brown curly-haired poodle—more like a small bear than a dog—would be in his accustomed place, stretched out across her desk.

'Please can we stroke Sinbad?' we implored our kindly teacher before lessons began.

'Give him a biscuit—just one, if you like,' she would reply, rummaging in a large tin.

If our work, during the previous five days, had been satisfactory, Miss Elmes would take down a heavy volume from the shelf above her desk and, as a reward, read aloud, enthralling us with dramatic tales from the Arabian Nights. The exploits of Sinbad the Sailor, Haroun el-Rachid, Ali Baba and Aladdin captivated us until the bell rang for lunch. Images of flying carpets, vast treasures, dreamy palaces, spells and Jinns teemed in our brains as we made our way to the dining room. Another favourite was Leigh Hunt's poem, 'Abou Ben Adhem', which Miss Elmes had learned by heart.

Magical, I thought, each time that she recited the poem, but who was Abou Ben Adam? What a strange name. Young children can find new names difficult and I am reminded of the story of the mother who took her small son for a walk in the country. Coming across a dead rabbit, she pointed and said, 'That's dead.'

'Hello, Dead!' replied the little boy

Little did I realise how stories from Arabia and other dusty lands would, in due course, become part of my life and influence me enormously. It would be some years before I learned about the occurrence, in Arabic, of the application of consonant roots (two, three or four)—BRK in 'Baraka' for instance—that provide a huge range of associated words or phrases that can build up a mosaic of powerful or poetic images. To my knowledge, there is nothing in Western literature that approaches this concept in terms of sophistication.

Music, taught by a petite bird-like lady called Miss Ticehurst, played an important part in the curriculum. My first formal musical education commenced with beating the triangle and tambourine in the percussion band while she bashed out Mozart's 'Turkish March' on the piano. Fun indeed;

and it was not long before I made friends with Benjie Harrison who had entered the school at the same time as I had and also enjoyed music. His mother had a friend who would visit regularly and who liked nothing better than to while away the afternoon at the piano. This fascinated me and she introduced me to simple pieces. She also recommended a series of books written for children by Opal Wheeler and Sybil Deucher (Faber & Faber) that described the lives of famous musicians. Over the years, I collected these biographies and have them to this day. They have quaint titles such as *Sebastian Bach: The Boy from Thuringia, Handel at the Court of Kings* and the very non-PC *Joseph Haydn: The Merry Little Peasant.* Appropriate examples of their composition were included. This was 1954, and senior boys, who had noticed my books when I read them in bed or in the library and had seen me at the piano, found this all rather 'wet', which led to unpleasant teasing, even bullying, but when—horror of horrors—they found that I possessed a book on ballet, that was the very last straw.

My parents were keen on ballet and we had been to see *Coppelia* and other productions in London. Fortunately, the bullies never discovered that, at my mother's behest, I had taken ballet lessons in Rochester with another boy called Rodney. I wonder how he turned out. My spine tingles in horror at the thought of such a revelation.

Several of the bullying incidents occurred while I plodded across the fields on my way back from the lake. On the first occasion I was tricked into taking hold of the wire of the electric fence that kept cattle out of the woods.

'Don't worry, it won't hurt,' the boys said reassuringly.

'If you grab the wire *through* your wet bathing trunks, you *won't* get a shock!'

A few weeks, later some older boys accused me of giving them 'cheek' and ritually 'bumped' me in several slushy cowpats. I was covered in shit from head to toe but on that occasion I got my own back. Resisting the immediate urge to shed my soiled boiler suit and take a bath, I crept down to the stream where the big boys had been building elaborate dams in the mud. Viciously, I destroyed every vestige of their creations while they were back at the house, as was usual at that time of day, scoffing sticky buns and slaking their thirst with lemonade from opaque plastic jugs, oblivious to my vengeful acts.

I don't remember the names of all the boys involved. I quickly scarpered, and no one to this day knows that it was me, but I met one of them at a party in London, years later.

'I don't think we were very nice to you,' he said. 'I am so sorry.'

Boys in groups can turn nasty, as was graphically described by William Golding in his novel, *Lord of the Flies*, which was published at about this time. I don't know why I was picked on, except to say that gangs look for a scapegoat, the music and ballet did not help, and I was a bit of a fumbler, for reasons that would soon become clear.

The most colourful member of the staff was Lewis Creed, the art master, a man with curly hair, a pointy face, and a sharp tongue when provoked, but whose enthusiasm for his subject was boundless. It was not long before he was encouraging my class to experiment with poster paints and lino cuts and he also initiated us to the mysteries of the potter's wheel. We started to churn out all sorts of clay artefacts that he dutifully loaded into the school's Dodge for the weekly trip to the kiln in Horsham. All this activity spawned presents that proudly and inevitably turned up for parents and others at Christmas and birthdays and were cherished for years to come!

Creed's energy also led elsewhere. When the playing fields were sodden and unusable, a notice would appear outside the dining room, in his unique black broad italics, announcing a 'Creedo ramble'. Conducted at a good pace; this was an excursion into the surrounding countryside where much of the terrain was interwoven with muddy brooks flowing into Hammer Ponds, the woodland lakes that had played an important part in the Sussex Weald's iron-smelting industry for 2000 years. Dressed in blue shorts, rugby shirts and plimsolls, the intrepid Creedo taking the lead, and yelling, 'Keep up the back—keep up the back' at the top of his voice, we charged along lanes, across fields, down slippery banks and through bogs and streams, often finding ourselves up to our thighs in water and mud. Finally, soaked to the skin, and with our legs and arms bloodied by briars, brambles and branches, we arrived back at school and tumbled into a hot bath, thoroughly satisfied by our exertions. No 'risk assessment' and 'health and safety' there. Thank God!

The terms were punctuated by 'Exeats', when my parents scooped me up in the Hillman Minx, where I was greeted by Billy Brock who licked me all

over. We made for Brighton where we spent too much money in the amusement arcades on the pier!

These days always ended with floods of tears and heart-rending farewells
as we stood in the driveway back at Ashfold. Although I had become reasonably happy at Ashfold, these occasions flooded one's consciousness with the
familiar 'home' world that I had left behind—hence the tears.

I wondered what Mrs Matcham was thinking.

Important weekly events were the opening of the tuck shop on
Wednesdays and Saturdays. This was not strictly a shop, but twice a week
lines of colourful boxes appeared on the scrubbed tables in the dining room
and we were allocated a few pence from our pocket money to buy sweets.
After years of rationing, we overdosed. God indeed knows what they did to
our teeth, and I would pay dearly!

When the evenings drew in, there were regular film shows in the panelled English Room. Small boys like me were supposed to sit on the hard
wood floor in the lotus position but we still enjoyed our introduction to the
Marx Brothers or thrillers, with Raymond Huntley playing an urbane policeman as his black Wolseley—like the one that Gawky drove—squealed and
swerved through the streets of London.

I vaguely recall a film called *Never Take No for an Answer* (1952), which
featured an Italian orphan boy and his donkey's visit to the Pope, and the
1950 version of *King Solomon's Mines*. Another hit which appealed to our
burgeoning sense of true Brit grit was the Technicolor feature film *Scott of
the Antarctic* (1948), starring John Mills. A little-known actor, named Barry
Letts, who later directed the *Doctor Who* six-part television adventure *The
Enemy of the World* in 1967, played the part of Apsley Cherry-Garrard, one
of the youngest members of Scott's ill-fated team. Cherry, as he was widely
known, wrote *The Worst Journey in the World*, arguably among the most
famous and successful travel books ever written, which went on sale in 1922
for a few guineas and a first edition, in good condition, can now command
thousands of pounds.[2] When I relayed the nail-biting events of Scott's tragic
saga, as I had seen them on film, to my mother, she pointed out that the
Cherry-Garrards were linked to our family by marriage.

'Apsley's parents attended Gawky and Baba's wedding in 1907', she informed me.

Every November, there was a spectacular bonfire in the grounds and
as parents, boys and staff munched on jacket potatoes and gobbled up hot

chipolatas, we ooed, ahhed and cheered as rockets, thunderclaps, Catherine wheels and all kinds of incendiaries exploded over the south terrace.

In November 1955, at Sunday assembly, Mr Harrison, dropped a bombshell of his own. To our huge surprise and immense shock he announced, before the whole school, that the lease had run out on the estate; 'Smith's place', as he called it. Ashfold as we knew it was to close and reopen in January at new premises in Buckinghamshire. That night, autumn gales blew hard from the south-west and the sturdy 'Signature Tree' bowed and creaked as the wind whipped across the Weald. In the dorm heavy wooden venetian blinds, a legacy from the wartime blackout, swung out across the sill, and the tooth mugs and their contents cascaded on to the floor. It was whispered that the ghost of Mrs Matcham was at large. Perhaps she was sorry to see us go.

Not long afterwards the fine house, in an act of unspeakable criminality, was razed to the ground.

Concurrent with the school change we also moved, from Rochester to London. My mother had never felt really at home in Albany Road, which was something that increasingly worried my father, and when an opportunity to move presented itself my parents acted. They released some capital from her grandmother's trust and my father was able to buy himself into Davies's Tutors Ltd which administered several schools in London, Cambridge and Brighton. He became a company director as well as a schoolmaster. In later years, I concluded that the former role did not suit him at all, although he made a valiant effort.

We moved into a spacious flat on the top two floors, above Sussex House Preparatory School in Cadogan Square. My mother was now in her element and although the flat came with my father's job, I doubt if it occurred to her that she lacked the income to match living at one of the smartest addresses in London. She just felt happy to be back in the stylish world that had been denied her for too long. After all, we were not that far from the Monkey Club, the fashionable finishing school in Knightsbridge that she had attended and Berkeley Square where she had so often danced the night away during grim times in the 1940s that, ironically, provided some of the happiest moments of her young life.

Several weeks after we moved to Chelsea and two months before my ninth birthday, my father and I were walking down Pont Street when he pointed up to the guttering on the newly constructed St Columba's Church. The date 1955 was inscribed in gold on each of the hoppers.

'Can you see that date?' he asked idly.

I strained my eyes to try and read it.

'No! No!' I stammered, somewhat alarmed.

It suddenly and dramatically became obvious that my vision was poor and an appointment was made for an eye test. It was soon confirmed by the oculist that I was long-sighted and had an astigmatism. Several weeks later, when my wire-rimmed NHS spectacles were fitted and the surgery door closed behind me, I was astonished to register the chips in the tarmac in the street and to observe details in familiar objects that I had not noticed before.

'You'll never get into the Navy now,' my mother told me.

'Daddy is very disappointed.'

It was a comment that surprised me. Aged eight, I had never shown any inclination to follow a naval career. In fact, it was the last thing that I would have wanted to do.

I was also hurt. Somehow this incident had exposed a gulf between us which pained me. Years later, a friend of mine who taught at Marlborough College threw out the line, 'naval fathers are always the most difficult!'

In hindsight, I often wonder how this situation was allowed to occur and why my poor sight had not been noticed previously. I had certainly suffered because of it but, of course, routine medical tests were not conducted on children as they are today. Wearing glasses revolutionised my life and for the first time I was able to see the blackboard clearly. Reading, writing and other schoolwork rapidly improved. Years later when educational psychology became more advanced and I was able to study such things, particularly the work of Robert Ornstein, it became apparent that while my spatial and imaginative capacities had developed normally, arithmetical ability and other areas that depended on close work, especially if it did not particularly excite me, had lagged behind. I have come to believe that this was why I had suffered so much pain in the classroom in the early days and because the urge to escape from those situations became a habit, I needed to apply myself, harder than most, when studying subjects that I found especially difficult. In modern terminology, I tended to be more right-brained than left-brained. My days of fumbling the cricket ball were over, but I had to be more careful when ragging and scrapping with friends.

The mother of my chum, Christopher Olgiati was not infrequently on the line to apologise to my mother and to offer to pay for damage when my spectacles had been flattened in a brawl. As my mother had been quite content for me to wear NHS glasses, I don't expect much expense was incurred.

In January 1956, I travelled to the now defunct Dorton Halt from Marylebone station. The new Ashfold was in a fine Jacobean mansion and had been completed in 1626. It featured huge rooms with oak-panelled walls and long corridors whose wide floorboards creaked underfoot. The house was six miles from Thame, at the end of a long drive, near the dreary hamlet of Dorton (which was registered as Dortone in the Domesday Book or Book of Winchester).

There was an attractive old church in the grounds, used for worship by the school, converted stables with a clock over the arched entrance that housed larger workshops for the music and carpentry departments, and a quick-flowing stream that ran through the property. Creedo adapted his rambles and carefully housed a new kiln in the art school, but otherwise the routine continued as normal.

I had a new teacher, Crispian Graves, and was introduced to the Dalton Plan, whose chief feature was to allow one to write one's own timetable by completing a chart at the beginning of each week. This suited some boys— the more organised ones—better than others. Boys were also encouraged to write reports on their teachers at the end of term, a practice which I found rather odd—how honest could one or should one be?

I remember Mr Graves as a truly dedicated and kindly schoolmaster. His nickname, 'Sausages, Crisp-in-Gravy' would be of no surprise and he memorably introduced me to Shakespeare's *Henry V*:

> 'And Crispin Crispian shall ne'er go by
> From this day to the ending of the world,
> But we in it shall be remembered.'
> (Shakespeare, *Henry V*, act IV, scene 3).

His style of teaching seared vivid images into my brain. Scenes of small boys climbing over piles of desks and chairs as we acted out Horatio's gallant defence of the bridge, described by Lord Macaulay in the first verse of his 'Lays of Ancient Rome', are unforgettable.

'Lars Porsena of Clusium
By the nine gods he swore
That the great house of Tarquin
Should suffer wrong no more.'

Stirring words and that name, Tarquin—I would return to Macaulay in later life, in circumstances that could not possibly have been foreseen.

Graves also encouraged sport and before long I was a member of the under-eleven football team. Initially, there were no swimming facilities at the new Ashfold. This did not concern me as, I was pleased to discover that an uncultivated area had been set aside for boys to construct small gardens in our spare time. Inspired by my grandmother, I started to plan and dig with vigour; my main aim being the production of a crop of vegetables. In due course, lettuces, radishes, carrots and beans were poking up through the chalky soil. Enthusiasm getting the better of me, I sent off a magazine coupon and postal order to Carter's Tested Seeds in Rayne's Park, whose premises we often passed when driving to Lodsworth on the A3. Expecting a few selected packets, I was hugely embarrassed when a lorry trundled up to the house and the driver appeared with several sacks of industrial-quality sugar beet seeds with my name on the labels.

One day, during the summer of 1956, while exploring the nearby terrain, I fell over a barbed-wire fence, ripping a large patch of skin from my thigh. It was very painful and I still bear the scar. Showers and baths were banned for a week and it necessitated a course of daily penicillin jabs, deep into my backside.

'Trousers and pants, off', demanded Doctor Beer, the school's medical practitioner, who was very attentive; unforgettably so, given his proclivity for chewing raw garlic. Neither is his basset hound forgotten, who followed him faithfully around the grounds.

My friend Lorne Nelson tried to cheer me up.

'How about coming to stay with me in Argyll during the holidays?' he said.

I couldn't believe my good fortune. 'Wow! That sounds fantastic! Can't wait,' I exclaimed. 'I'll have to check with my people but I'm sure it will be fine.'

At the end of term, my father took us to Euston and we boarded the night train to Glasgow. It was all very exciting as we approached the wheezing, snorting leviathan standing at the platform, and the cosy twin-berth compartment was just like the description in 'Skimbleshanks', my father's favourite from *Old Possum's Book of Practical Cats*. I had heard T.S. Eliot's poem so often that I could recite it verbatim, and did so in the dorm at Ashfold.

> Oh it's very pleasant when have found your little den
> With your name written up on the door.
> And the berth is very neat with a newly folded sheet
> And there's not a speck of dust on the floor.
> There is every sort of light—you can make it dark or
>   bright;
> There's a button you can turn to make a breeze.
> There's a funny little basin you're supposed to wash your
>   face in
> And a crank to shut the window if you sneeze.
> Then the guard looks in politely and will ask you very
>   brightly
> 'Do you like your morning tea weak or strong?'
> But Skimble's just behind and was ready to remind him.
> For Skimble won't let anything go wrong.
>
> 'He gives one flash of his glass-green eyes
> And the signal goes 'All clear!'
> And we're off at last for the northern part
> Of the Northern Hemisphere!
> (T.S. Eliot: 'Skimbleshanks')

We slept soundly, and waking at dawn, I released the window blind to find that we were in wild, open hilly country and startled rabbits with white bobbing tails were scampering away across fields close to the line.

We changed trains at Glasgow, but were soon on our way again, and the next few hours were thrilling as we travelled deeper and deeper into the

Highlands. At one moment we were passing through wooded glens, the next climbing the foothills of granite-faced mountains. We could feel the train straining as it mastered steep gradients before clattering over a score of bridges that spanned frothing mountain torrents. Seconds later, we were on the shoreline of a beautiful blue loch or chugging through yellow gorse and heather-strewn moorland.

We finally arrived at our destination, the village of Taynuilt, a dozen miles from Oban. Lorne's father, who proved to be very much the laird, had sent one of the estate staff to collect us and we squeezed in among the hay bales in the back of an ancient Land Rover for the short journey to Muckairn. Turning off the main road we bumped along the drive for several miles before arriving at the house, which was a huge stone manse, built in the traditional Scottish style.

'Welcome to Muckairn,' announced Lorne's father, who was standing by the front door holding a fishing rod. 'If you've not been to Scotland before, you're in for a treat.'

He was right. The next ten days, spent with Lorne and his sisters Caroline and Kirsty, were to be some of the happiest of my childhood. Every morning, except Sundays of course, began with a stroll down to the gurgling burn where we hauled in a few small brown trout for the breakfast table.

As we swallowed our porridge and munched on fish and drop scones, prepared by the cheerful cook, Loch Etive stretched out before us and on a fine day the snow-capped peak of Ben Cruachan shimmered in the distance. Not wanting to waste a moment, we were soon scampering away from the table. There were literally thousands of acres to explore and we headed up on to the moor or plodded through boggy meads by the edge of the Loch. There were deer in the glens and in many of the more remote parts of the estate. On several occasions we were ordered into the Land Rover to lend a hand in collecting a fallen stag. The deer had been stalked over miles of rough terrain and eventually shot by Lorne's father. It was a shock, on the first occasion, to see a huge, beautiful, noble beast lying motionless in the long grass. Heaving it into the vehicle, we drove back to Muckairn where it was carried, in triumph, to the game room located in the basement of the house. It was like the scene from *The Queen,* the 2006 film starring Helen Mirren where Her Majesty is left alone with a huge stag, hanging in the game room at Balmoral.

We were not invited to shoot, but Lorne had an air gun that provided entertainment as we roamed the property. I am ashamed to say that we threw a stash of old light bulbs into the loch, where they provided admirable targets as they bobbed about in the waves.

The main line to Oban ran through the grounds and we spent a good deal of time waiting for trains to pass. There was a steep cutting, not far from the main road, and it was hugely exciting to linger in the undergrowth until the unmistakable chugging—maybe a whistle—was heard in the distance. We verified that a train was on its way, and from which direction, by lying on the ground and pressing one ear to the cold metal track. As the rail started to vibrate, big pennies were quickly placed in the train's path. Suddenly, the whole might of a huge roaring, hissing and spluttering iron horse burst through the gap in the hillside. Towering above us, smoke and steam belched in every direction and hot cinders cascaded from on high, setting wisps of dry grass alight as it passed by. The pennies flipped and spiralled across the blackened sleepers. In no time at all, engine and carriages were gone and we delved among stone chippings to see just how flat and shiny our coins had become.

One morning, as we sat idly on the railway embankment, Caroline made an unexpected announcement.

'I know where babies come from,' she said.

'Storks bring them,' I rejoined.

'They come from mummies' tummies,' Caroline continued emphatically.

'That's right,' said Lorne. 'After a man and a lady are married they go into a back room and the man shows her his willy. Then they have a baby.'

'Girls don't have willies, see!' butted in little Kirsty as she pulled down her knickers to prove her point.

A few minutes later a train whistled in the distance.

Not many days had passed before we were invited to fish on the River Awe, a swift, wide, rocky stream that runs between Loch Awe and Loch Etive. Donning waders and other traditional gear, I struggled to stand firm against the powerful current as it swirled around deep pools and broke over gigantic boulders. Casting my first fly I was thrilled when, within an hour, I had landed a glistening sea trout. That evening one of the ghillies invited us to his cottage, which smelled of smoky peat and griddled bannocks, where we enjoyed a hearty supper and several hours singing Scottish folk songs.

March no more my soldier laddie,
There is peace where there once was war.
Sleep in peace my soldier laddie
Sleep in peace now the battle's o'er.

My ten days had flown by and on the last night we went to Oban to see the newly released film *Reach for the Sky* (1956), with Kenneth Moore playing the war hero, Douglas Bader. Any schoolboy would have been thrilled as Lorne and I were, although the hospital scenes, when Bader has his legs amputated, gave me nightmares for weeks to come. This was far worse than the big bad wolf that had featured on Gawky's cushions back in Lodsworth.

I was fortunate to make another trip to Muckairn the following year but sadly, when I left Ashfold, Lorne and I lost touch and have not seen each other since 1957. During the 1970s, I learned that Caroline had married Lord Egremont and I like to think that if the path of true love were to tear one away from magical Argyll there could be no finer destination than Petworth, the jewel in the Sussex countryside.

Far away from Scotland or Buckinghamshire, for that matter, trouble was brewing. On 26th July, Colonel Nasser had nationalised the Suez Canal, prompting military action by the Israelis, British and French in the following autumn. During the early period of my life the British Empire had gradually ceased to exist as former colonies and dominions were granted independence. The Suez Crisis was the final nail in its coffin while the Commonwealth was in the process of being born. It had been formally constituted by the London Declaration in 1949.

Military and economic dominance had already passed to the Americans but, by a happy coincidence, Britain was saved from circumstances that could have been so much worse. As Sir William Rees-Mogg and James Dale Davidson say in their book, *Blood In The Streets* (1988), '... the shift to new arrangements was so friendly as to be almost seamless.' What I find particularly fascinating is their further comment:

'What saved matters was a coincidence, the historical equivalent of a coin landing on its edge. For the first time and probably the last, the dominant power was succeeded by another speaking the same language, with a common culture, common legal heritage and very nearly common political and economic ideals.'

In Hungary, also during the autumn, the population had risen against their Soviet masters. The tanks were out and there was fighting and bloodshed on the streets of Budapest. Two hundred thousand refugees left their country, many never to return.

Tucked away in the rarefied atmosphere of a preparatory school, these international events and the tensions of the Cold War largely passed over our heads. We had no access to a television and the newspapers in the library were hogged by the older boys. However, my father, who had lived through two world wars, became alarmed as the clouds of conflict gathered. When petrol rationing was planned—in response to the crisis in the Middle East—he prepared for a threat to our lifestyle, restrictions on travelling and even the possibility that he and my mother would be unable to motor down to Ashfold. In the event, the new limitations did not last long and by May 1957 the Suez Crisis had passed but the Prime Minister, Anthony Eden, had resigned.

For me, however, it was too late. Lunching, one November day, at the Mitre Hotel in Oxford, which was a much smarter establishment than it is today, my parents dropped yet another bombshell. They told me of their decision to withdraw me from Ashfold.

'I'm afraid you will have to leave at Christmas', they informed me.

I was horrified by the news and not at all happy about moving again, but had no say in the matter.

'But what about all my chums?' I implored.

It was no good.

'You'll make new ones,' they said.

It would be many years before my parents wavered from the hard line: 'Mummy and Daddy know best!'

I was to be sent to a prep school in Sussex. In hindsight, I think that the international situation was an excuse, not the real reason. Sussex was where nearly all my relations lived, so we could depend on support from the extended family but it was a preferred venue, anyway, and money may have played a part in the decision. The new place was probably cheaper. In addition, because my father was a strict disciplinarian with a puritanical streak, I think he felt that the tone of the common room at Ashfold was a touch too boozy and convivial for his liking. He avoided the cocktail parties, commenting unfavourably on the lingering waft of stale ale emitting from the common room that greeted him whenever he arrived in the front hall.

We had only been in Buckinghamshire for three terms and although I had suffered some homesickness and unhappy moments in my two and a half years at the school, I was enjoying life there and had made some good friends. Creedo's words, as I climbed into the railway carriage at the end of term, still ring in my ears. He said: 'It's a shame. We have got to know and like you and now you have to go!'

I couldn't have agreed more.

With roots going back to 1808, Fonthill had become a school by 1820, initially in Salisbury and then at Fonthill Gifford (of Beckford fame) in Wiltshire. Initially known as Radcliffe's after its founder the Reverend Dr George Radcliffe, the name Fonthill was established at a later date, and the school moved to East Grinstead in 1885. This is was where I would receive my education for the next four years.

It was 7:15 a.m. on the first day of the Lent term in 1957, and I could hear two servants moving noisily down the corridor outside the dormitories. Inside my new dorm, another 'Blue', nine boys were lying in their iron beds, also awakened by the clatter. At the foot of each bed was a wooden stand with a marble top that supported a large china bowl and jug that was full of cold water. A towel and flannel hung on rails to one side and there was space for a soap dish and mug for toothbrush and paste. Some of the chinaware was plain but a few pieces were pleasantly decorated. These washstands were of the type that can now be picked up in antique shops if you are prepared to pay a pretty price.

Marco and Giuseppe, two young Italians, entered the room carrying large metal watering cans from which they proceeded to fill each boy's bowl with steaming hot water. Their departure was our signal to rise and to move to the washstand where we soaped and rinsed our faces, hands and underarms. Once this ritual was complete, I filled my mug with cold water from the jug and cleaned my teeth, spitting into the dirty soapy water. Some time later, the Italians would return, drain the bowls into buckets and clean the surfaces.

There were no showers and no communal washing facilities in the entire building except in the stone-floored basement, where six cast-iron baths served the whole school. These were only available to the boys in my dormitory on twice weekly 'bath nights'.

These facilities, or lack of facilities, epitomise the extraordinary place in which I now found myself, and the contrast with Ashfold defies description. It was a school that even in the 1950s was still coming to terms with the arrival of the twentieth century, let alone preparing children, both in pastoral and educational terms, for anything approaching the 'modern' world. Compared to the cosy school I had left behind in Bucks, I might as well have been in a time warp and, if my father was seeking a puritan influence, he need have looked no further.

I never knew why my parents chose Fonthill. My mother had been engaged to a man called Richard Carey, a sapper who was killed in Italy during the war. He had attended Fonthill in the '30s before winning a scholarship to Winchester. Perhaps it was a case of what was good enough for him, was good enough for me.

But worse was to come.

An expression in common Fonthill parlance was the 'squits'. This could be used to refer to the most junior boys—and also to the lavatories used by those boys. The latter were always in a disgusting condition. They smelled foul, there was inadequate lighting, and they were usually an inch deep in water—or something. Health and safety? Don't even mention it.

Following breakfast, a matron would be positioned outside the 'squits'. 'Have you been?' she would ask, noting the reply on her clipboard.

The headmaster was an Anglican clergyman by the name of Walpole Sealy. He had been a boy at Fonthill, attended Marlborough (B1 1897) and Oriel College, Oxford and, following his ordination, had returned as chaplain in 1908. After marrying Mary Radcliffe, the daughter of the school's owner, he and his wife had run Fonthill for nearly fifty years and he was seventy-five by the time I enrolled. Thin, of moderate height and with white hair that parted in the centre, he always wore a grey flannel suit, crumpled white shirt, collar and a greasy Old Marlburian tie. Nicknamed 'the Boiler'—why? I know not—he tended to peer through wire-framed spectacles at any small boy that got in his way, muttering 'squits, squits' under his breath.

Administering a strictly authoritarian regime, he was known to give a good wallop with the rung of a ladder if one was unfortunate enough to be summoned to his study for some misdemeanour.

A lesser punishment was to endure 'the Boiler walk'. This meant placing one's head under his arm. Then, pinned close to his side by his elbow and bent double, one was expected to hobble along quickly, keeping pace with 'the Boiler'. Conducted with an element of humour and to the great amusement of bystanders, who were happy to add a sharp whack on the bum, I can hardly say that I enjoyed these demeaning occasions.

'No! No! Sir! Not 'the Boiler' walk, Sir!' the miscreant would beg.

Oh dear! Kurt Hahn, where were you? Hahn regarded corporal punishment to be the very last resort as part of his experiential philosophy.

However, 'the Boiler' had some endearing practices. In the winter terms, because he was too old to run along the touchline, he employed a 'squit' to follow him with a chair. This allowed him to settle at various points during each game. He must have suffered frustration as he had been a keen sportsman in his youth—his father had been an FA Cup-winning football player—and he told me that he had played cricket with Sir Arthur Conan Doyle in the 1890s at Westward Ho! In the summer he could be seen, before breakfast, labouring in the strawberry beds. Then, when all ninety boys were assembled in the schoolroom, he would emerge with a basket brimming with fruit. Each boy would file past to receive one strawberry. If there were any left the older boys got two. One winter's night in 1963, he died in his bed, just across the landing from where my brother was sleeping.

May he rest in peace.

The school's life revolved around the huge first-floor Schoolroom. This was in the Victorian part of the house, and had a high wooden ceiling that ascended to a glazed and leaded folly, far above the roofline of the remaining building. In the centre of the room was a very large mahogany table, and the walls were lined with benches and open shelves where boys kept their personal belongings. It was here that the post was distributed in the morning. Telephone communication was non-existent, so letters from home were eagerly awaited and my mother wrote on Sundays, catching the early evening collection, and on Wednesdays, which meant that a letter would arrive, without fail, on Mondays and Thursdays. My father wrote once a term and on one such occasion, in the winter of 1957, he informed me that his father had died aged eighty-eight and that he would be travelling to Lancashire to attend the funeral. I was not especially affected by this news as I hardly knew my grandfather, a distinguished artist and Royal Acadamician. We had once visited him at his home in Bardsea and he used to come to London for an annual dinner at the Royal Academy, prior to the opening of the Summer Exhibition. My father would collect him from Euston station while my mother shivered in her shoes at Cadogan Square. The gruff, eccentric old boy, aesthete though he was, used to terrify her as he ambled around the flat puffing on his pipe which he kept supplied with a pungent mixture of tobacco, and for reasons of economy, flakes of dried raspberry leaves from his kitchen garden. After staying the night he would return whence he had come. *The Times* obituary which appeared on 6th December recorded that: 'As a landscape painter in oil and watercolour, and as an etcher, Hall had a distinct style of his own … an excellent … draughtsman, particularly in realising the structure of ground and the growth of trees.'

The next headmaster, Kingsley Storey, was a very different character. He unfortunately suffered from Dupuytren's contracture so when we shook hands after prayers at night his gnarled, bent fingers dug into our palms. An untidy man in his late fifties with sandy hair, sallow complexion and freckled arms, he was invariably dressed in an unbuttoned blue aertex shirt, and belt missing several loops in his grey baggy trousers. He smoked a pipe that he frequently placed in his jacket pocket while it was still alight, precipitating the inevitable result. When he did remember to extinguish the embers, in a spectacular pirouette movement he knocked the bowl violently on the heel of his shoe.

For some reason, which is now lost in the mists of history, he was nick-named 'Chore' and, for the most part, ran the day-to-day affairs of the school. He was a kindly man but could explode with a fierce temper. He was strict, and if the general behaviour of the school had upset him he would launch into a fierce tirade, in the schoolroom, after prayers. These 'pie jaws' could be an ordeal as he ranted on, for over an hour, about how dreadful we all were.

He would conclude with the words: 'Now go to bed, you wretched boys and remember what I have been saying!'

We trouped out of the schoolroom and retired to our dormitories. The Italians emerged from their top-floor flat, emitting wafts of garlic and other exceptionally pungent cooking aromas, and turned out the lights. They placed small blue and red enamel oil lamps at strategic positions around the house that flickered in the darkness, casting a warm glow on the walls and ceilings and shadows across the main staircase. I don't think any of us, in a building where only the most rudimentary safety equipment existed, had considered the risk we all faced of being burned alive in our beds.

From time to time, when in a benign frame of mind, 'Chore' would visit a dormitory and, sitting on the end of a bed, tell stories or reminisce about the war and the Battle of Britain that had been fought in the skies above the school. He relayed details of 'red letter days' when shrapnel or a piece of enemy aircraft landed in the grounds, and spoke of Archibald McIndoe, whose work with badly burnt pilots, his 'guinea pigs', at the nearby Queen Victoria Hospital in East Grinstead he greatly admired.

These yarns struck a particular chord with boys who had been reading *Boldness Be My Friend*, by the intrepid Yorkshireman, Richard Pape; one of the more dramatic wartime adventure stories that were doing the rounds in the senior dorms. Richard Pape had been one of McIndoe's guinea pigs and he wrote of the airman's 'indomitable courage and remarkable endurance' in the introduction to Pape's book.

This was the England in which I was raised. As Rupert Brooke wrote in 'The Old Vicarage, Grantchester':

> 'For England's the one land, I know,
> Where men with Splendid Hearts may go.'

If Chore was in an exceptionally teasing frame of mind, he would rag a boy and tickle his ribs until the poor child was close to tears. In an age of innocence, we all joined in the mirth. Today, he would probably be locked up and I know who would be the losers: 'Honi soit qui mal y pense.'

The third headmaster was Ronald Stawt, a tall, bald, austere man; a mathematician, with tiny wire-framed specs, who played a lesser role in the day-to-day running of the school. In later years, he would remind me of P.D. Ouspensky. He was particularly interested in Pythagorean theory and the patterns observed in plants and trees. I chiefly remember him for his practice of keeping a selection of cheeses in a covered china dish together with a few dry biscuits, on the sideboard in the dining room. At lunch, when everyone else had finished their Irish stew, prunes and custard or whatever the good Lord had just provided and for which we duly thanked him, Stawt alone reached for his dish and delicately consumed choice morsels of cheddar or double Gloucester as we all filed from the room.

A kindness that he and his wife performed, was to donate a trowel and fork to help me develop the only boy's flower and vegetable garden at the school, of which I was justifiably proud.

'Capability Hall! We really admire your enthusiasm', they said.

Gawky had given me some dahlia quorns, crysanthemums and pansies so, building on my experience at Ashfold, my horticultural endeavours were becoming more adventurous. In time, I established an impressive little garden in a corner of the estate where no one bothered me.

There were other members of staff who each exhibited a measure of eccentricity and taught in their own distinctive style. Mrs Drinkall was in charge of the juniors—the Fonthill equivalent of Miss Elmes. From her, we learnt everything by rote. My knowledge of the towns and rivers of the British Isles, the countries and cities of Europe, the industries associated with certain towns, the counties, kings and queens (including their dates) of England were all drilled into me by this pleasant and meticulous lady in her sunny classroom. She was friendly with Mr Jeffereys, the maths and junior games master; a large, bluff, good-natured chap with close-cropped white hair. Jeff—as he was known—had fought in the Great War, been in India and travelled a bit. He liked to encourage boys at all times and his booming voice could be heard ringing out across the games field.

'Jaldi, Jaldi,' he would yell, echoing years spent in the subcontinent and spurring us on to greater efforts. He was generous too, and always carried a stash of Crunchie bars in his coat pocket with which he rewarded excellence on the pitch or in the classroom. Oh dear! My teeth did suffer.

The middle-school boys were taught by Miss Wright, a lady of advanced years, frequently encountered in the grounds, furiously pedalling her bicycle with a woolly hat drawn firmly over her forehead. We used nib pens and there were inkwells in all the desks. The spilling of ink could trigger a furious outburst from Miss Wright. Ink and small boys was a dangerous mixture, and it seemed that there were always pools of wet blue liquid on the desk or on the floor. It got on our hands and our clothes, even our faces, constantly making a mess and causing trouble.

My favourite teacher was Michael Cooper, who taught the senior boys history and geography. 'Kips', as he was known, was short, with a huge kedge-belly, accentuated by his habit of wearing tight blue or green shirts that often lacked a button or three. A talented mimic, his jet-black hair and a stub moustache lent themselves to hilarious impressions.

'Please, Sir! Do your Adolf Hitler impression!' We implored him when he was in a good mood.

Educated at Marlborough (C1 1927) and Cambridge, he had spent time during the war at Bletchley Park and being of the generation whose careers had been interrupted by six years of hostilities, I suspect that he found post-war Britain an uncomfortable abode. Like Jim Prideaux in John Le Carre's *Tinker, Tailor, Soldier, Spy*, it was probably inevitable that he became a prep-school master, but he was a brilliant communicator and we sat enthralled when he demonstrated some of the techniques for constructing or break-ing codes. He also adored teaching history and spent hours preparing notes and drawing maps on the blackboard using a wide range of coloured chalks. Then, with the umpteenth cigarette lodged between his yellowing fingers, he would expound on the chosen topic of the day. I particularly remember a whole term spent detailing the course of the Great War. I owe him a debt of gratitude for lessons that awakened a fascination with times past, and still have the notes that he provided.

One day, as a prank, I slipped a tiny 'banger' into the end of one of his cigarettes while the packet lay open on his desk during break. Such devices were available at any shop that sold tricks, party jokes and novelties. When he returned to continue his lecture the whole class waited with bated breath and, as he lit his first cigarette, there was a sharp pop and grains of tobacco cascaded all over his papers.

Kips was none too pleased.

'Who is responsible? Own up,' he scowled.

I spent the next Saturday afternoon laboriously producing 500 lines that read:

I MUST NOT TOUCH ANY TEACHER'S PERSONAL PROPERTY.

'That was a bit of a bish!' I confided to my friend, Nicholas Parks.

When classes were over for the day, he was off, gently swaying on his white Lambretta—a hilarious sight indeed—to spend most evenings at the Dorset Arms, from whence he returned late. One exception to this routine was when, as the bats ('fluttermice' in olde Sussex) flitted from the eaves on summer evenings, he played croquet with the older boys on the lawn behind the house. He was a dab hand at this apparently sedate occupation, which can turn quite vicious, and would prepare for the games by consuming a bottle or two of stout that he kept concealed under straw, in the wooden Jaques box where the equipment was stored.

Latin and Greek were taught to the older boys by Chore, in his lair at the top of the house. This small classroom, which reeked of pipe tobacco, was piled high with papers of every description and festooned with used Roneo stencil sheets that were hanging out to dry. In one corner, among old Common Entrance and Greek scholarship papers, he kept a couple of swishy canes. On one occasion when he was away for the weekend, a friend and I thought it amusing to fence with his canes. Unfortunately, another boy sneaked on us when he returned. Summoned to his room he barked, 'I hear you have been playing with my canes.'

'Yes sir, just having some fun,' I replied.

'In that case, I shall have some fun and use one on you. Come back after evening prayers.'

One of the worst aspects of receiving a beating—and it wasn't the first or last time—was the agonising wait in the corridor, prior to execution, more often than not dressed only in thin cotton pyjamas.

'One ... two ... three ... four ... five ... six.'

'Yow! That hurt!'

I slipped out of the room with my tail between my legs.

The payback was showing off the six livid purple wheals on one's bum at bath time.

Considering the lack of facilities we kept remarkably busy and extraordinarily cheerful and I became quite fond of the place. But with the benefit of hindsight, it beggars belief that any parent would have sent their child to such a weird establishment and I wonder if some eccentricities rubbed off on me. In my time, there was no science on the curriculum, bicycles were not allowed, there was no tree-climbing, only rudimentary carpentry and art, no orchestra or percussion group and no Guy Fawkes parties. The only recreational amenities were extensive games fields, a sizeable swimming pool and a handicraft room tucked away under the eaves on the top floor. This was used for classes in basket-weaving and became a secret rendezvous for smoking. In the absence of cigarettes we puffed away on short lengths of thick raffia.

Someone always kept 'cave', but it is probably because Marco and Giuseppe and their splendid wives were invariably making such a din while they concocted their evening meals, releasing gut-wrenching culinary odours into the corridors, that we were never discovered and it was another miracle that the school was not set alight.

The schedule on weekdays was tight. After prayers and breakfast there were lessons until lunch with a short break at eleven that gave us the opportunity to drink the free, government-supplied milk that arrived each day in crates. This was the practice that Mrs Thatcher stopped for seven-year-olds and above in November 1971, causing huge political ructions. She was the Secretary of State for Education at the time and earned the sobriquet of, 'Margaret Thatcher, Milk Snatcher'. After lunch a rest on our beds was mandatory, followed by games. More work and prep followed as the day went by.

Sunday was different. After breakfast we were obliged to read the Bible or learn the catechism before matins in the pretty wooden chapel on the edge of the wilderness. The service was conducted by 'the Boiler' and attended by the whole school.

We also had visitors from Standen, a magnificent house that was only a mile away and set in lovely grounds overlooking Weir Wood reservoir. It was built for James Beale between 1892 and 1894 by the architect Philip Webb, a lifelong friend of William Morris. Beale had accumulated a fortune from his legal work for the burgeoning late Victorian railway companies. Standen provided a splendid home for his seven children and in the late 1950s his two unmarried daughters still inhabited the house. The prim Misses Beales used to walk over from their fine property to attend our chapel services. When they eventually died, the estate was gifted to the National Trust and it now a shrine to the Arts and Crafts movement and William Morris in particular. It is well worth a visit. Morris attended Marlborough College (JH) from 1848–1851, where he later installed a fine stained-glass window, designed by Sir Edward Burne-Jones, in the chapel. Beale sent one of his sons to Marlborough and several grandsons followed. Burne-Jones sent his son, Philip, to Marlborough (C3 1874).

After the service, boys could go out with parents providing that they were back for evensong. For those remaining there was always ice cream for lunch and then, on winter afternoons, after compulsory letter-writing, we lined up in a traditional crocodile for a walk down the lane. This led us past Saint Hill Manor that was owned by the Maharaja of Jaipur, whom I used to see playing polo at Cowdray Park. He was soon to sell the property to Ron Hubbard's Scientologists and I believe they still own it. Eventually we reached Weir Wood reservoir where we climbed on the steep sandstone outcrop of rocks that towered above the lake. Across the water and some miles into the Ashdown Forest lay Prime Minister Harold Macmillan's country estate at Birch Grove. When the Conservatives won the General Election in 1959, it was announced in the schoolroom.

'I think we should go over to Macmillan's place and cheer,' enthused 'the Boiler'.

The Tories' return to power, had been a foregone conclusion as the country was passing through a phase of post-war prosperity; a fact that Macmillan emphasised in a memorable speech at Bedford on 20th July 1957. He said: 'Let's be frank about it; most of our people have never had it so good.'

Games were banned on Sundays, but in the summer we were allowed to play in some rough ground to the side of the playing fields where boys had painstakingly constructed miniature mud tracks for racing the sort of Dinky toys that, if kept in their original packaging, would now be worth a fortune. On a hot day I would concentrate on watering my flowers and vegetables, a laborious duty as the nearest tap was five hundred yards from the garden.

The only other approved activity was 'strolling' around the games pitches, hardly an occupation that would appeal to modern youth.

One sultry afternoon in 1959, I was 'strolling' with my friend AT. Bored out of our juvenile minds the conversation turned unexpectedly smutty.

'Have you ever tried rubbing your cock when it's stiff?' he enquired, lowering his voice.

'No! Never! Should I?' I replied, somewhat shocked and wondering where this was going.

'Try it,' he continued. 'Give it a firm rub for a few minutes and you'll get a lovely sensation from head to toe.

He went on explain what that was all about. That night, after lights out, feeling decidedly guilty, I tried it. He was right.

Adieu, innocence.

'I'm a man! A real man!' I muttered to myself as I drifted into a deep sleep.

After 'strolling', television was becoming popular and at 5 p.m. we crowded into a small room to watch *Crackerjack*, *Juke Box Jury*, *Dixon of Dock Green*, *Wells Fargo* or *The Lone Ranger*. The tales of *Jennings and Darbishire* was a favourite although this may have been because the series was filmed by the BBC at Fonthill and some of us took part as extras.[3]

Back to chapel, we attended evensong. As the sun set beyond the stained glass windows, the singing of 'Abide with Me', 'The Day Thou Gavest, Lord, is Ended' and similar hymns engendered that mushy religious feeling that I came to distrust in later years. It would take a touch of 'the miraculous' to get over that one.

Attending evensong was compulsory but on one occasion, Jonathan Mills missed the service. Later in the evening, as monitor of the day, I was handed a note. It read: 'Please excuse Jonathan for missing evensong. We were unavoidably detained by Mr Walt Disney', and was signed 'John Mills'.

Jonathan, a flaming redhead, was our token celebrity and his sister Juliet was a favourite pin-up. Their sister Hailey had made her film debut as an infant but came to prominence in *Tiger Bay* (1959) and shot to superstardom in *Pollyanna* in 1960, the year I left Fonthill. My brother was friendly with the family and tells me that Hailey was the first girl he kissed.

On one occasion the famous actor attended an entertainment, during which I had recited some poetry. After the performance he came up to me and praised the clarity of my delivery. Perhaps I have missed my vocation.

It was the Lent term of 1960. Three years had passed since I had arrived at Fonthill as a 'squit' and if things went to plan this would be my last year. Aged thirteen, I was due to take Common Entrance in the autumn and, providing that I averaged 70%, I would pass into Marlborough. My brother Richard had just joined me and I was now Hall Major, and a monitor, while he was Hall Minor, a lack of distinction that must have irked him.

An age gap of four and a half years caused tensions. It seemed that I was always just leaving one developmental stage as he was growing into it. While I had been at boarding school for five years, he was still at home with my parents. However, I was pleased that he was now at Fonthill, not least because I was often able to persuade him to pump the bellows for the chapel organ. Thanks to Chore's encouragement, and Dennis Hunt's enthusiasm (when I was at home in Chelsea), I had started to play the 'king of instruments' and took every opportunity to scuttle over to chapel for a practice.

My general confidence grew and I acquired the sobriquet 'Bumptious'.

In many ways I had cause for confidence. My best friend was head boy and all my other pals were monitors. During the years I had gradually honed my games skills and after many a damp or freezing afternoon on the playing fields I earned my colours for hockey and football. I played on the right wing, in both sports, and was considered to be exceptionally fast. We all enjoyed away matches and Fonthill organised these in typically eccentric style. No stuffy coaches for us; the teams were chauffeured around the Sussex countryside in antiquated black taxis, hired from a local firm. When visitors came for home matches we always provided the best tea on the circuit and a crunchy cake made of a concoction of chocolate and cornflakes was a speciality. Sometime my parents came to watch a match and after a muddy game and a decent shower at Brambletye or Ashdown House we went for high tea in East Grinstead. These occasions were only marred by excruciatingly painful chilblains that were aggravated on cold days by woolly games socks and open fires. The condition became so acute that I had to be given injections to stimulate my circulation. Autumn evenings, with parents in town, might suggest a visit to the cinema but this was forbidden. There was always the fear of bringing germs back to the school and starting an epidemic. Matron kept a sharp watch on our health and anyone who was poorly was required to queue for a daily dessertspoonful of gooey brown malt extract. Notwithstanding the embargo; I recall that, on one occasion, my mother led my father and me astray.

'Come on', she said, egging us on. 'No one will see us. There's a good picture playing'. So, we slipped into East Grinstead's Radio Cinema to see Dick Powell, Robert Mitchum and Kurt Jurgens in *The Enemy Below* (1957), a powerful war film.

The First Eleven cricket, football and hockey teams were run by Mr Fox who played an active part as umpire or referee. An Old Etonian, inexplicably known as 'Chox', he occupied a comfortable house on the edge of the playing fields that he shared with live-in servants. He seemed much richer than anyone else and was always immaculately attired in dark tailored suits, drove the smartest and most comfortable car and smoked large cigars whose expended stubs could be found and gathered at the wicket, on summer evenings, when the match was over. He had a small grey moustache and his slicked-back hair was smarmed down with a pungent preparation, the fragrance of which lingered wherever he went. He did not appear to have any job besides running our games, although it was rumoured that he dabbled in the stock market. On days when there had been a match, he attended evening prayers in the Schoolroom and, standing with his back to the fireplace, presented a short report. He took a lot of trouble with these observations and would describe the game in detail. An extract might read like this:

'... and then Stan, dribbling down the right wing, neatly outmanoeuvred the opposing back before deftly scooping the ball into the centre, ready for Nicholas Parks to slam it between the posts.'

Who was Stan?

It was Fox's nickname for me, after our hero Sir Stanley Mathews, the first professional footballer to be knighted, the 'wizard of dribble 'and Stoke City's star player for thirty-three years.

One dark evening in February 1958, he suddenly appeared in the Schoolroom wearing a smart full-length overcoat.

'I have something very sad to tell you,' he announced, and then went on to relay the news that seven members of the Manchester United football team—the Busby Babes—had been killed in a plane crash at Munich. Things like that weren't meant to happen. We were shocked and trailed off to bed in silence.

In November, the day finally arrived for my chums and me to take the Common Entrance examination. This reckoning had loomed for a long time, but was now upon us. I was fairly confident—even though the required pass mark for Marlborough was one of the highest in the public-school system at the time—but in the event performed exceptionally well in my best subjects but dismally in Latin, maths and French.

After an anxious week, I was given the results and told that Marlborough wanted to interview me before making a decision. Clearly, they found it difficult to reconcile an outstanding performance in history, geography, English and scripture, together with my musical and sporting ability, with some other really dreadful marks. I travelled to London by train and the next day my parents and I drove down to Wiltshire. Spotting the Pelican Inn at Froxfield, on the Bath Road, seven miles from Marlborough, my mother—always up for a drink—blurted out:

'Hey! There's a pub. Let's stop for a brandy—it will do us all good!'

We quaffed down the strong liquor, shivering in the cold as I was too young to enter the bar, and arrived at the Master's Lodge with the taint of alcohol upon our breath. Whether this was noticed, I shall never know, but I was interviewed by Reginald Jennings, the tall, awe-inspiring registrar who had occupied every conceivable office at the College since his arrival in 1927, and Douglas Quadling, the aptly named Head of Maths. Quadling, without doubt, loved Marlborough, which he had got to know as a boy when billeted in the town with the Johnson family, following the evacuation of his own City of London School from the war torn capital. I was to get to know Alf Johnson, a remarkable character, in due course.

A decision was eventually reached. It was agreed that I would bene-fit from a Marlborough education. Since my IQ was considerably higher than 115, which was the minimum required for a boy to hold his own at the college, we were not surprised. If, as occurred, the result of my grilling by Quadling and Jennings was favourable, we had hoped for a tour of the College and perhaps even to be introduced to those who would be respon-sible for my future welfare. But it was not to be—an attitude, in hindsight, that indicated trouble ahead. Without further ado, we piled back into the car and headed for London.

'Home, James! We'll open a bottle for dinner tonight!' my parents cho-rused. They meant half a bottle, of course; a bottle would be far too extrava-gant—and I would be allowed half a glass.

What we did not know at the time, which is a pity as my mother would have capitalised on it, was that in Adderley, a fine panelled room, only yards from where I had been interviewed, hung the largest portrait that Gainsborough ever executed. The subject of this picture, painted in 1764, was George Byam and his wife and daughter, who were ancestors of ours through my mother's paternal line (Mathew and Mathew-Lannowe). George Byam's sister, Mary, had married Daniel Mathew, High Sheriff for the County of Essex and grandfather of Sir George Mathew, who had married Anne Hoare in 1836. The Gainsborough had been donated to Marlborough College in 1942, apparently with no strings attached, by benefactor, Turkish scholar and tennis enthusiast H.C. Hony, who also traced his family back to the Byams.

Hony's daughter, Dr Dinah Baxter (who caused a stir when she left the quiet confines of Wiltshire, married a distinguished Jamaican radiologist and produced four coffee-coloured children, as she told me with characteristic candour), has described how the huge portrait was transported through the streets of wartime Marlborough on the back of a hay cart.

This stunning work was sold by the College in 1999, amid considerable controversy and to the horror of the Hony family, to raise funds for a new performing arts centre and swimming pool, and is now on permanent exhi-bition in the Holburne Museum at Bath.

My return to Fonthill was something of a triumph and I was glad to find that all my friends had passed into their chosen schools. I arrived back at the school with cake, half a pound of butter and a pot of honey together with several packets of muffins that we toasted on one of the open fires located in every classroom. A few days later Chox held a splendid dinner for the First Eleven and before we knew it the term had ended and we were saying our goodbyes, swearing eternal fealty.

Sadly, I have to record that almost without exception I never saw any of my chums again.

The next day, as I waited for the taxi that was going to take us to the local station, 'the Boiler' came over to shake my hand and wish me well.

'There are two things that stick in my memory about Marlborough,' he said. 'The first, is the time I managed to hitch a lift in the driver's cab at Savernake station. By the time we got to Marlborough, which is only five miles up the branch line, I had learned to pull the right levers to get the train up the steep gradient, knew how to blow the whistle, and shovelled a few hefty loads of coal into the fire.' He then went on to tell me how he got covered in soot as they went through the new tunnel under the forest that had been opened in 1898 and how the house 'dame' had spotted him, as he crept back into his boarding house, after dark.

'I was "gated" for a month, which meant that I could not leave College property or walk down to the town,' were his last words on the subject before going on to tell me that his chilblains disappeared once he got to Wiltshire. 'I think it was the water from the chalk downs,' he added, thoughtfully.

I was to have the same experience. My chilblains vanished during my first term at the College.

As I climbed into the train at East Grinstead station, Chore presented me with two books. One was a transcript of all the chants used in chapel services that he had laboriously copied in his own hand, and the other was Leslie Bailey's *The Gilbert and Sullivan Story*, in which he had inscribed the dedication, 'Thank ye lad, thank ye, Ruddigore (adapted).'

Two years later, when I visited Fonthill; Chore showed no interest, whatsoever, in me or in anything I was doing. It was a salutary experience to discover that his affections had clearly passed on elsewhere.

Neil aged 4 at King Alfred School

Skating at Plön, 1949 (Paul French: former pupil)

Return to the Quarterdeck in the rain! 2008

Neil aged 5 in Trafalgar Square

Holly Cottage, Lodsworth

Fonthill Frolics, 1958

Neil (left) with Richard and Mother, 1959

Oliver Hall RA (right) with Uncle Gray (Claude Muncaster)

Sussex House (John Evans: former teacher)

Chapter 3
Marlborough

Old Bath Road you have conquered regions
Fenced with forest and sunk in swamp
Rung 'neath the tramp of Roman legions,
Borne the pageant of Norman pomp.
But today from city and town and shire
Hither you bring to your cherished school,
Youth, that may learn the things that are higher
Than Norman splendour and Roman rule.
(C.L.F. Boughey, 'The Old Bath Road' first sung at the
   summer term concert, 1923)

MY NEW LIFE started on the 16th of January 1961, with the familiar firm handshake, and 'good luck, old chap', from Father, and a surreptitious peck on the cheek from Mother, as I bade them farewell on the platform at Paddington.

'Write soon and tell all,' she implored, turning away as tears brimmed from her swollen eyelids. I disappeared into the cramped carriage and at nine minutes past five the Marlborough College Special pulled out of the station and into the cold January night.

A fresh green tweed jacket, pressed black trousers, grey shirt with starched, white, detachable collar and a brass stud that dug into my Adam's apple, and whose keen edge was already etching a red rim around my neck, marked me as a 'new boy'. These items had been purchased at Gorringes in

Victoria, the school outfitters, where tedious shopping trips were relieved only by a visit to the tea rooms for a knickerbocker glory, an exotic fruit concoction topped with a flourish of whipped cream and a bright red cherry.

Once on the Marlborough train, I cast around for a kindred spirit, but to no avail. The half-dozen boys in my warm compartment all seemed to be chums, and were chattering away at the top of their voices. I felt isolated, and with a deep sense of foreboding in the pit of my stomach I feverishly wiped away condensation from the smutty window with a freshly ironed white cotton handkerchief and stared into the abyss. The rooftops, dimly-lit streets, and small, deserted parks of west London were galloping by, punctuated by streams of sparks from the engine.

Some ninety minutes later, as the convivial atmosphere among the old hands became more subdued, we arrived at Marlborough's low-level station on the edge of the brooding dark acres of Savernake Forest. Clouds of steam, smoke and glowing embers swirled into the freezing Wiltshire night sky and several hundred youths disembarked on to the platform. We trudged down the hill in silence, resembling a battalion on its way to the front in 1914. Hockey sticks and squash racquets were silhouetted against yellow streetlights like rifles on parade, and kit was carried in cumbersome canvas bags. Patches of snow piled by the roadside or under hedges gleamed sulphur-white in the semi-darkness.

Eventually, we reached the bottom of the steep incline and, passing across Duck's Bridge, where the Pewsey Road crosses the River Kennet, we approached the College. With no idea of where I was going, except that I was aiming for my boarding house, Elmhurst,[4] I continued; joining the Bath Road at the gates to the Master's Lodge, which I recognised from my visit in the previous autumn. I soon passed under the arched red-brick footbridge, built in 1911—a landmark on the journey from London to Bath. The main gates were a few yards further on, and I sought directions.

'Three hundred yards, on your right and then up the drive,' the uniformed porter at the Lodge informed me. Breathless, I eventually arrived at Elmhurst and rang the bell. A man whom I had never met before, but correctly assumed to be the housemaster, came to the door.

'Ah, you must be Hall, come in.'

He led me into the house and introduced me to his wife. 'This is Hall,' he said. 'He came down from Paddington on the Special.'

'Hello, Hall!' she replied. 'High tea is being served in College; you had better follow the others.'

In those days, the College operated a Junior House system, which meant that the first year was spent with one's own age group, before moving to Senior House where, in a sense, one became a new boy all over again. Elmhurst housed a dozen or so thirteen and fourteen-year-olds, the smallest community in the school, split into two dormitories. Everyone else had assembled by the time I arrived, and off we went together, back through the main gates, for high tea in the College dining hall. This huge building, not dissimilar to a Victorian railway shed, with tall iron pillars and girders supporting a wooden roof, had been built in 1846, three years after the founding of the school.

In April 1846, Thomas Burn, a boy at the College whose letters I was to come across in the museum at Rugby School thirty years later, writing to his sister, had said, 'We actually had tea in the new dining room and we had breakfast and dinner there today. The new hall is an immense place with a vaulted roof, it looks very nice indeed.'

Entering the crowded, noisy building, a sour odour struck us. This, I later discovered, emanated from splattered rancid butter spats that generations of Marlburians had mischievously knife-flicked into the grooves and crevices of the ceiling.

The hall's days were numbered and it was soon to be torn down, rendering Court, the central open area of the College, a building site for several years to come as its replacement (the Norwood Hall) was built. A tall building with high ceilings, the rancid butter disappeared forever.

After tea and a long tiring day, new boys gathered in the music school for a voice test. It was there that I first met Anthony Smith-Masters (ABS-M), the portly, silver-haired Assistant Director of Music. This meeting was significant, but I never imagined, at the time, that he was to have an important influence on my musical career and upon other aspects of my life as well—my quest for 'the miraculous', for instance. The poor man had a minor speech impediment and was universally and affectionately known as 'Ithy-Pithy'. When my turn came he played a chord on the shiny, black grand piano and asked me to sing the top, middle and lower notes. This exercise was repeated several times before I was dismissed. I had not performed well enough to be invited to join the choir, but my skill, as a boy whose squeaky voice had not yet broken, was good enough for the Choral Society.

This was a large group composed of College boys and staff, together with a strong contingent from the town and surrounding villages. In tandem with the College orchestra, the Society gave an annual performance of a major choral work.

Following breakfast the next morning, I endeavoured to get my bearings in the company of RP; a tall lanky boy whose chronic acne rivalled the tortured barnacles on a conch shell that I had found on the seashore during the holidays. RP had been designated as my 'sponsor' until it was time for Chapel.

'Do you know that the "Hot Line" between Downing Street and the White House lies beneath this tarmac?' he announced as we crossed the Bath Road and entered the main gates.

'Are you serious?' I replied.

'Yup! Macmillan and the President could be talking to each other and their voices reverberating along the wires below our feet at this very moment.'

I was impressed. 'We are at the *centre* of the universe!' I joked.

'I expect there is a lot to talk about. Kennedy is being inaugurated later this week, you know.' I added.

In the years before satellite communication, the existence of the underground cable was considered to be of immense significance and it would be referred to on many occasions.

We were now in Court, and the fine seventeenth-century mansion once owned by the Seymour family (the Dukes of Somerset) rose immediately ahead, beyond a double row of lime trees.

'That's the original College building,' announced RP. 'It was once a private house and later became the Castle Inn, one of the most popular coaching hostelries on the route from London to Bath. Are you interested in the history?'

I nodded.

RP, who clearly knew his stuff, continued. 'The inn had been patronised by many famous people. Thomas Gainsborough used to stay on his way to Bath, where he painted portraits of his wealthy clients. William Pitt, Earl of Chatham, took a room for a fortnight in 1767 and the Duke of Wellington sought shelter overnight during the great Christmas snowstorm of 1836. With the arrival of the railways the Castle was sold and acquired by the College in 1843. That's why we come to be standing here today.'

Dropping his voice and pointing to the house, he went on. 'The days when teams of proud horses that drew fine coaches up to those eight Ionic columns, which make up the mansion's porch, live on for those who have witnessed the ethereal "phantom coach" that still drives around Court at night. Legend has it that one foggy night, many years ago, Doctor Fergus, the resident medical officer, through frantic and urgent entreaties just managed to dissuade a College boy from climbing aboard. So look out!'

I grimaced in mock horror.

The mansion was known as C House, and each of the lime trees in the avenue that led towards the house had a circular wooden bench at the base of the trunk, providing a pleasant spot to pause during the frenetic school day and rearrange one's kysh—a sort of padded cushion with pockets for books. The trees were felled during my time at the College—when the new dining hall was built—and never replaced, which I consider a great shame.

RP and I stood in the centre of Court, taking in the view and sniffing the country smells that emanated from the nearby farm and distant woodlands. 'Pretty impressive, don't you think?' he said.

The Chapel, with its elegant fleche rising more than one hundred feet, creeper-clad Victorian classroom blocks, the Memorial Library, and a small theatre known as the Bradlean lay before us. RP had whetted my appetite, and in due course I would bone up on further history. The Bradlean was named after G.G. Bradley, Master of the College from 1858 to 1870 and protégé of the great Dr Thomas Arnold of Rugby.

There were also two boarding houses, A House and B House. I soon learned something of their history, the former being notorious for its primitive and ugly features. Designed in 1845 by Edward Blore, who had built Abbotsford for Sir Walter Scott, and Lodsworth House and restored Lambeth Palace, but who was rumoured to have also constructed prisons, it featured a central well that ran from the basement to the third floor. Tall railings, accentuating a sense of incarceration, protected those on the surrounding landings from accidentally dropping to the stone floor far below. This feature gave rise to the cruellest bullying in the early days of the College. Small boys were taken forcibly from their dormitories and trussed up in bed sheets by their peers. Then, as horrendous screams and cries rose from the wriggling bundles, they were hung over the railings on the top floor of the well. It has been recorded that some victims of that particular torture were unable to mention the word 'Marlborough', even after forty years, without a shudder.

Towering behind A House, were the spindly trees on the 62-foot-high Mound; recently carbon-dated to 4500 years old, which was the site of the wooden motte castle, rebuilt by Roger, Bishop of Salisbury, following instructions from William the Conqueror (and where, some say, the wizard Merlin is buried).

'*Ubi nunc sapientis ossa Merlini?*' (Where now are the bones of wise Merlin?)

Over the ensuing decades, a stone castle developed on the Mound—the Keep—which became a significant venue for the mediaeval Court. Henry I spent Easter there in 1110 and Henry II spent Christmas there in 1170. The area, which we knew as the Wilderness, had been the Bailey of the castle, and housed a hunting lodge in the 11th century. King John was known to have maintained his hunting lodge, and in 1267, Henry III summoned his nobles, to the castle, for the signing of the Statutes of Marlborough, which I am reliably informed were as important as the Magna Carta. In the Middle Ages Marlborough was, without doubt, a very important town. 'The centre of the mediaeval universe!' I thought to myself when I had digested all this information.

During the eighteenth century, as part of the mansion's ornamental grounds, the Mound had been developed into botanical gardens with spiral paths leading to the summit. However, these had fallen into disrepair, and scruffy trees and scrub now covered the steep incline. With the exception of the open-air swimming pool, which followed the curvature of the mediaeval moat and where boys skinny-dipped on warm summer evenings, the Mound and Wilderness were definitely off limits, and all signs of the castle had completely disappeared.

It was not always thus. Thomas Burn, writing to his sister again in the winter of 1846, said, 'Mr Wilkinson [the first Master] preached a beautiful sermon last Sunday and Cobb took me to the Mound, a beautiful little hill with a walk all round it by which you get gradually up to the top where there are a good many snowdrops.'

At ten to nine the Chapel's single bell started to toll, as it would do every weekday.

'Get a move on!' exclaimed RP as he grabbed my elbow. 'It's time for Chapel!'

The bell resounded for five minutes over Court, echoing across the rest of the College and down the Kennet valley. There was then a pause for one minute, followed by a single stroke. Every boy was expected to be within the Chapel precincts by 'stroke', or woe betide him. The prefects were waiting to take the names of offenders. Staunch they stood, and stalwart hearted, to echo the school song ('The Old Bath Road'). To me they looked more like men than boys and, on Sundays, dressed in green woollen suits, colourful waistcoats and white ties, they were, indeed, very splendid.

We pressed into the glorious Chapel of St Michael and All Angels, built of sarsen stone in 1886, but in fourteenth-century Perpendicular style. RP disappeared into the crowd and 'new boys' were herded, like cattle, into the gallery at the west end. There was insufficient room in the wooden stalls to even bend forward in prayer, as every row was packed.

However, as we looked down over hundreds of heads, the sight in front of us was awesome. The entire school was assembled in pews that faced each other and stretched into the distance towards the golden reredos. Seated in stalls, on each side, behind the boys, were the beaks (masters) in their gowns and hoods, and as they were Oxbridge, virtually to a man, the lines were flecked in the white and red silk of resplendent academia. In 1961 there were no female members of the common room, with the exception of a few musicians. As the organ swelled and the morning sun shone through the stained glass windows, a thousand voices rose in unison and the hairs tingled at the back of my neck. It would be difficult to resist a sense of pride in being part—albeit an amoebic part—of a truly great school.

> Praise to the Lord! O let all that is in me adore him!
> All that has life and breath, come now with praises before
>   him!
> Let the Amen
> Sound from his people again!
> Gladly for ay we adore him.
> (Joachim Neander: 1680, English translation by Catherine
>   Winkworth, 1863)

In 1961, the College was still rooted in traditions that went back to its inception. It remained an institution where the Chapel played a dominant part in the daily routine. After all, the College had been founded 'for the sons of clergy and others', and many of the boys were still from parsons' homes.

Every visit to Chapel reaffirmed the record of countless Old Marlburians (old boys) who bore witness to service in every corner of the globe. From Uganda to Melbourne, the Punjab to the Crimea, Malaya to the Gold Coast, gilded on red panels, the names of bishops, soldiers, administrators and achievers of all kinds were scrutinised daily by the assembled congregation. The administrators must have been effective, perhaps because they were sent out with instructions to 'pray to God and keep your bowels open,' as the British Empire, supposedly, employed fewer bureaucrats than it now takes to run the National Health Service.

Years before my trip, not a few Marlburians had ridden through the Khyber in the Afghan Wars; some to achieve glory as did Reginald C. Hart (JH 1860), who received a Victoria Cross in 1879 for saving a private under fire; and some never to return, such as Robert B. Reed (Preshute 1851) who died of cholera at Landi Kotal in June 1879.

Forty-three Old Marlburians died in the Boer War; 749 (almost the equivalent of an entire generation) in the Great War and 415 in the Second World War. Decorations awarded have been numerous, including thirteen Victoria Crosses and one George Cross. The names of those who gave their lives are carved in stone on the walls of the Memorial Hall.

Many could echo this unfulfilled prayer:

> God grant, dear Voice, one day again
> We see those downs in April weather,
> And sniff the breeze and smell the rain,
> And stand in C House porch together.

After Chapel, 'new boys' went to the Master's Lodge, a large building behind C House with gardens that ran down to the Kennet. We were to be addressed by the Master (headmaster).

I do not recollect everything that the gently lisping Tommy Garnett had to say on that occasion, but his final words, before we were dismissed, still ring in my ears. 'Make every effort. Use your time wisely and never for a moment forget that boys in your mould have passed this way before.'

Did I catch myself muttering, 'We'll soon see about that'?

Later in the day the housemaster, David West (B1 1935), directed me to the sanatorium, where the fierce Doctor Hunter peered at me through his monocle.

'Strip!' he barked.

He took a firm hold of my testicles.

'Cough!'

'Cough again!'

'Again!'

Next, with my dignity already severely compromised, we were off to the gym, where about fifty boys were seated on benches around the walls dressed only in their underwear. At one end of the large room' two beaks stood next to a set of scales and a device for measuring one's height. Each boy's name was called in turn.

'Forward, Hall!'

I dropped my pants, and stark naked, advanced across the floor, before pausing for measurements to be recorded. It was a much disliked ritual, especially for the less mature boys who were made to feel conscious that their physical development lagged behind their hairier peers. Would a light pair of cotton Y-fronts have really messed up the statistics? I wondered.

These days, a great deal is known about indoctrination and the process required to subjugate an individual. Years later, I found *The Manipulated Mind* by Denise Winn (Octagon Press 1983) especially insightful. In hindsight, I believe that an agenda was at work on my first day at Marlborough College, and three steps could easily be identified. First, emotions were raised (in Chapel) and an uplifting sense of the 'group' established. Second, a 'message' was delivered (by the Master), reinforcing the group identity, vanquishing any notion of individuality and introducing a sense of guilt, lest one might betray the group. Third, one was stripped and humiliated (weighing and measuring), a process similar to that adopted in prisons or political indoctrination camps. Whether this process was deliberate, I don't know. Perhaps it had just become routine—the medium had become the message. Certainly, by the time I returned to my glacial dormitory on that first night I had been thoroughly 'cooked'. Forget individuality. The only possible way forward was to eagerly pursue the objectives prescribed for staunch members of the tribe into which I had just been initiated—or indoctrinated.

I smothered questions as to where all this was leading. I was now a pupil at one of the greatest—at the time, perhaps, *the* greatest—English public school. God was in his heaven; all was and would be right with the world, and as the Old Marlburian poet, Siegfried Sassoon (Cotton House 1902), put it, 'sausages for breakfast'.

Classes began the next morning and I found myself in Shell. This was the first step on the education ladder, and some twenty of my peers waited in a classroom for the arrival of the form master. Two things struck me. The class was much bigger than I had been used to at Fonthill—nearly twice the size—and the cast-iron framed desks must have been a hundred years old. With mounting curiosity, we ran our fingers over the woodwork. Gouged deep into their heavy oak lids were the initials of generations of boys. So vandalised had they become that it was impossible to write without some form of intermediary to provide a smooth surface. Eventually the form master, Geoffrey Chilton, arrived.

'All rise,' he announced as the door swung open, and with gown flowing proceeded to the front of the class. We shot to our feet like robots.

He too was of an advanced age and reminded me of a Spy cartoon of a Victorian schoolmaster that my father had in his study at home. Only the mortarboard was missing. We soon discovered that he had been hauled out of retirement to look after Shell for the Lent term. Chilton was proud of his Marlborough roots, having entered the College as a boy in 1910, returned to join common room in 1920, and later served as a housemaster for more than twenty years. Tall, gruff and proudly sporting another greasy striped Old Marlburian tie; I viewed him with grave apprehension.

Chilton would be in charge of our studies for the foreseeable future. However, it soon became apparent that scholarship was secondary to success on the games field. The captains of cricket, rugger or hockey were indeed gods. Exceptions existed, but to become a prefect, achievement in sport was almost a prerequisite. I find it curious that even today, in the wider world, when enquiring as to why an individual has been promoted to an influential position, the answer is so often, 'and of course, he played rugby/hockey for England.'

Steven Connor, in a lecture at Sussex University (2009), pointed out that while:-

'Dr Thomas Arnold was no adherent of the cult of games: this has been his legacy and that of his school,' and it was Lytton Strachey, the author of *Eminent Victorians* (1918), who reminded his readers that 'we have almost come to believe that an English public schoolboy who wears the wrong clothes and takes no interest in football is a contradiction in terms.'

Every prefect and many other senior boys, who had their own study, could rely on the services of a 'fag'. He was a junior whose duty was to fetch and carry, clean and sweep studies, prepare tea, make toast and generally wait on an older boy. Flogging by beaks was common, as was the delivery of a sound caning by a prefect. The drawing of blood was not infrequent. Fortunately, the nineteenth-century incident when a boy's thrashing was so severe that his shirt had been fragmented and pulped into his back, requiring the immediate delicate skills of the school doctor, has never been repeated.

Domestic facilities were still sparse. Dormitories had no carpets or curtains and windows always remained open. Cold baths were run at night before lights out and stood ready for a plunge on rising in the morning. In the very coldest weather, ice formed on the surface. At least, this was the theory. As often as not, we 'forgot' to run the baths before turning in!

The 'woods' (WCs) had no doors and were in the open. In the dead of winter, coal braziers kept the frost off—not for our comfort but to stop the iron pipes bursting. Icicles formed far above our heads and cold water dripped on us as we carried out our business.

'What the hell is that?' I demanded silently, as trickles of freezing water ran down my neck on one of the first days of term.

Although there was harshness in the regime, steeped in elitism and the knowledge that only four per cent of the population was educated at public school, a collective pride also permeated throughout the College, and an element of this harked back to the days of Empire. But much was about to change. In retrospect, it is clear that the boys who assembled on that cold January morning were members of a pivotal generation. The opening of the M4 would more than halve the four-hour drive from London. The telephone became an accepted medium for communication, whereas in my day there were, to my knowledge, only two public phone boxes available for 800 boys. In 1968, girls entered the College in the sixth form.

By then, fagging and corporal punishment had virtually ceased, and addressing students by their Christian names became the norm. The role of Chapel was to evaporate to almost vanishing point. Domestic comfort and food improved to such an extent that a visit today would remind one more of a good hotel than an academic institution, and it is heartening to report that extensive arrangements—barbeques and garden parties—are now made to facilitate the smooth assimilation of new arrivals. The idea of a tired, small boy, turning up in the dark; to be met by an authoritative member of staff whom neither he nor his parents knew from Adam, would be greeted with profound dismay.

Can you imagine what Princess Eugenie, The Duchess of Cambridge, her siblings, Samantha Cameron or Sally Bercow (all Old Marlburians) would have thought about that?

Pastoral care, extensive communal support, and tutorial attention have also, of course, improved out of all recognition. In 1961, we were indeed at a crossroads, not only for the school but also for the world, but many of those who were to be responsible for my education were unaware that their lives were still rooted in an age that was about to vanish as quickly as a conjuror's rabbit. Between the time when Geoffrey Chilton entered Marlborough College (C2 1910), and returned, as a beak, ten years later (1920), twenty-one of his contemporaries, from an intake of eighty-five, had been killed in action or died of wounds in the Great War.

Within ten years, my peers (1961) would have witnessed man on the moon and supersonic flight, flirted with pot and Eastern mysticism, raved about the Beatles and Rolling Stones and experienced Harold Wilson's 'white heat of the technological revolution'. Their sisters would idolise the fashion icons; Mary Quant, Twiggy and Jean Shrimpton, and they and their boyfriends could cavort amorously in the sure knowledge that they were protected from unwanted pregnancy with the arrival of the contraceptive pill.

Within a few days the chaplain, Perceval Hayman, took Shell for the first time. Morale improved rapidly with his enthusiastic and robust approach.

'I am going to teach you about the Marlborough countryside,' he announced. 'You will be given every opportunity to discover its secrets.'

This was more like it. Marlborough is surrounded by chalk downland, where ancient communities lived, well above the valley bogs and marshland. We were soon studying the local Ordnance Survey map, learning to take map references, and plotting excursions by deciphering the detailed contours of the terrain. But best of all, we were indeed encouraged to explore.

'We're off to Avebury this afternoon, sir.' I announced at the end of one session.

'Splendid!' he replied. 'Why not write up your trip for prep tonight?'

There was plenty of time for adventures, and with my new freedom I soon lost interest in formal games. At Fonthill I had been a big fish in a small pool, but now many of the boys were bigger or much better at sport than me. We were required on the games pitch most afternoons, but there were half-days and weekends; as the days lengthened my new friends and I took every opportunity to mount our 'grids' (bicycles) and head out into the surrounding countryside.

Soon we were panting up Sun Lane, past the old workhouse (a House of Correction for vagrants was established in 1578) and golf course, and leaving the town with the fresh wind streaming in our hair, freewheeled into the valley towards Rockley and Old Eagle. This was freedom. No risk assessment, health safety and helmets nonsense here. This was in the blood, or should I say the DNA!

In A.R. Stedman's 'Marlborough and the Upper Kennet Country' (1960) he says:

> The scientific study of the distant past really began with
> Sir Richard Colt Hoare [*my four times great grandfather*],
> whose labours resulted in the publication of his South
> Wilts in 1812, his North Wilts in 1819 and his Roman Era
> in 1821, followed by the first five volumes of that history of
> Modern Wilts which however, remained uncompleted at
> his death in 1838.

Within minutes, history was staring us in the face as we passed the sign to Temple Farm, close to where the military arm of the Knights Templar— founded in mediaeval times to protect the roads to Palestine and the Holy Places—had a house. Pedalling vigorously, we climbed the steep down to Hackpen. Pen means 'height' in Welsh or Cornish, and only in England would a steep hill be called a 'down'.

Hackpen Hill is at the edge of the escarpment where we crossed the Ridgeway, an ancient route that ran from the Marlborough Downs, across the Berkshire Downs and Chiltern Hills and on into East Anglia. On a clear day the Welsh mountains were visible to the north-west.

Soon we were hurtling down zigzag bends and into the valley of the Winterbournes (winter streams).

> And gliding through the Winterbournes was peace:
> Calm as canoeing were those winding lanes
> Of meadowsweet and umbelliferae.
> (John Betjeman: 'Summoned by Bells', 1960)

Within a short time we found ourselves within the ramparts and great stone circle at Avebury. The ancient monument, far older than Stonehenge, extends over twenty-nine acres and is almost a mile in circumference. The first encounter was spellbinding as we made our way between the huge sarsen megaliths that make up the circle and the smaller internal groupings. The stones of the great circle stand about six yards apart. Some are twenty feet high, weighing sixty tons and of an alternating male and female character.

But how much more impressive must it once have been? Of the original—some say six hundred—stones, many had been broken up for building purposes, and chunks of sarsen could be identified in the walls of nearby houses. A small conical concrete block marked the position of each missing megalith, and the main Devizes to Swindon road wound through the circle. The village had partly developed within its bounds and beyond the site an avenue of megaliths and conical blocks extended a mile or so down the valley towards the Bath Road.

We left our grids and wandered around, drinking in the atmosphere of this extraordinary place. While it was not 'spooky', and of course, no one knows why it was constructed, it certainly provided an interesting venue for a ride out from the College, and I was to visit many times.

We were required to be back at the College before dusk, but this was to prove a close-run thing as the sharp bends of Hackpen were too much for us on the return trip. Panting heavily, we dismounted and wearily pushed our grids to the top under the watchful eye of the chalky-grey White Horse etched on the hillside. Reaching the summit, the view eastwards was spectacular. Miles and miles of rolling downland stretched into the distance, and in the haze of the late afternoon light only the occasional smudge of a remote farm building indicated anything of twentieth-century civilisation. An iota of imagination could cast one back across the millennia.

What was that—the flash of sunlight on steel—could it be the king's party returning to Marlborough Castle?

Perhaps my illustrious ancestor, John of Gaunt, engaged in a hunting foray from his lodge at nearby Upper Upham. We can all trace a line back to John of Gaunt—can't we? Perhaps Cromwell's men, mustering for battle in 1642. Certainly anyone unfamiliar with the topography would be unaware that tucked away and, invisible in a fold of the hills, was a lush river valley, a famous college and a town of some five thousand souls.

'We certainly enjoyed our trip, sir,' I announced, handing in my essay the next morning. It had recorded everything we had seen—or imagined that we had seen.

The essay was good and earned me an alpha plus.

Marlborough, with its red roofs and tiled, gabled facades, was still a charming market town in the early 1960s although huge lorries, bound for London or Bristol, rumbled down the high street in increasing numbers. The grey tower of St Peter and St Paul's church reverberated continually, and not infrequently loads of merchandise spilled on the sharp corner where the Bath Road passes B House. I know not how often the motley-coloured brick garden wall, which conceals the small memorial to Richard Corfield (B2 1896) and the Camel Corps from the main road, required rebuilding, but the evidence is still there for all to see. Perhaps it was this constant vibration that caused human bones and other remains to surface among the roses in the flowerbeds that are still a feature of the churchyard at the College end of the elegant high street.

'Alas, poor Yorick!' declaimed my new pal, RP, one afternoon as he picked up a piece of battered skull.

Thought to be the widest high street in England, this had not always been the case, because buildings once occupying what is now the middle of the road were destroyed by the Great Fire of Marlborough in 1653. On two Saturdays in every October, the high street was closed to traffic for 'Mop Fair', a reminder of the mediaeval trade fairs and a tradition that continues to this day. They are colourful, noisy and bustling occasions spiced with the whiff of frying onions, hamburgers, fish and chips and diesel exhaust when all and sundry pour into the town to make merry until late into the night.

'Who's for the dodgems?' a gang of Elmhurst chums shouted above the fairground noise as we charged down the street, with loose change burning a hole in our pockets.

In the shadow of St Peter's tower, Mrs Kennedy ran her excellent tuck shop, renowned for exotic milkshakes, and in my mind, an attractive red-headed girl who worked there on Saturdays. However, with only a score of seats available, space was limited and many, wishing to augment the less than appetising College meals, preferred to 'brew' on primitive gas rings in house or study. Bread, jam, butter (of both the dairy and peanut varieties), baked beans and other goodies were purchased after lunch, when the town was briefly accessible to College boys. Next to Kennedy's, Crosby and Lawrence the sports shop carried on a brisk trade and further along the high street, opposite Mr Vincent Head's gentlemen's outfitters, was Maynard's, the family newsagent. Early every Sunday morning a boy was despatched from

Elmhurst to purchase the Sunday newspapers. The 'lads', it hardly needs saying, made a point of ordering *News of the World* or *Titbits* and then, back in the dorm, proceeded to shock us with the lurid details of the latest scandal! I expect it was all rather tame by today's standards.

St Mary's smaller tower punctuated the east end of the high street, to the left of the town hall, which opened in 1902. A leisurely stroll from tower to tower, eastwards along the high street, led one past Duck's toyshop. It was here one wet afternoon that I saw two ducks solemnly mounting the steps of the shop. They were, obviously and sensibly, seeking shelter from the horrendous rain.

Most of the town's businesses were in the hands of established local families. Chandlers were the saddlers and Stratton Sons and Mead the seed and grain merchants, from whose premises a wonderful aroma of newly ground coffee would waft down the high street. Mundys supplied footwear and Flux and Co were the stationers. Mr R.H. Baker, the chemist at 133 High Street, must surely have been one of the first subscribers to the telephone service, as his number was Marlborough 4. W.H. Smith was located at number 132 in the building now known as the Merchant's House—a glorious restoration of a seventeenth-century silk merchant's residence.

In the days when Britain had a native car industry, for those with a larger investment in mind, Hillmans, Sunbeams, Humbers and Triumphs were on display at Bridge Garage, Austins at Dobson's Garage, Rovers at Bell's or, if a Morris were more to your taste, highly polished models could be inspected at Herd and Leader in the high street. The first Morris Mini had come to the market in 1959 for less than £500.

Many of the tradesmen's names were inscribed, in gold, on panels in the town hall, which hosted King George VI and Queen Elizabeth in 1948 and the Prince of Wales in 2004, when his visit commemorated the granting of a charter to the borough by King John in 1204. Besides following their calling, these men were the aldermen and mayors who had guided the fortune of the town for decades, and the names of some College beaks also appear. One of these was my kindly, chisel-faced teacher, Jake Seamer, who had served in the Sudan, where he rose to the position of Deputy Governor and befriended the explorer, Wilfred Thesiger.[5] Back in England, he was elected Mayor of Marlborough on two occasions and was one of only seven people ever to be made a Freeman of the town, representing the optimum partnership of town and gown. Another family, the Maurices, linked by marriage to the

Honys and Byams, had been doctors in the town since 1792, and members of that tribe held mayoral office on ten occasions. Members of the Free family, who originally came to the town as stonemasons, have occupied the office of mayor on twelve different occasions.

Beyond tall arches that led off the high street, the ostlers' call, the 'ter-rum-ti-ta' of coaching horns, the rattle of metal-rimmed wheels and hooves on cobbles, now lived on in the mind rather than the stable yard, although a sense of past times was still exuded by hunting prints and brass curios within the comfy confines of the privately owned Castle and Ball Hotel and Ailesbury Arms.

A popular place, where oak tables and display cabinets stacked with éclairs, meringues, homemade cakes and confections of every description greeted visiting parents, was the Polly Tea Rooms, although they suffered a serious fire shortly after my arrival. I think the redheaded girl's mother worked there.

Marlborough and the Kennet valley was a centre for brewing in the eighteenth century, and beers emanating from the clear chalk stream and downland barley were found in hostelries throughout England. In the 1960s, if you fancied something stronger than tea or coffee, there were still sixteen pubs scattered around the town, but these were strictly out of bounds to College boys, as was the cinema. Infringement of such regulations merited a sound thrashing and, on a second offence, possible expulsion. Perhaps the most striking and memorable public house sign in Marlborough was the Five Alls at 13 London Road, and I am indebted to Margaret Wharton for recording the detail in her charming memoirs, *Marlborough Revisited* (1987):

> The King—I rule all
> The Soldier—I fight for all
> The Lawyer—I plead for all
> The Bishop—I pray for all
> John Bull—I pay for all.

The Five Alls closed for business in 1998. Together with the offices of the long defunct *Marlborough Times*, the distinctive black and white wooden façade of the White Horse Bookshop, the grammar school, with its clearly marked porches, 'Boys' and 'Girls', where William Golding's father taught and where the author and Nobel prize-winner was a student in the 1920s, all these businesses and facilities contributed to the unique ambience that was Marlborough when I first knew it. They exemplified the best qualities of an English country town, which have now largely disappeared, and I was glad to be part of it. In fact, the contrast between my life within the confines of the College and life outside created a certain amount of tension that would add to further troubles later on.

William Golding is commemorated by a blue plaque at 29 The Green, and I wondered if *Lord of the Flies* stemmed from his experiences at the grammar school. It is just down the hill from Silverless Street, where Jewish moneylenders lived and traded until they were expelled in 1275. Formerly Silver Street, the 'less' was added after their expulsion. I only became sensitive to this history when I went into business with a Jew later in the decade.

Beyond the Parade, which was the seediest quarter of the town and also off-limits to College boys, and past Mr Sumbler the butcher, who recently won the Countryside Alliance 'Best Rural Retailer' (Wessex) award, was the Pelham Puppet factory, home of Sooty and Sweep, Marlborough's contribution to industry.

For those beaks who wanted a break, a day in 'town', or a brief visit to their Oxford College, the train was standing at the platform below the edge of ancient Savernake—that is, until 9th September 1961 when it was closed permanently to passenger traffic by Dr Beeching, the chairman of the British Railways Board.

The great forest, whose name (Safernoc) first appears in a charter made by King Athelastan in 934, stretches south-east from Marlborough to Great Bedwyn and almost to Burbage. It has been administered by the Kings' Wardens, who have held this office, in an unbroken hereditary tradition, for nigh on 900 years. Members of the family include the Earls of Cardigan and Ailesbury, and Esturmys, Seymours, Bruces and Brudenells. The forest provided an enticing venue for hunting deer throughout the centuries and in an early history of Marlborough College there is an illustration that features boys with catapults climbing trees. It is by F.S Baden-Powell and entitled 'The Last of the Squirrel Hunters'. However, although one would be more likely to encounter camper vans and cyclists in the Grand Avenue during the twentieth century, no one could deny the forest's outstanding beauty.

In 1761 Susanna, the daughter of my ancestor Henry Hoare of Stourhead, married Thomas Bruce Brudenell, the Marquess of Ailesbury. This happy union not only secured the line to the present day but also provided the opportunity for Henry Hoare to actively encourage the development of the forest. It is thought that he introduced the eminent landscape designer Lancelot ('Capability') Brown.

Writing to his son-in-law, Hoare wrote:

I feasted my eyes with an exquisite beauty and did homage to the king of all oaks and to the queen of all beeches and I had a delicious day's ride, everything to a wish but the want of your Lordship's presence.

In 1804, grammar school boys cut the White Horse that stands guard over the Kennet valley into the turf on Granham Hill which rises to the south of the College.

If you had happened to be travelling on the steep road that rose above the 'horse' one Sunday morning in the winter of 1961, you might have spotted two boys in jeans and striped 'house' sweatshirts endeavouring to drive their bicycles against all the forces of gravity. Our appetite whetted for further exploration, I had teamed up with my pal Gus Low and we were heading for Stonehenge, a round trip of nearly sixty miles. Neither of us had 'gridded' so far before, so it was a bit of an adventure.

Leaving Elmhurst, we had made our way around the perimeter of the College grounds and down the rough path that ran parallel to the Kennet before meeting the A345, just beyond Castle Mill, at Duck's Bridge. The lane was known to generations of Marlburians and townsfolk alike as 'Treacle Bolly', on account of some long forgotten miller who invariably addressed his barrel-shaped pony crying, 'Come on, get up there, old Treacle Belly'.

We continued pedalling as hard as we could, past quaint cottages that nestled by the railway embankment; their thatch protected by sheets of corrugated metal from glowing sparks that sometimes blew on to the roof when a train passed. Finally, rising nearly a thousand feet above the Pewsey Vale, we arrived at one of the highest points on the Marlborough Downs. Then, under the shadow of the ramparts and earthworks of the chalk peak at Martinsell, we sped into the valley, exhilarated by the release from effort, as trees, bushes and the small village of Oare whizzed past.

We crossed the Kennet and Avon canal that was opened in 1810 but whose locks were rotting and waterway silted just as a large rat slithered from the towpath into the stagnant water.

'I don't fancy falling in there!' I gasped.

Also gradually deteriorating were the concrete pillboxes, built at intervals along the canal that formed part of the country's defences in 1940. This construction work had been undertaken by 'sappers', supervised by Richard Carey, my mother's old friend who was killed in the Second World War, but it would be a long time before the canal was restored to the thriving thoroughfare that now connects Bristol and Bath with Reading and London. It is now the venue for the annual Devizes to Westminster canoe race.

Soon we reached ancient Pewsey, associated with King Alfred, King of Wessex, who is commemorated by an attractive statue in the centre of the town, unveiled to celebrate the coronation of George V. There is also a plaque a few miles to the south of the town which reads:

HERE IN THE YEAR 871
THE FUTURE KING ALFRED THE GREAT
MET HIS ELDER BROTHER KING AETHELRED I
ON THEIR WAY TO FIGHT THE
INVADING DANES AND EACH SWORE THAT
IF THE OTHER DIED IN BATTLE
THE DEAD MAN'S CHILDREN WOULD
INHERIT THE LANDS OF THEIR FATHER
KING AETHELWULF.

As we proceeded away from the town, following the course of the Wiltshire Avon, we passed the church of St John the Baptist, so old that the foundations were probably laid by Saxons. White clouds scudded across blue skies and the waxen February sunlight sparkled on the river where swans were gliding among withered sedge.

'That scene reminds me of a poem by Keats that we are studying,' I mentioned to Gus as we paused for a break.

As we cycled on, the sound of church bells, rising and falling, wafted across the valley, calling the good folk of Wessex to worship. Each fold in the landscape brought us within earshot of a new peal, in the parishes of Rushall, renowned for its Norman Font, Upavon, which nestles below the biggest prehistoric fortress in Wiltshire, Netheravon, where my great-uncle, Blatchford Oldrey, attended Cavalry School in the early years of the twentieth century and Figheldean, where my cousin Brigadier Ernest Oldrey had retired to a thatched cottage and enjoyed his fishing rights on the river.

We paused at his pretty cottage.

'Maybe, they'll give us a cup of tea,' I suggested.

'Or even breakfast,' replied Gus—ever hopeful.

But it was no good. There was no reply.

'They are probably at church, or gone fishing!' I concluded.

I have fond memories of Ernest and his wife, Audrey, as they used to provide a good lunch on the occasional Sunday when they collected me from the College and then, having spent the afternoon inspecting the Avon's flora and fauna or listening to Wagner's 'Meistersingers' on their thoroughly modern gramophone, they returned me to my house following a sumptuous tea at the Polly.

Soon we found ourselves on the A303. Gus had gone ahead and I soon saw him punching the air with his fist and shouting: 'Yippee! Yippee!!' as Stonehenge came into view.

Much has been written about this 4500-year-old collection of massive grey megaliths, which stood before us on the bleak winter hillside, and new information and new theories surface regularly. What was important to us, on that day, was that we had arrived at our goal. Both Gus and I had been there before, so we had a quick wander around the stones and then took a break for lunch.

A bitter easterly wind had come up and the sky was leaden. We sheltered behind one of the thousands of flinty tumuli (burial mounds), found all over Wessex, which resemble extra-terrestrial molehills, and devoured our packed lunch, relishing a cold, greasy pork pie and apple generously supplied by the College caterers. We then headed back, taking the A360 towards Devizes, crossing Salisbury Plain, surrounded by evidence of military activity. Larkhill was in the distance and, striking out in all directions, across the grassy down land and traversing the main road, were the muddy tracks of tanks and other heavy armament. Being Sunday, no red flags were flying and no guns booming, but the ranges were clearly marked.

Further along was the sign to Imber. In my copy of Arthur Mee's *Wiltshire*, part of a series that was first published in the 1930s, the section on Imber reads: 'It is at the end of a long and desolate road, a lonely and lovely place, with pretty cottages splendid trees and a thirteenth-century church.'

No longer. In 1943, the 135 villagers were evacuated with only for-ty-seven days' notice, never to return. Initially, American troops from the Third Armoured Division required the village for training in preparation for the D-Day landings in France. Deserted and destroyed, public access was allowed on one day a year.

We continued to head north through the village of West Lavington, where the fine manor house now serves as a boarding house for Dauntseys School; Potterne, with its splendid timbered properties and Devizes, whose name lends itself to a naughty limerick that starts with the words: 'Two pretty girls from Devizes ...'

Skirting the town, we were on the home run and the view from Bishop's Cannings Down, one of the finest in the West Country, came in sight. The fifteenth-century spire of St Mary the Virgin's church stands starkly against the long line of chalk hills, the steep escarpment where the Marlborough Downs drop into the Pewsey Vale.

The wind had dropped but a thin, cold rain was falling as we gridded furiously on the long easy downhill stretch to Silbury Hill, the largest arti-ficial and pre-Roman mound in Europe. The drizzle on my specs obscured my vision like frosted glass and my clothes were quickly soaked, but I sud-denly felt immensely exhilarated and started singing at the top of my voice as we returned to the Kennet valley and finally arrived back at Elmhurst, wet, tired but thoroughly satisfied with our day's efforts. Sassoon, who lived at Heytesbury, not far off the route we had just taken, put it better than I can in this extract from his poem 'Everyone Sang' (1919).

> Everyone suddenly burst out singing
> And I was filled with such delight
> As prisoned birds must find in freedom
> Winging wildly across the white
> Orchards and dark green fields; on; on; and out of sight.

Winter passed into spring, and my parents came down from London for my fourteenth birthday. They stayed at the Castle and Ball and we visited Avebury, just as the first daffodils felt brave enough to battle with March gales. It was a treat to have a good dinner and a luxury to enjoy a full English breakfast. There was nothing really wrong with College food except that it was dull, with no choice of menu, and interminable servings of treacle sponge and custard—known as 'College Bolly'—became monotonous. In the hotel dining room other boys sat with their parents, holding intense conversations as to 'how things were going'.

There was an awkwardness between College boys when they were with 'their people', as on the occasion, at breakfast, when we found ourselves sitting at the next table to PC. He and his pretty mother and suave father smiled sweetly at us over the toast and coffee. Could that be the same PC—the little shit—who had 'borrowed' my hockey stick the previous day just when I needed it, and landed me in bad odour with the games master?

As the end of term approached, I found myself in the sanatorium with a nasty dose of mumps, although I was well enough to take the train back to London for the holidays. The next event of note was the arrival of my first school report. This would be the mother of all 'how things were going.'

With the exception of classes taken by Perceval Hayman, my studies had not gone well. Geoffrey Chilton and I did not get on from the first day. Maths continued to be a source of anguish and even tears. Latin was taught by Slimey M, who wrote nasty things about me, and my first encounters with science (unlike most of my peers, who had received a grounding in the subject at their prep schools) bewildered me. Thwarted by theories I did not understand, I fooled around in the labs, housed in the concrete and glass building that was designed by W.G. Newton, an Old Marlburian (C1 1899), completed in 1933 and now officially Listed. Notably, on one occasion, I placed a geometric compass across the terminals of a Nife battery. The compass turned white hot, flew into the air and, narrowly missing my head, landed on the work counter, exuding a puff of smoke as it burned a deep hole in the wood. My housemaster gave me a thousand lines and called me a pain in the neck. He was right. This was a stupid and childish act that in no way enhanced my reputation. All I can do is plead frustration and boredom.

> And when on whistles and toy drums
> We make a loud amusing noise,
> Some large official seraph comes
> And scolds, and takes away our toys,
> Bids us sit still and be good boys.

And when a baby laughs up here
Or rolls his crown about in play,
There is a pause. God looks severe:
The angels frown, and sigh and pray,
And some-one takes the crown away.
(Rupert Brooke: 'Song of the Children in Heaven', 1907)

On one bright spring day, I wasn't so lucky. David West was waiting for me when I returned to the house for lunch, following a French class held by a pleasant enough beak who rejoiced in the name Ivo Payne. 'Go into my study, I'm going to beat you,' he said.

'What for, Sir?' I replied, thoroughly shaken.

'For failing miserably in this morning's French test; you scored gamma minus,' he continued.

'How do you know about that?' I queried.

'Haven't you heard of the telephone?' he chuckled.

By that time we had reached the study.

'Now bend over ...'

My father shook his head in profound dismay as he read my report, and sternly exhorted me to double my efforts when I returned for the summer term. He was keen, above all else, that I should excel in the classroom, and envisaged my following in his footsteps to Cambridge. Devastated, he would not have entirely agreed with the words of old Squire Brown as related by Thomas Hughes in *Tom Brown's Schooldays*:

Shall I tell him to mind his work, and say he's sent to
school to make himself a good scholar? Well, but he isn't
sent to school for that—at any rate, not for that mainly. I
don't care a straw for the Greek particles or the digamma;
no more does his mother. What is he sent to school for? ...
If he'll turn out a brave, helpful, truth-telling Englishman,
and a Christian, that's all I want.

Unfortunately, I had acquired a taste for activities outside the class-room, and formal study became increasingly irksome. It would not be long before I found a new outlet for my energies and enthusiasm.

My friend Richard Inglis, now a county court circuit judge (2012), was the son of a clergyman and a keen bell-ringer. He began to recruit a small team to practise this art, whose origins go back to mediaeval times. It would be difficult to find a location better placed to pursue our new hobby, and with enthusiasm at fever pitch we were soon off on our grids to tour the church towers of Wiltshire. I cannot imagine what kind of reception we would receive today, but the locals took our visits, and in many cases the less-than-expert dinging and donging, with commendable complacency. No one ever complained as we regularly disturbed the countryside on weekday afternoons.

The first step in learning to ring bells in England is to master control of the bell. This is easier said than done, as each bronze bell can weigh from a few hundredweight to several tons and is housed in the bell chamber, at the top of the church tower. Swinging easily on bearings that are set in stout—often ancient—oak frames, the bells are controlled by a handmade rope that drops from a wooden wheel, attached to the bell, through the floor and down to the ringing chamber that may be many feet below. The number of bells range from up to four or five in a small church to perhaps six, eight or ten in a substantial tower. Most cathedrals have twelve bells.

The ringing chamber is usually hidden away and reached by a spiral staircase within the tower, although I have clambered up many a steep ladder. A degree of anonymity suited pious worshippers in times gone by, as ringers were sometimes unruly and given to drink. Ringing is performed at ground level in some churches, or even in the nave where there is a central tower, which is the case at the great wool church of St Mary the Virgin at Fairford in Gloucestershire and at St. Sampson's in Cricklade.

The normal resting position of the bells is down, and ringing starts by taking hold of the sally, the familiar, colourful, woolly section of the rope, with one hand and the 'tail' with the other and gently swinging the bells. Then, with each tug, they move faster and faster until their increased momentum brings them up with their mouths facing heavenward. The bells are stopped from tipping over the top by a wooden 'stay'. From then on, each stroke of the clapper requires a 360-degree revolution of each bell. Every ringer controls his own bell and great care must be taken not to break the 'stay', or overthrow the bell, in which case the full weight of the bell would cause it to tumble over and over, pulling the ringer up to—or even through—the ceiling with catastrophic results. That is, unless he or she has been quick-witted enough to let go of the rope.

The ringers in one Wessex church have been encouraged in their behaviour since 1746, when these lines were painted on a board in the ringing
chamber:

Pull off your hats, your belts, your spurs
And when you ring make no demurs.
Sound out the bells well if you can
Silence is best for every man.
But if a bell you overthrow
Six pence unto the Clerk you owe.

Ringing a bell up, requires one to exert considerable energy and is one
good reason why campanology used to be known as 'the exercise'. However,
once in position the bell is delicately balanced and can be handled by a ten-
year-old or an octogenarian.

Once up, the bells are in position for 'rounds', which means that each
bell follows the next; round and round in a circle—the familiar do, ti, la, so,
fa, mi, re, do.

Once bell control has been mastered, the next step is to make the sound
more interesting. This is achieved by the Captain of the Tower, who calls for
changes in the order of progression. Following a string of commands—moving to the right—do will follow ti, then la, then so, *ad continuum.*

The next development is for the ringers themselves to follow a pattern
that they hold in their heads. This is known as 'hunting a plain course' and
means that each bell will follow a different bell on each stroke, working
through a set pattern. Once this has been learned the ringer can exercise
mental agility by studying complicated method ringing and equip him- or
herself to ring a peal. A typical peal is just over 5000 changes, with no se-
quence repeated, taking several hours to complete.

Considering that for every stroke the bell passes through 360 degrees
and also, for every stroke its position in relation to the other bells changes,
ringing a peal successfully is no mean achievement.

Many methods have curious names. These may, like Stedman's, denote
the name of the originator of the method, or the name of the place where
it was first rung, as in Cambridge Surprise. Names with Minor (Little Bob)
or Doubles (Grandsire) or Triples (Single Oxford Bob) denote a technical
aspect of the method, as does Bob. A single error will disqualify the peal

attempt, but there are plaques in churches all over the country commemorating successful peals, the names of the ringers who participated and the
event celebrated. These are usually for coronations, jubilees, royal weddings
or a local occasion; perhaps a ringer's significant anniversary or in memory
of long-standing service. For a funeral, bells are rung half-muffled, which
is achieved by tying a leather thong to one side of the clapper, and the
clear call of the bell followed by an echo signifies this world and the world
beyond.

The first peal in England was rung in 1715, and I think most people agree that the sound of church bells, rung by real experts, is beautiful.
Knowing something of the skill employed adds an additional dimension.

In 1961, John Betjeman (B2 1920) came to the College for a public reading of his newly published autobiography, *Summoned by Bells*. We thought
him brave to do so, as his description of his time at Marlborough, commencing with these much-quoted lines of blank verse, was somewhat ambiguous.
Did I agree with his sentiments? I think anyone reading these pages would
conclude that the answer is yes—and no.

> Luxuriating backwards in the bath,
> I swish the warmer water round my legs
> Towards my shoulders, and the waves of heat
> Bring those five years at Marlborough through to me,
> In comfortable retrospect: 'Thank God
> I'll never have to go through them again.'

His enthusiasm for the sound of church bells, however, remained unabated throughout his life.

Our new hobby opened a completely new perspective to the exploration
of the Wiltshire countryside. We enjoyed every minute as we scrambled up
steep spiral staircases and cleared away pigeon droppings to read inscriptions
on ancient bells. The message borne by the seventeen-hundredweight tenor
at St Mary's, Bishops Cannings, cast by John Wallis of Salisbury in 1602,
that read: 'Feare God: Honour the Kinge', was typical, but others were more
flamboyant. We also noted the architecture, observed stunning views from
windswept towers, and chatted to local people far removed from the rarefied
confines of the College, from which we were only too pleased to escape. It
was fascinating to meet folk who would not consider themselves especially

well educated, but who were skilled practitioners of an art that was enshrined in the annals of English history and who encouraged us at every opportunity. The names of Donald Lee and Alf Johnson come to mind. They rang at St Mary's church in Marlborough during the 1960s and continued to do so until recently. It had been Alf's family who provided Douglas Quadling with a billet during the dark days of the Second World War, and at the time of writing Alf is Marlborough's beadle and town crier.

I was fortunate enough to have a cup of tea with him and his kind wife only the other day, sitting in their cottage on the London Road, which has a pretty little sign by the front door which reads 'Town Cryer'.

'I remember you and your friend Richard Inglis,' Alf said, as he passed me a slice of delicious home-baked cake.

'We were grateful; you taught us a lot.' I replied.

In every direction there were bells to ring and churches to explore. We glided down the exquisite Kennet valley on our grids, passing the little cross on the bank outside Mildenhall (Minal to the locals) that commemorated the death of A.H.P. Watts on 12th April 1879. His was the first fatality involving a motorcar in Wiltshire. Within minutes we discovered the jewel of St John the Baptist, with its forest of 'Gothick' box-pews in the finest oak and a light ring of six bells (tenor: seven and a half hundredweight) rung from the ground floor. A little further down the valley, on the hillside, was the site of a Roman camp at Cunetio (Black Field) where Caesar's coins could still be found with relative ease. We continued beyond Ramsbury Manor, then owned by the Rootes—the motor trade—family, where fat trout basked in a wide, shallow reach of the river and the Kennet slithered over a bubbling weir, to the church of Holy Cross, whose massive thirteenth-century tower dominated the village. Ramsbury, whose origins were recorded before the Norman Conquest, was once a cathedral city and boasts a suffragan bishop within the diocese of Salisbury. Gridding on, we passed the great elm in the high street. Of indeterminate age, it must certainly have pre-dated the restoration of 1660, but with a girth of more than twenty feet finally succumbed to disease and with much ado was felled and replaced by an oak tree in 1986. At about the same time a mulberry tree (*morus nigra*), which came from a cutting taken from the tree planted by John Milton at St Paul's School, in London, was planted in the churchyard of Holy Cross.

We soon reached the pretty church of St Mary at Chilton Foliat, whose bells, unusually, are rung anti-clockwise and whose history is linked to a gruesome murder at nearby Littlecote Manor, where Wild William Darrell killed his child.

Occasionally, strapping a tent, sleeping bags and rudimentary cooking utensils to our grids, we ventured further afield. Passing the smallpox isolation hospital on the A346, we pressed northwards and discovered the great Tudor tower of St Sampson's at Cricklade; on another occasion the dog-toothed Norman tower of St John's at Devizes. This was the church where Sergeant Troy was due to marry Fanny Robin in John Schlesinger's hugely successful film adaptation of Thomas Hardy's novel *Far From the Madding Crowd* (1967). By contrast, as we plunged down the wooded outer chalk escarpment we came across the delicate, pinnacled fifteenth-century tower of St Peter's at Clyffe Pypard. Here, in this remote corner of north Wiltshire, where little had changed for several hundred years, the only sound was the caw-caw of the rooks in tall trees above eighteenth-century monuments and the nearby manor house—until the bells started clanging.

We discovered so much of interest during our exploration of the churches of Wiltshire that I produced an analytical study that also drew comparisons with ecclesiastical buildings in London. This latter section featured glorious St Bartholomew the Great in Smithfield, the only surviving Norman church in the city (besides the Tower of London), but also churches that markedly contrasted in architectural style from their rural cousins. Examples were Sir Christopher Wren's work and W. Butterfield's Tractarian masterpiece (All Saints), tucked away among the drapers and furriers of Marylebone's Margaret Street. My essay was submitted, together with a collection of photographs that I had taken with my Brownie Box camera, for the Master's prize. This was a prestigious competition that encouraged junior boys to document a project of their choice. No one was more surprised than me when my name appeared on the Master's Notice Board in Court announcing that I was the winner. However, the prize of a box of chocolates was disappointing. As my mother observed, 'even a death-watch beetle would have been more imaginative'.

Perhaps a lack of imagination worked in our favour with respect to our capers in the various belfries. Our mentors back at the College were not privy to the details of our adventures, and today's health and safety officers would undoubtedly suffer cardiac arrest.

Worse was to come when we realised that the eight bells of St Peter's in Marlborough High Street were un-ringable and in urgent need of repair. To restore the bells in the church where Thomas Wolsey had been ordained in 1498 presented an exciting challenge, and my friends and I were soon climbing all over the inside of the tower, like so many ants, cleaning away years of muck and rubbish and smashing up worm-infested floorboards. This involved delicate and precarious manoeuvres as we balanced on the few remaining wooden supports and narrowly avoided falling to the floors below. Once we had restored some semblance of order, given the ringing chamber walls a lick of white paint and splashed gallons of preservative over the rafters, beams, floors and ourselves, we attended to the bells. Sections of the wheels were broken and needed expert attention from a carpenter, the ropes were rotten, and worst of all, the bearings had cracked and needed replacing. A matter of concern was that the bells were set in open bearings, which meant that they would be prone to jumping out of their frames. The idea of the thirteen-hundredweight tenor, or any other bell, crashing through the bell-chamber floor, a hundred feet from ground level, was very scary.

But help was at hand in the form of the intrepid Captain Mansfield-Robinson of West Overton, who provided rope and tackle so the bells could be raised from their sockets and temporarily suspended from the timbers in the roof of the belfry while the bearings were replaced and the position secured.

This all took quite a long time and, naturally, we did not want to rush things. The project provided an admirable excuse to not do whatever else we were supposed to be doing in the afternoons. However, we were eventually able to ring all eight bells and did so for the first time on Prize Day, which coincided with a visit from Geoffrey Fisher, the Archbishop of Canterbury (C2 1901), to whom we were presented. We felt pretty chipper about this, but I remember wondering why the archbishop was called a 'primate'—defined as the highest order of mammals or an archbishop—according to my dictionary. Very confusing for foreigners.

Unfortunately, the bells proved to be out of tune and made a truly horrible din. This could not have been foreseen but some years later they were removed, coinciding with the redundancy of the church, which was to become an arts and crafts centre.

These activities led to my becoming friendly with a young chaplain in the parish. His name was Gavin Fargus and he had been in the habit of using the tiny room above the church porch as a study. It was reached through a small door leading to the well-worn spiral stone staircase that ran up the inside of the tower. However, this facility no longer suited him, and he asked me if I would like to take it over. It had a couple of sticks of furniture, and the small leaded window overlooked a hawthorn tree that blossomed, red and white, in springtime. In those days, only very senior boys had their own study and the rest of us had to put up with huge communal halls where we spent free time, did prep and kept our books. Life on a winter's dark Sunday afternoon, when Alan 'Fluff' Freeman's *Pick of the Pops* was belting at full blast on the radio, could be pretty bloody.

Plus ça change, plus c'est la même chose.

Nearly 120 years previously, Thomas Burn, writing one of his chatty letters to his sister, had said: 'The only place for writing a letter or reading here is in the School Room ... in which there is a most tremendous row.'

The kindly curate did not need to ask twice. This was an opportunity for a haven, a headquarters for the bell-ringers and a retreat where my chums and I could brew a cup of coffee and relax. I even had a stab at composing sonnets when alone in that peaceful place. They have now been lost or were destroyed, but I recall these few lines written when I was sixteen:

> And here I found another place for quiet.
> Beneath the ancient tower. Below the bells.
> Away from College boys, and ribald riot.
> In this the tiniest of latticed cells.

There was certainly no better venue to discuss the topics of the day, or the news as it filtered down to us in October 1962 following the discovery of Russian missiles in Cuba.

'I bet the Hot Line is buzzing! Do you really think we are about to be blown to smithereens?' muttered our leader, Richard Inglis. For a few days a mushroom cloud of fear hung over us all.

'My parents are coming down for the weekend,' announced EC, another member of the team.

'They want us all to be together if the balloon goes up!'

'Gavin's study' remained our secret and sacred retreat for a year or so until one of the beaks realised what had been going on. He assumed nefarious practices and banned further use of our hideout. We were shattered. He was wrong, of course; our minds were on other things. There was no buggery in the belfry.

Unfortunately a culture of suspicion between beaks and boys lingered beneath the surface. Perhaps it was always thus, and is best exemplified by the story of the revered Doctor Farrar, Master of Marlborough College (1871-1876), author of *Eric or Little by Little* and subsequent Dean of Canterbury. When walking in Savernake Forest with a junior member of his staff, the Master pointed to the fallen autumn leaves. 'Alas,' he is reputed to have remarked, 'these leaves are like boys, fair without, but corrupt within.'

Farrar was another protégé of Dr Thomas Arnold, who once said, in a famous sermon: 'None can pass through a large school without being intimately acquainted with vice; and few, alas! Very few without tasting too largely of that poisoned bowl.' Farrar's attitude was therefore hardly surprising.

Indeed, the concept that public schools are a hotbed of wickedness is widespread, but I came across very little wrongdoing—a term it would be difficult to define today—at Marlborough. There was a certain amount of illicit smoking and drinking, and woe betide the culprits, if they were caught. Drugs and pornography were unheard of. On one occasion, a boy shot a deer in the forest with homemade gunpowder and a miniature cannon he had forged in the metal workshop! There was also the usual hanky-panky of a sexual nature found among male adolescents who relished opportunities to proudly demonstrate their newly acquired manhood and potency. Such incidents usually occurred, not behind the bicycle sheds, but after games, when evidence of competitive onanism remained in sticky damp patches among discarded jockstraps on the changing-room floor. I sometimes wondered if, for some obscure reason, the authorities encouraged this behaviour. We were certainly expected to take baths together, two at a time, which provided opportunities for experimentation.

'Just like the boys in College!' Jake Seamer was heard to remark at the end of a production of Ben Travers' bed-hopping farce, *Thark*.

I never came across anything of a coercive or sinister nature. Occasionally, one was aware of a frisson between an older boy and one of the pretty young boys known as 'lush' boys. Robert Graves, in *'Goodbye to All That'*, describes being caught up in just such a relationship while at Charterhouse which, he implied, tended to stem from misplaced romanticism rather than carnal desire and was innocent and idealistic. Am I naïve? Perhaps; but it would surprise me if such feelings continued, among boys, once the girls arrived. My evidence for this is the frequent crushes that developed between some boys and the few attractive daughters of certain beaks. Dishy nurses up at the 'Sani' did not escape attention either.

I left Elmhurst at the end of my first Christmas term, having amazed David West by being the first boy in his house to organise enthusiastic carol-singing forays into the town to raise money for charity.

The housemaster in Summerfield, my senior house, was a delightful man but untidy, forgetful and eccentric. His name was F.L. Coggin, and he and his wife were very kind and habitually invited small groups of boys to Sunday lunch. The cooking was basic, served on a threadbare white tablecloth, and the mustard was kept in a discarded bottle with the 'Quink Ink' label still in place. The boys were expected to leave by 3 p.m., in time for the Coggins to enjoy the afternoon concert on the BBC's Third Programme. 'There are some good stories about "Cogs",' one of the boys in the house told me, on my arrival. 'Have you heard the one about how the housemaster once drove to Reading, where he left his car in the car park and boarded the train for London? Later that evening, returning directly to Marlborough on the Paddington train, he discovered that his garage was empty. Naturally, he reported his "stolen" car to the police.'

Another exceptional and memorable beak was Alan MacKichan, whose teaching of English literature was inspirational. Alan was married to a gorgeous young lady named Gillian, whose photograph, at the time of their engagement, was prominently featured in *Country Life*. Many years later, my wife and I were staying at a B&B in the village of West Overton, where I understood that Gillian MacKichan had recently become the rector. When our hostess explained that breakfast would be a little late on Sunday, as she wished to attend communion, I remarked on the fact that Gillian's husband had taught me at the College.

'As far as Gillian goes, she was a corker and we boys lusted after her wickedly,' I added with a salacious grin. Coming down to breakfast in the morning, I politely enquired whether the service had gone well and was met with the reply, 'Oh yes—and I told the rector what you said!'

During my early teenage years I became very religious. My idealism was inspired by the prophet Isaiah (6:v8):

'Also I heard the voice of the Lord saying, "Whom shall I send and who will go for us?" Then said I, here am I, send me.'

Was I already seeking a higher reality—'the miraculous'? Maybe; but in the meantime I opened myself to the instruction that was available, and when the time came for confirmation into the Anglican Church I took preparation seriously. I attended Perceval Hayman's classes in his poky study in C House. He was a fortunate choice, being the beak who had befriended me when he first inspired my interest in the Marlborough countryside. A man of unfailing sympathy and amiability, his house, Halfacre, 'became a refuge for boys—Bruce Chatwin (B2 1953) among them—who were not enjoying their time at the school.'

Those words appeared in his obituary, in the *Daily Telegraph*, when he died in 1997. It also noted that Tommy Garnett regarded his appointment as the most important that he made during his time as Master, and that John Dancy, his successor, would take advice from Perceval that would not be acceptable from any other source. A tall, but slightly stooped, burly pipe-smoker, I found his avuncular presence to be a huge source of encouragement. Probably because my relationship with my father, and my mother too, for that matter, was far from close, I sought attention from father figures. Hayman, Fargus and ABS-M were examples.

The Master, writing in his report in July 1962, said of me: 'Happy when he has the attention of a grown-up ... maybe due to lack of self-confidence.'

It was, therefore, disappointing to learn, early in 1963, that Hayman was to leave Marlborough to take up an appointment in Sussex. On a memorable day, during that harsh winter when snow and ice forbade use of the playing fields for the whole of the Lent term, ABS-M and several of my chums set off to attend his induction as vicar of Rogate. Squashed into Ithy-Pithy's tiny Austin A30, and wrapped in our duffle coats, we drove for several hours across a white landscape and through lanes where huge drifts had frozen in great waves, completely obscuring the hedgerows. On the return journey, hares were spotted cavorting in the moonlight over the snow-encrusted fields.

Eventually, following a specially conducted 'Quiet Day' at the church of Holy Cross in Ramsbury, and supported by my parents, I was confirmed by the Bishop of Salisbury in Marlborough College Chapel on 2nd June 1962. My father presented me with a fine leather bible with my initials inscribed in gold, and wrote inside: 'From henceforth let no man trouble me: for I bear in my body the marks of the Lord Jesus' (Galatians 6:v17). From then on, for several years without fail, I attended Sunday Holy Communion at 8 a.m., and quite often the early weekday services too.

Sometimes, my friend John Henry Bowden and I would get up very early and cycle to Sunday communion at a church in one of the more remote villages. On such an occasion, I recall gridding along the pretty road that runs west from Lockeridge, past the sunken meadow with its plethora of sarsen stones or 'grey wethers', and below West Woods, which is the only spot where I have ever seen adders in the wild. 'Wethers' is a local Wiltshire name for sheep, which resemble sarsen stones as they lie out in the open country, although according to the *Reader's Digest Oxford Dictionary* the term means 'castrated ram'.

We slipped through Wansdyke and dropped into the vale at Knap Hill as the sun came up over Martinsell. It was a nice thing to do, although I fear that nature, beauty, spirituality and attempting to purge away some unspecified guilt by effort, in pursuit of unattainable purity, were all mixed up in our adolescent minds.

> The Old Marlburian Bishop thundered on …
> … 'Be pure,' he cried
> And, for a moment, stilled the sea of coughs.
> 'Do nothing that would make your mother blush
> If she could see you. When the Tempter comes
> Spurn him and God will lift you from the mire.
> (John Betjeman: *'Summoned by Bells'*, 1960)

It was only when I studied certain esoteric teachings, later in the decade, that I began to be freed from this brand of torture. In the meantime, I became a server in Chapel, was seriously considering the priesthood as my chosen career, and actively arranged a discussion group in Summerfield that dealt with moral and theological issues. Despite every consideration, a memory that will remain with me forever was walking back from evening services in Chapel across Broadleaze, to Summerfield, late on summer evenings. I am quite incapable of putting into words the glory, the majesty and the vastness of those huge, radiant Wiltshire skies.

> As o'er each continent and island
> The dawn leads on another day,
> The voice of prayer is never silent
> Nor dies the strain of praise away.
> (John Ellerton: 'The Day Thou Gavest', 1870)

Alongside other activities, I was making some progress with my music. I took piano lessons with Gertrude Enoch on a splendid grand piano in her spacious flat at the top of the sanatorium. Gertrude was another eccentric, and one of England's experts on handheld pipe instruments. However, a real excitement was when I started lessons on the Chapel organ, a four-manual, electro-pneumatic instrument that had recently been renovated.

My teacher was the same ABS-M whom I had met on my first day at the College, during the voice test, and with whom I quickly established a rapport. In fact, it was not long before I became responsible for the Chapel music and sat on the organ bench, to assist the organist, during services. This appointment was made by the extremely likeable Director of Music, Robert Ferry, who besides being a first-rate musician (he had been the soloist in a piano concerto with the City of Birmingham orchestra under Sir Adrian Boult, while still a boy) had also flown many sorties as a navigator for Pathfinder Mosquitoes during the war, earning himself the Air Force Cross.

A milestone was turning the pages for the renowned organist, Simon Preston. He was still in his twenties when he came to Marlborough, and rapidly making a name for himself. In 2007, he returned to the Chapel for the inaugural recital of the new Beckerath organ, built by organ builders from Hamburg. After a spellbinding performance, I made my way to the organ console, managed to shake his hand and proffer thanks, and remind him of our brief acquaintance nearly half a century ago.

'Oh! It was you!' he grinned, gripping my hand warmly.

'Come again soon!' I implored the youthful sixty-eight year old as I backed away. 'Don't leave it for another forty years!'

The main reason why my parents had selected the College for me was its musical reputation, although one facility that it spectacularly lacked was, access to quality musical recordings in congenial surroundings. There was a Gramophone Society, but this only provided a meagre collection of records and a very basic instrument, kept in the basement of the old music school. One of my abiding and formative musical experiences was hearing J.S. Bach's double violin concerto in D minor (BWV 1043) for the first time, while sitting on a mouldy carpet in a scruffy room where the wallpaper was hanging off the walls and the only light provided by a naked bulb. Bach became something of an adolescent hero, although chums chided me. 'Why not Stravinsky, Prokoviev, Shostakovich or even Stockhausen?' they would tease.

Nevertheless, more than forty years would elapse before I visited Leipzig and Bach's tomb in the Thomaskirche. Someone was playing the cello. It was a poignant moment.

However, standards were high in both the choir and orchestra and there was also a splendid 'Brasser', run by Bob Peel from a building that the boys had constructed for themselves. The breeze-block building, in a remote corner of College property, enabled budding horn players, trumpeters, trombonists and saxophonists to practise without fear of disturbing their peers, which reminds me of one of the politer definitions of an English gentleman: 'He is one who *can* play the bagpipes but desists.' I learned this from a teacher at a famous school, years later. She was describing her boss. 'If only!' she added.

Jazz and light entertainment groups performed regularly, and the cadet corps boasted a vigorous band that 'beat the retreat' annually in Court or in Marlborough High Street. ABS-M and his colleague Michael Davis wrote light operas that pre-dated Andrew Lloyd-Webber. One of these, *Daniel*, was performed in 1962. It was terrific fun and much enjoyed by performers and audience, although the vigorous set piece with the whole cast jumping up and down and the chorus belting out, 'There are no flies on Solomon the Wise!' raised a few eyebrows. ABS-M was certainly an outstanding organist and accomplished musician who had studied with Nadia Boulanger, in Paris, between the wars. Boulanger had herself been taught composition by Gabriel Fauré, who had been taught by Saint-Saens, a friend of Franz Liszt.

What an amazing pedigree. What a privilege, I thought to myself one day, as I climbed on to the organ stool for another lesson, exhorting myself to work harder; much harder. This would prove to be a course of action—verging on the obsessional—that I would pay for, dearly.

ABS-M had originally trained as a scientist, so he bridged 'art' and 'science', which was unusual at the time when compartmentation was the norm.

Today, he would be regarded as a polymath, and among other skills, he built up an impressive stamp collection. Later, in 1968, he decided to sell, and I accompanied him to Stanley Gibbons auction house just off the Strand. The auction was very exciting and the net proceeds allowed him to purchase Nowell House, a small, modern house at the top of Kingsbury Street in Marlborough, and thereby to move out of College accommodation.

Several of my contemporaries started to make a name for themselves and I recall their adolescent efforts. Notably, these were Crispian Steele-Perkins, the acclaimed trumpeter (taught by Bob Peel), and Humphrey Carpenter, son of the Bishop of Oxford, who wrote a controversial biography of Archbishop Runcie. 'Humph' was a versatile musician who played piano, tuba, bass saxophone and double bass at the College and in 1983 founded a band called Vile Bodies that specialised in playing 1930s music. The group performed at the Ritz for many years. Humph died far too young in 2005. Boys who were to see their names in lights and who displayed talent at a very early age were the Shakespearian actor Michael Pennington and Paul Brooke. The latter appeared in *For Your Eyes Only* (1981) and has often been seen in television dramas, having acquired a knack for playing obliquely sinister characters.

Recently, my wife and I attended a superb performance by Michael Pennington, acting with Susan Hampshire and Anna Calder Marshall, in *The Bargain*, a play about the relationship between Robert Maxwell and Mother Theresa. Maxwell's sons had attended the College. Their housemaster (Barton Hill) would draw them aside at the end of each term to warn them of any likely repercussions following Maxwell's receipt of their reports. It was said that he was prone to react violently when faced with less than satisfactory assessments of his sons' work.

Examining the contemporary register, it is apparent that scores of Marlburians of the early 1960s vintage have become high achievers in almost every conceivable field, although few names are widely known. There must be many unsung heroes.

Further exceptions that I recall are Mike Griffith, chairman of MCC and former Sussex County cricketer who also played hockey for England; Philip Pagnamenta, a producer of *Panorama*; Alistair Jackson of the Countryside Alliance; Christopher Martin-Jenkins, the cricket commentator; Sir John Kiszely, the distinguished and decorated Falklands veteran; Alistair Ross-Goobey, the economist; Sir Christopher Clarke QC, the lead counsel for the Bloody Sunday enquiry, reputedly earning himself a cool million or four; William Wyldbore-Smith, esteemed lawyer and High Sheriff of the County of Wiltshire (2013); Redmond O'Hanlon, the travel writer; Lord Alastair Goodlad, the Tory chief whip and Governor of Australia; Anthony Burns-Cox, the talented organist and Mark Phillips, the international equestrian and former husband of Princess Anne. No doubt there are more but these are memories; I have not employed a researcher.

With regard to beaks; Richard Pollock, the linguist who made strenuous efforts in the tortuous matter of my attempts to translate *Julius Caesar*, appeared on our television screens in the late 1980s, interpreting for Mrs Thatcher when negotiating with Mikhail Gorbachev. Ian Beer and Donald Wright distinguished themselves as Headmasters of Harrow and Shrewsbury respectively; and Dennis Silk, the Warden of Radley College; established himself as a legend in public school circles. Rumour has it, that when Tommy Garnett wanted to recruit Silk to Marlborough's common room, he tracked the illustrious cricketer down to his rooms in Cambridge. Silk was taking a bath at the time, and the interview and appointment took place while he remained clad only in a towel. Garnett was a skilled talent-spotter, and ten of his appointees went on to become headmasters.

Driving snow was caught in the powerful beam from the Lambretta's head-lamp as we headed up the Pewsey Road. Protected from the elements by duffle coat, scarf and helmet, I was riding pillion, having agreed to play the harmonium for the Lent evening services at a tiny church in the remote hamlet of Clench Common that nestled on the north side of Martinsell. This was to be in exchange for dinner and a glass of red wine at the Ivy House. It seemed an excellent alternative to Wednesday prep, and only a few hours beforehand I had thrust a chit in front of 'Cogs' that read: 'Permission to play for evening services and to ride on Gavin Fargus's Lambretta'.

There was no difficulty in obtaining a signature.

Now, every schoolboy knows that exploiting a situation is an art form. So, on various occasions, as the term progressed, when the College beagles were meeting some distance away, nothing seemed more natural than to hitch a lift with my friend, the Hunting Parson. After all, written permission 'to ride on Gavin Fargus's Lambretta' had been obtained, so it seemed an excellent, albeit lazy, way of following in the family's hunting tradition. Reflecting attitudes of an earlier time, I had been 'blooded' at the Opening Meet at Savernake on 30th September 1961. Cutting down on travelling time also provided the opportunity to enjoy a lavish farm house tea and to mingle with the local yeomanry before returning to College. I did relish those opportunities to escape!

The College beagles had been introduced in 1952, by Tommy Garnett, a true countryman, who had been working on the school farm at Charterhouse when news of his appointment at Marlborough broke. The beagles played a natural role in the school's activities and there were plenty of boys who enjoyed mucking out and generally looking after them. They were housed in kennels on the edge of the playing fields, near the Victorian cricket pavilion, and their yapping and barking could often be heard, especially at feeding times. How many times did I, together with a chum, push a huge wheeled urn from the kitchens up to the kennels, brimming with every conceivable leftover from fried sausages to porridge and ice cream for the hounds' enjoyment? Some boys, notably the farmers' and landowners' sons, took hounds home in the holidays, became hunt servants and learned many of the skills of field craft. The meets, which provided a vibrant link between the College and the rural community, took place several times a week during the season, usually within a ten-mile radius of Marlborough.

Trudging across flint-flecked furrows in the chalky plough, or stubble fields littered with 'grey wethers', was good exercise and offered another opportunity to discover the wilds of Wiltshire. John Masefield captured something of what we learned to appreciate in *Reynard the Fox*.

> As he raced the corn towards the Wan Dyke Brook
> The pack had view of the way he took;
> Robin hallooed from the downland's crest,
> He capped them on until they did their best.
> The quarter-mile to the Wan Brook's brink
> Was raced as quick as a man can think.
>
> Down he went to the brook and over,
> Out of the corn and into the clover,
> Over the slope that the Wan Brook drains,
> Past Battle Tump where they earthed the Danes,
> Then up the hill that the Wan Dyke rings
> Where the Sarsen Stones stand grand like kings.

It was exhilarating to climb from steep muddy 'bottoms' or clamber through straddling spinneys that embraced long lines of tall beech trees. Standing stark against the skyline, those noble features of down landscape served as windbreaks and held back drifting snow in the years when we had real blizzards and proper winters. Since I first wrote those words, we have, again, had some severe winters, so perhaps things are changing—global colding!

To tramp along ancient tracks running milky white in wet weather, lined with sloe-bearing blackthorn, wine-leaved bramble and scarlet rose-hip, all combined to provide a deeply ingrained love of the countryside that would have been difficult to achieve in any other way. It has never left me.

Some say that beagling, the pursuit of hares with hounds, is the poor man's hunting. If so, it certainly provided a taste of the real thing, and I am convinced that the discipline, the stamina, the teamwork, the sheer guts that hunting requires has stood many men and women in good stead for what-ever befell them in life—'Self-cultivation, with due regard to others'. After reading Sassoon's *Memoirs of a Foxhunting Man;* I question whether he would have survived the agonies of the trenches that he later described in *Memoirs of an Infantry Officer* without his earlier experiences in the field.

One afternoon, a choice: to go beagling or to attend a music lesson; each vied for pride of place. Juggling those various activities could be stressful. An attempt to negotiate with ABS-M produced a flash of temper, 'then take your A-levels in bloody beagling,' he barked.

What is it about music that appeals? I have often asked myself. I like the sounds. I like a good tune—even a pop tune! I was attracted to the power of playing the organ—producing a fabulous noise, all alone in a great build-ing—not only with the hands but also the feet. I find the emotion stirring, but not all music in all circumstances. For instance, I would never go to a performance of the St Matthew Passion in a secular building, but surely that is nonsense. I like some music as background, but, for example, never the Elgar cello concerto, Stravinsky's Symphony of Psalms, a Bach cello sonata or his Passacaglia and Fugue in C minor. They require total concentration. I like structure; a Beethoven violin and piano sonata, perhaps, at the end of a harrowing day. As far as the rudiments of music go, I am hopeless. I under-stand the basics and can read music, but as for more advanced technical as-pects of composition, I have never taken the time for study. I'm sure I would appreciate music even more if I had.

In time, there were changes at the College that would have serious reper-cussions, not only for the development of the school, but for me personally. Tommy Garnett, the Master, with his leather patched tweeds, untidy hair and down-to-earth attitude, who kept pigs at Charterhouse and was twice mentioned in despatches while serving with the RAF in Burma, had been appointed headmaster of Geelong Grammar School in Australia, where he was destined to play an important formative role in the education of Prince

Charles. The Prince spent two terms at Timbertops, the school's outback offshoot, which he hugely enjoyed and which was generally regarded as the making of him.

'I went out with a boy and came back with a man,' is how his equerry, Squadron Leader (later Sir) David Checketts, put it.

The Governors now appointed John Dancy as Master of Marlborough College. Tall, bald, scholarly and exuding a grave demeanour, he was cast in a very different mould to that of his predecessor. Undeterred by a pronounced limp, caused by an earlier bout of polio, the new Master could frequently be seen striding across Court in dark suit with black gown billowing behind him.

Soon after Dancy had arrived, I bumped into my chum RP. He pointed towards the Chapel.

'There's Dancy,' he exclaimed. 'He looks a bit like a raven from the Tower of London, don't you think?'

John Dancy commanded an immense sense of awe and respect, and no one remained seated when Dancy entered a room, not even the Common Room. Wykehamist and scholar of New College, Oxford, he was said to communicate at the family breakfast table in classical Greek. His reputation as a tough headmaster preceded him and, if the truth be known, the beaks at Marlborough were shivering in their shoes long before he arrived. His antics at Lancing were referred to as 'Dancy's Inferno', not least because he had sacked several staff when appointed there eight years previously. Talking to a very senior man at Winchester College some forty years later, I mentioned that I was an Old Marlburian.

'Winchester has an apology to make to Marlborough,' he said.

'What is that?' I enquired.

'John Dancy,' he rejoined. Unkind, perhaps, but a point of view.

I sometimes wonder if he saw himself as a latter-day Dr Arnold whom, it was foretold by the Provost of Oriel, would 'change the face of education all through the public schools of England', prior to his being appointed to the headship of Rugby at the tender age of thirty-three. Certainly, Dancy's *Public Schools and the Future* (1963), the book in which the new Master outlined his vision for the independent sector, was considered a pioneering effort by some, but many Marlburians felt betrayed. Henry Brooke (Littlefield 1916), a future Home Secretary and one time Chairman of the College Council, was to comment, 'John Dancy does have ideas. They aren't all equally good, but he goes on having them.'

In the preparation of this work I have received comments that these views are jaded. Others admired Dancy enormously, have described private conversations that revealed the man's sensitivity and hailed him as a hero with regard to his vision for the future of Marlborough College. He introduced girls, and that certainly and irreparably altered the character of the College, and he reformed Sunday worship by splitting the school in two. The junior half continued to attend Chapel, the remainder went to St Peter's Church, since it was no longer required by the parish. Once broken, the traditional place in the life of the school that Christian worship held could never be restored.

Formal, communal religious activity has almost vanished from the corpus of school life today. Maybe it all had to be—Marlborough is not the brutal place it was and I am sure Dancy, in part, can be thanked for that—but further words that John Betjeman placed in the mouth of the Old Marburian Bishop in *'Summoned by Bells'* were certainly no longer true.

> The centre and the mainspring of your lives,
> The Inspiration for your work and sport,
> The corporate life at this great public school
> Spring from its glorious Chapel.

There are no buildings at the College named after John Dancy, which seems a shame since his was a pivotal tenancy of the Master's Lodge (1961-1972); perhaps a girl's boarding house would be appropriate.

At Summerfield, the eccentric but endearing 'Cogs' also accepted a post at Geelong and I was faced with a new housemaster. This was to be the third time that my pastoral care had been placed with an individual whom neither I, nor my parents, had previously met, and needless to say, they never encountered (with a couple of brief exceptions) any of my other teachers either. The new man, appointed by Dancy, was known by the unfortunate sobriquet of 'Slug', however in contrast to an aspect of his character that this nickname implied, he was soon making rapid changes.

The days of crude containers for condiments in the dining room had definitely passed. Thick pile carpets and designer curtains appeared on the private side of the house, a luncheon club was formed that regularly invited distinguished guests to a splendid repast and plans were drawn up to improve some of the less salubrious aspects of the boarding facilities. Parents were invited to cocktails after matins on Sunday, an innovation that appealed to many. Marlborough College was a country school in a market town, and the early register confirms a substantial intake of country parsons' sons and those of local squires and gentry. But things were changing. The majority of fees were still paid, as were mine, from 'old money' rather than income but now parents came, increasingly, from industry, commerce, accountancy, marketing and other occupations where income alone could meet the rapidly rising cost of school fees.

It could have been predicted that there would be tension. No one of my disposition would have chosen a scientist, let alone 'Slug', as his housemaster, and he viewed my activities with deep suspicion and my efforts in the classroom with disdain. Glancing through my recent reports at our first meeting, he manifested extreme disapproval.

A chemist by training, you would be as likely to find the man out hunting or turning a bell as you would find a beagle in a belfry. For my part, I was stubborn and a round peg in a square hole. There was going to be trouble ahead.

Some say that for every negative there is a positive, and friendship with my organ teacher, ABS-M, was growing. We saw each other most days, in Chapel, and our conversations began to widen beyond musical topics. ABS-M was keen to encourage boys to think for themselves and frequently made outrageous remarks or acted provocatively. On one occasion, he had prepared a complicated voluntary to be played at the end of matins on Sunday. As everyone trooped out of Chapel, chattering away as usual and not paying any attention to the splendid music, he turned off the organ, which fell silent while he continued to play on a dumb console. Astonished, we asked him what he was doing.

'It makes no difference as to whether the pipes are speaking or not. No one is listening!' he groused. At which point, he thrust the music into my hands and stormed out of chapel.

In hindsight, he sometimes reminds me of the teacher, Mr Keating, in the film *Dead Poets Society* (1989). By coincidence, the boy who commits suicide in the film was played by a young Robert Sean Leonard, who was to become a good friend of my son, Alexander.

In 1963, Dr John Robinson (C1 1933) published his book *Honest to God*, which produced cascades of derision from the press, who referred to him as the bishop who did not believe in God. The *Sunday Observer* wrote: 'Bishop says the God up there or out there will have to go.'

Robinson had already achieved notoriety in the 1950s by defending the publication of D.H. Lawrence's raunchy novel *Lady Chatterley's Lover*. His son Stephen was in C House and one of my best friends.

ABS-M saw Robinson as a man who paid far too much attention to Christian theology and the Greco-Judaic tradition while disregarding—as he put it—'the wider aspects of man's spiritual inheritance'. ABS-M was well read in classical mythology and traditional stories. Did he know the tales of Sinbad the sailor, Haroun el-Rachid and Leigh Hunt's poem, 'Abou Ben Adam', I asked him when we first started talking about such things. Of course, he did. He was also knowledgeable about all sorts of faiths and teachings. One of his friends was the Chief Druid, no less. ABS-M used to make trips to London to visit Watkin's bookshop in Cecil Court, just off the Charing Cross Road, and returned to Marlborough with fascinating tomes on esoteric matters. In this era of multi-faiths, it takes an effort to remind oneself that in those days Watkin's was virtually the only place where such publications were available in the whole of the UK, and to find a public school beak on friendly terms with a druid was in itself pretty remarkable. All this was intriguing to a small group of ABS-M's pupils, and we persuaded him to allow us to form a society for the express purpose of discussing unusual ideas. Wary that the society might be considered subversive in a Christian community, ABS-M suggested that we call it the Jung Society—a tamer, more conventional name and something of a smokescreen. He invited me to be the secretary. There was a huge collection of societies, ranging from stamp collecting to mountaineering (not to mention the Campanology Society) and to be appointed a secretary was an honour that carried with it the right to carry an umbrella—a significant status symbol.

Without making heavy weather (forgive the pun) of this point, it was another step in the tribal indoctrination process to keep everyone out in the rain unless they had achieved some level of distinction. A society secretary, captain of games, member of the upper fifth and above, prefect or head of house are examples. I was keeper of the Chapel music and secretary of the Jung Society, so scored on two fronts.

The discussions at the Jung Society were stimulating, and mostly centred around questioning assumptions and adopting an analytical approach to teachings that one might normally be expected to accept on faith. On one occasion, ABS-M took a few of us on a trip to Glastonbury, Wookey

Hole, and Wells where we discussed the architecture of the sublime Chapter House, in particular, and legends associated with those ancient sites.

The idea of Jesus visiting Britain with Joseph of Aramathea, and the mystery of the Glastonbury Thorn, were especially fascinating to our young minds.

On another day, we went to see the supposed evidence of an alien landing, near Shaftesbury. When we arrived in a muddy Dorset field, it was a surprise to find the venue closely guarded by a detachment of soldiers, and even more astonishing to be told that the so-called landing site registered high radiation levels on a military Geiger counter.

The best part of these trips was that they ended with a splendid cream tea, courtesy of ABS-M.

> In childhood once we crouched before our teacher,
> Growing content, in time, with what he taught;
> How does the story end? What happened to us?
> We came like water and like wind were gone.
> (1967 translation of *The Rubaiyyat of Omar Khayaam*,
>   Graves/Ali-Shah)

In due course, he became an enthusiastic raconteur of the tales of the mythical Mulla Nasrudin, sometimes known as the Hodja, whose jokes pervade the teahouses of the Middle East. The 'jokes', he explained, often reveal, on closer analysis, unexpected dimensions in the human thought process. Later in the decade, he even put on a production in the Bradlean with boys acting out traditional tales. The title of the entertainment was *Not So Much a Stage Play; More a Way of Life*, which parodied the name of one of those popular television satire programmes of the '60s that systematically debunked almost anything of value in the British way of life. The first joke on the menu was especially appropriate for a school audience:

> The Hodja said something ungrammatical to a pedant whom he was rowing across a pond.
> 'You've clearly never studied grammar,' said the pedant. 'You must have wasted half your life!'
> A few minutes later the Hodja addressed him.

'Can you swim?'

'No!'

'Pity. We're sinking. All your life is wasted!'

Stories like these and related tales would have a significant influence on me for the rest of my life, but a reputation as an intellectual I certainly did not possess, so my involvement with the Jung Society further roused Slug's deepest suspicions. The fact that ABS-M and the Master, both scholars, both Wykehamists, only tolerated each other did not help. Dancy had actually fagged for Ithy-Pithy at Winchester.

An unhealthy dynamic was developing between those who liked me and wanted to help me, and those who considered me to be a weirdo. One of my staunchest supporters was Reg Sainsbury, the College porter. Never a day passed when I did not pause to chat with this splendid diminutive character, in his smartly buttoned uniform, as he shuffled about with the post or tolled the bell above the porter's lodge. He had come out of the trenches in 1918 and faithfully served the College ever since. When I finally left Marlborough, he wrote me a charming and much valued letter.

As time moved on and my sixteenth birthday approached, I seemed to be caught in a whirl of activity. There was bell ringing and beagling, duties for the Chapel music and chaplaincy, house discussion groups and running the Jung Society. I was keen on arranging outings, which included a visit to the newly launched English Bach Festival in Oxford, the Whitechapel Bell Foundry and the House of Commons, where we heard Harold Wilson, still in opposition, speak on higher education. Wilson used to say that he considered the founding of the Open University to be his highest achievement. Some might say it was his *only* achievement.

I played percussion in the orchestra, with questionable success, and struggled with the bugle in the CCF band under the excellent lead of Bob Peel. I also organised the group of boys who carried out charitable work in the town. In particular, I visited several blind ladies on a regular basis. One of these, a Miss Beech, who lived at 104 London Road, had been blind since birth and was totally fluent in Braille; the technique invented in 1829 by Louis Braille, a blind Frenchman. I found her skill and spirit to be quite extraordinary.

Against this background my studies suffered, and in the summer of 1963 my O-level results were disappointing. My poor father, faced with another bad report, was beginning to despair and in the autumn, when we returned from the long holiday, I felt the grip of Slug's imposing hand on my collar. To him, what mattered above all else was classroom performance, resitting failed O-levels, exercise by taking regular 'sweats' to Four Mile Clump, and supporting 'the house' on the touchline.

Slug's opinions ruled. He was the College establishment incarnate; I was an oddball and it seemed clear to me that we had developed a mutual loathing—a case of the institution versus the individual. What was it that Kurt Hahn said? 'It is the sin of the soul to force young people into opinions—indoctrination is of the devil ...'

I have recently read *MARLBOROUGH—an open examination written by the boys* (1963) and for the first time it has really come home to me that a cult of games and 'house spirit' existed in which I felt sure that 'Slug' was the prime mover—as far as I was concerned. As with any cult, woe betide an individual who steps out of line or shows disrespect. Unwittingly, and as an unconventional rebel, I trod a dangerous path.

My interests, hobbies and preoccupations encompassed none of the things that were dear to 'Slug', and I began to suspect that in the eyes of the man responsible for my pastoral care, all my activities amounted to meaningless vapour. Even when, at the end of one summer term, I gridded, solo, the seventy-six miles to Fittleworth in West Sussex, where my parents had recently acquired a small farmhouse, I have no doubt that 'Slug' regarded this not as an enterprising and perhaps even courageous act, but as just another symptom of eccentricity.

True, my studies were important and I was underperforming academically, but I began to sense that 'Slug' was starting to view everything I did with hostility. A trivial incident exemplifies what I mean. On one occasion, I left my grid leaning against the sanatorium wall. It slipped, and snapped the 'earth wire' for Miss Enoch's radio that ran down the side of the building from her flat. A huge row erupted, as it was immediately assumed that I had engineered this unfortunate episode, although I cannot imagine what motive I would have in upsetting my friendly piano teacher. Careless and ham-fisted I may have been, but destructive—no.

On another occasion 'Slug' approached me in the Norwood Hall when I was eating with my chums.

'I have been hearing things about you,' he announced in a loud voice. 'Come to my study immediately after lunch.'

It struck me that he relished embarrassing me in front of my friends. It also strikes me as amazing that I remember those precise words spoken fifty years ago. What an impact they must have had.

Who had been saying things, and what things? I wanted to know.

Maybe, John Whiteley, the new chaplain's, off the cuff comment: 'Well, Hall, if you can't hack it here, it will be Marlborough's loss,' revealed that far too much chattering had been going on. Even public school common rooms can deteriorate into gossip shops, and people can get 'things' about people. Tension was rising and, sadly, Gavin Fargus, my one confidant outside College circles, had also left for pastures new.

None of this was conducive to my wellbeing, and as 1963 drew to an end I felt torn apart and became increasingly unhappy. During November I was trying very hard to perfect a difficult Bach organ fugue ('The St Anne' BWV 552) for the music competitions. This aroused within me a real passion to achieve that I had not discovered before and, obsessively, I grabbed every spare moment for practice.

In marked contrast, 'Slug's' seemingly unwarranted impositions thwarted me, threatened me, provoked my pig-headedness and created excessive stress, but at least I did not suffer the onslaught endured by Siegfried Sassoon when his housemaster publicly castigated him, saying: 'I know why you play organ, you play organ to get out of playing games, you wretched brute!'

Oh dear! The cult of games and 'house spirit'.

In hindsight, it all seems rather silly, no more than any group of teachers should have been able to handle. Today, of course, there are elaborate plans in place to redress the balance between the institution and the individual; such matters have come full circle. Forty years later, I met the late Alan MacKichan at an Old Marlburian reunion. I had not spoken to him since leaving the College.

'I think Marlborough College owes your generation an apology,' were his parting words. I was astonished by his candour.

At a following reunion, less than a handful of OMs, out of an intake of 200 (1961), attended the day's events, so MacKichan may have had a point. However, in the autumn of 1963 my situation bore the hallmarks of an impending crisis and my parents were becoming concerned by the tone of my letters. I had even discovered the telephone, so they drove down to Marlborough to discuss my position. It was shortly after the Beatles' first appearance at the Royal Variety Performance in the presence of the Queen Mother. A vibrant can-do generation was upon us, while we remained incarcerated at the College in grey shirts with stiff, starched detachable white collars and all that implied.

My parents booked into the Ailesbury Arms and in the afternoon we all went beagling. As we plodded across the muddy fields, I tried to explain how I felt and they attempted to understand my point of view, but it seemed beyond them. I was unable to explain how the juxtaposition of my inner world and preoccupations—the 'God bug' that had bitten me didn't help—with the pressures exerted by the College, manifested by 'Slug', was tearing me apart. I was signalling an imminent nervous breakdown.

> Our birth is but a sleep and a forgetting:
> The soul that rises with us, our life's star,
> Hath had elsewhere its setting,
> And cometh from afar;
> Not in entire forgetfulness,
> And not in utter nakedness,
> But trailing clouds of glory do we come
> From God, who is our home:
> Heaven lies about us in our infancy!
> Shades of the prison-house begin to close
> Upon the growing boy ...
> (William Wordsworth: 'Intimations of Immortality',
>   1807))

My parents suggested that I consult a psychiatrist, so this was arranged by the College and an appointment made with Doctor O'Grady in Oxford. I clearly remember taking the train from sullen Swindon to the city of dreaming spires, where I was due to meet my mother before going on to see the consultant.

It was 23rd November, a wet and windswept day. Autumn leaves blew down Broad Street as I made my way to our rendezvous, and newspaper hoardings, flapping in the strong breeze, featured details of Jack Kennedy's assassination. This was the news that had reached me in the Memorial Library, at Marlborough, on the previous evening, although I felt curiously detached from this world-shattering event. I had been raised on huge doses of *The Lone Ranger*, *Wyatt Earp*, *Wells Fargo* and *Davy Crocket*. Shooting each other was what Americans did—right?

The next episode was to follow on the 24th, when Jack Ruby shot Lee Harvey Oswald (Kennedy's supposed assassin) live on television.

My mother had come down from Paddington, and after a quiet cup of tea we had time to pause in New College Chapel. As the clouds broke and the late afternoon sun's piercing rays lit the hallowed recesses of the ancient building, I played the 'St Anne' and Bach's chorale prelude 'Liebster Jesu, Wir sind hier' (BWV 731) on the fine organ.

The meeting with the psychiatrist proved to be a waste of time and money, providing no solutions. O'Grady asked me lots of questions and seemed especially interested in finding out whether I ever masturbated. I am not suggesting that he was perverted in any way, but if this exemplified Freudian analysis, his enquiry seemed rather beside the point. If life was made more agreeable from time to time, by what the comic actor Kenneth Williams once called 'a visit to Barclays Bank', was it any of his business?

I also understand, from anecdotal comments, that one of the bachelor house masters at the College, when first interviewing fourteen-year-old boys, asked the same question. On one occasion, meeting a chum who had just come from that particular housemaster's study looking a little flushed, I asked him if he was OK.

'Just come from my first interview with PP,' he retorted. 'He asked me a whole lot of questions. Then just as I was about to leave he peered at me over his half-rimmed specs and, staring hard, said: "Are you in the habit of masturbating?"'

'Oh, that!!' I exclaimed. 'Didn't anyone warn you? He always tries that one. I think it gives him a cheap thrill! Dirty old man!'

Needless to say, we were young and impressionable, and one cannot read too much into these things, but it did make us wonder. It was certainly an odd way to initiate a relationship, and we wondered if question and answer were duly recorded. I dread to think how it would be regarded today, but at least 'Slug' spared me that kind of embarrassment.

Several weeks later, the day of the music competitions arrived and I duly performed my party piece on the Chapel organ. It went surprisingly well and I achieved a good ranking in line with my age and experience. I even beat my close friend Richard Inglis, who had submitted 'The Giant' (BWV 690), another great Bach fugue.

The next day, Sunday, I had been invited to lunch with distant cousins in Nether Wallop. Colonel Peter Hammond and his wife, Beryl, were splendid folk. Beryl (née Oldrey) was a pioneer in treating speech impediments. (I wonder if she knew Lionel Logue, King George VI's therapist) They came over from Hampshire to collect me after the morning service and we spent a happy day. At teatime, I reminded them that I should be getting back to College when suddenly headlights shone in the drive, a car drew up and my parents appeared at the door. This was a shock in itself, but when they explained that it had been decided that I was not returning to Marlborough, I was absolutely shattered. Apparently, they had been to Summerfield during the day, collected my belongings and then drove over to Nether Wallop. They had decided that Marlborough was too much for me and that I should be removed.

Blubbing all the way back to London in the dark, hot tears rolling down my cheeks, my greatest anxiety was that I would never see my friends again. I need not have been concerned on that account, as a stream of sympathetic letters arrived in the next few days from various beaks and friends: ABS-M, Robert Ferry, the Director of Music and especially Reg Sainsbury, the porter, who said, 'I was so sorry to hear the sad news that you have left the College, I always enjoyed our chats in the lodge. I will miss you a lot but do look in if you are ever passing this way.' Which, of course, I did.

Several friends have read this chapter, while in preparation, and suggested that there must have been more sinister reasons why I was taken away. There were not. I was just a teenager in a tizz who was behind with his studies and at odds with his housemaster. My parents made the decision and I was not consulted.

I often wonder if being wrenched away from Marlborough had a long-term adverse effect. I used to think it had, and that not completing the cycle had given me a sense of inferiority. My parents were embarrassed and felt let down by the College, but not by me. However, with the benefit of hindsight, I think my departure opened new doors, and since my whole life has been a cacophony of ever-changing circumstances, many quite abrupt, it was probably destined.

Marlborough College has now changed out of all recognition, and for the better. It is currently (2013) in robust form with a new Master—Jonathan Leigh. I continued to see ABS-M until his death nearly forty years later. His funeral took place in St George's, the pretty church at Preshute, close to the water meadows on the west side of Marlborough, and I was invited to deliver the eulogy from the pulpit, which I did, surrounded by, among others, a number of his former colleagues and my now aged mentors. How that came to pass is a very long story.

Read on, dear reader, read on!

> When to Marlboro', old and worn
> We wander back like ghosts,
> And see some rascal now unborn,
> Running between the posts.
> Ah! Then we'll cry, thank God my lads,
> The Kennett's running still,
> And see! The old white horse still pads
> Up there on Granham Hill.
> (J. Bain: 'All Aboard! (The Leavers Song)', first sung at the
>   Christmas concert in 1912)

Footnote

In 2011, by kind permission of the then Master, Nick Sampson; Lucinda, and I organised a two-day seminar at the College in aid of Afghanaid and Hoopoe Books entitled *'Understanding Afghanistan'*. It was well attended and voted a great success. One notable member of the local community e-mailed me with these words: 'the most inspiring event I've been to at the College'. Speakers included an MP; Major-General John Lorimer (C1 1976); a Commander RN; an Oxford Professor, a film maker (*The Boy Mir*) and several notable writers including Bijan Omrani the co-author of *'Afghanistan: a Companion and Guide'*.

Chapter 4
High Days and Holidays

We must not say these were our happiest days,
But our happiest days, so far.
(Dorothy Reynolds, *'Salad Days'*, 1954)

I HAD BEEN at boarding school for nearly ten years. This meant that between the ages of seven and seventeen, fewer than forty-eight months had been spent with my family. Because my birthday fell on the Ides of March, I never spent a birthday at home during the greater part of my childhood.

Most of the holidays were spent at our huge flat in Chelsea, which occupied the top two floors above Sussex House Preparatory School—but more of that later.

Sussex always provided a bolthole. We would often drive down on a Saturday, passing through Fulham where houses that fetch six or seven figure sums today run in neat terraces, back from the New King's Road. This is where many of the servants who attended families in Knightsbridge and Kensington lived, in the days when the capitol was still predominantly populated by English people.

Much of my grandparents' life revolved around the equestrian community, which is not surprising as Baba had been a cavalry officer and international polo player with a high handicap. Both sides of the family had a long connection with 'the turf'. It could be said that it was in the blood.

Gawky's family, the Oldreys, were of Devonshire farming stock although her grandfather, Robert Foale Oldrey, moved to London and made a great deal of money after he embraced a career in the City, during the mid-nineteenth century. In 1877, at the age of forty-seven, he retired to Harpole Hall, a substantial property in Northamptonshire, and it is there that the link with racing began. Although he had owned horses for some years, in 1878, under the nom-de-course of 'Mr Devon', he registered the handsome colours of black, orange sleeves and cap that had become available on the death by suicide of Lord Ribblesdale in 1875. It is ironic that Robert Foale Oldrey himself committed suicide some years later.

Iris Oldrey (Gawky) was herself a keen horsewoman and I have a charming photograph of her riding sidesaddle, taken in 1908, shortly after her marriage. Her two brothers, Blatchford and Vivian, were also accomplished horsemen, polo players and point-to-pointers. Their mother, a strikingly handsome Irish redhead, was the daughter of Robert Foale Oldrey's trainer. It must have been some achievement for her to make it into the Big House at Harpole.

Blatchford was exceptional. Representing England at the Olympic Games in 1908, in the presence of King Edward VII and Queen Alexandra, he was presented with a gold cigarette case by the King that is still in the family's possession. Blatchford, a captain in the 4th (Irish) Dragoon Guards, had introduced Iris to my grandfather, a fellow officer, but on 29th October 1914, aged thirty-one, while commanding two squadrons, he was killed at the battle of Neuve Chapelle. He is buried in the Canadian War Cemetery (No. 2) in the Pas de Calais. He had actually been promoted to major, but his promotion had not been gazetted at the time of his death. His brother, Vivian, died of pneumonia five years later while on active service in Egypt. He lies in the War Memorial Cemetery in Cairo.

Memorials to both of these gallant young men, my great-uncles, can be found in what Wilfred Owen called 'sad shires'—but again, more of that later. Gawky's nephew, David Oldrey, has continued the family's equestrian tradition, as have other family members. He recently won his hundredth race (spread over fifty years) and achieved places in the Derby and King George while his horse Halsbury won the Cesarewitch in 1981.

David was steward of the Jockey Club for some years, achieving the office of deputy senior steward from 2000 to 2003, and for five years was president of the Thoroughbred Breeders Association. In collaboration with Christie's, the fine arts auctioneers, he completed a beautiful catalogue and history of the paintings and furniture at the Jockey Club Rooms in Newmarket, something that had not been undertaken before.

In the spring, we all met at point-to-points arranged by the local hunts, and these were held at Parham and Cowdray or Peperharow. I used to love the informal atmosphere of the race meetings that started soon after we had parked in a field close to the course and spread out rugs on the ground for a picnic. After demolishing a cold chicken salad, my parents each downing a glass of dark stout, we were off to study the form and place our bets. Billy Brock came with us, straining at the lead.

Gawky's grand-daughters, my first cousins, Tessa and Jill, both rode and over the years they won several cups and dozens of gaudy rosettes. In 1958, aged only nineteen, Tessa married the National Hunt amateur jockey John Stuart Evans at the little pre-Conquest church of St James at Selham where we used to take the train to London before Dr Beeching tore up the line. John became a successful trainer and trained Code of Love for my aunt, Susan Maxwell, which won seven races.

Years later, my son Tarquin learned to ride Texas-style when he worked as a cowboy for several months.

'Do you ride 'long'?' enquired Susan, at a family gathering.

'Oh yes!' he replied. 'For hours!'

Tessa and John's progeny continued the tradition in horsemanship. Their son and my godson, Nicky Evans, bearing what he regarded as the 'Baba mantle', became a useful polo player himself.

In 2006, Tessa called me.

'Guess what?' she said. 'My grand-daughter, Molly, has won an exciting victory'. It was true; as she went on to explain. The fourteen year old, with her six-strong team of Scottish riders and ponies, had won the championship at the DAKS International Pony Club Mounted Games Championship at the Royal Windsor Horse Show

Betting was fun and visiting the paddock to note the runners' finer points and choose a winner was taken seriously, although I was more inclined to bet on a horse whose name appealed—or on Tessa and Jill, if they were racing. A fine beast named Lobo Lad did me a few good turns over the years.

Some placed their bets at the Totalisator, and others with flamboyantly dressed bookies who, sporting every conceivable form of attire, were perched on rickety stands signalling tic-tac, their special sign language, and chalking up the odds on blackboards. In the distance, under the scudding white clouds of March and April skies the bright green of the racecourse stretched out over the hillside and the smell of spring and fresh grass hung in the air. Sometimes we met Cal Bradley-Williams, my godmother's eccentric son, who would haul us up on to a friend's hay cart to watch the races propped up on a bale of straw, binoculars at the ready, while Cal and the local farmers passed round flasks of sloe gin or port.

Point-to-points could be very exciting, especially as most of the riders and owners were from the immediate neighbourhood. As the horses thundered twice round the course, taking the huge brushwood jumps in their stride, we strained every muscle to keep our favourite in view. After all, even half a crown at eight to one could prove very profitable.

When the races were over we totted up our winnings. Then, along with dozens of other cars, churning up the field and spattering mud over the windscreen, we headed home. If my parents were up on the day we stopped at the Bear in Esher, which provided a good dinner in those days.

When the point-to-point season ended, the polo season began and this time we were off to Cowdray Park or Ambersham. Baba was still umpiring in the 1950s and we had seats in the members' enclosure. Everyone knew everyone and retired colonels with their wives and dogs mingled with the local gentry and the occasional exotically attired maharajah with his family.

'Why is that little girl black?' I asked, on first encountering an African child. It made a big impression. My memories of South Africa had faded. I can still visualise her today.

The Queen and Prince Philip were frequent visitors, together with Charles and Anne who, in the early days, could still be seen on a leading rein.

Between chukkas the elegant crowd descended on the pitch to 'tread in' fragments of turf torn up by the horses' hooves. They methodically worked over the ground and when the bell clanged loudly for the next chukka the terrain was fairly smooth and ready for play. It was a vivid and lively scene, made no less exotic by the presence of a few colourfully turbaned Indian grooms. One of the more enthusiastic, if overweight, players was the popular radio comedian, Jimmy Edwards who, sporting huge handlebar moustaches, perched precariously on his polo pony.

At the end of a tournament the Queen, accompanied by Lord Cowdray, would present a chunky gold cup and individual trophies to members of the winning team.

'Why has Lord Cowdray only got one arm?' I asked my aunt Susan, who was a friend of his.

'It was the war—ssh! We don't talk about it,' she replied.

If we got bored, Richard and I would head for 'the ruins', the sprawling remains of the Tudor mansion that had burnt down in 1793. Here, a few hundred yards behind the grandstand we could climb fragments of staircase, peer up massive chimneys and imagine ourselves in great kitchens or ballrooms that had been open to the skies for a hundred and sixty years.

Following our return from Schleswig-Holstein in 1952, we visited north Cornwall each summer for nine years and remained there from mid-August until the second week in September. We were drawn to Cornwall because my mother's family, the Mathews, traced their direct male line back to the sixteenth century when they lived at St Kew and the nearby fortified manor house of Tresungers which was rebuilt in 1660.

In the nineteenth century, my great-grandfather, Brownlow Hoare Mathew, had added the name Lannowe to become Mathew-Lannowe. Lannowe is a farm in the parish of St Kew. King Arthur was said to have had two castles in that part of Cornwall and the remains of prehistoric earthworks could still be seen. Anyone familiar with those parts will know the deep valleys, thick with English beech and oak, that stretch inland from the wild Atlantic coast, the streams and windblown hillocks. At the time of my family's early records the area was largely populated by sailors, fishermen, farmers, hunting parsons and squires. I wonder if there was considerable poverty, but it is tempting to conjure up a romantic image of secret liaisons, nautical adventures and smuggling associated with remote homesteads, inns and hidden tracks and pathways. The family's West Country roots and later involvement with the New World has led me to wonder whether there was any connection with John Cabot and his West Country crew who sailed in the *Mathew* from Bristol in 1496 and discovered Newfoundland.

Long before the construction of the motorways, our eagerly awaited holidays kicked off with arduous car journeys, crawling through Slough and Maidenhead and, once beyond the Home Counties, through small market towns dotted along the way. For amusement, we made sure that we carried a stock of I-SPY spotter's guides, which were produced by the now defunct *News Chronicle*. There were dozens of subjects, such as *I-SPY Churches*, *I-SPY*

Cars and *I-SPY On the Farm*, which were useful educational tools as well as time-killers. Another diversion was to count the number of AA motorbike patrolmen with their sidecars, who saluted us as they passed. They could see that my father was a member because of the shiny yellow chrome insignia fixed to the Hillman's bumper, and officers observed this charming practice, which started in the early years of the twentieth century and continued until 1961.

Sometimes we went through Marlborough, and in the early years, my mother would say: 'One day you may go to school here.'

In other years, we stopped at Stonehenge, pulling into a field by the side of the A303; something you would not be able to do today, and ran across the grass and between the megaliths, glad to be able to stretch our legs.

'I-Spy the Butt of Sherry', we intoned in unison, as we passed the landmark pub in Mere, knowing that we had broken the back of the journey.

All roads led to Taunton, where we stayed the night with Denise Bell in her terraced house in Staplegrove Road. Denise had returned from Pietermaritzburg in South Africa, where she had nursed me after my birth, and she now worked as a chiropractor. Short, with grey hair tied in a tight bun, red shiny cheeks and sparkling eyes, she would provide a cheerful welcome after our long journey and, sitting us down for supper, serve a hot chicken casserole cooked in the hay box that she kept below the wooden draining board in the kitchen. A devotee of this quaint method of cooking, whereby the food was preheated and then left to cook itself in an insulated box surrounded by hay; she argued that it saved on fuel bills and was convinced that food tasted better and that more nutrition was retained. My parents found this lengthy process rather eccentric, I recall, but the meals were delicious.

Denise, who had been imprisoned for demonstrating against apartheid and standing up for blacks in South Africa, had attained something of the status of a guru in my parents' eyes. On one occasion, I asked her how she had survived conditions in a South African jail.

'All you need in life is your own toothbrush!' she chortled.

She was certainly not afraid to speak her mind and was particularly fond of me, having been present in those dark days following my birth. She would remind me of the passage in Psalm 91: 'With a long life will I satisfy him, and shew him my salvation'—it had given her strength at that time.

'You will need to work on yourself,' she would say and if, as the years went by, she observed undesirable traits in our characters, she would say so.

'Avoid negative emotions' was a frequent dictum, and following my habit of saying 'sorry' at any opportunity she scolded me harshly:

'Why say that? It is lying, you're not sorry at all!'

She was keen that I exercised my eyeballs to improve my poor vision and suggested rolling them in their sockets for five minutes every day, up, down and to left and right. Fingers, for piano playing, also need to be strengthened by strumming rhythmically against thighs. I don't think she spared my parents either, but not in front of the children. She was a bit 'sussy' and we were slightly scared of her. Some years later I heard that she had expressed anxiety that my room in our London flat was haunted. I am not sure how she had come to this conclusion as I do not recall her visiting us in Cadogan Square and I certainly was not aware of any ghostly presence. However, not long after Denise had died my future mother-in-law—who was also a bit fey—swore that she had seen a white-haired lady on the staircase when, to our certain knowledge, there was no one in the building. Long after our family left Chelsea, several other strange incidents occurred and an exorcist was consulted.

In the 1970s, the years just preceding her death, she remained a good friend to my brother Richard and me, and lent us books about the Masters of Central Asia—the *Khwajagan*. We never discussed the matter in any depth, however, in hindsight, I wonder if she had been in touch with some form of mystical tradition—a touch of 'the miraculous'.

The following day, bidding our farewells, we set off early and the next very exciting event was at our journey's end, when we spotted the sea.

'Who's going to see the ocean first?' my parents would clamour in unison.

'I see the sea! I see the sea!' Richard and I shrieked from the back of the car.

This was an annual game but, of course, over the years, we got wise to the lie of the land and the gaps in rough stone walls where the first glimpse of the Atlantic would appear.

Our destination was Doyden, a huge grey forbidding building on the cliffs above Port Quin. It belonged to my maternal aunt's brother-in-law, Donald Maxwell, who had converted it into spacious self-catering flats.

Ugly it may have been, but we adored Doyden and were soon racing up the staircase and staring out over what became a familiar and much-loved view across the bay to Rumps Point and the Mouls. Over the years that glorious panorama would, like an accomplished thespian, adopt the mantle of every varying weather condition. Sometimes a thick mist or driving rain obscured even the closest contours. At other times, the full fury of an Atlantic gale thundered in deep recesses within the cliffs and torrents of spume and spray shot over the headland. Once the storm had subsided, a strange silence settled over the grey water, only shattered by the shrill sound of seagulls, and a somniferous swell would break gently, flecking foam against the black slate cliffs. On a glorious day, white clouds raced and birds soared across a blue sky. The sea swirled around 'the Cow and Calf,' a rocky outcrop that rose like a bovine monster above the surface at low tide and, huge patches of the palest aquamarine, the deepest cobalt and radiant lapis stretched out over the seabed, right across the bay.

There was a small cove immediately below Doyden and each year, at the earliest opportunity, we scrambled down the hillside, eager to explore old haunts, while Billy Brock was off across the springy turf sniffing at the entrance of earthy burrows for loitering rabbits.

We had been cooped up in the car for two days and Richard and I tended to bicker, which irritated our parents, so this was supreme release.

Standing high above the rocky inlet, approached by a stony track, a small folly with turrets and weather-beaten battlements, boasting Spartan accommodation, was available as a holiday let to adventurous families or those of a romantic disposition.

It would be some years before the tower became familiar to viewers of the BBC television series *Poldark*, in which locals appeared as extras. Around the corner was the hamlet of Port Quin, where seven or eight slate and granite cottages nestled in the valley alongside farm buildings. The houses also belonged to Donald, who rented them to holidaymakers.

'Come along,' he said to me and my brother one afternoon, leading us into the old barn at the top of the cobbled slipway. There he related the heart-rending story of how the village had been a busy fishing centre until one wicked night, years ago in the days of sail, the whole fleet was destroyed in a ferocious gale.

'All the men were drowned, wives and children were left penniless and the village was abandoned, leaving no trace of their passing,' he related. 'But there is a secret,' he continued, pointing into the dim recesses of the barn, where we could just make out a long length of heavy timber, like a mast or huge flagpole, that disappeared into the darkness at the very end of the stone building. 'Known only to a few,' Donald continued. 'That is the oak bowsprit of one of the ships that foundered on that dreadful night!'

Geoff Provis, in his fascinating book, *The Seafarers of Port Isaac* (2011), casts some doubt on this legend but he concedes that there is no firm evidence either way. However, there is a photograph in the book of a schooner named the *Madeleine* stranded on the rocks at Port Quin in 1911. It has a fine bowsprit—the very one to be found in the darkness of the barn? I wonder.

At low tide the cove was, under normal circumstances, a perfect place for children to play. A bubbling stream ran down from the hills across a thousand quartz-encrusted boulders and rocky pools, brimming with tiny shrimps that darted among limpets and red sea anemones that were replenished at every tide. Two smugglers' caves ran deep into the cliff side, and it was thrilling to penetrate the interior where the constant drip of water from the roof, splashing on to rocks and into puddles, echoed and blended, in the semi-darkness, with the muffled sound of children's voices. Huge boulders, wedged against the sloping ceiling in the furthest corner of the cavern, protected treasure beyond our wildest dreams—or so we told ourselves.

But there was danger too. Atlantic coves could be subject to flash torrents, and further up the coast at Lynmouth and Lynton, twenty-eight people were killed when a wall of water crashed down the ravine in 1952. On our first holiday at Port Quin a teenage girl dived into the sea at high tide, unaware of the rocks hidden beneath the surface. She broke her neck and died on the beach a few minutes later. I can still see her ashen face as she lay there stretched out across the pebbles. That was more than sixty years ago and I sometimes wonder who she was and how her family have coped with their loss.

Occasionally we ventured over to Polzeath, a resort that was considered a bit downmarket, although Beaks' Cove, an inlet off the main beach, was so named because of its popularity with public school masters (beaks). Awesome surf rolled in from the Atlantic, and 1930s-style pebble-dashed pink, white and blue villas clung to the cliff side.

'My God! There's one of my teachers in his bathing trunks!' I exclaimed, on one occasion.

I drove through Polzeath recently. Superficially, it has changed little in sixty years although beaks are today more likely to be found in Crete or Carnac than Cornwall and the older properties have been done up with stainless-steel balconies and huge plate-glass windows that facilitate spectacular views. New owners would have paid many hundreds of thousands of pounds, or even millions, for a property that could have been picked up for a schoolmaster's salary in the early '50s.

Be that as it may; sand still blows from the beach and drifts in little eddies across the grey tarmac road and children in swimsuits still queue up for Cornish ice cream or to hire surfboards. The same café serves fish and chips, while brightly coloured buckets, spades, shrimping nets and beach balls are piled up on the pavement outside the newsagents. Further technological advance is evidenced by the bustling emporiums that sell or rent out wetsuits, in all weathers, for those who wish to enjoy the excellent surfing.

Around the headland, to the west side of the beach the River Camel flows into the ocean across the Doom Bar. Rising on the slopes of Rough Tor (Rowter), one of the highest peaks on Bodmin Moor, the river runs through wooded valleys and in full spate gushes over granite outcrops and gurgles through deep channels. It reminded me of the burns I had seen in Scotland.

Just above the pleasant town of Wadebridge, whose stone bridge, founded on woolsacks in 1485, spans the Camel, the river broadens into a wide tidal estuary where mud flats provide a paradise for ornithologists. At high tide, on a sunny day, long tentacles of blue water, like an octopus, stretch into the surrounding countryside between lush green or corn-golden fields. Dinghies with red, white or blue sails tack between the shorelines and, as the tide recedes, sandbanks appear, eventually transforming the valley into one gigantic sandpit. In the distance, the old railway line has been converted into the Camel Trail, an idyllic venue for cyclists and walkers, but before Beeching got his way in 1967 steam trains chugged over an iron bridge, chuff-chuffing into Padstow; the last stop on the line from Paddington and home of the famous Hobby Horse. I have read that this ancient Cornish custom can be linked back to the Moors in Spain and was once part of a Sufi ritual or teaching system

A ferry ran regularly from Padstow to Rock. This was the centre of the sailing community and as we grew older we spent more time there. Eventually, to be closer to the boats we decided to hire a house each year, instead of going to Doyden.

Trevena, our holiday home, was situated at the top of the village almost opposite the Rock bakery where the Swiss baker rose early every morning. His huge mixer could be seen churning fresh dough as we entered the shop, setting the cow bells tinkling on the back of the door and our noses twitching at the delicious aroma of freshly baked bread, scones, pasties and other delights.

My father enjoyed sailing and much admired his brother Gray, the artist Claude Muncaster, who as a young man had worked his passage back from Australia on the clipper *Olivebank*. He recorded this thrilling adventure in his book *Rolling Round the Horn* (1933).[6]

Moored in the estuary were all kinds of small craft, many of which could be hired by the hour. My father used to keep a pint milk bottle on his bedroom mantelpiece in Cadogan Square and each day when he returned from work he would empty his pockets and drop any loose sixpenny pieces or threepenny bits into the bottle.

I enjoyed learning to row and spent my father's coins and my own pocket money pottering around in a dinghy at half a crown an hour. The local boat-builder, Kempthorne Lee, constructed 'Rainbows', which were wooden-hulled, Bermuda rig sailing craft designed for conditions on the Camel. It was in these that I learnt to sail, and my father and I spent many hours negotiating the sandbanks and currents of the estuary. These were some of the more enjoyable times I spent with him and a huge release from the tribulations of boarding school.

The tidal race could be merciless, especially at spring tides, and we often saw boats running before a force five westerly, with the mainsail stretched out across the water at ninety degrees from the hull and the jib goose-winged but, actually slipping backwards, unable to make headway upstream against the outgoing tide. Woe betide a vessel without an engine if it slipped beyond the Doom Bar and into the Atlantic surf. Fortunately, a lifeboat was housed close by, in the little Victorian boathouse with its steep slipway, across from lovely Daymer Bay. The boathouse has now been converted and was home to the actor Edward Woodward for some years.

Moored off the point where the ferry crossed from Padstow, a pretty sailing dinghy called *Louise* was often to be seen, bobbing about in the water. 'Every little breeze seems to whisper Louise,' my father would whistle through his teeth and we would wave cheerily to the owner as we sailed by. His name was Ken Duxbury who, after a career in the Royal Navy and five years demolishing wrecks around the coast of Great Britain—a dangerous task involving huge quantities of high explosive—earned his living by giving sailing lessons. Superbly fit with a fine physique, there never seemed to be a shortage of strapping young sirens waiting to improve their nautical skills.

I met him again, years later, under totally different circumstances. Still trim, lithe and looking a lot younger than his actual age, he told me that after years of sailing he had turned to writing and could boast several published works including *Lugworm on the Loose,*[7] a humorous and thoughtful narrative that describes an extensive adventure on the Aegean and Ionian seas in an open dinghy. His career also included thirty years as boat test feature writer for the *Sunday Express* before he taught himself to paint in 1987. Now based, with his wife Brenda, in his granite-built studio home on the edge of Bodmin Moor, he spends his time executing very commendable watercolours of local beauty spots and places of interest. A few years ago my wife and I were actually on our way to treat ourselves to one of his pictures in a little gallery at Porthilly. It was a surprise to find his old green Mini parked outside and, as we drew up, an unexpected pleasure to see him clambering out of the driving seat.

'Hello, Ken!' we chorused. 'What a nice surprise. We are here to buy one of your pictures!' He was delivering a new picture of the view across the moorings at Rock, and we are now its proud owners. Having lunch with Ken and Brenda recently, I told him about this book.

'You are part of my nostalgia,' I said.

An old barn that has now been converted into a posh yacht club and features in Ken's picture stood on the wharf, and above the beach was a thick wall whose broad slate top provided an excellent place to pause at the end of the day. Collecting a drink from the Rock Hotel across the road, we frequently gathered to watch the sailing boats racing and fishing trawlers returning from a day's work as the sun went down over the estuary. One evening, a rather portly fellow, a flash Harry who owned one of the first speedboats to regularly break the silence of the estuary, was sitting on the wall with his back to us chatting away to his friends without an apparent care in the world. Unfortunately, engrossed as he was, he failed to notice that one of his testicles had slipped out below the hem of his tight shorts. My mother spotted this indelicacy and within a few moments she and the rest of the crowd were giggling and smirking, hardly able to contain their mirth while the poor man continued his conversation, oblivious of his predicament and the entertainment he had created. At the time, I was rather shocked by my mother's exuberance. It was unlike her to be coarse, although echoes of her days mucking out with Sussex grooms sometimes surfaced, especially when she had downed a couple of brandy and gingers— her favourite tipple.

Gawky and Baba booked into the Rock Hotel for a fortnight at some point during our holiday. The high point of their stay was 'Gawky's treat'. This annual event meant rising at six in the morning and venturing out into the Atlantic with one of the fishing boats. Nothing in our whole holiday was more fun than riding the ocean rollers, way out beyond the Doom Bar and Pentire Point.

'Yipee! Haul away!' we cried again and again. Words were lost in the wind as we spotted the flash of silver in the fizzing emerald waves. We quickly reeled in the line and that night fresh mackerel was on the menu at Trevena.

St Enodoc golf course provided a further source of enjoyment. Stretching from Rock, along the shore of the Camel estuary, with the Atlantic surf pounding the beaches beyond the green fairways, this is one of the most beautiful sports venues in the British Isles. At the far end of the links is the 800-year-old church of St Enodoc that had lain under the sand dunes for many decades. Once a year a priest and clerk and possibly some parishioners too, were let down through the roof to hold a service, thereby sustaining the tithes. John Betjeman is now buried in the blustery churchyard beside a protective row of intrepid leylandii.

> Come on! Come on! This hillock hides the spire,
> Now that one and now none. As winds about
> The burnished path through lady's finger, thyme
> And bright varieties of saxifrage,
> So grows the tinny tenor faint or loud
> And all things draw towards St Enodoc.
> (John Betjeman: 'Sunday Afternoon Service in St Enodoc
>   Church, Cornwall')

My father had a good handicap and enjoyed his annual games. There were several friends he met regularly, including the secretary of the Cadogan Estate and the headmaster of Ashdown House. Each of these gentlemen arrived in their own Rolls-Royce, which added zest to the occasion.

I learned something of the game at glorious St Enodoc, but preferred delving for lost balls among the long, wispy stems of couch grass that pervaded the sand dunes before selling them at the nineteenth hole. The early signs of a wheeler-dealer, perhaps.

There were so many other things to do during our precious four weeks. We enjoyed casting a fly among the shady pools on the upper reaches of the Camel and visiting Port Isaac, where dozens of homemade lobster pots, their multi-coloured, ragged pennants flapping in the breeze, were stacked against the rough stone harbour wall. Tar-soaked fishing nets were spread out to dry on beached boats at low tide and a piscean pong permeated the port, luring us to the fishmonger where we purchased fresh seafood.

Richard and I undertook long hikes on the moor or along coastal paths, carrying a primus stove and sausages, bacon and eggs in our rucksack so that we could make a day of it.

In the evenings I caught up with a pile of books, mostly Cornish legends. The Legend of King Arthur was a favourite, as we were only a few miles from his castle at Tintagel, and I loved the stories of local saints such as St Piran, patron saint of Cornwall and tin miners, who discovered the silvery metal while making a fire on a slate ore-bearing slab.

On Sundays, passing the tall Ogham stone which is inscribed with the most ancient, indecipherable Gaelic writing, we all trooped through the churchyard and into the church of St James the Great at St Kew.

The first entries on my family tree, certified by the Windsor Herald of Arms, inform me that on 23rd August 1633, Abednego Mathew had been baptised at St James as, in due course, were Meshack, Shadrack, Nicholas, John and William, his five brothers. No doubt the carved angels, still poised in the wagon roofs, looked down on the scene below while light poured through the fine Bodmin glass of 1469, as it has done throughout the centuries.

Abednego became a colonel in the army and Governor of St Christopher in the West Indies. His sons and grandsons held office in St Christopher and the Leeward Islands, and the Mathews retained a significant presence within the West Indies for three hundred years.

Abednego's great-grandson, Daniel, became High Sheriff of Essex and Johann Zoffany's delightful picture of him and his family hangs at Clandon Park in Surrey. Daniel's younger brother, also Abednego, was Member of Parliament for Corfe Castle in the mid-eighteenth century, and the youngest of the brothers, Edward, was Chief Equerry to George III. His son, Daniel

Byam Mathew, was married by the Archbishop of Canterbury to the daughter of Sir Edward Dering at Lambeth Palace in 1783, a year before the following proclamation was posted in the ringing chamber at St Kew.

> We Ring the Quick to Church the Dead to Grave.
> Good is our ufe such ufage let us have.
> Who here therefore doth Damn, Curfe or Swear.
> Or ftrike in quariel tho no Blood appear.
> Who wears a Hat or fpur or turns a Bell.
> Or by unfkillful handling fpoil a pail.
> Shall fixpence pay for every fingle crime.
> Twill make him careful againft another time.

A number of members of the Mathew dynasty were buried in the churchyard at St Kew and there is a brass plate on the wall, in the south transept, commemorating Baba, together with his grandfather, father and brother. While on a visit to Cornwall in 2006, I took the opportunity to ring for the Sunday service and meet the local bell-ringers, which seemed a nice way to connect with the family history that runs, appropriately enough, like a stream of molten tin through the hills and valleys of north Cornwall.

All too soon, our holiday came to an end and the return to boarding school loomed. The last day was marked by lunch at the Three Beares.

Miss Beare, Miss Beare and Miss Beare lived in a large Victorian house (now known as Laburnums) in the centre of Trelights, and by prior arrangement, with charming old-world hospitality they opened their dining room for home cooking. This provided a fitting end to each holiday, usually coinciding with my brother's birthday on 10th September, and if it were not so memorable would I recall to this day those delicious meals, when green beans and potatoes tasted of real vegetables and the meat was succulent? Catching sight of an elderly gentleman working in his garden, while on a recent visit to the village, I attempted to draw him into conversation.

Did he remember the three sisters? I asked. What were their Christian names?

'Oh yes,' he replied. 'I knew them Miss Beares but we 'ad no famil'arity. Ev'one was Miss or Mister or Missus—no names—in them days.'

It was not the answer I had expected.

On 11th or 12th September, we set out on the long trip home, occasionally by way of Sherborne in Dorset where our formidable cousin, Jacobina Earle, would put us up for the night. This fierce lady lived in Priestlands, a substantial stone residence with a gravel drive near the town centre where children were most unwelcome and preferably neither seen nor heard. She eyed Richard and me with evident disdain as we scrambled out of the car.

'Take the boys upstairs!'

Her imperious command rang out across the cold, marble floor as soon as the front door had closed. We were ushered to the top-floor nursery by the maid and remained there, like the princes in the Tower, taking our meals on a tray until it was time to leave in the morning.

'Oh! My God! What an old bag! This is worse than school,' my brother would mutter.

We then continued along the A30 to Salisbury, which boasted a nice shop near the cathedral where my mother invariably bought her Christmas cards. Three months later, when Christmas was upon us, we more often than not spent the festive day at Lodsworth and for many years fourteen of us would sit down for lunch. The party would include my grandparents and parents and other members of the family. Some army friends called Toddy and Tree were also invited. By the early 1960s, Toddy had survived more than forty years on half a lung following a gas attack in the Ypres Salient. This piece of information amazed and impressed me.

Our day followed tradition, with presents around the tree in the drawing room and a pause for the Queen's broadcast. We rose to our feet for the national anthem.

Baba, who celebrated his ninetieth birthday during my second year at Marlborough, would slump on the sofa with cigar ash dropping on to his chest. At least this was one day when he need not worry about getting his Pools coupon into the post. My grandfather had lived an extraordinary life, much of it spent serving the Colours. As well as the Distinguished Service Order, his medals included the Mons Star, the British War Medal, the Victory Medal and other notable reminders of conflicts in far-flung corners of the empire. I was expected to address him as 'Sir' and, never really got to know him. I would dearly love to have a conversation with him today.

An exceptional horseman and polo player, he had taught both British and foreign royalty, but the only time he ever gave me advice was one morning when he must have heard me go into the loo. Rushing out of his dressing room, he banged loudly on the door and bellowed: 'Always put a flat sheet of "Bronco" on the surface of the water before you sit down. It will stop any splashing and save your bottom from getting wet!'

If you visit the recently renovated restaurant at Peter Jones today, you can admire a westerly outlook that is very similar to the superb view from what was once my bedroom window. The celebrated store is just a few hundred yards around the corner from where we lived, and little has changed in the last fifty years. Brompton Oratory, the Victoria and Albert and Natural History Museums and the green cupola on the top of the tower at Imperial College punctuated the skyline, as they do today.

On some hot summer evenings, we sat on an iron platform that formed part of the fire escape to the rear of the building, enjoying a drink while the sun went down as a flaming fireball over the shimmering roofs of Kensington and Earls Court. In the distance, the grey hump of the famous Exhibition Hall, which we christened the 'mountains of Wales', rose above the urban sprawl.

Immediately behind us, with its two clanging bells, stood the church of St Simon Zelotes whose vicar, I recall, had bright red hair. My father was a churchwarden and we regularly attended services. It was the only church I knew that smelt more of mothballs than the usual musty combination of furniture polish and damp hassocks, and I put this down to a congregation largely composed of wealthy women who took good care of their luxurious fur coats. My mother had her own beautiful fur that she wore in winter. In the late spring, it was collected and taken to Harrods where it remained in a deep freeze, hibernating like a grizzly bear, until the autumn.

Our fine property in Cadogan Square was leased from the Cadogan Estate. It had been designed by Norman Shaw, the renowned architect, born in Edinburgh in 1831 and was positioned alongside an elegant array of adjoining houses rising five or six floors from the street and built in 'Pont Street red brick' at the end of the nineteenth century. Almost every building was uniquely designed and some were quite exotic. There was one house that was separated on each side, from the rest of the square, by the width of a brick. Apparently the original owner felt that it was beneath him to be 'connected' to his neighbours' property. The gap that ran down each side of this building had largely filled with rubble, over the years, but could just be detected—if you knew where to look.

From the front of the flat, in summer, we could just spy pleasant lawns and the tennis court through thick leafy green foliage. Elderly residents who had a key to the private gardens shuffled along the gravel paths with their poodles or Pekinese. In winter, the scene was entirely transformed and during the day the full extent of the square was clearly visible through a lattice fretwork of the smoke-blackened branches of London planes. At night, flickering gas lamps cast long shadows. This was some years before the Clean Air Act and views to both east and west quite frequently disappeared beneath thick smog known as a pea-souper. We continued to burn fossil fuels until the late '50s, delivered weekly by men with coal-dust streaked across their faces, wearing grime-encrusted overalls and black leather jerkins. They heaved bulging sacks onto their backs from a cart, drawn by an old nag that worked its way from house to house, before tipping the contents down a hole in the pavement, outside the front door. Here it was stored until our caretaker shovelled the shiny black lumps of anthracite into brass coal scuttles and carted them up innumerable flights of stairs to our flat. Thousands of ornately engraved iron plates, that provided access to the damp coal-holes, still punctuate the London pavements, although most of them have now been firmly sealed or stolen by metal thieves.

There was an intimacy in Chelsea during the late 1950s and early 1960s that has long vanished. All the tradesmen whose services one might require could be found close by, and the streets echoed with the clip-clop of horses' hooves and the cry of the rag and bone man.

'Eny ol' iron or lumbaa? Eny ol' iron or lumbaa?' This sound, familiar to my ear, often reverberated between the rows of red brick houses. It sounded much like the cries that can be heard in cities in the Middle East.

In Milner Street, there was Oakshotts the grocer and the United Dairy whose little electric carts emerged through a tall arch from a back yard, to deliver milk, cream and butter around the neighbourhood. Next to the small hardware emporium with its buckets, ladders and bins spread across the pavement, large letters that read 'Miss E. Watson' had been sign-written in gold on panels above the front windows of the local stationers. The interior smelled of blotting paper and 'Miss E', as we referred to her, a diminutive lady with short grey hair, peered suspiciously at her customers through wire-framed spectacles from the back of the small, dingy corner shop. She sold Basildon Bond writing paper, rolls of string and brown gummed paper, pencils, fountain pens and bottles of ink, among other useful items.

In nearby Walton Street, there was an excellent bakery whose gooey jam doughnuts proved very tempting when taking Billy Brock for his morning walk. Across the road from Peter Jones, the cheerful straw-boatered men who worked in MacFisheries were continually sloshing water and ice over white marble slabs where salmon, trout, plaice, kippers, crustaceans and every manner of cold-blooded sea or river-based vertebrate was displayed to catch the eye of passers-by. The water ran away across the pavement, forming scaly rivulets in the gutter, and the stench of fish hung over Symons Street.

'Never buy fish on a Monday,' my mother would say. The days of large-scale food freezing had not yet arrived and she suspected that it had been lying around over the weekend. She also avoided the fishmongers on Fridays in case she was thought to be a 'left-footer', as Roman Catholics were sometimes known.

Around the corner in Cadogan Street, there was a pharmacist with large coloured bottles in the window and where ranks of wooden drawers with brass handles lined the walls. No doubt good builders, electricians and window cleaners traded in the vicinity, and of course the most famous plumbers in Chelsea were Thomas Crapper and Company Ltd, established in 1861, whose name was to add colour to the English language.

In the King's Road, Bathgates, the greengrocers, were always good enough to provide a box of overripe fruit and tired cabbages to feed the elephants whenever we went to the zoo. Further down the road, Andrew's the butchers were more than willing to deliver a few lamb cutlets for our supper, courtesy of a lad on a black bicycle, who still had a long climb ahead once he reached the school's front door at 68 Cadogan Square.

My mother would have placed a telephone order as part of her daily routine. This commenced at seven o'clock, when she went in to the kitchen to make a pot of tea, which she took back to the bedroom with her. An hour later, before he left for work, my long-suffering father, like a hotel waiter, delivered a tray with coffee, lightly boiled egg, toast and half a grapefruit to her, while she remained in bed, attending to correspondence. An avid letter-writer, she wrote regularly to her mother and childhood friends and to my brother and me when we were away at school. We eagerly anticipated her letters, written in her familiar flowing hand with the marbled-emerald Parker pen that she cherished for her entire adult life.

From her bed, she would phone her stockbroker and bookmaker and attend to any business matters with solicitors, doctors and so on. On a red letter day, she might book a holiday with Erna Low, the Austrian émigré whose offices were nearby and who was cashing in on the burgeoning package holiday market. An early brochure read: 'To sun and snow with Erna Low'.

I never knew why she remained in bed so long. It could be irritating if one wanted to get on with the day. Perhaps she had picked up the habit from her mother, but her habit it certainly was. At ten o'clock Mrs Dixon, our Cook, would arrive and Mother would put on her dressing gown and go into the kitchen to give Cook her instructions.

'Now, Mrs D, I think we'll have lamb cutlets for lunch today'.

She would then take a bath, dress and soon be ready for the day.

Mrs Dixon was not a married lady, but was given the honorary title 'Mrs', as was customary, like 'Mrs Bridges' in the popular television series *Upstairs, Downstairs*. Her duties were to provide lunch for the family, and sandwiches and cake for tea, which she left sealed under tin foil, and to prepare the evening meal. Having cleaned up, she would depart at three in the afternoon. She was the most excellent cook, having come with references from Lady Ravensbourne, and her tour de force was to provide two scrumptious chocolate cakes for Richard and me to take back to school at the end of each holiday.

Walking in the streets was pleasant, and it would not be unusual to spot the artist Augustus John striding along, an earring gleaming in the sunlight. The parking meter had not yet been invented, the streets were uncluttered and the likes of the publicity-seeking Sir Bernard and Lady Docker were often spotted in their glamorous Daimlers; as was the eccentric Conservative MP Sir Gerald Nabarro. Known for his exuberant moustaches and flamboyant dress on Budget Day, he owned a fleet of cars, the number plates of which read NAB 1, NAB 2, NAB 3 *ad continuum*.

One day my brother Richard and I were crossing Pont Street. The traffic had halted at the lights and we were weaving our way through a line of stationary vehicles. Suddenly I recognised the occupants of the car in front of us.

'Do you see who that is?' I nudged Richard.

The Queen was at the driving wheel and Prince Philip was in the passenger seat!

'We saw the Queen! We saw the Queen!' we boasted when we got home.

She has, of course, been a constant presence in my life. A glorified mother figure, I suppose. I even dream about her, although not so much these days. How will we all react when she dies? I wonder.

On 5th April 1960, General and Madame de Gaulle arrived in London for a state visit. My mother, brother and I, on our way to the spacious swimming baths at Dolphin Square, ambled over to Victoria Station in time to see the French President pass by, in an open carriage, accompanied by the Queen.

'Vive la France! Vive La République!' Mother shouted at the top of her voice.

The General turned and waved.

Coincidentally, de Gaulle had lived at Dolphin Square during the war when it was still the largest block of flats in Europe. I don't think the great man enjoyed his enforced sojourn with the English. On one occasion Churchill famously declared, *'Si vous m'opposerez, je vous get-ridderai!'*

Later that night, I was woken by the sound of massive explosions. Convinced that the Third World War had started, I rushed to the front windows and drew back the curtains but was reassured to see rockets rising in the distance and streams of coloured stars bursting over the rooftops. It was a fireworks display at Buckingham Palace, celebrating the de Gaulles' visit.

Harrods was a ten-minute walk away and here, they said, one could buy anything—even an elephant. The special attraction for my mother was the lending library, where she could indulge her passion for biographies, but afternoon visits also meant lingering in the television department. Not having a set at home until 1965, she would position herself in front of the largest screen, and propped up by her shooting stick, as if she were at Sandown Park or Ascot, remain glued to the racing.

Another attraction was the fabulous food hall. In the days when French and Italian delicacies were, otherwise, only available in little shops that reeked of exotic cheeses, and ground coffee, tucked away in Soho; Harrods provided a viable option. Besides, it saved a return trip on the number 19 or 22 bus and purchases could be put 'on account'. In the late 1950s, an Italian delicatessen opened on the corner of Cadogan Street and Draycott Avenue and—oh, unbelievable!—remained open until noon on Sundays. Culinary innovation was in the air and it wasn't long before Justin de Blank (Preshute 1940) opened his emporium in nearby Elizabeth Street, although a widely based restaurant culture had not developed at that time. My parents would occasionally go—alone—to a smart restaurant for a very special occasion but meals with friends would be in their homes, not at a restaurant. I recall one family outing to an Indian establishment in the King's Road, but that was the exception rather than the rule.

For me, membership of the Harrods children's library was a terrific bonus. I devoured all the *Swallows and Amazons* books, *The Scarlet Pimpernel* by Baroness Orczy, *Biggles*, the Famous Five and Secret Seven books, and as I grew older, Stevenson's *Treasure Island*, *Kidnapped*, *The Eagle of The Ninth* by Rosemary Sutcliff and a particular joy, Cynthia Harnett's *The Woolpack*. This exciting adventure, concerning fifteenth-century merchants in the Cotswolds, won the prestigious Carnegie Medal in 1951. It never fails to entrance, and I have read it again recently.

It was always fun to wander through the grand banking hall at Harrods, to take the 'moving stairs' or to ride in the metal-grilled elevators.

'Ladies' underwear!' sang out the uniformed attendant as he brought the lift to a halt with a sort of cranky handle, just when I had other things on my mind.

There were very few children living in Cadogan Square, although a small group did get together to kick a ball around in the gardens, from time to time. In consequence, friends were made at boarding school and life during the holidays, tucked away in my fifth floor eyrie, could be a touch lonely. I was certainly aware that we lived a refined existence, but it would be a long time before I began to react to my sheltered background and question whether it had been good for me. Given a rainy day with nothing much to do and having explored the Children's Basement at the Science Museum *ad nauseam,* I headed for the gramophone department at Harrods where the kindly assistant thought nothing of supplying me with a pile of records to play in a little private soundproof room. After Christmas or a birthday, I might have a ten-shilling note, or even a one-pound record token, to add to my savings and was in the exciting position of being able to buy a record. I was given a gramophone when I was nine and was gradually building a collection. 'Peer Gynt', 'Hans Christian Anderson' and 'Tubby the Tuba' were favourites.

Richard and I would regularly have our hair cut in the children's hair-dressers, and while waiting our turn, poke our fingers through the cage of a doleful rabbit, sleepy hamster or an excitable puppy in the pet department. Before leaving the store I would cast envious glances at the Grundig tape recorders in the electrical goods department, fantasising that I would soon be buying one of the very latest glitzy models.

Life tended to revolve around Knightsbridge and Chelsea, but my father had responsibilities elsewhere. Davies's owned several schools in Holland Park and he also oversaw the general educational requirements of the students at the Ballet Rambert, at the Mercury Theatre in Notting Hill Gate. Needless to say, I was not performing there. When I returned from Marlborough on the Special, at the end of term, he would be waiting at Paddington's Platform One, close to 'The Letter from Home', a poignant statue that depicts a 'Tommy' in full battle-gear. It commemorates some three thousand men and women of the Great Western Railway who had been killed in the two world wars.

Combining the chore of collecting me with a visit to those west London venues, we would drive through the back areas surrounding Westbourne Grove and Portobello Road. This was a very different London. There were a lot of black faces, properties were generally neglected and some streets could be defined as slums. Many years later, Rose, a secretary of mine described life, as it was, when she was brought up in those terraced houses.

'We was poor,' she said. 'But front doors were always open, and we kids, played safely and 'appily in the street.'

I rather enjoyed those short trips with my father; especially pass-ing through the Portobello area during the week before Christmas when costermongers' barrows, packed with mouth-watering produce, lined the roads. There were exotic fruits, and piles of apples, oranges and tangerines glistened in the bright lights emanating from a hundred naked bulbs, strung untidily from stall to stall. Spanish chestnuts grilled slowly on smoky braziers at street corners and huge bunches of mistletoe hung from the electric wires. Sweet-smelling Christmas trees of all sizes were piled on the pavement, closely guarded by old men in thick overcoats and children wearing balaclavas. It was a cheering sight on a grey December morning.

Following the Blitz, parts of London still lay in ruins. One day, my father visited a warehouse in the East End to buy a job lot of second-hand school desks and I accompanied him. It was in the late 1950s and we were shocked to find the Isle of Dogs utterly devastated. Most of the buildings, still standing, were without roofs, windows were gaping black holes, and loose sheets of creaking, corrugated metal swung in the breeze. It reminded me of scenes I had previously witnessed in Hamburg and Lübeck that were indelibly engraved on my memory.

Human damage was also in evidence on the streets of London, as the war-wounded could frequently be seen hobbling around. My brother attended Faulkner House, a pre-prep school in Kensington. One summer, sports day was held at Wellington Barracks on the King's Road. Field Marshall Montgomery, the hero of El Alamein, resplendent in full dress uniform, presented the prizes and a few red-coated Chelsea Pensioners and a contingent of wounded ex-soldiers were specially invited. It was humbling to see this group of cruelly damaged human beings from both world wars walking with the aid of crutches, or propelling themselves in ugly and ungainly invalid carriages. Most had lost more than one limb (41,000 men lost at least one limb in the Great War alone), some could hardly see, others, who had yellowed skin, bore the traces of poison gas.

As the years went by these men, and many others like them, mobile memorials to the murkiest days of the twentieth century, vanished—but I will never forget that day when, as an impressionable Baby Boomer, I spent time in their presence.

> The Bishop tells us: 'When the boys come back
> They will not be the same; for they'll have fought
> In a just cause: they lead the last attack
> On Anti-Christ; their comrades' blood has bought
> New right to breed an honourable race.
> They have challenged Death and dared him face to face.
>
> 'We're none of us the same!' the boys reply.
> 'For George lost both his legs; and Bill's stone blind;
> Poor Jim's shot through the lungs and like to die;
> And Bert's gone syphilitic; you'll not find
> A chap who's served that hasn't found some change.'
> And the Bishop said: 'The ways of God are strange!'
> (Siegfried Sassoon: 'They', 1916)

As London grew, many of the outlying villages became absorbed in the metropolis and Chelsea was no exception. Its high street was the King's Road and westwards from Sloane Square, past World's End, there were an increasing number of antique shops where some real bargains could be had.

There were three cinemas in the King's Road. The Classic was on the corner of Markham Square and matinee seats were available for children for less than a shilling.

Further along were the Odeon and Essoldo. We all enjoyed a trip to the flicks and many good films come to mind. *Genevieve* (1953), *The Cruel Sea* (1953), *The Dam Busters* (1955), *The Ladykillers* (1955), *Oklahoma* (1955), *High Society* (1956), *Gigi* (1958), *The League of Gentlemen* (1960) and lots of others, especially a whole genre of films spawned by the Second World War. The beach scenes in *Dunkirk* (1958), starring John Mills and Richard Attenborough, were filmed near Rye, on the Sussex coast, and we had wandered among scattered tanks and battle debris on a day out from Fonthill. In 1956, we went to the Astoria in Charing Cross Road to see *Around the World in 80 Days* starring David Niven and shown on Todd-AO, an exciting new wide screen format. The next year Cecil B. de Mille's *Ten Commandments* was showing at the Plaza in Lower Regent Street. I had been taken by my friend Christopher Olgiati and we sat in the front row of the royal circle, gaping in the darkness as the Red Sea parted before our very eyes. In 1962, brother, Richard and I went to see David Lean's *Lawrence of Arabia* which enthralled us.

Sometimes my parents went to the cinema in the evening and I recall them returning shocked, exhilarated or scared stiff when they had seen films like *Rear Window* (1954), *The Bridge on the River Kwai* (1957), *Saturday Night and Sunday Morning* (1960), *Psycho* (1960) or *The Servant* (1963). *The Servant* starred Dirk Bogarde and James Fox and was filmed in Royal Avenue. A few years ago, strolling along the King's Road past Bywater Street—home of John Le Carre's George Smiley—and reaching Royal Avenue I pointed out the film's location to my son Alexander, who was home on holiday from his job in Hollywood and is something of a movie buff. Suddenly, I spotted a rather elderly Bogarde.

'Do you see whose coming?' I managed to enunciate as the famous actor passed us by. We were heading for John Sandoe's iconic bookshop in Blacklands Terrace—a favourite haunt of mine.

There was plenty of other entertainment. My parents particularly enjoyed light opera and ballet and in 1961 when Nureyev defected from the Soviet Union my mother quite lost her heart to him. Traditionally we marked her birthday, Boxing Day, with a visit to the Savoy for a performance by the D'Oyle Carte Opera Company of a Gilbert and Sullivan opera.

My first visit to the London theatre, was to see the *King and I* at Drury Lane with Herbert Lom and Valerie Hobson, the beautiful star of *Kind Hearts and Coronets* (1949) and future wife of John Profumo, the Cabinet minister whose affair with Christine Keeler was to rock the Tory establishment in the early 1960s. However, my most memorable early thespian experience came in 1956. Somehow, Julian Slade and Dorothy Reynolds' *Salad Days*, which we attended on a warm evening in London's Theatreland, with its light, catchy tunes and silly, whimsical story about a piano that gets lost in the park, caught the spirit of a time which in hindsight seems a naïve but golden age. It epitomised an era when school and university were followed by a lifelong career, often arranged by an obliging and influential uncle.

The musical proved hugely popular, running to 2283 performances at the Vaudeville, and finally closing in 1960. As was customary, each evening concluded with the audience rising for the national anthem. Another 'hit' was an original show called *At The Drop of a Hat* in which two men, bearded polio victim Michael Flanders in his wheelchair, and Donald Swann at the piano, held the audience spellbound for several hours. Their hilarious songs—'Gnu', 'Glorious Mud', 'Madeira', and the one about the marriage between 'a right-handed honeysuckle and left-handed bindweed'—would be heard on the airwaves for years.

My mother particularly wanted to hear the violinist, Yehudi Menuhin. 'He relaxes by standing on his head, you know', she had informed us.

On another hot summer's evening, we packed into the Royal Albert Hall and heard the maestro play Mendelssohn's violin concerto in E-minor. I read that the Hungarian composer Joseph Joachim had told the guests at his seventy-fifth birthday party: 'The Germans have four violin concertos. The greatest, most uncompromising, is Beethoven's. The one by Brahms vies with it in seriousness. The richest, the most seductive was written by Max Bruch. But the most inward, the heart's jewel, is Mendelsohn's.'

What about J.S. Bach? I ask.

It was a memorable occasion. Before the performance we spotted a fiddler at the main entrance, scraping away with his bow, hoping to earn a few shillings. When Menuhin arrived, the virtuoso paused at the door, asked the beggar if he would like to attend the concert, and invited him into the hall. Years later, I would visit the Yehudi Menuhin School in Surrey, which was an education in itself. It was much smaller than I expected, with only seventy talented students.

There was always something to do in the capital, which I grew to love as much as the country. Christmas in Chelsea dictated brisk walks around the Serpentine, whose invariably unruffled waters reflected the wide London winter sky like a huge mirror. Tarmac paths were choked with children showing off their first bicycles or roller skates and pretty girls with ponytails displayed new winter coats while attempting to avoid the clouds of dust whipped up by horses on Rotten Row. Disciplinarian as my father was, he encouraged me in the 'Spencer-Chapman Walk,' which meant taking in a deep breath when walking, and holding it for as many paces as possible.

In the spring, an afternoon walk could mean a visit to Peter Pan's statue in Kensington Gardens or a stroll down the Flower Walk admiring April blossoms, and on long summer days we sometimes took a boat out on the lake. Throwing bread to the ducks as they dodged between the model sailing boats on the Round Pond was a perennial activity, as was circumnavigating the cohorts of uniformed Norland nannies wheeling their small charges in unwieldy black and chrome prams.

Returning to Cadogan Square in time for orange juice, cake and marmite sandwiches, we always paused in South Kensington and, parting with several copper pennies, picked up a copy of the *Evening Standard* or the *Evening News* from the friendly vendor at the entrance to the tube station. My mother particularly looked forward to the literary reviews, read avidly while she hid behind her newspaper with her habitual cuppa. Many years later I met the then editor of those columns. He indulged in an unusual and interesting hobby—lion taming.

As we munched on sandwiches and honey cake, the tranquillity of our nursery world was occasionally disturbed if threatening headlines caught our attention, as in April 1956 when two Soviet hoods, whom the press had labelled 'B and K', visited London on a so-called 'goodwill mission'. The trip was marred by the disappearance of Commander 'Buster' Crab in Portsmouth harbour. It was thought that he had been snooping below a Soviet cruiser, and the incident provoked a major diplomatic row in true Cold War style. More than a year later, his headless, handless and mauled body was found in the water and many theories still abound as to what had occurred.

The dreadful 'K' (Nikita Kruschev) was to dominate the news again when he took off his shoe and banged it on the podium at the United Nations in 1960 and, two years later, he was to frighten us Baby Boomers, and everyone else, when he and Kennedy confronted each other over the nuclear sites in Cuba.

In 1961, as a fourteenth birthday present, my parents had arranged for me to have riding lessons on leafy Wimbledon Common which I much enjoyed and, in the time available, made good progress. On occasions like this, or when we were off on some chore, I would inevitably spend a good deal of time alone in the car with my father. He used to take these opportunities for serious talks about work, my school report, my future, or the birds and the bees. In fact, I began to dread those earnest moments, which were frequently embarrassing and always pre-empted by long silences and a certain amount of deep breathing on my father's part—or 'huffing', as my brother called it. During one trip, the familiar routine had started and I braced myself for what was to come. Suddenly, as we crossed Battersea Bridge he took a deep breath and exploded: 'Do you know what a beatnik is?' he asked.

'No!' I replied, wondering if I was in for a long harangue.

In that instance, fortunately, a brief explanation sufficed.

This episode had been triggered by the imminently expected 'Ban the Bomb' march from Aldermaston in Berkshire during the Easter holidays of 1958. The protesters would be passing down Sloane Street, a stone's throw from Cadogan Square, on their way to Whitehall, and my parents had no sympathy whatsoever for the campaign or its supporters.

'Bearded weirdos who intone passages from the Manchester Guardian like Old Testament bible thumpers' was how my father described the men, and his description of the women was similarly unflattering. 'Promiscuous harlots with dirty knickers, small breasts and overactive brains' was what he said about them!

Years later, I made friends with the then feminist, novelist and active marcher Doris Lessing. I dread to think what she would have thought of my parents' views.

It was rare for my father to exhibit emotion, and it would take a win on the horses or, in later years, a 'weepie' on the telly, for my mother to unbridle her feelings. I never knew either of them to raise their voices to each other—which does not mean that tensions did not rise to fever pitch, but the boil was never lanced. I have no idea what a good row between them would have been like, and in hindsight, I'm sure it would have been good for them.

Regular visits to the dentist involved dreary car journeys through Battersea, Clapham, and Streatham en route to unfashionable Tulse Hill. It was there that John Hall, my great-grandfather, brought up his family in the second half of the nineteenth century. He was a silk merchant who was reputed to have run a profitable line in black crepe and the censuses of 1871, 1881 and 1891 make interesting reading. Other residents in those burgeoning Victorian streets included a provisions merchant, a manufacturing ironmonger, a civil engineer, a wholesale confectioner, a telegraphic engineer, a brush and umbrella manufacturer and a corn merchant, together with their attendant cooks, maids, gardeners and coachmen. I would like to know more about my father's family but have never been able to access sufficient information.

I don't recall why my mother chose a female dentist who practised in dingy basement rooms in south London, but I think she was a friend of a friend. She was certainly no friend of mine, and during every holiday monotonously drilled and filled cavities, pulling out teeth she considered beyond repair. I was paying a heavy price for over-indulging at the tuck shop, and the concept of dental hygiene as we now know it was light years away. With regular fluoride and flossing, my own children would escape these horrors.

The frequent extractions were performed in the dentist's chair under general anaesthetic and were pretty ghastly. 'Open wide!' the dentist would say before jamming a rubber block into my mouth, and the smell of the mask, whiff of gas and taste of rubber still remain in my sensory memory like some gruesome experience in the torture chambers of Rochester Castle. Be that as it may, the result was that by the time I was sixteen my jaw was in danger of collapsing and had to be restored with extensive and expensive gold bridgework. But by that time we had moved to a practice in Kensington, although my teeth caused me trouble for years to come.

My brother had better luck when it came to medical attention. At the age of eight it was decided that his tonsils and adenoids should be extracted. Recalling my unpleasant experience at the Midhurst Cottage Hospital, my parents decided that the operation should be performed at home. The required equipment was transported from St George's Hospital at Hyde Park Corner and the nursery was briefly converted into a theatre, awaiting the arrival of the surgeon, anaesthetist and assistant. God knows what it cost, but the operation was a success and Richard awoke with the cosy gas fire glowing warmly behind the brass fender in one corner of the room and surrounded by Bear, Golly, Rabbit and his other soft toys.

He did not always attract such tender loving care. One day, Richard thought it amusing to chuck potatoes out of a top-floor window, which smashed down on cars parked in Cadogan Square. Unfortunately, my father was talking to some parents on the pavement at the time and they only narrowly escaped the hail of organic missiles that rained down from far above. A very sound thrashing, with a long-handled hairbrush, followed.

In the Christmas holidays I attended ballroom dancing lessons. These were held in the hall behind St Saviour's Church in Walton Street under the meticulous eye of Mrs Hampshire, and were designed to teach young ladies and gentlemen the waltz, Gay Gordons, polka, foxtrot, and other dances. If I had been a girl, my mother would have expected me to 'come out' as a debutante, even though the custom of being presented to the Sovereign ended in 1958, but as a boy, I was to be provided with a passport into acceptable social circles. Mrs Hampshire, whose daughter Susan was to become a famous actress, gave lessons every morning for a week and then on the Saturday night a ball was held in Belgrave Square, providing the opportunity to exercise our newly acquired skills. Donning a dinner jacket at the age of thirteen for the first time, I felt very nervous although there were compensations in that I met two delightful girls, Robina and Charlotte and, fortified by apple juice, we danced the evening away. At midnight our parents came to collect us, and Charlotte, a tall pretty girl with a cute snubbed nose, who had forgiven me for trampling on her toes, promised to keep in touch. A few days later, following the mandatory ritual, my mother telephoned Charlotte's mother, only to discover that my new friend's father was 'in trade' which didn't go down too well. Nevertheless, the next day Charlotte and I caught the 137 bus bound for Oxford Circus for a visit to Studio One to see *The Swiss Family Robinson* (1960), a tropical island adventure starring John Mills. After the film, we popped into Joe Lyons Corner House, one of a popular chain of teahouses, for an orange juice and slice of cake. My mother's parting words came to mind: 'Give Charlotte plenty of time to powder her nose,' she had said, but I kept wondering just how much time was required.

On my return from my second trip to Scotland, I was horrified to find my father in bed with a badly damaged leg. He had been thrown from a prime stallion in Richmond Park that had subsequently rolled on him. By the time I returned, the worst was over. He was propped up with a pile of pillows, wading through back numbers of *Horse and Hound*, and soon recovered. At any rate, he was not past ticking me off for not writing while I had been away. When I got home, I also found that my mother had discovered something called the 'never, never', and from her attitude, I reckon that I could be forgiven for thinking that this was a means of buying things without paying for them. She had just purchased a transistor radio from King's Radio in Sloane Street. It embodied the very latest in technology and she proudly carried it around the flat, placing it in just the right position to obtain quality reception and generally showing off the portability of her new toy. She was a talented flower arranger and could be found by the kitchen sink with one of the BBC's eight light orchestras playing 'Music While You Work' in the background. Failing this, another favourite was 'Mrs Dale's Diary', the daily events in the life of a doctor's wife. At a quarter to two she would take her transistor into the nursery for 'Listen with Mother' and we would gather by the radio as the cheerful signature tune, the *'Berceuse'* from Fauré's *Dolly Suite,* was broadcast.

My father was also delighted to have the new radio as he could listen to the Archers in his bath, and we all laughed along with contemporary comedies like 'Life with the Lyons', 'The Clitheroe Kid' or 'The Navy Lark' on Sunday, after church, while the joint was cooking. Bisto gravy sizzled on the stove and 'How Much is that Doggy in the Window?' or the popular American singer Doris Day's rendition of 'Que, Sera, Sera!' blared across the kitchen. On Sunday evenings, I soon got into the habit of broadening my musical education while tucked up in bed with a mug of Ovaltine, courtesy of Alan Keith's 'A Hundred Best Tunes' on the BBC's Light Programme. It was a safe, cosy and secure world and a million miles from the battles and shenanigans that raged at boarding school.

Chapter 5
Trust in God but Tie your Camel.

Youth, what man's age is like to be doth show,
We may our ends by our beginnings know.
Sir John Denman (1615–1669)

AFTER MY CAREER at Marlborough was abandoned in the late autumn of 1963, decisions had to be made. However, I spent the weeks before Christmas catching up with friends. Perceval Hayman and his wife invited me to stay at what is now the Old Vicarage in Rogate, a striking property not far from the common where P.G Wodehouse used to walk his dogs when staying at the Lodge, before the war, and half a mile from Terwick Church. It was there, between St Peter's and the A272 that a strip of land was donated in the 1920s by Thomas Hodge, a local landowner. His express wish was that the field should be maintained and sown with lupins, which is why a splash of vibrant summer colour greeted travellers for many years as they passed along the main road. They were in striking evidence on that day, when I gridded past on my way home from Marlborough, although unfortunately, in the age of pesticide sprays the generous benefactor's instructions are no longer followed and when I was last there not a single blossom was visible.

Perceval's study, on the west side of the vicarage, had French windows that led out to a walled garden and was of special interest. It was lined with bookshelves, displaying tomes on every subject under the sun, and besides these I particularly admired his splendid collection of antique musical boxes, housed in finely polished oak or mahogany chests. One afternoon Perceval invited me into his lair. Puffing away on his pipe, he sank deep into a comfy leather armchair that had seen better days and motioned me to a small sofa in the centre of the room.

The Haymans had treated me with extraordinary kindness and hospitality, and no attempt was made to grill me about my time at the College. However, on this occasion, ever positive and encouraging, Perceval opened up the conversation with a piece of advice.

'You've had a rough ride,' he said, as clouds of smoke rose above his head, 'but you can put that behind you. May I suggest that you think long and hard about how your education should now continue and do not allow yourself to be led along any path that makes you feel uncomfortable.'

I was grateful for his words and pondered them on the journey back to London.

A recent television documentary about his grandson, his only daughter's son, Orlando Montagu (Summerfield 1984), surprised and interested me. The young man had, with great ingenuity, taken his father's title, the Earl of Sandwich, as the trading name for his flourishing catering business.

Soon after returning from Sussex, I received an invitation to stay with my friend Stephen whose father was the Bishop of Woolwich. My mother was impressed and the next day I took the train that winds its way through dreary southeast London and alighted at Lewisham. It was a foggy afternoon and I was apprehensive because there had been a bad rail smash at the station in 1957, but soon cheered up when I saw Stephen standing on the platform. Leaving the train was a cumbersome if not dangerous process, as anyone who travelled on suburban railways in those days will recall. It was impossible to open the compartment door without lowering the window and leaning out to turn the external brass handle. As it unfastened, the heavy door would fly open, pitching one on to the ground, unless you reacted quickly to restore your centre of gravity.

I was to stay for a few days in the Robinsons' large modern house near Blackheath. Again there was no raking over old coals and I spent much of the time accompanying Stephen and his sister, Catherine, on the piano. His oboe technique was excellent, as was her virtuosity, and we made a fair showing of Bach's Oboe and Violin concerto in C minor (BWV 1060).

Stephen and his mother and sisters were a kindly, noisy bunch as I discovered when we gathered in their sizable kitchen to prepare the evening meal.

'Pass the olive oil! Lots of garlic!'

'Mushrooms! Green peppers!'

'More onions! Tomatoes next!'

Commands rang out and excited voices rose in crescendo.

'More salt and pepper!

'More salt!'

'Needs much more pepper!'

'Where's the parmesan?'

We sliced and chopped and tossed colourful ingredients into the hot pan of sizzling mince that stood on the Aga, and soon a delicious spaghetti bolognaise was ready for our consumption. This was not the sort of food we ate at Cadogan Square, where the kitchen was strictly Mrs Dixon's domain, so the whole experience was a refreshing delight. The younger members of the family were excited because the bishop was to appear on television, the next morning, in *Breakfast with Frost*. Their mother seemed to view the occasion with a degree of indifference, although everyone knew that to receive such an invitation was a sign that one had arrived. Even bishops, I surmised, were not immune from competing in the social jungle.

In fact, there had been concern that the bishop's clothes were a bit shabby.

'I think we need the services of Messrs Marks and Sparks,' announced Mrs Robinson, so we all trooped down to Lewisham high street where a pair of new grey flannel trousers was purchased. When I subsequently related this episode to my mother she was profoundly shocked and disappointed.

'What? No gaiters?'

The idea of an Anglican bishop jostling in the Christmas crowds in search of cheap garb, was too much for her. If those people represented the new 'Southwark religion', the new Christian formulation inspired by the Bishops of Southwark (Mervyn Stockwood) and Woolwich (John Robinson), she wanted no part of it.

In contrast to the rest of the family, I could not establish any rapport with John Robinson. He seemed a cold fish. There was an unkind story that circulated at Marlborough relating to the day in 1961 when he took Stephen to the College for the first time. Striding into the housemaster's study he extended his hand, episcopal ring gleaming.

'I am the Bishop of Woolwich,' he announced. Then, turning slightly, he continued: 'and this is my wife, and this is my son.'

Poor Stephen; he had a lot to live up to, but I particularly liked his sister, Catherine, and we went to a few concerts together.

When I got home, my parents were full of it. They had attended a reception in St James's on the previous evening.

'It was a grand affair,' my mother boasted. 'Prince Philip was there, wearing an admiral's uniform!'

In my innocence, I idly wondered what the admiral had been wearing.

Once Christmas was over it was decided how I would continue with my education. My parents had been severely shaken by the events at Marlborough, especially my father who, as a headmaster himself, felt that the College had let me down badly.

I was encouraged to make my own decision.

Anthony Chenevix-Trench, headmaster of Bradfield, who later went on to Eton where he was known as 'Chummy', interviewed me and offered me a place, as did the headmaster of University College School Hampstead. However, following Hayman's advice, I was not prepared to take on all the palaver that attending a 'proper' school involved, and opted for the senior crammer that was part of the Davies's group. This meant that I could live at home for a year or so to complete my A-levels and retake a couple of Os.

The next question was how to continue with my organ studies. My father knew Professor William Lloyd-Webber, who agreed to hear me perform. We visited him in his dingy flat in South Kensington and I played the 'St Anne' on his study organ. Following his appraisal, he recommended me to Richard Latham, the organist and choirmaster at St Paul's, Knightsbridge. Within a few days, I started lessons on the splendid Father Willis at that fashionable church in the parish that had been formed as Belgravia was first developed in 1843

Classes were also held on one of the practice organs at the Royal College in Prince Consort Road. These are located high up in the 'gods' that feature in the film *Shine* (1996).

The final part of the reorganisation of my life was to find a sensible person with whom to discuss any emotional problems. My mother felt that I might be depressed, or at any rate, a bit 'mixed up'—a very '60s expression!

I did not feel unhappy or confused, but lacked motivation when faced with a future that apparently led, by way of a trail of exams at school and university, to some sort of professional career and a job for life. I often sensed that something significant would happen that would change my life and in due course it did—a touch of 'the miraculous'—but not yet.

Fortuitously, while on holiday, my parents had met a Chinese psychiatrist who rejoiced in the name of K.C. Yeo, and I drove with my father to St Ebbas's Hospital in Epsom to meet him.

Fearful that I had been consigned to the loony bin, I cheered up when I met K.C., whom I liked very much, and during the spring and summer of 1964 regularly made the journey to Surrey. It was a pleasant trip from Victoria, in one of those green electric trains that clickety-clacked past parks decked out in pink and white chestnut candles and suburban gardens where lilac and buddleia bloomed. Arriving at his consulting room, we chatted about nothing in particular and, after an hour, I would return whence I had come. The only specific suggestion made was that I should study spiritual texts on a regular basis, as K.C.—a staunch Christian convert—felt that they would strengthen me and guide me as my life developed.

'Take these,' he said, handing me a couple of pamphlets. 'Read them and let Christ enter your life!'

I used to peruse his little meditation books in Joe Lyons at Hyde Park Corner, while enjoying a nice cup of tea before my organ practice, but I cannot say that I found them to be of much value. After a few months it was agreed that the chats had fulfilled their purpose and they were discontinued, which reminds me of a story that I recently heard.

There was once a man who had suffered mental illness and spent time in a psychiatric hospital. When considered to be cured he went for a last interview with his consultant.

'How do you feel about going home?' the doctor enquired.

'A bit nervous,' came the reply.

'Why's that?' the doctor asked. 'You know that you're not a mouse now; you've completely recovered!'

'*I* know that I'm not a mouse,' the patient spat out scornfully. 'But does our *cat* know?'

I sometimes wondered what happened to K.C., whom I never saw again. It was therefore a surprise, in 2004, when I saw a picture of him and his wife on the obituary page of the *Daily Telegraph*. He had just died at the age of a hundred and one. It was only then that I discovered what an extraordinary man he had been. Initially imprisoned and kept in solitary confinement by the Japanese in 1941, he had the chance to escape, but remained voluntarily to run Hong Kong's medical services. After the war, he carried out important work in the fight against tuberculosis and malaria, and founded a leper colony on Hayling Chao Island. He then became Professor of Social Medicine at Hong Kong University and was appointed CMG before retiring to Britain in 1958. I recall my parents relating two details of the Yeos' lives. First, although they were both Chinese, they spoke in entirely different dialects and could only communicate in English. Second, they took a holiday in Japan after the war, to consciously purge themselves of any lingering enmity.

Hopping on a 46 bus to go to school in the morning was a novel experience, as was the routine at Davies's. The crammer was housed in a rambling Victorian mansion in Addison Road. It had formerly been the residence of David Lloyd George and boasted a lovely garden, with a mulberry tree and huge weeping willow. There were no games, just lessons on a one-to-one basis until four o'clock and the other students, both boys and girls, were a mixed bag. Two Etonians (or possibly Harrovians—my memory fails), befriended me. They were both titled, one being the son of the governor of the Bank of England, and the other the son of the Marquis of Lansdowne. During the lunch break we slipped into Au Caprice, a little restaurant on Holland Park Avenue, not far from Wedgie Benn's house at number twelve with its pointedly *red* front door. The previous year Anthony Wedgwood Benn had been one of the first hereditary peers to disclaim his peerage (Lord Stansgate) in order to remain in the House of Commons as a Labour member, and could be seen at the autumn conferences enthusiastically belting out 'The Red Flag'.

My father provided four and sixpence each day that procured bangers, peas and mash followed by sponge pudding and custard. The 'Etonians' were good company, but on Fridays they went off to country estates while I took the bus to Knightsbridge for my organ practice. In contrast there was a rough gang that included Gerald 'my jewellery is crap' Ratner, and what they got up to at weekends, if corridor conversations could be believed, would certainly have made my mother blush. A bonus was that I met and rekindled a friendship from Ashfold days with Christopher Olgiati, who was to become a brave and imaginative documentary film-maker. Even at school he had ideas for projects that were far ahead of his time. His pretty blonde cousin,

Elizabeth, attended some of our classes and I immediately developed a huge crush on her.

We were glad to escape London's heat and oppressive atmosphere in the summer of 1964, which was spent quietly at Limbourne farmhouse in Sussex. It was set in a solitary and romantic setting; near Fittleworth, below Bedham, where, Edward Elgar had retreated to a cottage called Brinkwells, after the Great War. Elgar knew Oliver Hall, my grandfather. The lovely woods that covered the sandstone ridge surely inspired some of his music, as he once told another friend: 'This music is what I hear all day. The trees are singing my music—or have I sung theirs?' Our house was at the end of a long lane, half a mile from our nearest neighbour and hidden behind old barns, derelict pigsties and an apple orchard.

I was learning to drive and my parents bought me a second-hand Lambretta.

Having wheels, gave me the mobility that any seventeen-year-old craves and, more importantly, the ability to get around and earn money. I was soon booking in to the local fruit farms to pick red and black currants and touting around the neighbourhood for jobbing gardening. One day, the Lambretta's engine was spluttering and backfiring and finally cut out altogether near some farm buildings just outside Petworth. The noise had attracted the attention of a swarthy youth who emerged from the milking shed where, in the sudden silence, I could hear the electric pump chugging away.

'Need any 'elp?' he enquired. 'Sounds like dirt in the carb'rettor.'

I shrugged my shoulders. 'I'll give it a wipe and try and make it to Etherington's garage in Fittleworth. Thanks anyway,' I responded.

'Is that where you live?' he continued.

'In the holidays, how about you?'

'This is Dad's farm but I'm away soon.'

A quizzical expression must have crossed my face.

'Yeah. Just 'ad me results. I'm off to Cambridge in the autumn. Got a scholarship from Mid'urst Gramma'.'

I was dumfounded and it probably showed.

'Congratulations!' I stammered. What are you going to read?'

'Microbiology and genetics!' he beamed.

I gave the scooter a kick-start and with unexpected verve the engine sprang to life. Waving over my shoulder and bellowing 'good luck', I zoomed off down the road.

His achievement amazed me. My Marlborough background had not led me to expect that level of education from 'those sort of people' and I had the same reaction when Gawky told me that Harriet's daughter had passed more O-levels than I had.

To be fair, a quiet but systematic revolution was taking place—but it was an important lesson I needed to learn.

Towards the end of August, I developed a wheeze for generating extra cash. Gawky was an expert jam maker; in fact, she had mobilised the local Women's Institute in 1940 to make tons of the stuff for the war effort. I drove my Lambretta over to Lodsworth for a lesson in jam production and she taught me her secrets at the kitchen table. Limbourne was surrounded by fields where hedges were thick with brambles ripe for picking, and the boughs in our orchard groaned with juicy apples, so it was only a question of organisation and effort before huge pans were bubbling away in the old bakehouse. The sweet sticky red liquid needed careful attention to prevent it from boiling over, and constant testing to ensure that it set at the required consistency, but a wonderful aroma soon permeated our home. Within a few days, dozens of jars of red jelly and jam stood, neatly labelled, ready for sale. My marketing skills would now be tested, but I found that with a little persuasion the local farm shops were happy to order and, more importantly, to provide repeat orders. I really enjoyed the process of gathering the fruit, and then making and selling a product. Unfortunately, the season was limited but my coffers were temporarily replenished.

While I was developing a taste for business, my brother Richard was playing cricket in the local villages and chasing the girls. My opportunities for meeting the opposite sex were confined to swanky dances held in private houses and I was glad of skills taught by the intrepid Mrs Hampshire.

'What's that hard thing in your trouser pocket?' questioned one pretty young lady as we danced cheek to cheek in the candlelight.

Be that as it may. The full impact of the 'swinging sixties' had still not percolated to rural Sussex, and my idea of a 'date' was to take one of the few young ladies that I knew to a performance of the St Matthew Passion at the newly constructed Guildford Cathedral. I also enjoyed evenings spent with our generous friends, the Boxfords, who had a lovely house nestling beneath the South Downs at West Burton. Happy hours were spent there as the bonfire's embers glowed and the moon came up over Barlavington Down while someone strummed on the guitar and provided a passable rendition of 'Where have all the Flowers Gone?'

A visit to Chichester's new theatre to see Olivier as Othello was also a memorable occasion, in 1964. I did, however, make time to pass my driving test, largely thanks to Gawky, who encouraged me to drive her maroon Wolseley round and round the polo ground at Ambersham while she walked the dogs and picked autumnal mushrooms.

She was pleased to hear that I had passed, although deeply saddened by the death of Baba, aged ninety-two, at the King Edward VII Sanatorium; the hospital in the pine woods near Midhurst that had been opened in 1906, primarily to treat cases of tuberculosis. His ashes were interred at St Kew alongside those of his father and other forebears.

Soon it was autumn and time to go back to school, but a treat was in store. The newly launched BBC2 was showing *The Great War*, a groundbreaking documentary and, since we still had no television, I was fortunate to be able to watch it at my cousin Charles Earle's flat, a few doors away in Cadogan Square. Charles was a retired colonel in the Grenadier Guards who had been awarded a DSO during a distinguished career. Tall, stiff-backed, moustached and reticent, I chiefly remember him because of the ashtray he kept in his beautifully appointed drawing room. Fashioned from a slab of marble broken off a piece of furniture in Hitler's bunker in 1945, and kept as a war trophy, it bore a small brass plate detailing its provenance. The documentary brought all those Fonthill history lessons vividly to life although recently, when the series was repeated, I was amused to note that among the researchers was one, Max Hastings. As President of the Campaign to Protect Rural England, I had only been listening to him a few weeks previously in the depths of rural Wiltshire.

The autumn of 1964 also meant that a general election was imminent. The writing had been on the wall for the Conservative Party ever since the Vassall (1962) spy scandal and the seismic politico-sex scandal in 1963, when kinky, real sixties-style capers at Cliveden and the lurid lifestyles of Christine Keeler, Mandy Rice-Davies and Stephen Ward made daily news. John Profumo, the Secretary of State for War, was also implicated when it became known that he had shared Keeler's favours with the Soviet naval attaché and he resigned after admitting that he had lied to the House of Commons.

Lied to the House … Extraordinary!

Now battle lines were drawn between the traditionalist Sir Alec Douglas Home, who had renounced his peerage (14th Earl of Home) to take over from Harold Macmillan at Downing Street and Harold Wilson, socialist and academic. After thirteen years of Conservative rule, there were many who could not believe that Britain might soon be run by the likes of Harold Wilson (described by Sir Alec as the fourteenth Mr Wilson), George Brown and Jim Callaghan.

On election night, I was invited to a performance of Gounod's *Faust* at Sadlers Wells by Norman Davis, my father's best friend. The opera was conducted by his brother Colin (now the late Sir Colin) and we were privileged to sit in a box. Colin Davis had achieved his first major break five years previously in a performance of Mozart's *Don Giovanni* at the Royal Festival Hall, when he replaced Otto Klemperer who had suddenly become ill. In 1960 he had been subject of a profile in *Time* magazine which hailed his exceptional promise.

At the end of *Faust* we met the maestro and some of the performers at a pub in the Angel. I was shocked to discover that men and women whom I had heard singing sublime classical opera only minutes earlier, were speaking in quite rough and common accents like Bill Sykes in *Oliver*. The incident again reminded me that there were people in the world who were talented and high-achievers who had not gone to public school or entered the services.

Jumping into Colin's car, we drove to Trafalgar Square where he left us as the first election results that were already pointing to the decisive Labour victory were coming up on huge screens. I am sure that Davis hoped for a Labour success—his obituary (in the *Daily Telegraph* in 2013) refers to a description of him as a quintessential angry young man at the time, but I don't know whether his politics changed in later life. We met again at a lunch party in Kent, many years later and I have followed his career with interest. Born into a musical family and educated at Christ's Hospital, surely a genetic predisposition led him to a very successful career in his chosen field. But, what about his big break? Was that destiny or chance? This is a subject that interests me greatly.

The 15th October 1964 was a defining moment. With the new government a whole new era was about to begin. On a personal front, a very significant event was also about to occur. I had kept in touch with ABS-M and he recommended my reading a book by P.D. Ouspensky called *In Search of the Miraculous,* subtitled *Fragments of an Unknown Teaching.*

I purchased the weighty volume from Watkin's bookshop and immediately read it twice, from cover to cover. A paragraph on the very first page made a dramatic impression.

When leaving Petersburg for the start of my journey I had said that I was going to seek the 'miraculous'. The 'miraculous' is very difficult to define. But for me this word had a quite definite meaning. I had come to the conclusion a long time ago that there was no escape from the labyrinth of contradictions in which we live except by an entirely new road, unlike anything hitherto known or used by us. But where this new or forgotten road began, I was unable to say. I already knew then as an undoubted fact that beyond the thin film of false reality there existed another reality from which something separated us. The 'miraculous' was a penetration into this unknown reality. And it seemed to me that the way to the unknown could be found in the East. Why the East? It was difficult to answer this. This idea was due partly, perhaps, to the perceived romance of the East, although it may have been due to my absolutely real conviction that, in any case, nothing could be found in Europe.

The book, which goes on to provide intricate details of the teachings of George Ivanovitch Gurdjieff, the mesmeric and mysterious Georgian who had turned up in Moscow in 1914 and died in Paris in 1949, precipitated a radical rethink. It profoundly—yes, profoundly—changed my attitude to religion and to life. I had found 'the miraculous', a source of knowledge that introduced me to the concept of conscious evolution and service known as the Work. This was the route to 'Self-cultivation, with due regard to others'.

At an early opportunity, I mentioned my new-found interest to a friend, a Christian priest, who poured scorn on the whole idea.

'That eastern stuff is a load of rubbish,' he ranted. 'If I were you, I'd stick to what you have been taught!' This struck me as a strange reaction, coming from one who had dedicated his life to Jesus of Nazareth.

However, there were more pressing matters to attend to and, in January 1965 I found that A-level exams were only weeks away. It was during that month, as I passed by Hyde Park Gate on the 46 bus, that I spotted a small crowd gathered in the street. My newspaper informed me that this was where Sir Winston Churchill lay dying and on 24th January he passed away.

The lying in state followed, in St Stephen's Hall, so I suggested to my father that we go over to Westminster to pay our respects. I was surprised when he declined, so I went on my own. It was a cold night and joining the queue on Westminster Bridge, I shuffled patiently for three hours in the darkness as members of the public snaked along the southern embankment, back over the Thames at Lambeth and through Palace Gardens before we passed the great man's catafalque.

On the following Saturday, our family watched the state funeral at home on television as the event had finally moved my parents to rent a set. Few people who witnessed the occasion will forget the moment when the launch, carrying Churchill's coffin upriver on his last journey, passed cranes in the Pool of London which dipped their derricks in silent tribute.

At the end of the winter, once my exams were over, and while awaiting the results, I decided to further investigate Gurdjieff's work. ABS-M had suggested that I read *Witness,* the autobiography of John Godolphin Bennett, and this led, by chance on my eighteenth birthday, to Coombe Springs, a massive nineteenth-century property on Kingston Hill. Hidden from Coombe Lane and approached through huge gates, the house was set in seven acres of landscaped gardens. It was strikingly beautiful on that fresh March morning. Springs rose from the hillside and bubbled down carefully contoured, shrub-lined channels and lawns stretched away from the house below the rose garden. At the lower end of the property was the Spring House, where a series of underground pools allowed sediment to settle before pure water flowed along lead pipes to Hampton Court, three miles away. Fabulously cool in hot weather, it had been constructed at the time of King Henry VIII.[8]

Coombe Springs was the headquarters of the Institute for the Comparative Study of History, Philosophy and the Sciences, whose director was John Bennett, a colossus of a man both in physical and intellectual terms. I wondered how many of those attributes were inherited from his mother's New England genes. Already in his late sixties, white-haired and standing well over six feet, with broad shoulders and a powerful frame, I found him digging in posts for a children's mini-zoo that was being prepared in the grounds. It was in the shadow of a mighty oak tree reckoned to be five hundred years old.

He extended a large grubby hand.

'Welcome,' he said smiling broadly, with a reassuring twinkle in his cornflower-blue eyes. He took me aside and while we strolled past patches of nodding daffodils and through the rose garden, he explained that a community of about twenty people lived on the property, together with his wife and four young children. Everyone had their own accommodation in various buildings around the place but met in the big house for communal meals. The majority had jobs nearby, leaving in the morning and returning at night, but there were some retired people and young mothers with children. Everyone had an interest in the teachings of Gurdjieff and Ouspensky and some were members of the quasi-religious movement known as Subud. There were various study programmes that people joined and he also gave lectures from time to time. On designated weekends, other members of the Institute would visit Coombe Springs to take part in the activities, to look after the gardens and perform regular chores. He said that the human race existed on earth in order to learn, develop and evolve. That was the meaning of a spiritual path, but 'withdrawal from the world' was not encouraged; in fact, it was frowned upon. From time to time, I have recalled that conversation that echoes the words of Haji Abu al Yazdi: 'He makes Self-Cultivation, with due regard to others, the sole and sufficient object of human life.'

An essential requirement of the teaching was to maintain a practical relationship with the environment in which we found ourselves, and to use our life experiences as a catalyst for further study.

'This is hard, very hard indeed,' he said, 'and the "Fourth Way", as it is sometimes called, is no easier than the other three. To follow this Way, you must also be viable in the world; to be in the world but not of it.'

I had learned from Ouspensky that the three Ways to which he referred were the Way of the Monk, the Way of the Yogi and the Way of the Fakir, traditional but outmoded paths in spiritual development.

At this point, he looked at his watch and excused himself because he needed to get back or his project would fall behind schedule.

'Wander round, make yourself at home. You are welcome any time and speak to my secretary, Joan, about the weekends,' he said, waving goodbye as he tramped down the hill. I found his attitude refreshing and pragmatic and a far cry from the plethora of platitudes that had, in my experience, so often passed for spiritual instruction. Had I, indeed, found my own route to 'the miraculous'? I thought I had.

I resolved to further investigate the Fourth Way and, a few weeks later, when I had another opportunity to visit Coombe, I called Joan[9] and arranged to attend a 'Work Sunday'.

The main tenet of the Gurdjieff teaching was that man is asleep. He needs to be awakened. While man sleeps, he drifts through life, he is ineffective, he cannot 'do'. Like a sleepwalker, man is oblivious of his situation; he needs to 'remember himself', or, as another teacher said; 'he thinks that he is alive but has in fact fallen asleep in life's waiting room.' The activities, which in my case provided a chance to learn new skills such as simple decorating, gardening, organising the estate and cooking for large numbers, were also designed provide an opportunity for service and to help us work on ourselves. One exercise was called 'STOP'. While we were engaged in any activity, whether it was peeling potatoes or pruning roses, the director would shout 'STOP', very loudly, and we would freeze. This was designed to focus attention on our bodies, how they were transfixed, and whether physical actions were being conducted economically. It was also applied to draw our attention to where our minds had wandered and whether we were lost in daydreams. In other words, it was meant to wake us from our somnambulant state. I found all this very interesting and was appalled to discover how frequently I was quite unaware of the manner in which my body was being put to use and how often I was dreaming. The exercise reminded me of the almost unbelievable story, related by Ouspensky, of a man who was boasting to a group of friends that he had given up smoking, blissfully unaware that he was at that very moment lighting up.

Lunch was held in silence in the attractive dining room overlooking the rose garden and neatly clipped yew hedges. Roast lamb, with lashings of garlic, frequently appeared on the menu. This was an experience in itself, as we never cooked with garlic at home in those days. The silent meal gave us further opportunities to observe ourselves, and to particularly observe our 'mechanicality'. After the meal Bennett would sometimes talk or read from Gurdjieff's *All and Everything,* the first of his writings, which was subtitled *Beelzebub's Tales to his Grandson.* These were quite remarkable and I confess I found them largely incomprehensible. In contrast, a fascinating talk comes to mind in which Bennett expanded on the concept of the 'present moment'. He drew our attention to the 'present moment' of a baby, who is only aware of instant stimulation. As we grow up our 'present moment' expands, but the human concentration span is limited and this is reflected by our equally stunted 'present moment'. He went on to talk of the possibility of a more developed 'present moment' that can be acquired; citing the builders of the gothic cathedrals and great mosques as an example. Their 'present moment', he explained, encompassed a vision of work that they would not see completed in their lifetime and the effect of endeavour that might last a thousand years. He spoke of higher forms of consciousness, referring to teachers whom he believed were sent to guide human progress, and finished by referring to the Greatest Consciousness, the Absolute, the Alpha and the Omega, the Ancient of Days; A consciousness whose 'present moment' engulfed all time and all space.

After tea the visitors would leave.

Driving down from the rarefied atmosphere of Knightsbridge on my scooter and passing through the gates on Kingston Hill was like taking a cold shower. Today, it might be described as culture shock, and in the sense that the Institute was in the business of administering deliberate psychological shocks, it was effective.

The other people I met were of all ages, both men and women and from many backgrounds. It was certainly the first time I had worked in close proximity with the fairer sex, and I found the whole experience exciting and original.

The oldest inhabitants were Olga, a Russian who had escaped from the Bolsheviks in 1917, and Mr Kaminski, a white-haired Polish refugee. Others included a Norwegian, two Swedes, a German count, several Americans, an Australian, an Anglo-Indian and other English people from across the social spectrum. This eclectic group included labourers, artists, designers, architects, accountants and businessmen. One particular character who had made his home at Coombe was the controversial artist Gerald Wilde. Gerald (sometimes erroneously thought to be a son of Oscar) had, and perhaps this is where the rumour started, been put through art school by Lord Alfred Douglas, known to history as 'Bosie'. He had made a name for himself when he and a group of students from Chelsea School of Art exhibited at the Bloomsbury Gallery in 1935. There were also research fellows of the Institute with university doctorates who worked with Bennett on some of his academic projects.

Educated at King's College School, Wimbledon, Mr B., as he was affectionately known, had been severely wounded and nearly died on the Western Front in 1918. In his biography *Witness*, he described the experience as death and rebirth. Following the Great War he rapidly learned Turkish and became a Liason Intelligence Officer in Constantinople. This was followed by a meteoric rise in industry, and at the beginning of the Second World War he found himself as Director of the British Coal Utilisation Research Association, the largest industrial research association in England, serving coal, the basic industry of the war effort. Searching for research premises led him to Coombe Springs and the fine gardens, which had hosted a whirlwind social life, patronised by royalty, in former years. Mr B. was able to negotiate a lease on the property and continued his research work, while building up his community, until 1946, when he purchased it outright. A man with outstanding intellectual capacity, he was a mathematician, linguist and author. His *Dramatic Universe* in three volumes, which expands on Gurdjieff's doctrine of reciprocal maintenance and explores the connections between the mechanical and other worlds, is still considered by some to be a work of genius. He had a reputation for being able to play, and win, a dozen chess games simultaneously.

I felt that I was in limbo during the early months of 1965. What would my exam results be, and what options would I have? It seemed sensible, but contrary to my instincts, to apply to a couple of universities and before the words 'degree in theology' could be enunciated I was on a train to Exeter. One of Norman and Colin's sisters kindly gave me a bed for the night and in the morning I attended a tedious and distinctly uninspiring interview. A couple of weeks later, I repeated the process in Durham, staying overnight at St Bede's. I had never been through the industrial heartlands before, save a trip to Lancashire in the early 1950s, and on that occasion, when visiting my grandfather, Oliver Hall, we were shocked to see people wearing wooden shoes and children running barefoot in the streets.

I travelled alone to the northern university but on the return journey the carriage was packed with other aspiring students. As we passed through Bishop Auckland and Darlington where rows and rows of identical little houses clung to the hillside, and carbon-copy (no pun intended) wisps of smoke poured from their chimneys I started intoning:

> Little boxes on the hillside, little boxes made of ticky-tacky,
> Little boxes on the hillside, little boxes all the same.

There's a green one and a pink one and a blue one and a
  yellow one
And they're all made out of ticky-tacky, and they all look
  just the same.
And the people in the houses all went to the university ...

Suddenly and with unexpected and alarming vitriol my companions
rounded on me.

'Who the hell do you think you are?' they demanded.

For my part, I felt that I was just airing Malvina Reynolds' popular song
(1963) and being descriptive, but I still appeared to be a toffee-nosed public
schoolboy, which was an image that I desperately desired to shed.

Back in London, I felt less inclined than ever to pursue further academic
study. I knew that I had to be viable in the world, and I was very attracted
by what I had heard and seen at Coombe, but how all this was to fit together
was a huge dilemma.

My results arrived. They were reasonably satisfactory although to secure
a university place I needed to retake them to achieve higher grades. That
meant returning to school for the summer term and then what? I was deeply
demotivated. I did not want to study in class. I wanted action! No more
classrooms.

As I was ruminating, my eye spotted an advertisement in the newspaper. The London Symphony Orchestra was looking for a young assistant
to the Personnel Manager, who would now be known as Head of Human
Resources. That sounded more like it. I applied and was shortlisted but didn't
get the job.

As a friend said, 'You won't be jumping on that bandwagon!'

I was back to square one.

Time was drifting. April had become May, and May, June. My parents
were remarkably phlegmatic. I think they had learned that I was best left to
my own devices, but the start of the summer term came and went and I was
not in the classroom. Soon I was back in Sussex, looking up my old customers for jobbing gardening.

I had been reading *Witness*, John Bennett's autobiography, and was impressed by his description of how he taught himself Russian. He was in Paris
at the time and made long lists of vocabulary that he forced himself to learn
while moving from one bench to another on the Avenue des *Champs-Élysées*.

He learned ten words on each seat, totalling two hundred words on the first day. Using this technique, he learned five hundred words in a very short time. Following some of the conversations held at Coombe I had become interested in learning Arabic and wondered if the same technique would work for learning the alphabet. I duly set out all the letters on little white cards and took them with me on my gardening sorties. Every time I took a break, leaning against a shady tree, or sitting outside the Three Moles at Selham, where they served scrumptious cheese and tomato sandwiches, I would shuffle the cards and test myself repeatedly. Within a couple of weeks I had the alphabet down pat.

Nature abhors a vacuum and suddenly, in what amounted to a significant U-turn, I came up with a new idea, something to satisfy my desperate craving for an identity and a solution to the conundrum as to where my life was going. I decided that I would go up to Cambridge and read oriental languages. Yes, I thought to myself as I hoed another row of carrots; that would be absolutely splendid.

I duly wrote to the faculty and received a letter by return, inviting me to an interview. Before the month was out, I was sipping a very dry noon sherry in Peter Avery's study, overlooking the Backs, at King's. I explained, as I spun myself a new image, that I had read some Rumi and Attar in translation, which was true, and would love to be able to read it in the original text, which was a half-truth, although my vision of myself as an accomplished Arabist was developing with remarkable ease. I also told him that I had been reading Arnold and Guillaume's *The Legacy of Islam*. Avery was impressed. He voiced concern that there were not enough Arabic and Persian scholars, or indeed, students of Islam in England. Since Mecca was generally thought to be a dance hall in Leicester Square, Granada a television company, The Alhambra a theatre in Bradford, and all dervishes were wild murderous fanatics, his comments did not surprise me. Furthermore, I recalled that most people had little or no knowledge of England's great nineteenth-century explorer, the Sufi and Arabic scholar, Sir Richard Burton, who translated the *'One Thousand and One Nights'* and much else. He was described by Lady Burton as 'the greatest Oriental scholar England ever had and neglected'.

He lies, forgotten, together with his wife, in a tent-like mausoleum in the churchyard at the Roman Catholic Church of St Mary Magadalen in Mortlake where the coffins, together with a few chattels, are clearly visible through a small window. The name 'Richard Burton' had become indelibly linked with the silver screen among the population at large.

Despite all this, I was astonished when Peter Avery immediately offered me a place at the university but regrettably, a few days later, the College wrote to say that although the faculty would be only too pleased to admit me, I would need higher qualifications to meet College entry requirements.

Yuk!

That meant more time at stuffy Davies's, so I passed on the opportunity. This was, perhaps, a shame as there is a wealth of evidence pointing to the fact that English schoolboys whose abilities in the classroom are less than satisfactory easily pick up several oriental languages once they are exposed to them in North Africa, the Middle East and beyond. Maybe there is a significant degree of Orientalism in our collective English DNA.

Frank Gardener, who left Marlborough (Littlefield) in 1979 with almost as dismal an array of academic credentials as I did, and went on to build a multidimensional and successful career based on his seasoned knowledge of Arabic, is a recent example, as is his friend and my second cousin, Peregrine Muncaster. Gardener's life was put in jeopardy when eleven bullets were pumped into him by Al-Qaeda in the summer of 2004. However, his life story and the chronicle of his courageous road to recovery and rehabilitation as the BBC's Security Correspondent, together with his reflections on the current, lamentable state of affairs between Islam and the West is chronicled in *Blood and Sand* (Bantam Press 2006). I found this book moving and poignant. It was made even more so when I reflected that for the indeterminate future, possibly for the rest of his life, Gardener, who like me had once drawn strength from his ability to roam across the Marlborough countryside, would only be able to 'sniff the breeze and smell the rain and stand in C House porch again' with some difficulty.

But in 1965, I was back to square one.

Fortunately I was delivered from this perturbation by a chance conversation with John Henry, my old friend from Marlborough. He suggested a cycle tour in northern France. I thought this an excellent idea, if nothing else it might exorcise memories of an unpleasant fortnight spent at St Jacut-de-la-Mer in Brittany. It was in 1962, when I was sent to a Parisian family's holiday home to learn French, although the only part I enjoyed was observing the daily routine of an old woman milking her only cow in the orchard below my bedroom window and the night ferry crossings on the *Falaise*, the vessel that had borne Guy Burgess and Donald Mclean into exile in 1951. Buddy Holly's 'Peggy Sue', blaring from the gramophone, is forever associated with that unhappy holiday.

With regard to my career, I promised both myself and my parents that I would make firm plans upon my return from France, and it seemed no time at all before John Henry and I were puffing and wheezing as we pushed our grids (bikes) up a steep hill outside Rouen, heading for the ancient Abbaye de St Wandrille. I had written to the Abbott, asking if we might stay, and received a favourable reply before leaving England. Legend records that the monastery had been founded by a seventh-century count who, along with his wife, had renounced all earthly pleasures on the very day of their wedding. It did seem a terrible waste.

It was 16th August 1965 and our aim was to cycle for ten days or so, starting in the Seine valley before striking south towards Chartres. We would then skirt Paris, visit *Fontainebleau* and return to Dieppe via the capital, but we did not foresee the novel means by which we would make our first entry into the great city. Our bicycles were loaded with a tent, sleeping bags, change of clothes and cooking utensils.

We kept a diary and, on that first evening, after attending the service in chapel, I wrote:

> Although too late for supper, we were given the most excellent meal at the Hostel of St Joseph opposite the monastery. We had cider, noodle soup, cauliflower au gratin, potato omelette, yogurt and grapes. We then discovered—all this for eight francs! We were invited to Compline. The simple rounded chapel was full of black robed monks and the service was sung in Gregorian chant. We both noticed how beautifully each man seemed to be singing and, as a section finished, the last note was held like the hum of a bell. After Compline and a hot shower we turned in and slept fitfully between coarse sheets as a clock chimed outside the window every fifteen minutes.
>
> The next morning we consumed bread and butter, washed down with huge cups of café au lait, in the refectory. We then

bought a big pot of tasty honey and thanked the monks for their kindness before heading for the ferry at Caudebec.

Having crossed the Seine, we soon came across a beautiful wooded valley. We passed through Bourneville and Montfort without incident except for our first puncture, which we mended by the roadside. At Conches we approached a farmer and in our appalling schoolboy French, requested permission to camp on his land. This was freely granted and as the diary records, 'we went to sleep with the sound of animals eating instead of bells'.

The next day we headed across a flat plain, with the wind in our faces. The cathedral at Chartres could be spotted as a tiny blob on the horizon long before we reached the city. Every turn of the pedals was an effort but the nearer we got the larger it became until, late in the afternoon, we found ourselves below its massive towers and buttresses. The facilities provided by the campsite could best be described as sordid, although we cheered up once we had located the public baths and enjoyed steaming hot showers. We then treated ourselves to steak and chips at the brasserie in the main square.

Sunday was spent exploring the cathedral and city. It is widely known that the mediaeval glass is beautiful but predominantly a very dark blue that leaves the images difficult to decipher. We took the tour up the tower and along the terrace above the flying buttresses. The architecture was breathtaking and the countryside stretched for miles below, reminding us of our efforts, when crossing the windy plain. Back on terra firma, we lingered below the west front admiring the sculptures and shimmering stonework, which exuded such a vibrant quality that it felt almost alive. Who built Chartres Cathedral? I wondered. Were these the people with a greater 'present moment', to which Mr B. had referred?

The next day we travelled east and, after a trying haul across another bleak and windswept plain, only interrupted by a further puncture and pause for lunch, we reached the Forest of *Fontainebleau*. I wanted to find the *Prieuré* where Gurdjieff had taught in the early 1920s when it became a centre for well-to-do English people and others with an interest in esoteric matters, who earned the sobriquet 'the forest philosophers'. John Bennett had spent time there, Katherine Mansfield died there, and the stories that abounded relating to Gurdjieff's extraordinary behaviour and bizarre teaching methods are all part of the folklore that grew up before and after his death.

We were taking turns to complete the diary, and John Henry wrote:

> The last few miles were through the pleasant Forest of
> Fontainebleau. When we got to it we were rather tired and had
> some difficulty in finding the campsite, which was so revolting
> that one of us felt that we must move on, as did the other after a
> glass of lemonade. We heard that the next site was past the *Prieuré*
> but looking for the *Prieuré* and the site and buying supper took
> another hour, so one of us was in a thoroughly bad temper by the
> time we reached the site (on the banks of the Seine), which was in
> fact quite nice. After a meal we felt better and slept well following
> a tiring day.

The next morning the river traffic woke us and we were soon on our way
to the *Prieuré*, where we met someone who allowed us to walk around the
grounds. They were not in a good state of upkeep and the eighteenth-century
château could have done with some repair. There were certainly no sign of
the Russian Bath or Study House that feature in memoirs of past disciples,
nor was there anything to be seen associated with activities that took place
more than forty years previously. After an hour we left the *Prieuré*, and cycled up the hill to Avon in search of Gurdjieff's grave. It was difficult to find
although the gatekeeper pointed us in the right direction. There was no in-
scription, just a neat patch of turf bordered by red flowers and a sarsen stone
standing at each end—at least, they looked like sarsen stones to me. I'm not
sure what John Henry made of all this. He was too polite to suggest that I
was showing signs of having joined a cult.

Leaving the cemetery, we returned to the campsite to collect our belongings and pack up the tent. For the next few days we enjoyed an entirely
different mode of transport and this is how I logged the events as they occurred all those years ago:

> We made our way downstream to the first *écluse* (lock) to pick
> up a barge if we possibly could. We hoped for a lift *vers* Paris. We
> were lucky as a number of barges were about to enter the *écluse* and
> the third bargee accepted us after consultation with his wife. Our
> bikes were hoisted on to the top of the cover over the barge hold

and we set off, our backs to the wheelhouse and our legs stretched out in front, eating our *déjeuner*—much to the amusement of the bargee and others. This particular barge was empty and was on its way to Rouen from Montargis, a journey of five or six days. We realised almost immediately that an adjustment would be necessary in our level of patience—the bargee must be the most patient man in the world because it depends almost entirely on the time it takes him to get through the locks as to how long the journey will last. Above Corbeil the locks are only of single capacity, and if a queue of barges is waiting to go through, one might have to wait for two hours. We averaged about fifty minutes per lock and enjoyed ourselves by just admiring the river, despite John Henry's hat being blown away in the first gust of wind. We reached Melun, an attractive town, marred by a prison on the island in the river. It had high walls upon which were built little boxes for guards, aided by searchlights. A couple of prisoners were peering through their cell windows.

At the next lock, it was feared that something below the water might puncture the boats and a diver had been sent down. A queue of barges grew steadily and we waited for three hours. At eight o'clock we set out for the next lock, where we were to spend the night. We munched on fruit, cheese and bread and watched the gathering dusk and lights on the water. After about an hour we tied up at Corbeil and pitched our tent near the railway and beside the road. We were due on board by six-thirty a.m.

We were up as the first barges started to move through the locks. It is the opening of the locks that brings the river to life each day and wherever we camped by the Seine it was the renewal of the chugging of the barges that awoke us. We packed up quickly and walked down to the lock in search of *café au lait*. The first bar we entered was full of workmen swigging brandies and crème de menthe, but we soon found somewhere a bit more sophisticated. We were underway by eight-thirty and spent time chatting to the bargee and his wife. Their life consisted of the run between Rouen and Montargis and although his father and grandfather run barges they never left that route. We presumed that his sons would carry on in the same manner.

We were in Paris by noon, having come through an extremely industrial area. One thing that struck us was the extraordinary smells that greeted us as we passed each factory. We tied up between the junction with La Marne and Le Pont National. Having said our goodbyes, we cycled through Paris and arrived later in the afternoon at the most nauseating of all campsites—Le Bois de Boulogne. The stench of the 'pissoir' permeated the whole area.

Years later I discovered that we had passed the jewel of a small estate at Tilly (St-Fargeau-Ponthierry) where Jane Lecomte, my future sister-in-law, and her husband, Rémi were living.

For the next two days we explored Paris, cycling down the Rue de Rivoli, up the Avenue des *Champs-Élysées*, around the Arc de Triomphe, wherever our whims led us. We visited Notre Dame, where I was bowled over by the rose window in the south transept, and we carefully navigated the narrow streets on the Rive Gauche. Friends of mine in London, knew some Americans who ran an antiques business—Au Troubadour—in the quaint Cour de Rohan so, hoping to introduce ourselves, we made a detour, but found that the shop was closed for the August holiday. A young man who was house-sitting in the flat above, reached by a pretty spiral staircase, told us that the owners were in Turkey collecting *objets* for their business. As we paused for a coffee in the Boulevard St Germain, we encountered the 'Rat man', who terrified tourists with his fake, long-tailed rodent. He skilfully handled this wooden creature in such a deft manner, keeping it moving all the time, so that one had the illusion it was running over café tables and slithering up customers' bare forearms and across their shoulders. People shrieked in terror before realising that they had been totally fooled. The trickster then passed his cap around and was surprisingly well recompensed for his deception!

On our last day, we fastened our bikes to some railings and wandered along the banks of the Seine. Feeling hungry, we clambered on to the balustrade of the Pont Neuf, and sitting facing each other with our legs astride, opened our knapsack and tucked into the inevitable brie and bread that we had brought with us. Suddenly, and without warning, a large bunch of red grapes was plonked down in the space between us by a pedestrian, who continued on her way without even a glance over her shoulder.

On Thursday 26th August, we felt that it was time to make our way home and in the afternoon we took a train to the suburb of St Germain where we camped by the Seine for the last time. The next day, with a fine drizzle coming in from the north-west, we headed towards the Channel. It was a long hard push to the coast, and we had several punctures, but we were within easy reach of Dieppe when we pitched our tent for the night. The next day, we crossed to Newhaven and by teatime were sitting with John Henry's parents in the rectory garden at Highbrook near Ardingly. It had, of course, never occurred to us to phone our respective parents from France, so the rector and his wife were all ears as we relayed our adventures. My parents had taken Richard away for a holiday and I had only the faintest idea where they were.

John Henry's last entry in the diary read: 'During the boat trip we calculated the total mileage to be about 280—not as far as we expected—but what does it matter? We have done all we set out to do.'

September arrived, and having made various decisions I wrote to John Bennett to ask him if I could live at Coombe. If he agreed, I would leave home and find a job. A phone call produced an invitation to go down to Kingston and Mr B. told me that I was welcome to come and stay for a few months. He warned me that becoming involved with the Work should not be taken lightly, and that I would be required to make a huge effort to shed any preconceived notions, but I would not understand the real significance of the teachings until I was much older. My teenage expectations were running high and I was disheartened by what he said, but his words have often echoed in my mind.

Later that week I left home with few regrets. As you will recognise, years at boarding school had conditioned me to take a pretty independent stand. In time, my father appointed a young Cambridge graduate, Nicholas Kaye, who took my room with the stunning view and as I write (2013) he has now been the school's very successful headmaster for nearly twenty years. Sussex House has just won the *Tatler* 'Best Prep-School Award'.

I moved in to a tiny ground-floor cell in the Fishbowl, a converted laboratory behind the main house at Coombe. The roof leaked and I was separated from my neighbour, Richard Maxwell, by a piece of thin curtain. He was up at six every morning to do his ablutions—a mandatory requirement for those living at Coombe—before catching a bus to the local brewery where he humped beer barrels all day.

My immediate task was to find a job to support myself—a requirement of the Fourth Way—and pay rent to the Institute. My father had promised to contribute £1 a week so I reckon he got off pretty lightly. I went down to New Malden, parked my Lambretta in the yard at Luff's Landscapes, the local garden contractors, and knocked on the door of what appeared to be large shed. As I entered, a bald man with glasses, incongruously wearing a neat suit with white shirt and striped tie, peered at me from behind an untidy desk.

'Yes,' he responded to my request, they could do with an extra labourer and they paid five shillings an hour for a forty-hour week. 'Come back tomorrow morning at eight,' he concluded. This was just what I was looking for, not only in monetary terms but because it would enable me to mix, at length, with the kind of people I had never worked with before. It wasn't so much a case of 'seeing how the other half lived' but an opportunity to muck in with men who represented a huge percentage of the working population in my country. Military conscription had once provided this type of experience although it was abolished in the UK in 1960.

The next day, as instructed, I was waiting by the gates when the boss arrived. My autumn would be spent mowing lawns, trimming hedges, raking leaves, pulling out bedding plants, mixing cement, carting paving stones and generally learning the gardening business. Our customers were mostly on Kingston Hill or in Sheen and Richmond, but we once went out into the Surrey countryside to work for the comedian Terry Scott. There were about ten employees, some of whom were very skilled and, as I was eager to learn, I watched carefully when they laid crazy paving or constructed brick walls. Others, like me, did the labouring and provided support.

> Our England is a garden, and such gardens are not made
> By singing:—'Oh, how beautiful!' and sitting in the shade
> While better men than we go out and start their working
>   lives
> At grubbing weeds from gravel paths with broken dinner
>   knives.
> (Rudyard Kipling: The Glory of the Garden)

I especially remember Bert. He was of medium height, probably in his forties, with long hair that curled up from beneath his brown cloth cap. He wore wire-framed NHS glasses whose lenses were so thick that I marvelled that he could see at all and blue dungarees whose trouser legs were kept permanently rolled within his wellington boots. He spoke with a strong south

London accent, was friendly enough and a knowledgeable gardener but one day, while we were both working on a landscaping project, I discovered that he was also a keen amateur photographer. To my delight Bert was happy to impart his knowledge. Whenever the Surrey rain poured down and pitter-pattered on a potting shed or green-house roof, where we had taken shelter, another lesson unfolded as my assiduous teacher drew diagrams with a stubby pencil on the back of seed packets and took me through the theory of apertures, shutter speeds and focal length.

One Friday afternoon in November, I was helping a group of men lay out a new terrace in front of a beautiful Georgian house in Ham. Through tall windows I could see the warm lights of the drawing room, fine pictures on the walls and elegant furnishings. Our clients, like the opening scene from a Noël Coward play, had just entered and were sitting down for their afternoon tea, as my parents would be doing in Cadogan Square. A wave of nostalgia swept over me, although I instantly reminded myself that I had consciously turned my back on that world, even if it was to be only temporary. I picked up a gritty, wet shovel in the semi-darkness and got on with mixing the cement. Soon it was time to go home and we piled into the truck. Dropping Mike, one of the labourers—whose brains were kept in his Y-fronts—at the station, I called out, 'Enjoy your weekend!'

'Fucking joking?' he yelled. 'It's 'er bloody rag days, innit!'

I remained at Luff's until the end of the year.

The community at Coombe Springs was welcoming and I found the after-dinner chats over coffee with people from so many different backgrounds stimulating, as was much of the rest of my stay there. I was certainly caught up in the spirit of the place. What I did not notice at the time was an intensity that could be oppressive. There was a 'work face' manifested by people 'remembering themselves', and because this became part of the sub-culture its oddness went largely unnoticed. In hindsight, I became aware that the Institute bore all the characteristics of a cult although the people were kindly and well-meaning, somewhat puritanical; almost religious in their gravity. Morality was high and promiscuity, drugs and other liberal behaviour that was infecting the wider culture, remained outside the wooden fence that surrounded Coombe Springs.

I befriended an earnest young Iranian, Ardalan Panahi-Azar, who had recently arrived from Cincinatti where he had been studying architecture. Over the next few months we took weekend trips around England visiting cathedral cities and prehistoric monuments. On one of those occasions—it was 21st October 1966—I switched on the car radio only to hear news of the mud-slide at Aberfan, where twenty-eight adults and 116 children died. This was a horrendous catastrophe that affected the whole nation and led to much soul-searching and recrimination.

Eventually, I lost touch with Ardalan who returned to Iran, but was shocked to hear that he had become a devout follower of Ayatollah Khomeni, following the abdication of the Shah in 1979. A little-known fact that I have established to be true, from several sources, is that Khomeni's father was Welsh and his surname was Williams. Presumably he had converted to Islam at some point and changed his name, rather like Cat Stevens (Yusuf Islam).

One activity that was taken very seriously was the Gurdjieff movements. These were bizarre dances that Gurdjieff had developed at the *Prieuré* with the musician Thomas de Hartmann. They consisted of adopting extraordinary poses and contorted positions in time to music. I could not really discover what function the movements fulfilled, except that they followed the wider programme of self-observation. It seems that they were what later commentators referred to as a mechanical repetition of rituals that were significant in some vague, undefined way. However, participating was enjoyable, they provided good exercise, apparently improved the functioning of various internal organs, and I liked the music very much. Not only the dance music, but the other compositions have an unusual quality which is why my ears pricked up in February 2005 when, for the first time, I heard de Hartmann's music played on Classic FM.

The movements were held in a nine-sided wooden building that had been constructed in the late 1950s with the encouragement of Frank Lloyd Wright. It had been inspired by Bennett's travels in Asia Minor, especially by the Sema Hané in Konya, Turkey, which had been built by the Seldjuk kings in the twelfth century. He aimed to establish a haven at Coombe where psychic energies could be concentrated and it was named the Djamichunatra, a word taken from Gurdjieff's *All and Everything* which describes a place where the soul takes its spiritual nourishment. I am not qualified to comment on the presence or otherwise of psychic powers but felt, as I think we all did, that the building was peaceful and had a certain beauty. Besides the dance movements, it was used for meetings and individual meditation.

One day we were all summoned to the Djamichunatra for what was to be a remarkable occasion. Bennett explained that, for many years following the death of Mr G. (that is how Gurdjieff was often referred to, in deferential terms—the true sign of a cult) in 1949, he, and others, had carried on the Work as best they could but he now knew that the time had come to terminate this operation, which had fallen into the realms of 'mechanicality'. As he saw it, the teachings of Gurdjieff and Ouspensky were now outmoded, had become atrophied, and it was time for something new. It was a defining moment, and raised strong emotions for those who had known Bennett and Coombe for decades. In some quarters there was open hostility and a programme of quiet contemplation was instigated. However, towards the end of the year at an Extraordinary General Meeting a vote was taken and the work of the Institute for the Comparative Study of History, Philosophy and the Sciences at Coombe Springs came to an end. A few weeks later, I attended the last dinner under the old regime and it was no surprise that Gurdjieff's favourite Georgian recipe, chicken with walnuts in a garlic sauce, was served. It was delicious and the meal ended with traditional toasts to all the Idiots.

Bennett's last words to me provided encouragement to pursue my own search for understanding of the Fourth Way, which he now referred to as the Way of the Sufi; in a new direction. I read *The Sufis* by Idries Shah, closely followed by *The Teachers of Gurdjieff* by Rafael Lefort and also *The People of the Secret* by Ernest Scott. These works made a huge impression, and led me to follow this particular interest along refreshing lines. Any romanticism regarding 'the miraculous' was replaced by a more solid approach to the search for knowledge.

In the meantime, as Saturday's child, I had a living to earn.

In January 1966, when I needed somewhere to live and was looking for a challenging career opportunity I noticed that *The Times* personal column was advertising the position of assistant manager at the King Charles, a family-owned hotel. No previous experience was required and accommodation with full board was offered. I applied and was called for an interview. It was no coincidence that the King Charles Hotel was in the Cromwell Road, at the Earls Court end.

I met the owners, Hugh and Pam Neil, who explained that having built up trade at the King Charles over many years they had now bought Highbullen,[10] an estate in north Devon, which they planned to develop into a country club style hotel. They would continue to own the King Charles although the day-to-day running of the place would be carried out by

Christopher, their manager. I must have made a good impression, as they concluded the interview by offering me the job as his assistant. Christopher, a tall man with black wiry hair, exhibited the posture of a wannabe matinee idol. An out-of-work actor, he was a bit of a smoothie whose claim to fame was 'sleeping' with Julie Christie in the film *Darling* (1965). I was excited by the job offer and nipped round to Cadogan Square to break the news. My mother was suspicious and thought I would just be a dogsbody.

'You'll have to clean the guests' shoes every night!' she warned, although she was good enough to buy me a new jacket and cotton shirts in traditional style. However, when I moved in on the following weekend I felt that I was at the centre of swinging London.

Twiggy dominated the front covers of magazines in the hotel lounge and miniskirts, promoted by the fashion designer Mary Quant at her two shops in Knightsbridge and Chelsea, were just beginning to turn heads. The exuberant disc jockey Tony Blackburn was frequently seen at the pumps on the garage forecourt in Earls Court Road and Millie, a black singer who lived in a flat next door, twittered her suggestive hit 'My Boy Lollipop' over the airwaves from the pirate radio station Radio Caroline.

I was the only member of the management team to permanently live on the premises and my tiny room was in the basement where traffic rumbled past the window, day and night. Huge lorries bound to and from Covent Garden, where the fruit and vegetable market was still located, were especially noisy at five o'clock in the morning.

My daily routine started at 7 a.m. and if there was any job that would knock the corners off lingering social inhibitions and put paid to a snotty public schoolboy persona, this was to be it. Greeting people at all hours, regardless of age, sex, colour, nationality and background, straight off the street, or, as they emerged in the morning from the lift, bleary-eyed, rushing for a taxi and in no mood to discuss their account, was going to be an education in itself. Making up bills, taking payment, operating the corded telephone exchange, relaying messages, calling for cabs, confirming bookings, dealing with the post, and listing departures for the chambermaids, was all part of the early-morning mêleé.

I soon discovered that, Delia, the breakfast cook, was unreliable and, with a crowd in the dining room looking forward to their eggs and bacon, it often fell to me to don an apron and get stuck in. If, or when, Delia did eventually turn up, panting and all in a dither with her woolly cap at a rakish angle, she would mumble and mutter in her Irish brogue, 'It was the bus, mister Neil … the bus was not to be arriving!'

By ten o'clock things would have settled down and we took a break. A daily chore was to balance the books and we did this over a cup of coffee in the dining room but trying to balance a ledger (pre-decimalisation) manually, recording forty room charges, each with a possible range of extra items such as dinner, bar, room service, telephone, newspaper, laundry, snacks and so on, could be exasperating. The columns needed to balance both vertically and horizontally and if an error occurred if was unbelievably difficult to spot. We sometimes sat staring at the figures for what seemed like hours. It could reduce one to tears but the trick, when really foxed, was to get someone else to take a fresh look and they would usually see the mistake immediately.

The next chore was to stock the small bar, which was in a pleasant room with gold and green striped wallpaper and matching furnishings, whose French windows opened out on to the terrace and pocket-sized back garden. All the empties had to be carted away and bottles of beer, wines and spirits replenished from a store in the cellar. Occasionally a beer barrel had to be changed. This job and serving in the bar at night taught me a lot and the names of European vineyards and those of Scottish malts were soon rolling off my tongue.

One evening Bill Rhoads, an American whom I had met at Coombe turned up unexpectedly. 'How yer doin'?' he enquired, poking his Puck-like face around the office door. I took him down to the bar and bought him a drink.

'If you want to make a good barman and keep the cash till ringing,' he said, 'recall your customers' names and remember what they drink. Make a note if you have to!'

He recounted how he and his wife Emmie had once dropped in to a tavern in Colorado on their way to California. Three months later they retraced their steps, and as they approached the saloon bar, the attendant greeted them with these reassuring words:

'Good evening, Mr and Mrs Rhoads, nice to see you back with us. Will that be a Jack Daniels on the rocks and a sweet Martini?'

Bill was born in Illinois where he studied art and design before serving in the infantry during the Korean War. He then worked at the American Embassy in Paris while moonlighting as a photo-journalist. He was in the process of moving to London and was working as a producer and designer in the film industry when I first met him. Some twenty years later his first novel, *Baudoin's Moustache* was published by Weidenfeld and Nicolson, and my wife and I are proud to have an inscribed copy. It is set in Paris and the central theme springs from the venerable French system of property acquisition by which the buyer guarantees the vendor—usually an elderly person— an annuity in exchange for the vendor's property upon his or her death. This unique system has sometimes been regarded as an incentive for murder. A reviewer at the time of publication, referring to Bill's work said, 'I very much admire this elegant, spare, ironical novel.' It serves as an inspiration to any aspiring writer and would make a good film

I enjoyed serving in the bar in the evenings and tried to put into practice what Bill had taught me, but I was often on duty alone so any chit-chat was repeatedly interrupted by the telephone or the bell on the reception desk.

All through the day new guests would arrive, and I soon realised that the hotel had an extensive clientele. In fact, as I had written to many of them confirming their bookings, stumbling with two fingers as I learned to tame the typewriter, some names were already familiar before they came through the door. An important corporate client was the Australia and New Zealand Bank, which booked holidays for their retired clients who were visiting the 'old country'. These people were always exceptionally pleasant. They invariably stayed for a couple of weeks to see the sights, taking in the Chelsea Flower Show and Trooping of the Colour. Then they were off on a tour of Scotland or some other part of the British Isles. Two more weeks at the King Charles, during which they took day trips to Windsor, Oxford, Cambridge and Stratford-upon-Avon, would be followed by other tours and finally they returned home. I used to get to know them quite well, as they relayed their adventures, invariably culminating in how they had found a gravestone in some remote country churchyard and after removing the thick, silvery lichen identified it as the last resting place of a revered ancestor. When they finally set off on the long trip back to the antipodes, it was sad to think that they would almost certainly never grace these shores again.

Other regulars were from the BBC in Scotland, staying overnight for a meeting at the Television Centre or Broadcasting House, and it was not unusual to see the reporter Fife Robertson or other familiar faces at the breakfast table. Moira Anderson was staying with us at the time that she got her first big break.

I grew wary of a particularly well-known television presenter and tried to avoid giving him Room 18 because it was just above mine. He appeared to have an insatiable appetite for horizontal exercise and had unfortunately developed a liking for that particular room—or should I say bed.

A quietly spoken guest who stayed every other Tuesday night, whose demeanour suggested such activities to be the last thing on his mind, worked for the National Savings Office in Bootle and in the summer. Wimbledon tennis players would patronise the King Charles. I recall Roger Taylor as an especially charming guest.

In the autumn and winter the place was packed with businessmen from the Motor Show or Boat Show at Earls Court or Olympia. On one occasion I was chatting to a guest whose name I cannot recall. This is perhaps for the best as she told me that she had an influential friend, who was always on the lookout for enterprising young men who could do with a 'leg up' in their career. Would I like to meet him? She enquired.

'What's his name?' I said.

'Jeremy Thorpe,' she replied.

I thanked her and said that I would give her offer of meeting the celebrated MP some thought but the opportunity passed. On 12th August, there was bad news from Shepherd's Bush—just down the road. Three City of London policemen had been shot dead, the worst incident of its kind since 1911. We were all profoundly shocked, but at least the chief perpetrator, Harry Roberts, was caught and sentenced to life imprisonment. I am not sure why he was not hung, as capital punishment was not abolished in England until 1969.

I never did have to clean the guests' shoes, but getting the evening meal cooked was as problematic as breakfast, even though we offered a simple menu. Most residents preferred to enjoy the gastronomic delights of the capital. I would have thought that finding someone who could rustle up a bowl of soup, unfreeze potted shrimps, cook a steak or chicken and make a salad would be easy, but we were often let down. I found a solution by arranging for the hotel to employ my friends. Whenever one of my chums registered a need to earn extra cash I persuaded him to commit to the kitchens for a few weeks. Christopher Olgiati was one of that select band who supported the amenities of the hotel and also provided me with company when I was on duty in the evenings. I also became surprisingly popular, and friends were always popping in. A sirloin steak from Mr Stone, the excellent butcher in

Barnes, and a bottle of Nuits-St-Georges went down very well. My employers were easy-going. My meals were provided as part of the job, so all I had to do was cover the basic cost for my guests. It made the long hours pass more quickly, because I was often on duty until midnight. After that, since there was no night porter, a phone link from my bedside to the front door served those who had forgotten their key or even thought they would try their luck at getting a room. One night as I was locking the front door some people were climbing the steps from the Cromwell Road. They turned out to be an Iranian family.

'You have room?' a bearded man quizzed me.

'No, I'm sorry, we're full!' I replied.

He tried again. 'Please, you have room, all hotel full?'

I pointed to the corner of the street. 'Try Earls Court, many hotels.'

I was breaking into pidgin English.

'All hotel full,' he repeated. 'Please, sir, I have childs.'

Indeed he did; three small tired faces were looking up at me together with four adults. I felt myself giving way.

'OK, you can sleep in the lounge,' I said, beckoning them inside.

I led them into the spacious lounge and after pointing out the loos brought in a pile of pillows, blankets and eiderdowns.

'You sleep on sofas or chairs; children on floor,' I said, waving my hands. Then I beat a hasty retreat, wondering if I would regret my impetuousness. Early the next morning they were sound asleep, sprawled all over the place. I quickly awoke them, charged a nominal fee and shooed them out of the hotel before anyone else was around.

When Christopher was away for the weekend I was in charge. Today, it would be inconceivable that an unqualified nineteen-year-old would be given twenty-four-hour responsibility for a London hotel, with some fifty guests and resident maids.

I certainly enjoyed the job, made good money, had few expenses and was able to save. I even bought a state-of-the-art Hacker radio. However, after nine months, towards the end of the summer, I began to get restless and wonder if all this effort could not be better directed. Why work so hard for someone else, I thought to myself, why not run my own business?

As soon as the idea struck me I got really excited. I had seen what it was like for the Neils to own and run a hotel, so why shouldn't I run my own show—although a partnership might be more practical?

The idea was thrilling. 'Be more—do more', rang in my ears and left my head spinning, which kept me awake at night. The buzz of the swinging, can-do '60s had got to me. Anything was possible.

I went in search of Leon Flamholc, a friend from Coombe Springs to whom I had been giving driving lessons on my days off and who now lived in digs in Kingston. I broached the idea. He was all for it—keen on us working together—but in what kind of business?

We drove to Borscht 'n' Tears, the dynamic new bistro in Beauchamp Place, and devoured bowls of steaming red borscht followed by spicy chicken Kiev as we tossed around ideas and tossed back a few vodkas at the same time. On a superficial level, Leon was the last person anyone would have expected me to team up with. He was a few years older, and shorter than I was at about five foot seven, and boasted a Jewish background, having a Polish father and Russian mother. He had been born in a concentration camp during the war although the family moved to Stockholm in 1948 where they became naturalised Swedes. Leon had arrived at Coombe at about the same time as I had in order to study with John Bennett.

Instinctively, I must have felt that we could work well together, and even though his English was poor, he possessed a keen wheeler-dealer mentality that could complement my style. I was still wet behind the ears. He was far more streetwise, had knocked around France and Germany a bit and possessed various skills. Today he would be described as a polymath, but was at a loose end, looking for something to get his teeth into.

'Vy not start a restaurant?' Leon proposed.

'We have no capital. We need to make money. Then we can open a restaurant,' I suggested.

'So, vot shall ve do? I sink a place dat sells only vine and cheese vud do vel, like dey haf in Paris,' said Leon.

'No money and we wouldn't get a licence,' I replied with mild irritation. 'People go to pubs in this country if they want a drink and to restaurants if they want to eat and drink. There is nothing in between,' I continued, but even as I spoke I realised that Leon had hit on a very good idea, which proved to be ahead of its time. As yet, no one had opened a 'wine bar' with the possible exception of 'Gordon's' in Charing Cross.

The conversation went back and forth like ping-pong.

Eventually we came to the conclusion that there was one enterprise we could start with the least amount of capital and the minimum of skill—a painting and decorating business—so that is what we agreed to do.

We ordered more vodka and drank 'to enterprise'.

'You never know, once we are in business, other opportunities may also come our way,' I chimed in as we settled the bill. At that moment a fellow diner—a kindly-looking man who was impeccably dressed—interrupted us.

'Excuse me,' he said, passing me his card which read, Dr Ari Sheldon. 'I couldn't help overhearing your conversation. I think the idea of running your own business is great. Do you know, when I first came to London, stony broke, I started a steak and kidney pie round in Chelsea pubs. I make excellent pies and after three months I sold my round for a thousand pounds. This is the way you have to think! After that, one thing followed another and my life, in England, has developed in many directions!'

Dr Sheldon then bought us each another vodka and went on enthusiastically for about half an hour about the virtues of 'running your own show', as he called it.

'Why report to others? Be your own masters!' he chuckled.

We had no idea who he was, although I suspect that he was originally from the Middle East or even further afield. However, by the time he had finished, we were so fired up that we knew nothing would stop us from getting on with the job, and his inspirational words came back to us from time to time in difficult days ahead.

When I told my parents what was planned they were horrified, viewing Leon, whom they had met briefly, with deep suspicion. His being a foreigner was bad enough, but shacking up with a Jewish immigrant was not what they expected of their Marlborough-educated son. However, our decision set me on a learning curve that would be thoroughly absorbing, fill every moment of every day and provide me with an income for the next seventeen years. It also set me on an indeterminate course, in respect of my net earnings, that would continue, month by month, for the rest of my working life.

St Peter and St Paul's, Marlborough

Marlborough College, Main Gates

Marlborough College, Memorial Hall

Port Quin Bay, North Cornwall

John Godolphin Bennett

Vietnam War Demonstration, London, 1968

Chapter 6
The Painter of the World I

Next came the golden Peacock, with feathers of a hundred—what shall I say?—a hundred thousand colours! He
displayed himself, turning this way and that, like a bride.
'The painter of the world,' he said, 'to fashion me took in his
hand the brush of the Jinn.'
(Farid ud-din Attar, *'The Parliament of the Birds'*, twelfth
century)

IT WAS ONE of those hazy golden October afternoons, the weakening
sun reflected off glossy stucco-work as shadows lengthened across London
squares. Leon and I parked in Bayswater and, although it was late in the day,
we were about to take the first step in our new enterprise. I had handed in my
notice at the King Charles in September and taken a room in Kingston for
five pounds per week. With one hundred pounds in the bank, a second-hand
Austin A30, recently purchased for less than half that sum, and a pair of
stepladders secured to the roof rack, we felt equipped for business. We left the
car, and scattering crisp autumn leaves that littered the pavement, started to
make our way around Kensington Gardens Square, knocking on doors and
asking for decorating work. To our surprise, we received a positive response
after only a few minutes. A woman who must have been in her late thirties,
who had both legs in plaster, hobbled to the door.

'As it happens,' she said, 'I do want my bathroom painted.'

She invited us in to give an estimate. I had done a bit of decorating at
Coombe, but did not have much of a clue. Fortunately Leon was more experienced. We looked around the scruffy little bathroom; wet clothes were
draped over a wire above the bath and the Ascot heater leaked rusty water
down the far wall. Leon stroked his chin, appearing to be in deep thought.

'Sirty pownds,' he said. We looked at the lady wondering what would
happen next. 'Done,' she replied. 'When can you start?'

'Tomorrow,' I blurted out. 'How about ten o'clock?'

This was agreed, and once we had determined that she wanted a white
gloss finish, we left. She had pressed ten pounds on us, as a deposit and to
buy the paint. Naturally, we were over the moon. We had our first deal and
enough cash to buy paint, brushes, filler, white spirit, sandpaper and a couple
of dustsheets.

We stopped at the Boileau near Hammersmith Bridge and toasted our
new enterprise.

Our first job was completed satisfactorily over the next couple of days
and when our customer was out of earshot, Leon gave me a few tips on using
filler and how to get the best results when applying oil paint.

It occurred to me that Leon fancied her.

I dink she is frustrated—could do with a good screw,' he grinned, sala-
ciously. Here was a different Leon than the one I had seen before and would
see more of as the months passed.

Now we needed another job.

We popped into Cohen's, an estate agent in Queensway and explained
what we were doing. 'Come with me,' barked a tall Irishman, rising from his
desk which bore a little sign that read 'Mr Patrick Calverson'. Calverson led
us down Queensway and into Porchester Road. He stopped under a mews
arch just before we got to the iron railway bridge and, opening a door, led
us up a few stairs in to what was clearly a bedsit. Beyond the smoke-grimed
windows, we could just make out a train pulling into Paddington Station.
The large room was in a disgusting condition, made worse by plaster from
the high ceiling that had collapsed and lay in chunks on the floor and all
over the grubby furniture. There was a foul smell that emanated from soiled
linen on the bed, as well as the dozen or so half-empty milk bottles whose
contents had gone green and mouldy weeks ago. A pile of greasy dishes and
cutlery were stacked on the draining board. The sink was full of dirty water.

'How much to do this place up? Emulsion on the walls and ceiling and gloss on the woodwork, two coats,' growled Calverson. 'I want it let in ten days,' he added menacingly. Leon said that we would take some measurements and give him a price after lunch.

'OK, see you later. Slam the door behind you.'

He left us to it. We made a few notes on a pad that Leon had brought and estimated the time and materials needed.

'Richard Maxwell's good at plastering, he can help us,' I said. 'We better put on twenty quid for him, and we'll need to hire some tall steps and boards.'

'Good sinking, dat should make about £250,' Leon rejoined. We scratched our heads.

'Calverson will probably try and knock us down, so let's go for £295 so we've got some leeway,' I suggested. We agreed and went off to have lunch in the Danube Café in Queensway, an excellent establishment that served good coffee and apfelstrudel with freshly whipped cream, and whose walls were lined with blow-up photographs of old Vienna and Budapest. During the meal and not for the last time we got cold feet before settling on a price, although we certainly wanted the job.

Calverson hardly looked up from his desk as we entered his office.

'How much?'

'Two hundred seventy-five pownds,' Leon volunteered.

'Two fifty,' he barked.

'Two sixty,' Leon replied.

'Two fifty,' Calverson repeated firmly.

We reluctantly agreed. Rising to his feet, he gave us the key.

'Starting tomorrow?' he queried.

We nodded.

'Good, I'll drop in and choose some colours, so have a card with you. Remember, I want that shit hole ready to let by the end of next week—don't let me down.'

We assured him that the work would be finished on time and to a good standard, then left the office wondering just what we had got ourselves into. For the next ten days we slogged away. Our first tasks were to thoroughly wash the woodwork with sugar soap, strip the walls, leaving a pile of wet gooey paper on the floor and get rid of all the filth, debris and carpet as further instructed by Calverson. Then Richard gave us a hand with the plastering. Once the preliminary work was complete, the place slowly began to take shape and, as the deadline approached, we felt pleased with ourselves. Magnolia walls were offset by white gloss that gleamed on tall box shutters and the other woodwork. The bedsit was being transformed, but there was still a lot to do and we found ourselves working later and later, grabbing fish and chips in Westbourne Grove, before returning to Kingston well after midnight.

Finally, the day came to hand back the key to Calverson, who arrived pulling out a wad of notes from his back pocket. We turned down my paint-spattered Hacker radio which was belting out the Four Tops' chartbuster, 'Reach Out, I'll Be There', as he counted out the cash.

'There you are, two hundred pounds.'

'Hang on, we agreed on two fifty,' we both chimed in.

'*You* said you'd do a *good* job—just look at those runs on the shutters,' he argued.

'That's ridiculous, they were there already,' I said, getting shirty.

'Ever heard of fucking sandpaper?' he sneered.

'And what about the plastering? I can see the join with the old ceiling,' he added. He had us there, but it would have been impossible to produce a seamless finish in such an old building.

'Look here,' we blustered, 'we've transformed this place, you'll let it to the first applicant.'

'Take it or leave it,' he concluded.

'Bastard!' we both intoned, picking up the cash which he had left on the draining board. We retreated to the Danube, crestfallen.

'What a con—he saw us coming,' I groaned.

'Yep! I bet every decorator in Baysvater has Mister Patrick Bloody Calverson in his sights,' Leon replied.

We went back to the car, parked up by the Athenian grocery in Moscow Road, took out some leaflets that we had just had printed, and started to work along some of the small streets near the Greek Orthodox Church. After a couple of hours, a man opened his front door and shouted, 'What are you two up to, touting for business? Piss off!'

He slammed the door in our faces.

That was it—we'd had enough—back to Kingston.

For the next of couple of days, we adopted the same routine but with little success. Blocks of flats seemed a good bet. If we could sidle past the janitor, unobserved, and take the lift to the top floor, then, by working our way down to the ground, we could push leaflets through several hundred letterboxes without leaving the building.

'Vot ve should do is bribe de buggers, not avoid dem,' said Leon, so we started to present our card to the porters, with the promise of a generous backhander if they got us work. It was a tiring and dispiriting activity and we were frequently tempted to pop in to the Danube to shelter from the November chill and while away an hour chatting to Harry, the amiable West Indian with a global smile who served behind the bar and operated a noisy contraption that emitted clouds of steam and produced a hot frothy drink called a cappuccino.

On the third day we struck lucky; a middle-aged couple in Bedford Gardens wanted their elegant drawing room painted. They chose a soft duck-egg tone and our price was accepted. We were back in business. Our customers proved to be a tall, handsome white-haired retired Wing Commander, who was also a director of Beefeater Gin, and his wife. They were hospitable, brought in numerous cups of tea and biscuits on a tray and generally encouraged us. From time to time, the lady of the house paused for a chat. She always appeared neatly dressed, like the Queen, in pleated skirt, soft woollen blouse and a single string of pearls adorning her ample bosom, but she was obviously worried about her daughter who had recently eloped with a German condom salesman. She was also interested to know more about us and clearly found me and Leon a curious duo. I was skinny, fresh-faced, about five foot ten, clearly 'public school' and happy to lay on whatever charm I could muster, while Leon was the elder and assumed the role of 'business brain'. He spoke a number of languages and was only too happy to talk about his Jewish roots and the circumstances of his birth.

'In nineteen terty-nine my farder vas living vith parents and bruder near de Polish border vith Germany,' he explained. 'Ven de bombing started de town vas destroyed by blitzkrieg and de family split up. My uncle vent vestvard and vas never seen again. Ve heard dat he died in Auschwitz. My farder fled east and vas picked up by de Red Army. He vas sent to Karabalty in Kyrgyzstan vitch vas a place far avay from de front vere a lot of people ver evacuated from parts of de de country dat de Germans had occupied. He met my mudder dere and dat is vere I vas born.'

Ours was, indeed, a curious symbiosis; two opposites that provided the energy and will for things to happen. I wonder what 'Slug' would have thought.

When we finished at Bedford Gardens, the Wing Commander and his wife were pleased with their newly painted room and promised to have us back in the spring to paint the exterior of the house.

Arriving back at our digs, there was a message from a lady who wanted a flat decorated for a tenant in South Kensington. Perhaps one of our leaflets had come up trumps, we thought, so I rang her and arranged to meet. However, we had identified a problem. While we were working, on site, there was no opportunity, and little energy to look for new business. The knack was going to be to juggle our time to try to establish continuity. Negotiations with our new contact, whose flat in Harrington Road was only yards from the mansion that W.S. Gilbert built for himself in 1882, were successful; things were looking up, but who was going to hang the wallpaper?

After another couple of weeks of rising early and working late, Mrs Telfer-Smollett, the owner of the flat, was pleased with our endeavours and my efforts with the wallpaper passed anything but the closest scrutiny.

'Not bad,' said Leon, 'I could not have done better myself!'

I popped round the corner to buy a tin of Quality Street or a box of chocolates, as a friendly gesture for the incoming tenant. This proved to be a problem.

'Not Quality Street, sir,' responded the turbaned assistant in the first shop I entered. 'This is Gloucester Road.'

Mrs Telfer-Smollett told us that she managed several properties, as well as working in her antique business in the Portobello Road, and would be in touch in the January. Just before Christmas we received a boost. The novelist Doris Lessing asked us to redecorate the sitting room and staircase in her eighteenth-century terraced house in Ossulston Street, behind St Pancras Station. This was the same first-floor room where I had been introduced to her during August, when a group of friends had gathered to plan a big party. On that stiflingly hot Sunday, there were not enough seats for everyone so I had stretched out on the coarse coconut matting that covered the floor. The urban jungle, beyond tall dormer windows, basked in sultry, breezeless late afternoon sunshine. In contrast, we arrived for work on a freezing December morning and found most of the house in shambles, occupied by more cats than humans, but by beavering away until late every evening, supported by endless cups of tea by the kindly Doris, we completed our assignment in time for seasonal parties.

As Leon prepared to leave for a holiday in Sweden we reflected that, over the first few months, we had paid our way, learned a few lessons and even acquired customers who might provide regular work. We treated ourselves to dinner at Borscht 'n' Tears, wondering if we might bump into our friend, Dr Sheldon. By chance, he was just settling his bill and on his way out.

'How nice to see you again', I said, greeting him.

'Me too', he replied. 'How's it going?'

'Going vell, but steep learning curves! rejoined Leon.

'That's good. No pain, no gain!' he chuckled and slipped out of the front door.

'I do like that guy', I said as we sat down. 'Do you remember how enthusiastic he was about our new business?'

Leon nodded.

'To enterprise!' We clinked glasses, toasted the future, and called for more vodka.

Early in January of 1967 I received a phone call from Jane Weston, a distant cousin whose maiden name was Sharpin, as was the mother of the explorer and author Apsley Cherry-Garrard, to whom I have referred earlier and to whom she was related. She and her husband, Mark, had heard about our business and wanted their flat decorated when they went skiing. I called round to see them in Clifton Place. Leon was still away, but I felt confident enough to give them a price and execute the work on my own. We had not met before and I immediately liked them. They ran a firm called the London Window Box Company which pioneered contract plant supply and maintenance for homes and businesses.

Nowadays, London is brimming with plants of all types in shops, offices, hotels, window boxes, balconies, terraces—but in the 1960s, this was not the case and I felt myself empathising with the Westons' innovative operation. He had boundless energy and was up at five every weekday to visit the flower-market, still located in the bustling streets between the Royal Opera House and St Paul's church in Covent Garden.

They asked me to carry out the work on their flat and I was secretly rather pleased to be able to report an operation successfully completed when Leon returned.

'You English rely too much on charm. I dink you learn it at your public schools,' he once told me. 'Ve Jews have little charm. To survive, ve have to deliver!'

I had found the fortnight working alone at Clifton Place a lonely task, but Donovan telling me repeatedly over the airwaves, that he was 'mad about Saffron', and Nancy Sinatra raving about her boots—the ones 'made for walking'—had kept me company!

The Westons were delighted and in the spring they asked us to decorate their shop followed, several years later, by their house in Hampshire. Leon returned with a Volvo Amazon 122 that his parents had given him for Christmas, which was useful as it secured us independent transport. They were generous folk and could afford to spoil their only son. Leon's father had become a successful tailor, patronised by Swedish royalty, and his mother was in great demand teaching piano in Stockholm. We immediately agreed to hold a serious planning meeting and went to the Mardi Gras Café in Harrington Gardens for a working lunch. I liked the Mardi Gras because it served an especially tangy Italian vinaigrette and the avocado pears always seemed just right. This delightful fruit (imported from the kibbutzim of Israel) had only recently become commonplace in London restaurants. Mardi Gras was also one of the few venues where, at that time, you could sit in the open—even in winter.

As soon as we sat down a large bird shat on the railings close to where we were sitting.

'Bloody crouw!' exclaimed Leon.

'Actually, CROW … C-R-O-W … rhymes with SNOW,' I sniggered.

We both laughed. Leon began to outline the future, as he saw it.

'Ve have made a good start,' he said, 'but de time has come to get men to vork for us. Ve vil never break out from being de two-man band, living hand and mouth, unless ve take some risk and expand. Believe me, I know how dese sings verk.'

I agreed, and pointed out that our aim had always been to run a business rather than just slog away 'on the brushes'. My concern was that if we were really serious, leaflets with 'Hall and Flamholc: Painters and Decorators' and an obscure telephone number in Kingston was not good enough.

'We need a registered address, a proper business name and a telephone answering service. Ideally, we should have an office in central London,' I concluded.

Leon thought this was a bit ambitious and probably expensive, but we agreed that I should see what was available.

'Vile you look for de office I'll explore de labour market,' he promised.

As it happened, finding a base proved easy. In the window of Gordon's estate agency in Paddington I saw a tiny office advertised. It was about seventy square feet and on the second floor at 102 Queensway, bang opposite our friend Mr Calverson who still owed us fifty pounds. I would continue to remind him of the fact, for years to come, whenever we passed in the street. The rent was affordable at eight pounds per week, and we arranged for a lease to be drawn up. We also arranged for a telephone line (Bayswater 1909) and signed an unexpectedly costly contract for a Telstor answering machine, one of the first new brands on the market. We were very excited by these developments and after visiting a local junk shop, moved in with a trestle table, two chairs and a grey metal filing cabinet. My father presented us with an old Olivetti typewriter that the school no longer required.

We liked Queensway, which runs from Kensington Gardens to Westbourne Grove. It combined seediness with rising multiculturalism and a faded elegance. At the top of the hill, on the corner of the Bayswater Road, stood the Coburg Hotel with its brass cage lifts that ascended, with imperial grace, to spacious bedrooms. These rooms enjoyed views towards the Round Pond and Kensington Palace and the tallest spire in London, soaring above St Mary Abbott's Church (rebuilt by Sir Gilbert Scott in 1869–72), drew the eye, across the park, and into the distance. On the opposite corner, diners at Le Mignon, a Hungarian restaurant, would be entertained by a lively gypsy fiddler, with red spotted kerchief knotted jauntily around his neck and, further down the hill, the popular ice rink that opened in 1930 attracted energetic skaters from far and wide.

At the bottom of Queensway, all sorts of merchandise could be purchased in the Victorians' favourite store founded by 'the universal provider', William Whiteley, in 1863. An ambitious young Yorkshire man, he had come down to London with £10 in his pocket but by 1896 his achievement had earned an unsolicited warrant from Queen Victoria. Sadly, he was murdered in 1907 by a man claiming to be his illegitimate son. His customers who, like Eliza Doolittle, were sent 'to Whiteleys to be attired' (*Pygmalion*) came from all over the metropolis but many had lived in the huge houses that made up the squares and terraces of the surrounding area. For the most part, with the demise of the domestic servant and other sociological changes, following two world wars, these grand properties became impossible to run as single family units. They had been converted to bedsits where paint peeled from external stucco-work, clumps of grass sprouted from cracks in the balconies and faded curtains drooped across open windows. Sixties pop blared and a sense of smouldering anticipation hung in the air on hot summer evenings.

A further customer for 'the universal provider' would undoubtedly have been another ambitious young countryman with an entrepreneurial turn of mind: my forebear Robert Foale Oldrey who, putting his farming background behind him, had come up to London from Slapton in Devon and was creating a fortune for himself in the City. By 1866 his affairs had sufficiently prospered to enable him to take a lease on 7 Notting Hill Terrace, together with coach-house and stables.[11]

Curiously, this was only a ten-minute walk from the new office in Queensway where Leon and I were planning the next steps in our pursuit of 'enterprise'.

Sandwiched between the Coburg Hotel at the top of Queensway and Whiteleys at the bottom were an array of shops, eating places and businesses. Bertorelli's, a busy family restaurant, served Italian food, where patrons dined off quality china served on crisp white tablecloths. In the basement a few doors away the Artist's Palette contributed London's muted response to Pigalle. There, customers enjoyed a high standard of cuisine, although attention was easily diverted to scantily clad ladies, posing on chaises longues, whose flirtatious charms they were encouraged to capture in charcoal or pastel. Leon and I liked the Danube Café or Monsieur Pechon's Patisserie Francaise at number 127, but occasionally the whiff of frying onions and the thought of hamburgers and chips lured us into the Wimpy Bar. That was, until we learned better when the real product arrived from the States. Greasy Wimpys were, to a finely chopped juicy steak burger with all the relishes like a bowler hat is to a native American's head-dress.

Our business routine now started early in the morning when we arrived at the office to plan our day. Parking in Porchester Gardens, a street still free of meters at that time, we would pass Mr Harris, who had just finished laying out fresh fruit and vegetables on stands in front of his corner greengrocer's. He never failed to bid us a cheerful good morning while sauntering up and down, proudly admiring his produce and puffing on a fat cigar. Invariably, we detected the exotic aroma even before our portly friend, who somehow resembled Mr Toad, came in sight. Then, having crossed Queensway, and slipping past the neighbouring newsagent's board where cards advertised services ranging from French lessons, massage, correction, rubber goods and dancing lessons with Gay Gordon, we climbed the stairs at 102. The first-floor office was occupied by two quantity surveyors whose door was frequently left open, so we could see them sitting at polished oak roll-top desks, already hard at work. Hats and coats hung on a wooden stand, jackets had been discarded and they toiled in white shirts and braces, each puffing away at his pipe. There were small sets of brass scales on the desks for weighing the post, together with several ashtrays and an array of ancient staplers, hole-punchers and card index files. The yellowing walls and brown stained woodwork had not seen a lick of paint for decades and the room was stacked high with papers. It would not have surprised me to learn that they had followed the same routine for thirty or forty years and we considered that the time must soon be approaching when they awarded each other a gold watch and began to draw their pensions.

The next item on our agenda was to choose a business name. During my browsing through translations of Persian poetry, I had come across the lines that introduce this chapter. They are a direct quote from *The Conference of the Birds* (Mantiq Ut-Tair), an allegory in which thirty birds embark on a quest in search of the Simurgh, their mystical king. Simurgh, in classical Persian means 'thirty birds', so the analogy actually works better in the original. This long, complicated poem was written by Fariddudin Attar, who died more than one hundred years before the birth of Chaucer, and some authorities have drawn a connection between Attar's birds and Chaucer's thirty Canterbury pilgrims. Certainly the *Pardoner's Tale*, related as the party wend their way to the tomb of Thomas à Becket, features in the Persian's work.

We named the business 'Peacock Decorators' because Attar's description of the Peacock seemed remarkably appropriate.

'Are you sure that people won't think that you decorate peacocks?' my smartarse friend, Richard wondered; a comment that was treated with the contempt it deserved. What a pity I did not study oriental languages, I thought to myself as I wrote these lines. Not too late—I suppose.

The next step, starting to build a team of craftsmen, was going to be far more difficult. Although we now felt that we were a real business with premises and an image, professionally designed business cards and even a van (which used to belong to the Post Office) instead of my A30, we had no working capital. We would only continue to exist on a day-to-day basis unless we could make a breakthrough. Were we going to generate enough jobs to support ourselves, let alone other workers? On the other hand, if we could achieve sufficient continuous work the profits would be there for expansion. One thing we agreed on was that we needed bigger jobs so that we could then start planning a month or two months ahead.

We pondered these problems long and hard, but, in the meantime, with a birthday to celebrate, we dropped by Granny Takes a Trip, a dimly-lit boutique at Worlds End in Chelsea. Here, perfumed candles flickered, joss sticks glowed in brass receptacles and smoky aromas of an indeterminate nature, together with shadowy figures whose sexuality was ambiguous, lingered in dusky recesses. The most outrageous clothes were on sale in this exotic '60s den and we procured an expensive purple silk shirt as a present for our friend Alan Tunbridge, who had designed the Peacock logo and stationery.

To overcome our problems we decided on a division of labour. Leon, who was now thoroughly proficient, would continue to do the painting and wallpapering but would start to integrate a couple of other decorators into our team, hopefully running more than one job at a time. I would concentrate on finding work and estimating. The latter was, of course, a skill in itself, and it was not customary to charge for estimates even though they could take a long time to prepare.

Every new proposition required assessment in terms of materials and time. Materials could be quantified quite easily by adopting regular formulas and using manufacturers' guides. Taking accurate measurements was essential. Judging the time a job would take required careful consideration and that rarest of commodities—common sense. As I soon began to realise, standards—and therefore the price—for work in a Knightsbridge flat would not be the same as those for bedsits in Bayswater and although I never met the notorious Rachman I did meet a few Rigsbys in my time. Peter Rachman was a racketeer, and Christine Keeler's lover (on a daily basis, apparently), who operated in the Notting Hill area during the '60s and whose name has crept into the English language to describe landlords who buy up slums to fill with immigrants who are charged extortionate rents. Rigsby was the landlord in a rundown apartment building, hilariously portrayed by Leonard Rossiter in Yorkshire Television's black comedy series *Rising Damp* (1978). Much of this type of property, north of the park, was very poorly maintained and in some cases dangerously so. There were several disastrous fires in cheap hotels and on one occasion, in Kensington Gardens Square, a guest leaped from an upper floor to escape the flames, only to be impaled on the iron railings beneath. There is, more than forty years later, still a gap in the row of spikes where the fire service cut through the metal to free that unfortunate individual before taking her to hospital.

I had a nasty experience myself in a smart flat behind Harrods when invited to estimate for some work. While taking the usual measurements I had popped to the loo, but unfortunately, in my haste, my foreskin caught in my trouser zip and I was riveted to the spot. Not life threatening, but I was convulsed in agony. It was just too painful to move, and visions of delicate surgery flashed through my mind. As I was about to summon up all my courage and stagger into the corridor in search of help, my tormented member released itself from the teeth of the zip, leaving me sore but mobile.

Standards varied widely from customer to customer. It would be some years before we undertook work for the Cadogan Estate, however when I received specifications from their office, the quality of preparation expected far exceeded the norm and they were prepared to pay for it. Estimating also required making judgements with respect to the location and ease of access to the job. Waiting for deliveries could be time-consuming and therefore a consideration. The time needed to protect carpets and furnishings and move furniture and cart away rubbish should all be taken into account. Exterior work might require scaffolding, cradles or extension ladders, and prices from subcontractors had to be obtained. When assessing work on the outside of shops or water-damaged buildings, special skills such as sign-writing or asphalt work could be required. Here it would be prudent to build in a provisional costing rather than wasting too much time obtaining an exact price for a contract that might not be awarded to us. There was, in short, a whole range of criteria that entered into the final analysis and determined the price, and it was a skill that I would hone for the next ten years. The state of the order book and likely competition could be a deciding factor, as was also the general amenability of the customer. If a potential customer was especially wealthy or in a rush—before Christmas, for instance—I would take the opportunity to add on a few bob. After all, business is the licensed process of getting cash from the other guy's pocket and into one's own bank account—a bit like Robin Hood.

Some customers employed professional advisers. I would learn to deal with architects, surveyors, designers and town planners, the latter being— in my opinion—an especially strange breed. This was brought home to me when an architect of my acquaintance presented the local planning officer with some preliminary sketches for a gazebo in a London square. A note came back that read: 'Looks all right to me, but where will the animal's food be stored?'

To generate enquiries, I placed adverts in the local paper, continued distributing leaflets, had trade boards painted that were placed outside Peacock work sites and took the Morris van to be sign-written. Calling on shops and offices to leave a card and generally promote Peacock Decorators, I developed a useful gambit. If a shopkeeper gave us some work—a hairdresser in South Kensington was an example—then I called on other barbers and hairdressers. I pointed out that we had just completed work for a competitor in the vicinity, and when they were in the market for painting and decorating, we would be delighted to provide an estimate. I always added that we were prepared to work outside normal business hours. This all took time, but by harnessing every ounce of initiative, positive results were achieved.

Several years later, we decorated a fish restaurant in Poland Street by organising relays of painters over a forty-eight-hour period.

Leon was also making headway. He had taken on a couple of Cockneys from Forest Gate in the East End. Frank and Sid were good decorators and hard workers, but they were hungry; it was going to take all our efforts to keep them busy or they would be off. They were paid cash by the day. We were also going to have to change our attitude and review how potential customers perceived us. One day, I was asked to estimate for repainting a house in the corner of Wellington Square, just off the King's Road. It was, by our standards, a big undertaking so I took Leon with me to have a look. We worked out a price and I went back the next day. It was accepted.

'Thank you,' I said, 'We'll bring our men around on Monday.'

'Oh no, you won't, I want you and your friend to do the work,' our potential customer replied. This put us in a bit of a fix and would undermine our strategy so regrettably we had to pass on that job. At about the same time a Scotsman, who had come down to London to earn more money and had seen one of our adverts, appeared in the office. He was very nervous and we did not really have anything to offer, but he seemed keen, so we decided to try him out on a small job in a pretty top-floor flat that looked out over Regent's Park. It was near 13 Hanover Terrace, the house where H.G. Wells had lived, and died in 1946. Our zealous Jock was on his own and started well, whereas on the second day Leon criticised his workmanship; there were no serious problems but a few areas where improvements could be made.

'Don't be afraid to use de sandpaper, mate, and votch dose runs!' Leon implored him. He seemed a bit crestfallen and we left him to it, but the next day he had vanished: his tools, kitbag, everything had gone. Leon was apoplectic. He smashed his fist down on the paste table and kicked an empty paint can across the room.

'Vere de hell he's fuckin' gone? Bugger'd back to Glasgow, if I'm not mistaken,' he raged.

This caused some disarray and I had to pitch in to finish the job before our customer returned from holiday. These setbacks, although not catastrophic, were frustrating and tempers could rise at 102. On more than one occasion, the surveyors on the first floor knocked on our door and asked us to keep the noise down. Experience taught us, early in the course of the enterprise, never to discuss business when we were hungry as that fuelled our irritability, and we tried to hold to that principle. Anyway, pangs of hunger and rumbling tummies provided a good excuse to leave the office and decamp to the Danube where a plate of frankfurters and mash and a Pils soon sorted us out.

One day in April we reviewed our position again. We felt that we were making progress, but the figures were not adding up. Although Leon and I had the minimum of personal expenses, three men could not support four, in addition to the overheads that we had taken on. To be viable, we really needed at least four men working for us, ideally six, then Leon could continue as a sort of floating foreman and I would continue with my tasks. The unresolved question remained. How was this to be achieved? That evening, I popped in to the King Charles Hotel to catch up with the gossip and found that Christopher was desperate for a new assistant manager because my replacement had not worked out. He virtually begged me to return, at least for the summer. This gave me an idea which I was anxious to discuss with Leon. Late the next afternoon, I drove over to St John's Wood where Leon was working at the home of Russell Page, the internationally renowned garden designer.

Frank and Sid were packing up for the night and stopped for a ciggie and a chat. Just at that moment a smart car drew up in the drive next door. An attractive woman wearing a mini skirt stepped out.

'Fuck me!' said Frank, turning aside.

'See 'er?' I nodded. 'I know 'er, she's an arkitec'.

'OK,' I said.

He leaned towards me and lowered his voice. 'She shagged every roofer on site where I was working last summer!!'

Shocked, I told him that I didn't believe it.

'Gospel,' he said 'Likes it rough, that one—a right little screwball!'

At that moment, Leon turned up and the others went on their way. I told him about the architect.

'I could do vith a bit of dat,' he spluttered.

He and I dropped into the Warwick Castle in Little Venice, a pleasant pub that backed on to one of the few nursery gardens (Clifton Nurseries) in central London; a forerunner in an industry that would grow like Topsy, over the ensuing decades.

We ordered two pints of Guinness and I told Leon what I had gleaned at the King Charles.

'What if I went back for a few months?' I suggested. 'You could carry on with Peacock, and I could continue with the marketing in my free time. It would save me drawing money from the business and we would buy time to build our customer base and workforce.' I continued, 'They need me down there so badly that I am sure that I can negotiate extra time off in the afternoons.'

Leon thought this was a brilliant turn of events and in no time at all I was back in my little room, the lorries rumbling by at night, as before. In fact, everything was much as it had been when I left eight months previously. The occupant of Room 18 was as energetic as ever and regular customers greeted me like a long-lost friend. The gang of trainees from Martin's Bank, who lived there semi-permanently, had even forgiven me for falling asleep in the television lounge, during the 1966 final of the World Cup, the previous year. It was pleasant in London that early summer; Scott McKenzie exhorted those going to San Francisco to wear flowers in their hair; I could afford to buy purple shirts and salmon-coloured trousers at Harrods' newly opened boutique, Way In; and a brief romance blossomed with Carol, the girl from Baltimore in Room 38.

As the months passed, Leon, Frank and Sid worked well together and I got bolder. I started looking for a better quality of work altogether and realised that an appropriate source might be the interior decorators in

Knightsbridge and Chelsea. These designers were nothing without a reliable team to execute their work.

I called on David Mlinaric, Dudley Poplak, Jon Bannenberg and John Siddeley, all doyens of their craft, who received me graciously and although they could offer nothing immediately, each agreed to retain our card. One afternoon, I dropped by the showroom of a firm called Plus Two in Walton Street and was greeted by a very attractive young lady—'well stacked', as they say in the building trade—whose name was Patsy. Again, there was no immediate work available, however she was to play a significant part in the Peacock story some years later.

Nosing around Knightsbridge, I left some leaflets in Thurlow Square. This proved to be fortunate as Kathleen Tynan, the new wife of the controversial critic and playwright, Kenneth, who had uttered the 'F' word for the first time on television in 1965, and was to give us the erotic review *Oh! Calcutta!* (1969), called our office to request some estimates. As night follows day, this led to a stream of work at number 20 that continued for several years. The Tynans gave numerous lunch and dinner parties in their crimson dining room and Lord Snowdon, Peter Hall, Roman Polanski and other important theatrical people were always popping in and out. Leon and the team enjoyed working there and on the occasion of their daughter Roxana's birth everyone was thrilled and took the opportunity to toast her future. Returning to Kingston one evening, we bumped into a writer friend who was sharing our digs. He asked us how things were going.

'Ve're vorking for Kenneth Tynan,' said Leon.

'Don't mention my name to him,' retorted our chum. 'I once knocked him out in a brawl at an Oxford party!'

We'd love to have known what was behind that but he was somewhat evasive.

Peacock Decorators' reputation spread around the square and we were soon working for other residents as well. One eccentric lady proved to be breeding mink and her basement was crawling with the little creatures, which was quite a shock, but the mirrors on the Tynans' bedroom ceiling that could be adjusted to virtually any angle won the trophy for surprises.

> 'Writing about "the subject" makes me reflect again how infinitely more varied in its excitement is sado-mas than straight sex ... Really, there is no sport to touch it: it is

not just a nocturnal relaxation, it is a way of life' (*Kenneth Tynan's Diary:* 1973).

As the wallpaper dried and gloss paint glistened it was difficult to detach from images akin to Dante's inferno. Becoming increasingly aware of Leon's hunger for sexual adventure, I sometimes wondered if he returned in the evenings for a bit of fun. Maybe he did. I must ask him.

Another afternoon's wanderings, this time in Victoria, were to prove very rewarding. I spotted a brass sign on some railings that read 'Problem Ltd' and curiosity led me down an iron staircase to the basement where I rang the doorbell. Once inside, I met a gregarious Canadian by the name of Garran Patterson and his partner, Robina Lund. They ran a club that aimed to solve any problem; the epitome of the can-do culture. Members of Problem were assured that if their dog devoured the turkey on Christmas Day an immediate replacement would be found, unobtainable theatre tickets would be obtained, locks whose keys were lost would be opened at two in the morning, champagne—or anything else, for that matter—could be delivered anywhere at any time to anyone.

I introduced myself and Garran told me that his members were always asking for reliable decorators. If I could supply a couple of references and was prepared to pay commission he would be happy to recommend us.

Bingo! Very soon, this entirely new source of business started to provide customers, many of whom were to prove to be what are now called high-profile. Certainly the directors of Problem were well connected and I believe that Robina had previously worked for Paul Getty. As important, was our growing confidence that by the beginning of 1968, when I planned to leave the King Charles Hotel permanently, we would be able to run a team of at least five professional decorators and that our 'leapfrog', or what my friend, Tahir Shah calls 'zigzagging', strategy and persistency had paid off—not without a good dollop of luck.

In the meantime, our 'enterprise' took a completely different turn.

I once had a stockbroker friend named John Drage who enjoyed doing a little trading on the Portobello Road—'keeping my hand in', as he called it. He would start at the top of the hill on a Saturday morning with fifty pounds in his pocket and expect to have doubled his money by the time he reached the costermongers' barrows at the bottom. I never adopted such a robust attitude and certainly did not possess his skill, but had dabbled a little myself. One crisp autumn morning, when it was cold enough to see your breath and the market was in full, vibrant swing, I spotted a man in a pure white reverse-sheepskin jacket. I really liked the look of it and asked him where he had bought it. 'Istanbul, the covered market,' he told me.

My burgeoning entrepreneurial brain went into fifth gear. Was this an opportunity to make a killing? Coats like that, I thought to myself, would sell well in London during the winter. The King Charles owed me ten days' holiday and Leon had plenty of work to keep the team going so, before you could say 'Topkapi', I had bought a forty-pound return ticket to Istanbul.

The Tauern Express left Victoria for Turkey late one afternoon. We crossed the Channel from Dover, arriving at Ostend in darkness then, having passed through the Low Countries while I slept tucked up in my couchette, reached Germany early the next morning and Munich at noon. A scheduled break of several hours in the Bavarian capital gave me time to take a leisurely walk through the clean streets and into the pretty park bordered by the River Isar. I got back to the station in time for a hot chocolate, consumed as demure German ladies with large bottoms and huge hats sat gossiping while they dug into sizable cream cakes at the next table. Then, boarding a new train, we set off through the night, halting at Salzburg and Ljubljana before arriving at Belgrade the following morning. As we approached the capital a pretty young English girl, who was preparing to disembark, pointed out President Tito's palace. She told me that she was madly in love with a Yugoslav and they were to be married. In the troubles that followed in that war-torn country, I have wondered what became of her.

For the rest of that day, the train passed through spectacular country. Wide valleys with sparkling rivers and a shoreline of white boulders, thatched cottages and smallholdings where peasants in colourful costumes paused to watch the train go by. White rocky precipices that soared above us, all merged into a seemingly endless panorama. Much of the line was single-track, and it was fun sitting on the steps of the carriage with the door open and my legs dangling a few feet from the ground which sped along below me. There were not many passengers to talk to and the only Englishman that I met was from Bognor Regis. We struck up a conversation and I enquired what he did for a living.

'I am a commercial traveller. I travel in rubber goods,' he replied.

Keeping a wary eye on my companion at the other end of the compartment, I was glad that I had picked up a book at Victoria Station, which helped to while away the evenings. It was *Secret Societies* by Arkon Daraul, and I was surprised to find a chapter called 'The Order of the Peacock Angel Cult' which described a quasi-religious/mystical movement that I had never heard of whose members held meetings in Putney. They claimed links with the Yezidis of Iraq. There were also several sections relating to the Knights Templar, whom I had come across in Wiltshire. The remains of one of their medieval estates lay near Marlborough.

By way of Sofia we reached the Turkish border on the third morning and, a few hours later, the Sea of Marmara came into view as we chugged through Istanbul's ancient city walls and ramparts. My first task was to find accommodation as I was expecting to stay three nights. The district of Sirkeci, where the station was located, was pretty rough with shady-looking characters lurking in the side streets, but I soon found a cheap hotel. There were three or four iron beds, customary in what was effectively a dormitory, and I dreaded whom my companions might be. As it happened, I was fortunate enough to be left alone.

Eager to find the covered market (*Kapaliçarşi*), I left the hotel and wound my way up Ankara Caddesi towards the Sultan Ahmet Mosque and Santa Sofia. Tempted as I was to do a bit of sightseeing, those glorious buildings would have to wait; there was business to be done.

Entering the *Kapaliçarşi* for the first time was truly breath taking. In every direction, stone arches that supported soaring roofs and a hundred small domes melted into a kaleidoscopic jungle of shimmering lights. The even-handed Turks had a history of welcoming all races and creeds, especially when it came to business. A sprinkling of Coptic Christians, Jews, even Greek and Armenian hawkers, graced stalls packed with gold, silver, jewellery, trinkets, antiques, curios, and as one penetrated further, surely every conceivable form of merchandise that anyone could desire. It took a while to find my sheepskin coats, but they were there all right; hundreds of them. By this time, it was getting late and the market was about to close so, after a cursory look around, which proved difficult because I was immediately spotted as a punter, I resolved to return in the morning.

I wandered back down the hill and as the sun set over the minarets behind me the haunting call of the *muezzin* caught my attention for the very first time. I found it strangely beautiful. Pressing on, an appetising redolence lured me to the side of the Golden Horn where I was heartened to find fresh fish being grilled by fishermen who had set up their glowing braziers on the quay or even on the decks of their boats. After parting with a few dinars, I munched on mackerel, wedged with a slice of lemon between layers of naan, as I returned to my squalid quarters.

At each street corner, voices rang out from the depths of the shadows.

'Sir, sir, you like girl … boy … womans?'

'Sir … Sir, best hashish, good price.'

I do not quite know what I was expecting when I returned to the coat stalls the next day. At the back of my mind I had planned to purchase half a dozen sample coats and establish a rapport with one of the traders so that we could subsequently order from London. Unfortunately the Turks did not see things like that.

I was a punter with pounds or dollars in my wallet; how many coats did I want, and what 'best price' was I prepared to pay? That was all there was to it. They were not the slightest bit interested in my long-term plans. They wanted cash, then and there.

Eventually, after dodging from stall to stall and examining several dozen coats, I seemed to have made a friend of a young stall-holder named Ayhan. His products were of good quality, the white skins unblemished and the wool thick and curly, so after several cups of apple *çay* (tea) and the inevitable haggling we settled on a price. He promised to parcel up six coats and I would collect them in two days' time.

Well satisfied with my endeavours, I had forty-eight hours to explore the city before my train left for London. Tourism had not reached Istanbul in 1967. The few travellers that existed were hippies en route for Afghanistan, who sold their blood to hospitals as a means of providing an income, adventurers driving Mercedes Benz or Land Rovers to be offloaded profitably in the Middle East, or tough nuts driving ex-army trucks and attempting the land route from London to Singapore and thence to Sydney.

An exciting revelation and my first contact with Islam was visiting the Sultan Ahmet Mosque, which was built in 1609–1616 by the sultan's chief architect, Mohammed Aga, and known as the Blue Mosque. It looked like a space ship. I peered through the portico of the Palace of Topkapi, ogled the mosaics of Haghia Sophia and then took a stroll over the two-tiered Galata Bridge that was constructed on pontoons and spanned the Golden Horn. The top level carried the road and pedestrian walkway while a lower level housed shops and restaurants. It would be years before the great suspension bridges were thrown across the Bosphorus, and the romantic in me could not resist a boat trip to Asia Minor. The ferries, together with dozens of smaller vessels and huge ships bound for the Black Sea or Mediterranean, packed what was one of the busiest seaways on earth. The return crossing was frenetic, noisy, thrilling and sadly unrepeatable, as most of the traffic now goes by road and the Bosphorus is a much calmer place. Once at Usküdar, I made for *Haydarpaşa* railway station where lunch consisted of tender lamb kebabs and *patlican* as I eyed the trains bound for Baghdad, Damascus and Erzerum. I was itching to jump on board. After I had eaten, this urge became almost irresistible as I peered through compartment windows where plush, richly embroidered seating caught my eye and I imagined myself travelling in style to far and distant lands. Sadly, time passed all too quickly, but I knew that I had not come for sightseeing. It was to be twenty-five years before the opportunity arose to really acquaint myself with Constantine's great city (Konstantinyye), and that would be under circumstances that could not possibly have been foreseen; circumstances that pose a question. How did it come to pass that my huge, ginger English cat found his last resting place in Galata, at the centre of the city?

Read on, dear reader, read on!

On my last night, I sauntered up Istiklal Caddesi towards Taksim, where the big international hotels were located. Flashing lights outside a small side-street bar attracted my attention and beneath the glittering neon strips a few steps led to a softly-lit basement lounge. Soft music played as I sat down at a table, discreetly positioned behind some stunted palm trees, and ordered a beer. Almost immediately a stunningly beautiful Turkish girl with long black hair and piercing eyes came and sat on the bench beside me. She ordered an orange juice which I paid for and we started chatting in broken English. Eva, for that was her name, seemed pleasant enough and showed interest in what I was doing in the city, but gradually I realised that she was getting closer. She began to gently stroke my thigh. I was not particularly averse to this familiarity; in fact, it quickly dawned on me that I might be in for a bit of naughty fun, so I made no effort to resist her advances. The stroking intensified.

It was not long before she was snuggling up against me, and taking my hand, she gently inserted her index finger within my loosely curled fist. Moving it rhythmically in and out, she whispered, 'you like fucky fucky?'

It was at that precise moment I realised two very large Turks were standing by the palm trees, behind me.

'Lady only drink champagne,' one of the men informed me abruptly. 'I bring two bottles. First you pay one hundred dollars.'

Glimpsing the staircase; I bolted, and hardly pausing to draw breath tore down Istiklal Caddesi, scrambled down the long flight of steps below the Galata Tower that I had so laboriously climbed only an hour before, and kept going until I was halfway across the pontoon bridge. Only then, breathless as I was, did I turn to see if I had been followed but, of course, the coast was clear; no one was going to bother to trail a silly twenty-year-old tourist who had nearly fallen into a honey trap.

The next day I went back to the market and collected my parcel from Ayhan. I noted all his business details and assured him that orders would soon be flowing from London.

'Inshallah,' he said, smiling, as he warmly shook my hand.

The return journey was uneventful and I took the opportunity to read Isaac Asimov's *Foundation*. As we approached Ostend, I began to wonder how to get my coats through customs without incurring tax. It occurred to me that if one was wearing a sheepskin coat and it was clearly one's own property no charge would arise. Fortunately, on the train, I had been chatting to a group of delightful American girls and when I explained my predicament they were only too eager to assist!

Before very long six pretty girls, each adorned in a spotless white coat, were tripping through the customs hall.

At the earliest opportunity, Leon and I started to hawk our coats around the boutiques in Carnaby Street, Chelsea, Kensington and Hampstead. Almost immediately, on another cold Saturday morning, we attracted some interest in the King's Road at Mates, one of a chain of trendy clothes shops which throbbed with loud music and eager punters. Leon and I pushed through the mêlée and approached a young man wearing jeans and a leather jacket half off his shoulders. With his tousled hair and chunks of gold flashing on his fingers, he was clearly in charge. He stood out from the crowd and was energetically hustling for sales, so we approached him with our samples. He took a good look at the coats, gave us a once-over and pressing a business card into my hand said, 'Be at my office at five o'clock on Monday,' and continued with his sales pitch. Leon and I retreated. The name on the card read IRVINE SELLAR.

Monday afternoon came and we found ourselves in Mr Irvine Sellar's plush offices in Kilburn. Now, his shoes shining, wearing a finely tailored suit and his hair smoothed down with a fashionable preparation, he welcomed us. We could hardly believe that it was the same man whom we had seen only a few days before, cleverly working the crowd, like Del Boy in the BBC comedy series *Only Fools and Horses*. He ran his hand over our coats, fluffed up the woolly fleece and asked a few questions about their origin. After some tough bargaining, we agreed a price and he ordered fifty coats, assuring us that there would be more deals if they sold quickly. We wanted to fulfil this order as soon as possible so, sensing that we were onto a good thing, Leon agreed to fly to Turkey and bring a hundred coats back with him. This should convince Ayhan that we were serious businesspeople. However, our perennial problem emerged. How were we going to finance all this with Peacock Decorators still in embryo?

I racked my brains and finally approached Gawky to lend me a hundred pounds. This she readily agreed to do, but it made my parents nervous. They did not understand my interest in business and felt that borrowing was somehow getting something for nothing, despite my mother's enthusiasm for the 'never-never'! Their attitude was irritating, but understandable, as no one in the family had been involved in money-making activities for several generations. Anyway, the plan worked; Leon was soon back from Istanbul, and we got down to fulfilling Irvine Sellar's order and flogging the rest of the coats.

However, on 19th November, the very day that Leon had landed in Turkey, the Prime Minister Harold Wilson did something that caused us problems; he devalued the pound by 14%. I am not sure that anyone was convinced when Wilson went on television, saying, 'It does not mean that the pound here in Britain, in your pocket or purse or in your bank, has been devalued.'

This severely cut our margins, and although we appeared to have diversified into a new business, would it be profitable? Were we really in a position to sustain this enterprise, fun though it may have been?

As soon as we were paid by Mates, I had to repay Gawky's loan, which left us short of capital again. However, our bank, the old Westminster, came to our rescue when we convinced ourselves that ordering another hundred coats, by letter of credit, would work. We awaited the next delivery eagerly, dashing to the airport when it arrived. You can imagine our huge disappointment when we opened the sizable cardboard boxes and found every single coat in shreds, riddled with revolting, wriggling maggots. The whole consignment had to be dumped.

We had now run out of time and money. But for years to come, wherever I went, men and women, boys and girls, were wearing 'must have' white reversible sheepskin coats and jackets. No doubt, with his considerable nose for business, Irvine Sellar and other entrepreneurs had stepped in and cornered the market. Could you blame them?

Sellar was a clever cookie, clearly destined for a great business future, although I was staggered to read that, having sold Mates (which had ninety stores in 1981) and, developed a property empire, he—the very same Irvine Sellar, now in his late sixties—was the brain and the money behind the Shard—Europe's tallest and most exciting new building—which opened in 2013.

He was one of the new breed of hardworking English entrepreneurs, during an exciting period of revived UK enterprise, whom I was fortunate enough to bump into and who provided me with salutary lessons from time to time. We put elements of this particular episode to good use some years later when Leon and I imported Bedouin dresses from Jerusalem in a small and profitable operation.

In January 1968, we were now ready to take the business further. Besides the Cockneys, Frank and Sid, we had three more painters and decorators working for us; two Irishmen who lived in the scruffy streets off Ladbroke Grove and a Geordie who crashed out in a bedsit in Finsbury Park during the week and returned to his family in Newcastle on Friday nights. We had also built up good relations with other tradesmen whom we could call on when necessary, and I was glad of my experience at Luff's Landscapes which held me in good stead in the situation that I now found myself.

We had established lines of credit with suppliers and were at ease with our banking arrangements. Leon left Kingston and I left the King Charles, for the last time. We found a flat to share in Victoria, for ten pounds a week. It was at the Dolphin Square end of St George's Drive and very grubby. Soot deposits rained down on us from Battersea power station, driven by the prevailing wind that howled through the vent in the tiny bathroom and blew out the pilot light in the water heater. This resulted in a pervasive smell of gas that seeped throughout our dingy apartment.

Our various sources of work were also developing nicely and the first job we did that year was for the Bs, a wealthy family based in Harley Street. The main source of income appeared to be generated from fees earned by Dr B, who spent a great deal of time on film sets—James Bond locations in particular—in foreign parts where he was contracted to attend the stars. At the time of which I write, when the British film industry was booming, he had just returned from an exotic shoot in Zanzibar.

The doctor's wife, the daughter of a lord and a woman who knew her own mind, was employing us to renovate a penthouse, for her daughter, in Swan Court, Chelsea. She also demanded the highest of standards.

'I hope you're up to scratch,' she said when she first met Leon and me. 'We usually use Colefax, but Problem recommended you very highly.'

Who the hell was Colefax?

Leon and I were learning fast.

When we came to be paid, our client opened a large, alligator bag which she invariably carried with her. It was stuffed with receipts and documents, a sort of mobile office, and from its depths she produced a crinkly roll of pristine banknotes.

Leon's jaw dropped as he took the notes, which had acquired an exotic aroma while nestling among silken folds within the bag. The Bs would remain customers for years to come. As we left Swan Court, two men from Harrods were delivering a colour television. This was the first time that we had seen one in a domestic environment and we were mightily impressed. The cost of a small colour television in 1968 was approximately £250—a hefty sum today. That kind of technology has become much cheaper in the intervening years.

As our confidence grew we started to attract bigger jobs and in the early spring of 1968, undertook external repainting of a huge house in the Boltons. This made me realise that many leases on the estates that were still owned by private families, such as the Grosvenors, Cadogans and de Waldens, stipulated a regular outside repaint and when we saw other contractors working on what must literally have been acres of vertical high-gloss paint work in Belgravia and elsewhere we devised mailshots to secure some of those contracts. It was an ambition of mine to paint the exterior of the Afghan Embassy at the top of Exhibition Road, and although we provided an estimate—it certainly needed painting at the time—we were unlucky. It would be some years, in totally different circumstances, before I would enter those premises again.

It was not long before we were working in Eaton Place and Chester Square. We also started to get enquiries from some of the interior decorators I had contacted the previous summer which raised our horizons dramatically. Our little business was not only paying the bills but our upward mobility was providing a fascinating insight into other worlds. One day I was asked to provide an estimate in Eaton Place, for a gentleman who rejoiced in the splendid name of Magnifico. At the appointed time a smart car with diplomatic plates drew up and a man got out. I approached, extending my hand. 'Signor Magnifico?'

'No,' came the reply, 'I am 'is right 'and man.'

He led me into the house and in due course the Italian embassy accepted our estimate and we executed a great deal of work on their behalf. However, when we came to be paid, Signor Magnifico, whom I had got to know, together with his delightful wife and children, said, 'I prefer to pay in whisky. At embassy we have access to excellente Scotch and that is good currency.'

Taken aback, I remonstrated by saying that this was a lovely idea and a couple of bottles of the hard stuff wouldn't go amiss but I could not pay my men in Scotch or balance my books. Fortunately, he did not pursue the matter further and a cheque was soon produced.

In March, my father lent me the Great Hall in Sussex House for a party to celebrate my twenty-first birthday. Mai Watts, an artistic American friend, decked it out with netting, huge silver fish and painted crustacean to capture a Piscean theme and I invited a wide range of friends and relations. It was all good fun and we danced the night away, although a gift, from Leon, of goldfish in a bowl did not fare too well after being left on the ledge above an exceptionally hot radiator. By 2am the water was approaching boiling point.

I spent much of the evening with DT, a beautiful South American lady, who was one of my customers. She was divorcing her husband at the time and she and I had built up what I thought was a close relationship. A few days later, Leon and I were discussing the party and business matters. Not surprisingly, her name came up.

'She has a lovely flat,' he said.

'How do you know? I didn't know you had been there. That's one of my jobs,' I replied, giving him a quizzical look.

He reddened, and shrugged his shoulders. I stared hard at Leon. The penny dropped. He turned away.

'Christ! Christ Almighty!!' I exploded. 'You've been bloody screwing her, haven't you?'

He smiled sheepishly and shrugged again.

'You bastard! You little shit! You c***!'

'Ven … you've finished!' Leon began to raise his voice. 'Screwing her? The vay that little minx moves it was more like her screwing me. But den, you'd know all about dat,' he concluded sarcastically.

'The fucking little whore! The fucking whoring bitch! Who'd have thought it?'

I stormed out of the office and headed for the park to cool down.

Work, meals, the flat and other interests I was prepared to share, but not DT. It hurt, and that was the end of her, as far as I was concerned.

My parents gave me a Praktica 35mm single lens reflex camera for my birthday, so if I had any hankering to emulate David Hemmings, who was attracting huge cinema audiences in the semi-erotic mystery drama *Blow Up* (1966), directed by Michelangelo Antonioni, I was at least partly equipped to do so. Hemmings played the role of a trendy photographer with long hair and tight white jeans, who spent his days wandering between East End doss-houses and his studio before parking his white Rolls Royce outside Chez Nicole, a prim little restaurant that I knew, in Chelsea. The film, among other things, captured the 'anything is possible' attitude to business that was spreading like wildfire at the time. We were learning that you did not have to be an old fart to become rich!

'You really are becoming a dirty capitalist!' joked my friend, Bill Rhoads, one weekend. Was I? Perhaps so.

My Praktica was the same camera that was brutally torn off my neck by a London policeman later that year when I was in Grosvenor Square taking snaps of a Vietnam War demonstration. It disappeared under ten thousand feet but fortunately I just managed to scoop it up, dented but otherwise un-scathed, before it was lost forever.

In England, we lived with constant reminders of the Vietnam War from 1955 until 1975 because brutal, live, bloody battle-scenes were frequently shown on our television screens, which is something that had never happened before. But it was not our war, and with the demise of conscription it was never likely to be. Leon and I had other battles to fight and, if the truth be known, most of the population of the UK knew little and cared less about the reasons for, and conduct of, the conflict. However, as the bombing increased in parallel with heavier casualties, protests escalated during the '60s and '70s. The voice of the Peace Movement refused to be silenced and crowds taunted American President Lyndon Johnson, who had succeeded Kennedy.

'LBJ! LBJ! How many kids have you killed today?'

Various singers, notably Joan Baez and Bob Dylan, wrote bitter lyrics condemning the war however these are the words of a popular song at the time by Country Joe McDonald:

> Come on mothers throughout the land,
> Pack your boys off to Vietnam.
> Come on fathers, don't hesitate
> Send your sons off before it's too late.
> You can be the first one on your block
> To have your boy come home in a box.

Meanwhile, Leon and I were enjoying ourselves in spite of the fact that, working and living together, we could get on each other's nerves, and despite the interlude concerning DT. We were learning a great deal and meeting lots of different people. One day, when we met for dinner Leon had come straight from Sir Michael Redgrave's flat in Knightsbridge.

'I have just met another famous Englishman—a Shakespearean actor!' he informed me. Leon's command of the language was improving.

I had been with a Greek shipping millionaire in Mount Street, and on the previous day, not wishing to let Problem down, had taken on a small job myself, painting the central spiral staircase for Stirling Moss in his funny little modern house in Shepherd Street, Mayfair.

As single guys we habitually ate out in the evenings, which we could now afford to do. Cruising the streets of London in Leon's Volvo, we felt ourselves to be what a later generation might call 'cool dudes' and we accumulated an array of favourite restaurants. Our choice of venue tended to be dictated by choice of menu. If we were in the mood for boeuf stroganoff or spaghetti bolognaise, together with a carafe of the house red, we settled on the Chelsea Kitchen in King's Road which teemed with mini-skirted 'dolly birds' and other devotees of swinging London. At one time, half the young bucks in the capital seemed to be dressed up as Lord Kitchener, aping a trendy new boutique named I was Lord Kitchener's Valet. In a satirical age, the shop mocked the Field Marshall, whose face was familiar on account of the famous recruiting poster, 'Your country needs YOU', that had appeared during the Great War. Now, it was reproduced *ad nauseam* with little sensitivity to the circumstances in which it was originally published. In the last forty years, a new awareness has developed in respect of those who fought and died in that war and indeed all subsequent wars. It is, perhaps ironic that while we now live in remarkably liberal times, louche '60s behaviour would be unacceptable today. As Gurdjieff maintained: 'Everything becomes its opposite'—known in his system as the Law of Seven or Heptaparaparshinokh.

Lord Horatio Kitchener was drowned in 1916 while on a secret mission for the British government, when *HMS Hampshire* went down with all hands on its way to Russia. But no one cared a toss about that: the '60s slogan was 'make love, not war', and there were plenty of opportunities to do so. Young men no longer sidled, furtively, into barbers' premises and shops advertising 'rubber goods' in Praed Street, the Commercial Road, and anonymous suburbs where they were unlikely to be recognised, to obtain a packet of 'johnnies' passed over the counter in a plain brown paper bag. There was no need. These aids to free love, rebranded as condoms, became available for half-a-crown per pack at the point of sale in every high street chemist. But crucially, women could now take charge of contraception by taking the readily available contraceptive pill.

As the title to the 1973 rock 'n' roll revival film, featuring Chuck Berry, Fats Domino, Bill Haley and a plethora of ageing rockers declared: 'Let the Good Times Roll'!

A craving for modish attire also stemmed from David Lean's Oscar-winning film, *Doctor Zhivago*. Inspired by images of the bloody Russian Revolution of 1917, elegantly dressed folk in black capes, matching boots and red, Lenin-style, corduroy caps flitted through the streets of SW3.

Red corduroy caps?

Oh yes—I had one of those.

If the idea of a prawn cocktail followed by coq au vin appealed, we strolled around the corner to Grumbles, a splendid bistro in Pimlico, where Wilfred Bramble, who co-starred with Harry H. Corbett in the BBC's black comedy *Steptoe and Son* and appeared as Paul McCartney's mischievous uncle in the Beatles film *A Hard Day's Night* (1964), was often seen dining alone. Despite being a comedy actor, we got the impression that he led a sad and lonely existence.

Leon and I adored Luba's Bistro, one of the very first restaurants of its kind to open in London. Situated in a converted garage in Yeoman's Row, the tables sported chequered red plastic covers and curtains were in matching gingham. Oil and pastel portraits of the indomitable Luba, a large cheery Georgian lady and Gurdjieff's niece, hung above the diners. Strings of onions, garlic and bunches of dried flowers and herbs festooned every vacant wall space. Candles guttered in old wine bottles, invariably of the squat variety shaped like a mandolin that had contained the fashionable Portuguese Mateus Rosé. If you wanted wine you brought your own. My favourite dishes were *piroshki* (finely ground mince in a rolled pancake) with salad, and *crèpe à la reine*, a delicious chicken concoction in a lemon pancake with rice.

For an entirely different atmosphere, when we were in the mood for wiener schnitzel, sauerkraut and pommes frites followed by apfelstrudel, we drove to Swiss Cottage and ate at the Cosmo. This Viennese style establishment on the Finchley Road boasted a 'posh' restaurant with uniformed waiters and starched white linen tablecloths, but beyond a curtained archway there was a café which also had an entrance to the street. We usually patronised the latter, whose regular clientele was largely composed of intellectuals from nearby Hampstead, or Jewish immigrants who had arrived in north London before the war and now owned a string of rundown tenements from which they derived a meagre income. The latter were mostly Germans and Austrians and resembled elderly men, in their characteristic homburgs, and ladies in large hats, that I had seen in Munich. They lingered for hours over coffee and cream cakes, breaking off to gossip and catch up with the *Ham and High* or *Jewish Chronicle*, popular local newspapers.

One evening, Leon and I were tucking into a sumptuous plate of summer strawberries, topped with a dash of sugar and lashings of thick whipped cream. Our neighbour at the next table, who closely resembled the Latin American Marxist, Che Guevera, suddenly set aside his copy of the *Socialist Worker* which had held his attention for the last thirty minutes. Freezing us with a glacial stare, he addressed us:

'Dig in, comrades. Stuff yourselves like the pigs that you are. Time is running out. Long live reparation! Long live the revolution!'

At which point, he rose, scattered a few coins on the table and disappeared on to the Finchley Road.

From time to time we visited Au Troubadour, a bohemian café in the Brompton Road. It was there that we met Matt the glazier. Matt was a charming cockney, with a real twinkle in his eye, but one of the ugliest men I have ever met.

He had a hobby at which he excelled. Every night, after working all day in a glass works in Shepherd's Bush, he would set himself up at a table in the café with a mug of strong coffee and wait for an opportunity to chat up 'a bird'. Subsequently, if 'a bird' was not in his bed by midnight he felt his evening had been wasted. He lived a few doors away and boasted an awesome score of conquests.

'Once I ge' a bird back a' my place,' he confessed, 'I ge' 'er on the bed, put me tongue down 'er throat and massage 'er titties. Then, I 'ave a good sniff-about—like, —ge' me inquis'tive little fingers in 'er draw'rs—know wot I mean? If I like wot I smell—I'm down on 'er—ther's no stopping me! Mind you,' he leered, 'some o' these birds go wild when my thick, throbbing rod, gets going, but major'ty are pretty damn useless. They lie there like cod fish, while I 'ave me wicked way!'

Leon and I sat with our mouths open. Matt was unbelievable. When we first met him, his tally was running at something like a hundred women in the previous six months and still counting. In fact, his reputation was such, and I bear witness to this, that young girls, mostly Scandinavian au pairs who worked in Kensington and Chelsea, or tourists who had landed up in the Earls Court area—approached and begged for his services. I am sure that any red-blooded young male would have been tantalised by his escapades and I was certainly gobsmacked. However, although my visits to Au Troubadour and elsewhere were not lacking in opportunities to exercise youthful lust—temptations for a virginal public schoolboy were never far away—I did not develop an overwhelming urge to become a '60s Casanova. The same could not be said about Leon. Matt's ability fascinated him.

'If Matt can shag all those women, why can't I?' he moaned.

'Why not go down to the Swedish church after the evening service', someone advised. 'You'll find plenty of young girls—mostly au pairs—who are emotionally aroused and in a suggestible state of mind—it's a good moment to pounce!'

On one occasion we did pick up a couple of Swedish girls. They didn't know that Leon spoke their language so we were able to monitor their intentions, which were wicked enough. In respect of our business, carnal ambition increasingly distracted Leon during the ensuing months and, in hindsight, I would come to realise that the first drum roll that ushered the break-up of our partnership had been sounded.

One morning, he staggered into the office at noon. With great shadows under his eyes, he was looking pretty shattered. I looked at him with a question written all over my face.

'That was unbelievable!' he managed to enunciate. 'Two birds—two gorgeous, lovely birds—one black and one white—in bed at the same time! Wow! Look out Matt! I'm after you!'

I gaped at him. My Anglican conditioning was being eroded slowly, day by day. As if that wasn't enough, a few days later, Leon opened a small package in the office.

'What's that?' I said, spotting the word 'MAGNAPHAL' printed on the label.

'Er … it's a treatment to enlarge my prick,' he replied, deadpan.

'Is that a problem?'

'Not really, but I'd like to have a bigger organ—much bigger. More fun, eh!' he grinned. 'How about you? Do you want to try it?'

'No thanks!' I replied. 'I'm hung quite well enough … or, at least, no one has complained, to date!'

As I said, and no pun intended, my Anglican conditioning was being eroded inch by inch and my relationship with Leon, this strange foreign fellow, was introducing a symbiosis I would never have dreamed of. Some years later, long after I was married, I ran into Matt who told me what had befallen him. Apparently he had become tired of his addiction to sex, which was beginning to make him ill, so he left London and went down to the south coast for a complete break. When he returned he decided to avoid the Earls Court area and went to Hampstead. Sitting in a café on Haverstock Hill he started—old habits die hard—to talk to a young girl sitting at his table. But this time it was different. For the first time in his life he fell hopelessly in love. One thing led to another, the couple were married and after the wedding his new wife's family solicitor requested that they visit him at his office. There it was explained, and it was news to both of them, that on marriage his wife had inherited substantial wealth that included a fine house in central London. I haven't seen Matt since that day, but I hope that good fortune continues to shine upon him.

At one of our regular reviews, Leon and I agreed that the work Problem was generating for us was very welcome, but we did not want to become too dependent on that source. It was a major consideration that we were obliged to pay commission, thereby cutting profitability or reducing competitiveness. By the summer of 1968 we had six men on the team and we reckoned that keeping two busy with Problem customers was about right. Sometimes, keeping Problem happy could be disruptive. On one occasion we had to pull a man off another job when the playwright, Alan Bennett, wanted someone for a day to help him dissolve layers of distemper that had gunged up the fine lace-like plaster cornice in his new house in Camden Town. I knew exactly where he lived, opposite the homes of Jonathan Miller and George Melly, whom I had met previously.

As we arrived at the open front door, the Yorkshireman called down from his perch on the top of a pair of tall steps where he was pressing the spout of a steaming kettle into the ceiling moulding with one hand and scraping away with the other.

'Kum right in, lads, an' give us un 'and,' he yelled.

It was a scene to relish for years to come, and when *Talking Heads* or one of his plays appeared on television I would be reminded of him, his unique style and exquisite powers of observation. Occasionally he could be seen on his bicycle, pedalling earnestly through north London, a woollen scarf invariably trailing from around his neck.

To maintain turnover, we intensified our mailing campaign and considering the state of our trade, at the time, this was considered innovative. We rather enjoyed composing snappy letters, and as the response from advertising agencies, one of our target markets, was disproportionately high, we must have been doing something right. The advertising industry was booming in the 1960s and was largely populated by ex-public schoolboys, who no longer had an empire to run, and boasted a wealth of pukka contacts with whom they enjoyed long boozy lunches followed by afternoons spent in their studios designing pretty posters and dreaming up pithy slogans. By and large they were a decent, relaxed crowd, and when we were commissioned to paint the entire offices of Geer Dubois in Mayfair, with the silver paint used for

Christmas decorations, it did not seem extraordinary. Even when the paint rubbed off on passing shoulders, elbows and bottoms, no one seemed to care.

During July 1968 we redecorated Rupert Chetwynd's offices, just off Fleet Street. Once again we found the partners particularly nice people to work for. Our instructions came from Rupert's wife, although they were divorcing at the time, and when we had completed painting the hall and three-storey staircase in two coats of a violent crimson gloss and were clearing up, a passing executive whispered in my ear: 'Antonia's revenge!'

One of the agency's clients was Abbey Life, the new insurance company with offices opposite St Paul's, and a director of Chetwynd's suggested that I go and talk to the Abbey people. He was impressed by my 'get up and go' attitude and thought I would make a good salesman. Following his introduction, while slogging up Ludgate Hill and passing under the old railway bridge, I was reminded of a cold winter's day in 1964 when I heard the civil rights activist Martin Luther King preach in the cathedral. He was on his way to Oslo to collect the Nobel Peace Prize.

Finding the offices with no trouble, I went in for an interview but soon decided that it was not the sort of thing that interested me and that a career change was not on the agenda. Perhaps, I should have been born several generations later and then I might have competed as an apprentice to Sir Alan Sugar.

Abbey Life was the brainchild of Mark Weinberg (now Sir Mark) who, together with his friend and colleague, Mike Wilson (now CBE), was to achieve great things in the financial services industry. I sometimes wonder whether I met Mark or Mike on that day in 1968, as they would feature in my life thirty years later.

As the year went on, we seemed to be dashing all over the place. A bit too much dashing resulted, one summer afternoon, with Leon turning over the van in Maida Vale, and like a scene from a Laurel and Hardy movie he emerged, together with one of the painters, covered from head to toe in white emulsion. As we say in England, 'It could have been worse.'

We suffered—as others did—when skills that we had not entirely mastered were called upon. One weekend, we sanded the wooden floors for a dentist's practice in Harley Street but the partners were not overjoyed when they arrived on Monday morning to find every inch of their consulting rooms, including all their delicate equipment, covered in a fine layer of dust. It took two days to clean up.

A few days later, Garran Patterson called me to say that, Mr Harbinson, a customer, had complained about some tiling that one of my men had done in his bathroom. He and I agreed to meet on site week to inspect the work.

A few days later, standing with Garran in the reception area of a smart block of flats in Mayfair I spoke to the porter.

'We arranged to meet Mr Harbinson at ten o'clock, but he doesn't answer his doorbell. Have you seen him?' I enquired.

'Don't 'spect he does, mate,' he replied. 'He died on Friday.'

'Oh, boy! That workmanship must have been bad,' growled Garran as we left the building.

Apart from the odd spot of bother, Problem continued to refer celebrities and we undertook extensive work in Bramham Gardens for Robert Beatty, the Canadian actor who made more than sixty films and numerous television appearances in a career that spanned fifty years. We were in his apartment for about three weeks and it was very odd, as he constantly referred to his wife as 'the princess' but she never made an appearance. I did not discover if she really was a princess and why she remained in her room. Was she an invalid? Perhaps someone knows the answer to a puzzle that has mystified me for more than forty years.

Beatty was pleased with the results of our efforts, but as we were clearing away our last pieces of equipment Alan, one of our best men, drew me aside and whispered almost inaudibly, 'Ere, take a butcher's.' He was pointing at the wallpaper in the hall.

''Ung upside down,' he said.

I took a good look. It was true. Roses were climbing down, rather than up. We slammed the front door behind us and scarpered. Perhaps our gaffe was never noticed as we heard no more about it.

By August, as we approached the end of our second year of trading, our turnover was approaching £2000 a month. After accounting for a wage bill of about £700 plus materials and overheads, Leon and I retained a reasonable profit and we considered that Peacock Decorators was healthy, despite cash-flow limitations that meant we survived on a month-by-month basis. The fact that the business we had created now provided a living for not only ourselves but our workmen and their wives and children too gave some satisfaction. We felt that it was time to take a holiday.

Leon took a short break in Sweden and returned with a new girlfriend in tow. I then decided to go on another European train journey, this time through Paris, Milan, Venice, Belgrade and ending up in Thessaloniki. On the first stage of the trip, I met some jolly girls from Ifield Road in Fulham and we spent forty-eight hours drinking, singing and generally behaving disreputably. When the train divided at Belgrade they encouraged me to accompany them to Corfu, however I declined their invitation; a decision I later regretted as my holiday turned out to be a rather lonely adventure. Considering my somewhat irresponsible attitude towards women—the legacy of an all-male boarding school, I surmise—I wonder how life would have panned out if I had followed those mischievous girls to Corfu.

On my first night in Thessaloniki, I failed to find a hotel—and the reason for that only became clear twenty-four years later (see chapter twelve)—so I stretched out on a stone bench in the station. My days at Coombe Springs, when we were encouraged to make 'conscious efforts', had left their imprint and I regarded this as a 'test' to see if I could force myself to sleep through the night undeterred by discomfort and distractions. I only achieved partial success, but it was an experience I recalled when I found myself in similar circumstances in Karachi more than twenty years later.

Greece was very hot, which was not to my liking, and on the return journey, as we passed through Skopje, the Yugoslav city that had been utterly devastated by an earthquake in 1963, news broke of the Russian invasion of Czechoslovakia. It was 20th August and the Soviets had decided to put an end to Alexander Dubček's liberalisation programme, known as the 'Prague Spring'. The violation of the Czech border and the movement of Warsaw Pact troops, only a few hundred miles to the north, were matters of deep concern and I wondered if destiny would confine me within the train's stuffy compartment while World War III erupted around us. When we arrived in Paris I lingered for a couple of days on the Île de la Cité, where hairy hippies hung out, keeping their transistor radios tuned to hourly bulletins.

Dubcek was initially imprisoned, then released, but was soon forced to resign. In 1970 he was expelled from the Communist Party. The Soviets installed their own 'puppet', Gustav Husak, and a programme of 'normalisation' was initiated. The West turned a blind eye. During the Cold War, we Baby Boomers and others, lived in the constant fear that an over-reaction to any incident, by either side, would lead to mutually assured destruction (MAD), which is not to deny that a cat-and-mouse game was played between the leading protagonists, day and night, for the best part of fifty years—I'm sure that it still continues.

Returning to London and back in the office, I found a message to say that Leon and our gang were working in a large house in Belgravia. It was in Gerald Road where there was a police station, and it is said that the bobbies from that particular constabulary, who made up the choir of St Michael's church in nearby Chester Square, provided the inspiration for *The Pirates of Penzance* when Sir Arthur Sullivan was choirmaster in 1861. Be that as it may, as I approached the property, up the garden path, between tightly packed cotoneasters, I heard, appropriately enough, a woman's powerful voice belting out an aria from *Carmen*. The front door stood wide open and our newly acquired customer, Regina Sartori, was poised on the oak staircase practising her art. She was a splendid American lady, built as a female opera singer should be, and married to a much sought-after international tax lawyer from New York. His spacious office, which we were also to renovate, was in Waterloo Place, where the fine statue of Florence Nightingale could be seen from the windows. On his polished desk there was a small wooden plaque upon which these memorable words were inscribed in gold: 'The first thing we do, let's kill all the lawyers' (Shakespeare, *Henry VI*, Part 2, act 4, scene 2).

As we left Gerald Road at the end of the day, it dawned on me that Peacock Decorators was facing a crisis. Leon was clearly preoccupied with Danielle, his girlfriend, and it was obvious that she wanted to go back to Stockholm and would not go without him. Matters soon came to a head and in September Leon faced a stark choice. It was to be Peacock or Danielle. I had mixed feelings. Leon's love life had begun to take up a lot of his attention and I was getting more and more confident at running the show. On the other hand, he was immensely valuable and we had been through so much together.

In the end Danielle won.

My predominant emotion was disappointment. I was begrumpled but we parted amicably. I gave Leon all the money in the bank, which must have been about £1000, and the business became mine. The dream of opening a restaurant, or even a wine bar, together, was over.

Leon Flamholc went on to develop a career in film and television after attending film school in Stockholm. He had always responded to the allure of adventure and it had been all we could do to dissuade from going to fight for Israel in the Six Day War of June 1967. In the 1980s he visited Russian-occupied Afghanistan and, with immense bravery, made a documentary that was shown all over Europe, with the notable exception of the United Kingdom. (We Brits must never be beastly to the Russians.) It is now available on Facebook.

In 2003, his documentary following Tahir Shah's expedition in search of Paititi, the lost Peruvian city, home to the treasures of the Incan empire, was shown on Channel 5.

Just after the London Tube bombings in July 2005, I read in *The Times* that he and his son David had spent sixteen days in a Pakistani jail. They had been arrested in the North West Frontier Province and falsely accused of links to terrorism while developing another project with Tahir. Fortunately they had friends in high places and were eventually released. The full story is told in Tahir Shah's *'Travels with Myself'* (Mosaique Books 2011).

Chapter 7
The Painter of the World II

Oh, London is a fine town,
A very famous city,
Where all the streets are paved with gold,
And all the maidens pretty.
George Colman (eighteenth century)

I WAS INTRODUCED to Aubrey by a mutual friend, who felt, since I was now on my own, that it would be beneficial to have occasional chats with an experienced businessman.

Aubrey, who was slim and about five foot ten, grey-haired with a trim moustache and wire-framed spectacles, must have been in his mid-sixties at the time of our first meeting and had run his family firm of hop-brokers ever since his elder brothers were killed in the Great War. He was wearing a dark suit, collar and tie and pale green pullover when he welcomed me, with the quiet confidence of a prosperous Quaker, at the door of his spacious house in central London. We proceeded down the hall and into a large, sparsely furnished room, with wooden shutters that took the place of curtains. I started to tell him about Peacock Decorators and as our conversation progressed he seemed very interested in what I said and in my future plans. I remember him making one particular point.

'One of the advantages of having a business that has traded over several centuries, as I do; is that you can look back and see how they handled previous difficulties,' he said.

'It was only the other day that we had a problem and from the records we could see identical circumstances developing in the 1820s. This knowledge helped us to avert a crisis.'

It encouraged me to know that Aubrey could draw on that depth of experience and was there in the background. He encouraged me to call him if I needed any advice and we met many times over the next twenty-four years. I greatly valued those meetings, which were always kept very formal. I would arrive at his house at six in the evening and we would draw up two cane-seated, wooden hoop-backed chairs, facing each other in the centre of the same big room on the ground floor. We would talk about the business for about an hour, raising any issues that came to mind, and then I would leave. We never digressed, although sometimes I wondered if he would offer me a drink or a cup of tea, however that never occurred. It was not Aubrey's way, perhaps in line with his Quaker tradition, and occasionally we remained seated in total silence for what seemed an eternity. Soon after our first encounter he realised that I required working capital, especially since I had given Leon what little we had accumulated, so he offered me a loan of £1000, interest free, to be repaid on demand but not for at least five years.

'You'll have to learn to make a sustained effort,' he said as he handed me a cheque. It was a sting in the tail, although right on cue reminding me of school reports that branded me a 'gadfly'.

The loan was just what I needed to buy a Volkswagen van, one of the new models with sliding side doors, and it was soon sign-written with Peacock Decorators' logo.

One advantage of Leon's departure was that I was now the sole occupant of the pleasant flat in Elgin Avenue to which we had recently moved. However, as I began to adjust to my new circumstances and my business continued to expand, I felt the need to rely on my team more than had been previously necessary. We had hired a smart young man named Dominic O'Halloran, whose brother Julian was making a name for himself at the BBC. Dom, as he came to be called, impressed us enormously by chain-smoking Rothmans King Size while we, like a couple of Bohemians, tended to puff away on smelly Gauloises. Occasionally, when feeling ostentatious I bought a packet of gold-tipped Black Russian Sobranies. His job was to purchase materials, help with deliveries, fetch and carry and execute all the general chores that the business generated. Once Leon had left he became an invaluable pillar of the firm and his Irish charm was much appreciated by customers and workmen alike. It was also clear that the days of my tapping away at an old typewriter were over. I would just not have the time to deal with the estimates, invoices, mailshots and other correspondence. Feeling brave, I decided to hire a secretary and a friend suggested that Jenny might be just the ticket.

I don't know what it was about me and Jenny, but we just did not hit it off, and the relationship only lasted a few days.

'You're bossy and boorish and I hate this beastly little office!' she announced after a week as she picked up her coat and slammed the door behind her. Secretarial work was clearly not her bag. This was confirmed in my mind, a few years later, when I saw her face staring at me from a poster in Waterstones.

They were promoting a new novel by the celebrated author, Jenny Diski.

I decided to muddle through without a full-time secretary for a while but had been doing some writing, recording my European railway journeys, and needed to have it typed professionally. Whenever I did something really interesting or unusual, I experienced an irrepressible urge to write it all down, although it would be a long time before I published anything. On this occasion, my intention was to send an article to Nova, a new '60s-style magazine which had recently featured a naked (wearing fig leaves), picture of Adam and Eve in full Technicolor on the front cover. How tame that sounds in 2013. When my copy fell out of my overnight bag, it had startled and deeply offended the passport inspector on the train as we crossed from Yugoslavia to Greece in the dead of night.

Some friends told me about an American girl called Cindy Briggs who had just arrived from Paris, where she had been living for four years, and was now looking for ways to earn extra money. While waiting for a permit, she was working as an au pair for the film animator Richard Williams (*Christmas Carol* and *Who Framed Roger Rabbit?*) and his wife, in St John's Wood. I went round to see her in Springfield Road and found her engrossed in conversation with Richard's elderly mother, who was showing her some of the exquisite copies of Persian miniatures that she had recently completed. I explained about the typing, which she was happy to do and when I called to collect the manuscript a few days later I suggested dinner. Cindy, or Lucinda, to confirm her baptismal name, seemed a bit surprised to be dated by a man who could do with a haircut and was wearing what she called 'salmon-coloured pants', but accepted gracefully. On our date we dined at Luba's, and she recounted her experiences during the Paris riots which had occurred earlier in the year. She spoke good French and had been living in a mediaeval building in the Rue Chanoinessse, on the *Île de la Cité*.

Danny (Cohn-Bendit) the Red's 22nd March Movement of leftist students and workers, had caused mayhem earlier that summer (1968), and while on the way to the OECD (Organisation for Economic Cooperation and Development), where she worked as a secretary in Dr Alexander King's Department of Education and Science, Cindy, had braved the pitched battles that raged between revolutionaries, the police and the army.

'It was really, really, scary!' she said. 'Chunks of pavement and cobblestones wizzed past my head, just missing me, and the tear gas that hung in the air, stung my eyes and made me feel nauseous.'

All this had occurred a long way from her native Boston, and staring into her deep brown, kind eyes, I was full of admiration.

After our meal, we took a walk past the window displays at Harrods before ending up at a basement discotheque in South Kensington. I knew the venue, because I had been there with DT and several other girls on a number of occasions. On the way home, my second-hand two-tone Austin Mini with blue tinted glass, of which I was justly proud, overheated and had to be abandoned in Dorset Square. We took a taxi and I dropped Cindy off at Springfield Road.

While in Paris, Cindy had been introduced to an extraordinary Afghan by the name of Omar who later went into partnership with Richard Williams and was also involved in Sufi activities. By coincidence, Cindy had also become fascinated by those ideas. We therefore had this interest and a group of friends in common. Cindy had first met Omar while he was tinkering with his Jaguar, up to his elbows in grease. He had received driving lessons from Stirling Moss and was reputed to be a general in the Afghan army, besides being a civil aviation pilot, businessman and Persian scholar.

As November came and went, the business ticked along and Cindy and I saw more and more of each other. I even lured her to Queensway to help with the paperwork, introduced her to my favourite eating haunts and we went to the cinema. A smutty film called *Sixteen* was popular during that autumn, as was the award-winning *Closely Observed Trains*. We also enjoyed *The Knack ... and how to get it*, the iconic film about how to seduce women starring Rita Tushingham and Michael Crawford.

Cindy's sister, Jane Lecomte, had recently separated from her French husband and was living in a nice garden flat close to the canal in Little Venice with her two young children, Edouard and Alexandra. Cindy, who adored her nephew and niece, used to babysit and I called round to keep her company while she rattled away with her knitting needles. She also came round to my flat, bringing her knitting and spools of coloured wool, and we cooked supper.

Just before Christmas, Cindy and I went down to Marlborough and spent the day with ABS-M, whom I still saw from time to time, and on Boxing Day I collected her from Woodman Court, Omar's house in Godalming where he had recently moved. Since Cindy was many miles from her home in Massachusetts, Omar and his wife had become good friends and taken her under their wing. I think she was glad of the opportunity for a break as one of the other guests had been repeatedly playing the Beach Boys' 'Good Vibrations', with the sound turned up, next to her bedroom wall.

We stopped at Petworth and had a lovely walk in the park. Standing on a wooded knoll that provides a magnificent sweeping view of the South Downs, I realised how much Cindy was beginning to mean to me. I believed that those feelings were reciprocated.

It was my mother's forty-ninth birthday and we soon headed for Bury, where she and my father had recently bought a thatched cottage. Arriving in time for a Black Velvet party and celebratory lunch, I was pleased to have this festive opportunity to introduce Cindy for the first time.

John Galsworthy, who also knew my grandfather had lived in Bury. Galsworthy, Elgar and Oliver Hall; did they get together? I would have loved to have been a fly on the wall.

At one minute past midnight on 1st January 1969, Cindy and I were toasting the New Year at a glamorous Arabian Nights party in Kent. Friends teased me later, saying that I had been following her around like a love sick puppy. It was therefore no great surprise when we announced that we were to be married and that we had a baby on the way. The un-planned pregnancy was something of a shock and was certainly an act of carelessness. We pondered our options long and hard, and considered a termination as so many couples do. I even booked an abortion at a clinic in Harley Street and paid a deposit. Cindy's sister Jane suggested that we consult Omar, who pointed out that if we planned to continue our relationship, terminating the life of our baby might leave a long and bitter scar—the 'after thought' as he called it..

We decided to make the commitment and, as we left Omar's house on a dark January night, he said, 'We'll have a big bash here in my house; tell all your friends and arrange the marriage ceremony for Saturday week!'

Our heads were spinning as we drove back to London but we felt a profound sense of gratitude to Omar—and also to Jane—for helping us on our way. Clearly in a state of excitement, I returned to Harley Street the next day and cancelled the abortion.

'We are going to keep our baby!' I announced, my face wreathed in smiles.

Did I get my money back?

Did I hell!

My parents took our surprise news well, and Cindy's mother flew over from Boston. We were married in Chelsea Registry Office on 25th January, followed by a splendid party, held at the fine house in Mark Way, Godalming, where Cindy had spent Christmas. The bright winter sun shone through huge south-facing windows, wedding cake was cut and eaten, my father made a speech in which he said that I had not been fishing long but had clearly landed a prize catch and Omar, our host, toasted 'togetherness'. The Mormon Tabernacle Choir's rendition of 'The Battle Hymn of the American Republic' boomed from loudspeakers in the gallery.

As we were leaving, Omar turned to me. 'When things get difficult, remember today,' he said.

I was startled by his words. He had said 'when' not 'if'; however his advice has held us in good stead.

After the party, friends and relations, including my brother Richard and his girlfriend Annie, who were attending the nearby Guildford Art School, waved as we disappeared down the drive, covered in confetti and with tin cans trailing along the ground secured to the car's bumper. We drove to Bury because my parents had lent us their cottage for a few days. Someone had been there earlier because we found the fridge was stuffed with goodies and there was champagne on ice to greet us.

In the final analysis, I considered Cindy brave in taking me on although we had been fortunate, not least because our backgrounds were similar. My father was a Cambridge man. Cindy's father, a professional musician, was in his time, probably the youngest ever entrant at Harvard. We both had a litany of professionals in our extended family and ancestry, many interests in common and some friends too. A few said that our linguistic and behavioural heritage might prove more of an obstruction than a bond, and I was indeed miffed when I found my trusted travelling alarm clock had been thrown out, a few weeks after our wedding, 'because it was old',

However, it is nearly forty-five years since these events and like any other couple who have been together for a long time, there have been waves and troughs, highs and lows, plateaus and valleys, many of which are recorded in this narrative. Building friendship and retaining a sense of humour is key.

Two men were travelling from New York to Boston in a railway carriage. The younger man turns to the much older man, saying, 'Scuse me, do you know what time it is?'

The older man stares at the younger man. 'What? You don't have a watch. Why no watch? No, NO! I am not going to tell you the time.'

'What do you mean, you're not going to tell me the time?' replies the younger man, indignantly.

'I will not tell you the time because if I do ... if I do ... we might get to chatting,' the older man continued. 'We might have things in common. We might get to like each other. When we arrive in Boston I might ask you to my home to meet my wife. You will like my wife and she will invite you to dinner. My daughter will join us. My daughter is very beautiful. You will certainly fall in love with her and soon you would ask me for permission to marry her. And then what would I say? I would have to refuse and things would end badly—because how could I allow my daughter to marry a man who doesn't even own a watch?'

We also both enjoyed the *Exploits of the Incomparable Mulla Nasrudin*[12] by Idries Shah, which had been published in 1966 and tried to absorb its wisdom.

Attending a friend's wedding later in the year, DB, an old chum from Marlborough, questioned me. 'What's it like living off your wife?' he asked. Cindy was an American therefore she was rich. It was a misconception that surfaced regularly.

Returning from our brief honeymoon and soon immersed in Peacock business, while Cindy took a temporary job with a City bank, my mind turned to the future and I asked myself why I was now running the firm. It had been something of an adventure—even a lark—but a new sense of commitment had crept in. I now had a wife and there would be a child to support before the autumn.

Our Polish landlady, probably concerned that she might soon have sitting tenants with a baby on her hands, gave us notice to quit the flat in Elgin Avenue but we just managed to squeeze in a breakfast birthday party in March. My parents, sister-in-law Jane and various friends came over and Cindy celebrated my twenty-second birthday by giving me the New Seekers record featuring 'I'll Never Find Another You'. I was delighted.

Finding a decent home, at an affordable rent, was a priority so I got up early every morning to search through the announcements in *The Times;* a practice that had served me well in the past, and as the fruit trees were blossoming in leafy Barnes a suitable unfurnished ground-floor flat turned up. It was just across the elegant suspension bridge, built in 1887, on Castelnau, the main road out of London from Hammersmith and a few doors down from where Errol Flynn attended school in the early part of the century. It had two large rooms, a smaller bedroom, a big kitchen and a conservatory that led into a small garden running back from the house towards the reservoir. At the bottom of the garden were some allotments and several prefab garages where a classic car enthusiast tinkered with an old Riley at weekends. We begged, borrowed or stole a few sticks of furniture, but our housing problem had been solved and we remained there for more than two years.

Back in Queensway, I put the engine into full forward thrust and we landed some juicy contracts with Interior Decorators. One was for a beautiful house in Egerton Crescent, a few doors away from the Vesteys, where we had worked at an earlier date. The decorator was Dudley Poplak and our wealthy clients were a young director of Sotheby's and his wife. It was spring, and if I arrived early, the study door leading to the garden would be open and a magnolia grandiflora, in full blossom, was clearly visible. Seated at the harpsichord, our customer always played something from Bach's 'Das Wohltemperierte Klavier', before leaving for the Bond Street showrooms. It seemed to me an idyllic, dreamlike existence and I was saddened to hear of his early death a year or two later. Part of our assignment was to paint the huge drawing room on the first floor. It was a fine, light room with high ceilings, an ornate cornice and magnificent marble mantelpiece. French windows opened out on to trees and gardens both to the front and rear. The room was to be painted white. After we had applied two coats, Poplak arrived.

'*Too* white', he pronounced. We added black tint and applied another coat. The same thing happened. We repeated the process with the same result. We tried again, and although I would be prepared to go to my grave swearing that I could not detect the slightest difference, it took another two coats to satisfy the maestro. We weren't bothered; each coat meant more money, although I felt sorry for the clients. As we were tidying up and clearing away, we buffed up the highly polished oak floors and laid out exquisite Persian rugs that had been carefully set aside while work was in progress.

Alan turned to me. 'Wot's this shit?' he whined. 'Why don't these geezers 'ave wall-to-wall, like ev'won' else?'

Our next high-profile design contract was for a Greek shipping magnate. The designer was John Siddeley (Lord Kenilworth) and the work, in Albion Gate, involved building intricately designed rosewood cupboards inlaid with tiny strips of mirror. Fortunately, I knew a brilliant Maltese cabinet-maker from the East End by the name of Louis Fenech, who was qualified to execute the work. The only problem that Louis had was that he was going prematurely bald and was the only man that I have known, or should I say known that I have known, to have undergone a hair transplant. Unfortunately, it was not a great success and Louis worked away with a little black beret pulled down firmly over his head. My task was to find the finest rosewood and it took a long search. After visiting numerous wood yards I finally tracked down timber of superb quality at merchants in Hackney Road. Louis did a first-rate job but in the process we needed to make some alterations to the original design. A meeting was held with Siddeley, his Greek client, Louis and me. While we ironed out the details I chipped in with a 'bright idea' that ran contrary to what the designer was suggesting. My idea was, however, adopted. Once the client had left, Siddeley slammed the door and exploded. 'NEVER, NEVER, contradict me again in front of a client!' he bawled.

I never did get another opportunity, and I wish I had known then that he was an Old Marlburian and had even been in Summerfield (1938), my house.

Our work was predominantly painting and wallpapering, but it was inevitable that all sorts of other little jobs crept up. Shelves needed to be altered, sinks repositioned, locks fitted, tiles laid, gutters fixed, floors screeded, brickwork pointed. We needed a jack-of-all trades and found one in Derek, who became an indispensable member of the workforce. In fact, if there were not enough odd jobs I sometimes took on work, as a loss leader, to keep him busy and stop him from straying. I knew when he was on-site because a grey 1955 Rover 90, whose tyres appeared to be permanently deflated, would be parked close by. He kept his tools and all sorts of bits and pieces in the boot. There were nails, screws, lengths of pipe, flex, bags of quick-drying cement, strong fixative, almost any imaginable item that could just come in handy. Even if I hadn't spotted the Rover, the red bobble hat that hid thinning sandy hair poking up from behind a cupboard or fence betrayed his presence. He invariably greeted me with a broad smile, watery blue eyes twinkling as he took the pencil that resided behind one ear to make a mark on wood or wall. On Saturdays his young son, Pete, would be scampering around not far away.

With Derek on the team, it did not seem an entirely unreasonable course of action to go one step further and take on some building work. Our first opportunity to do so, was provided by my generous friend George Kasabov, the son of Bulgarian immigrants, who practised as an architect in north London and it wasn't long I found myself involved in a small construction project for the writer B.S. Johnson.

One day, I was talking to Derek on the pavement in Dagmar Terrace, Islington, outside the house where we were working. We became aware of a dull roar in the sky, quite different to anything we had ever heard before. Looking up, the awesome sight of Concorde streaking across the blue sky came into view. We were mightily impressed.

The Islington contract proved to be a steep learning curve, but when the chance to undertake a full-scale conversion came my way, I could not resist the challenge. The opportunity was offered by interior decorator and erst-while 'debs' delight', David Ashton-Bostock, who was also, in my opinion, something of a dandy. I, again, asked Derek to price the work and we were awarded the contract. Since this was the biggest job that Peacock Decorators had undertaken I opened a bottle of champagne in the office. It was something I would never do again. Because of the events that were about to un-fold, I have not celebrated any kind of deal from that day to this—at least, not until the cheque has been banked and cleared.

Our task was to entirely renovate a house in Charlwood Street, Victoria, for Ashton-Bostock's personal use. Two problems emerged quite early on. First, the work had been ludicrously under-priced and, second, it required roofers and other trades that I had not worked with before, certainly not on that scale, so it was difficult to exercise quality control. Derek was nominally the foreman but lacked the personality to manage headstrong workers. An incident relating to the roof illustrates my predicament. After we had been working on-site for about two months a new roof had been constructed, however the plumber omitted to connect the roof's central gully with the conduit that was to carry rainwater to the down-pipe at the back of the building. Arriving after the wet August bank holiday, we discovered that, as a result, water had poured through the centre of the house over the weekend. Several ceilings had collapsed and when Jones, the plumber, eventually turned up I demanded an explanation.

His reply still rings in my ears.

'Mister 'all,' he said. 'For this I must apologise.'

Apologise? I was apoplectic.

'Apologise!' I screamed. 'Apologise! Get off this site and NEVER darken my door again!'

As the hot summer continued, the work at Charlwood Street dragged on. We had plenty of other contracts whereas the conversion haemorrhaged money and at one point the wages for twelve men had to be found on a Friday. By September, our turnover had surpassed the total for the whole previous year, but our profits were being drained away.

I sometimes thought that the project would sink us, and to cap it all Ashton-Bostock adhered to an irritating practice of carrying out inspections, which he expected me to attend, at nine at night or very early in the morning. The sole reason for his untimely visits was that he did not want builder's dust to settle on his bespoke suit and hand-crafted shoes. One day, I told him that I was struggling to complete the work within the agreed price.

'That's why I gave you the job, you were cheap,' was his only comment and it became blindingly clear that the only way I could get more money was for genuine 'extras'. I learned the hard way that turnover did not equal profit. Secretly hoping that Aubrey would stump up more cash to get me off the hook, I arranged to see him. However, that wasn't going to happen either. He was kindly but firm, and as he showed me to the front door he said:

'You got into this mess and you'll have to get yourself out of it.'

As I ran down the pavement towards the van, a violent thunderstorm erupted and torrential summer rain lashed the plane trees in the square, soaking me to the skin. I began to learn that 'being in the world but not of it' was no excuse for shoddy thinking and conditioned expectations.

The heat of that summer was particularly trying for Cindy as the due date for our baby's arrival came closer. She would squeeze on to a number 9 bus from Barnes that took her to the old Charing Cross Hospital for her tests and I would then try and find time to collect her. The Americans were about to put a man on the moon, and we wondered if the birth would coincide with that event. As it happened, the moonwalk occurred more than a month before our baby was born.

On 20th July, we watched Neil Armstrong take those historic steps and plant the Stars and Stripes on the surface of the moon. I thought of Gurdjieff's pronouncement that man was 'food for the moon' and wondered how that all fitted together in the scheme of things. The next morning, I met Garran Patterson to discuss some proposed work. We stood in the sunshine, in Belgravia, swapping impressions of the momentous pictures we had seen on our television screens and the moving words uttered by Neil Armstrong. We did not, of course, know at that time the story of Armstrong's further comment.

For a long time it had been rumoured that when Armstrong stepped on to the moon, as well as his famous 'giant step for mankind' statement, he was also heard to mutter, 'Good luck Mr Grodzinsky!'

These words were picked up by NASA but no one understood what they meant. None of the US or Soviet observers knew any Mr Grodzinsky. It was a mystery, and remained so. From time to time, journalists pressed Armstrong for the meaning of those strange words, if indeed they were ever uttered. His lips remained sealed. But finally, quite recently, when pressed for the thousandth time, he relented, and this is what he said.

'I can now answer your question because Mr Grodzinsky and his wife have both passed away. They were once neighbours of mine. When I was a small boy I was kicking a football in the back yard. The ball bounced across the grass and came to rest below an open window in the Grodzinskys' apartment. Suddenly I heard a woman's voice shouting. It came from the open window. She yelled "SEX! SEX! All you men want is SEX. I tell you, there will be no SEX until the boy next door walks on the moon."'

Years later, I attended a business meeting where Neil Armstrong was the guest speaker. Being in the hall with the man who had made 'one small step for man, one giant leap for mankind' somehow brought a tear to the eye.

On 3rd September, Cindy went into hospital. My parents hoped that the baby would be born that day since, for them, it would exorcise the memory of the outbreak of the Second World War. Thirty years to the day, a birth might transform a sad anniversary into a happy one. They had lost many friends and my mother had lost a fiancé. However, Cindy's labour was long and difficult and I remained in the hospital all night to be with her, sleeping on a couch in the waiting room. I had taken her some books, *The Cruel Sea* by Nicholas Monsarrat and other war novels including *They Have their Exits* by Airey Neave, who would come to political prominence in the 1970s before his murder by the Irish Republican Army (IRA) in 1979. It was some time before it occurred to me just how inappropriate that reading matter was and how remarkably insensitive I had been.

What a wally. I still had much to learn.

At lunchtime on 4th September, my parents arrived, hoping for good news, but there was nothing new to report. I was dog-tired and unshaven and they took me across the Strand for lunch at the Charing Cross Hotel. We were not overjoyed to be turned away from the restaurant, because I was not wearing a tie and the management appeared incapable of providing one, so we decamped to the Marquess of Granby in Chandos Place and wolfed down minute steak sandwiches before returning to the hospital. At 3 p.m. Cindy delivered a ten-pound baby boy. Cindy was completely ramfeezled but otherwise mother and child were fine. We named him Tarquin, the name I first came across, courtesy of Lord Macaulay, under the tutelage of Crispian Graves at Ashfold. I had promised myself that if we had a son, this would be his name. Browsing through D.H. Lawrence's *Etruscan Places* earlier in the summer had only reinforced this intention.

'Well, that's a bit different', was Omar's comment when I rang him with the news.

The next day Dr Jolly made his rounds, surrounded by a group of white-coated student medics. With the exception of the actor's legendary whiskers the scene would be recalled when we watched *Doctor in Trouble* (1970) with Old Marlburian James Robertson Justice (Cotton House 1921) starring in the role of Sir Lancelot Spratt. Pausing at the end of Cindy's bed, our beardless paediatrician took hold of Tarquin by the ankles and lifted him high in the air, like a team captain at a league cup presentation.

'Now, here's a fine specimen,' he chortled.

'Mum did well,' added Matron—a Hattie Jacques lookalike. 'At one point we thought she wasn't going to make it!'

A string of friends trooped up to the maternity ward. They included Oliver Hoare, whom I had known at Ashfold and who had dated Cindy in Paris. He was wearing an exotic wide-brimmed suede hat and smoking a long cigar.

'We can do without that!' said Matron, who grabbed the offending item and swiftly relegated it to a slop pail. Meanwhile, there was no paternity leave for me during those balmy September days. I had eight men painting the exterior of a huge hotel complex in Marylebone.

A few days later I drove Cindy and Tarquin back to Castelnau. The door of the flat closed and I put on a record. It was the soundtrack of 'The Graduate' by Simon and Garfunkel. Before bedtime, we related the story of Mushkil Gusha—the remover of all difficulties—to Tarquin, as I gently rocked him. This ancient tale carries an embargo. All who hear it should repeat the story on Thursday nights and help the work of the mysterious Mushkil Gusha.

The next morning, I left Cindy to sleep on and pushed Tarquin's pram down Lonsdale Road and around the block. I was twenty-two years old and felt very self-conscious.

However, work soon beckoned me back to Queensway and Cindy settled into life as a young mum in Barnes. Every day, she took Tarquin through the centre of the village and up to the pond where other young women with babies fed the ducks. She also prepared for her second English winter and got to know some of our funny little ways. Asking for a pair of sneakers, meaning plimsolls, raised eyebrows, as did requesting a kilo of oranges in the greengrocers. We agreed that the latter reflected her four years in Paris rather than the eighteen she spent growing up in Massachusetts. Like most young dads, I was eager to get home for bath time and particularly wanted to finish early on a Friday, but something always seemed to delay me. More often than not, it was a knock on the office door at about four o'clock. Pat and Danny, two of the painters whose childhood had been spent in the wilds of County Cork but now lived close to the concrete pillars that supported the elevated section of the M40 in North Kensington, were outside.

'Could you sub us thirty quid?' they would ask.

'Did I not pay you two hours ago,' I would reply.

They looked sheepish.

'All gone on the horses, eh?' I sighed.

'We had a good tip, but he fell at the third!'

I had heard it all before. It was years before cash machines were invented. Where the hell was I going to get thirty pounds with the banks closed? I did pity their wives.

The autumn sped by, but as a grey November descended into frosty December things were looking grim. Charlwood Street was still bleeding away oodles of cash, and a new secretary had walked out, snitching a pile of notes that had been set aside for wages. There was no exterior work on account of the winter weather, and our order book resembled Mrs Hubbard's cupboard. To make matters worse, I had acquired more points on my driving licence and a summons to appear before the beak at Marylebone in January meant an almost certain ban. Three weeks before Christmas, we were down to a matter of days before I would have to lay off my workforce and face the consequences. It was agonising.

The team that I had built up over three years included craftsmen who were as good as any available in London. Once gone, how would I replace them, and if the firm collapsed how were we going to eat and pay the winter bills? The men were oblivious of the truly dire situation that all our families faced, and I tried to keep the true nature of our plight from Cindy who was looking forward to the first Christmas of our marriage, when Tarquin would be nearly four months old.

I sat alone in the office with my feet up on the desk, staring at the wall, puffing on Gauloises and racking my brains. Suddenly the phone rang. Robert Slotover was on the line from Knightsbridge. He reminded me of the estimate that I had provided to decorate his entire six-floor house in Montpelier Square, some weeks previously. Of course I remembered, I told him.

He sounded slightly embarrassed and explained that my price had only exceeded our nearest competitor by one pound. He had, however decided, now much to his regret, to take the lower bid. The other firm had quickly proved to be dreadful and he had just sacked them.

'Is there any possibility that Peacock Decorators can take over?' I heard him say.

Was there *any possibility*? Struggling to keep calm, I assured him that we would do our best and I would have workmen at his house on the following

Monday morning. Almost beside myself with relief I figured that the contract, worth the best part of a thousand pounds, would keep everyone busy until well into January. It was also a nice, clean, simple job; just lining the walls and painting all the surfaces, and I had liked the Slotovers when I met them.

In business terms, 1969 had been a roller-coaster. We had expanded recklessly and although our turnover reached £40,000, our profits were right down. The events of the last few weeks had given me a serious fright. It had been a close shave and I was no longer in a position to take such risks.

We entered 1970, the year that the Conservatives were returned to power under Ted Heath (dubbed 'Grocer Heath' by the satirical magazine *Private Eye* because of his negotiations on food prices at a Common Market conference in 1962 and his election promise to reduce grocery bills), resolving to continue to grow steadily but only with easily manageable, profitable work.

The points on my driving licence had accumulated over the years: parking too close to a zebra crossing, driving a van that was in a dangerous condition and speeding. They were all offences committed while trying to cut corners, and I had already been banned for three months in 1968. On this occasion I stood up in court and explained my position: I had a young baby; I was self-employed; families relied on me and so on. I was fined, but not banned. It taught me a lesson and with the exception of a couple of very minor speeding infringements my licence has been clean for the last forty-three years.

Once that threat had been dealt with, I looked for a new secretary and was lucky when a young American called Georgia knocked on the door clutching a note from the agency. Georgia and I got on famously, and Cindy liked her and her boyfriend Paul. She remained at Peacock Decorators for several years. As the new year progressed, our list of high-profile customers increased. The names of Alan Bates, George Melly, Adrienne Posta, Patrick Wymark (whose daughter Jane partners John Nettles as Inspector Barnaby's wife in the television series *Midsomer Murders*), Zena Walker, Ivan Foxwell, Bernard Braden, Michael York, Mark McCormack, Madame Prunier, Mrs Kashoggi, Rachel Billington, Herbert Lom, Osbert Lancaster, Anthony Sampson, Hugh Whitemore, Eve Boswell, Barry Took, Colin Clark (Alan's nicer brother whose relationship with Marilyn Monroe was featured in the 2011 film *A Week with Marilyn*), Jane Asher, Sir George Solti, Paul Jones, Vidal Sassoon and several members of both Houses of Parliament were soon in our invoice ledger. The producer, Tony Garnett, who worked with Ken Loach on *Kes* and *Cathy Come Home,* the ground breaking '60s BBC 'Wednesday Play', was a customer, and his friend, Roy Battersby, invited Cindy and me to play the love-making scene in his film *The Body* (1970). We declined.

Drat! I could have become a porno stud!

However, famous did not always mean easy, as we discovered when we decorated a small flat in Knightsbridge. The client was the manager of a sexy black singer. He agreed to our price of £250, providing the work was completed by noon on a certain Tuesday. I thought it would be a doddle, but as it happened, we had some problems with the wallpaper, which delayed us. When the deadline arrived, we had completed the work and cleared the flat with the exception of an hour's 'snagging'. Our client turned up and presented me with a cheque. He had deducted £70.

'What's this?' I asked.

'You're late; read what's on the back,' he replied.

I turned it over and read the following typed note. 'This cheque shall only be cleared if endorsed by Mr Neil Hall of Peacock Decorators as full and final settlement for work undertaken at 33 Knightsbridge.'

I did not appreciate being bullied, but endorsed the cheque and left the premises with my Celtic temper at boiling point.

As the old man in a bookshop looking for a good holiday read said, when offered a romantic novel: 'Just the thing, no sex!' Blatant sexual activity did not feature much in our wanderings around the capital. This might seem surprising, considering the fact that we spent a great deal of time going in and out of people's houses, especially their bedrooms.

On one occasion, we had to wait while a group of young men piled out of various bedrooms in a Mayfair flat. It was clearly some sort of homosexual den and they weren't shy about the photographs they left lying about. Referring to my customer, a theatrical agent, Alan spat out:

'Wot's that Gerry do then? 'Es 'as bent as a nine-bob bit!'

Alan was a born-again Christian and frowned on what he perceived as immoral practices. When we were working in a house in Chelsea for a distinguished art dealer, Alan spotted Barnaby, our male customer's young lover, shaving his legs in the bathroom.

'Got a sore botty today, Barnaby?' 'Is our bum a little tender this morning?' muttered Alan whenever he thought there was a good chance that he *would* be overheard. When the art dealer came to settle up, he was distinctly tetchy.

No two days were ever the same, and life was full of surprises. Working for a solicitor, near the Albert Hall, was one such occasion. I had only ever met him dressed in a pinstriped suit, starched shirt and regimental tie. He appeared the epitome of the smart young man about town and retained the stiffest of stiff upper lips. It was, therefore, something of a shock when a cupboard door flew open and literally hundreds of sealed condoms tumbled to the floor. They were the sign of a man planning to enjoy life.

In contrast, another solicitor left his house in Clarendon Place each morning, looking neither to right nor left as he passed my men doing exterior work for him. He never even bid them good day; clearly they were as dirt under his feet.

'Old stuffed shirt,' was one of the politer comments I overheard.

My chaps' lives brightened up when they moved to a huge exterior re-paint that backed on to Hyde Park Gardens Mews. On most mornings, a tweedy lady in jodhpurs left her little house, far down below the scaffolding. She was off for a ride on nearby Rotten Row, returning several hours later, and must have had a host of admirers. Nearly every afternoon, a different car drew up, one of a string of young men would descend and the front door opened. A few minutes later the upstairs blinds would be pulled down and, after an hour or so the whole process went into reverse. Someone else was enjoying life!

Further entertainment was supplied by a titled divorcée of a certain age in Cadogan Gardens. Returning from a liquid lunch at the Admiral Codrington in Mossop Street with her blue-bloodied companion, she flew into a terrible tizz because a valuable diamond and emerald ring was missing. All work immediately ceased as we searched the flat, pulling up dustsheets, moving the furniture and rummaging in every corner. We never did discover precisely how, after several hours, the ring turned up in his lordship's coat pocket.

Moving the furniture in a bedroom in Chester Square produced another surprise. Something fell out of the bedside cabinet and rolled under the bed. It was making a buzzing noise. Closely watched by Danny and Pat, I bent down to retrieve what turned out to be a sort of pink plastic tube that came to an elliptical point. It was vibrating in my hand.

'What the hell's this?' I spluttered.

'Take it home and show it to the missus,' piped up Danny.

'She'll know what to do with it!' Pat added with a smirk.

One day, in the early 1970s, I was called to a house in Orange Street behind the National Gallery and a stone's throw from the Royal Academy at Burlington House, where my brother Richard was now studying. There was a little lighted doorbell on the street, clearly marked 'LULU'. I pressed the plastic button and made my way up the stairs. On the first floor an elderly lady was waiting; she ushered me into a small flat, and if I did not know it already, it soon became clear that I was in a brothel. As I hastily explained the reason for my visit, the old woman, who had started to rustle up a prawn and lettuce salad for herself and Lulu in the little kitchen at the back of the building, offered me a 'Rosie Lee' (cup of tea). She then showed me to a tiny cubicle where a punter could wait his turn, unobserved, for the services on offer. A pile of smutty magazines lay on the floor. After a few moments Lulu, an unexpectedly attractive young French woman with a slim waist, tight powder-blue blouse and pink mini-skirt, arrived and showed me into the bedroom. She recalled our earlier telephone conversation, further explaining that that she hoped the flat could be painted over the coming Easter weekend.

'Ze reception, kitchen and shower room should be white', she said, 'But I want an 'igh-gloss red ceiling and 'igh-gloss dark-green walls in ze bedroom'.

I assured her that my men would be keen to earn extra money over the holiday and sat down and worked out a price that was immediately accepted. Several weeks later, Dom delivered the men and set them up for the weekend and on bank holiday Monday I dropped by to see how things were going. All was well, although the men sniggered and made coarse jokes as they pointed out the chains fixed to the king-size bed.

Tarquin was about five years old when this incident occurred. I am sure he would appreciate the irony if I tell him where I went when I left him in the car that day. He waited for me for about twenty minutes before we continued en route to the Astoria cinema to see the film *Mary Poppins* (1964).

After the holiday I went to Lulu's flat to get paid. She counted notes into my hand, which I then checked by laying them in small piles on the bed.

'NEVER,' she scolded. 'NEVER put ze money on ze bed. It bring much bad luck!'

I left Lulu and walked back through Leicester Square to Wardour Street where I had managed to find a parking space, just outside St Anne's Church.

This was the source of a hoary (no pun intended) old chestnut because at some time in the past gilded letters were inscribed on the notice board in the churchyard that read:

'IF YOU HAVE SINNED ENTER THE HOUSE OF THE LORD'.

Below these words, someone had scrawled in large black lettering:

'IF YOU HAVE NOT—GO TO 27 GREEK STREET.'

My old friend Richard Burton (CBE) had teamed up with two pals, Peter Ahrends and Paul Koralek, to form an architectural practice in 1961. One project which, because of lack of funds, did not did not proceed was to rebuild St Anne's Church. Kenneth Powell, who has written the history of the firm, says that it 'would have unquestionably been one of the most remarkable British churches of the post-war era'. Nevertheless, the firm prospered and built extraordinary buildings in Britain, Russia, Israel and Ireland. Peter, Richard and Paul were a remarkable and very likeable trio who were good enough to give us work from time to time. Years later, when Prince Charles rubbished their design for the National Gallery extension, calling it 'a monstrous carbuncle on the face of a much loved and elegant friend', I felt extremely sorry for them but they survived, and went on to construct many other buildings, including the British Embassy in Moscow.

One of my most trusted men, another Irishman, had been blessed with the name of Attila. He was to have bad luck when, on a stormy March day, while burning off old paint from exterior window frames, flaming flakes flew under the eaves of the house where he was working and set the roof on fire. In minutes, a blazing inferno had developed in the rafters, which was especially unfortunate—to put it mildly—as the house was Sussex House and the roof was immediately above my parents' flat and within inches of the ceiling of my old bedroom. A call came through to the office, and when I got to Cadogan Square, fire engines were blocking all approaches.

It was most embarrassing.

There were questions as to whether blow torches should have been used, considering the weather conditions; however, the men were hardened professionals and the insurance company coughed up. My father, who used to give us work whenever an opportunity came along, was remarkably phlegmatic. Perhaps he was secretly pleased to get a new roof at someone else's expense.

Attila soon redeemed himself, when his skills were tested during the redecoration of a spacious flat just north of Hyde Park for the glamorous young

Earl and Countess of Woodborough. The couple had recently married and
Lady Woodborough was keen to experiment with some of the new decorative finishes that were becoming popular. Consequently, I visited a specialist
supplier in Theobald's Road, and purchased scumble glazes and unusual-
ly-shaped brushes for Attila to set about dragging, stippling and mop-rolling.
The work took several months and included extensive carpentry executed
by my old friend Louis. It turned out to be a huge success and when I was
rummaging in the archives (the loft) recently, I found this letter, dated 20th
December 1970, which I reproduce with apologies.

> Dear Mr Hall
>   Enclosed our cheque for £3,560.
>   We are both thrilled with the finished product, appsolutely no
> complaints at all. All the decoration and carpentry is first-class,
> and also all your men were very nice and pleasant.
>   We'll certainly recommend Peacocks.
> Yours sincerely
> Victoria Woodborough

I was suffering at the time, having contracted glandular fever. It made
life very wretched, as the firm had to be kept going despite my weakness,
fratchiness, depression and soaring temperature. Against our doctor's advice,
I spent alternate days in bed or being chauffeured by one of the men, and
was not back on my feet for several months. I doubt whether it did my long-
term health much good; my fuse seemed shorter and Celtic temper increasingly mercurial, which probably contributed to one outburst of rage that
the family has never allowed me to forget. Undoubtedly induced by a trivial
domestic incident, I once took a leg of lamb that Cindy was preparing for our
Sunday lunch, and charging into the bathroom, threw the raw meat with all
my might into the lavatory pan, where it hit the water with a sobering splash.
I sometimes wonder how poor Cindy—let alone my two sons—has put up
with me for all these years.

Lady Woodborough was not the only member of the aristocracy keen
to subscribe to new design trends. We had undertaken work for a certain
Lord B, who had discovered an embryonic company who were designing
and hand-printing exciting and innovative ranges of wallpaper. We drove
over to a small workshop in Chelsea where one of the directors, Sir Peter

Osborne, came out to welcome us. He was wearing brown overalls, like the foreman in a ball-bearings factory, and providing Lord B with a pile of samples went back to wrapping up bundles of wallpaper on a wooden bench in the back room. It took about ten minutes for my customer to make his choice. He made out his cheque to 'Osborne & Little', which was destined to become a famous brand name and once Sir Peter (whose son George would become Chancellor of the Exchequer in the Coalition government in 2010) had handed over six beautifully produced twenty-eight-inch wide rolls that featured a striking design, together with the recommended adhesive, we were off. Lord B asked for a lift to Westminster, because he was running late for a meeting at the House, and as we drove through Eaton Square he spotted a book lying on the back seat of the car.

'Are you reading this?' he asked, turning to pick it up.

It was *Caravan of Dreams* by Idries Shah. I nodded.

'Hmm … the Sufis, they *are* the business!' was his thoughtful response.

Half an hour later, I stopped at Mardi Gras for a spot of lunch. Opening Shah's book at random, my eyes alighted on a piece headed 'In Spain'—an extract from Gibbon's *Decline and Fall*—which vividly describes the fabulously opulent Medina al-Zahara in Spain. Yes, I thought to myself as I tucked into avocado vinaigrette; that does put our decorating into perspective.

Alongside all our efforts relating to family and business, we continued to read matters relating to Sufism and the Fourth Way and mentally bounced the stories and other material off our day-to-day experiences. Applying life experiences, as a catalyst for further study, was how Bennett had described the process of the Fourth Way. As far as stories and fables go, we were inordinately lucky to receive the rich abundance of literature that was provided and remains available to all. One reviewer referred to Shah's *Tales of the Dervishes* (1967) as 'a jewel flung in the marketplace'.

ABS-M had pointed out that certain stories, entertaining as they may be, carry extra psychological dimensions. These 'teaching stories', became familiar to us and together with the supporting literature provided by Shah's publications, a whole raft of instruction became available and continues to remain accessible through The Idries Shah Foundation.

In the summer of 1971, we took the decision to get out of rented accommodation and buy our first house. After lengthy discussion, we agreed to remain in Barnes which we had grown to like and where Tarquin would soon attend playschool.

There is evidence of human habitation in the Barnes area going back more than 6000 years and the Manors of Barnes and Mortlake were established before the Norman Conquest. From the time of Elizabeth I, extensive market gardens developed, serving a burgeoning demand for organic produce in the expanding London metropolis. Much of the merchandise was transported by river until the construction of the first Hammersmith Bridge in 1827. From then on, scores of loaded wagons dispensed fruit and vegetables to customers as far away as Covent Garden. Towards the end of the nineteenth century, developers increasingly appreciated the residential value of the land and the market trade dwindled away. Many gardens in the newly constructed estates had once been part of larger orchards, and dozens of gnarled old fruit trees remained, adding to the charm of the neighbourhood. Wild asparagus, parsley and rhubarb sometimes sprouted unexpectedly, a legacy of bygone days. Some of these gardens belonged to fine houses, built by one, Major Boileau, at the time of Queen Victoria's accession. These properties, with their own drives, were set back from Castelnau, the road named after the major's estates in France. Those on the east side backed on to the reservoir, and because of the raised level formed by a steep embankment, the first-floor windows commanded a spectacular view across a wide stretch of water. You could almost feel you were by the sea, and it was easy to understand why the actress Diana Rigg and other celebrities moved there. In the house opposite hers, Peacock Decorators had carried out work for the Kerrs, an eccentric colonel and his wife. When I received the letter accepting my estimate it was headed: '8th May 1971: being the 26th anniversary of VE Day.' There were, it seemed, a lot of people around whose lives were still deeply scarred by memories of the Second World War, however these were pleasant folk to work for, despite Mrs Kerr's tendency to disappear just when she was needed.

'Has anyone seen Mrs Kerr?' I would ask, on arrival at the house. Invariably, she would be found in her greenhouse, potting cyclamen and geraniums and exuding a wickedly pungent aroma as she puffed on a briar pipe.

After a couple of false starts, we settled on a three-up, two-down in the vicinity that the estate agents had recently dubbed 'Little Chelsea'. This was situated in west Barnes, separated from Mortlake by White Hart Lane where traditional brick terraced houses, once gentrified and the garden privy removed, were painted in assorted colours so that the streets began to resemble

Neapolitan ice cream. It was an interesting area, changing rapidly, although populated at that time by a wide social mix. The local postman, who bred racing pigeons in his shit-spattered shed, lived next door, and our garden backed on to a property where Bernard Hepton and his wife resided. Hepton was about to make his name playing the Kommandant in the BBC Television production of *Colditz* (1972–4) and when we visited Schloss Colditz many years later we were duly shocked by the grim reality of what the Allied prisoners must have faced. Memories of the remarkable exploits depicted in the series flooded back, and his was one of the faces that most readily came to mind.[13]

Around the corner, close to a stable where a rag-and-bone man kept his horse and brightly painted cart, lived the bluff North Countryman Colin Welland. Many will remember him from his acting days in the television series *Z Cars*. Some will recall how he went on to write the screenplay for *Yanks* in 1979 and *Chariots of Fire* in 1981. It was for the latter that he won an Oscar, famously, and perhaps rashly, remarking at the Hollywood ceremony that 'the British are coming!' Since he later became a customer of mine it seems reasonable to boast that his is the only Oscar I have actually held in my hands—so far.

Financing the new house meant getting a mortgage, which was a lot harder than it is today. Being self-employed with a dubious track record invited difficulties. However, the good Wing Commander, one of our first customers, referred me to James Sanders, another ex-RAF officer and one of the 'Few', who was reputed to have destroyed sixteen enemy aircraft during the Second World War. He was now working for a Canadian Assurance Company. He was a splendid character whose sales pitch included inviting Cindy (whom he always referred to as 'your beautiful wife') and me to his box at the Albert Hall, not once but several times, and exhorting us to enjoy life.

'Why, I was up at five o'clock this morning to pick asparagus,' he told us. 'I prepared it with, butter, lemon, a touch of salt and pepper and then— yum … my wife and I gobbled it up for breakfast while we were still in bed. Never miss a moment, I say, what?' Perhaps it takes a war to engender that spirit.

James fixed us up with a mortgage and life assurance and we were all ready to go when disaster struck. I was expecting to obtain £1500 of 'key money' for our flat in Castelnau in exchange for passing on the lease to new occupants. This cash was earmarked to provide the deposit on our new house, and although demanding a premium was not strictly legal, it was common practice at the time. It would more than recoup money we had shelled out two years previously. Unfortunately, our landlord's agent had heard that we were charging a premium, and blocked the process. Someone, who had been pipped at the post for the flat had shopped us.

'You can't do this; it is illegal and I won't allow it,' said the little man in his dingy office near Hammersmith Bridge. I remonstrated fiercely, but to no avail. Then I switched tactics.

'Come on,' I begged. 'I'm only doing what everyone does, trying to get ahead, making a home for my wife and son. Anyway, we need to move—we have a new baby due in February.'

Surely that would do the trick. I was greeted by stony silence. However, as CJ in the *Fall and Rise of Reginald Perrin*, the 1970s television comedy created by Old Marlburian D.G. Nobbs (Cotton House 1948) would have said, 'I didn't get where I am today by surrendering to a troublesome estate agent.'

Only one course was left open to me.

'How about a deal … a split?' I suggested.

'Now you're talking! Seven hundred and fifty!!' the little shit exclaimed.

'Five hundred!'

'Six!'

'Done!'

Somehow we got over the cash shortfall, and moved into a little house in Thorne Street in September. At Christmas, we moved out again for the holiday because we wanted the two ground-floor rooms knocked into one, and this required installing an reinforced steel joint (RSJ) on brick piers. It was a messy business and the house was a building site for several weeks. Derek acted as the foreman for a team of my men, and reversing roles, I became a labourer. It all worked out well, and in early January 1972, Cindy, Tarquin and I moved back in time to prepare a small room on the first floor for the new baby.

> 'London is the only place where the child grows up into the
>   man.'
> (William Hazlitt (1778–1830, 'Londoners')

Hippies in Paris, 1968

Lucinda and Gawky, 1969

Lt. Col B H Mathew-Lannowe DSO, 1916 (Baba)

Philip Hall, 1973

Chapter 8
Peacock of Barnes

Now mark me well—it is provided in the essence of things, that from any fruition of success, no matter what, shall come forth something to make a greater struggle necessary. (Walt Whitman, 'The Open Road')

There is nothing so stimulating and rewarding as trying to create something new and better. Profit is often used as a measure of success. But profit in itself should not be the real motive. The motive should be to create something better and different.
(Sir James Dyson)

THE PURCHASE OF our little house in Barnes coincided with the fifth anniversary of the day Leon and I had started Peacock Decorators with only one hundred pounds in the bank, and I felt some satisfaction with what we had achieved. In 1969, I had nearly come to grief but had recovered and, by the autumn of 1971, we were trading steadily with a turnover of about £40,000 a year with a manageable workforce of between six and eight men.

However, I was beginning to feel that we had sailed into the doldrums. The pioneer spirit of the 1960s was running out of steam and external factors were providing additional burdens that slowed business momentum. New tax legislation for self-employed people in the building trade; increased parking restrictions and the spread of traffic meters; IRA activity in London (the Post Office Tower was bombed in 1971) and industrial action in the electricity and postal services; all combined to generate inertia. In the early 1970s, power-cuts across large sections of London, lasting several hours, were not unusual. I felt that we needed to expand, but had learned from experience that vertical development without a broader base would lead to disaster. I was encountering my perennial problems; lack of capital and, if I were to seek a new partner, the absence of anyone I could really trust. Ever since Leon had left, I had shouldered all the management functions, which included dealing with the accountants and tax liabilities, keeping the vehicles on the road, organising our marketing strategy and juggling all the other activities I was involved in on a daily basis. Most evenings would find me preparing estimates while seated at the dining-room table before participating in family life or relaxing as we watched episodes of *The Onedin Line* or *The Brothers*. *The Onedin Line* told the story of a nineteenth-century family who ran a shipping company in Liverpool, while *The Brothers* was a series about a family running a transport business, starring, amongst others, Derek Benfield, who turned out to be one of our neighbours in Barnes, and Gabrielle Drake, whose brother Nick, the guitarist and songwriter, had been a contemporary of mine at Marlborough (C1 1962). Both those series combined nail-biting commercial life with drama on the home front. We especially identified with those programmes and, in due course, *Dallas*—hair-raising tales of a Texan oil family—came along too. They shed vivid, if exaggerated, light on the workings of business within a family context. There were few days when Cindy did not get an earful of my problems during our evening meal so, in a sense, we were a family business too. I took her stoic support too much for granted at times. She certainly deserved a medal.

What was needed was a management structure in larger premises so that I could get on with what I was best at; dealing with customers, attracting new contracts and maintaining a good relationship with the workforce while delegating other responsibilities. However, without substantial capital or a reliable partner, I was impotent. This conundrum weighed on my mind and, driving around each day, I endeavoured to come up with a solution.

In the early 1970s all sorts of new decorating materials were becoming available and—more importantly—becoming fashionable. Disposable incomes were also rising. Specialists like Osborne & Little with their hand-printed wallpapers and John Oliver, who produced a range of easy-to-apply emulsion paints with alluring names like Gretna Green, Kinky Pink and Bedouin Brown, were revolutionising the London decorating scene. There was a craze for covering walls with colourful hessians and felts and expensive imported grass cloths and cork. Metallic finishes of various kinds were popular as well. I had certainly noticed that my customers were obtaining lovely wallpapers from America and Europe that they asked us to handle, and then they proceeded to go elsewhere for their curtains and upholstery fabrics. The general public was becoming much more design-conscious and there was an increasing tendency to match or blend paintwork, wall-coverings and furnishings.

The problem was that there were very few outlets for this kind of merchandise and, with rare exceptions. they were all in central London. Suddenly, as I mused over my dilemma, I spotted an opportunity. I would open a retail shop selling all the kinds of things I mentioned above, for a proven market, but it would be in the heart of a residential area where property prices were rising rapidly and houses were being renovated. In fact, if I could find a suitable shop, why not in Barnes? The more Cindy and I considered the idea, the more we liked it. Expanding by a combination of lateral thinking and what I call 'leapfrogging' seemed the right approach. We would call the shop—Peacock. It would broaden the basis of my operation and, because we would employ a manager, probably with a part-time assistant, it would increase revenue without overstretching me. I hoped that both Peacock Decorators and the new shop would cross-fertilise each other in terms of increased sales, while providing a furnishing service was a natural progression.

The first step was to start thinking about staff and the second was to find an appropriate location. Finding a manager was simple because I already employed a suitable, trustworthy candidate. His name was Roger Bates and he had taken over from Dominic as the van driver and general dogsbody for the decorating business. Replacing someone to carry out that function would be relatively easy. Roger was as much a Cockney as one could wish for, although I doubt that he was actually born within the sound of Bow Bells, and we had already worked well together for several years. Short, in tight jeans, ginger-moustached, chirpy and quick-witted, everyone liked him, especially women, who found him sexy. When I raised the idea of his managing Peacock he jumped at the chance.

In early 1972, I started to scout around for a vacant shop that might suit our purposes and almost immediately struck lucky. Driving along Mortlake

High Street one day and almost at the point where Turner painted his famous picture *'Mortlake Terrace: Early Summer Morning'* in 1827, I spotted a sign advertising a shop to let. It was in just the right location, close to the river, on the corner of White Hart Lane and The Terrace in Barnes, and available at a competitive rent of £2000 per annum. With no parking restrictions and in an exposed corner position, it was well placed to catch passing trade. When I realised that the new business would be within half a mile of the site of the famous Mortlake Tapestry Works, founded in 1619 under the patronage of James I, I felt that this could only be a good omen. Some people might think that the question of finance would be the primary consideration here, but I was so used to flying by the seat of my pants with the motto 'where there's a will there's a way', that it was only at that point that I sat down to do my sums. I calculated that sufficient working capital to cover the rent and wages for three months, plus additional sums to install a telephone, the minimum of furniture, carpeting, lighting and other bits and pieces, would be £3000. My men could paint the shop and hang wallpaper and our intended suppliers, whom I had started to approach, would provide reasonable credit for sample books and other display materials. At the end of three months I hoped to be self-financing, although I would not draw any salary until we were profitable.

It was now time to visit my bank manager to request a loan, and here I discovered something interesting. Although my relationship with the bank had been amicable and they were aware of how close to the abyss I had come in 1969, I was nervous when presenting my plan. My concerns proved to be without foundation.

'No problem,' responded the manager. 'After all, you're a man of property now!'

He was right and, what was more, the equity in our house had increased by several thousand pounds in only a few months. Obtaining a loan was a doddle so everything seemed to be falling into place. Before finally committing myself, I went to see Aubrey to tell him about the new project. As usual, he listened attentively, understanding all my reasons for enthusiasm, and concluded our meeting with the comment, 'I always think that if a horse is running well, back it!'

In early February, I drove Cindy to Charing Cross Hospital, with a major section of West London blacked out by another scheduled power-cut. On 8th February 1972 our son Alexander was born. On this occasion I attended the birth, which proved less traumatic for Cindy than Tarquin's delivery, but I am not convinced that the father's presence at such a gory event is such a good idea. The traditional veil of privacy strikes me as more appropriate. However, mother and child were in fine fettle, ably cared for by the admirable Dr Shimshek (Turkish for 'lightning'), an American doctor studying in London. Naturally, all the family were delighted and I recall that we recited the story of Mushkil Gusha, again, once we were all together in our little house in Thorne Street.

A few months later, we took Alexander down to Sussex to visit my beloved Gawky. Sadly, this was to be the last time I saw her, as she was killed in a road accident the following October. She left the splendid grandfather clock which stood in the hall at Holly Cottage to me—a memento that I much prized—but unfortunately left the house to my Aunt Susan, who promptly sold it. Naturally, this infuriated my parents, and the two sides of the family hardly spoke to each other for years.

During the evenings when Cindy had been in hospital, Roger and I started to sort out piles of samples and prepare for the opening of Peacock. We aimed to make the shop colourful, comfortable and, above all, fun. Leaflets that I had printed announcing the opening proclaimed: 'PEACOCK IS FUN'.

Gone were the days, as far as we were concerned, of dingy, cold, linoleum-floored wallpaper and paint shops packed with cumbersome sample books filled with dreary designs. In our small way, we felt ourselves to be revolutionaries.

The last few weeks before we opened were hectic as we finalised arrangements with our main suppliers. They included Warners, Bakers, Osborne & Little, John Oliver, Parker Knoll and Coles. These names were less well known than they are today and more would follow, like Sartor, the exclusive importers of artefacts from the Far East run by Lady Victoria Weymouth, who sadly died so young.

We decorated the shop, laid a pleasant blue carpet, installed a large centrally positioned chunky pine table and hung lengths of colourful fabrics especially chosen to catch the eye of passers-by when we left the spotlights burning until midnight.

Just in time for our launch party, I felt that we had created the right atmosphere, at least to be going on with. Cindy, Roger and I hosted a very jolly occasion one evening in April when friends, trade associates, local pressmen, our bank manager and others gathered to toast Peacock and wish the business every success. When I got home that night I burst into tears. It must have been a release from all the tension that had been building, but next morning Roger was in his place and the cash till began to ring.

A new routine developed that hardly varied for the next five years. I would leave home, struggling with the traffic over Hammersmith Bridge, in time to arrive at Queensway by 8.30 a.m. When the boys were old enough I would drop them off at school en route. They were lucky to go to a super little playgroup on the common in Barnes, where two kindly ladies, Margaret Oppé and Phyllis O'Kelly, took good care of them. Later, they progressed to Allendale School in Kensington, which was also run by two dedicated women. I would then continue with Peacock Decorators' work until about five o'clock, when I would call in at the shop and review the day's events with Roger. I worked in the shop all day on most Saturdays, and an immediate requirement was for me to learn more about interior design, a skill that had not been previously required. Now, I found myself being asked for advice with regard to colour and material coordination and, over the ensuing years, I like to think that I became quite good at pointing my customers in the right direction. Initially, it was more a knack of being familiar with the thousands of samples that we stocked, and interpreting what the customer was looking for, rather than imposing my own views and taste, but as my confidence grew I felt able to take the lead.

If I had known of its existence at the time, I might have taken comfort from this letter in the *House Furnisher* of 1871:

> The greatest evil in our trade is the multitude of patterns: we all have shelves and counters loaded with books from every manufacturer in the trade, and as ladies never tire of looking over samples the selection of papers for a house becomes frequently a very bewildering and tiring business: we are generally too glad to finish the transaction to think of upsetting our customers' choice by any remarks as to incorrectness of taste in the design choice.

There was another hurdle to cross. I needed to find curtain-makers to whom I could subcontract our work. However, one day who should walk into Peacock but the glamorous Patsy, whom I had met on one of my marketing forays in Walton Street five years previously. Patsy had called to leave a business card describing curtain services that she and her boyfriend, Donald Cameron-Clarke, provided.

'Oh, it's you!' she said, surprised to find that I was the owner of Peacock, and recalling our previous acquaintance. This was just what I was looking for, and we immediately began to build up a good business relationship. For the next eleven years, Donald and Patsy handled all the furnishing work that Peacock generated; an arrangement that undoubtedly benefited everyone involved.

For the next few years, both of my businesses traded successfully despite continuing industrial action and the three-day week that was called by Edward Heath for 1st January 1974. Those restrictions, which drastically reduced the nation's man-hours and productivity, lasted until the General Election in February when Harold Wilson was returned to Downing Street for the third time. However, the Labour Party was seventeen seats short of a clear majority, resulting in a hung parliament, and another election was called in the autumn. At the election, held on 10th October, Labour was returned with a majority of three but remained in power until trounced by Margaret Thatcher in 1979. Indeed, reflecting on life in the 1970s, a constant battle was raging between alternate Conservative and Labour governments and the unions who were dominated by the likes of Jack Jones and Hugh Scanlon ('the terrible twins') and Joe Gormley. In 1974, when Harold Wilson was returned to power, a poll recorded that 'Emperor' (Jack) Jones (General Secretary of the Transport and General Workers' Union) was considered by the majority of Britons be the most powerful man in the land. According to an article by Peter Oborne in the *Spectator* (November 2009:'A poisoned legacy from which Labour has never quite recovered'), he 'was a paid agent for the USSR, and in receipt of cash hand outs from his Soviet handler Oleg Gordievsky as late as the 1980s'.

Gordon Brown (his protégé) and Tony Benn admired him hugely.

I was standing one dark evening in Peacock during the three-day week. The shop was packed with stalwart customers, all endeavouring to choose wallpapers by candlelight, when the front door opened and a voice called, 'Is my wife in there?'

'What's she feel like?' came a wag's instant reply.

The shop's turnover increased exponentially, although Roger left after six months because he found the travelling from south-east London too much. I replaced him with Anna Driver, who came to us from the furnishing department at Peter Jones and who worked well with our part-time girl, the actor Stephan Chase's wife, Jane. Both girls had considerable artistic flair, which went down very well with the customers. The decorating business continued much as before, although I had found a new source of business.

It was the practice at that time for the Chase Manhattan Bank to purchase houses or apartments in London for their executives who were on secondment for several years, and were responsible for the bank's activities throughout Europe. These sizable properties were usually in fashionable parts of town and required complete redecoration and furnishing. A quiet revolution had taken place. Large houses that had become unmanageable after the Second World War were once again being occupied by single families because the introduction of efficient central heating, double glazing, economic washing and cooking facilities and other mod cons meant that the minimum of staff were required. A Swedish au pair and one Spanish cleaner could easily suffice.

Who better to finance the transformation of these properties to their former glory than the Chase Manhattan Bank, and we secured a number of lucrative contracts. An added bonus was that the bankers and their families had simple tastes, were friendly and not in the least demanding. One senior man, a New Yorker of Italian extraction named Jo Ferrigno, even invited me to the first *real* American hamburger bar, which had just opened in Chelsea.

'My! Do I need to educate you!' he said when he discovered that my idea of a hamburger was a greasy Wimpy, although, if the truth be known, I think he was a bit lonely after his wife and children had pushed off to Cape Cod for the summer. As we chatted away, I could not help wondering if I was missing out, confined as I was to my little fish bowl, while Jo roamed the globe, intoxicated by the world of international corporate finance. On his part, surprisingly, did I perhaps note a tinge of envy? Could it be possible that he would have gladly swapped places with me, to enjoy running a little business with his family always close at hand rather than facing a return to Wall Street after five years and possible executive burnout at the age of forty? As Petula Clark sang in her 1968 hit, 'The Other Man's Grass is Always Greener!'

On another occasion, in a large house, north of the park, I heard an exchange between my American customer who worked for CBS News and Eddy, a Geordie, and the fastest wallpaper-hanger I ever met.

'Hey, Eddy,' exclaimed the Yank. 'Goddammit, I can't understand a word you say!'

'That's fooni,' came the reply. 'Ev'one speaks like me where I kum from!'

One morning I was visiting a job and needed to talk to Derek. He was not on site so I walked around the block to see if he had parked further away. There was no sign of my jack-of-all-trades, nor his Rover, which always reminded me of the much-publicised scandal concerning Dr Bodkin Adams. It was the sort of car the rich Eastbourne doctor enjoyed driving. In 1957, many local people believed that the wealthy bachelor and car enthusiast had murdered twelve women patients following suspicions, aroused by the number of legacies he received. On 26th July, he was actually charged with the murder of Edith Morrell, but acquitted at the end of a sensational month-long trial. Struck from the medical register for less grievous demeanours, he returned to practice four years later but, apparently, still continued to receive substantial gifts from wealthy women for years to come. It was the sort of yarn that made an impact on a ten-year-old Sussex schoolboy. Did he actually kill any women? I don't think anyone ever knew; but it seems that I am not the only one to be interested in the story. In 2013 John Murray published *The Curious Habits of Dr Adams* by Jane Robins.

Thinking that Derek must have got held up in traffic, I hung around a bit longer before calling his home. His wife answered and informed me that he would not be coming in to work and gave me a number where I could reach him. A crackly line and an incoherent Derek left me none the wiser. All I knew was that I had rung a call box in County Sligo. I never saw Derek again and why he had done a bunk—perhaps he was on someone's hit list or the police were after him—I shall never know. What skeletons were in his closet? I wondered, but I was sorry to lose him as we had worked together for some years and it left me without my carpenter and chief fixer.

Fortunately, it was not long before I heard that Greville, an eccentric friend of ours, was looking for work. We gave him a call and he came round for supper clutching a bottle of his homemade wine. I quizzed him a bit about the kind of things he could do.

Wig-making was a speciality, but not quite what I had in mind. He was, however, a good chippy and tiler so I outlined details of a couple of projects that needed urgent attention and he happily agreed to take these on. A few weeks later, we were enjoying an early evening beer in the public bar at the Plumber's Arms in Lower Belgrave Street, the pub where Lady Lucan had sought help following the murder of her nanny Sandra Rivett in November 1974, when Greville said:

'You know, Neil, while you were giving me the Gestapo inquisition about my skills I was reminded of this story. Maybe you've heard it.

There was once an Irishman looking for work and he knocked on the site manager's door where a construction project was in progress.

"Do you have work for a bricky?" he asked.

"Now, one moment," came the reply. "Things are not as easy as that; I need to test your knowledge."

"Test my knowledge? All you need to know is that I'm a bricky, and I need to know if you have any work!"

"Please yourself," said the manager. "No test, no work," and he started to head for the door.

"OK," the Irishman shrugged his shoulders, "fire away."

"Right, this is the first question. What is the difference between a joist and a girder?" asked the manager.

"Did you say Joyce and … Goethe?" The Irishman scratched his head. "Joyce … and Goethe? Why, yes! Joyce wrote *Ulysses*, and Goethe wrote *Faust*!"'

'I think that deserves another pint,' I responded, quickly moving towards the bar as Greville puffed on his Disque-Bleu, dusted excess sawdust from his grimy trousers and fiddled with the buttons on his shirt. Greville, who was about fifty years of age at this time, qualified for that overworked expression 'a character'. He lived in a caravan style mobile-home near Tonbridge that contained three rooms and the usual amenities. Incongruously, the sitting room was packed with heirlooms, including several fine pictures inherited from his father, who had been a respected doctor in Barnet. Greville had been educated at Aldenham and there had once been family money through Duckham's, the oil people. His shambolic bedroom defied description and copies of *Playboy* and *Penthouse* were strewn across the floor. The third room, which should have been a dining room or spare bedroom, was in fact a Heath Robinson apparition where Greville spent most of his time, brewing beer or fermenting wine, although he also enjoyed making imaginative masks or wigs or building super sets for the Oast Theatre in Tonbridge. In this context the provenance of Aldenham School was distinctly appropriate. It had been founded in 1557 by Richard Platt, 'Cityzen and Brewer of London', for the free education of 'children of poore people inhabitinge in the Parishe of Aldenham and the children of Freemen of the Companye of Brewers, London'.

Cindy was particularly fond of Grev and the boys were too, probably because he was addicted to making rude jokes about bottoms and farts. We would sometimes take a picnic down to the caravan and he would invariably be watching out for our car, leaning against the brightly painted railing on his balcony, his bushy blond hair blowing in the breeze and proudly displaying a T-shirt that read, I LOVE BREWSTER: NEW YORK. As we approached, a huge welcoming smile would engulf his face. The balcony, reached from the ground by mounting a couple of steps, was no ordinary construction. It was a Greville-designed mock-up of something you might find in Bokhara or Samarkand. A painted wooden screen with mathematical designs and arabesques cut into fretwork ran the length and breadth of the caravan and at intervals there were brightly coloured pillars embellished with miniature domes and turrets. I don't know what the neighbours thought, but it was an amusing addendum to the Kent countryside.

Occasionally, to save travelling or when there was urgent work for Peacock Decorators to attend to, he would stay the night with us, usually falling asleep at the supper table. His head would loll forward and his wispy beard end up in the gravy. Then, waking with a start and greatly embarrassed, he would toddle off to bed. Poor Cindy, she had a lot to put up with. Sadly, Greville suffered from bouts of depression, and he occasionally ended up in mental institutions. It was very sad when I visited him in several of these places and in hindsight, it was even more wretched when these episodes proved so unnecessary. Eventually his brother Barry, who had emigrated to up-state New York, came to the rescue, and Greville was treated for a chemical deficiency in the United States. This treatment proved successful, if only he remembered to take the tablets. Because of these problems, his work for me was limited and irregular although he took off time to build a wonderful treehouse for our boys some years later when we had moved to Wiltshire. It was tragic indeed when we heard that he had been killed in a motor accident.

Exercising his many talents, he had worked as a social worker and also as a designer and creator of furniture and ornaments. Sometimes I see what we call 'Greville mirrors' in gift shops. Constructed with small pieces of ceramic tiles, coloured glass and silver and gold paper, they were years ahead of their time and unsaleable in the 1970s. Now you see the style everywhere. Fortunately, we are the proud owners of some of his work. Greville's genius also extended into the prolific and irreverent production of limericks and doggerel, but some good verse too.

An extract from the following poem is included in memory of our mischievous friend.

'Electric Soup'

Hand me down, my honey, my automatic hat,
My stereophonic trousers and a plain baroque cravat:
Don a false moustache or two, be real and join the troupe
And tonight we'll sing the pleasures of Electric Soup.

Stimulate the intellect, discuss aesthetic cake
And analyse the flavour of a paranoid beef steak;
That's the stuff to give the lads! They'll all be cock-a-hoop,
So wire me to a plateful of Electric Soup

Now, some soups come in packets and others come in cans,
They sometimes come in kitchens, where they serve it up
    in pans,
But which soup comes in batteries, each spoonful scoop by
    scoop?
The one that tastes of POWER—vote: Electric Soup.

One morning, early in 1974, I received a telephone call from the Ambassador's secretary at the Moroccan Embassy. She explained that extensive refurbishment of the residence in Bishop's Avenue was planned and that they would like me to attend a meeting with His Excellency on the following Monday. If I did not speak Arabic or French it would be better, she suggested, if I brought along someone who did, so that the proposed work could be discussed in detail.

I called my sister-in-law, Jane Lecomte, who was working for Slendertone in Baker Street, had been married to a Frenchman, and spoke fluent French. She agreed to accompany me. Arriving at 6 p.m. at a huge house in one of the most desirable avenues in north London, we were ushered into the drawing room where the Ambassador, M. Abdullah Chorfi and his charming French wife, were waiting. After greeting us in French, which Jane duly translated, he explained that all the curtains and upholstery were to be replaced in red and green velvet, the Moroccan national colours. This was quite an undertaking, as there must have been six sofas and several large windows that would probably require several hundred metres of fabric. Pound signs started to dance before my eyes, but this was not all. My clients led us into a magnificent reception hall that had been recently added to the main building, where decorative tiles and embellished plasterwork closely resembled the interior of parts of the Alhambra. The Ambassador informed us that this huge room required a new carpet. More pound signs were bouncing around in my head; exhibiting a marked state of anticipation, which was probably not lost on their Excellencies.

We returned to the drawing room and a very large whisky and soda, sparkling in a heavy-cut glass, was deposited in my outstretched hand. Slightly taken aback by the impact of the strong liquor, I managed to assure my clients that we would be able to undertake all this work, plus some additional items that they were in the process of mentioning. I would return, I said, with an assistant to the take necessary measurements before the end of the week. We took our leave and before driving home I bought Jane dinner in Hampstead as a thank you. Christmas, it seemed, had come early that year.

In the post, the next day, arrived a gilt-edged card, inviting me and a guest to attend an evening reception at the residence. Thrilled by this turn of events, I gave Cindy enough money to buy herself a plush new dress for the occasion. However, when the great day came and after we had been announced at the main entrance we were disappointed to find that most of the guests appeared to be professional freeloaders on the diplomatic cocktail circuit.

'I come to a do like this most nights,' explained one little man as he emptied a plate of chipolatas into a paper napkin and stuffed it into his jacket pocket. 'It saves a fortune in housekeeping,' he guffawed.

Over the next week, Donald and I visited Bishop's Avenue and prepared estimates and samples, which we sent to the Ambassador. I respectfully pointed out that we would require a substantial deposit since the cost of materials ran into thousands of pounds. Everything was agreed by return of post with the exception of a cheque as this had been 'requested from Rabat and would follow shortly'.

Naturally, I took the Ambassador at his word and ordered all the materials. When they arrived, we hired a van and returned to the residence to pick up all the furniture. Three weeks later I found myself in a tricky position. Donald had all the Moroccan furniture in his workshop, which left the Ambassador with very little to sit on, and I had several hundred metres of the best velour on the shelves at Peacock. There was still no sign of any cash and I did not want to commence work until the materials had been paid for. I rang M. Chorfi's secretary, who assured me that money would be available very soon. Another week went by and nothing had come from the embassy. I called again, requesting an interview with the Ambassador to 'discuss the progress of the work'. We agreed to meet the next morning at 9 a.m. although I felt at a disadvantage because Jane was unable to attend. I was nervous despite the fact that I suspected Chorfi's English to be much better than he had let on. However, by an extraordinary coincidence, as I was driving through Swiss Cottage, feeling very twitchy, I spotted an old boyfriend of Cindy's standing by the traffic lights. It was Julian Hayter, the son of William Hayter, an early member of the Surrealist Group and one of the most influential twentieth-century printmakers. Julian had recently moved to London from Paris and I knew he was a professional translator. I slammed on the brakes and, leaning out of the car window, hailed him and outlined my predicament. Could he possibly accompany me, I asked. He readily agreed to do so and within seconds we were heading north up Fitzjohn's Avenue and soon arrived at the residence. The immaculately attired Ambassador was descending the stairs, adjusting his gold cufflinks as the front door opened, and a waft of Eau Sauvage swept across the hall. If I had been told me that he had just bathed in the exotic green liquid I would have believed it. I introduced Julian but sensed immediately that Chorfi was adopting an entirely different tone to that of our first meeting. 'Where is my furniture?' he demanded. He could not entertain, there was nowhere to sit, and I was responsible came the message, loud and clear.

'Excuse me, your Excellency,' Julian translated, 'we are waiting for money from Rabat.'

'Ah, money!' He was all smiles. 'Please return my furniture immediately, with work completed, and all money will be paid.'

'That is very difficult,' I rejoined.

'Please,' he reiterated, 'you have my word as Ambassador to the Court of St James.'

Indicating that the interview was over, he headed out of the front door and climbed into the back of his chauffeur-driven black Mercedes. I drove Julian to the Finchley Road, where we had met.

'You've got a problem there!' was his only comment.

I decided to go and talk to Aubrey and explained the position I was in.

'You have to get up very early in the morning to outwit an Arab,' he reflected. 'You can strike a deal with a Jew and he'll keep to his side of the bargain, but to an Arab you are an infidel! It is his God-given duty to strike you down.'

'But what do I do about his furniture?' I said, struggling to smother my exasperation.

'Hang on to it, he'll pay, you'll see!' was all he said.

A few days later, I was working in our tiny office in Queensway when I heard Rita, my new secretary, giving the address to someone over the telephone.

'Who was that?' I enquired casually.

'The Moroccan Embassy,' she replied.

'Christ!' I exclaimed. 'What have you done? They don't know about this office, only the shop in Barnes. Why do they want the address?'

I paused. 'Someone must be coming round. They'll probably be here any minute!'

I peered out of the window and, sure enough, the black Mercedes was parking in the street below and two hefty Arabs were getting out.

'Bloody hell! What are we going to do?' I screamed.

There was no escape. Rita made as though she was about to dive under the desk. The men were pounding up the stairs and within seconds there was a sharp knock on the door. Two men, whom I recognised as members of the Embassy staff, entered. They were courteous, but announced firmly that the Ambassador wished to see me immediately; would I please come with them. They drove me to the Embassy in Queen's Gate Gardens where I was frogmarched into Chorfi's office on the first floor. There he subjected me, in perfect English, to an extraordinary display of ranting and raving that culminated in his threatening to report me to the Foreign Office. With Aubrey's words ringing in my ears, I stood my ground.

'No money, no furniture,' I repeated several times.

Suddenly and unexpectedly, the Ambassador made a signal to his secretary, who produced a cheque for the total value of the contract. He endorsed it, and without a word, handed it to me, gesturing to his henchmen to return me to my office.

In due course the full contract was completed, although not without a last-minute hitch. When my contractors had laid the massive carpet in the reception hall the dozen or so metal doors to the driveway and garden would not close. The carpet and underlay were too thick. The only solution was to take all the doors off their hinges and transport them to an engineering works, several miles away, where a sixteenth of an inch was shaved off the bottom of each door. They were then returned and rehung. Fortunately, the Ambassador was in Rabat. He had already suffered for two months without furniture and I would not like to have been around if he turned up to find his grand hall with no doors and his luxurious and extremely expensive new carpet exposed to the elements. When it was all over, I breathed a huge sigh of relief, although I remained puzzled about what all the fuss had been about. In a strange way I felt grateful to M. Abdullah Chorfi, who had eventually paid me in full and taught me some useful lessons. I would be better prepared if the same set of circumstances occurred again. Despite the dramas, we had made a good profit from our dealings with the Moroccans, and I thought it was high time I took my family to the United States for a holiday.

Cindy and the boys flew to Boston a week before me, and I travelled on 17th June 1974. Mine was a long exhausting journey, as the TWA flight from Heathrow to New York was followed by a four-hour delay, before the connecting hop up the Eastern Seaboard. It was a great relief to see Cindy's welcoming face, wreathed in smiles, waiting to greet me at Logan Airport. The dry heat of the Massachusetts night struck us when we left the terminal building, as it did again as we emerged from our air-conditioned car among the sweet-smelling pines surrounding her parents' house in Wellesley. It was, of course, my first visit to America and I was fortunate to have acquired an extended family who lived in such a pleasant region—only an hour's drive from the state capital. The wooden, clapboard, colonial-style house at 171 Benvenue Street was painted a rust-red colour and nestled in the woods just outside the small town that revelled in the worldwide reputation of its famous ladies' college and whose charming central square featured the Wellesley Inn, an eighteenth-century hostelry—now sadly demolished to make way for new housing.

Having slept late, we rose to find waffles, maple syrup, eggs fried sunny side up and coffee being served on the deck. Cindy's uncle Bob joined us.

'I want to meet the boy,' he announced in his soft New England drawl.

The treetops below us basked in the fierce June sun and on the steeply sloping back yard there was a small vegetable patch where my father-in-law was attempting to produce a few lettuces and beans in arid, sandy soil. While we were eating, the question of how I should address my in-laws arose because, for the first five years of our marriage, they had expected me to address them formally, on the telephone or when they had visited England.

'Please call us Mr and Mrs Briggs,' they intoned together.

Cindy explained that this would be unacceptable in England, and that she called my parents by their Christian names while I still called them Mummy and Daddy. Embarrassed, I nodded in agreement. Eventually, after further discussion a compromise was agreed and from then on they would be 'Granny' and 'Grandpa' to us all. After brunch we hastened, barefoot, up the blistering tarmac road, avoiding trickles of sticky, melted asphalt that shimmered in the heat, towards a fine property where Cindy's parents had permanent access to a large swimming pool. On arrival at the honey-coloured brick house, I was introduced to the owner, Mrs Isa Livingstone, another real New Englander, wearing a battered straw hat to protect her from the sun. She welcomed me and ushered us across her manicured green lawns, as the boys danced in the glistening fountains that rose from her water sprinklers.

What George Wright Briggs, my father-in-law, lacked in horticultural skills he made up for in enthusiasm for tennis and squash, and the next day we were off to the Harvard Club to watch him competing with his buddies, followed by an excellent lunch in the Club's splendid dining hall. Memorials to renowned alumni and, perhaps more importantly, to benefactors of Harvard University surrounded us. The most distinguished of these, at the time of its founding in 1636, was John Harvard himself, who was born in Southwark and christened at St Saviour's Church, close to the family's butcher's shop, on 29th November 1607. He was educated at Emmanuel College, Cambridge (England) which coincidentally was my father's alma mater.

After our meal we started to explore the city, which was founded in 1629 and named after Boston in Lincolnshire from whence the Colonists had come, but we returned on several further occasions because there was much to see. Ill-fated Boylston Street, Boston Common, the attractive Beacon Hill area, the Charles River, Harvard Square, the notorious and dangerous

'Combat Zone' and the site of a certain celebrated 'tea party' (1773) had become familiar sights by the time we completed our excursions. On several evenings we attended Boston Pops, the light concerts associated with Arthur Fiedler, although 'Briggsy', as my father-in-law was nicknamed by his musical chums, occasionally stood in as guest conductor. He wrote a biography of his close friend, the composer Leroy Anderson (famous for 'Sleigh Ride', 'The Typewriter', 'The Blue Tango', 'Forgotten Dreams' and others), which has recently been published under the title *Leroy Anderson—A Life in Music*.

We also witnessed the appalling traffic problems that the city suffered, leading to the 'the Big Dig', the huge project that involved extending the Massachusetts Turnpike (toll motorway) through a tunnel beneath South Boston and Boston Harbour to Logan Airport, which was completed more than thirty years later in 2005.

At the weekend, we set out early to drive to Cape Cod, pausing on the way to enjoy Plimoth Plantation, a replica of a seventeenth-century stockade village. This was a 'live' museum that covered several acres with lanes, houses, vegetable strips and smallholdings where goats, pigs, chickens and other farmyard animals were doing what such creatures do best—albeit noisily. The staff were actors who arrived every morning from the nearby town, donned seventeenth-century garb and then for the rest of the day played the part of cowherd, shepherd, seamstress, cook or dairymaid to add authenticity to the scene. The remarkable thing was that they remained in character, even when provoked. While sheltering from the rain in a tiny cottage whose distempered white plaster walls were springing away from the timber lathes, we endeavoured to engage a young lady in 'contemporary' conversation, but she was not to be drawn; she feigned ignorance of what a cinema might be and only replied in simple sentences delivered with a strong Somerset accent.

After an hour, passing several fusiliers, we emerged from an area that would have adequately served as a defensible wooden fort and returning, as if by magic, to the twentieth century, climbed back into our automatic, air-conditioned Avis hire car to continue on the next leg of our trip. This took us over the Sagamore Bridge that carries the main road to Cape Cod and past one of the biggest thatched roofs in the world; soon to be restored by Adrian Ward and his team of English thatchers from Wessex, whom I happen to know. It dawned on me then, that in this vast country there really was space for anyone to do anything they wanted, anywhere.

Not long after encountering this landmark, we found ourselves among extensive, colourful cranberry bogs. Pausing for a picnic on the springy turf, Grandma insisted on tying a rope around two-year-old Alexander to stop him from straying or falling into the water. He was intrigued by a miniature railway that transported tourists around the fruit-growing areas and we promised to return for a ride at a later date. The early settlers jealously guarded the newly discovered wild cranberry and in 1773, it was decreed in Provincetown that 'any person should be found getting cranberrys before ye twentieth of September, exceeding one quart, should be liable to pay one dollar and have the berys taken away.'

As the road continued we passed more Kentucky Fried Chicken and other fast-food outlets than I imagined existed in the whole of America, each establishment advertising their goodies in a cacophony of neon lights and plastic, so we were glad when we reached the turning to Hyannis Port, the home of the Kennedy clan, as this signalled our imminent arrival at the quiet town of Chatham. Here was our journey's end, near the lighthouse on the brink of the ocean, where Cindy's maternal grandmother, Mrs Marjorie Nickerson, resided in a fine, grey wooden house with the Stars and Stripes fluttering from a flag post that stood close to the porch in the sandy driveway.

The Nickersons are an interesting tribe and I felt privileged to have married into such a colourful family. In 1637, William Nickerson, a streetwise Freeman of the City of Norwich and brave worsted-weaver, sailed for Salem, Massachusetts, together with his wife Anne Busby, her parents and their four children. No doubt they yearned for a better life, their own land and an improvement in living standards. As it happened, like others, they had fallen out with Bishop Wren of Norwich. Unusually though, all the Nickersons and William's in-laws survived the Atlantic crossing and another five children born in the colonies grew to adulthood, married and the family multiplied. Considering their situation and the time in which they lived, this family was exceptional in being so healthy and having such strong immunity. In 1641, a complaint by the Church was lodged against William when they said that he was 'a scoffer and jeerer of religion', but no reason is known for this accusation. Buying land from the Monomy Indians, thanks to a friendship with Chief Mattaquason, but without the consent of the Pilgrim authorities, landed William in hot water once again. Perseverance prevailed, however, and William went on to set up the Nickersons in farming and other trades, founding the town of Chatham in Massachusetts. Much evidence of the family can be seen on Cape Cod, including a museum and the 'Nickerson House', and many Nickersons still remain in New England.

Over the decades, William and Anne's descendants have increased exponentially and today, almost every state in the Union boasts someone genetically related to them.

When Cindy learned about William's stubborn libertarian streak and thought back to the line of her strong-willed, entrepreneurial relations, the pieces of her particular puzzle fell into place.

I had not been in the habit of booking extensive holidays so, after ten days, it was time for me to return to England. I did, however, take the opportunity offered by Louise Noyes, an old school chum of Cindy's, to stay overnight with her and her husband, Jock, at their home near New York, so that I could do a little sightseeing. With some regret, I said goodbye to the family in Wellesley and caught a fast train to Grand Central Station, where I was greeted by Jock, a city financier whom I had not met before. He quickly explained that the afternoon would be spent at a barbecue in New Jersey. Settling down in the car, his next words were, 'I'm on thirty thousand, what are you on?'

Soon, I found myself among a crowd of Wall Street businessmen, together with their wives and children, enjoying a hot Sunday afternoon. It was four o'clock and the martinis were flowing; T-bone steaks and hamburgers sizzled on the grill and a large table groaned under dishes piled high with chicken wings, cold ham, corn on the cob, sweet potatoes wrapped in silver foil, and salads. To one side, there was a further display that included tasty apple and cherry pies, along with bowls of freshly whipped cream.

Jock and Louise introduced me to their friends and colleagues, and I soon realised that I was something of a novelty.

'Keep talking, we love your accent!' How many times did I hear that?

The next morning, Louise and I took a train on the Hoboken railway into the Big Apple. The carriages were full of city workers who read their newspapers folded vertically, instead of horizontally as we do in the UK, and I tried to think of a pun about being 'divided by a common language', but it didn't seem to work. On arrival in the city we left my luggage at the Yale Club, and set out on a sightseeing spree.

New York was buzzing and like millions of visitors before and since, I was overawed by the skyscrapers that panned to east and west along an interlocking network of numbered streets where, for the most part, the sun's rays rarely or briefly penetrated. As we made our way towards the shoreline at Manhattan, I soon realised what people meant when they spoke of the energising effect of the metropolis. Standing in the shadow of the recently completed World Trade Center, it was thrilling to be at the heart of the capitalist world. Certainly, as our ferry drew out into the Hudson, making its way to Ellis Island and the Statue of Liberty, one could understand the draw of America for 'huddled masses yearning to breathe free'.

We lunched in Wall Street with Jock, but it was soon time to leave. Collecting my things from the club and bidding Louise farewell, I headed to Kennedy Airport for my flight to London. It would be four years before another opportunity came along to further explore New York, and almost thirty years before Cindy, Alexander and I found ourselves booked in for a few nights at the Yale Club.

Impressions flooded my brain during the homeward journey. The United States was an extraordinary country and its people hugely generous. Spacious, thriving, driving—perhaps driven—modern and expansive yet, in some ways, curiously old-fashioned. This was brought home to me by the way older people were treated and there seemed to be an increasingly dangerous divide between 'college kids', or 'college bums', as Nixon famously called them in 1970, and the old folk. I had initially been expected to address my in-laws in a formal manner because none of Cindy's chums, who had known her parents all their lives, would have dreamed of calling them anything but Mr and Mrs Briggs. Another instance of an almost quaint attitude was when I was pulled up on a Cape Cod beach by a lifeguard for being indelicately attired. I was wearing standard European bathing trunks, but was expected to appear at the seaside in long shorts that came down to the knees.

American business methods might be slick, but in many of the shops there was still an old-world charm. In Wellesley, a man was employed to help carry customers' purchases out to the car, a practice I had not observed in England for years and was not to see again until our sojourn in Istanbul in 1992. The adaptation of technology was also a maze of idiosyncrasies. The people who had put man on the moon drove around in huge, gas-guzzling automobiles that lumbered down the highways at fifty miles an hour and, those who worked in glitzy new supermarkets during the day and were entertained by the latest movie technology in the city's numerous cinemas in the evenings, returned to homes where the electrical, plumbing and telephone systems were still in the dark ages (no pun intended). The streets of New York and elsewhere were festooned with wires and cables and bulky junction-boxes dangled precariously from tall buildings. The country where peace, freedom and liberty were deeply cherished, and yet so many had access to a gun, struck me as a land of profound contradictions.

Squeezing back into our little house, with two boys still under the age of five, was a shock after enjoying the wide open spaces of America. We hankered after a larger property and, within weeks of our return, on the day that Richard Nixon resigned from the presidency following the Watergate scandal, we put the house on the market. Despite the fact that the garden had recently been professionally renovated by our old friend Bob Gates, it took a whole year to sell, but we eventually found a pleasant house behind Castelnau, in Madrid Road. It even had a small garden that sported wild rhubarb. Across the road lived the Watkins family and it would not be long before I was surprised to see a familiar figure walking up the garden path.

'I know that man.' I said to Lucinda, when we happened to be looking out of the first floor window.

It was none other than the aged proprietor—known to the family as 'Watty'—of Watkin's Bookshop in Cecil Court, which specialised in esoteric subjects and where I had purchased so many volumes. His son, wife and grandson Tristan lived in the house and Tristan would become a good friend to our children, as would his brother Alastair when he was a little older. By chance, the scholarly Dr Ensor Holiday and his wife, who were old friends of ours, lived next door. She was the daughter of Sir John Rothenstein (the longest-serving director of the Tate Gallery) and one of Ensor's notable achievements was to have invented Altair Design: pads of printed mathematical patterns, based on a fundamental formula discovered by Arabs in the tenth century. These were available from bookshops and specifically designed for children who were encouraged to colour in the patterns. Altair Design became very popular and gave huge numbers of people, of all ages, scope to exercise their imagination, sometimes with mind-boggling results.

My shop had been trading for three years, which meant I now had two sources of income. It was establishing a reputation over a wide area, spread by word of mouth and because I could afford to advertise in some of the smartest magazines. Peacock was increasingly recommended as a source of materials in articles designed to help readers with their interior decoration requirements, and these subscribers eventually found their way down to Barnes. Anna, the manageress, was doing well and I now had two part-time staff, both sophisticated in design matters.

We felt quite settled living in Barnes and saw ourselves remaining there and raising our family, at least for the foreseeable future. During the latter part of the 1970s, the older working-class residents were either dying or moving out and I was shocked when a lady of our acquaintance, when she heard that we had moved to Madrid Road, said, 'Much better; how did you stand living with all those dustmen and riff raff?'[14]

As properties were bought up and renovated, Peacock played a part in the change and profited from it, but we had rather liked the mixed community and were sorry to see Barnes becoming a sanitised middle-class neighbourhood. It was all part of the process of much wealthier foreigners, particularly Arabs, infiltrating central London, forcing the indigenous population out to the suburbs. The picture restorer Reggie Hoare, with whom I shared common ancestors, was an example. He and his family had moved from a huge house with a private drive in Holland Park to a less grand property in Barnes. I am sure he was able to cope with the adjustment, since he had been a fighter pilot in the Second World War. After being shot down, he was incarcerated in Stalag Luft III and took part in preparations for the Great Escape. Bitterly disappointed when he was not drawn to go down the tunnel, it was a quirk of fate that probably saved his life, as so many of his fellow prisoners were captured and executed in cold blood.

There was also an influx of film, television and theatrical people into the south-west suburbs, many of whom were to become my customers. I have already mentioned some familiar names but others included Julian Glover, Polly James and Nerys Hughes (*The Liver Birds*), Jocelyn Dimbleby, Ninette de Valois, Annette Crosbie, Terence Alexander, Edward de Souza, Alan Price, Clive Dunn, Sir Jeremy Child, John Pertwee and William Franklyn (who famously advertised Schweppes on television for many years: 'Schh! You know who!'). Across the river at Strand on the Green, lived the upwardly-mobile young heart-throb, Trevor Eve, who was making a name for himself in the television series *Shoestring* and who turned the legs of the girls in my shop to jelly whenever he came in search of furnishings for his new house. Donald Pleasance, who played the part of a blind escapee in *The Great Escape*, for whom we did some work, also lived in Chiswick, as did Richard Briers who once turned up with a curtain whose hem had been seriously molested by a mouse.

'Do you have anyone who can repair it?' he enquired sadly.

The annual Oxford and Cambridge boat race, which finished just up the river at Mortlake, was a colourful occasion that I turned to commercial advantage. On the day of the race we closed to normal business, and piled remnants and old fabric samples on trestle tables, both inside the shop and on the pavement at the front of Peacock. As the hordes descended, en route for the tow path or the White Hart, which is one of London's few riverside pubs, discerning punters often picked up some pretty attractive bargains, swelling our coffers and adding value to our good will. When the helicopter carrying the television cameras reached Barnes Bridge, it was a signal for us to pop across the road and watch the exhausted rowers pass by. In the spring of 1978, Tarquin and I were standing right opposite the spot where the Cambridge boat came to grief.

'Dad! Dad!' cried eight-year-old Tarquin, clutching my hand. 'Dad! They're sinking!'

And sink they did, much to our horror. Two years later, we watched Cambridge lose the race again, unaware that one of the oarsmen, Hugh Laurie, would become a famous actor and that our son, Alexander, would work with him in Hollywood for six years during the first decade of the twenty-first century.

I associate the White Hart with another notable occasion in 1992. While enjoying a pint on the balcony overlooking the river with my talented, Argentinian designer friend, Jorge Centofanti, news of the invasion of the Falkland Islands reached us. We learned that Parliament was to sit on a Saturday for the first time in many years, but viewed the matter as a trivial incident that would soon be sorted out by the politicians.

'What are you Argies up to?' I teased.

Poor Jorge; it particularly irked him if I referred to his country of birth as 'the Argentine'.

In the end, a task force was sent to the islands to oust the invaders, and bloody conflict continued until mid-June. Television reports became compulsive viewing with Max Hastings, the first journalist to enter liberated Port Stanley, making a name for himself. When the British task force recaptured South Georgia, Mrs Thatcher broke the news to the media with the words,

'Just rejoice at that,' but it was a close-run thing, and the names of Bluff Cove, Goose Green, Fitzroy, Colonel 'H' Jones VC and the bravest of the brave, Welsh Guardsman Simon Weston, who survived 49% burns when his ship *Sir Galahad* was destroyed by enemy fire, passed into the annals of British history.

Later each year, the local UNICEF branch organised a cricket match between 'the stars', who were composed of actors and media people, and Barnes Cricket Club. Cindy, an American, was on the committee, which included an eclectic group of individuals. The actor Edward de Souza, the cheerful chairman, whose wife presented *Blue Peter* on BBC television, was of Portuguese, Indian and English extraction and there was an Italian aristocrat, married to a university professor, an Irish lady and Mrs Rigg, who had spent many years in India and was the mother of Diana (widely known at the time as Mrs Peel in ITV's *The Avengers*). This is not to mention a few English people, one of whom was the local bank manager. Was this a typical circle to be found in a suburban house? It most probably was.

We had bought our house from Greeks and there were French, Germans, more Americans and Nigerians living in our road. There were also a number of Swedes in the immediate neighbourhood, following the founding of the Swedish School in Lonsdale Road. It was close to St Paul's, the famous public school, which had moved to Barnes from Hammersmith in 1968.

The cricket match made a fun day and was held on the local playing fields known as Barn Elms. The venue was of particular interest to me as it had been the home of members of the Hoare family. Sir Richard Hoare, my umpteen-times-great-grandfather, lived there when he was Lord Mayor of London, at the time of the Jacobite Rising in 1745. Subsequently, the manor house was taken over by the fashionable Ranelagh Club where my grandfather, Bunny Mathew-Lannowe, ran the polo after the Great War.

One of the prime attractions at the match was Diana Rigg herself. Decked out in hot pants and tight sweater, she was invariably asked to bowl the first ball. Taking an eye-catching and excessively long approach, her fabulous long legs thundered towards the crease, speeding up, with her arms raised to deliver as she reached the wicket. Most assuredly, the blood pressure of male observers rose in equal measure at the same time.

I was invariably assigned the task of running the crêpe stall, ably assisted by Tarquin and little Alexander. One year, after the match, we attended a good party in Barnes High Street. At the end of the do, on our way out, a young man mentioned, rather sheepishly, that he did not have the fare to get home.

'You can always sell your shirt!' I chortled, so that's exactly what he did.

He stripped off; I parted with five pounds, and a nice blue silk shirt was mine.

I was happy, he was happy, but he was not The Happiest Man in the World. To discover who earned that title you will have to continue with this saga!

Other notable members of the community were Sir John and Lady Pilcher, our immediate neighbours on the corner of White Hart Lane. They had recently returned from Japan where he had served as British Ambassador, following two years in Vienna, and was now retired from the service. While Sir John was a small man, Lady Pilcher was huge and towered above him. They cut a striking picture when observed trudging along from the bus stop following a shopping expedition to the West End. He would lead, eager to get home, bowler hat firmly in place, rolled umbrella in one hand and Harrods bag in the other, while she glided behind, burdened by packages, like a stately galleon under full sail. They were always happy to drop in for a chat, and honoured us with their presence at Christmas gatherings and other special occasions such as the evening film shows we arranged, depicting various aspects of design and production in the furnishing business. Sir John was at his most amiable at parties and welcomed any opportunity to provide an imitation of peacocks screeching in the imperial gardens in Tokyo. He was in a more serious frame of mind on the day that I met him returning from lunch at Buckingham Palace. He had been advising the Royal Family in respect of Prince Charles's imminent visit to Japan. It might have coincided with one of the times that Peacock Decorators were painting the outside of the Chilean Ambassador's residence in Eaton Place. One day at noon all work had to stop, as the Santa Cruz family was entertaining the Prince to lunch. Lucia Santa Cruz was reputed to be his first lover. Cradles were raised, ladders lowered and the men took off to the Nag's Head in Kinnerton Street, one of London's smallest pubs.

We undertook a lot of work for the Chileans over the years, both at the residence and the Embassy in Devonshire Street. Sometimes there was uncertainty with regard to who was in charge, as the country was prone to regular regime change, although I dealt with a delightful lady named Miss Schweppe.

Of those who gave Peacock business, there were few more memorable than Howard Strowman. With long straggly black hair, a pronounced nose and a broad Cockney accent, he bore all the characteristics of a Jew born and bred in the East End. Howard had clearly made a fortune, and when he was not drawing up in the Rolls he was parking his state-of-the-art BMW motorbike. That is, if he was not driving his bright orange VW van which was fitted out with a radio telephone—a remarkable innovation for the time. The way he made money, he explained, was to drive the van up to the north of England, starting at dawn, and then load up with second-hand photographic equipment, mostly bankrupt stock. On the way home he would use the radio to place his acquisitions, and it was a bad day if he netted less than ten thousand pounds. As he became richer he moved to grander houses and fortunately bought materials and furnishings from Peacock. One day when I went to his house, near Marlow, to collect a cheque, I learned an important lesson. Flamboyant entrepreneur he may have been, but every single transaction was recorded in detail and every cheque photocopied and filed. He was a businessman who exercised total control over his financial activities, so it is not surprising that I have seen his name on lists of the richest individuals in the country. However, my staff and I felt that there was one thing missing.

'He seems a bit lonely,' we would confide to each other when he had left the shop, and were pleased when the news broke that he had married. One morning, looking ghastly, his complexion drained and his long, black, windswept locks more frenzied than ever, he turned up at the shop. He explained that he had been up all night for the birth of his son.

'You'll have to put him down for Eton,' I teased as he was leaving.

'On my "to do" list,' he scoffed as he jumped on the BMW and shot off down the street, narrowly missing a number nine bus.

One day in 1975, a smartly dressed woman appeared in the shop and started rummaging through patterns and samples. After a while she introduced herself as Helen Pilkington and explained that she had come over from Eton, where her husband was Conduct; the college's head of spiritual matters. He had recently been appointed headmaster of the King's School, Canterbury and, once extensive refurbishment was complete, they would be moving into the official residence. Over the next few weeks she was always popping in, discussing colour schemes with Anna and collecting samples. They got on well and as soon as the Pilkingtons had arrived in Kent, Donald and I went down to take measurements and discuss the work on site. Little expense was to be spared, which meant that it would be not only an interesting, but also a very profitable, contract.

As we moved around the house we eventually reached the study where Canon Pilkington was working. We knocked and as we entered I found that I was shaking like a leaf from head to toe. Desperately seeking an explanation, I realised that this was the first headmaster's study I had entered since my troubled days at Marlborough, twelve years previously. I was clearly having some sort of nervous reaction but with huge effort, hoping that no one had noticed, I managed to compose myself. A few minutes later the headmaster rushed out of the house, muttering under his breath, 'The only trouble with this job is the boys!' I would hear similar words again at Repton School, some years later, in a different context.

After a month, and once all the curtains and loose covers had been made, Donald went down to King's to complete the installation of tracks and to hang and dress the curtains. I took a train from Charing Cross to coincide with the completion of the work, to give him a hand and to check that everything was in order. It was while we were having a cup of tea that I got chatting with the housekeeper. Pointing through the kitchen window to the cathedral, a short distance away across the green, I commented that it must be nice to work so near such a glorious and historic building and that she must know it well.

'Never been in there,' was her reply.

Not believing my ears, I questioned her. 'Are you saying that you have never been inside the cathedral? How long have you known Canterbury?'

'Born and bred, forty years,' she replied.

'Forty years and you've not entered those doors? Why on earth not?' I reiterated, trying not to sound rude.

'Never felt the need,' was her last word as she left the room, shrugging her shoulders. I turned this conversation over and over in my mind all the way home and could only come to one conclusion. It appeared that the housekeeper had developed some kind of fixation that led her to believe that something dreadful would happen; she would die or the world would come to an end if she ever entered those hallowed portals. I found it extraordinary.

In early 1976, I appointed a new manager, as Anna had moved on to other things. Esther Stebbings, my new manager, was energetic, enthusiastic and diligent. She was to prove to be an excellent choice and my confidence in her remained unabated for years to come.

At about that time, Cindy and I were invited to dinner by my old chum Count Tassilo Wolff-Metternich and his wife Cecilia. I had been an usher at their wedding at St Patrick's Church in Soho Square in 1968 and they had been to ours the following year. The Metternich wedding reception was a very special occasion, partly because it was held in the British Museum where Cecilia's father, Basil Gray, was Keeper of Oriental Antiquities and Acting Director. It was also uncomfortably memorable for some guests in respect of the smoking ban that applied to the premises. The museum's grand reception halls were in marked contrast to the distinctly bohemian, messy bedsit in Hampstead's Fellows Road where I had visited Tassilo on the night before his marriage. The ramshackle tenement building was owned by an eccentric called Henry who lived in the basement and bred handsome bloodhounds whose sole, lucrative purpose in life was to appear with Clement Freud in television advertisements for dog food.

We had continued to keep in touch with Tassilo and Cecilia and enjoyed visiting the large house in Putney, which had a garden that ran down to the river. Tassilo was immensely rich, eventually becoming a tax exile in Guernsey and, besides administering family interests that included a vineyard in the Rhineland, I never knew him to have a job. His father had been killed on the Russian front during the Second World War and Tassilo was educated at Gordonstoun, which he had loathed. For many years he was one of the most eligible bachelors in England, although he could justifiably have been described as a hippy before hippies were invented. With long hair, centrally parted, exhibiting the broadest of foreheads, he roamed around barefoot in whipcord slacks, occasionally deigning to put on a pair of sandals if he was going into town. However, he was far from being a dilettante, and excelled at all sorts of pursuits. An accomplished painter, he had studied at the Byam Shaw School of Art, and was a brilliant photographer, a collector of oriental antiques, especially embroidered Suzanis, and a devotee of any kind of technology relating to film or sound. Besides these interests, he was capable of sailing a sizable yacht, single-handed, across the Atlantic. Essentially a loner, we sometimes felt sorry for his wife, a fine photographer in her own right, whose sister had married Oleg Prokofiev, the composer's son. Tassilo always referred to Cecilia as 'Seagray' because Miss C. Gray was the name by which he first knew her when he studied the attendant's list at the start of a 'culture tour' of Persia, arranged by Sothebys.

He could also be boorish and was once heard to say, at the breakfast table, 'Seagray, life would be infinitely more agreeable if only the toast were pressed!'

Sadly, they eventually parted and Tassilo died—far too young—at the age of sixty-one, on 24th July 2002. He was buried at sea and on the appointed day, bearing his coffin draped in a favourite Suzani and with the Metternich coat of arms emblazoned on a flag flying from one of two masts, a fifty-foot schooner drew out into deep water, away from the shipping lanes, off the coast of Alderney. Before and after the committal, dolphins and four pilot whales were seen circling near the vessel and the other boats that made up the burial party. A few days later we received a message that concluded with these words:

'The combination of whales and dolphins is quite unheard of and Tassilo had both! It all seems so unreal—I can't quite believe it really happened. Lots of love, Cecilia.'

The other guests at that dinner party in 1976, where Tassilo effervesced cordiality and excelled as *mein host* while he served wine from his own vineyard, were an unlikely couple, and meeting them was to precipitate an important change in my business activities. Mogador Empson was the son of the poet William Empson and his South African wife Hetta. The poet named both his sons, as he said, 'each had to have an English name, an Afrikaans name and the name of a town captured by the allies on the day he was born.' Mogador's brother's name was Calais.

Catarina, Mogador's girlfriend, enjoyed high-level connections in the interior design world in Sweden and this was of interest to me within the context of expanding trade at Peacock. By 1976, small retail decorating shops similar to Peacock had sprung up all over the country. To expand and secure a competitive edge over these other retailers, it would be a natural progression for us to either design, print and distribute an exclusive range of wallpapers and fabrics ourselves, or to obtain an agency from a foreign manufacturer with exclusive rights to distribute in the UK. The latter course would be less risky and require less capital.

Mogador and Catarina, as it turned out, were agents for DURO, a Swedish wallpaper company, and they had recently granted distribution rights for a range of designs to Osborne & Little and also a further range to a new company trading under the name Paper Moon. I knew that both those lines were selling well and I pricked up my ears. At the end of the evening, we exchanged telephone numbers and a few days later I called Mogador. He confirmed that DURO had many more design ranges that could be imported and invited me to make a trip to the factory at Gävle, in Sweden, to see if there were any products that would suit us.

The Swedish Chamber of Commerce had vacancies on a subsidised flight in February, so Cindy and I took the opportunity offered. We flew to Stockholm, which was in the grip of winter. Perhaps the word 'vice' would be more appropriate since neither of us had experienced such biting cold since we had been children in Massachusetts and Schleswig-Holstein, respectively. The next morning we rushed over to NK, the famous store, to buy ourselves warm woolly hats. A fast train then took us some hundred miles up the coast towards the Arctic Circle, where we had reservations at the Baltic Hotel in Gävle. When I awoke the next morning and peered out of the window, it was dark and the only sign of life was dimly-lit trams swishing through slushy streets. It looked a grim place to me. Who would want to live there? I thought. After a breakfast of cheese, ham, cold herring and coffee we were collected by Nille Kjestensson, the managing director of DURO. He was tall, cheerful, welcoming and the best thing that had happened to us since we arrived in that depressing town. It was only a few minutes before we were parked outside his factory. To my surprise, he then took a lead from beneath the bonnet of his state-of-the-art BMW and, his feet crunching in virgin snow, plugged it into the factory's electrical system. He explained that a device in the engine, now activated, would keep the motor from freezing.

A tour of the spotlessly clean factory gave us the chance to admire all sorts of bright and colourful designs which were in marked contrast to the gloomy streets outside where the sun never appeared for months on end. These designs were of the kind people associate with modern Swedish décor, including those I had already seen selling through Osborne & Little and Paper Moon. However, we found a range of wallpapers that was entirely different. They were reproductions of hand-printed designs taken from old Scandinavian houses and we thought they would suit our image very well.

Transported into the world of Ibsen and Strindberg, we particularly liked a paper based on primitive botanical drawings of dandelions, with long green stems and soft yellow flowers, and also admired a clover design that came in pinks, greens and blues. That evening we were invited to the Kjestenssons' modern apartment, where we enjoyed an excellent dinner cooked by Nille's wife, Gugge. As we sipped schnapps in their warm dining room where the walls were papered in the very dandelion design we had admired earlier in the day, we stared out through large picture windows, over a bleak white landscape to dark fir trees that surrounded the property.

With regard to the business in hand, agreement was soon reached—confirmed by telephone with Mogador—that Peacock should be granted exclusive rights to distribute the old Scandinavian designs in the UK. This was exciting news and we raised our glasses to toast the new venture! The next day we returned to Stockholm, passing through the university town of Uppsala,..and were greeted at the station by my old friend and business partner Leon Flamholc who to our surprise had married Eva, an attractive Swedish girl. What had happened to Danielle? We did not like to ask.

Leon's parents, Salic and Rosa, had invited us to stay the night and were extremely hospitable, providing red Russian caviar and pink champagne to accompany a magical meal. A lot of water had passed under the proverbial bridge since they met in the wartime concentration camp in Kyrgyzstan and it was only later that we realised just how kind they had been, having given up their own bed for us while they slept on sofas in the living room. Well into their nineties, they died in 2013.

May they rest in peace.

The next day, a bitterly cold but bright Sunday, we were treated to a sightseeing tour and as we enjoyed *smorgasbord* at the top of the *Kaknästornet* (television tower), we followed the antics of energetic skiers and colourfully clad families with toboggans in the park, far below. As darkness fell, Leon dropped us off at Arlanda Airport, and we returned to London.

My next task was to prepare for the arrival of hundreds of rolls of wallpaper and several dozen pattern books. After ten years' experience in the building trade and four years in retailing, I was now going to learn about wholesaling and the art of stock control. Every roll of paper represented potential profit. Rolls sold in my own shop provided extra revenue as there was no need to provide a third-party discount. Some patterns were going to move faster than others and some not at all; the latter represented dead money and the skill was to keep the stock moving without incurring additional transport charges from DURO. Fortunately, we had recently taken over the shop next door, doubling our frontage onto the street and providing additional storage space. There was no excuse to be disorganised.

I needed special containers for packaging rolls of an attractive art-deco frieze that formed part of the new collection, and my search for a cardboard-box manufacturer led me to Whitechapel. The firm that produced what I was looking for was run by a Jewish family, and as the young proprietor was completing the paperwork I quizzed him about his business. He explained how he ran sales and his brother dealt with manufacturing, and that the business had been started by their father shortly after arriving in this country from Poland in 1946.

'And how about your father?' I asked. 'What does he do now?'

'Oh, he is on the other side,' came the reply.

'Accounts?' I queried.

'No, no,' he reiterated. 'On the OTHER side ... we buried him in Willesden last summer.'

I much admired Jewish business acumen which I had, of course, experienced directly when in partnership with Leon and I particularly enjoyed Stephen Aris's book, *The Jews in Business* (Jonathan Cape), when it was published in 1970. Years later I was to read *Rothschild: A Story of Wealth and Power* by Derek Wilson (Andre Deutsch), which also fascinated me. This was especially true, because by that time, I was involved with a company founded by Lord Jacob Rothschild. This weighty volume charts the fortunes of the Rothschild family from the sixteenth century when they lived in *Judengasse*, the Jewish ghetto in Frankfurt. Their house was identified by a *rot schild* (red shield) above the door.

One day I was talking to JW, a particularly successful Jewish businessman, in the panelled boardroom at his headquarters in Berkeley Square. Soft wall lights were reflected on the polished, cherry wood conference table which dominated the scene and which was surrounded by plush leather-backed chairs. A good portrait of my customer's father, in his rabbinical robes and *yarmulke*, framed in chunky gold, hung at the far end of the room. JW and I, were discussing some business when, without warning, he kicked off his shoes, shed jacket and tie, unbuckled his belt, dropped his suit trousers and slipped into some blue jeans and trainers he retrieved from a corner cupboard. Then, slinging a canvas bag over his shoulders, he made for the door.

'Must go. Plane to catch,' he muttered.
'Important meeting in Jo'burg first thing tomorrow.'
I thought that was real cool.

The summer of 1976 was one of the hottest in living memory. The heatwave started on 23rd June, just days after the England v. West Indies test match at Lords had been rained off. At least it did not snow as it had on 2nd June of the previous year. London basked in burning sunshine for months, and people said that the parks would never recover—which of course they did, quite rapidly, when rain eventually fell.

By good fortune, we had planned a holiday under canvas in Brittany where an American friend owned a property. The small estate—Le Cosquer—we were warned, consisted of a collection of tumbledown farm buildings and a few acres of land. There was a well and an earth box but no other facilities. We drove from London and took the ferry at Newhaven, accompanied by Louise, a young girl whom we had employed to help with the children. After camping for one night on the way, we arrived in darkness but could not for the life of us find Le Cosquer, even after driving around in circles for several hours. Everyone we asked seemed to point us in a different direction and, becoming increasingly tired, hungry, exasperated and very bad-tempered, we eventually decided to sleep in our little Renault 5, although Cindy preferred the grass verge. Waking at six in the morning, we found ourselves parked close to a driveway entrance. A rough sign slung between granite posts read 'Le Cosquer'. Within minutes we had covered the last hundred yards and were greeting our friends and various cousins.

This was to be a real family holiday. Our friend Jack MacDougal, a huge American from a Boston suburb with giveaway Irish white hair had known Cindy and her sisters back in Wellesley. He had worked his way through Harvard and now ran a very successful English language school in Paris. He was married to Suzie, a beautiful auburn-haired Argentinian, and had three children from a previous marriage. These children, Leo, Catherine and Johnny, were soon showing us where to pitch our tents and introducing us to the sparse facilities. Other kids at Le Cosquer were Cindy's half-French nephew and niece, Edouard and Alexandra Lecomte, another niece, Catherine, from San Francisco and Simon, Jack's nephew from Boston. In all, there were nine children and nine grown-ups, including Jack's brother, sister and sister-in-law and Edouard and Alexandra's father Rémi. With such a vibrant group, of which I was the only Englishman, wonderful weather, splendid surroundings and fresh meat, fish and vegetables obtained from local markets daily, it could have hardly failed to be the terrific holiday it became. We swam in the Atlantic, visited the causeway at Carnac and the nearby towns of Auray and Vannes, played endless games of baseball and sat every night, after the barbeque, under an azure sky as the fire's embers faded and shooting stars streaked across the heavens. On Thursday nights we told the story of Mushkil Gusha.

Our ten days passed quickly and it was soon time to pack up and make for home. On the last day we were highly amused, when little Louise, who had earned the sobriquet 'Louise the Breeze', strung a length of string from her tent to the nearest tree and solemnly pegged ten pairs of multi coloured panties to her makeshift line, one for each day of the holiday! Nor was Louise spared some leg-pulling. On the last night, Rémi, thanked her for her efforts when sailing the dinghy. 'She was ze bes' crew I 'av ever 'ad,' he solemnly pronounced.

We liked Rémi, who sadly died too young in 1997. He had visited us in Barnes in 1975 at the time of the Common Market referendum. Asked for his opinion he said, 'If you join the Common Market you will all work twice as hard for a great deal less money.' How right he was.

On the way home we took the new bridge across the Seine at Caudebec and stopped at St Wandrille. This was the Benedictine monastery where John Henry and I had stayed eleven years previously. We spent an hour or so looking around and bought wonderful honey, as I had done before. I watched the monks tilling the earth where they were growing vegetables on one of the terraces, and could not help reflecting on just how much had happened since that first visit when I was still a schoolboy. Now I had a family, a house, even a ginger cat and a canary, and business interests in London with an annual turnover approaching £200,000. The very thought brought me back with a jolt. There would be much to do on my return.

However, one sweltering evening before I returned to work, my parents took Cindy and me to see *1776*, the Broadway musical, at the Albery Theatre in London's West End. From what I recall, it was a light-hearted entertainment that we much enjoyed but my chief reason for remembering the occasion was because we spotted Jack Mayer sitting right behind us in the audience. He was an old friend of Cindy's from her days in Paris and another of the plethora of extraordinary characters that I want to record. Jack, an American from Memphis, Tennessee, had volunteered to serve with Bomber Command during the Second World War and was reputed to be related to the legendary Auntie Mame. Short, rotund and bald—a Carlo Ponti lookalike—and a chain smoker, he exuded mesmeric charisma. I only met him a few times, but he was not the sort of person one would forget, and he was particularly knowledgeable about art. He spoke fluent French, had once run a gallery in Paris and held a responsible and politically sensitive job commissioning the annual Christmas card range for UNICEF. This was a task that took him all over the world, so it was a nice surprise to bump into him. My mother, always wary of an equally strong-willed character, invariably referred to him as the 'Christmas card man'. More of Jack later.

Holidays provided an opportunity to take stock. In fact, I used to dread the return of my employees from an extended break as this was often the moment when they asked for a rise, gave notice or raised other matters relating to pay and conditions. It made me feel insecure and I sometimes overpaid in return for a quiet life. When I got back from France the shop was trading well, the distribution of wallpapers to other retailers was picking up nicely and Peacock Decorators was plodding along like the ponderous beast it had become. One of the problems was that the best men, the ambitious ones with families like Eddie, Allan and Attila, had left to set up in business on their own. This was partly because they could not stomach the recently imposed PAYE deductions. I was left with the rump of my splendid team, a herd of mules who were skilled enough but were more interested in what happened after work and at weekends than achieving targets. Another problem was increased traffic so that operating in the centre of London was becoming tortuous, and events like the IRA's siege at Balcombe Street, which lasted for six days, and the Black Liberation Front's siege of the Knightsbridge Spaghetti House in 1975, added to a sense of unease.

Urban terrorism was becoming an established part of modern life and my godfather Major General Richard Clutterbuck had published his books *Protest and the Urban Guerilla* in 1973 and *Living with Terrorism* in 1975. These were followed by other works, including *Guerillas and Terrorism*, which appeared in 1977. Following a spectacular military career in which he served as a sapper in Germany and Italy in the Second World War and in Palestine and the Far East after the war, he took a PhD in politics on retirement in 1972. This immediately led to his appointment as a lecturer in political conflict at Exeter University, where he established himself as a world authority in his field. Following his death in 1998 at the age of eighty, Paul Wilkinson wrote in the *Guardian*:

> As if these achievements were not enough for one lifetime, he also helped to pioneer the development of the Control Risks Information Service, briefing business and industry on political violence around the world. The success of this work can be gauged by the number of security companies and businesses which depend on the methods of security analysis and briefing that he developed. Richard was that rare combination; an intellectual former soldier who made a major contribution to a fresh field of academic study and succeeded in the wider work of public education through his books and contribution to the media.

He died before 9/11, and I would dearly loved to have discussed that pivotal event with him, because he was certainly aware of the creeping effect of urban terrorism on my Baby Boomer generation. Urban surveillance, airport events' security which cause delays for citizens going about their business, data protection, the ramped-up protection levels required to shield the Royal Family and other high-profile individuals are some effects of this insidious development. 9/11, of course, took violent urban incidents to a new level, triggering off wars on an international scale, the results of which we still live with. On a personal note, I wish I had known him better as he only paid the rarest of visits to our flat in London. He had been deeply saddened when my mother's fiancé, Richard Carey, was killed in Italy while under his command. My mother must have written to him on the subject as late as 1993, because this is how he replied.

> Yes, perhaps he might have been a great poet rather than a general— or, like Wavell, both. But, of course his life was not wasted. Apart from leading the advance of the army, he inspired all the rest of us

and he will have influenced the lives of the soldiers in his troop as he has forever influenced yours and mine. Does any other face ever come into my mind during the silence on Remembrance Day?

    With much love

    The other Richard

Curious. But for a twist of fate, I might never have been—but I guess that is always the case.

As it happened, in the autumn of 1976, I landed the biggest painting contract we had ever secured. It was a huge job for a major institution in north London—I'll call it X—and estimating had been made easier when my contact at the premises in question had dropped a heavy hint as to the price he was prepared to pay. It would provide work for months and I expected it to be very profitable. On the back of this opportunity, I decided to give Peacock Decorators a last chance to expand. After all, my business activities were much more broadly based than when I had addressed the problem of business development in 1971, so I felt that I was in a position to take the risk of trying to find someone I could trust who would act as my second-in-command.

The offices in Queensway were therefore closed and we took larger premises in Putney while I advertised for a manager with wide experience in the building trade. It did not take long before Bruce, a short, fiery, red-faced son of a Glaswegian policeman, with greasy hair, turned up. A qualified building surveyor, he seemed to be just what I was looking for. I hired him immediately, bought him a second-hand Alpha Romeo and within days the firm was buzzing. As works manager, he expected to be able to crack the whip, tell workmen exactly who was in charge—and in his fierce brogue—call a spade a spade. This was fine with the recruits he employed for new work, but I soon became scared that he would upset the established staff, who were conditioned to a gentler regime and whose work at X was underpinning the whole 'kick-start' operation. What if they all walked out?

I went to talk to Aubrey, who shared my concerns.

'Will you be able to control Bruce?' he asked.

I decided to keep him away from my employees at X, but gave him a free hand elsewhere and for a time it seemed to be working, so I took the opportunity to take my contact at X out to lunch. I will call him Dick. Business lunches have never appealed to me, and the outcome of this one would certainly not encourage me to reverse the habit of a lifetime. C.J. (the ebullient character created by D.G. Nobbs in *The Fall and Rise of Reginald Perrin*) would say, I'm sure:

'Mrs C.J. and I didn't get where we are today by taking people to lunch!'

However, in this case I felt that it was expected. It was a way of saying thank you for a huge piece of business, and perhaps for more to come. During lunch at a smart hotel, Dick told me more about his job and I talked about my business. Towards the end of the meal, as we sipped coffee and brandy, he leaned over and gently but deliberately told me that he had authority to sanction any cheque below one hundred pounds without referring higher.

'Right; you have a responsible job,' I said, not sure what he was getting at.

'I do,' he replied, continuing, 'Now; say you invoiced the department, from time to time, for ninety pounds for paint or such like, I could draw a cheque in your favour—no questions asked.'

For a few seconds neither of us spoke as the implications of what he was suggesting sank in.

'We could then—' I made signs with my hands indicating that we would split the proceeds. He nodded.

'Hmm, an interesting proposition; yes … I'll give that some thought,' I murmured, trying to catch the waiter's eye and desperately hoping that the bill would arrive. As soon as the meal was finished, we walked back to the building where my men were hard at work and I thanked him for his suggestion, promising to respond soon. He applauded me for lunch, we shook hands and parted. Of course, I had no intention of getting involved in Dick's crooked plan, but what should I do? Nothing irregular had actually occurred, and if I reported our conversation it would be his word against mine and I would have made an enemy. The painting contract had barely begun and he could make a lot of trouble. I decided to do nothing, except to avoid Dick as much as possible and in the end, at least from my point of view that turned out to be the best course of action.

As the weeks went by, Bruce's talent for procuring new enquiries, and pricing and organising work increased business beyond all expectation. A good example was when we were executing a small decorating job for some Americans in Hampstead. Bruce learned that these customers wanted their long garden wall rebuilt. I would have passed by the opportunity, as it was not the kind of work we usually undertook. Not Bruce; within hours he had got a price from subcontractors, slammed on a profit for us and by jingo—before

I knew it—we had another lucrative contract on the go. It was exciting but chaotic, and it made me very nervous.

As I had learned from Howard Strowman, taking risks was one thing, but lack of financial control spells disaster. Nothing was being properly documented and I was required to shell out huge sums on Fridays to pay workmen whom I had never even seen. I was particularly anxious to know whether all the paperwork, absolving me from any tax liability, were being completed correctly. I had no idea if what appeared to be very desirable activity, and just what I had been hoping for, was in fact profitable or likely to explode in my face and land me in Carey Street. That could even threaten the existence of the shop.

The men did not like the diminutive Bruce, who bullied them, swaggering around in his camel coat and puffing on cigarettes. His strong accent did not help and they made fun of him behind his back but, while there was money floating around, he was tolerated. If things went wrong, there would be no loyalty, and off the workforce would go. My first prerequisite in any expansion programme was to find someone I could trust. I had broken my own self-imposed constriction. Bruce was a loose cannon, he drank heavily and, as Aubrey had surmised, he was soon out of control.

One night, in November, disaster struck. I received a late phone call at home. It was the Richmond police to say that an Alfa Romeo registered in my name had collided with a lamp-post. Needless to say, Bruce was at the wheel. He was not badly hurt, but he had failed the breathalyser test and the car was a write-off. This was the last straw and the next day as I drove Bruce to a meeting at Cat Stevens' (Yusuf Islam) house in Walham Grove, to discuss a building project in which we were already deeply embroiled, I felt very depressed. My works manager would soon be banned from driving, and where would we all be then? Over the Christmas break, I mused over my predicament and with enormous regret came to a sad decision. I had a perfectly good business in Barnes that was profitable and ripe for expansion; why jeopardise it with exhausting, risky and time-consuming shenanigans? After eleven years it was time to cease trading, and over the next few months I ran the business down, finally giving the staff and my secretary their notice in March 1977. This was a painful process, but it had to be done, and I do not recall my thirtieth birthday on 15th March being a happy occasion. My men were sorry to lose their jobs. They had enjoyed their time at Peacock Decorators. They had all worked for interesting customers and often in fascinating places but now realised that it had all been a bit too cosy. Lilly, my once loyal and trusted secretary, was livid that she had not been offered a job at the shop, but there was no place for her there. It was the first time that I really learned the meaning of the expression 'a woman scorned'. Hysterical and abusive phone calls at home, when I was trying to eat or spend time with the family, were not something I had bargained for, and they continued for months. Even, her young son got on the phone.

'I hate you, Neil! You've made my mum cry', he yelled.

The first half of 1977 was extremely unpleasant, and I felt sore and battered. I was also considerably out of pocket as the redundancies, settlement of rent obligations and other expenses had cost more than I expected. However, by the time of the Queen's Silver Jubilee celebrations in June, we had turned the corner and I was once more looking forward to the future. We took a short holiday at Cellardyke on the Fife coast, where we rented a fisherman's cottage. At the end of the street the baker sold freshly baked bannocks and scones from early morning, and a swimming pool that was replenished by the tide twice a day was easily accessible. One dip was enough for me. The North Sea, even in August, hardly encourages salt-water frolicking. Fortunately, the sands at St Andrews and lochs at Pitlochry were within driving distance, so we had a refreshing break.

I was now able to put all my energy into developing the shop and furnishing business. We designed new marketing material featuring a beautiful peacock whose tail swept graphically across half-page advertisements in the glossy magazines. I even bought a stuffed peacock with exotic plumage that had come from a Norfolk game park. It was much admired. One Sunday, I took the bird down to the towpath with Tarquin and Alexander. We thought it would be amusing to photograph it standing with a few autumn leaves scattered around its feet and with the Thames as a backdrop. The stuffed creature stood motionless as I fiddled with my camera, taking shots from various angles. After a few minutes a couple walked by, and to my utter disbelief, I heard a woman's voice saying, 'Just look at that peacock, the vain thing, standin' there 'avin' its photo taken!'

Over the next few years, Peacock of Barnes, as it came to be known, attracted increasingly high-profile customers and it was a red letter day when we received an order from Shepperton Studios for a dozen rolls of one of our Swedish papers for a set for the film *The French Lieutenant's Woman*. Turnover increased rapidly, but the fact that the headline inflation rate was standing at 25% in 1977 contributed, not a little, to the sense that business was booming. In fact, this was a nightmare scenario because our suppliers constantly increased their prices. Hardly a day went by without a new price list arriving in the post and, as we dealt with forty or fifty wholesalers, we were overwhelmed by the task of constantly re-labelling our samples. I even had to take on extra part-time help to deal with the problem, and quoting for contracts with a fixed price became untenable.

Concurrently, house prices were rising as never before and property developers were among our best customers. One day a very beautiful, slim Egyptian girl with tight white jeans and long blonde hair arrived at the shop. I only ever knew her as Miss Sami. She spoke impeccable English, had been educated in Switzerland and over the next year or so purchased an enormous amount of merchandise. She was acting on behalf of Arab investors, spearheading a new wave of foreign businessmen who renovated London properties with very little concern for expense. One day, Miss Sami took me to a house in Eaton Place, next door to where I had worked for Signor Magnifico some ten years previously and not far from the fictional home of the Bellamy family in the television series *Upstairs Downstairs*. All seven floors had been gutted, and in the subterranean equivalent to where Mrs Bridges, Rose and Hudson laboured in kitchens, sculleries and parlours, there were palm trees and a magnificent, aquamarine tiled swimming pool with gold-plated accoutrements, set within white marble surrounds. The walls throughout the whole building were covered in the finest silks and woven materials, which we had supplied.

Soon after my trip to Belgravia with Miss Sami, I delivered a dozen boxes of expensive and assorted wall-coverings to a large house in Strand on the Green. They had been ordered by another glamorous young lady who had been in the habit of visiting Peacock on a daily basis while planning her design schemes, and invariably arrived in a silver blue 350SL Mercedes convertible that she parked a few yards up the road. The house had, clearly, just undergone major renovation, was clean and dust-free, and the decorators were about to move in. The unmistakable tang of a central heating system that had recently been turned on for the first time hung in the air. Since the front door had been left open, I wandered in and soon found a swarthy fellow with his sleeves rolled up poking about in a kitchen cupboard.

'If that's the wallpaper f'r Mrs Jones, mate, pu' it in the front room,' he called over his shoulder.

I did as he suggested before returning to report completion of my task. By this time the plumber, for that is whom I took him to be, was standing by the sink, testing the hot water.

'All done,' I said. 'She'll be jolly pleased when this is finished!'

Then curiosity got the better of me.

'She's a bit of a cracker. What does her old man do?' I heard myself blurting out in a low conspiratorial tone.

He turned, smiling, and replied with a twinkle in his eye. 'I am 'er ol' man.'

The decorating scene became increasingly active in the last few years of the seventies. Osborne & Little opened extensive premises on the King's Road opposite newcomer Tricia Guild's flamboyant emporium, and there were other new names, such as Mr Stone in Muswell Hill, Maurice Brown in St John's Wood, Paper Moon in Hampstead and Mr Topp in Fulham. These companies vied for trade that was stimulated by satisfying an increasingly design-conscious population, the rise in property prices and in our case the transition of the middle classes out of central London. They were actively innovative in design, rivalling established houses such as Coles, Sanderson, Colefax and Fowler, Hammonds of Sloane Street and Home Decorating. The latter still proudly exhibited a photograph of the Queen, demurely dressed in the style of the time, visiting their Knightsbridge premises in the early years of her reign.

Many of the new decorating businesses also acted as agents, as we did, for foreign wallpaper and fabric manufacturers whose gala trade fair, Paritex, was held annually in Paris. Cindy and I took the opportunity to visit this glamorous jamboree on several occasions. We left the children at a lovely Victorian house, near Pooh Bridge in the heart of Ashdown Forest. The Old Rectory belonged to our chums, the Swingles, whom my sister-in-law, Jane had first befriended in Paris. Ward Swingle, originally an American, had studied at Cincinnati Conservatory and also under Walter Gieseking in Saarbrucken. Following an early career as both piano soloist and accompanist he had launched Les Swingle Singers in 1963. Originally an A Cappella Choir that only performed Bach—the vocal response to Jacques Loussier's instrumental—'Play Bach'—they soon extended their repertoire to motets, madrigals and folk songs. The group's unique arrangements became hugely popular and they performed before delighted audiences all over the world. At the time we visited them in Sussex, Ward was establishing his new group, Swingle II, in England. We knew that the boys were in good hands, and had three girls of similar age to play with, as we left to fly from Gatwick to Le Touquet on the Flèche d'argent and thence by train to La Gare du Nord.

In Paris, we stayed with our American friend Jack MacDougal in his spacious apartment close to the Luxembourg Gardens. Like a scene from *Maigret*, it was reached from the street, through huge ornamental doors, and past a curtained entrance where the concierge discreetly eyed those entering or leaving the building. We would then squeeze into a brass cage lift before rising to the first floor. The flat was well-lit, with several glass-paned and mirrored connecting doors, entirely decorated in black and white, including a chequered carpet throughout. As a token of thanks for his generosity and hospitality, I had taken Jack a bottle of Armagnac on the camping trip to Le Cosquer, which I felt he had appreciated. However, for some unexplained reason, he thought it hilarious when I turned up with another bottle each time we visited Paris. Jack was very suspicious of English men—he thought we were all closet fags. One, not unpleasant, duty to be fulfilled when staying with Jack was to attend a business lunch at La Hulotte ('the tawny owl'), a restaurant in the Latin Quarter where excellent food was served and, with rough tables and sawdust on the floor, diners enjoyed a memorable ambience. The purpose of these lunches was to entertain adult students from Jack's English school. Our job was to eat, drink and be merry, but to speak only in English to the men or women who were undergoing a saturation language course. On such an occasion, when the wine had been flowing, I tried a riddle:

'What is the difference between a bad archer and a constipated owl?' I asked one of the students at my table. The upwardly-mobile Frenchman from IBM, although desperately anxious to master the English language, looked at me, nonplussed.

'A bad archer shoots but cannot hit; a constipated owl hoots but ...'

It was no good; my coarse Anglo-Saxon humour fell on stony ground and my companion showed no reaction. After lunch, Cindy pointed out Jack Mayer's gallery and reminded me of the story he loved to repeat of how one day he had raised his eyes from his desk only to find himself staring into those of the ravishingly beautiful Brigitte Bardot, who was peering through the front window. She smiled sweetly before continuing on her way.

The Paris exhibitions halls were light and airy and in every way superior to dingy old Earls Court, and Olympia where we had once taken a stand. As you would expect, the catering facilities, housed in pretty surroundings carpeted with, bright green plastic grass, provided food that far outshone greasy hot dogs and stale sandwiches washed down with pints of effervescent—'the beer that works wonders'—Double Diamond!

One year, we discovered a fresh range of wallpaper and fabric designs called 'La Campagne'. It featured bees, chickens, starlings perched on telephone wires and other rural motifs. After negotiation, during which Cindy's excellent French came into its own, we obtained the exclusive UK rights.

Before returning home we slipped into the church of St Sulpice. Organ music greeted us, reverberating through the early eighteenth-century building. Here, where Charles Marie Widor had been the organist for more than sixty years, a young performer was displaying his own skills and demonstrating the versatility of the great five-manual organ built by the master Aristide Cavaillé-Col (1811–99). French, German and English organs each emit very varied sounds and combinations of tone—rather like the people who build them.

I was reminded of a story which describes how Widor had been seated at that very instrument in the autumn of 1893 when Albert Schweitzer, who later became a famous doctor, humanitarian and biographer of J.S. Bach, approached and asked if he could play.

'Play what?' Widor asked.

'Bach, of course,' the young Alsatian replied.

I would have answered in the same vein but was reminded, sadly, of how organ playing had slipped off my agenda under the pressure of family and business life. Maybe I would take it up again one day.

In 1978, we undertook another holiday in Massachusetts. The family was to go two weeks ahead of me and, having dropped Cindy and the boys at Heathrow, I returned to Madrid Road, feeling terrible. I had developed a high temperature and was breaking out in spots. It was chickenpox! For a week I nursed myself and, as I began to recover, the girls from Peacock brought round shepherd's pie and other nourishing dishes.

'Are you all right?' they would whisper through the letterbox, before depositing my rations at the front door. Fortunately, I was well enough to travel a week later on Skytrain, Freddie Laker's innovative airline that was to revolutionise the cost of long-haul flights. The hot July sun soon dried up my last spots.

ABS-M, my old music master from Marlborough, who had become a close family friend and Tarquin's godfather, also travelled to Wellesley, a few days ahead of me. We were curious to discover how he would react to the New World, as his only experience of travelling abroad, as far as we knew, was war service in North Africa and Turkey, and trips to Paris when he studied with Nadia Boulanger in the 1930s. There was not enough room at 171, so Isa Livingstone kindly put him up at her house and as soon as I arrived we all strolled up the road to take a dip in the pool and see how he was getting on. We found Isa in her garden, still laughing about an incident that occurred when he arrived, hot and exhausted from his London flight.

'I offered him refreshment,' she told us, 'and he asked for a long, cool squash. Well, to me that means a long, cool vegetable, like a pumpkin whose name comes from the Narragansett Indian word 'asquutasquash'! But we got there in the end!

My, he was thirsty!'

We all giggled, enjoying the little joke at ABS-M's expense.

One of the excitements of the trip was to go in search of dolmens—megalithic constructions of great antiquity—with Jimmy Whitthall, an archaeologist and close friend of the Briggs family. ABS-M was astonished and fascinated, as we all were, to learn that such things existed in New England.

We spent a day visiting Mystery Hill and other puzzling sites and had to pinch ourselves to ensure that we were not in fact wandering through the Kennet valley, back in deepest Wiltshire. Needless to say, the topic raises questions that are outside the scope of this narrative, and plenty of published material is available for those who wish to learn more.

During much of the holiday, we retraced steps we had taken in 1974 and Alexander got his trip on the miniature train that ran through the cranberry bogs. We relaxed over hamburgers and clam chowder at the Howard Johnson's restaurant in Wellesley Square and managed short trips to Martha's Vineyard and New Bedford, a town with strong Portuguese influence, before visiting the property in Westport where Cindy used to go for long summer holidays. She showed us the clapboard house with its 'widow's walk', the turret-like window in the roof where wives could watch for a sailor's return. The Stars and Stripes flew from flag posts in every garden. While we wandered along the shoreline and down the wooden jetty where a tiny shop sold lobsters, swordfish, quahogs and littlenecks (both types of clam), she recalled the great hurricane in the 1950s, when all the boats were smashed and the sand dunes blown away.

Our delightful friend Louise, invited us to stay with her in New Jersey and, taking two cars, we drove south. While still in Massachusetts, we were amused to see a sign informing us that we were entering a 'thickly settled area', but continued on through the states of Connecticut and New York. Stopping in the small town of Madison, Louise pointed out a delightful church, built in colonial times.

'Now, you must look at this really old church,' she said.

'Louise!' I replied pompously. 'You shouldn't say things like that to an Englishman!' Years later, I got my revenge when she visited London and I showed her around St Bartholomew the Great in Smithfield, which was founded in the twelfth century. The next few days provided opportunities for sightseeing, so we took the ferry to the Statue of Liberty and visited the United Nations. Cindy and I were especially moved by the little chapel, within the main building, that commemorated Dag *Hammarskjöld* (known to have been directly influenced by the Sufis) who was killed in a plane crash in the Congo and posthumously awarded the Nobel Peace Prize in 1961. I remember the day he died, because it was one of the few times that I saw my father visibly dismayed by an international incident.

Time spent in the city also gave us the opportunity to visit the Frick gallery with Jack Mayer, which was to be last time that we would see him, as he died shortly afterwards. He reminded Cindy of a trip to the Louvre, before she and I were married, when he had pointed out several Renaissance paintings, mentioning that some artists implanted coded messages in their work. Neither of us understood the implication of what he was saying at the time. It was a treat to see Turner's *'Mortlake Terrace: Early Summer Morning'*.

ABS-M was to return to London directly from New York. On his last night we went for a celebration meal at a rooftop restaurant above Central Park. It was a splendid occasion; the food was excellent, the service superb and the Big Apple panned out in front of us. However, just as we savoured our coffee and the boys were stuck into their second round of ice-cream sodas, we noticed an unseemly rustling and agitation at the one table that divided us from the huge plate-glass windows. We suddenly realised what was going on. The attractive young couple dining in front of us, who were facing each other, were making strenuous efforts to reach under their table and rummage in each other's underwear—all silhouetted against the neon lights of New York City.

God Bless America!

1979 was to prove a turning point in many respects. Early in the year, the opportunity arose for us to purchase the freehold of 3 White Hart Lane. This seemed a natural progression, as I was a sitting tenant with a lease on the ground floor and there was a pleasant flat on the two floors above. My eccentric landlord, Bill Fitzhugh, had moved away, which was a shame, as he was good company and we used to have a drink together from time to time. My abiding memory of him was during the bi-centennial celebrations of American independence, when he departed for Boston in full eighteenth-century military attire, together with a three-cornered hat and dress sword.

Brian Fleming, a property developer and one of my customers, was also keen to add the building to his investment portfolio, but after knife-edge negotiations that resulted in a race to complete the paperwork, I clinched the deal at a purchase price of £30,000. It just happened that, at the moment, Brian was booked on a flight to Majorca leaving me free to exchange contracts, by courier, in his absence. When he returned, I took him to lunch at the Dorchester as consolation, which was to pay off at a later date. The occasion coincided with my thirty-second birthday. I now owned two properties in Barnes, and although we were all pleased to have the added space for storage, office work, business meetings and lunch breaks, I began to wonder how the flat could be best utilised in the long term. Before anything else, however, it needed a new roof, which proved to be expensive.

On 4th May, Margaret Thatcher won the General Election and became Britain's first female Prime Minister. Only months had passed since the Labour government had been forced to beg a loan from the International Monetary Fund (IMF) and Britain had suffered the Winter of Discontent (1978/9), when rubbish up piled in the streets and bodies were stacked in mortuaries awaiting burial. One of my customers was Denis Thatcher's sister and she later told me that in 1979, when strikes were rife, Mrs Thatcher had considered the country to be virtually ungovernable.

Draconian monetary policies, including the raising of VAT, were to follow. These were aimed at reducing inflation, but exacerbated a deep recession brought about by that summer's international oil crisis. It would not be long before unemployment was over three million. The years of riding on the crest of inflation, which suited a businessman like me, who had very little underlying capital, would soon be over. However, although I have met a lot of business people whose firms suffered under Mrs Thatcher's policies—some terminally—I have yet to meet one who did not feel that the price was worth paying, to put the 'Great', as they saw it, back into Great Britain. The population at large, particularly in the north of England, would not all agree with that point of view.

In the summer Cindy, the boys and I attended a splendid weekend shindig at a country house. The theme was 'time machine' and everyone dressed up in amazing costumes reflecting the past, present and future. I went as Henry V and had ordered printed T-shirts for Tarquin and Alexander that read 'Tarquinius Superbus' and 'Alexander the Great', respectively. Our particular contribution was to cook 'The Rakes' Breakfast' on Sunday morning to revive the previous night's revellers. Scrambled eggs, toast and bucks fizz were served in the garden.

Throughout the weekend there were numerous diversions. Acrobats, conjurors, portrait-painters, story and fortune-tellers occupied stalls around the grounds. Cindy visited a palm reader, an old lady from Willesden Green in gypsy dress. Taking her hand she looked straight into Cindy's eyes and said, 'You have great courage, but you will have to learn to live with uncertainty.'

How right she was, on both accounts.

We felt as if we were on the crest of the wave—but perhaps the rolling surf was about to break as the party seemed, in some undefined way, to foretell difficult times ahead. However, the immediate future entailed taking our new metallic blue VW Passat estate car to Scotland, on the Motorail from West Kensington, for a family holiday. ABS-M came along too, and the sixty-three-year-old astounded us with his stamina when trekking through the Scottish glens. Arriving at Perth at six in the morning, we drove across the Highlands all day, passing Ben Nevis in the early afternoon and stopping off here and there before we reached the Kyle of Lochalsh late in the evening. As we crossed to Skye, by ferry, the sun dropped behind the Cuillin hills, shooting rays that emblazoned fluffy clouds in such vivid pinks, crimson and tinges of scarlet and rose that we were left breathless. Truly, it was the most magnificent sunset that we had ever seen or have ever seen.

We had planned to have a cheap holiday at a Bed and Breakfast recommended by a neighbour in Barnes, but our eager anticipation soon turned to disappointment. Rooms with paper-thin walls and supper consisting of green hard-boiled eggs and limp watery lettuce forced us to rethink our plans. The next day we returned to the mainland and booked in to the Kintail Lodge Hotel. This was a terrific establishment with wonderful cuisine. As we entered the loch side dining room each day, a freshly-caught salmon lay displayed on a large silver platter and through the windows a lone piper could usually be seen. The bright red in his tartan tunic stood in sharp contrast to the pine-covered mountains rising beyond. We were all thrilled by the delights of the Kintail Lodge and I was secretly relieved to know that they would accept my American Express card at the end of the holiday. The only black spot in a delightful fortnight was when I turned over one of the hotel's kayaks in the loch. Never having entered such a craft before, I was overdressed for the adventure, even wearing wellington boots, which immediately filled with water. As I sank, I began to panic but Tarquin was close by in a canoe and towed me to the shallows. The only real casualty was my Jaeger-LeCoultre watch that my mother had bought me in Amsterdam when I was sixteen.

'You idiot! You could have drowned!' screamed Cindy as she found me, soaked through, wiping my specs and staggering across the beach. She was right.

We spent the rest of the time walking, fishing, pony-trekking, watching seals and generally enjoying all that Scotland had to offer. One windy day, when a turbulent grey sea flecked with white horses was running between Skye and the mainland, we took a boat up to Camusfearna, the site of Gavin Maxwell's adventures that feature in *Ring of Bright Water*. It was outstandingly beautiful and of special interest to me as his sons, whom I remember as particularly nice boys, were my contemporaries at Marlborough.

At the end of the holiday we drove back to London, arriving late on 27th August. As we crossed Hammersmith Bridge, Cindy spotted two Union Jacks silhouetted against the evening sky on top of the Harrods depository. They were flying at half-mast. As soon as we got home we turned on the television and learned that Lord Louis Mountbatten, together with other members of his family and a young friend, had been murdered by the IRA earlier that day.

As the leaves began to turn and dahlias and chrysanthemums bloomed in our garden, family life settled down for the autumn. Alexander was still at Allendale in Kensington, and Tarquin started at Sussex House. My father had recently retired as headmaster and was pleased when the Duke and Duchess of Kent enrolled their son, Lord Nicholas Windsor, during his last year. Tarquin was lucky to have Margaret Cowlishaw as his teacher. She was wonderful with children, and once told me of a particular boy who seemed beyond hope when it came to discipline and learning ability. This was until she discovered that he was mad keen on football. Margaret, a spinster in her late fifties, had no interest whatsoever in the game but took the trouble to swot up on details of teams, players, leagues and matches and in no time the boy was like putty in her hands. Sussex House was fortunate indeed to have such a brilliant teacher, as was Prince Charles, whom she had taught at Cheam. Both our boys were beginning to develop distinct interests of their own. Tarquin, who had a good voice and was in the choir, also started to play the piano. He took lessons with Frances Saville, a remarkably enthusiastic tutor. Alexander continued, when not climbing trees or tearing around the park, to be fascinated by film, a passion that was born when we all went to see *Star Wars* at Twickenham Cinema in 1977. Little did we know what we had started.

The shop traded steadily through the months leading up to Christmas. I was working a six-day week, but fulfilling the role of hunter/gatherer, it was fun for the whole family when I brought home a heap of cheques on Saturday night. I listed these, sitting at the dining-room table, in preparation for banking and the boys were highly amused by some people's surnames. Funny names were a running family joke and any Smellies or Ramsbottoms produced peals of mirth while the all-time prize went to the Wyser-Prattes (with apologies).

Some days at Peacock could be quiet but sales, almost uncannily, maintained a consistent momentum. There were anxious moments when the expected turnover for a whole week had still not been reached and we were into the last few hours of Saturday trading. Suddenly, our target could be achieved with one spectacular order, such as a suit of furniture or a deposit for curtains for an entire house.

Merrie Pryor, a clever designer and cheerful soul who lived up to her name, left Peacock to start a family and I replaced her with Anne, a pretty girl with an infectious smile and member of the Warner family. High-quality wallpapers and fabrics were supplied by their family business. Anne's father was soon to become a High Court judge but was based in Luxembourg at the time. We were rather envious when she slipped over to Europe to visit her parents for long weekends. She possessed considerable design flair, as did Wendy Burton, our useful, part-time member of the team who was married to an account executive at the Oxford University Press. As the status of the business increased, in terms of the quality of customer we attracted, I was also able to seek out experienced, sophisticated staff to serve them, although the face of one smartly dressed, upwardly-mobile young lady turned vermilion whenever her husband called in for a chat. He was the local fishmonger, invariably on his way back from Billingsgate, reeking of fish.

As 1979 drew to an end, I may have been aware of the financial tensions lurking in the background, but I do not remember. As we headed towards Christmas, we felt confident and relaxed, and I recall that Cindy and I threw a rather good party. Nothing had therefore prepared us for news of events that occurred many miles away on Christmas Eve. In fact, it was to be some time before we digested the information broadcast on the news bulletins. Nevertheless, something had happened that would impact hugely, both in personal and international terms, from that day to this.

The Russians had invaded Afghanistan.

As the early months of the New Year passed, the implications of this monstrous act sank in, and Mrs Thatcher announced a boycott of the Moscow Olympics. She only received half-hearted support. There was still a feeling in Britain that we should, on no account, be beastly to the Russians, and the media insisted on referring to the *mujahideen*, freedom-fighters who were organising resistance from bases in mountainous regions of Afghanistan, as 'the rebels'. These Afghans saw the treatment they were receiving from their oppressor in an entirely different light.

My friend Amina Shah wrote these words:

'The Questioning Child'

Why do we walk, my mother's mother through the mountains and the pass?
Why do we leave Mother and Father, silent, hidden in the grass?
Where are all our sheep and horses, why do our empty bellies swell?
Why do the flying gunships bomb us with the flames as hot as Hell?
Hush, male child of seven summers, walk on o'er this snowy hill,

Afghan hearts are strong, and willing to take on the good
and ill.
Grow strong, grow strong as Afghan eagles; shelter till you
are a man—
And then with risen Men of Freedom, win your fields back,
As you can!

My whole Baby Boomer generation had lived under the shadow of the
Bomb, but suddenly the world was looking a very dangerous place. Powerful
and hostile dynamics were emerging. As a student of the Great Game, I knew
that an aggressor who occupied Afghanistan could easily pour through the
great passes, invade the subcontinent and reach the ports of the Indian Ocean.
This appeared to be one objective of the Soviet government, which was led by
desperate old men who relied on ageing military technology that they could
ill afford to replace. Other objectives were to plunder huge mineral resources,
access the rich opium trade and, perhaps, even capture the gold of Ahmad
Shah. On the other side of the world the odds were that a strong Republican
president would succeed Jimmy Carter, following elections in the autumn of
1981. In Europe, tensions were rising in the shipyards of Gdansk where Lech
Wałęsa, a founder member of Solidarity, the free trade-union movement, was
poised to challenge the communist government.

In London, we became aware of increased concern for the need for protection in the event of nuclear war. A 600-page book entitled *The Effects of
Nuclear Weapons,* published by the United States Departments of Defence
and Energy was available, and we purchased a copy.

But how did all this fit in with my family and business life? First, Cindy
and I were beginning to feel that it was time to move to the country, to
give the boys an opportunity to enjoy rural life. We had noticed that children of our acquaintance in London appeared to mature very quickly. But
this was at a price. They seemed to skip through the teenage years, missing
the leisurely enjoyment of what should be the best days of their youth. We
wanted Tarquin, now eleven, and Alexander, eight, to have time to do boy-
ish things while they were still young. We had also taken to heart Richard
Clutterbuck's *Protest and the Urban Guerilla* and Doris Lessing's novel
Memoirs of a Survivor, in which she painted visionary pictures of a bleak and
violent urban life. The nuclear threat added an impetus for change.

Second, our house in Madrid Road had doubled in value, giving us some twenty-five thousand pounds of equity. I did not particularly relish dinner parties where the prime conversation centred on how much your house was worth and, anyway, the general view was that prices had peaked. But a 100% gain in only five years, was at that time, a unique phenomenon. My view was that this unexpected dividend should be used, and I was considering ways of cashing in. We came up with a drastic strategy that caused us to agonise for several weeks but the possibility of securing a tax-free windfall and resolving our other concerns proved irresistible. We planned to sell 39 Madrid Road and move to Wiltshire, which I had loved since my time at Marlborough, where we would rent a suitable property. I would then invest the capital we had released, by renovating the flat at 3 White Hart Lane, primarily to serve as a showcase for Peacock but also as a *pied à terre*. The family would enjoy rural life and the boys would go to a local school but I would stay in the flat during the working week. If this all worked out, we would eventually buy a house in the West Country.

In early May, I booked a time to see Aubrey, whose loan I had now re-paid. I arrived late, having been diverted from my usual route as the terrorist siege at the Iranian Embassy in Kensington, which had lasted for six days, while images of smoke and hooded figures clambering over Victorian balconies filled our television screens, had only just been resolved in a dramatic raid by SAS commandos.

Aubrey nodded with approval when he heard our plan, but—added a caveat.

'One thing I can assure you,' he said. 'It won't work out as you imagine.'

He was, of course, to be proved right. The first part of the project went surprisingly well. We sold our house quickly and by August had settled into a cottage in the Pewsey Vale on the very edge of Salisbury Plain, along with Nimr, our striped ginger cat. Nimr was a huge cat by any standards; even as a kitten he was big for his age and we had named him Nimr, which translates as 'tiger' (*nmr*) in Arabic. The property included a couple of acres of land and we bought bicycles, an air gun, basketball set and football, ready for the kind of life we had planned. On our very first day, red flags were raised at the top of the hill above the house and howitzers boomed on the ranges where the army were practising. This became a common occurrence, which rattled the windows and jiggled the crockery on the kitchen shelves. When the prevailing wind blew from the west the sweet smell of swine drifted through the house. We had failed to notice the pig farm just across the lane.

In September Tarquin and Alexander were booked to start at a local prep school named The Old Ride. . It would prove to be manned by eccentrics, as my prep schools had been, and was not as forward-thinking and modern as we would have liked

'Goodness me! I used to play The Old Ride', I exclaimed, when I saw the name. 'They must have moved from Bucks'.

For once, I had thousands of pounds in the bank and after a couple of weeks at the cottage, I returned to Barnes and started to renovate the flat above Peacock. With a talented team behind me, we produced what one customer described as 'a work of art' and in the autumn customers, neighbours and friends were invited to an open house that showed off our ideas and the quality of our workmanship. For upholstered sofas and chairs, I had found a mews workshop just off the Tottenham Court Road. It was run by George and Arthur Kelly, two brothers, both elderly with thinning hair and grey moustaches, who could always be found on their shop floor dressed neatly in white shirts, ties and waistcoats, with dashing braces and their sleeves rolled up. They would be gently tacking webbing to the kiln-dried beech frames of their furniture with a small, magnetised hammer or cutting heavy fabric with huge pinking shears in preparation for the upholsterer. I learned that, before the Second World War, when visiting customers, each would have a white carnation in his buttonhole. Attired in top hat and tails, they would draw up in their Rolls-Royce outside Harrods, Maples, Whiteleys, Derry and Toms (the store with an extensive garden on its roof), and other quality retailers. Those were the days.

Once the novelty had worn off and the flat had been decorated, our first country-based winter proved less than easy. I did not enjoy being alone in the week and the weekends were too short to catch up with family life. I was frequently tired by the time I had driven back to Wiltshire in the dark, and tensions rose. Cindy found the school run too long, especially when caught up behind a herd of cows. The lanes were often muddy, slippery and dangerous, particularly on frosty and misty mornings. Farm lads careering along on motorbikes or in old bangers added to the hazards. It was one of those difficult times that can make or break a marriage. But we got through it, and I am sure the experience tested and strengthened our friendship.

After a year in the Pewsey Vale, we decided not to renew the lease at the cottage and to move nearer the Old Ride. The Grange at Hilperton was available at a low rent, with the proviso that tenants looked after the extensive garden. The property was to be let by a naval family who were off to SHAPE at Mons for two and a half years, and we immediately fell in love with it. The house, which was 500 yards from the Trowbridge to Devizes road, commanded a spectacular southerly view to Salisbury Plain and the eye was drawn across a dreamy landscape, into the far distance, by a plume of white smoke invariably billowing from the tall chimney at Westbury cement works. This was a familiar landmark to passengers on the Great Western line. After we had completed our negotiations, the family kindly invited us to a cocktail party to meet the neighbours. We wandered across the croquet lawn admiring the ancient mulberry tree, asparagus bed and extensive fruit cage while glasses of champagne, sparkling in the early evening sunshine, were set out on a huge raised millstone, similar to the one in Gawky's garden at Lodsworth. We eagerly anticipated future meals seated around this stone slab, savouring the view from beneath a magnificent copper beech. Everyone was in good spirits; it was 29th July 1981, the wedding day of Prince Charles and Lady Diana Spencer, and we drank to their health. Our time at the Grange was to include some of the happiest days I can recall, just the sort of life we had hoped for when we left London—and in marked contrast to the royal couple's tragic story.

One of the blessings of the Grange was that it had a 'granny annexe' above the garage, to the side of the house, and behind a massive cedar of Lebanon. We invited ABS-M to come and live there and help with the children. In due course, I became especially grateful to him as I felt that he was able to supply aspects of the boys' education for which I was either not qualified or lacked the time. He was quite happy to take care of the boys, ferry them backwards and forwards from school and became a sort of proxy grandfather. My parents had retired to Sussex and were not able to fulfil that role. He adored Tarquin and Alexander, who in no time were darting in and out of the flat, clambering up on to his balcony or spending hours playing Monopoly, canasta, cribbage and numerous card games with him. They also played hunt-the-unicorn, a game that ABS-M had designed but, unfortunately, was never able to produce commercially. To this day, Alexander will defy anyone to beat him at Monopoly.

When not playing games or watching Laurel and Hardy or Harold Lloyd on the television ABS-M worked at his cassette business, which involved recording and distributing traditional stories from all over the world. Needless to say, the boys spent hours mesmerised by his cassette player, enthralled by stories from Arabia, India, Persia and China or the exploits of King Arthur, Sinbad the Sailor, Alexander the Great, Moses, or Jason and the Argonauts. I was reminded of my days at Ashfold with Miss Elmes, and an increased awareness of the power of stories became an even stronger part of our family culture. We all took turns in practising the art of storytelling. Lucinda was able to add a whole range of experience from her own background including Brer Rabbit, Johnny Appleseed and tales of the West recounted by Laura Ingalls Wilder. On one occasion, we took part in a twenty-four-hour live broadcast 'storython' organised by the newly-founded College of Storytellers and Radio London. As far as the boys' future careers go, a very strong influence can, undoubtedly, be traced back to these times.

ABS-M's presence enabled Cindy, who had recently decided that she wanted to be known by her baptismal name, Lucinda, to spend mid-week with me in London. Life became much more agreeable and when the weekends arrived we were ready to enjoy croquet, make bonfires, attend to the garden, pick blackberries and sloes in due season and, above all, nip up to the Old Ride to watch the boys play football, rugby or cricket and participate in other activities. Alexander, in particular, was establishing a reputation for speed on the sports field, and was voted Man of the Match at an inter-school rugby sevens competition played at Bryanston. He also made his mark playing the lead part in *The Thwarting of Baron Bolligrew*, the school's production of Robert Boult's amusing play. Sadly, the headmaster had not arranged for official photographs to be taken, so we have no record of it apart from our own proud parental snapshots.

Our friendship with ABS-M held some interesting moments. Glued to the screen in a Bath cinema for a performance of Richard Attenborough's *Ghandi* in 1982, we were shocked when ABS-M stood up and yelled 'IT DID NOT HAPPEN LIKE THAT!' during the graphic depiction of the 1919 Amritsar Massacre. The darkness hid our blushes.

During the following couple of years we made the very best use of the Grange. In the summer, we invited friends and relations from across the Atlantic and elsewhere to come and stay, and on many evenings we were still pacing up and down the croquet lawn, gin and tonic in hand, as the evening sun sank in the west. While we enjoyed ourselves, Nimr stalked mice in the fields below the property. During the winter, log fires roared in the ground-floor rooms, lights twinkled on a tall tree in the hall and the scene was set for a traditional family Christmas. In 1981, when my parents arrived from Sussex, thick snow covered the garden, weighing down the netting on the top of the fruit cage and the huge branches of the cedar. During spare moments, when we were not throwing snowballs or building a snowman, the boys and I were gainfully employed keeping the wood shed piled high, frequently re-minded of the saying: 'Chop your own wood and it will warm you twice.'

My parents enjoyed their visits to the Grange and several years after my father's retirement, they moved to Bath which brought them closer to us and Richard's family, who had also moved to Wiltshire.

The Grange lent itself to all sorts of gatherings. One dark October night we held a splendid Hallowe'en party. Ghostly figures could be seen flitting across the lawn, ghoulish wailing emanated from the bedrooms and out-buildings, while murderous shrieks rose from the bushes at the edge of the property. After the bewitching hour, we danced in the dining room as Abba boomed on the stereo, rocking the house from the cellar to the eaves. On another occasion, members of the College of Storytellers stayed the night en route to a session at 'The Hole in the Wall', a popular restaurant in Bath, and on a very hot August afternoon we held a fete in support of CLIC, the can-cer charity. This was arranged with Henry and Maureen Boys, longstanding friends whose son was suffering from the disease, and we were pleased to help raise a tidy sum. Henry, who was wearing a flamboyant hat on that sunny day, had a few stories to tell. He had been a member of a privileged group who had regularly visited Gurdjieff in his tiny flat in the Rue des Colonels Renard in Paris during the years that led up to his death in 1949 and had helped John Bennett edit *The Dramatic Universe*. Maureen was one of those people who could give useful tips on all sorts of practical matters, like how to feed the asparagus bed, planting caper spurge to keep away moles, spreading coffee grounds on flowerbeds to deter slugs and snails, and how to encourage moss and lichen to grow on new cement work by smearing it with a mixture of live yoghurt and manure. They were also both gifted musicians.

With chilling irony, our Hallowe'en party was soon followed by a grue-some event. We had taken the opportunity to invite new friends, including parents of other children at The Old Ride. One such couple seemed pleasant enough, so, a few days later, it came as a tremendous shock to hear that the wife had allegedly taken a shotgun and blasted her husband's brains all over his study wallpaper. At the end of the summer term I was seated next to her at an Old Ride dinner party. She was out on bail, pending trial, and I confess it was difficult to make bright conversation about plans for the impending summer holidays. Within a few weeks she was locked up in Holloway.

In September 1982, as members of the Nuclear Protection Agency (NUPAG), we were invited to take part in an extraordinary experiment. We were to spend seventy-two hours in a private nuclear fallout shelter deep below the English countryside. The trial was to be made as realistic as possible, although we would be in radio contact with 'observers' above ground, so the only element missing was the certainty that atomic bombs were not actually falling from the sky above us.

Ivan Tyrell (the talented artist who had redesigned the Peacock logo used in our successful advertising campaigns) had introduced us to NUPAG, where he was the information officer. In an interview with Tom Pocock, published in the *Evening Standard* (16th November 1982) he said:

> Other countries take (nuclear fallout shelters) seriously today, so why shouldn't we? North Vietnam showed the way by surviving the heaviest conventional bombardment yet launched by digging a vast labyrinth of shelters.
>
> Russia has incorporated civil defence into its overall defence policy and values it so highly that they would not allow it to be used as a bargaining factor in the SALT negotiations. China has enormous shelters beneath its cities with long escape tunnels radiating out to the suburbs in all directions so that exits up-wind of a nuclear fallout should be used. The Swiss have the most sophisticated shelter system of all; the Scandinavians are building them, and the Finns can now offer protection to 85% of those in Helsinki and 60% to those outside. They are even digging shelters in Baghdad.

Reading the last sentence again after nearly a quarter of a century induced a wry smile, but perhaps a friend's comment at the time is still amusing: 'Imagine a world only populated by the Swiss, Swedes, Norwegians and Finns.'

Lucinda, Tarquin and I had agreed to bury ourselves underground for a long weekend and we were all apprehensive about how we would behave.

As we trooped down the concrete steps at 4 p.m. on Friday 3rd September, I took a last packet of Gauloises from my jacket pocket and tossed it into a nearby waste bin. This required imposition was certainly real enough.

Once our group had entered the shelter, thick steel gates were locked from outside and the blast-proof doors sealed. We found ourselves in a dimly-lit pipe-like concrete capsule that just allowed a man to stand full height. There were some very basic toilet, washing and cooking facilities near the entrance, two tiers of bunks stretched out on each side, as one passed down the tube and air-purifying apparatus was housed at the far end. The whole shelter was about fifty feet in length—and we were to be cooped up until Monday afternoon. During the first few hours we introduced ourselves and began to get to know our companions, some of whom already knew each other. There was a doctor and his wife from Essex, both of whom must have been in their sixties, and a heavily bearded antiques dealer of about the same age from London. There were two young women, one a writer and the other a teacher from Liverpool; two American businesspeople and a single lady who worked as a stained-glass designer in Dorset and who recalled the London Blitz. Besides the three of us, last but not least, a Maltese computer and electronics expert completed the group. He regaled us with shocking tales from the Second World War of the bombardment of Valletta in Malta, and life in the labyrinth of tunnels within the great fortress that guarded the Grand Harbour. Twenty-five years later we took the opportunity to visit that astonishing place for ourselves. I do not know if this 'Bunker's Dozen', as we nicknamed ourselves, presented a true cross-section of a likely group seeking safety from nuclear attack, but it was a good effort. We were all white Caucasians except for the young teacher who was black.

I am sure you agree that it would be beyond the scope of this narrative to reprint the entire log but perhaps a few excerpts, kept by one of the female participants, provide a flavour of what occurred.

Day One
Housekeeping and introductions.

Day Two
Washing and dressing in toilet area takes too long.

08:30—Breakfast. Discussed dreams. N. said he dreamed of the Queen. Apparently he often does. Discussion opens up to others.

10:30—Clean up. Disinfect loos. R. and N. play chess. C. wraps T.'s birthday present.

13:00—Lunch. Discuss why we volunteered.

S. 'I thought being closed in with 11 people would be absolutely horrible so I wanted to see how I would cope.' Others agree.

Call in to 'observers' on radio. They say the experiment seems to be going so well that they will extend it to 7 days. Howls of laughter.

15:30—General chatter mostly in whispers. Some reading. J. tells joke about Queen Mother. Sudden feeling of 'real shelter life'.

16:30—G. (who is nominal leader) asks group to address themselves to topics that will form part of the report on the experiment. J. says she is surprised at lack of stress after no fags. G. thinks we are all stressed in our own way. C. and J. discuss the need to wash knickers and their hair. Should have brought disposable panties.

21:30—'Observers' call to wish T. happy birthday. He is 13. Cake brought out and consumed. We all sing 'Happy Birthday'!

22:30—Settling down. S. always helps without being asked. C. has look and manners of Victorian lady. J. is a night owl.

Day Three

07:30 Feel down because of inability to concentrate. Grit my teeth to 'see it through'. Everyone cheerful—if not, they hide it.

10:00 Open meeting about how it is all going. N. makes heated plea to curtail any introspection—we are just here to observe how chores are carried out and to test the equipment. G. seems to feel inadequate as a leader. All get a bit emotional. Adjourned.

18:15—Meeting continues; everyone in a better humour. T. is a pretty remarkable addition to the shelter. Seems to have matured before our eyes. Fancy having your thirteenth birthday party in a fallout shelter!

20:30—Dinner actually tasted good. Beef Chow Mein—stock pot.

24:00—Climb into bunk. It's been a bit of a party—a bit too much booze. Could be a problem if real shelter. Probably will have a hangover.

Day Four

09:50—Bleeper goes on. We've reached high carbon dioxide level. L. turns on manual ventilator. R. and G. still discussing leadership. N. wants reassurance that his outburst was called for and everyone still likes him. J. very dozy.

11:00—R. talks to us all about improving the soft furnishings and having bags for personal property.

12:15—Lunch—some new stock pots. Fair.

14:15—Everyone packing. Excited. Hot and steamy.

14:30—L. agitated says he is glad the experiment is over as generator is overheating and becoming dangerous. It will have to be redesigned.

14:40—Everyone leaves. N. and T. test the emergency exit.

After seventy-two hours we emerged into the autumn sunlight and weeks later, when we completed our reports to NUPAG, the participants noted their feelings on returning to the 'real world'. These are some of the comments that were recorded:

'I was shaking like a leaf when I left the shelter … felt tearful.'

'Felt disorientated on returning home. Peculiar dreams. Elated. Had a good cry!'

'Agitated dreams to do with people.'

'What struck me most about emerging was the quality of the light … smells, too, were very strong.'

'Felt weak. Patchy sleep. Distinct revulsion at going back into shelter.'

'Felt as if I had just come out of hospital … weak … tired … battered. Felt I must wash everything; as if someone had died.'

'Great relationship with all the other people. I found it very emotional leaving them.'

It was an extraordinary few days, something that Lucinda, Tarquin and I will never forget, and I think we all felt privileged to have taken part. The snapshot provided by the log and the quotations supplied require no further comment from me; suffice it to say, I have not touched any nicotine product since that day. Did our adventure prepare us in any way for the ultimate disaster? I am not sure. Thankfully, we Baby Boomers and the rest of the population have not had to endure the real thing and I hope the threat, as far as England is concerned, has now passed.

Back on terra firma, as it were, some hard truths were facing me. For the first time in ten years, Peacock's exponential sales development had seriously stalled. In the summer of 1982 turnover was heading for the same level as the previous year (£220,000) but 10% of sales could be accounted for by one contract alone. We had been asked by Chris Evert, the tennis champion, to supply all the furnishings for the house she and John Lloyd had purchased on Kingston Hill, which was to be their base during Wimbledon Tournaments. This was a lavish and very successful undertaking, closely supervised by Anne Clark, a talented new member of our team, and we were delighted, but as I inspected the completed work and ambled around the house admiring the beautiful curtains, quilts and wall-coverings, and noting the tennis memorabilia and piles of sports' videos, I wondered where my business was going. Over the following months things got worse, and in March 1983 the monthly sales figure suddenly fell to 50% below the average. This was a major crisis.

The reasons for this were not hard, to find as the slump in the housing market and the wider recession was taking its toll. Things had come to such a pass in the construction industry that some architects who had been overwhelmed with work a few years previously were now driven to suicide. All this had a knock-on effect on Peacock.

Competition was also making trade more difficult, not only because there were now far more interior design and home improvement retailers, but also because an insidious practice had developed in the trade that was killing my business. This practice involved so-called 'interior designers', many of them women, who for the most part operated from their own homes outside London, offering substantial discounts to the general public. It was easy for them to do so, as the same fabric houses and wholesalers who supplied Peacock and other high-street retailers were quite happy for them to open accounts on equal terms. As far as the wholesalers were concerned, no qualifications were required of these 'upstarts' and no protection or pricing agreement was offered to longstanding customers, such as ourselves, who had substantial overheads to meet. They simply adopted a policy of 'the more the merrier'; business was business and it did not matter where it came from. In a way, we found ourselves in the same position as independent bookshops are in today with the competition supplied 'on-line'.

The way that this worked in practical terms was that these 'interior designers' advertised in glossy magazines offering large discounts on designer ranges of wallpapers and fabrics. These operators did not carry anything like the range of samples required by bona fide retailers, and they therefore encouraged their customers to visit shops like mine, pick the staff's brains, note the manufacturer and pattern number of their choice, and phone the order through. There was no need for them to even meet their customers. Posing as a potential customer, I recorded a telephone conversation that verified this procedure. This practice grew from recession-driven market forces, but it meant that the cost of running our premises, my girls' time and the endless supply of samples were not being met. In an attempt to bring this matter to a head, I wrote to as many fellow retailers as I could, most of whom I knew personally, pointing out the destructive implications of what was happening, but by the time we had agreed to coordinate pressure on the wholesalers it was too late, as far as Peacock was concerned.

As any businessman knows, an antidote to falling sales is to slash overheads. But in retailing this is not easy. Confidence is an essential ingredient, and a high street shop is very exposed. Cutting back on staff or lowering standards could be interpreted as an indication of underlying financial weakness. No one was going to give us a decent furnishing contract if they thought we were about to go bust, but as the hot summer continued, that terrifying possibility raised its head. Part of the problem was that we operated on a gross margin of only 28%, which some might find ludicrously low. However, this was the standard rate for our type of business. If inflation was high, operating at this profit level was sustainable because of the illusion that everything was growing more rapidly than it actually was. Trading in a severe recession, however, when coupled with the other problems I have referred to, meant that Peacock was heading straight towards a brick wall—and several bad debts did not help. Trying to recover monies for goods and services supplied in good faith, withheld for no substantiated reason, only added to our frustration. Of course, all this was far easier to see in hindsight. At the time, I tried everything to survive.

Draconian action was required. I even sold the freehold of 3 White Hart Lane to my friend Brian Fleming and took a leaseback on the ground floor, but to no avail. Somehow, the harder I tried, the lower morale fell and the worse things got.

'I don't think I can stand the heat in this kitchen, anymore!' I mumbled to myself.

We were on the skids, and in September I decided to cease trading and to put the company into voluntary receivership. It was very sad and painful, but one aspect that really tore at my heartstrings was to see a business that I had cherished and nurtured reduced to so many numbers in the liquidator's job-book. Over the next few months, the financial aspects of the collapse of the business were resolved, and no blame was attached to my management. We had become a casualty of the times, and times had changed. The days of flying by the seat of one's pants with insufficient capital were over, although there was some consolation in knowing that the same fate, for similar reasons, had befallen Mortlake Tapestries exactly 280 years before. Eventually, two delightful sisters, Yannik Banks and Michelle Waldemar Brown, customers of mine, took over Peacock. With reduced overheads and a different management style, they traded for some years before selling on to others. The shop finally folded shortly after its twenty-fifth birthday.

I look back to the 1970s and early 1980s with a considerable degree of nostalgia. My sleeping hours are still punctuated, more often than I care to admit, by dreams of wallpaper, fabrics and paint, projects undertaken and the countless characters that had filled my life for seventeen years. But, as they say, 'When one door closes …'

Chapter 9
Tricky Days

Cease, Man, to mourn, to weep, to wail;
Enjoy thy shining hour of sun;
We dance along Death's icy brink,
But is the dance less full of fun?
('*The Kasidah*' of Haji Abdu El-Yezdi)

AN IMMEDIATE CONSEQUENCE of the demise of the business
was facing up to how the children were to continue with their education. As
I was brought up in the private system, the idea of the boys going to state
schools was anathema to me. In fact, I had never even entered such an establishment, and the prospect terrified me.

Tarquin, who was now (1983) Head Boy at the Old Ride, had won a
bursary to Bryanston, because he sang well, played the piano and had become a very good cellist. We had chosen Bryanston because it seemed less
harsh and smaller than Marlborough and several of our friends had children
there. Times had changed, but I did not want Tarquin to suffer what I had
endured only twenty years previously, and we also felt that the emphasis on
music and the arts would suit his disposition. Every week he and Lucinda,
together with his cello, had squeezed into our VW Beetle for the trek to
Coombe Down. It was there, in her little cottage set in a pretty garden, that
the delightful and eccentric Miss Doris August gave lessons. Tarquin and
Lucinda had first met her in 1981, at J P Guivier in Mortimer Street, when

we were desperately seeking a cello teacher; a chance encounter that proved a true blessing.

Doris, a brave woman who had suffered serious ill-health, really knew how to make music fun, and gathered her young students together in her front room for a jolly party every Christmas.

The thought of Tarquin not taking up his place at Bryanston in September was unacceptable, and we scrambled together enough cash to pay the first term's fees and also to keep Alexander at the Old Ride. With the boys away at boarding school, Lucinda and I turned our attention to the future.

One fine autumn afternoon, we drove from the Grange to Stourhead and as we walked around the lake and through the gardens we discussed our position. Stourhead had proved a refuge on previous occasions. Even in childhood, it sometimes provided a welcome break on the journey to or from Cornwall, although my mother got annoyed when she had to pay at the gate. She considered herself 'family' and reminded us that the portrait of her great-grandmother, Anne Hoare, hung over the mantelpiece at Lodsworth. I could claim that my fondness for Stourhead stemmed from the fact that the house was built and the gardens designed by my ancestors, and that I had a special affinity with the place, but the real reason was its overwhelming beauty, come rain or shine. It was stunning in the spring when green leaves were fresh and daffodils nodded in the breeze beside the Grecian follies, and in early summer when the rhododendrons and azaleas were spectacular. Autumnal colours were breathtaking too, especially those emanating from the huge variety of magnificent trees whose origins lay in distant lands and whose tones were reflected in the dammed waters of the Stour. But a truly memorable visit was on New Year's Day in 1979. On that occasion the stark branches of the deciduous trees were stripped naked, a wisp of mist hung in the cleft of the valley, and the lake lay unruffled amid an awesome winter stillness.

I was now thirty-six and unemployed but, being a cussed individual, was incapable of grasping the notion that I might not bounce back. After all, I had started two businesses, from nothing, which had supported me from the age of nineteen. At that moment, I considered that the only option for someone thrown from a horse was to get back into the saddle as quickly as possible. I had learned lots of lessons following the collapse of Peacock, but was not ready to accept that the days of running my own business were over.

As Lucinda and I ambled along the gravel paths, arm in arm, we pondered upon these things and promised ourselves that we would work together towards a full financial recovery. Continuing the boys' private education, which was high on our list of priorities, might be considered a sign of confidence that all would work out in the end, but it was to put us under immense strain. I seemed, however, to be programmed to follow that course so, in a sense, there was no choice.

One outcome of our discussion was a decision to put an advertisement in the personal columns of *The Times* along the lines of 'experienced businessman seeks new opportunity'. The only reply I received was from a Dorset business—Phoenix Kitchens—looking to franchise in the West Country. To rise above the ashes—the name alone attracted us, and the pressure to restore financial equilibrium, together with the abhorrence of a vacuum meant that, with the maximum of impulsiveness and minimum of critical analysis, we found ourselves, in March 1984, running a kitchen studio in the depths of Somerset. There were attractive ideas attached to the project. First, and most important, was that we would effectively be running our own business but could rely on marketing and technical support from the host company. Second, the average customer would be in the market for a whole kitchen rather than a few pairs of curtains or rolls of wallpaper, so time invested should be profitable.

Unfortunately, the day we opened our doors for business the parent company in Dorset, who were importing and distributing German kitchens, went bust. We did not bother to make too many enquiries, although there were rumours of fiscal skulduggery. All we wanted to do was keep our new business going so, with the intention of negotiating with the Germans, I flew to Hanover. A friend dropped me at Heathrow with these parting words: 'If you want to flatter a German, tell him you took him for an Englishman, and if you really want to lay it on thick, say that you thought his wife was French!'

Before leaving, I discussed the situation with Aubrey on the telephone. His advice was simple: 'Remember, you do not negotiate with Germans. You tell them what to do.'

Aubrey had attended Heidelberg University so I did not question his judgement. His words rang in my ears when, within half an hour of my arrival at the kitchen factory, I was sitting in the managing director's plush leather chair, while he paced up and down wondering how to reconnect his

UK market. Following several telephone calls to my bank and accountants in London, I soon felt that I was in a position to dictate the terms on which I was prepared to take on the UK agency.

It was all a bit of a shock, and back in the pretty market town of Frome we had a mammoth task ahead of us. Lucinda ran the attractive showroom that we had designed together, but without the support expected under the franchise arrangement, the business would have to be built from scratch. This meant that we needed to find a designer/salesman, fitters and a warehouse to store kitchens prior to installation. A significant factor was the nature of our clientele. Compared with the folk of south-west London, we could not have chosen a greater contrast. We were now dealing with people from an entirely different cultural background, a factor that we had, initially, failed to register.

Frome was a town where commercial life and the mindset of the population revolved around the agricultural community and local farms. On Wednesdays, a market was held; heralded by the rumble of cattle trucks, from which strands of loose straw blew across the wide concrete area in the town centre and down the high street, finding their way beneath the front doors of shops and offices. After the cows, pigs and sheep had been sold, a colourful produce auction commenced in a huge marquee. Item by item; every last sack of potatoes, each marrow, box of eggs, chunk of local cheese or bunch of dahlias went under the hammer and the whole town gathered to stock up at bargain prices. All this was very quaint, like a scene from *Far From the Madding Crowd* and conducted at such a speed that the auctioneers were, to our untutored ears, virtually incomprehensible.

The town was tucked away from the world in a valley drained by the Frome River and rolling hills, pretty villages and acres of cider orchards surrounded it. However, I came to believe that it was a better place for holidays than business. No major routes came near the town and property was more often than not passed on to the next generation rather than sold. There was a high rate of intermarriage within families and very little discernible middle class. Immediately prior to our involvement with the town, a policy of re-housing ex-convicts from the south-east had been implemented.

Running a successful kitchen business in that environment would be a Herculean task and the niceties of a public-school manner, let alone a transatlantic accent, would count for very little. In fact, they proved to be a serious obstacle. I had, however, been ruminating on Aubrey's warning that nothing is quite as you expect, when we struck lucky and found a good fitter and a young lad to work as his mate. The designer was a very different matter.

One day a man, I will call him Ashley, contacted me claiming to be an ace salesman. He said that he had worked for Phoenix Kitchens before they foundered and was familiar with the product. I invited him over and a day or so later a tall, smartly dressed individual emerged from a shiny new Jaguar with a glamorous blonde at his side. One could not fail to be impressed by his suave and charming manner, and a silk cravat and smart blazer with polished brass buttons only accentuated a favourable impression. He and I went off to have lunch at the Lamb in Bath Street and, being pretty desperate, I readily agreed to him starting the following week. It was at that point that something very strange transpired, something that has never happened to me before or since—a mental aberration. Without warning my perception of Ashley morphed into a hideous monster, a grotesque beast, like *The Picture of Dorian Gray*, right there in the pub, before my very eyes. This demonic apparition only lasted for a split second, and I was so keen to get my salesman that I dismissed the incident, driving it from my mind. Ashley had worked his magic on me, as he would do on many others over the ensuing weeks, and at noon the following Monday he turned up for work in a clapped-out Rover. I vaguely wondered where the Jag was. He had probably hired it together with the blonde.

Over the next month or so, a familiar pattern started to emerge. Ashley was on commission so he turned up at the showroom when the mood took him and noted any leads that we had developed or chatted to potential customers while they were inspecting our display. He would book sales meetings to be held at their home over the weekend, and always carried a crate of iced champagne in the back of his car. Announcing himself at the front door, this tall domineering man would stride into the house, turning off the television as he passed. Then, grabbing some glasses, he declared that he was there to toast the swift arrival of the new kitchen. This was before any details had even been discussed or any measurements taken. The good folk of Somerset were as putty in his hands and before the hour was out they had invariably parted with a substantial deposit or, if Ashley was on his best form, the total cost of a new kitchen in advance. It was reported to me later, that if he had any problems in closing the deal, he was quite capable of passing himself off as anything he pleased. It was said that he posed as an ex-serviceman, active sportsman, gentleman farmer, keen gardener, amateur archaeologist; whatever the punter wanted to hear, while remorselessly chipping away any resistance to the sale.

This was business in a totally unfamiliar guise. On Monday, Ashley would appear in the studio and I would casually enquire as to the results of his weekend endeavours. 'How did you get on with the Browns?' I asked.

Like a conjuror, he would pull a cheque from his breast pocket.

'And the Robinsons?'

Another cheque for a four-figure sum.

Within two months, we had logged sales in excess of £100,000 and Ashley wanted his commission on the nail. They say that having too many orders is a nice problem to contend with, but events were moving too fast. Once again, I had fallen into a situation where I was not in control.

I had taken on storage space in the little town of Mere, some ten miles away, but did not have enough fitters to deal with all these orders. The business needed to grow gradually—organically—while I built my team, but I was being bulldozed into a manic situation. What were my options?

I could take on more fitters to deal with the backlog, but where would I find craftsmen of the required calibre? I could sack Ashley, but a business cannot survive without a salesman. I could try to tame Ashley but, in reality, there was no halfway position. I had to either tolerate him or sack him, in which case I knew that he would be quite capable of causing havoc with my customers, who worshipped the ground upon which he stood. As Aubrey once pointed out, very few people are capable of admitting that they have been manipulated. Even fewer admit their own greed.

As it happened, events took over.

First, Nigel Lawson, the Chancellor of the Exchequer, announced that he would be extending VAT to home improvements. This created a stampede for more kitchens and the Monday-morning cheques cascading from Ashley's pockets beggared belief. Under the Budget guidelines, customers who paid for their kitchen in full before the deadline (1st June 1984) would be exempt from VAT but, of course, they also wanted results.

We arranged for those pre-payments to be lodged in a solicitor's client account but my problems were now exacerbated ten-fold. As if this wasn't enough, I was in for a nasty shock when I turned up at our storage unit in Mere one bright summer's morning, rolled open the front shutter and stared into a totally empty space. It was the antithesis of Ali Baba's cavern.

Every single cupboard, worktop, sink, dishwasher, oven and fridge had been stolen. Someone had driven a van into the warehouse and nicked the lot. In total disbelief, I wandered around kicking the dust on the concrete floor where the vehicle had left its tread marks, as if this would, in some mysterious way, restore my loss. The racket I made echoed in the emptiness and the torrent of expletives streaming from my mouth vaporised in the void. We now had no kitchens to fit except those already on site. It was a nightmare, but worse was to come.

As they say in dusty countries a long way from the rolling chalk downs where Wiltshire, Dorset and Somerset meet, 'Once the caravan has faltered a thousand demons fall on it.'

We needed to re-order the stolen kitchens immediately and, while I was insured for their full value, a national dock stoppage was threatened in sympathy with the miners' strike, led by Arthur Scargill, which was in full swing. This meant that if I could not get replacements very soon my fitters would have no work and I would have to let them go. I would also have half the wives in Somerset baying for their kitchens, their money, or my blood.

The only course that seemed viable was to hire a lorry and drive to Germany to collect the kitchens before the threatened strike hit the ports. I asked Frank, my fitter, and Darren, his mate, if they would like a trip to Hanover—all expenses paid.

'Where be that to?' came the earthy reply in broadest Somerset.

I explained that it was in central Germany, and of course, they agreed at once. We set off for Dover at noon the next day and as we drew out of Frome, 'Radio Ga-Ga', Queen's inordinately irritating hit, boomed over the radio in the closely confined cab. Taking turns at the wheel, we drove all night, crossing the Rhine as a dirty dawn broke and reaching the Hanover area at lunchtime the following day. In the afternoon, the three of us loaded the kitchens onto the van and started on the return trip. By the time we reached Antwerp, curtains of rain were sweeping across the cobbled streets. It was late and we were exhausted, so we booked into a scruffy little hotel that stank of cigarettes in the centre of the city. However, in the morning, I found it difficult to awaken my companions. Aroused by the temptations of the nearby red-light area, their weariness had proved short-lived and, at eight in the morning, they were dead to the world. Eventually, I managed to get some strong coffee inside them and we set off, avoiding the electric trams as we made our way to the tunnel that passes under the Scheldt. Following the route by which we had come, we arrived back in Somerset sixty hours after our departure but despite these efforts our problems—mega, mega problems—were still mounting. I had failed to introduce a quality control function between sales and execution. The result of this was that Ashley's silver-lined and liquor-loosened lingo proved to have been more believable than the accuracy of the measurements he had taken. Over the next few weeks, the kitchens we tried to fit were found to be riddled with design faults, and the cost of correcting these was ruinous. I certainly lost count of how many moulded work surfaces had to be scrapped because they were too short or too narrow. Frank did his very best, and each time a new error was discovered I tenuously asked him how he would get over it. He would put down his tools with a sigh, draw deeply on his briar pipe and exclaim:

'Mr 'all, all will be revealed!'

Those words still ring in my ears, but finally even his morale cracked, and in September, Lucinda and I felt that we had had enough and for the second time in a year called in the receivers. The horse that I had impetuously mounted twelve months previously had proved to be a bucking bronco. It seemed that my days of running a business were well and truly over. I am reminded of a telephone conversation that I had, some years later, with my son, Tarquin. He was on a ranch in Texas.

'What have you been up to?' I asked.

'I'm a bit sore, today—splitting headache!'

'How come?'

'One of the cowboys challenged me to ride a magnificent horse that none of the others could tame. I was very excited and couldn't resist.'

'What happened?'

'I was thrown off and hit the ground—very hard!'

Yes, Tarquin; I knew exactly what you meant.

The next year was to be one of the most difficult of my life, and was to test the family's resilience to the utmost. As the kitchen studio door closed behind me for the last time, I headed home, overwhelmed by a sense of foreboding. My state of intense anxiety was such that I stopped at a roadside coal merchant in the village of Wanstrow and, acting on impulse, loaded up the car with as many sacks of coal as I could muster, paying with the last notes in my wallet.

'At least we won't be cold', I assured Lucinda, when I got home.

Earlier in the year, the tenancy agreement for the Grange had expired and we had moved, for the seventh time in our marriage, to a sizable seventeenth-century house near Templecombe in Somerset. Monmouth House, as it was known, was within an easy drive of Frome but also only half an hour from Bryanston. We had felt this to be important so that we could keep in close touch with Tarquin. The house was built in typical Somerset sandstone with mullioned windows and a roof that was tiled with huge, moss-covered slabs of what looked like York stone. The date '1685' was carved on a plaque above the front door and it was believed by the locals that the ill-fated son of Charles II, the Duke of Monmouth, had slept there in that eventful year. It is the oldest house I have ever lived in, and I used to stare into the fire on a winter's eve, musing on how news of past events had been broken, perhaps in the very room in which I was sitting. The arrival of George, Elector of Hanover, in London in 1714; the loss of the thirteen colonies; the fall of the Bastille; Waterloo; the death of Prince Albert; the death of British officers in Bokhara in 1842; the relief of Ladysmith; the declaration of war in August 1914—my imagination worked overtime. The house had, in fact, been let over many years to an American who lavished money on the place. He used to drive down from London in his Rolls-Royce for the weekends, however the gardens, once splendid, had long since gone to seed. The only evidence of past glories were half-hidden grassy paths, rarely perfumed roses that continued to produce huge blooms among rambling overgrown hedges and stretches of miniature cyclamen and lily of the valley that blossomed in the shade of the beech trees at the end of the lawn. The American was said to have once entertained a distinguished senator as a house guest. His initials were JFK.

Our landlord, the Count de Pelet, lived on his estate in a house called Inwood, two miles away. How this Frenchman's family had come to inherit a huge swathe of land on the Somerset/Dorset border was shrouded in mystery, and since he was a kindly gentleman, always immaculately attired when he passed us each day on his fine horse, it felt indecent to be seen to be nosy. However, there were rumours, gleaned from the tradesmen, of a 'changeling' arrangement and in my Baily's Hunting Directory of 1933–34, a Miss Guest is recorded as the occupant of Inwood and also the master and huntsman of a private pack of foxhounds founded in 1913. Sadly, the old count eventually died and his son Richard, the Christie's agent for the West Country, inherited the title. I expect those who need to know the whole story, undoubtedly do.

Fortunately, there was a self-contained flat within Monmouth House, so ABS-M moved in and continued to play his role as proxy grandfather to the boys. He kindly offered to pay Tarquin's fees at Bryanston for the time being, as he could see that we were in no position to do so, and several other good friends chipped in as well. The headmaster of the Old Ride generously waived Alexander's school fees as an extended IOU. Alexander had been making a name for himself as the fastest runner the school had ever known, and was also a useful rugby player.

Staring into the fire and dreaming of times gone by was not going to get us out of our predicament. I had always seen myself as the family provider, ably and stalwartly supported by Lucinda, but had dismissed the notion of starting any new form of business. I had not been an employee since the days of the King Charles Hotel, most of our friends were self-employed and I now felt like a king deprived of his kingdom. Where on earth would I look for a job?

In October, I spotted an advertisement in the *Daily Telegraph* advertising a diploma course in accountancy and finance for non-accountants. It was a TOPS training course, which meant it was a scheme run by the government for the huge numbers of unemployed, especially from the professional classes, that had accumulated in the mid-1980s. Students would be paid a weekly wage. I was attracted to this idea and sent in an application together with my CV, even though the five-month course would be held in Doncaster. Within a couple of weeks, I was called to an interview at the Metropolitan Institute of Higher Education and made my way from Templecombe to South Yorkshire via King's Cross. The interview went well. I don't think that the lecturers in the Department of Business Studies had met anyone with my sort of track record.

'Do you really mean to say that the business you started with one hundred pounds, aged nineteen, lasted for seventeen years? I'm staggered,' piped up the kindly David Smith, the chief interrogator.

'In one form or another,' I agreed.

Although several hundred people had applied for this nationally advertised opportunity, I was confident that I would be offered a place. I was, however, not taken with the city of Doncaster. It appeared to me, on that grey November afternoon as I returned to the station in a filthy, graffiti-covered bus, to be what an old school chum would have described as the 'arse of the earth'. I bought a local paper and on the way back to London studied the property rentals to get an idea as to what might be available. The details of every flat or room to let ended with an instruction to call 'Don' on such and such a number. Perhaps I had ODd on Francis Ford Coppola's film *The Godfather*—I was certainly ramfeezled and clearly paranoid—but could not help wondering anxiously, as the train clattered along, who this 'Don' was. He seemed to own every property; a real tough, big-cheese Yorkshire businessman, who might end up being my landlord. Then, with considerable relief, it dawned on me—'Don' was short for Doncaster. Call Doncaster 1234.

Back in Somerset, confirmation of my place, commencing in January 1985, soon arrived.

'What do you think?' I questioned Lucinda at breakfast.

'Could open a whole new world', she replied with characteristic encouragement.

After further discussion, we agreed that it seemed a sensible step and an opportunity not to miss, despite all the difficulties it entailed. I felt that after nearly twenty years of 'flying by the seat of my pants' with no family business background, here was the chance to learn business theory. A little late, one might say or, as someone commented graphically, 'What's this; sackcloth and ashes?'

Christmas was soon over, and the day after my parents had arranged a visit to the pantomime at the Royal Theatre in Bath, where John Nettles was playing Wishy-Washy in *Aladdin*, I was back on the train to Yorkshire, sadly waving goodbye to my family as they stood in the bitter cold at Gillingham station. Tarquin and Alexander would soon be off to Bryanston and the Old Ride, respectively, and Lucinda planned to close down our part of Monmouth House and go to stay with Jack MacDougal, in Paris, for a couple of months. This was indeed a brave decision. He always needed help with his language school. We did not expect to be together again until Easter.

I arrived at Doncaster in darkness; across the city the fine nineteenth-century tower of St George's Church, the only recognisable landmark, rose silhouetted above the yellow streetlights. Dirty slush soaked my shoes and clogged up the gutters outside the station where I hailed a taxi, and thick snow lay in the fields and on the rooftops of the better-insulated houses as we drove to a drab pub on the outskirts of the city. It reminded me of my first night at Marlborough. I had booked accommodation for a couple of nights and as soon as I was safely in my room I dived under the skimpy bedcovers. The room was cold and I drew the blankets tightly around my body, to keep warm, and to blot out a world that engendered waves of homesickness and apprehension. I soon fell into a fitful asleep, but after an hour's kip went down to the bar for a mixed-grill supper. The television was showing the final episode of *The Man from Moscow*, a drama about the Russian spy, Penkovsky, and Greville Wynne, whose son had been at Sussex House. I had seen the previous episodes and it provided welcome relief, just the sort of thing to distract me from my worries. Such a comment is, of course, obscene considering that both Wynne and Penkovsky suffered dreadfully for their services to the West. Wynne was eventually released from prison, in a classic Cold War exchange with the Soviets, but Penkovsky was executed by the KGB with a bullet to the back of the head on 16th May 1963. Perhaps I was 'gridding' with pals in the Marlborough countryside at the time, totally unaware of such dramas.

The next morning, I managed to get a lift to the Department of Business Studies, which was situated in a modern building in the suburb of Scawsby, and at around nine o'clock found myself seated in a classroom for the first time in twenty years. I had previously met the course director, David Smith, whom I liked, and as was customary the twelve members of the group were each asked to stand up and introduce themselves. There was a wing commander who had just left the RAF, a retired major and an engineer from the Red Arrows team who wanted to equip himself to make more money. When he told me what he earned, and the long hours he worked in the group's huge hangers, I sympathised with his motives. There were several middle-aged businessmen who had been made redundant, a couple of university graduates and two housewives. I was the only one who had actually run a business and was immediately regarded as something of a curiosity.

David outlined the syllabus that we would be studying over the next sixteen weeks, interrupted by an Easter break at the end of March. There was a lot to cover and he assured us that it would be very intense. A diploma in accounting and finance would be awarded after examinations in the summer.

My next task was to find digs and fortunately the engineer had neighbours who let out a room from time to time. The husband, Alf, worked as timekeeper in the coal mines, although he was currently on strike, while his wife, Ginny, was a chambermaid at a local hotel. They had a young son. I went round to meet them in their little modern house on the outskirts of Doncaster and was soon fixed up with a room that contained a single bed, desk and clothes cupboard for thirty pounds a week including breakfast and an evening meal. This was very convenient as I could hitch a lift with George, the Red Arrows man, each day and a routine was soon established. On the first night, my mother rang to see how I was getting on and Ginny answered the phone.

'It seems strange talking to someone in whose house you are staying when we haven't been introduced!' Mother declared. Poor Mother, life had changed so much from the days of empire.

Classes started at nine, there were a couple of breaks for tea, and lunch was available in the crowded cafeteria that we shared with the sixth-form college students. I got back to my little room at about five and there was always evening work to be completed. I also had to deal with my post as there were domestic bills to be paid and a considerable amount of correspondence regarding the defunct kitchen business. Alf and Ginny were friendly enough, but I resisted the temptation to watch TV with them in the evenings, certainly in the early weeks. Winter weekends were dreary, although I forced myself to take a grubby yellow bus into the centre of town on Saturday mornings and then to walk back to my digs. My heart lifted once the daffodils were blooming in the parks and along the side of the dual carriageway in early spring, but within days they were cut down by vandals and lay on the grass in decaying heaps. By my reckoning, there were only four good things about Doncaster: the Metropolitan Art Museum, which was free; the racecourse, which I could not afford to visit, and the pub on the way back to Bessacarr where I indulged in a couple of pints of John Smith's ale once a week. In addition, a five-manual organ built in 1862 by Schultze was located in the parish church. This famous German organ-builder was known to have been influenced by the Silbermann family, contemporaries of J.S. Bach. While I sipped Tadcaster brewed bitter, I regretted a missed opportunity. My technique was far too rusty to take on that formidable beast.

As the weeks progressed, I found it difficult to concentrate because of mounting money worries. It was true that I was able to support myself on my TOPS allowance and the family were currently not incurring any expenses, but that would change when we all returned to Somerset in the holidays. Bills arrived daily, mostly relating to our continued tenure of Monmouth House, where heating and basic services had to be maintained. Unexpected liabilities stemming from the old businesses also kept surfacing, like untreated sewage. One evening, on my return from Scawsby, when faced with yet another pile of brown envelopes I burst into tears, and to Ginny's horror rushed upstairs to my room. By mid February, the financial landscape had become as depressing as the wretched town in which I found myself. Reluctantly, I came to the conclusion that it was quite impossible to continue in the same vein. The only way out was to make a clean breast of my position and declare myself bankrupt. At least I could then make a fresh start. On the very day—yes, the very day that I decided to take this awesome and irrevocable step and contact the relevant authorities—another brown envelope arrived addressed to me in a haphazard handwritten scrawl. It contained a cheque for one thousand pounds together with a request to keep this gift a secret. I knew the donor, but have no idea how my dire financial plight had come to the attention of an old friend. I have always honoured the request for secrecy.

'My God!' I thought to myself. 'Unbelievable! I can pay outstanding bills and live to fight another day.

As the course progressed, I made friends with fellow students from nearby, who invited me to dinner and introduced me to their families, and with others who were also a long way from home. Several owned cars, so on Sundays we sometimes took the opportunity to drive to neighbouring places of interest. I had never been to the city of Lincoln where William Byrd was supposedly born in 1543, or to its fine gothic cathedral where he became the organist twenty years later. This proved an enjoyable excursion, although all the pews had been taken out of the magnificent building, giving it an empty look and the semblance of a deserted railway station. Driving across the flat Lincolnshire countryside was an education in itself, and visiting Boston's fourteenth-century church of St Botolph, said to be one of the largest and grandest of parish churches in the realm, was a special treat. We climbed its famous 'Stump', the loftiest church tower in England, and looking out across the Wash, I idly wondered where, precisely, King John had lost his treasure. If only.

I was particularly keen to visit York where an ancestor's tomb had recently been returned to its mediaeval splendour. Toby Mathew, the 66th Archbishop, lies in the Minster, behind the high altar, and on his death in 1628, his wife donated his collection of 3000 volumes to the cathedral library. During his lifetime, he was 'respected for his great learning, sweet conversation, friendly disposition and sharpness of wit', while he and his wife, Frances, remained on good terms with Queen Elizabeth I who apparently gave her 'a fragment of a unicorn's horn'. Frances Mathew established what must be a rare achievement in being the daughter of a bishop and having four bishops as brothers-in-law and an archbishop for a husband.

Following the disastrous fire in July 1984, repair work was still in progress in the south transept at the time of our visit, but we managed to 'do' the Jorvik Viking Centre and the National Railway Museum as well, which kept us busy and provided a relaxing day away from our studies.

Other excursions included a trip to the North Yorkshire Railway at Pickering, the National Museum of Photography, Film and Television at Bradford, and Castle Howard, one of the locations for Granada Television's production of *Brideshead Revisited* (1981). Something that particularly intrigued me on the staircase at Castle Howard was a marble statue of a lion attacking a bull. I wondered where it had come from and how it had been acquired. It was a scene straight out of the selected fables of Bidpai that have been retold in the most delightful manner by my clever friend, Ramsay Wood (*Kalila and Dimna*, Octagon Press, 1980). The scene in question is when King Lion attacks Schanzabeh, the bull, following scurrilous intrigue instigated by the two despicable jackals, Kalila and Dimna.[15]

Perhaps the most amusing of my classroom companions was Harry, the retired major, who continually regaled us with amusing anecdotes from his experiences in the army. The blackest of these was when, during a recent fireman's strike, he had been called out to drive a Green Goddess. He and his team were instructed to rescue an old lady's cat from the top of a tree. Needless to say, the old dear was distraught when they arrived, with floods of tears pouring down her cheeks, but once the furry ginger bundle was successfully returned to ground level everyone was invited in for tea. A newly baked cake was produced, the best china taken down from the dresser and their grateful hostess, wreathed in smiles, went around shaking everyone's hand. After half an hour Harry and his gang were called to another assignment and, stuffing the last morsels into their mouths, they cheerily waved goodbye and climbed back into the Green Goddess. As Harry pulled out from the kerb he glanced in his mirror and there, squashed flat in the road, was the ginger cat. He had just run over it.

When Easter came, I hitched a lift to London with one of the other students, and we dropped Harry off at his home in Peterborough. It was good to be back with the family and to catch up with everyone's news, but unfortunately I became very ill. The months in Yorkshire had certainly been a strain, however I was convinced that I had become weakened by vitamin deficiency. Ginny was a kindly and well-intentioned lady but the food that she served was very poor in nutritional terms. I shudder to think of the long-term effect this diet had on her family and am convinced that Jamie Oliver is right to conduct a crusade aimed at revolutionising the nation's eating habits. Weeks of meals from tins or packets, white bread stripped of every iota of goodness and roughage, a menu that lacked fresh vegetables and fruit, had taken its toll. I had not even enjoyed more than a couple of glasses of red wine since leaving Somerset in January. As John Keats put it in his 'Ode to a Nightingale':

> O for a beaker full of the warm south!
> Full of the true, the blushful Hippocrene,
> With beaded bubbles winking at the brim,
> And purple-stained mouth ...

By the time I had recovered, it was time to return north, and this time I drove the 'Jeans' Beetle that we still just managed to run. Lucinda was planning to stay with friends in London for the six weeks that remained of my course, as she had found a job with Intermediate Technology in Covent Garden, and the boys would go back to school. Alexander was particularly looking forward to the athletics at which he excelled.

On the first day back, we immediately noticed that Harry's place was empty and within a few minutes David Smith informed us that he had died during the holiday. He had suffered a heart attack while reading the Sunday newspapers. It was then that I noticed something unusual. Harry had invariably been accompanied by a distinct odour; not particularly unpleasant, but noticeable. We had put it down to the medication he was taking. A few minutes after David had made his announcement my nostrils caught that very smell for a few seconds, in the classroom and later, when I mentioned it to Joan, one of the housewives who sat next to me, she confessed that she, too, had noticed it, but had been reluctant to say anything.

The miner's strike had ended in March and Alf returned to the pits. One Sunday morning, he took me to his local Working Man's Club. We sank a few beers, and he introduced me to some of his mates, but I spent most weekends revising everything we had learned, glad to be entering the home stretch.

In May, the term ended and the surviving course members gathered for a get-together in the local pub. The wing commander had left soon after the Easter holiday as he had got a job managing a shopping centre in Nottingham, which seemed to please him. I was reminded of the fall-out shelter experiment as we faced release from daily incarceration and the world beyond. Emotions were running high and Mike, one of the young undergraduates, invited me to be the godfather of his firstborn. One of the lecturers presented me with a Blythe Cricket Club tie which was a kind gesture but I thought it a bit odd, as I have no interest in the game. The rest of us swore that we would keep in touch which, of course, we never did. The next morning, I started on the long haul down the Great North Road, and as I left South Yorks, the land of the slag-heap and pit head derrick, I heaved a huge sigh of relief. It was a good moment to reflect on what I had got out of those months in Doncaster.

I had certainly been exposed to a great deal of business theory. It had confirmed in my mind that many of the things I had done during the previous eighteen years, mostly learned as I went along or picked up intuitively, were not far off the mark. There really is only a limited range of options at any given time, which reminds me of the occasion when a friend of my wife's criticised her husband for not being better prepared for any eventuality.

'What have you been doing?' she enquired the next day. 'You've been on the phone for hours.'

'Well, I took you at your word,' her husband replied. 'I called the plumber in case the boiler breaks down and the electrician, anticipating a power cut, and the RAC in case the car fails to start and the doctor in case I get ill and, of course, the undertaker because I might pass away!'

If I had known about the things that were to trip me up, I would probably never have started in the first place. Not appreciating the effect of lack of capital was certainly a factor, and this meant that I endured the affliction suffered by many small entrepreneurs. This debilitating condition is the belief that one can do everything while the truth is that every function in the business process takes a minimum length of time. Running around in circles and trying to perform every role—from selling the product, to managing the accounts, to putting the dustbins out, while vaguely imagining that the business is bound in some way to expand, is often the lot of the small businessman. For this reason, lacking capital to address the situation, he or she so often eventually fails.

I used to say that running a small business was like playing chess, except that the board moved as well as the pieces. The course had also reinforced my view that, faced with radical changes in the commercial environment, the small businessman is rarely his own master. Directives from Whitehall—or latterly the EU—had impacted on my business dealings on several occasions and were going to do so again. However, I had certainly not become an en-thusiast of accountants running businesses. Spawning, nourishing, running and developing a successful enterprise requires skills that come from a differ-ent part of the brain than the skills required of a trained logician. Some may call this panache, flair, intuition, the pioneer spirit, even chutzpah[16] and it is an essential ingredient.

I think it was Lord Weinstock who coined the phrase, 'experts on tap but not on top', which to me illustrates optimum harmony. An individual who can command such a position is a true entrepreneur. As for all the detailed material with which I had been bombarded, most of it went in one ear and out of the other. I do not possess a good retentive memory for information that I am not using on a regular basis, and I wondered if I had much of a chance in the examinations. Once I got home, I would need to find a job and sort out the family and there would be no time for cramming. It would take longer to develop the perspective that led me to believe that the irksome months I had spent in Doncaster were not wasted. They provided an essential interlude, in the sense that they were a watershed between the years when I lived in my bubble, running small businesses, and my next career move. It had given me the opportunity to spend time with people who had held real jobs—some for years—or developed careers in fields of which I had no experience whatsoever. This would all prove very useful if I were to make the best use of an opportu-nity that soon presented itself. Meanwhile, as I continued south towards London, I noticed cowslips growing in profusion on the road side banks. This surprised me, as I had understood them to be virtually extinct in this country. I composed a letter to the Editor of *The Times* which was pub-lished under the caption 'More beds for Ariel' on 21st May 1985, a few days after my return to Somerset.

Sir, I have not seen cowslips growing in the English country-side for many years and had understood that the species was in danger of extinction. This month, however, I have seen large clumps growing on motorway banks in Yorkshire, Avon, Somerset and Hampshire. They have also appeared in my orchard and in the fields and hedgerows near this house. What is the reason for the return of this delightful flower? I have three possible suggestions:

1. An effect of the hard winter.
2. A change of policy with regard to the use of chemicals in the countryside.
3. Persons unknown are driving around England and scattering handfulls of cowslip seed.

Yours faithfully
Neil Hall
Monmouth House, Yenston, Templecombe, Somerset.

It gave rise to further correspondence that was of interest. I even received personal letters at home, including one from people who had lived at Monmouth House before the war. It was a subject dear to my heart and some years later, when I regularly traveled on the newly-constructed M40 and saw huge swathes of crimson poppies growing in the disturbed earth, as they did in Flanders' traumatised fields during the Great War, it also occurred to me that there was a connection between the release of seed that had long reposed deep in the earth and possibly the other factors, mentioned in the correspondence, that encouraged the species to re-establish itself. At the time of writing (2013) delicate, pale yellow cowslips in huge numbers are once again a glorious sight in the English countryside during springtime.

When I got home, the summer term was in full swing and there were plenty of opportunities to visit the boys at their respective schools. Alexander shone on sports day and won the Senior Athletics Cup for the second year running. Tarquin played a cello solo in the summer concert at Bryanston. The time had come, however, to dedicate every moment to finding a job. I was apprehensive because I had been keeping an eye on the appointments pages in the newspapers but saw nothing for which I felt qualified. However, one day in June, a large advertisement in the *Daily Telegraph* for Schroder Financial Management, a subsidiary of the merchant bank J. Henry Schroder Wagg, caught my eye. They were looking for business-minded people in the West Country, to seek out and service clients who might benefit from their investment and tax-saving products. Although a huge divergence from previous activities, this now seemed right up my street. I was especially attracted by the prominently displayed figure of £30,000 that was designed to whet my appetite and indicated the annual earning potential. A company car was also on offer.

'Hey! Look at this!' I interrupted the family, who were watching Wimbledon.

'Here *is* a good job. We *could* be on our way!'

Spirits raised, I applied for an application form which I returned, together with my CV and a personal testimonial from Sir John Pilcher. This set the ball rolling and I was called to an interview at Schroders' West Country office in Swindon. The manager, potentially my new boss, was a tall, ex-cavalry officer with a long thin nose, down which he peered at me with an air of detached curiosity. He was David Chapel, also an Old Marlburian (C2 1954), as were two members of his team. I discovered this when he dropped a broad hint about being close to my *alma mater*. Marlborough was only ten miles down the road. Had I fallen on my feet? I wondered as I drove home. The excitement led me, for the first and last time, to run out of petrol on the M4. But nothing was settled and I was soon called to a further interview in London. This time an even smarter chap gave me the once-over. He sported a deep purple silk handkerchief that flourished ostentatiously from his breast pocket and matched his suit jacket lining, which I noticed as he paced up and down recounting his fishing exploits on the River Test. When he had finished, he explained in more detail what my job would entail and took me through complicated figures about earning potential and targets. It rather went over my head. The only thing that interested me was, did I have a job or didn't I? At that point I had not appreciated that the whole thing was about *selling*. Anyway, he seemed positive, complimented me on the interesting career path I had pursued, and promised to be in touch. He must have realised that I was broke, since he offered to pay my train fare and as I left his office I discovered, to my horror that my mouth had filled with blood. Raised blood pressure during the interview must have caused it to seep from my gums, which were in grave need of attention.

As I waited to hear from Schroders, I arranged to discuss my new career move with Aubrey, whom I had not seen for more than a year. I somehow felt that my business failures had let him down, but if this was so he kept it to himself, and as we talked I sensed that he respected me for my efforts and considered that I had broken the mould of much of my childhood upbringing. I hoped this attitude would be passed on to my children. Aubrey, was a man who would have endorsed Rumi's teachings on conditioning, which are outlined in Idries Shah's writings.

Had I advanced along the Sufi Way? Had we absorbed the material available? Was I more perceptive? How about Self-cultivation? It would be hard to say. In fact, measuring one's own progress is impossible.

Always ready to provide considered advice, I never knew Aubrey to moralise, criticise or interfere. He would also have approved of Robert Graves' comment when he said, 'Advice is invaluable, interference is intolerable.' As ever, he was interested to hear what I was up to. As a Quaker, Aubrey was related to most of the big banking families, kept his finger on the financial pulse of the nation, and once told me that if he appeared in his box at the opera looking glum, the London stock-market would fall several percentage points the next day.

'Beware!' he warned in his usual way, as he ushered me to the door at the end of our meeting, 'There's a nasty smell in the city these days, so I would cross myself from time to time if I were you!'

That was in 1985—and look how things turned out.

With regard to the immediate future, when huge numbers of Lloyd's Names lost fortunes during the collapse of Lloyd's syndicates and various banking scandals surfaced in the late '80s and early '90s, following the deregulation of the City, known as the 'Big Bang', his words rang very true. It would soon become clear that the familiar world was disappearing for City gentlemen whose word was their bond and whose typical day started with furled umbrella at the ready and bowler hat firmly in place as they took a leisurely stroll to catch the 08:35 from Godalming station. These stockbrokers; who tended to work hard for most of the year and looked forward to the summer break, which began with the Chelsea Flower Show, when they adhered to the old adage, 'Sell in May and go away, buy again St Ledger Day', were now having to adapt.

The demise of Barings, the merchant bank, was another seismic shock that rocked the financial institutions, largely brought about by the unregulated activities of one, Nick Leeson, a rogue trader in the Far East markets and an exemplar of the new generation of sharp-witted wheeler-dealers who had infiltrated the financial sector. In this context, my friend, Ivan Tyrell's, name surfaced again in the public arena when he wrote a book with Leeson entitled *Back from the Brink: Coping with Stress* (Virgin Books 2005).

It seemed prudent to look at other companies in the same field and discover what else was on offer. I had no knowledge of unit trusts, investment bonds, stocks and shares or the burgeoning financial services industry, and my experiences would prove indicative of the state of the industry at the time. I went for three more interviews. The first was at a company in Exeter, which shall remain nameless, where a smarmy fellow talked for fifteen minutes about a couple of products that paid a huge commission and then suggested that I start work the following day. He proposed that I return to his office, make telephone appointments and 'get out to see the punters'. I remonstrated, saying that I really did not know what I was doing, but he assured me that I would learn as I went along and as a special favour he might accompany me for a couple of hours, if he had the time.

'Listen, mate,' he concluded, 'you gotta see the people, *see* the people. The sooner you stop pissin' about an' start sellin', the sooner you'll find that Christmas comes every day!'

It seemed a curious way to conduct business, but after Ashley at Phoenix I was pretty well prepared for anything. The next week, I attended an interview at a London hotel. The reception area was crowded with Japanese people chattering away among themselves and puffing on cigarettes. Suddenly, a diminutive figure appeared in the doorway, dwarfed by a huge palm tree. He clapped his hands loudly and, raising his high-pitched voice above the mêlée, made an announcement that was totally incoherent.

It sounded to me like, 'U wing wang fook kang lode chits'.

The crowd immediately rose as one and everyone proceeded in single file out of the room, across the reception area and into some coaches that were parked on the tarmac outside. I could hardly contain myself and was still giggling quietly when called to what proved to be a disappointing meeting.

My next stop was the Allied Dunbar office in Salisbury where I initially encountered a businesslike approach, and where someone gave me an isometric test that apparently produced commendable results.

'There's only one thing,' my bearded inquisitor concluded with a conspiratorial air before passing me on to the manager. 'Are you aware that you
have no ego?'

How do you answer a question like that?

A battered ego—maybe! No ego—unlikely.

The manager got very excited when he read the isometric analysis and,
like a brigand who had just captured a prize prisoner, put his big feet on the
desk, pulled a bottle of Bells and a plastic mug out of the nearest drawer and
started to tipple, while he explained that I was just the sort of person they
were looking for. I had, it seemed, all the potential for being really successful, and fortunately, my assessment analysis had not strayed into the 'purple
band'. This, I understood, indicated someone who would be capable of saying *anything* to secure a sale. On reflection, I was sure that Ashley at Phoenix
spent his whole working life in the 'purple band' and it occurred to me that
many politicians probably do as well.

After an hour or so I was offered a deal.

'Eight hundred smackers a month to start with and you'll never look
back! I reckon you'll be one of our "high producers" in no time at all. What
do you say?'

As I shook the manager's hand and promised to be in touch, he confirmed that I would be a self-employed agent and there would be no car. I
walked back to the Beetle, through the market square, and decided to wait
and see what Schroders would offer. That proved a long wait. For some reason the decision-making process dragged on. I started calling the secretary
in Swindon once a week to try and find out what was happening, although I
was scared of appearing desperate, which I was. However, I wanted to show
that I was keen and finally, after the umpteenth call, I was put through to
Robert Hunt, one of the Old Marlburians (C3 1959)

'Yes, you've got the job, details are in the post,' he said and put the
phone down.

The next day confirmation of my position as a financial consultant, at
a salary of £10,000 per annum plus a car and expenses, arrived. There could
also be 'on-target earnings' that could boost my remuneration considerably. I
should confirm my acceptance in writing and, subject to a medical examination, report to the offices in Portsmouth for a two-week residential course in
September. This seemed very professional. I was overjoyed and immediately
wrote, agreeing to the terms offered. As I stood by the rough stone garden

wall at Monmouth House, looking out over fields where sheep were graz-
ing on lush grass and wild mint (we called them the 'self-minting baas') I
wondered if all my troubles would soon be over. After all, I lived in a lovely
country house with my wonderful family, was now attached to a prestigious
merchant bank and would soon be a licensed dealer in securities—whatever
they were.

Life even looked hopeful on the international front as Mikhail
Gorbachev, the man with whom Mrs Thatcher expected to be able to do
business, had recently succeeded to the presidency of the USSR. It amused
us to hear that he had gone to Paris to meet the 'intellectuals' and we wondered who those folk were, and indeed who their English counterparts
might be. Bertrand Russell's name came to mind, but he was dead. Malcolm
Muggeridge or Bernard Levin—perhaps.

When Indira Ghandi visited Britain she asked the Iron Lady to arrange
a meeting with the country's intellectuals, only to be told that none existed.
Perhaps Kingsley Amis had got it right when he pronounced that a typical
intellectual was, 'some fearful woman who's going to talk to you about Ezra
Pound and hasn't got large breasts and probably doesn't wash much.'

The next day, we drove over the downs to Cranborne for a celebratory
lunch in the Fleur de Lys and visited the lovely gardens. The little Elizabethan
knot garden by the side of the mansion was especially enchanting.

I came down with a bump, a few days later, in the headmaster's study at
Bryanston, when I attended a meeting to discuss Tarquin's future. The problem was how to find the school fees, and although I had received considerable
assistance, there was some money outstanding for the summer term and the
September term's fees would be due during the holidays. I explained to the
head that I now had a new career, and I was confident that we would soon be
able to pay our way. Perhaps the school would be able to give us some time to
catch up. It seemed a pity to disrupt Tarquin's education, I suggested. He had
clearly discussed the subject with the bursar, as I had, and quickly brought
the matter to a conclusion.

'It strikes me that you no longer have the option for private education.'
he said, 'and it would be better if Tarquin left at the end of this term.'

This was a bitter blow and not what I had expected. Tarquin had
been doing quite well, although letting off a stink bomb in assembly
and locking the staff in the chapel compound had not impressed the
authorities.

Our concept of breaking the mould—Self-cultivation—did not necessarily include becoming an outright rebel. However, even though Lucinda and I were keen for him to continue, the matter was out of our hands. The decision had been made, but not by me. Echoes of my last days at Marlborough bounced around in my head. When I had an opportunity to relay what had transpired to Tarquin, he was equally disappointed, and of course we felt that we had let him down. Teenagers are not always aware of the efforts that are made on their behalf.

Salt was rubbed into the wound when I received a demand for September's fees, in lieu of notice, threatening court action. Needless to say, the debt to Bryanston was soon settled in full.

After much thought, we all agreed that Tarquin should attend the Tertiary College at Yeovil. This was not what we had planned and it was a wrench, but actually worked out very well. The teachers at the college were brilliant and excelled at teaching Tarquin, exam technique, which is what much of western education is all about. He took the bus every day, studied really hard, and notched up a respectable array of O-level passes the following year. It was good to have him at home and I was able to provide help in the evenings, particularly with Latin and the complications associated with the history of the Weimar Republic.

The news during the first week of September, when some twenty recruits gathered at the Hospitality Inn at Southsea for the start of Schroders' induction course, was dominated by the discovery of the wreck of the *Titanic*, and I was reminded of vivid accounts that my grandmother wrote of her life with Oliver. While reading one of her diaries, I learned of how a valuable, but uninsured, collection of his pictures, destined for San Francisco, had gone to the bottom of the Atlantic when the *Titanic* foundered in 1912.

The hotel was across the road from the pier, an excellent venue for a brisk walk before dinner and a terrific vantage point to watch the busy Solent. It was not an inappropriate place to reflect on the fate of the *Titanic*, and how it had remained hundreds of fathoms below the surface of the Atlantic for more than seventy years.

The next morning we decamped to the training rooms in Isambard Brunel Road, a name with a splendid ring to it, but it was a bit of a shock to be in a classroom again so soon. After routine introductions, we were addressed by the man whom I remembered sporting a purple silk hand-kerchief, although a flourish of lime-green now matched the lining of the jacket of the day. He told us how fortunate we were to be chosen to represent Schroders and that an exciting career, during which we would meet scores of fascinating people, was about to open up before us. However, he warned, the next two weeks would be gruelling. The first five days would be spent on learning to develop client relationships and then, after the weekend break, we would return to study financial products. At the end of the course our knowl-edge of these would be tested and providing that we passed all papers with 70% or more, our appointment would be confirmed. Only then would we be allocated our company cars. This was another shock. It never occurred to me that my new position was so tenuous, and we all felt a bit like the recruits in Joan Littlewood's *Oh What a Lovely War!* (1969). Poor sods, tantalised at the recruiting jamboree and egged on by the grinning, busty, female compère, mount the stage in eager anticipation to join up. Once behind the curtain, they encounter stern faces, harsh attitudes and the grim, brutal realities of an army at war.

The first step was to learn about marketing and finding 'prospects'. A 'prospect' was someone you hoped to do business with, we were informed. The company would provide some 'leads', but we were expected to take the initiative and generate 'activity'. Making appointments on the telephone came under that heading, and I soon found myself learning how to cold-call. I also discovered that an essential part of activity was known as 'asking for referrals' which, in broad terms, meant trying to access the address book of as many of the prospect's friends, relations and colleagues as possible. It re-minded me of the advice a friend of mine gave her teenage daughters: 'Watch out for boys!' she counselled. 'Every boy you meet will have one objective— to get his fingers into your panties!'

The next step was an introduction to the 'fact find'. This was to be the prime tool in learning about our prospect's financial circumstances and Schroders were, I believe, the first company in the UK to introduce this tech-nique. Skilled questioning and completing the 'fact find' led the prospect out of his or her comfort zone by exposing gaps in their financial armoury. Did they have sufficient life and illness insurance? Were they saving and were their investments tax-efficient? How would they educate their children? Did they have a retirement plan in place? Had they made a will? Those were the sort of questions to ask. Then, having thoroughly unsettled the prospect, the next step was to come to the rescue by providing financial products that filled those gaps. The entire sales cycle followed this course:

Prospecting
Making an appointment
Fact finding
Defining a need
Agreeing a need
Presenting the solution
Closing the deal

It could be very manipulative, and once again I was encountering commerce in an entirely new guise, and a world so very different from the one in which I had been brought up. But as the week progressed and we took part in numerous role plays, I learned to adapt. In time, as you will see, I also changed my attitude profoundly.

As we gathered for the second week, I heard of Laura Ashley's death. She had played a prominent part in a world that I had once belonged to so it was sad news indeed. The first green shoots of her business sprang to life in the 1970s, while she sat cutting pretty, rustic-style fabrics on her kitchen table and, catching the mood of the time, huge success followed. The company was then floated on the stock-market, shortly before her death, but appears to have been buffeted by commercial storms ever since.

When proceedings commenced on Monday morning, I could see within a few minutes that the week would be irksome because there was a lot of information to absorb. This ranged from details of products such as unit trusts, investment bonds, insurance schemes and pension plans to generic knowledge of tax planning, the stock market, state benefits and domicile.

I shared a room with Mik Taverner, an ex-concert pianist, and while he sat poised in the lotus position on his bed, dressed solely in his yellow stained Y-fronts, a practice that I did not emulate, we grilled each other over and over again. Until late into the night, we checked our knowledge of plan costs, bid/offer spread, annual management charges and all the other technical bits and pieces that would be tested at the end of the week. Fortunately, when it was all over, everyone passed, and following a farewell dinner, we dispersed around the country in our company cars, ready to start new our careers the following Monday.

The drive from Monmouth House to Swindon in September, over Salisbury Plain and the Marlborough Downs, was a pleasant start and end to a day and, once seated at my desk, I was keen to get going. All I now had to do, I thought, was make appointments on the telephone, follow them up, and generate loads of money. My initiation was sugared with a few leads and a long list of names, addresses and telephone numbers was also provided. I rapidly discovered that I was very good at making appointments and my diary was soon packed with scheduled meetings, although it has to be said that some prospects were just curious as to what Schroders, a prestigious merchant bank, was doing marketing in the West Country. The next couple of months, an Indian summer, were largely spent meandering through the lanes of Wessex interviewing wealthy landowners, businessmen, retired folk and professionals with families. I visited lovely houses and had some fascinating conversations.

'Why have you let me come and see you?' I asked one prospect.

'I was curious,' she replied. 'You see, your name is Neil Hall and I have a godson with the surname Neil-Hall; James Neil *hyphen* Hall.'

I asked her how much her house was worth. She replied curtly, 'I have no idea; this is my home.'

Refreshing.

Perhaps the most unexpected situation arose when, a rugged huntsman who lived at his kennels in Wessex, told me to get back to him later in the autumn as he would, by then, be in a position to invest a pile of cash earned from selling the skins of hunted prey and fallen stock.

Unfortunately, although I had more meetings than anyone else in our office, I was not selling anything. To me, selling was a matter of being affable and having an attractive tangible product. In the past, this meant dangling the vision of a freshly painted flat or even a new kitchen before a potential customer, or holding up a beautiful fabric and just waiting for the chequebook to emerge. This new business meant selling intangibles and there were lots of ifs and buts. It seemed a bit like smoke and mirrors to me.

The manager brought me up sharply. He told me to get my hair cut and to learn to close a deal.

A *manager*! I had never had one of those before.

'You're involved but you're not committed,' he barked, 'and if you don't know the difference, think about when you last had eggs and bacon for breakfast. The chicken was involved, but the pig was committed!'

Wielding a crowbar did not come naturally. I also needed to learn the jargon. The process of 'defining and agreeing the (client's) need', invariably meant writing a report for the client and that involved using the correct terminology. I had to learn phrases like 'bull and bear markets'; 'anticipated growth'; 'reduction in yield'; 'past and future performance'; 'with the expectation of a better return'; 'capital realisation'; 'earnings potential'; 'taxable gain'; 'money purchase'; 'funding for cash'; 'chargeable event' and 'fluctuating emoluments'. The latter sounded like an acutely painful condition of the small intestine.

This was a much tougher business than I had anticipated, and the pressure began to mount. A friend of mine provided a warning. He had been working for a merchant bank that was involved in a stock-market flotation.

'We'll need you to come in on Saturday to finish this work,' his boss informed him.

'Can't do that, I'm afraid,' he replied. 'We have an important family wedding.'

'No problem—enjoy the wedding—but don't bother to come back next week unless it is to pick up your P45!' retorted the senior man. And collect his P45 was exactly what he did.

'How many appointments have you got booked for next week?' my manager questioned as I was preparing to go home one evening.

'Five!' I replied.

'Not good enough—get back on the 'phone and don't leave until you have eight!' he snorted.

I endeavoured to toughen up, but retain a sense of humour, and this joke helped.

> Shortly after the war, Hitler was found in Argentina by some of his old comrades. They tried to persuade their Führer to return to Germany, assuring him that he could still command a huge following and would be welcomed by immense crowds. Initially reluctant, he eventually bowed to pressure.
>
> 'There is just one condition … just one,' he insisted.
>
> 'No more Mr Nice Guy!'

Gradually, as the autumn passed, I came to terms with my new situation and eventually made my first sale. This was followed by a process, designed to encourage competition between colleagues, which I found distasteful. Every sale, together with the appropriate commission, was marked up with a felt-tip on a large white board in the office, for all to see. My sale was duly registered with a commission of £500 logged.

I felt very pleased with myself.

A couple of hours later, one of the Old Marlburians, Richard Macfarlane (Cotton House 1952), congratulated me and idly asked what I had sold. When I told him, he questioned the level of commission.

'I think you'll find that's £50, old boy,' he said.

The administrator had got her decimal point in the wrong place.

Richard was a splendid fellow, but he did not enjoy selling. In retirement, he was appointed Private Secretary to HRH Princess Alexandra.

When I went back to my new friend at the kennels, I could see him stoking the fire in the sitting room as I walked up the garden path towards his tied cottage. A few minutes later, after a warm greeting, he took a roll of grubby notes from a rusty biscuit tin on the mantelpiece and stuffed them into my hands.

'You'll find there's three thousand,' he said. 'Buy me some units in your Japanese Smaller Companies Fund.'

Chapter 10
Pirates and Pathans

It is, it is a glorious thing
To be a pirate king
(Sir W.S. Gilbert, *'The Pirates of Penzance'*, first performed
  1879)

Travel, in the younger sort, is a part of education; in the
elder, a part of experience.
(Francis Bacon, 1561–1626)

IN THEIR RECRUITMENT campaign, Schroder Financial
Management had been clever to emphasise their connection with the merchant bank. This strategy formed part of a drive to establish a salaried 'officer
corps' within the sales force so, unlikely as this may seem, it was not until
Christmas that it actually dawned on me that I had joined the life assurance
industry. I also found that I was in competition with our own self-employed
direct sales force and brokers, who were free to sell Schroders' products, and
this situation sometimes produced an undignified and unseemly scrummage
for business.

The real position with regard to 'salary' and commission also became
clear. The theory had been explained, but reality was now staring me in the
face. The fact was, that the 'salary' proved to be only a payment of commission in advance and, if the 'salary' level was not justified by adequate sales,

an unacceptable debt would build up and contracts would be terminated. I was already developing a love-hate view of the industry however, I had got myself into it, had little choice and, taking the poet, Wilfred Owen as my inspiration, determined to make a success. Owen had viewed his early days as a soldier, following enlistment in the Artist's Rifles in 1915, with horror, but he stuck it out, eventually becoming a first-rate officer and earning the Military Cross.[17]

In the early months of 1986, I began to learn how to make the business work for me. I refined my prospecting so that I was seeing people with a genuine interest in reviewing their finances and, as I became confident with the products and the terminology, I learned to detect 'buying signals' so that the sale became part of a natural process. I also came to believe, when in a positive frame of mind, that genuine needs could be met by the industry and that I could perform a useful service and earn a good living in the process. Perhaps I had read Winston Churchill's view: 'If I had my way I would write the word "INSURE" upon the door of every cottage and upon the blotting book of every public man, because I am convinced for sacrifices which are inconceivably small, families and estates can be protected against catastrophes ...'

I was often overcome with nerves before attending a 'closing' meeting, akin to going on stage, but found that by adopting a more aloof stance and suppressing the pound signs that danced before my eyes when a 'close' was imminent, sales and income actually began to increase. Had I learned that people needed time and attention as well as financial products?

Schroders rewrote their contracts as they realised that a mounting debt, starting on day one, was not viable if they were to continue to recruit quality consultants dealing with wealthy clients. Unfortunately, just as everything was beginning to gel, a threat from an unexpected quarter threw an almighty spanner into the works. Once again Nigel Lawson would profoundly influence my business life. He abolished capital transfer tax in his March Budget. This was a huge blow as much of the business completed in Swindon involved products designed to mitigate this punitive tax. The immediate consequence was that the branch was closed. The consultants were given an ultimatum that, to my mind, required us to achieve a punitive level of business by the end of April or our contracts would be voided. If we succeeded in meeting the target, we were offered the option of reporting to one of Schroders' branches in Bristol or London.

'For God's sake, get out there and SELL something ... ANYTHING!' were the manager's final instructions.

So, Lucinda and I reflected, this was how big business worked. Top brass took strategic decisions, far from the front, and the little guys with wives and children got crushed in the trenches. In my case, although left high and dry at Monmouth House, I was determined to be the one to make the decision. Desperate situations require drastic measures and after a huge effort I squeezed in under the wire. Lucinda and I agreed that I should opt for the offices in Covent Garden.

The summer of 1986 found us, once more, in a precarious position. Tarquin was preparing for his O-levels. Alexander had left the Old Ride and was at school in Shaftesbury, following a brief spell at Sexey's School, the Somerset county school in Bruton, founded by Hugh Sexey, an ostler's son who became auditor to Queen Elizabeth I and King James. Lucinda was commuting daily to Street, where she attended a Training Opportunities (TOPS) course in computer skills. She was finding her return to the general working environment as daunting as I had in Doncaster, but the benefits of acquiring this knowledge would prove incalculable over the coming months and years. She was a brave girl.

Meanwhile, I was trying to keep all the balls in the air, primarily building a client base in the West Country, although now I was required to travel to London a couple of times a week. Clearly these circumstances could not continue, and once term was over we devised a plan. Tarquin went to stay with Jack MacDougal in Paris, to learn French, and Alexander visited his grandparents in Wellesley. The boys were certainly learning that business life could be harrowing, but I wanted to prove to myself that I really could make a go of the financial business. To do that, we needed to be in London, so we begged a room from our old friend Cecilia Metternich in Putney. Lucinda took a hugely stressful temping job with Laura Ashley in Chelsea and I planned to slog my guts out for six weeks in Covent Garden. An awful lot of water had flowed beneath the Thames bridges since we had abandoned the idea of buying a house in the country, but we told ourselves that if this experiment worked we would move back to London on a permanent basis. The day that we implemented the plan was memorable. Suzy Lamplugh, a glamorous young estate agent, disappeared after visiting a house in Fulham with a client. It happened just across the river from where we were staying, and she has not been found to this day. She was certified dead in 1994.

After six weeks, I came to the conclusion that, providing I kept up a relentless routine of prospecting, followed by initial meetings, followed by sufficient closing meetings, I would be able to earn a decent living. In addition, if Lucinda also worked, we could remain solvent and the family would survive. Having assessed the risk, we agreed that we would move to London in the autumn—but in the meantime we would have some fun.

Alexander's enthusiasm for film and the movie business knew no bounds and he had written a short film that he wanted to make. We were keen to encourage him and Lucinda, who had visited the set of *Bonanza* in Hollywood, as a child and whose father had been in the music business, proved to be his guiding light, energetically organising the project. The film was called *Going In, In Action*, the location Monmouth House and its environs, the actors ten of his school chums, and the general back-up and dogsbodies Lucinda and me. Alexander's friend, John Clarke—a Fleet Street journalist—lent him a video camera and one Thursday afternoon in August, everything came together. We spent the next four days with a house full of rowdy teenagers. Walls built of cardboard boxes were ritually smashed, dummies thrown from the roof, boys leaped over stone walls at unexpected moments and feigned death in the middle of the lane, and I seemed to spend every waking hour careering around the countryside in the company car. One minute 'actors' were being dropped off in fields or woods, the next moment I was revving the engine in a muddy farmyard while Alexander took close-up shots of wheels spinning before the chase and, finally, I was even given a part driving the getaway car, with revolver at the ready. While all this was going on, Lucinda alternately sorted out the sleeping arrangements, rustled up huge pans of delicious spaghetti bolognaise or manned the barbecue, stoking the coals and preparing juicy burgers, sausages and chops for the grill. Dozens of cans of coke and bottles of lemonade stood at the ready, not to mention whisky and wine for the caterers.

It was all hugely enjoyable, but on Monday morning some semblance of order returned. I had a business meeting at Usher's Brewery in Trowbridge that gave me the opportunity to return several of Alexander's friends to their parents and, while driving home, as was so often the case, I ruminated on our immediate plans.

'One thing is certain', said Lucinda as I aired my thoughts, upon my return.

'When we move, Alexander should go to a school with a good media studies department and preferably a video-editing suite'.

She started to do some research. In September we planned our move back to London, after six years in the country. Lucinda had discovered, by pouring over dozens of reference books in the library, that the only school that boasted the facilities we sought for Alexander was William Ellis Comprehensive in Kentish Town. She booked a meeting with the headmaster and managed to persuade him to give Alexander the last remaining vacancy for the autumn term. This was very good news and determined the neighbourhood where we should live.

After a couple of days slogging round Hampstead, we found an affordable, airy first-floor flat in Netherhall Gardens with good views over west London. It was a bit of a squeeze after our country houses and gave rise to a considerable amount of tension but we learned to adjust. Alexander would be able to walk across the Heath to William Ellis, which proved to be a pretty rough establishment. On one occasion, the gym was burned to the ground by a young arsonist, and there were instances of furniture being flung at the teachers. Alexander would say that he came from a prep school where the staff hounded him; to a comprehensive where roles were reversed and the children bullied and abused the teaching staff. A short Tube ride took me to Covent Garden, and we hoped that Lucinda would find a suitable job nearby. We returned to Monmouth House at weekends until our notice to the Count expired, and early in 1987 entirely severed our ties with Somerset.

As the New Year got under way, the stock-market started to rise quite rapidly. The FTSE 100 index in January stood at 1679 and had risen 18% to 1987 by the beginning of July. My job was to bring investment to Schroder's, and a spirit of bullish optimism spreading across the country made that task easier. As any salesman knows, targets are always under review and a new year presents a blank sheet that will have to be filled. However, I began to surprise myself and my boss, who continually threatened me with termination unless I achieved my targets; as clients confidently parted with five-or six-figure sums and the risk we had taken by moving to Hampstead seemed likely to pay off. Ian Hammond, my new manager, taught me a lesson that proved useful.

'When you are out selling,' he said, 'try to identify your potential client within these categories. Is he or she an Analytical, an Amiable, a Driver or an Expressive? The Analytical will approach financial concepts in terms of percentage returns and cold logic. He will be the one who studies the fine print and the statistics. The Amiable may be more intuitive, but will want to feel that you are his friend and that he is doing the right thing. The Driver will ask for information but make his own decisions. The Expressive will behave like a prima donna. Try and observe these tendencies, although most people exhibit a combination of these characteristics.'

Initially, I found his ideas rather odd but as time went by I came to value this psychological sales tool. Approaching an Analytical as though he or she were an Amiable would prove pointless. My prospect would think me an idiot and quickly show me the door. Conversely, eyes would glaze over if a warm-hearted Amiable were approached with loads of numbers. Selling to a Driver was easy, providing you presented enough information for a decision to be made. I learned that it was unwise to question that decision, even if, in my opinion, it was the wrong choice. In time, as an Amiable myself, I found selling to Analyticals to be very difficult. A school bursar would be a good example. They did not want to be told, invariably swamped themselves with too much information and usually ended up taking—in my opinion—the wrong course. I once asked the headmaster (a Driver) of a famous school how he got on with his bursar.

'Well!' he replied. 'When a project is mooted, I say, "Yes." He says, "No," and we learn to muddle through!'

One of my early sales was to an elderly Czech lawyer-cum-businessman who exhibited some of the characteristics described by my manager, and lived in North London. As he handed me his cheque for a substantial sum, he said,

'I know a good zing ven I see one. Did you know zat I invented ze Arctic roll?'

He sounded a bit like my old chum, Leon.

The Arctic roll; ice cream rolled in a thin layer of sponge cake with raspberry jam, was invented in the 1950s and became hugely popular for a time. In the 1980s, twenty-five miles of Birds Eye Arctic roll was sold each month.

Although it has been referred to as tasting like 'frozen carpet', my family found it very tasty, so, in time, we must have consumed a few hundred yards.

BD, another old man and one of my first clients, unexpectedly invited Lucinda and me to his eightieth birthday party. It was to be held in the spacious basement kitchens of Kenwood House in Hampstead. As I ambled along the terrace, I fell into conversation with a tall chap who was evidently on the guest list as well.

'I am very fond of BD. It was he who first got me interested in politics,' he explained to me.

'And has that interest continued?' I replied.

He chuckled and strode ahead.

At that moment Lucinda caught up with me. 'What were you talking to Peter (now Sir Peter) Bottomley about?' she enquired. 'You know he's a Tory MP and has been marked as a high-flyer!'

Whoops!!

Commissions rose rapidly, which enhanced our personal financial security, and Lucinda and I even wondered if we might qualify for an overseas holiday, one of the perennial carrots dangled before us. The next scheduled jamboree sounded tempting; it would be held on the Greek island of Rhodes but, in the meantime Lucinda, Alexander and I managed a short, overdue holiday in Sussex.

My cousin, Tessa Hall, lent us Broad Halfpenny, her charming cottage tucked away in the woods near Fittleworth, and we enjoyed one of the quietest and most relaxing few days I have ever spent. I even had time to read *Darkest England* (1987), a hilarious and astute analysis of the English and Englishness. Such a book by an Afghan was extraordinary in itself but, with Idries Shah as author, there are unexpected dimensions.

We slept late, gathered eggs for breakfast from the ducks that splashed about in the pond at the end of the garden, walked in the woods near Lodsworth, shopped in the pretty market town of Petworth, and one afternoon took a boat out on the Arun at Arundel. The river meanders sleepily through a gap in the South Downs at this point, below the magnificent Norman castle which towers above the town and valley. After messing about on the water for an hour or so, we drove the few miles to Littlehampton. Here, a favourite spot from my childhood, the Arun joins the sea and we sat with our legs dangling over the quayside munching fish and chips and watched the sun go down over the sand dunes beyond the yachts moored on the far side of the estuary. Once back at the cottage, we stayed up late to watch videos that Lucinda and Alexander had selected.

On my return to the office, I took the opportunity to digest developments within the company. Some months previously Schroder's had sold their subsidiary (Schroder Financial Management) to National Mutual, an Australian life assurance company, for a figure reputed to be close to £100 million. This was something of a personal blow and a further example of an individual's vulnerability in the face of corporate power. The elite Schroder name would be phased out and after three years we would be trading under the simple but less attractive title NM Financial Management. Several of the Schroder people, including the extrovert with the flamboyant breast-pocket 'kerchiefs, took fright and decamped to Flemings, a small but successful investment bank in the city. My contract was cancelled and I became a self-employed representative.

National Mutual had traded in the UK for many years. Their largest customer base was the Post Office workforce, and they were keen to move upmarket and enter the unit-linked business established by Schroders. Schroders themselves, must have been laughing all the way to their own bank. They not only amassed a huge profit, but managed to shed that part of their operation which was connected to an industry which would not only be hit by mis-selling scandals but was also about to enter a stranglehold regulatory regime that would be very costly to implement and supervise.

The passing of the Financial Services Act 1986 and the introduction of the Life Assurance and Unit Trust Regulatory Organisation (LAUTRO) were aimed at policing an industry that had failed to regulate itself. I had no doubt that this was for the general benefit of the consumer and also protected people in my position who were required to demonstrate that they were consistently providing 'best advice'. Many of those, whom Lucinda called 'the pirates', were brought to heel or left the country to trade with expats in unregulated territories.

Is there a tendency to larceny in many of us? I wondered. Perhaps some of us who were left, were *reformed pirates*. However, greed and fear, the engines of capitalism, are difficult emotions to tame, and occur on both sides of the counter. As the market boomed in the latter half of 1987, some people, who probably should never have gone near equities, continued to buy. A colleague put it succinctly:

'When your cleaning lady tells you she is going to buy stocks and shares, that is the time to get out.'

On the morning of Friday 16th October 1987 I curtailed an early phone call to a colleague with the words, 'Well, I'd better get off to the office,' and his reply was, 'I don't think you'll get very far!'

It was only then I learned that while we all slept soundly in our cosy beds in Hampstead, a devastating storm had passed right over us. A deep depression, famously missed by the forecasters, gave rise to a hurricane that wreaked havoc across the south of England. A few minutes later, taking my chances, I turned from Netherhall Gardens into Fizjohn's Avenue and realised what my chum meant. Fallen London plane trees lay, at intervals, blocking the road all the way down to Swiss Cottage. It was the same wherever one went and in the afternoon, walking in St James's Park with Tarquin, who had recently returned from Paris, it was distressing to see that beautiful trees had crashed into the lake and broken branches lay everywhere. During the evening we received a call from friends in the country. They told us it would take months to clear the debris and years to recover from the damage, and that the drive and front door of their house were blocked by the fall of a massive beech tree. However, it could have been a lot worse. The very top branches scraped down the front of their house, only roughing up the paint work and dislodging a few tiles, as it fell. We promised to help, and the next morning Tarquin and I set off down the Brighton road.

'Bloody hell, Tarquin! This is a disaster zone!' I exclaimed as we proceeded through the countryside.

We spent the whole weekend wielding chainsaws, stacking severed boughs and burning brushwood; while from gardens, woodlands and farmland all around came the sound of screeching petrol engines as the whiff of blue wood smoke drifted across the meadows. It became clear that not only had the force of the gale been greater than anyone could recall, but because it had been preceded by mild and excessively wet weather, tree roots had been easily loosened. The trees, still in full leaf, were vulnerable to the force that pounded them.

On the following Monday, there was a meeting at the Covent Garden office that all consultants were expected to attend. It started at 10 a.m but was soon interrupted.

Someone poked their head around the door.

'Markets are dropping! Big falls!'

The meeting was abandoned and we tumbled out of the conference room.

Checking our screens, we were soon greeted by the appalling news that the stock-market, which had peaked at 2302, had dropped by 11% during the morning and was still falling. It fell a further 12% the following day and it soon became apparent that clients who had recently bought equities had taken a massive hit. A colleague had invested £1m for a client only a few days previously, proudly chalking up some £30,000 commission on the office board. That investment was now worth less than £750,000.

Why had this occurred? Some said that it was because the stock exchange was only manned by greenhorns on that Monday morning. Experienced dealers were either unable or unwilling to get to London because of the storm, and once the prices began to fall there was no one available who knew what to do. Others blamed the new computer trading systems, which went into freefall. Certainly prices had been rising hysterically. Advertisements screamed from every billboard in the country, during that late summer and autumn, urging punters to buy, buy, buy!

A correction was inevitable; the fundamentals were entirely at odds with what was happening in the marketplace, but how many consultants were expecting it, or wanted it? In due course we came to appreciate that when J.K. Galbraith said, 'the only function of economic forecasting is to make astrology look respectable,' he was not far off the mark. The daunting process of fielding phone calls from anxious clients immediately began but, as far as I was concerned, these were uncharted waters. Old hands in the business started to mutter about a 'buying opportunity' but, by God, one would have been brave indeed, to have invested during those last weeks of October 1987.

However, there were such people. Perhaps they were schooled in Nathan Rothschild's directive: 'The time to buy is when blood is running in the streets!'

Those people, investing for the long term, prospered, but those who panicked and sold their holdings were the real losers. Over the following weeks the markets gradually recovered and the FTSE 100 ended the year, marginally higher (1713) than it had been at the beginning of the year. As I write in 2013 the FTSE 100 stands at 6673.

The last few months had provided a steep learning curve. It was sobering to deal with the mechanics of an effervescent stock-market rise followed by a crash, even though in the longer term the fall became perceived as a blip. But living with the reality that bull markets can falter and that prices can fall as well as rise was to colour my future approach, and was also to influence those of us involved in selling within the rapidly developing financial services industry. The events of October 1987 had provided a degree of 'baptism by fire' and were certainly going to strengthen the regulator's hand.

In January, following the sale of the company to National Mutual, the Covent Garden operation was closed and I moved to offices in Richmond, Surrey. This was not as disruptive as it might seem, because the Northern Link line ran from Frognal Station, at the bottom of our street, through London's western suburbs, and crossed the Thames at Strand on the Green. The journey took about forty minutes but the carriages were grubby, seats frequently soiled and walls and ceilings covered with graffiti. Daily travel on public transport necessitated frequent visits to the dry cleaners to keep business suits fresh and clean. In the mornings, it was convenient to leave clothes at such an establishment in the Finchley Road. A woman with bleached blonde hair and a pointy, heavily rouged face invariably served me. As she issued the ticket, without looking up, she always barked out the same question:

'Wot woz 'e name?' 'Wot WOZ 'e name?'

It drove me crazy. No pleases or thank yous, just, 'WOT WOZ'E NAME?'

I could have screamed but replied quietly, enunciating clearly:

'My name IS Hall—H-A-double L.'

It was to no avail; her manner did not change. I might as well have been talking to the proverbial brick wall, and so the ritual continued for nearly two years until we moved.

I wondered in the January of 1988, when loss of investor confidence prevailed, where future sales would come from. There were new targets to be met, a living to be earned, and a family to be supported. I analysed what my job was really all about, and redefined my role introducing a useful slogan at the same time. I was selling 'financial security'. This meant that I also sold life and illness assurance, something, initially, I was too coy to mention.

However, I was well paid to sell those products, so I got used to the idea and in due course experienced situations when clients or their families benefited from the policies I had sold them.

I also encouraged people to save. With Mrs Thatcher exhorting us all to adopt an attitude of thrift, and inflation running well below levels of the previous decade, saving to build financial security seemed a goal worth pursuing. The value of regular monthly unit trust investments could be enhanced by what was called 'pound cost averaging'. This was the means whereby units were bought at fluctuating prices thereby ironing out peaks and troughs in the market. After the introduction of Personal Equity Plans (PEPs) in January 1987 and Individual Savings Accounts (ISAs) in April 1999, tax advantages made this concept even more attractive.

Arguably, the longest-term form of saving is building a pension fund, and I found advising in that area difficult; the reason for this being that it was very easy—and profitable—to jump on the pension bandwagon and sell a label without making it entirely clear to the client the nature of the commitment they were undertaking. How many times did I meet someone who proudly claimed to 'own a pension', like they owned a car, when it turned out that they were only contributing twenty-five pounds a month? There was considerable ignorance about what funding for a pension meant. Some considered it a kind of magic wand. Sign here and expect an income for life.

Harsh number-crunching dictated that the target of a taxable annuity (pension) of say £50,000 per annum (assuming 5% return) on retirement would require a pension fund of at least £1m, and to achieve that, contributions exceeding £1000 per month for thirty to forty years would be necessary. How many people would be in the position to pay so much into their pensions for so long? Even if they were, funds were so often side tracked to other diversions or to fulfil a legion of expectations along the way that such sustained saving was unlikely.

'To hell with all that. I want to live NOW!' was not an uncommon response.

I was left in a quandary. If I explained the stark reality of the situation, potential clients, unless they had exceptional levels of disposable income, felt that whatever they did was a drop in the ocean and therefore not worth pursuing. If I pleaded the case of 'anything is better than nothing', was I really doing my client a favour by suggesting that they tied up their money in that way? In general, I found this serious topic, saving for old age against the background of a consumer culture, difficult to address, as has every government, right up to the present day.

Lump sum investment to build a portfolio was my preferred mode of business. Providing that the client's medium-to long-term aim had been established, it was easy to execute and with unit-linking, the client always knew exactly what his or her investment was worth. From the point of view of remuneration it was clean, in the sense that advisers could not suffer a 'clawback'. Clawbacks were dreaded by consultants because it meant that business had fallen off the books and commission would be clawed back, or reclaimed by the company. This only applied to what was called 'regular premium business', such as a life policy or pension, and for each case the commission could be vulnerable, on a reducing scale, for a minimum two-year period. Clawbacks were a hazard of the industry that rarely affected me. However, I have known advisers whose entire year's commission was wiped out by a huge cancellation from a previous year. It is easy to imagine the pressure to sell that such a person would be under, especially if they had spent their previously credited commission, but had failed to set aside funds to meet their tax liability. Those situations evolved from an industry that was not adequately regulated. The original sale was often—although there were justifiable exceptions—unsafe. That triggered a vicious circle that could only be sustained by further selling. The more desperate the salesman, the harder he pushed for the next sale.

My kit bag was primarily geared to provide protection, savings and investment. The question, once again, was, to whom? There was no point in casting around for prospects in every direction, so I decided to target people involved in activities that interested me or where I had direct experience. I had concluded that it was much easier to sell to people with whom one had some degree of empathy. In that way, prospects became clients because they perceived me as someone with a genuine interest, rather than as someone trying to sell them something. It was rather like the old adage: 'Don't marry for money—just knock around with rich people until you fall in love with one of them!'

Interior decorators and proprietors of established painting and decorating firms were an obvious choice. I went to the Summer Exhibition at the Royal Academy and contacted artists and sculptors. I went to the Chelsea Flower Show and contacted horticulturists and landscape gardeners.

'How about taking a stand at the Boat Show, next year?' the manager suggested.

'Good idea—but how much will that cost?' I replied.

I went to concerts and contacted musicians. I actively introduced myself to local retailers and other businesspeople. Not all those people had money to buy the services that I was offering, but they all needed to build financial security, and a sufficient number gave me enough business to establish a robust client bank. Gradually, over the next couple of years, I became one of the more successful consultants, which was important with respect to relationships within the company. Managers didn't see faces, they saw numbers, and were obsessed by what they called 'high producers'. I was reminded of my encounter with Jock Noyes, in New York, twelve years previously, as the culture of the financial sector became increasingly vulgar.

'Are you on target?' was a question that arose on a daily basis

If you weren't pulling in the sales you were dirt, but the more you sold, the more trinkets and baubles were showered upon you. I even qualified for overseas holidays, and in 1988 Lucinda and I did indeed go to Rhodes for five days at the company's expense.

Arriving at our luxurious hotel, we were impressed to learn that the Iron Lady had only recently departed after attending a conference for EU leaders. On the first evening, as we sipped retsina and nibbled on pistachio nuts, we stared out from our balcony across the Aegean to the nearby Turkish coast. We mused about Ottomans and Venetians; Romans, Greeks, Persians and Phoenicians, and wondered who, over the centuries, had passed across that stretch of water.

'Do you think Alexander the Great sailed into this very harbour?' I questioned.

'Probably—what a sight, that would have been. Cheers to Alexander!' Lucinda rejoined, raising her glass.

It was a romantic spot and reminded us of a visit to Churchill's favourite hotel in Tangier—the El Minzah—where our attention had frequently been captured by the sight of large vessels slipping through the Straits of Gibraltar. We had been on our way back from an exciting trip to Essaouira and Marrakech.

The next day, we hired a car and started to explore the island, to make the most of this opportunity and because we were anxious to escape from the crowd. Heading away from the city with its magnificent palace of the

Knights Templar, bustling lanes and colourful harbour once dominated by the legendary colossus, we explored coves and inlets, stopping for a bathe from time to time. When we reached Lyndos, I was reminded that this had been the location for the star-studded 1960s epic *The Guns of Navarone* (1961), although scrawny donkeys now carried portly tourists rather than boxes of ammo. Over the remaining days we enjoyed driving through remote, rocky areas dotted with tiny white chapels that shone like pearls on steep hillsides. Ranks of gnarled and crooked olive trees, some a thousand years old, hobbled across the landscape before disappearing into a dusty mirage. We stopped and gathered bunches of thyme, rosemary and sage, which we later stuffed into our suitcases and took home, where they added a piquant zest to our cuisine for weeks to come.

Although there were obligatory evening events that we were required to attend, our daily excursions eventually took us to the deserted beaches at the southernmost tip of the island. When I returned the car to Avis on the last day they were astounded to find that we had clocked up eight hundred kilometres, something of a feat as the island is only seventy kilometres from north to south and less than forty kilometres wide!

'So did you enjoy the convention?' Ian Hammond, who had been dumped, fully clad, in the swimming pool in a moment of excessive exuberance, enquired on my return to the office.

'Marvellous—we loved every minute!'

'What a pity you play the organ,' Ian said with a quizzical expression etched across his face. 'Playing the violin or cello would have made you a much better team player!'

He could have been right. Our conversation reminded me of this occurrence.

An acquaintance of mine, staying at a country house, was invited to go hunting. He hated hunting and he loathed killing things, but how could he refuse? Some days later I asked him how the hunt went.

'Very well,' he replied.

'Did you see any foxes? Did the hounds kill?'

'No, nothing happened at all—not a fox to be seen!'

'That can't have been much fun,' I rejoined.

'You don't understand. I hate foxhunting so no foxes suited me down to the ground!'

We attended several of these overseas conferences, as they were called and, on one occasion, won a fancy-dress competition for which we received a cup inscribed, 'The Most Imaginative Couple'. The theme for the evening was 'The Movies'. Lucinda, having addressed the challenge with ingenuity and skill and, having cleared the stock of bandages at our local Boots, had packed all the gear before we left England, which included old sheets and worn-out trainers that I had daubed with thick white emulsion. Somehow, she had managed to get it all together in our cramped cabin. Then, having bandaged every inch of our bodies except our faces, and sporting grotesque masks we appeared, amid hoots of laughter, as *The Mummy* and *The Mummy Returns*.

We each had mixed feelings about these events but much of the time was enjoyable, and we took advantage of every opportunity to visit places that we had never been to before.

The managers tended to spend a great deal of the holiday and a considerable amount of their own money at the bar and while we enjoyed the venues they seemed to be more interested in company politics and watching what the other guy was up to. This was in line with what I had come to expect from management, whose time was generally spent, not on managing the sales force but on engineering their own career moves. Having run my own business, I was frequently appalled by the effect of costly and inappropriate decisions while the instigator, far from being blamed, was more often promoted. In a small business, such things were impossible or the firm would collapse very quickly.

The conferences also cost a great deal and that expense was borne, in the final analysis, by clients. Those occasions really presented me with a conundrum that epitomised the financial services industry at the time. Were we salesman, with targets to achieve, who could be rewarded with glistening trophies like a sales force in any other commercial organisation, or were we closet members of the social services, constantly being obliged to make value judgements and living in fear of our lives or at least our livelihoods, less we had omitted to provide best advice and mis-sold a product? It struck me that this situation would continue until members of the public, at large, took more responsibility for their own financial affairs and while they remained apathetic about their future they were prey to commission-hungry salesmen. It would be some years, when all the 'pirates' had either emigrated or walked the plank and when the commercial and regulatory climate was more appropriate, before 'advice-led' rather than 'sales-led' businesses were able to operate within the financial services industry. Eventually, in 1992, one such company came into existence—The J. Rothschild Partnership (now St. James's Place Wealth Management).

Although I did not join that company until much later, my attitude to the industry was maturing. Rather like my change of perspective about Peacock Decorators following my marriage; when the business which had been as much a source of enjoyment as a serious enterprise, evolved into a very serious undertaking. So, my attitude to providing financial advice developed. I began to realise that what had been primarily—for me—a cash cow, reflected deadly consequences with regard to future planning. I became much more serious about the advice I gave and my clients appreciated this attitude. On one occasion, I lectured a young couple on the fact that they were attempting to educate their children privately when it was quite clear that they could not afford to do so.

'You can't afford it, and it will put a huge strain on your marriage,' I hammered on. (Where did I learn that, I wonder?)

They could not afford any of my products either so, with good grace, I left. Some months later the husband rang me with a question.

'By the way,' I said. 'What did you do about the children's schooling?'

'Oh!' he replied. 'You were quite right; we took them away from their private school at the end of that week!'

In contrast, a source of satisfaction was seeing the results of building substantial tax-efficient portfolios that provided additional, tax-free income when clients retired.

Several years later we visited Majorca. Palma, the capital, once again presented opportunities to visit places of interest away from the hotel. The cathedral is spectacular and there are beautiful courtyards nearby that trace their origin to the days of the Moors. We took the opportunity to drive around the island and, in the centre, not far from where the railway from Palma to Soller enters a tunnel through the mountains, we were surprised and delighted to find Arab gardens at Alfabia that boasted cool cobbled courtyards, fine trees and bubbling watercourses. They reminded us of our trip to *Andalucía* in 1983, when we had revelled in the dazzling glories of Moorish Spain. The Alhambra and Generalife at Granada, the gardens and Alcazar at Seville and the great mosque at Cordoba (Mezquita), which is now a Christian cathedral, stunned us with their exquisite beauty. Why should this be so? Because the Moors applied their deep knowledge of architecture, design, gardening, the application of light and shade, use of water and mathematics to construct a paradise on earth. Tahir Shah, in his extraordinary and surreal book *The Caliph's House* (2006), describes the Alhambra as the 'finest Islamic palace ever constructed' and it regularly features on lists of places you *must* visit before you die.

Following that conference, we remained for a further week after our colleagues had returned to England and rented a tiny stone-built house in the quaint little town of Valdemosa, right in the shadow of the hilltop monastery where Georg Sand and the ailing Chopin spent the winter of 1838–39. The nearby northern coast of Majorca was rough and there were few beaches so, early one morning, we were pleased to find a lovely stretch of sand not far from the town of Deja. We settled ourselves on the beach, expecting a relaxing day, but at about ten o'clock when other people began to appear we realised that we had made a serious mistake. Everyone was stripping off. We were on a nudist beach. Neither of us wanted to return to the car and start driving again so there we only had two choices: remain as we were, or strip. What would you have done?

Returning to Valdemosa at the end of the day, we stopped at the hilltop church in Deja, both curious to find where the poet Robert Graves was buried. After walking around the isolated cemetery for a few minutes, I looked down and saw his name staring up at me. To my dismay, I was actually standing on the great man's simple tombstone. Graves had interested me ever since my Marlborough days when the College Press produced a limited, hand-printed edition of some of his poems.It was then that I was inspired to read *Goodbye to All That*, the autobiography of his early life. Lucinda and I had met him on several occasions at a friend's house in the country, which was a treat, although I always kept close to Lucinda when Graves was around, especially in the garden. I did not want him adding her to his list of muses.

A little-known fact is that Graves had a double-jointed pelvis and when sitting on a garden bench he liked to perform his party trick. With a quick swivel of his bottom he dislocated the joint, thumping the base of his spine on the wood in a most extraordinary way.

'Did I hear you call your little boy, Tarquin?' he enquired after one alarming performance.

'Perhaps I can tell you something about the Etruscans that you do not know'.

Graves believed that the Etruscans had been capable of producing nuclear fission and referred to their advanced techniques for firing exceptionally durable pottery. Examples can be seen at the Etruscan Museum in Rome. He held the Etruscans in high esteem and stated categorically that the rape of Lucretia was a myth and part of Roman 'spin' to smear 'the great House of Tarquin'. As I write, a report has appeared, following a DNA study, that confirms an account in the 5th century BC by the Greek historian Herodotus that the Etruscan civilisation was founded by seafarers from western Turkey. And where had *they* come from? I wonder. All grist to a fascinating mill.

In the summer of 1988, Tarquin was approaching his nineteenth birthday. After his return from Paris, eighteen months previously, he had obtained a scholarship to Davies's, following in his father's footsteps. Some fees still had to be found, so he worked in McDonald's and the newly-opened TGI Friday to pay for them. Lucinda and I admired his tenacity and when he achieved good A-level passes the whole family was delighted. However, like father, like son, he felt unable to spend a minute longer sitting in a classroom and resolved to quit full-time education and spend time travelling. Lucinda and I sympathised, but were uncertain as what to advise. On the one hand, we felt that he should obtain further qualifications, probably at university; on the other hand why should he follow the herd? A period as a nomad, enrolled in the University of Life, seemed fair enough. The 'gap year' had not been established as *de rigueur* at that time. In fact, I am not sure if the expression had even been coined.

One warm evening, Tarquin and I sat in the garden of the Clifton Arms in St John's Wood and talked. He was adamant that he would never darken the doors of an educational institution again, and had his eye on photography and journalism as a profession. He resolved to travel, working his passage, and practise those skills until he could depend upon them for a living. When discussing this topic, Lucinda and I had been concerned that he would bum around the world, frittering away time, and would achieve nothing worth while. On the other hand, would a sustained period at a British university anaesthetise his imagination? In the end we agreed a compromise.

'Why not go to the United States?' I said, 'but, if in four years time, when you are twenty-three, you are unable to support yourself at your chosen vocation, promise me that you will enrol at a university'.

Tarquin nodded and we shook hands on it. Since he held dual nationality there would be no problem with visas or work permits.

We returned to the flat and reported our conversation to Lucinda. She readily agreed to the plan, delighted that Tarquin was to spend time in the country of her birth, and immediately started rooting around for the addresses of friends and relations from Boston to San Francisco. Tarquin was itching to get going but, before he left, we arranged to spend a day together. We both felt that we had not seen enough of each other in the recent past and I was more than happy to sacrifice a day's work. Lucinda would have liked to come too but another irksome temping assignment prevented her. We took a pleasure boat from Westminster to Greenwich and spent an enjoyable few hours exploring the National Maritime Museum and, after lunch, we climbed the hill to the observatory. It seemed fitting, as the unknown beckoned, for me to photograph Tarquin standing on the Prime Meridian.

Within a few days he was in New York and, from what he has subsequently told us, I am sure that arriving alone in the Big Apple was a daunting experience. But with admirable determination and guts, it wasn't long before he had found himself a room and a job at one of the smartest hotels near Central Park. Lucinda, Alexander and I were greatly amused to receive long chatty letters in which he described his 'bellhop' uniform and the duties that he had to perform.

Meanwhile, Alexander had finished at William Ellis, where long hours in the editing suite, under the guidance of the stalwart, ex-BBC, Laurence Halstead, meant that *Going In, In Action* had become a reality and we all had fun watching it and reminding ourselves of those crazy few days at Monmouth House. The process of putting the film together had taught him useful skills and, in addition, he found himself valuable work experience at Hackenbacker, a sound studio in Soho. His film career was beginning to take shape and he followed his brother to Davies's, in Holborn, to finish his studies.

Just before Tarquin left for the USA, we had found ourselves a small, purpose-built flat in Kew. After eight years, this put us back in the property market and we were delighted to be in such a pleasant area, close to the famous gardens and within a mile of my office. It was convenient for Alexander to take the Tube to Southampton Row and there was plenty of work for Lucinda in the vicinity. I enjoyed walking to the office in Richmond, but if I had been tempted to drive I would have been discouraged by a sign in a churchyard that I passed each day. It read:

PRIVATE CAR PARK
NO UNAUTHORISED PARKING
BY ORDER OF ST JOHN THE DIVINE
&
RICHARD ELLIS

For the next couple of years, life maintained a steady routine. I continued to build my client bank and kept the sales coming. Alexander pursued his art and media studies and Lucinda tended to work as a temp, which she found to be the most flexible way to contribute to the family income. She particularly enjoyed the odd stint at a small engineering firm in Richmond, where she befriended an Anglo-Indian girl by the name of Bernie, and working at Dr Rennik's psychiatric clinic in the West End, which was largely patronised by media and film icons. In addition she was in charge on the home front, so her hands were kept pretty full.

News from across the Atlantic was very positive. Once Tarquin had found his feet in New York, he bought a camera and started taking photographs. He also practised writing, and that included long letters telling us everything he was doing. After Christmas, he moved from New York and went to stay with Patti Schneider, an old friend of ours who had spent time in England, but recently returned to Texas. With her encouragement, he got a job as a cowboy on a ranch near Sweetwater, and as the adventures kept coming, so did the photographs and lengthy descriptions. Eventually, before leaving America, he spent a few months in San Francisco, working in a catering business and staying with the Rabins, his Aunt Deborah and Uncle David. These exploits, among others, were duly recorded in his first book *Mercenaries, Missionaries and Misfits*—but more of that later.

In the summer of 1989, Alexander and I flew to Paris for a long boys' weekend. It was his first visit to the French capital and I enjoyed showing him the sights, which included a trip on the Seine and a ride out to the newly completed La Défense. My former brother-in-law, Rémi Lecomte, lent us his apartment near La Gare du Nord and we made a pilgrimage to visit Jack, on the south bank, with the customary bottle of Armagnac in hand. Lunching nearby, we were amused, but also irritated, when a tall man in a black beret with a large white mouse on his shoulder came towards us, and leaning across our table, stole *pommes frites* off our plates which he fed to his greedy rodent.

'That reminds me of the 'Rat man', I interjected.

So, after our meal, we went in search of the rogue who had entertained John Henry and I and countless others, in the Boulevard St Germain more than twenty years previously, but he was nowhere to be seen. He had probably retired on a mischievously-acquired fortune.

Our trip to the Eiffel Tower was marred by the sight of a waiter slipping in the rain as he hurried across the wet steel plates on the *premier étage*. As his feet flew up into the air, the back of his head came down and hit the metal with a dreadful bang. He just managed to stagger away, brushing the grime off his white apron as he went, and was lucky if he had not cracked his skull. Leaving the tower, we wandered down the Quai D'Orsay in time to witness a man thrown from his motorbike as it slithered across wet cobbles. I was reminded of traditional tales where one disaster follows another until, at the end, a meaningful lesson is learned, but this did not seem to apply, and unfazed, we continued on our way over le Pont des Arts, through Les Halles and past the Pompidou Centre. The route to Rémi's apartment took us up the Rue St Denis where painted ladies hung out in doorways or leaned against lamp-posts. As they smiled and beckoned, I recalled my Hungarian actor friend Robbie S. who, when a teenager, was taken to a brothel by his father and ordered to 'get stuck in'. As far as Alexander was concerned, that wasn't quite my style.

After witnessing this litany of quirky incidents and having thoroughly enjoyed our few days, we returned to England.

Later in the autumn Tarquin spent a couple of weeks with us in Kew and we all attended my godson Nicky Evans' wedding. I had been asked to be his godfather when at Marlborough at the time when everyone expected me to become a holy vicar, so I have to confess that I failed dismally in my duties. Nicky, for his part, had become a first-class polo player and by coincidence his bride's family owned the Old Rectory at Trotton, which is where my mother's late fiancé, Richard Carey, lived before the Second World War. The wedding reception was held in that house, with its lovely gardens running down to the Rother. My brother sent a snap he had taken of me standing next to Lord Cowdray, and enclosed a cheeky note that said something about life insurance salesmen mingling with the great and the good.

Both boys were now entering an interesting period of their young lives.

Tarquin announced that he was off to Pakistan, and soon after Nicky's wedding we put him on a KLM flight at Heathrow. He was heading for the ancient city of Peshawar in the Indus valley, a short drive from the formidable Khyber Pass, one of the main routes in and out of Afghanistan. It could only be approached from the city by passing through tribal territories, terrain that resembled the American Wild West in respect of the absence of the rule of law, together with its gaunt landscape. The Russians had withdrawn from Afghanistan earlier in the year (February 1989) although the Communist President Mohammad *Najibullah Ahmadzai* remained in power until he was overthrown by the *mujahideen* three years later.

Peshawar itself, was bursting with several million refugees who had fled Afghanistan following the Russian invasion in 1979, although there was evidence that a further six million were still missing; a brutal holocaust that has been largely ignored in the West. The fugitives were mostly settled in camps but there were also, in the vicinity, a significant number of workers from the international aid agencies so the area swarmed with foreigners of all kinds. It might not have been in one's best interests to question why some of those people were there, as Peshawar had changed little over the centuries. Spies, it was said, lurked everywhere.

This melting pot of civilisations and crucible of turbulent history had attracted intrigue and adventure since the earliest times, and Tarquin sensed that there would be plenty of opportunities to develop his skills as a journalist and photographer. On arrival, he soon found himself teaching English to Afghans in the camps and worked on a project for the United Nations. This provided sufficient cash to support his meagre lifestyle, but it was not long before he was selling articles to the *Friday Times*, one of Pakistan's national newspapers. On 19th August 1990, I was sitting in our flat in Kew thumbing through *The Sunday Times* when I noticed a striking photograph of a young man holding a child. The background suggested it had been taken in the developing world. Idly, I looked to see who had taken this excellent shot and was thrilled to learn that the photographer was one, Tarquin Hall. It was his first sale in the West, made two years into our 'deal'. Lucinda and I agreed that things looked very hopeful.

In the meantime, eighteen-year-old Alexander was developing another project. He spent hours in his room, where the walls and ceiling were plastered with film posters and all kinds of silver-screen memorabilia; scribbling on sheets of paper and filling notebooks. Just to enter his lair, propelled one into the world of James Bond, Indiana Jones, Superman, the A-Team, Jaws and E.T. Shelves were laid out with Star War figures, Smurfs and all sorts of other collectibles, including piles of cards that illustrated scenes from the hundreds of movies he had seen. Each visit to the cinema was duly recorded in a diary, together with the entry ticket and appropriate comments. I have lost count, but seem to recall a point when he had seen *Star Wars* at least ninety times. He swore that each viewing taught him something new about film-making.

His new film would be on a more elaborate scale than *Going In, In Action*, and in partnership with his pal, Adam Schreiber, the son of old friends of ours. The two boys had already been through some adventures together and on one memorable day in 1989 they visited Pinewood Studios, bumping into David Putnam in the process.

Brothers in Arms would take eighteen months to complete, as both boys had to juggle schoolwork and part-time jobs that generated cash, with their activities on location. They were the producers, directors, actors and everything else rolled into two extraordinarily energetic teenagers. Much of the action, featuring a monster bent on devouring our heroes, took place, appropriately enough, during the holidays at Adam's home in Bridport on the Jurassic Coast. The boys required frequent ferrying backwards and forwards, together with their innumerable props which included huge sinewy bones from the local butcher that added colour to the grisly story. When we were allowed to see some of the rushes, we were shocked to discover that our friend's house had come close to being burned down, and that Alexander had set himself alight while filming a dramatic scene in a cardboard tunnel. Other filming was carried out on the A303, in the gasworks at Kew and in Mortlake cemetery. All this must have been thirsty work, because the final list of expenses features an entry for £67 spent on Coca-Cola. Eventually, the film was finished, Adam carried out the editing at Weymouth College, where he was a student, and during the Christmas holidays of 1989–90 the boys worked with Nigel Heath, the proprietor of Hackenbacker, who very generously created the ambitious soundtrack for *Brothers in Arms*. Heath's career subsequently blossomed, and he went on to work on as diverse projects as the Harry Potter and James Bond films.

Quite apart from the sheer enjoyment of putting all this together, the point of the exercise was to further the boys' progress in the movie business. Early in 1991, Alexander struck lucky when he met Robert Watts, who produced two of the *Indiana Jones* films and *Who Framed Roger Rabbit?* Watts watched *Brothers in Arms* in his office at Elstree and was very enthusiastic about what the boys had achieved, readily providing a quote for use in publicity and as a reference to advance their careers.

He said: 'A remarkable success in making a film of high energy and excitement.'

It was only later that I discovered Watts had attended Marlborough College in the early 1950s and was one of the first Masters of the College Beagles (C1 1952).

When I asked Alexander how he had first attracted Watts' attention he told me that it was because his CV recorded that he had been Head Goatman at the Old Ride.

Lucinda and I found these developments exciting, even nail-biting, but we were unsure where it was all going to lead. I, especially, felt a bit out of my depth, as the machinations of the movie business were, to me, totally uncharted waters. Undaunted, however, we arranged for a screening of the forty-minute *Brothers in Arms* at a trade cinema in Wardour Street, London, on 27th February 1990. Alexander had become adept at making contacts and together with a number of friends, we were able to invite a sprinkling of movie people. Lucinda and I were particularly pleased to have the opportunity to chat with Bruce Boa, whose face would be familiar to film buffs; notably from *The Omen, Superman, The Empire Strikes Back, Full Metal Jacket* and many television appearances. We were also fascinated to meet the legendary pioneer of special effects, seventy-year-old Ray Harryhausen, whose filmography includes *The Beast from 20,000 Fathoms, The 7th Voyage of Sinbad, Jason and the Argonauts* and *Clash of the Titans*. His comment on *Brothers in Arms,* duly recorded in the magazine *Film Review,* was that it was 'enterprising and remarkable'.

The next day, the *Daily Mail* published a high profile and complimentary article by Shaun Usher, their film correspondent, together with a photograph of Alexander and Adam, entitled 'the teenage shooting stars'. Several other articles followed, including in *The Ham and High* and *Bridport*

News, and Sky Television featured a short interview with the boys. Soon after this Alexander signed on as a film extra at Central Casting and, early one morning, he found himself carrying a spear in Burnham Beeches in Kevin Costner's *Robin Hood: Prince of Thieves*.

He was learning the hard way, but it was to be well over a year before his film career took a major step forward. In the meantime, having completed his final school exams, he spent the summer working in the Gap in San Francisco, where his Aunt Jane lived. Later that summer, an introduction by Robert Watts spurred his flight to Los Angeles, intent on applying for a job as a runner for Steven Spielberg's company, Amblin Entertainment. Stuart Baird, whose long film career included the editing of *Superman, Gorillas in the Mist and Skyfall* was good enough to accommodate Alexander in his apartment for a couple of weeks. His application was successful and Lucinda and I were very excited to think that he would be working in the heart of Universal Studios. We felt that all our efforts were bearing fruit, and that he would be able to develop the career he had set his heart on since his early childhood.

In the meantime, life for Tarquin in the North West Frontier Province was becoming very interesting. He was regularly providing material for the *Friday Times*, had interviewed Gulbuddin Hekmatyar, and was hoping to meet Ahmad Shah Massoud and other prominent *mujahideen* leaders. He had even persuaded Afghan loyalists to smuggle him into Afghanistan at the dead of night to file reports for the BBC World Service. At the age of only twenty, he was one of the youngest journalists to do so.

I had read a book by Peter King, *Afghanistan: Cockpit in High Asia* (1966), and also Idries Shah's only novel, the blockbuster *Kara Kush* (1986), which described the relentless Afghan struggle (under the leadership of the fictional Adam Durany, 'the Eagle') for survival during the occupation by the 'Russian Bear'. These volumes contributed, during the summer of 1990, to a burning desire to go and visit Tarquin in Peshawar. In addition, there were four more reasons for this. Primarily, I felt that Tarquin would be unlikely to remain in Pakistan forever, and here was an opportunity to visit a part of the world that I found fascinating. Second, my grandfather (Baba) had been posted to Rawalpindi at the turn of the century and served in the Tirah Expedition (1897/98) when the British fought the Orakzais and Afridis, so it would be interesting to follow in his footsteps. Third, the romance in me had been stirred by the 1959 film *North West Frontier* starring Herbert Lom,

Kenneth More, old Marlburian Wilfred Hyde White (B3 1917) and Lauren Bacall, although some of the grisly scenes of massacres following Partition in 1947 were far from romantic. Finally, I certainly wanted to find out more about what Tarquin was doing, much of which sounded highly dangerous, and to share some of his experiences, as this would strengthen the bond between us. Unfortunately, as we all agreed, it would not have been an appropriate place for Lucinda to visit at that time.

I procrastinated for several months. Saddam Hussein had invaded Kuwait in August and there was talk of an American-backed operation to depose him but, finally, on 6th November 1990, I was on a plane to Karachi. I had managed to leave a telephone message, on a very crackly line, at Tarquin's lodgings, announcing that I was on my way. The flight would take me further east than I had ever travelled and, as we rose steeply over golden autumnal forests, following a stopover at Frankfurt, I felt that an adventure was opening before me. The late afternoon sun rapidly disappeared behind us, casting a reddish glow upon alpine peaks, and the jet engines droned mercilessly as we passed over the waters of the Black Sea, scarcely visible in the semi-darkness. Soon, total night enveloped the huge plane as vast uninhabited stretches of Asia Minor slid past, 35,000 feet below. Occasionally tiny pinpoints of light were visible in the blackness. Who? Where? Why? These were questions I turned over in my mind as I peered through the cabin window, intent on deciphering any detail of remote and lonely habitations. Eventually the hazy orange glow of streetlights appeared and the ordered layout of Karachi suburbs quickly became defined as we descended towards the runway.

The heat of the night struck me abruptly as I trotted down the jumbo's steep steps, and pandemonium broke out the moment I cleared customs. It seemed that every scruffy porter in the vicinity wanted to carry my bags, and at one point I thought that the handles would be torn off in the struggle. Eventually, a swarthy, toothless baggage-wallah grabbed both cases and, elbowing his rivals aside, strode off in the direction I indicated. On reaching the area of the terminal designated for internal flights he dumped my things and, grinning from ear to ear, pocketed the handful of rupees I gave him as he returned to the mêlée.

Unfortunately, the flight to Peshawar was not due to leave for seven hours, and with nowhere to stay I had a long night ahead. I did not fancy venturing out into the street in search of a hotel, so there seemed nothing for it but to stretch out on the marble floor and try to catch some sleep. It reminded me of my sojourn in Thessaloniki station more than twenty years earlier. Other lone individuals and men, women and children in family groups, wrapped in the clothes they had been wearing, lay around the hall, although some had covered themselves in tribal rugs. As night wore on, it was reasonably peaceful despite the occasional grunt and fart, but it was certainly not comfortable. Prudence decreed that I arrange my luggage in such a way that I would be awakened if it was disturbed. When dawn broke and the early sun poured in through plate-glass windows, queues started to form for the Peshawar plane. This gave me the opportunity to witness a gathering of the most vibrant and extraordinary group of individuals I had ever seen.

In 'Paradise Regained', John Milton wrote of 'dusky faces in white silken turbans wreathed,' and so they were, except many of the faces were a great deal paler than I would have expected, and the range of head-coverings spectacular and unparalleled. All the women's heads were covered and some females were enveloped from top to toe in white or blue pleated burkas, which have famously been compared to giant shuttle-cocks. Others wore *salwar kameez*, a sort of loose shirt over baggy trousers. The variety of the men's headgear was astonishing. Short white tight-fitting caps and long thickly gathered scarves, known as *lungis*, abounded. The latter, in white, oatmeal, black or even woven in sombre-toned stripes, were wound round the head to form bulky turbans with the end, hanging loosely over the shoulders. Some, especially the boys, had beautifully embroidered caps in a multitude of colours, and many wore the grey or white rolled woollen hat—the *pukkal*—associated with the *mujahideen*. There was also a variety of fur or skin caps with flaps to protect ears from the cold, but from what animals they came I could not say—bear or wolf perhaps?

The men were of all ages and most wore a white or grey *salwar kameez*. Some had what looked like a blanket draped around their shoulders or a woollen sleeveless jacket made from goat's hair. Their skin colour varied from dark—and these I understood to be Punjabis—to very light, who could easily be taken for Europeans. Some might be descendants of Alexander the Great. There were even redheads, probably from Nuristan, and members of the Hazara minority, thought to be descendants of Genghis Khan's horde. Most striking of all was the magnificent collection of beards. White, grey, black, henna-coloured, some dropping down over their clothes like Father Christmas's beard, some brown and bushy others short and stubby. Most of the beards combined with luxuriant moustaches, and beady black eyes stared from beneath arched bristling brows. I was reminded of the words of Hakim Jami: 'If the scissors are not used daily on the beard, it will not be long before the beard is, by its luxuriant growth, pretending to be the head.'

This remarkable array of human beings waited in dignified silence. In addition to the Punjabis, Hazaras and Nuristanis, every tribe of Central Asia—Pushtuns, Afridis, Turkomen, Tajiks, Uzbeks, Sarts and goodness knows who else—must have been represented. Each individual displayed distinct physical characteristics, but I lacked the knowledge to match physique to tribe. By the time I left the North West Frontier Province I hoped to be better informed.

Accompanying this wonderful collection of individuals, piled on the terminal floor, were gigantic ghetto blasters and an array of securely-boxed and labelled examples of modern technology that would do any Western warehouse proud. Sony, Panasonic, Miele, Hoover, Philips, Zanussi—there were examples of every kind of television, video player, washing machine and dishwasher on their way to the remotest corners of the Punjab, Chitral, Gilgit, Peshawar and, doubtless, even Afghanistan. This was West meets East in a format that I could never have envisaged.

Eventually the aircraft, duly loaded with its motley array of passengers and merchandise, took off for Peshawar via Lahore. Some hours later, while I sipped green tea, the snow-capped peaks of the Himalayas came in view, standing guard beyond the northern plain. At the airport I was greeted by Peter Jouvenal, the television cameraman, who shared the house where Tarquin was, supposedly, staying and who came to prominence filming John Simpson's march into Kabul in November 2001.

'I'm afraid Tarquin is not in Peshawar, at the moment', Peter informed me, as we jumped into his Land Rover. 'He is somewhere in Afghanistan'.

Apparently, he had 'gone inside', as it was called in the secretive parlance that prevailed throughout the North West Frontier Province. He was engaged on a self-imposed, freelance/story-by-story mission, reporting to the BBC Language Services on the civil war raging beyond the Khyber Pass, and no one knew when he would be back. I was shocked and mildly irritated but blamed myself for being casual about my own timetable. Anyway, I soon learned that when dealing with Afghan affairs, a Western attitude to the passage of time proved pointless; what was much more important to those people was when the apricots would ripen or the tea would run out.

Nothing had prepared me for the journey up the dusty Jamrud Road to the house where Peter and several other journalists lived and where Tarquin had rented a room. Intermittently, on each side of the road were barrows choking with lettuces, beans, carrots and tomatoes, pomegranates, apples, peaches and freshly picked mulberries. Interspersed between these were rough wooden stalls piled high with gigantic green watermelons, some cut wide open to display their juicy red flesh, which glistened in the sunlight. Unusually dark-skinned Punjabis puffed on cigarettes and eyed prospective customers while keeping a wary lookout for scraggy goats that wandered the streets intent on taking a mouthful from accessible goodies. No poverty-stricken country this, I reflected as we passed butchers' shops sprawling out over the deeply rutted pavements where chunks of fatty meat hung from iron hooks, surrounded by hordes of black flies. Delicious *naan* was being prepared in cook-houses with piles of logs stacked by the entrance, and the pungent odour of freshly baked dough together, with a whiff of wood smoke, wafted into the cab as we passed by. At intervals, good Muslims could be seen praying on their roadside rugs in response to the *muezzin's* midday call which echoed from the mosques and reminded me of my adventures in Istanbul. These pious folk seemed oblivious of the dense traffic that passed dangerously close, avoiding potholes and flouting all regulations. Signals were ignored as hundreds of noisy Vespa rickshaws weaved in and out, intent on reaching their destination by the quickest route, no matter what side of the road they were supposed to be on. A reckless disregard for others also applied to the drivers of horse, or donkey-drawn carts, laden with straw or building materials, and huge lorries, piled high with heavy goods, exuding clouds of black diesel exhaust that overwhelmed the more enticing aromas lingering in the street. These lorries were the 'camels of the road', gaudily decorated with brightly coloured metallic paint and embellished with glistening bells and beads.

Eventually we reached our destination, a house close to a stagnant canal on the north side of the city. This is how Tarquin described it, a few years later, it in his book *Mercenaries, Missionaries and Misfits:*

> Our house on Peshawar's Canal road was surrounded by an immense twenty-foot-high wall, topped with bails of rusty barbed wire and slivers of sharp green glass. If from the street it looked more like a brigand's mountain retreat than

somebody's home that was the intention. The front door was made from reinforced steel and a ferocious dog that looked like a werewolf patrolled the courtyard and garden.

As we drew up, Peter leaned on the Land Rover's horn and the armed guard, the *chowkidor* Abdul Rahman, slid back the bolts of the steel door and we drove into the yard. Politely welcoming us, Abdul, a huge bull of a man, showed me to Tarquin's room. As he opened the door a grey mouse jumped off the table, where it had been feasting on half a loaf of stale bread, and scampered away across one of the two mattresses that lay on the floor. I slumped into the only chair, wondering what to do next. Soon there was a knock on the door, and Peter invited me to lunch. I was introduced to John Jennings, one of the other journalists, a tall thin American who had, apparently, been giving Tarquin some coaching. He gleefully reported that his writing skills were improving in leaps and bounds. Naturally, I thanked him before broaching the question as to when they thought my son might appear. They both shook their heads, explaining that, while they knew which group of *mujahideen* he was with, it would be far too dangerous to call him on the shortwave radio. Revealing the presence of a Western journalist 'inside' could precipitate a death sentence.

'All you can do is wait and see', they counselled.

'Peshawar is a fascinating city; take the time to explore it and why not join us at the American Club this evening?' they concluded.

That afternoon, after a short nap, I wandered off along the canal and. crossing the old railway tracks where trains had passed on their way to and from the Khyber in happier times, I soon found myself totally lost. I hailed a Vespa rickshaw whose driver seemed no more knowledgeable of the terrain than I was. After about fifteen minutes, he let me off near the edge of the city. Almost immediately, two burly armed men appeared and, grabbing my arms, bustled me through a door into a shabby outhouse. Inside, a clean-shaven man wearing a white *pukkal* was sitting behind a desk. A revolver lay before him. There were several automatic weapons and what I took to be a machine gun in one corner of the room. The men started to question me, in fairly good English. It was like the forest meeting between Strelnikov (Tom Courtney) and Dr Zhivago (Omar Sharif) in the film of that name.

'What are you doing in Peshawar? Where were you going?' they barked and demanded to see my papers.

'I'm just a tourist. I've lost my way.' I explained and showed them my passport.

'British, huh?' I nodded

After talking briefly between themselves they seemed satisfied and ushered me out, although I had got the distinct impression that being British, not American, had been to my advantage. It was all over in a matter of minutes and I was not really scared, whereas in hindsight it occurred to me that I probably should have been. There were dangerous and violent men around playing for high stakes in all manner of ways; politics, money, drugs, arms and, I hardly needed to remind myself, there was a war zone just across the border. As I eventually found my way back to the house on Canal Road, cursing that I had somehow lost my prescription sunglasses, I vowed to be on my guard.

Almost immediately, Peter invited me to hop on the back of his ancient khaki motorbike and within a few minutes we were parking in front of the American Club. I had abstained from alcohol for a month before the trip to get used to being in a 'dry' country, but I need not have bothered as here there was cheap whisky, juicy hamburgers with all the relishes, and American cookies and ice cream. English-speaking people from all over the world were playing tennis or seated at tables on the terrace, enjoying the warm evening. I soon discovered that most of them knew Tarquin and were curious to meet me. Ron B., an American and someone whom I had not met before, sidled up to me and introduced himself.

'We have friends in common,' he whispered furtively. Whom did he mean? I wondered.

It had been a long exhausting day but I could feel a party coming on.

The next morning the telephone rang while I was enjoying a cup of coffee and a slice of watermelon. It was Lucinda on a very bad line.

'The gas cooker has blown up!' she announced.

'What am I supposed to do about it? I'm in Peshawar,' I retorted, before the line went dead.

For the next couple of days I decided to explore Peshawar (which means 'frontier town'—*pesh awar*) and the origins of which can be traced back 2,500 years. It had been the capital of a thriving Buddhist empire two centuries before the birth of Christ. Ashes reputed to be those of the Buddha were discovered in 1909 and taken to the Peshawar Museum.

I crossed the canal and took one of the tree-lined streets that led through a pleasant suburb. *Bougainvillea* and jasmine sprawled over high walls and fierce dogs lurked behind huge gates, protecting properties that belonged to the relatively well-to-do. Within a few minutes I had spotted a large white sign with black lettering that read:

INTERNATIONAL COMMITTEE OF THE RED CROSS
ORTHOPAEDIC CENTRE FOR AFGHANS

Several Afghans were hobbling on crutches further down the road; one had lost a foot; another, a leg. Once I reached the Jamrud Road, taking my life in my hands, I hailed a Vespa rickshaw and headed downtown. Soon I was in the heart of the city in the renowned *Qissa Khawani Bazaar* (the Storytellers' Market). The folk who regularly recounted ancient legends had long gone, but times past were easy to imagine as snatches of English and what I believed to be Urdu and Pushtu could be heard, rising above the inevitable clatter of horses' hooves and the rumbling of passing carts. On all sides the most intriguing shops flourished. Many were stuffed with ornaments, jewellery, semi-precious stones and of course wonderful carpets from Bokhara and the central Asian republics. Everywhere there were reminders that the city had commanded an important position for centuries on the trade routes from China to Kabul and Samarkand. The sweet aroma of cardamom hung in the air together with the whiff of pungent tobacco emanating from the shiny hookahs that a group of men sitting outside a *chaikhana* (tea-house), were smoking. I soon found myself wandering into dark alleys. Each one seemed to open into a cavern packed with treasure. Small ateliers were hidden away where men beat intricate designs on copper or brassware, and dozens of colourful kelims hung from balconies above my head. I paused to refresh myself with green tea while a hawk-eyed trader tried to interest me in his wares, but eventually I found myself in the *Chowk Yadgar* (the Square of Remembrance), the central square, which was being dug out for some kind of building project. Lines of scrawny donkeys trailed up from the muddy depths of the excavation, burdened with wicker panniers full of heavy clay. Presumably, this was deposited somewhere nearby because the poor beasts soon returned with empty panniers ready for the next load. All around the square the money-changers sat, with piles of colourful paper currency on trestle tables in front of them. This seemed as good a place as any to change sterling into rupees so, taking a few green notes from my wallet, I approached a hook-nosed, turbaned individual who quickly worked out the conversion rate on his state-of-the-art calculator. By this time I was hungry so, sitting outside a cafe in one corner of the square, I relaxed and indulged in one of my favourite occupations—watching the world go by. A cheery young lad with a colourfully embroidered cap and matching waistcoat brought me meatballs in saffron rice and a Coca-Cola while he paused from turning *shashlik* over glowing coals on his roadside grill.

After a while, I began to wonder if Tarquin might have returned, so taking my chances again with a rickshaw I headed back to Canal Road. The late afternoon traffic was as frenetic as ever and careering round a roundabout I was not encouraged when I spotted a sign that read:

LIVE FOR EVER: DONATE YOUR EYES

Arriving at the house, I banged on the gate but could tell immediately from the expression on Abdul Rahman's face that there was no news. An evening at the club beckoned. Clutching a pad of lined paper and a pencil, I made my way to the terrace where I ordered a whisky, parked myself at a corner table and started to scribble some of my impressions of the trip so far. Half an hour later, John Jennings joined me.

'Ah! Do we have another writer in the family?' he exclaimed. I showed him what I had written.

'That is bloody good', he said. 'A brilliant description of your arrival in Peshawar!'

The next day I retraced my steps, pausing at the *Bala Hisar* Fort ('the high fort') built in 1530 by Zaheer-ud Din Babur and a symbol of the eminence that the Islamic city achieved under the Mughals. It was forbidden to photograph this imposing building with its ninety-two-feet-high walls, however I had become infected with the local disregard for regulations and happily snapped away. There was so much to see and I spent more time in the markets, especially the bazaars of the goldsmiths and the coppersmiths, and in addition discovered wonderful arrays of knives, swords and intricately decorated matchlock rifles. However, instead of returning to Canal Road by motorised transport, I decided to walk. I particularly wanted to

visit parts of the city inhabited by the British, who came to Peshawar in 1849
and remained there for almost a hundred years. A contemporary guidebook
stated categorically that there is 'capital hunting with the Peshawar Vale
Hunt throughout the winter', so those who indulged in the sport must have
felt at home. The hounds, mostly imported from England, hunted jackal
on Sundays and Thursdays from October to March and battle-hardened
soldiers who enjoyed the chase and eventually returned to the 'field' in
England took the imprint of their experiences in the North West Frontier
Province with them, as John Masefield records in 'Reynard the Fox' (1919):

> Then on a horse which bit and bucked
> (The half-broke four-year-old Marauder)
> Came Minton Price of th' Afghan border,
> Lean, puckered, yellowed, knotted, scarred,
> Tough as a hide-rope twisted hard,
> Tense tiger-sinew knit to bone.
> Strange-wayed from having lived alone
> With Kafir, Afghan and Beloosh
> In stations frozen in the Koosh.
> Where nothing but the bullet sings.
> His mind had conquered many things—
> Painting, mechanics, physics, law.
> White-hot, hand beaten things to draw
> Self-hammered from his own soul's stithy.
> His speech was blacksmith-sparked and pithy.
> Danger had been his brother bred;
> The stones had often been his bed
> In bickers with the border thieves.

The quiet avenues, neat gardens and parks of the cantonment, built for
the families of officials and troops that administered the Raj; the 'extras' in
the continuing saga of the Great Game, contrasted sharply with the pandemonium that reigned, night and day, throughout the rest of the city.

I thought of Kipling and Rikki-Tikki-Tavi, Mrs Rigg, Somerset
Maugham and John Masters. Most poignant was a visit to the British cemetery, where many of my fellow countrymen lay. It was astonishing to find
that most of the gravestones recorded death from cholera, typhoid or measles

but recalling Kipling's gruesome lines in 'The Young British Soldier' (1890) it would, perhaps, have been even more remarkable if soldiers killed on active service had been returned to the peaceful wooded cemetery in the British cantonment.

> When you're wounded and left on Afghanistan's plains
> An' the women come out to cut up what remains
> Jest roll out your rifle an' blow out your brains
> An' go to your Gawd like a soldier.

I reflected on the fate of my forebear, Richard Byam Mathew, a lieutenant in the 27th Madras Infantry, who had been educated at both Marlborough and Cheltenham and who died in 1857 at the age of twenty; he must surely lie in similar surroundings close to the fort at Vellore in Tamil Nadu Province. I do not know why he came to lie there, but I assume that he was killed in the Indian Mutiny which began as a rising amongst the troops of the Bengal Army but turned into a civil war.

Continuing my trek up the Jamrud Road, I was suddenly amazed to see a game of cricket being played by Pakistanis in traditional white garb on green lawns that ran back to an imposing building. A sign told me that I was passing Islamia College, built shortly after the Great War and now part of Peshawar University. I paused to watch for a while, but soon headed away from this oasis and 'Little England', narrowly avoiding being run down by a particularly large Bedford truck, loaded with sugar cane, just before I reached the safety of Canal Road.

There was still no sign of Tarquin.

I had heard of Darra Adam Khel, the smugglers' village at the very edge of the Indus valley, close to the Afghan border, and was determined to go there. I took a taxi and drove the twenty miles out of the city one warm hazy afternoon that reminded me of Indian summers when I had just returned to school at the beginning of the Michaelmas term, and found the ground too hard to play football or rugger. The dusty roads, dried-up riverbeds and rough terrain of the tribal territories, broken occasionally by verdant strips of irrigated farmland and boggy patches where water buffalo were attempting to keep cool, basked in the November sunshine.

Darra nestled below towering rocky crags and I asked my driver to wait while I ventured into the village. He had parked close to where someone had nailed a faded Stars and Stripes to a telegraph pole. It hung limply in the motionless air. As I walked up the only street, which was lined with small shops, each selling weapons or other military equipment, I soon realised that the whole village was essentially a primitive armaments factory. Many shops doubled as ateliers and men were busying themselves tapping away, turning out brass cases for bullets or shells, rifle barrels and other bits and pieces used in gun manufacture. There was one workshop entirely dedicated to reproducing exquisitely crafted Lee-Enfield .303 rifles and another that made lethal weapons disguised as fountain pens. The finished products were all available to be purchased by anyone with enough rupees, or preferably dollars, in their wallet. I wondered what Lucinda would say, were I to present her with a brightly polished Smith and Wesson revolver in full working order. As I turned to make my way back to the taxi, I spotted a small shop packed with what appeared to be Kalashnikovs. The owner, wearing a traditional *salmar kameez* and a fine hat made from tightly curled Karakul lamb's wool, invited me to inspect the weapons. Explaining that I was a tourist and could not possibly take such a thing on an aircraft did not deter him.

'Not buy; but shoot,' he said beckoning me to follow him. Once behind the building he pressed a Kalashnikov into my hand, slipping off the safety catch as he did so, and pointing enthusiastically to the cliff top immediately above us shouted, 'Fire! Fire!'

I lifted the gun, and aiming the barrel vaguely in the direction of the summit, pulled the trigger. A hail of bullets crashed into the hillside two hundred yards away, sending up a plume of white dust, frightening the life out of me and propelling all the crows in Darra into the air. I returned the gun to its owner and thanked him.

'No, I thank you; twenty dollars please,' was his reply. What choice did I have? You don't argue with a man holding a loaded weapon. I passed over the notes and, bidding him farewell, hastily made my way to the cab. As the driver started on the return journey, I noticed a blocked-off alleyway. On the wall at the far end someone had painted a huge red five-pointed star together with a picture of Lenin and several Soviet soldiers. The wall was heavily pitted with bullet holes. Thank God someone had the guts to stand up to the Russians!

The Berlin Wall had fallen the previous year. The end of the evil empire was at hand.

Once back at the house in Canal Road, I banged on the steel door. It was immediately opened by our *chowkidor*, who now had a broad smile on his face. Tarquin was standing right behind him. We greeted each other with warm bear hugs. My first impression was that he had lost a lot of weight and that a fattening-up regime was called for, so after half an hour or so we wandered down to the Club, where Tarquin was welcomed by everyone he met and I soon discovered who Ron B's 'friends in common' were. However, Tarquin warned me that because he had eaten very little over the last few weeks and also suffered from chronic diarrhoea it would be unwise to eat too much, too soon. That didn't stop me from devouring my umpteenth hamburger since I had been in the province, together with baked potatoes drenched in butter, but Tarquin nibbled on chicken breasts and sweetcorn.

'How about a scotch?' I suggested. 'That should kill a few bugs!

'Not sure about that, Dad. Thanks, but I'll stick to mineral water'.

We sat on the terrace and the evening passed in no time as I relayed family news and discovered a lot more about what he had been doing. His trip into Afghanistan had clearly made a huge impression and he recounted some of his adventures, which he later recorded in his first book. I was riveted when he described his visit to the luminescent lakes of Band-e Amir and every detail of the day he spent examining and photographing the great Buddhas carved into the living rock at Bamian. Years later they would be blown up by the Taliban in an act of vandalism. I am so glad that he had seen the statues for himself and told me about them.

Shortly after dark, the usual 'fireworks' to which I had become accustomed commenced. Streams of tracer streaked across the sky, followed by the ack-ack sound of machine-gun fire. 'What is all that?' I asked expecting a lengthy explanation about rival drug gangs.

'Total madness,' Tarquin replied. 'The local people get bored in the evenings so they step out of their houses, point their Kalashnikovs into the air and let rip. When their clips are spent, they go back indoors. The trouble is; bullets that go up also come down, and there have been some tragic accidents. Recently a doctor was playing tennis just over there,' he pointed to the courts below where we were sitting, 'and a stray bullet struck the end of his nose, causing permanent damage. A bridegroom was even killed at his own wedding—imagine!'

'Come back, John Wayne, all is forgiven!' I muttered under my breath.

Tarquin giggled.

At that point the nearest 'show' stopped abruptly, although gunfire continued in the distance. We sauntered back to the house and bedded down on the floor, both in need of a good night's sleep. The next day Tarquin wanted to show me some of his haunts, so we hopped into a rickshaw and headed for Saddar Bazaar; one of the less salubrious areas of the city. After yet another teeth-gritting encounter with the Peshawar madness, we paused outside a horribly run-down establishment that called itself a hotel. Close to the front door there were huge holes in the road. Rotting garbage and worse floated in storm water. Tarquin explained that this was where he stayed when he first arrived and before he made contact with Peter Jouvenal. A giant of a man with tattoos on his forehead and arms was just coming out of a side entrance. Tarquin quickly ducked out of sight and we continued down the street. 'That's the owner,' he confided over his shoulder when we had gone a few yards and as we passed a gaudy, plastic sign that advertised dental services. Huge, three-dimensional white teeth and shiny red gums grinned down at us from outside a first-floor window and a flashy poster featured forceps gripping a set of putrescent molars. A man hailed us from inside a doorway as we passed by. Perhaps he had noticed the widening gap between my two front teeth.

'Hazara,' commented Tarquin. 'You must have noticed his Turkic-looking features.'

We paused in front of a bookshop where Tarquin informed me that he had spent a few happy hours. The window display featured books on *buzkashi*, surely the roughest game in the world. Played on horseback, with teams that numbered about ten on each side, the objective was to place a headless goat within a white circle marked on the pitch. That is the comparatively civilised version. I had heard of tournaments in the valleys of Afghanistan where a hundred horsemen vied for the prize over a 'pitch' five miles square, and the goat had been replaced with a dead Russian.

We paused at a small Afghan restaurant for a dish of *kofte* (meatballs) and rice.

'For God's sake don't touch the salad—who knows where it was washed, or in what,' Tarquin advised.

I was curious about *buzkashi* and asked whether there was any chance of seeing a game.

'Maybe. I'll try and find out, but that could prove difficult. You can never be sure with these people. They will tell you that there is a game on Saturday and you turn up at the ground, but there's not a soul in sight. They may have meant some future Saturday, because games are usually played on Saturdays, or Saturday if Allah wills, or Saturday if it's fine, or Saturday if the horses are fit.'

'Or Saturday if the tea hasn't run out,' I chipped in.

'Exactly; they just don't think like we do and if they can't provide an answer they prefer not to have to say 'no'. They are the consummate diplomats. But let's see, maybe we'll get lucky.'

I dropped the matter for the time being and crossing the road we entered a small shop that specialised in lapus lazuli. It came in all sizes and was more expensive than I expected, but after a while we chose a small glistening blue egg to take home to Lucinda. I have it right here, on the shelf above my desk, as I write.

'Now, what tribe was he?' I asked Tarquin, as we left the shop.

'He was a Pushtun; did you notice his sloping forehead and large aquiline nose? They are the biggest minority group in Afghanistan and believe themselves to be the Bene Israel, one of the lost tribes of Israel. Come this way, I want to show you something.'

He led me through ever darker nooks and crannies that seemed to protect even more exotic treasures and I was glad that there were the two of us or I would have got totally lost.

'When I come down here,' Tarquin told me, 'I sometimes wonder if I have entered the world of *A Thousand and One Nights* and that Alla-din will suddenly appear or perhaps magic carpets float by, just when I am not looking.'

Eventually we entered a small workshop.

'You can have anything you want made here. I will order you some cotton shirts,' said Tarquin. 'They'll cost virtually nothing and be made in a couple of days.'

I thought this was an excellent idea and within a few minutes the proprietor had taken my measurements and I had parted with a few rupees.

'Another Pushtun?' I asked as we left.

'Yes, well spotted, although the British and Indians tend to say P'tan (Pathan),' Tarquin informed me. 'The last time I was here,' he continued, 'I met a Brazilian Aid Worker who had ordered a brass diver's bell to be constructed. It was a beautiful life-sized model, a perfect replica right down to the metal grate protecting the window in the helmet, but I never did discover why a Brazilian needed such a thing, in landlocked Peshawar of all places!'

As we made our way out of the labyrinth, we passed a stall crammed full of all kinds of headgear including a range of especially dashing Karakul hats. I asked Tarquin where they came from.

'Funnily enough, I have just been reading about them,' he said. 'I'll lend you my book.'

'Thanks, I rather fancy one,' I mused.

'They're not really you, Dad,' Tarquin responded. 'In Europe they are often called Astrakhan, but that is inaccurate, being the city on the Caspian Sea from where they are exported. They really suit people from this part of the world best.'

I took his advice.

I later discovered that the hats were from Karakul in Central Asia, a town some fifty miles from Bokhara. The delicate, tight curls of the pelt are obtained uniquely from sheep of the same name that are reared on a rare strain of wild corn only grown in Turkistan. If the Karakul sheep are moved to another area, the quality of the lamb's skins diminish immediately. New born lambs are slaughtered just a few days after birth and the skins are wrapped in salt and barley flour to preserve the curls. When I had read the gory detail, I was glad that I had not purchased a hat after all, but when I see pictures of the Afghan President, Hamid Karzai, or Muhammed Ali Jinna, the founder of Pakistan, wearing just such a hat, I am reminded of this incident.

We left the bazaars and found ourselves at Dean's Hotel, where the contrast in ambiance could not have been greater. Here lingered the faint nostalgic aroma of empire, and my first impulse was to order a Pimm's or a pink gin; strong liquor that would not have been available anyway. We sat on the veranda among a complex of Colonial-style bungalows with green corrugated roofs, drank tea and discussed the events of the day.

'What next?' I asked.

'I haven't been to Islamabad. Do you think we could go?' responded Tarquin. 'A daily shuttle runs from the airport.'

The next day, we relaxed at the club and Tarquin played a couple of games of tennis. In the afternoon, he invited some of his Afghan students to Canal Road and we laid out cups and saucers and plates of sticky *baklava* beneath a frazzled fig tree that lent shade to the sun-baked garden. Abdur Rahman brought out some rugs to make us more comfortable, and I was introduced to the half a dozen or so young men as they arrived. They all wore the familiar brown, black or white *pukkal* and seemed a nice crowd, speaking remarkably good English and eyeing me with fleeting glances that betrayed their curiosity. A cumbersome iron brace secured one arm of the youngest in the group. He had picked up a booby-trapped 'toy' left by the Russians near the Afghan town of Khost. The ensuing explosion shattered his hand and forearm, right up to his elbow, but he had managed to make his way over the mountains to Peshawar for treatment.

'Never trust the Russians,' I murmured under my breath.

I soon discovered that one of them, Jalil, a Tajik from north-east Afghanistan, was friendly with the local *mujahideen* commander, so I asked him about *buzkashi*. He promised to find out if a game was planned.

'I think they will play on Saturday,' he said, licking honey off his fingers.

Early the next morning, we boarded a small Fokker at the nearby airport and in what seemed no time at all arrived in Islamabad, the capital of Pakistan. Designed and built in the early 1960s by a firm of Greek architects, the city nestled below the Margala Hills. It was regarded as a more central location for administrative purposes than Karachi, the capital since independence in 1947, and had a comparatively benign climate. It was also near the army headquarters in Rawalpindi. Since we only planned to spend a few hours in this modern conurbation, we quickly made our way down pleasant avenues in search of Shah Faisal Mosque. Dedicated to the late King Faisal of Saudi Arabia and designed by the Turkish architect Vedat Dalokay it was, at the time, reputed to be the largest mosque in the world. It was indeed an awesome experience to stand before the massive building, set against the backdrop of the Margala Hills, with its eight-faceted concrete roof that represented a desert tent. Although forbidden from entering the main prayer area, we peered through huge stretches of plate glass and admired the white marble hall, decorative mosaics and enormous Turkish-style chandelier. Wandering away from the mosque, led us through what seemed like a separate village housing a café, library and small university before reaching the mausoleum of General Zia-ul-Haq, ruler of Pakistan from 1977 to 1988. He had been killed when the plane in which he was travelling exploded, and it has always been assumed that he was assassinated. As we passed a bookshop I saw *The Great Game* prominently displayed in the window. This was Peter Hopkirk's fascinating history of rivalry in Central Asia between the British and Russian Empires that had been published earlier in the year by John Murray. I promised myself that I would buy Tarquin a copy for Christmas.

Later in the day, we took a Morris Minor taxi to 'Pindi', as it was affectionately known by the British. I had hoped to find something to link my grandfather's time there in the 1890s, but the only evidence of the military we came across were smart sentries, with plumes in their turbans, guarding government buildings. After an early supper at the Pearl Hotel, whose menu, surprisingly, only offered fish, and rather dry fish at that, we returned to Islamabad airport for the short trip back to Peshawar.

While waiting in the departure lounge, we struck up a conversation with an elderly gentleman who, as he soon told us, had been born and raised in Karachi. I got the impression that he been a military man, on account of his dignified bearing and clipped manner of speech. He enquired where we were from and what had brought us to the Punjab. Learning that our home was in London and that Tarquin was a burgeoning writer he commented, 'I do admire the British, they are a scholarly people.'

When his flight was called and he was out of earshot I turned to Tarquin.

'That reminds me of the one about the impressionable Indian who had been to Paddington Station where he caught a train to the West Country,' I said. "The English love their books and have special compartments," he had told his companion, "Yes ... whole carriages are reserved for READING!"'

Tarquin grimaced.

Approaching the runway over the Jamrud Road, streams of tracer could be seen arching their way up from the cantonment. This prompted Tarquin to divulge the less than reassuring story of how a pilot in similar circumstances had recently become confused by all the flickering lights and, mistaking the shimmering water of the canal for the runway, had crashed the plane; killing himself and all the passengers.

John Murray's *A Handbook for Travellers in India, Burma and Ceylon* (published in London and printed in Calcutta in 1938) says: 'No one should leave Peshawar without seeing the Pass, if it is allowed.' I wanted to go, and it was allowed providing that I obtained a permit and travelled with an armed guard. This proviso was not unexpected since a young aid worker had been killed near Jamrud earlier in the year. Tarquin was not so keen. He was exhausted and, from the stories he told, I knew that he had recently experienced close shaves with the Pakistani police near the Afghan border. I decided to go on my own and went down to the Peshawar cantonment to make the necessary arrangements with the Political Agent: Khyber. Within an hour I was in a taxi heading out of the city once again; a grey-bearded Pushtun (Pathan) wearing a rather tired black beret sat in the seat behind me, rifle at the ready. As the car proceeded down the potholed highway, I was not convinced that the presence of the guard contributed to my security. He was no spring chicken and I wondered how effective he would be if we were ambushed. It also occurred to me that since he held an ancient loaded Lee-Enfield .303 calibre rifle, upright between his knees, which left the tip of the barrel hovering only inches from the back of my head, I was quite likely to have my brains blown out. I weighed up the chances of being murdered by wild tribesmen or the gun going off accidentally when we hit a meandering goat or were forced, by a manic lorry driver, into the deep ditch that separated the road from arid terrain.

Soon we reached the approach to the Khyber where Alexander the Great, Genghis Khan and Tamerlane once passed by, and where *kafilas* (caravans) had wound their way for thousands of years. The heavily loaded *kafilas*, which frequently stretched for up to two miles, consisted of strings of bullocks, asses, goats and Bactrian (two-humped) camels, together with their dogs, domestic fowl, attendant keepers, wives and children. These would have been the colourful and legendary Kochis—the nomads of Afghanistan—whose name is thought to come from the Afghan-Persian '*koch kardan*', meaning 'to sally forth, move out or travel far afield'.

I noted from Murray's handbook that they used to pass through the Khyber on Tuesdays and Fridays in winter and Fridays only in summer. When I read that information, I wondered, for a split second, if I had mistakenly picked up a National Trust guide to the opening times of one of the stately homes of England, but for some reason this was indeed their time-honoured practice. Perhaps Kipling saw them in the spring because in 1890 he wrote in 'Ballad of the King's Jest':

> When spring-time flushes the desert grass,
> Our kafilas wind through the Khyber Pass,
> Lean are the camels but fat the frails,
> Light are the purses but heavy the bales,
> As the snowbound trade of the North comes down
> To the market square of Peshawar town.

Soon we were approaching Jamrud Fort. At 1,500 feet high, built in 1823, it had ten-foot-thick walls. From a distance it could be mistaken for a battleship. It was here that the legendary Amir Dost Mohammed's son Akbar Khan defeated and killed the Sikh leader Sardar Hari Singh in 1837. We pressed on towards the highest point of the pass, which stands at 3500 feet above sea level and some twenty-five miles from Peshawar as the crow or vulture flies. Our route, however, wound round precipitous hairpin bends, bumpity-bumped over little bridges that crossed the Jam Nalar, and coiled in and out of sight of the now defunct railway line that passed through innumerable tunnels in the khaki-coloured hillside. The line stopped in the Pass near Torratiga as there was no rail network in Afghanistan. Other forts, including the Shagai, built by the British, the Bagiari and Ali Masjid, came into view and it was not difficult to imagine the glint of sunlight on steel between the battlements, the flash of red on the parapets, a dragoon's bugle call. For these were once the outposts of empire and housed the custodians of the jewel in the British crown.

Eventually we reached Landi Kotal, as scruffy a border town as you could imagine. Once we had passed this collection of dreary hilltop dwellings the driver stopped the car. I got out and stood by the roadside, the distant valleys and mountain ranges of Afghanistan stretched before me. The guard borrowed my camera and took some shots of me posing with his rifle and with the Khyber and several of the moribund rail tunnels in the background. I then reciprocated, snapping the guard and driver. Soon it was time to start the journey back, and as we faced east at the top of the steepest of the notorious hairpin bends the Indus valley, gateway to the subcontinent, opened out before us. At that moment, in a flash, I realised that beyond me lay the inestimable prize, the road to power and riches, the final trophy coveted by generations of political and economic rivals whose august agents were the intrepid players in that long, deadly and continuing contest known as the Great Game.

'Guess what? Jalil called to say that there *will* be a *buzkashi* game tomorrow,' Tarquin announced on my return. 'He will collect us at ten in the morning'.

'Fantastic! Terrific! … *Inshallah!*' I replied, holding up two crossed figures.

At the appointed hour a huge Shogun 4x4 drew up in Canal Road and Tarquin and I climbed aboard, not quite believing our luck. A *mujahideen* commander's base was to be the first port of call. Anne, an attractive young woman whose head was covered with a pretty scarf and who was sitting next to me, explained that she worked for the Red Cross and had business to discuss before we all went on to the game.

Mr Barri, the commander, lived in a small ranch-like enclave on the outskirts of the city, and both Tarquin and I were surprised by its sophistication. Several Land Rovers and another Shogun were parked outside and in one corner of the compound a group of Pushtuns were polishing saddles, mending girths and fiddling with an array of weapons. While Anne went in for her meeting, we were given a tour of the stables, passing a sallow-skinned Turkoman who sat cross-legged in a leafy courtyard, weighing golden corn for the horses on a pair of primitive scales. I would easily have mistaken him for Chinese, and his face broke into a warm smile as we approached. He had a short white beard flecked with grey, a pure white silk turban, and a spotless off-white padded coat with minutely thin black stripes running from top to bottom. In a corner of the yard, behind him, stood a finely groomed chestnut mare, and there were half a dozen other horses, all beautifully cared for, munching away in their individual stalls. After a while it became clear that *buzkashi* really was going to be played and that we would have the opportunity to witness the traditional game inherited from the Mongols; the national sport of the most renowned horsemen of Central Asia. We piled back into the Shogun and Mr Barri went ahead in one of the Land Rovers, accompanied by several of his children, who were festively attired in multi-coloured silk coats (*chapanes*), black boots and exquisitely embroidered caps.

It was only a stone's throw to the sports ground, which was the size of a rugby pitch and boasted several stands which reminded me of visits to Rosslyn Park in the 1950s. Spectators were rapidly filling these rickety wooden edifices, and if I had been surprised at Karachi Airport by the extraordinary collection of individuals that I encountered, it was nothing to what I now witnessed. There were no women, but there were men with beards of all lengths and colours, vibrant robes, elegant waistcoats, beautiful embroidery, baggy *salmar kameez*, magnificent turbans and sun-bleached hats that retained no colour at all. The faces were also extraordinary: there were Mongolian features, aquiline and hooked noses, sharp, hooded black eyes, redheads and every possible combination and variation in between.

The game began with a line-up similar to a rugby game and when the referee, a huge man sporting a scarlet corduroy jacket, gave the signal, it began. Within seconds, the twenty or so players, each gripping the reins firmly with one hand, thundered up and down the pitch. Crashing hooves sent earth and dust flying everywhere. The strength required by the horsemen, who were as splendidly attired as the spectators, to haul a dead goat's carcass from the ground to the saddle with their free arm, and then to gallop with it, must have been stupendous, and virility was matched by ferocity. Holding their whips between their teeth, they careered past the stands, jostling for position, while pulling on their decorated reins and bridles that glistened in the sunshine. White phlegm streamed from the mouths of both man and beast. The crowds, who far exceeded the stands' capacity, and now surrounded the pitch, cheered and shrieked and when the goat was deposited in the white circle, thereby scoring a 'goal', their enthusiasm knew no bounds. On several occasions players rode into the crowd, scattering spectators in every direction and leaving them choking, spluttering and covered in dirt. Tarquin and I watched in fascination, taking every opportunity to use our cameras and also, during a fleeting break, to grab kebabs, hard-boiled henna-dyed eggs and popcorn from one of the popular stalls near the entrance. After about an hour the winners emerged, and both teams gathered in front of Mr Barri. He presented a fistful of rupees to the man who had scored the most goals, declaring that he was the *champandaz*, the champion! Admirers handed him more money as he rode away from the pitch and a huge cry went up in Dari Persian:

'Allah is great! Long live Afghanistan!'

As the sun went down behind the poplars, it cast a watery light across streams of spectators returning to their camps and to the city. Clouds of dust churned up by powerful Land Rovers, Shoguns and Mitsubishi 4x4s hung in shafts of withering sunshine. Where do they get the money for these things? I pondered.

Tarquin and I drove back to Canal Road with Jalil and Anne.

'I wonder when they will play again,' I mused as Jalil navigated his way through the crowd.

'I think they will play on Saturday. Inshallah,' he replied.

As the time for me to return to London approached, Tarquin and I decided to visit Lahore, the capital of the Punjab. We planned to spend a couple of days in the city and then I would fly back from there. We went down to the station in Saddar Bazaar to book a couchette on the overnight express and as we stood in the booking office the clerk questioned us abruptly from behind a plate-glass window.

'What is your name?' he barked.

'Hall,' I replied.

'And what is his name?' he asked, pointing at Tarquin.

'Hall,' I reiterated.

'No! No! Two people cannot have same name,' he stammered.

I started again, enunciating clearly.

'My name is HALL and this is my son who is also called Hall.'

'Ah! He is son of Hall!'

In a flash, the light had dawned. The clerk completed his paperwork and we returned to Canal Road without further ado. Later in the evening, I thanked Peter and John for their hospitality, and collecting six beautifully tailored shirts in the bazaar on the way, we boarded our train. A neat label on the couchette door read:

Mister Hall

Mister Son of Hall.

As the train pulled out of the station, tracer rose across the city and gunfire stuttered in the distance. We glimpsed the bright lights of Saddar Bazaar as we gathered speed, before drawing the blind and settling into our cosy berths. I wondered if I would ever return to Peshawar or enter the 'God Gifted Kingdom of Afghanistan'. If so, it would certainly not be under the same circumstances. As became clear later; when Tarquin and I were there; after the Russians had left Afghanistan but before the refugees had returned to their ravaged homeland, to face further years of strife, war and the heinous rule of the Taliban, was a special moment in the city's history. I deem myself as being extremely fortunate to have made the journey.

The rattle of the train, crossing a steel bridge, woke us soon after sunrise. I opened the carriage door and sat on the steps gripping the handrail as the flat plain of the Punjab passed before me. Punjab means 'five rivers' in Urdu and it was beautiful in the early morning sunshine. A light mist hung over the countryside, men and women were already toiling in the fields and at the occasional road-crossing horses or oxen, together with their carts and dark-skinned drivers, waited patiently as the train thundered by. However, before long we were crossing the metal bridge over the wide Ravi River where I could see herds of water buffalo basking on the mud flats, and the train soon entered Lahore railway station, built like a fort for a scene in the *Lone Ranger*. In the station yard several scrawny camels were tethered to a peg in the ground, a sight that reminded me of this story. I wonder if you have heard it. Perhaps not, as it was transcribed by the Austrian writer Gustav Krist in 1936. He heard it from a storyteller in Central Asia, who claimed that Allah had revealed it to him in a dream.

It goes like this:

In the days of Tamerlane, there lived at the court of Samarkand a certain *mirza* (scribe) called Abdullah Bezdik. The *mirza* had a great love of animals and could not bear to see them suffer. He used to go around the *caravanserais* of Samarkand and buy up every sick or wounded camel he saw. One day the great Tamerlane heard of the *mirza*'s doings and sent for him. Tamerlane was seated on a throne with a circle of many *imams* and *mullahs* around him when the *mirza* came in and prostrated himself again and again before the mighty Ruler of the World. Then Tamerlane asked him why in the name of Allah he had bought up a lot of sick camels which, after all, had no souls and were worth even less than so many women. The *mirza* answered that animals also had souls and suffered pain. The *imams* and *mullahs* blanched at such blasphemy and challenged the *mirza* to prove that the camel had a soul. If he could not prove it he must die. The *mirza* replied that he could not prove it, since it was not possible to prove that even men had souls. Tamerlane was still more enraged at this reply and bade them strike off the impudent fellow's head. Before this order could be carried out, the court fool interposed:

'Tell me, mighty Timur, had the late Diwan Begi a soul or not?'

'By Allah,' cried Tamerlane, 'I shall execute any man that doubts it!'

'And shall you let the *mirza* go free, if I prove that camels have a soul?' asked the fool.

'By the beard of the Prophet, I promise to let him go free. But how wilt thou prove it, fool?'

'Right easily, thou favourite of Allah! Thou hast just now declared that the Diwan Begi had a soul and, how often, oh my Master, hast thou not thyself called him a camel!'

Tamerlane, the *imams* and the *mullahs* laughed until the roof threatened to fall in. The *mirza* was free!'

For the next two days, Tarquin and I unashamedly adopted the role of tourists. We booked into a cheap hotel and started to explore the sights of the city, whose heyday had been in the sixteenth and seventeenth centuries, at the time of the Mughal emperors. We soon found our way to the magnificent Badshahi Mosque built by Emperor Aurangzeb whose father, Shah Jehan ('the king of the world') constructed the Taj Mahal in memory of his favourite wife. It featured the largest courtyard in the world, and is an awesome example of the grandest style of Islamic architecture. Close by, we admired brightly coloured mosaics in the Lahore Fort and gaped in wonder at the walls and domed ceilings of the Palace of Mirrors, the Shish Mahal. Outside stood an ornate pavilion built in 1631 and here we were amazed to find semi-precious stones; lapis lazuli, garnet, jade and malachite embedded in the stonework of the building. Our wanderings took us through the Shalimar Gardens, where 450 fountains once sparkled providing a cool retreat from the frenetic city. Also built by Emperor Shah Jehan, in 1641, the gardens were in an advanced state of disrepair at the time of our visit. But perhaps the most beautiful sight that we encountered on our whistle-stop tour of that fascinating city was the tomb of Emperor Jahangir, built in 1633. The Emperor was Shah Jahan's father and died from the effects of drink and drugs at the tender age of thirty-six. Now at rest in a beautiful and peaceful mausoleum on the outskirts of Lahore, the tomb and its surrounds are sculpted in white marble, embellished with fine floral decoration and delicate engraving in the Naskh script that details the ninety-nine names of Allah. Muslims adhere to the tradition that knowledge of the one-hundredth name is vouchsafed to the camel alone, so perhaps those remarkable beasts do have souls after all. The likeness of Shah Jahan, his contemporaries and much of their history are minutely illustrated and documented in *Padshahnama*, a fabulous manuscript that was given to George III in 1799 and remains in the library at Windsor Castle.

On our way back to the centre of the city we passed Zamzama, immortalised by Kipling as Kim's Gun. This huge, large bore cannon with a barrel over fourteen feet long stood in the Mall, one of Lahore's most pleasant streets. It was cast in 1757 by Shah Nazir and used by Ahmed Shah in 1761 at the battle of Panipat and other campaigns.

On the following day, we explored the bazaars, not unlike those we had encountered at Peshawar, certainly in terms of the general pandemonium and with their own share of treasure-filled caverns. I found a wonderful shop full of brassware, and after delving around for an hour, followed by a spot of bargaining, emerged with some pieces to take home as presents. One item I could not resist for myself was a solid brass, 2.5x4-inch, six-lever padlock that weighs over two pounds and stands on my desk as I write.

In the evening it was time to leave.

'What a fantastic trip! Thanks so much for everything', I exclaimed, as Tarquin and I gripped each other in tight bear hugs at the airport.

'See you in London soon!'

'Love to mum and Alex!'

I climbed the steps to the small plane that would take me to Karachi before transferring to a jumbo for the flight to London. Tarquin had business to see to at the offices of the *Friday Times* and would then make his own way back to Peshawar. Two weeks in the North West Frontier Province had seared vivid impressions into my brain. Friends had warned me that I would suffer culture shock when I arrived in Peshawar. I didn't. What I actually experienced was aftershock. The bustle of the bazaars; the frenetic fut-fut rickshaws; the incessant honking of horns; the indescribably colourful characters; the beards and vivid hats and turbans and burkas; the piles of juicy fruit; the huge cauliflowers; the thundering of horses' hooves at the *buzkashi* game; the bleating of goats, braying of donkeys and bellowing of buffalo; the gaunt crags and winding hairpins of the Khyber; the rattle of gunfire; the call of the *muezzin*—all these tossed and turned and tumbled and jumbled around in my brain, night after night, for weeks to come.

Having not read a newspaper while I was away, it was something of a surprise, when I landed at Gatwick, to find Britain gripped in a political crisis. It was 20th November 1990, and the Conservative Party was tearing itself apart following Michael Heseltine's challenge to Margaret Thatcher's leadership. I arrived home to see the Iron Lady speaking on television to the BBC's John Sergeant. She was in Paris, where she had gone to attend celebrations marking the end of the Cold War, and had just received the disappointing results of the first ballot. A second ballot followed a few days later and on 28th November she was gone. Her tearful departure from Downing Street after eleven years was a poignant moment.

Tarquin returned from Pakistan just in time for Christmas. He had suffered a severe attack of dysentery and was looking so ill that British Airways had thrown him off the plane at Islamabad. Following a medical check, he was allowed to travel a few days later, but severe weight loss required a pro-gramme of carefully thought-out meals and Lucinda's refined cooking. It was nice to have him at home and we duly presented him with a copy of *The Great Game*, which had been reprinted three times in its first year of publi-cation. Tarquin devoured the weighty tome in no time. I noticed that he had become a voracious reader, and a chance remark elicited this response:

'Henry Miller once said: "If you wanna be a good writer, ya gotta be a good reader." At least that's what my friend Tommy told me when I was in New York.'

In the meantime, the gathering storm was about to erupt in the Middle East.

George and Bettina Briggs

The Nickerson House, Cape Cod

Alexander, Neil, Lucinda and Tarquin, 1974

PEACOCK, 1976

Chapter 11
'You've been to Peshawar?!'

Life without steep learning curves is no life at all.
(Tahir Shah: '*Travels with Myself*', 2011)

ON 16TH JANUARY 1991 the Gulf War started, and we endured six weeks of dramatic news, transmitted in seemingly endless live television broadcasts that appeared very real and instant as we watched in the comfort of our sitting room. One memorable scene showed John Simpson reporting for the BBC, while a missile cruised past the window in his hotel.

Tarquin spent the first few months with us in Kew, recuperating from the rigours of Afghanistan and Pakistan, by the spring he felt strong enough to continue on his travels. In early March, we found ourselves waving good-bye at Gatwick's Passport Control, as he left for Nairobi.

After my adventures in the North West Frontier Province, I set about re-organising my marketing strategy against a background of uncertain invest-ment sentiment, following conflict in the Middle East. By this time, I had become used to bouts of market jitters, but the war had affected my brother badly. Richard, had for some time harnessed his artistic skills in developing an Oriental carpet-repair business, run from his home in Wiltshire, where he established a reputation for being one of the finest restorers in the coun-try. His clients included many of the London dealing houses, the Victoria and Albert Museum, English Heritage, Osborne House and wealthy princes from Kuwait. At a stroke, his Middle East business was lost, which initiated a chain of difficulties. Unfortunately, his problems were compounded by alcohol and drug dependency, so both his business and marriage foundered. These habits had first developed in the madness of a drug culture which prevailed at art school in the 1960s, and over the years they caused huge problems in the family and divided loyalties.

This was especially true as my parents had a tendency to defend their youngest and dearest. There were long periods when no one felt able to communicate with one another. In due course, Richard moved to Cornwall, remarried and turned his life around. He is now a successful painter (Richard Lannowe Hall) and runs a charity for those who have been abused or suffered various addictions. His organisation is called 'Sailaday' and, building on his own experience and training, he takes young people on long sailing trips from Falmouth to teach them skills and self-confidence. It has been hugely successful and has received support from the National Lottery and St. James's Place Wealth Management. Better family relationships have been established.

I began to exploit a market where I had already achieved some success; having discovered that there was a special need for advice and for financial products among those who taught and often lived in public schools. With my background, not only as a headmaster's son who had lived in schools as a boy, also as one who had been through the system and was an experienced businessman, I was the ideal person to provide that service. I was certainly familiar with the lingo, as were few of my colleagues in the industry. I also found that many of the staff at what are now termed 'independent' schools were woefully ignorant of financial matters. I even came across a man who taught economics, but did not know what unit trusts were, which was alarming, and when a senior man—now the headmaster of a famous school—handed me a cheque with the words 'I don't suppose there are many people who can lay their hands on £3,000,' I was equally dismayed. This lack of knowledge arose partly because they were so caught up in their demanding and absorbing environment that they spared little thought for the wider financial world, and also because they were sufficiently well funded not to have to worry about money on a day-to-day basis. This was especially true of those who lived within a school in tied accommodation. It did not take me long to discover that when I asked schoolmasters what they earned, an astonishingly high percentage were unable to tell me. A long way from my friend Jock Noyes, in New York City.

My question invariably precipitated a rummage in a cluttered drawer to find an unopened payslip. When a certain Eton Master died, some years ago, not only were his payslips found unopened, but the cheques had not been removed from the envelopes either. During one meeting, a housemaster nodded off at the table, which showed just how much importance he attached to what I had to say.

However, this situation posed a serious threat to these individuals, because the day would come when they would have to move back into the 'real world', and they needed to know what standard of living they could then expect. It also posed the question of what safety net was in place for a family in the event of the breadwinner's premature death or serious illness. In such circumstance, as I was to learn, wives and children would be homeless and without an income.

Fortunately, people are now more sophisticated than they were in the early 1990s. More information is available today, than at the time when I first addressed these issues. Even if schoolmasters realised that there were matters to be dealt with, they were unsure where to go for advice, and whom to trust.

So the scene was set for circumstances to develop that were to prove beneficial for all concerned. There was a clearly defined need to insure, to save, and to plan in the longer term. It was also a market that suited me in respect of my qualms about pension advice, because all my prospective clients already belonged to the Teachers' Occupational Scheme. I understood the environment in which these people lived and worked, better than most, and sold the products they needed. It would prove to be my main source of business for the rest of my career in the financial services industry. At the last count, I had visited sixty-four schools.

But it was to provide more than a cash machine, because as I began to contact schools and schoolmasters, I began to travel to all sorts of interesting places, and this process of earning my living widened my education enormously. Within a relatively short time, I had visited some of the most hallowed environs within the private education system and gradually, from a unique viewpoint, acquired an insight into the world of what has been paradoxically termed the public school.

The passages that immediately follow present a bird's eye view—a whistle-stop tour—of some of the experiences that provided that perspective. I shall always be grateful to those who took me into their confidence and made this possible. I hope that I served them well.

Some people have shown surprise when I explain what I did—the development of a niche market.

'Surely these teachers had no money,' they said.

That was not necessarily true. They may not have had huge salaries; they were partly rewarded by the benefits of the environment in which they lived and worked, with few expenses and, therefore, had the disposable income to purchase products that enhanced their longer-term security. Some of them also inherited money or had wealthy families. Husband-and-wife teams were often in the strongest position. By and large, they were an extraordinarily decent and reliable crowd with whom to work, which were important factors in my business life and contributed to my ongoing sanity.

There were few clawbacks when dealing with schoolmasters.

As I began to develop my strategy, I wrote to members of the Common Room at various schools, inevitably starting at Marlborough. I must confess that I did suppress a wry smile when I found myself sitting with a housemaster, directing his financial future, only yards from where I had been flogged thirty years previously. My interview with a second beak was to prove more problematic, as his golden labrador was very ill and in fact died in the house, minutes after the meeting was prematurely curtailed.

I am sure everyone loves a labrador, but I could have been spared the experience of Bill, a black version, who farted with nauseating consequences during meetings with a staff member at Rugby, where I had begun to acquire clients. I had never been to the town before, and my initial visit was something of a thrill as I interviewed a beak in the very house where Dr Thomas Arnold had ruled from 1828–42. Large windows in spacious rooms overlooked the playing fields where Webb Ellis first handled a ball in 1823. A plaque commemorating the event was set in the perimeter wall that reads: 'with a fine disregard for the rules of football as played in his time (he) took the ball in his hands and ran with it.'

One thing I had not known was that Ellis went on to become a clergyman, eventually becoming rector of St Clement Danes in the Strand, where a further memorial has been erected by members of the Royal Air Force Rugby Football Union. My next meeting was at Sheriffe House, named after Laurence Sheriffe who had founded Rugby School in 1567. He was a wealthy grocer and in a codicil to his will left estates near London to the school. These eventually became absorbed into the city and I am reliably informed that the revenues derived from property in the neighbourhood of Great Ormond Street and Lamb's Conduit Street, in central London, still fund the development of the school. Opposite School House was a small museum, part of which was dedicated to Rupert Brooke, whose father was once a house-master. Brooke wrote memorable poetry, perhaps the most quoted and also prophetic being the following:

> If I should die, think only this of me;
> That there's some corner of a foreign field
> That is for ever England.
> ('The Soldier', 1914)

He attended Rugby at the beginning of the twentieth century but died of septicaemia on St George's Day 1915 and was buried in Skyros, Greece. A boarding house in Horton Crescent was named after him. The museum had in its possession a letter from one, Thomas Burn, who went to Marlborough in 1846, but after a year, transferred to Rugby. This is what he wrote concerning the comparative merits of the schools at that time: 'I like Rugby altogether very much indeed, there is no comparison between it and Marlborough.'

Perhaps this view is not surprising. Marlborough must have been pretty bloody in the days leading to the Great Rebellion of 1851—an event that stands out above all others in the early days of the College.

Burn subsequently returned to Marlborough as a beak, but in 1858 accompanied the then Master, George Edward Lynch Cotton, to India, as his domestic chaplain, following Cotton's appointment to the Episcopal See of Calcutta. Bishop Cotton, a severe man but of undoubted charisma, was immortalised as the 'grave young man' who inspired the hero in Thomas Hughes' famous tales of *Tom Brown's Schooldays*. He must surely have exerted a benign influence on his chaplain, who sadly died at the age of thirty, two years before the bishop himself, who met an early death when he slipped off a steamer's gangway in the dark and disappeared into the Hooghly River. I understand that there is little evidence to support the legend that he was subsequently devoured by crocodiles, although there are two small crocodiles carved into the choir stalls in the chancel at St Peter's Church in Marlborough, so someone must have believed the story at the time. Cotton was commemorated by having boarding houses at both Marlborough and Rugby named after him, and there is a fine portrait of him in the Norwood Hall at Marlborough College. A statue to Thomas Hughes stands on pleasant lawns in front of the library at Rugby.

On my visits, I always thought that Rugbeians, both boys and girls, were well turned-out and looked cheerful enough as they went about their business along the pavements of the Barby Road and Horton Crescent, a collection of large red-brick Victorian houses in a pleasant part of Rugby.

I was surprised, however, when a housemaster was called away during a meeting and returned a few minutes later looking decidedly glum.

'One of those meetings,' he muttered under his breath.

This was explained the following day when the story of a pupil, who clearly thought he would be happier elsewhere and had absconded to the West Indies, was plastered all over the tabloids.

Most of the rest of Rugby was industrial and dreary, but on Saturday nights the Bodger (Headmaster) could relax, as he knew that his staff were on the watch for troublemakers who came in from rougher neighbourhoods.

I particularly enjoyed visiting the towns of Oundle, Oakham and Uppingham, each of which boasted its own unique school. The road from Northampton to Oundle passed the village of Aldwinkle All Saints, the birthplace of the poet John Dryden in 1631. My mother used to quote Dryden's poetry, and these lines come to mind:

> I think and think on things impossible
> Yet love to wander in that golden maze.

If this was how she thought of me as a teenager, she may well have been right.

Dryden was educated at Westminster, but there was a boarding house named after him at Oundle School, and members of his family still lived at Canon's Ashby, a National Trust property on the other side of the county that is well worth a visit. The gardens boast a splendid mulberry tree and views across ancient fish ponds.

Approaching Oundle by road, the fine spire of St Peter's Church rose above the Nene Valley and could be seen for miles around. The school, like Rugby, dated from the mid-sixteenth century, and originated from a bequest to the Grocer's Company by Sir William Laxton, a native of the town. Do grocers ever die poor? *Plus ça change, plus ça est la même chose.*

The school buildings were integrated into the busy market town, and were especially frenetic on Thursdays when colourful stalls filled the small central square.

I have met some interesting staff members at Oundle, including one chap who gave me a signed copy of his 'do-it-yourself' book, and taught boys how to build road-buggies for as little as one hundred pounds. He was continuing the tradition of teaching engineering that had been implemented by the modernising nineteenth-century headmaster F.W. Sanderson. Sanderson, a pioneer in teaching methods, sought cooperation rather than competition, and also transformed school music by encouraging every boy to take part. 'Boys set forth,' he proclaimed in one of his sermons, 'to do their work as well as they possibly can—but not to beat one another.'

Memorable in the Common Room, were a husband-and-wife team whose combined qualifications for outdoor pursuits was mind-boggling. Their skills included skiing, mountaineering, diving, sailing, swimming and trekking. What an inspiration for the young! I also recall an especially nice young couple, whom I first met when romance was blossoming; they then married, and within a couple of years their first child came along, followed by another and then another. I gave them financial advice at each stage, and began to feel like some sort of fiscal vicar.

The man I got to know best, I will call D. We soon discovered that we had both studied music with ABS-M. He lived alone with his black cats and two pianos in a small house on the edge of the town. An eccentric English scholar with a passion for Gilbert and Sullivan and Victorian church music, he was also second in command of the Combined Cadet Force. His grandfather, a major in the Royal Army Medical Corps, had won the Military Cross in the Great War and met his grandmother at a casualty clearing station in the Ypres Salient. His own father, Roger, landed at Juno Beach in June 1944 and fought all the way into Germany, finishing near Belsen in April 1945. Roger died in December 2002 and the last time I saw D, he gave me a copy of the eulogy he had just delivered at his father's funeral. I was touched by this sharing of private grief, and when I read the first three words of his speech: 'Loyalty, integrity, generosity,' I wondered if, in some way, D was describing himself. Sadly, he had by this time contracted cancer, and at a meeting in January 2003 we reviewed his investments. He was content with the way things stood and was particularly pleased to receive the proceeds of a critical illness policy that I had sold him, but he was due to go for tests and confided that if things looked really black there would be enough money for him to enjoy a few treats before the end. Sadly, he did not live long enough to pursue those pleasures, and I was choked when informed of his death a few weeks later.

The road from Market Harborough to Uppingham that passes through Weston-by-Welland and Medbourne is one of the prettiest I know. The brook at Stockerston marks the boundary of Rutland, England's smallest county, and I wondered who the Ruts were. They seemed to have carved out a delightful neck of the woods for themselves. However, I was corrected in this line of thinking by my friends David and Katharine Gaine, who have both held senior positions at Uppingham School for many years. They pointed out that the etymology of 'rut', probably Saxon, was in fact 'red', on account of the colour of the local soil. Rutland is therefore the Redland.

David also pointed out that the Isle of Wight is now the smallest county—at least, it is when the tide is in.

If I was lucky, I could arrange meetings in such a way as to be able to pick up tasty homemade rolls at Baines, the tea shop in Uppingham High Street, and then park the car, at lunchtime, close to Eyebrook Reservoir. This lovely spot, is one of the few places in England where you can see ospreys. It is below the hamlet of Stoke Dry that clings to the hillside, and is now a preserve of birdwatchers, but in St Andrew's church, which has traces of Norman work, it was rumoured that the Gunpowder Plot was hatched in 1605. Whether this story is true or not is a matter of debate, but Guy Fawkes was the son of Everard Digby, hanged in 1606 for his part in the conspiracy, and there are several tombs containing members of the Digby family in this charming but unsophisticated church. Interestingly enough, Rutland has the largest number of mediaeval churches of any area of its size in Britain.

One of the most difficult aspects of my job was trying to fill my diary with meetings that coincided with clients' or prospective clients' timetables. Sometimes I was rushed off my feet, but at other times, there were long gaps between meetings. If I was in Uppingham those could be filled with chats to the delightful Mrs Baines in her second-hand bookshop, close to the school entrance. It was delving about in her shop and striking up amiable conversations that provided opportunities for me to learn something of the local history. On one occasion, I stayed overnight in the Garden Hotel, formerly the Capital, where the coachmen and chauffeurs were once put up while the gentry stayed in the Falcon. Coming down to breakfast, a fellow guest greeted me with the words, 'Did you know there's a big school across the road? Boris Karloff went there … and Rick Stein!'

Uppingham, set in beautiful countryside and a hundred miles from London, is a sleepy market town. The school was founded in1584 by Archdeacon Robert Johnson, but it is the ghost of Etonian Edward Thring that still stalks the corridors. Thring was Headmaster from 1853–87, and raised the school from a local grammar school into the thriving institution that we recognise today. An enthusiastic defender of boarding-school educa-tion, he wrote: 'Children leave home to go to school … In theory, they are sent to a place which is better than home, to be under men that train better than mothers and fathers … Every boy who leaves home ought to go to a better than home place.'

He founded the Headmaster's Conference in 1869, initially to defend public schools from government interference, but was, on one occasion, criticised for excessive zeal when he flogged some boys who had returned to school late after the Easter holidays. He was lampooned in *Punch* which wrote: 'Mr Thring seemed to know how to manage boys and, if he did not train their minds, he made them mind their trains.'

I have visited most of the boarding houses, which resemble small manor houses, set in splendid grounds, and it was easy to imagine the days when prefects ruled the roost and the housemaster was not expected to ven-ture beyond the green baize door of the private quarters. But things have changed. The flogging of boys is no longer acceptable, and attitudes to con-trolling bolshy teenagers are very different. I recently heard of an incident when a senior female member of staff, described as a 'feisty lady who speaks as she finds', was giving one of the boys a dressing-down in the privacy of her study. He was playing silly buggers and, her patience clearly exhausted, the high-pitched directive: 'DON'T FUCK WITH ME, YOU LITTLE SHIT!' could be heard through the less than soundproof door to her lair.

Surprisingly, I have found that a large number of the staff are ardent Francophiles. By contrast, there is one particularly charming man who, al-though coming up to retirement, had never been out of England. I was de-lighted to talk to him recently and to learn that his family had broken the habit of a lifetime and spent a few enjoyable days in Lille.

Forebears of mine attended Uppingham School and, family legend has it that at the beginning of the autumn term in 1880, Eustace Oldrey, the son of Robert Foale Oldrey, was being waved off at Northampton station by his mother when she dropped dead on the platform. One afternoon, more than a hundred years later, Lucinda and I combined a business trip with a long weekend break. Motivated by curiosity, we stopped at Harpole Hall, the Oldreys' former home, a few miles from Northampton, and making our way through iron gates and across the gravel drive I knocked timorously on the front door. The present owner, Mrs Vivienne Simpson, gave her unexpected callers a warm welcome and, inviting us in, appeared fascinated to hear of our family connection with her house. She has become a good friend, and staying at the Hall, where Iris, my dear grandmother (Gawky), was born on 17th October 1885 provokes a curious sensation. Sadly, much of the land has now been sold and housing estates occupy what were once the stable block and surrounding parkland, but the house is still much as it was when the young Oldrey family enjoyed it in the gay 1890s.

Both of Iris's brothers, Blatchford and Vivian (Old Uppinghamians), died during the Great War, as I have mentioned before, and they are commemorated on memorials at Turvey in Bedfordshire, which is where their mother lived following her remarriage to Dr Archibald Sharpin. Their father, Robert Blatchford Oldrey, had died at the age of thirty-six. However in 2004, at the instigation of English Heritage, the boys' names, together with several from other families, were added to the war memorial in the churchyard at Harpole. David Oldrey and I attended a short but poignant ceremony, honouring those dashing young men. I wonder how they had reacted to the call to arms in 1914. Did they concur with these inspiring words—Rupert Brooke again:

> Now, God be thanked who has matched us with his hour.
> And caught our youth and wakened us from sleeping,
> With hand made sure, clear eye and sharpened power
> To turn like swimmers into cleanness leaping ...
> ('Peace', 1914)

It was held exactly ninety years and a day since Blatchford had died at Neuve Chapelle, and on a morning that broke in damp autumnal mist. By eleven o'clock, the sky had cleared and the small congregation had assembled amid ageing lichen-encrusted gravestones in the watery October sunshine. It was a moment to contemplate the great loss of skilled, talented, experienced and even the most ordinary of men, that this country suffered, and from which it has never fully recovered, and the personal suffering that my grand-mother and others endured.

For a moment, I thought I saw Blatchford—whom I appeared to rec-ognise from a photograph—standing in the crowd. How could this possibly be? Surely I was just being silly. Driving home, I recalled a passage from John Bennett's autobiography *Witness* (1962) when he visits his old school and sees the names of the fallen on a monument.

> I knew why I had never returned: I had never reconciled myself to the loss of so many of my best friends. I was all alone on the great playing field; but, as I stood, I was no longer alone. All these boys were still there; still living with their powers undiminished ... An immense joy flooded through me. Past all understanding, it was yet true that premature death is not necessarily a disaster. Potentialities are not destroyed by death.

On 6th November 1914, following Blatchford's death, Captain Charles Hornby, who later commanded the 4th Dragoon Guards and was also a member of the regimental polo team, wrote to Mrs Sharpin at Turvey, from King Edward VII's Hospital for Officers in Grosvenor Gardens. He ended his letter with these words: 'I can't tell you how much I shall miss him; he was just one of the best. I only hope that knowledge of what he was to us may be of some help to you. With my deepest sympathy.'

A few miles north of Uppingham lies Oakham, another sleepy town and close to Rutland Water where Lucinda and I once spent a delightful weekend sailing our dinghy. The school was also a grammar school founded by Robert Johnson, also in 1584. It is understood that Johnson enjoyed the patronage of the Cecil family who resided at Burghley House near Stamford. The school applied for a direct grant from the local authority in the early years of the twentieth century, but became an independent school in 1970. Sadly, one of my clients at Oakham died prematurely. I shall call him P. He was the kindest of men, a real 'Mr Chips'. His funeral was an emotional ex-perience for friends and colleagues of all ages and the chapel was overflowing. As we left by the west door, a rainbow arched across the sky, high above the roofs and treetops of Oakham town.

My trips tended not to extend beyond the River Trent, but on one occasion I visited clients whose career path had led them to appointments in Yorkshire. A long and tiring excursion took me Giggleswick, the delightful school that had been founded in the reign of Henry VIII in an attractive valley near Settle on the edge of the Yorkshire Dales National Park, and also to Ampleforth, a bleak outpost on the edge of the North Yorkshire Moors. With a foundation that dated back to Benedictine monks in the early seventeenth century, Ampleforth College's present site dates from 1802. The countryside was beautiful enough, but I found it to be a cold and lonely spot and felt sorry for boys who were wrapped, supposedly for spiritual comfort, in what I consider to be the miserable doctrine of original sin. The actor Rupert Everett (Old Amplefordian) recalls being instructed that if he were to awake with a 'hard on' he should turn over and recite three 'Hail Marys'!

Repton School, by contrast, has a strong Anglican tradition. Close to the banks of the Trent, one of England's longest rivers, it occupies Repton village, once the capital of Mercia. The church of St Wystan boasts an ancient chancel, and I once had the opportunity to venture down the winding staircase past wreathed spiral bands to the Saxon crypt. Two headmasters, William Temple and Geoffrey Fisher, became archbishops of Canterbury and a further occupant of the see of St Augustine, Michael Ramsey, was once a pupil. Roald Dahl claimed that he was severely beaten by Old Marlburian Fisher during his time at the school. It was Fisher's wife whom I once heard interviewed on the radio. The topic was her long marriage and she was asked if she had ever considered divorce. 'Absolutely not!' was her emphatic reply. 'But MURDER ...?' Would Lucinda echo this sentiment? I have wondered.

When William Temple moved into Lambeth Palace in 1942 he complained to the then Prime Minister, Winston Churchill, that there were forty bedrooms for which he had no use. 'Forty bedrooms?' replied the great man. 'Archbishop, you do indeed have a predicament. What—with only thirty-nine articles?'

Repton, like so many schools, had adapted from the days when future archbishops stalked their corridors. Fewer members of the staff had been educated privately, and only a minority attended Oxford or Cambridge. From my observation, tradition had largely given way to supplying the local community with splendid and wide-ranging, albeit expensive, educational facilities. This was not true of, among others, the great boys' schools at Eton, Harrow and Winchester, which still drew on their historic roots, but many schools were now heavily populated by families who had not sent their children to public school before, colloquially known as 'first-time buyers'. They included Germans, Russians and Hong Kong Chinese, a tendency that started, along with the proliferation of co-education, when the books were failing to balance in the early 1990s. Some schools had totally moved away from their original function and this had been dictated by history. For example, the fine buildings at Haileybury (Imperial Service College) built for the East India Company in the early 1800s, whose sons were sent to administer the subcontinent, would look at home in Delhi or Lahore. Today, the old boys' list features scores of addresses in nearby Hatfield, Potters Bar and Welwyn Garden City. Marlborough, once the domain of the sons of rural deans and country gentry, now attracts children who largely spurn the activities of the beagle pack and are more likely to be found shopping in Monsoon, eating at Ask or gallivanting at the Pheasantry in London's King's Road. To be fair, many participate in adventurous and educationally beneficial expeditions to all parts of the world in their holidays and during their gap year.

'The only trouble with this job is the parents!' a delightful Repton housemistress once confided to my sympathetic ear. 'At the slightest hint of trouble, the mobile bleeps, Mum jumps into her Isuzu Trooper and in no time at all she's round here wanting to know what's going on. I've come across a parent ranting and raving in the girls' dorm before I have even heard of any kind of incident! How do you manage a situation like that?'

On one occasion, when Lucinda and I decided to combine work with pleasure and following on from a business trip, we arrived in darkness one Friday night in October at a caravan near Offa's Dyke in the Black Mountains. The vehicle was permanently sited, at least fifty years old, and belonged to Tommas Graves, our accountant, who as a kind gesture had lent it to us for the weekend. Almost immediately, we singed the ceiling by turning the gaslights up too high, but after managing to cook an evening meal we settled down on the floor for the night. In the morning, not only the windows but also the walls were streaming with condensation and we awoke feeling cold, damp and stiff. This was not the relaxing break we expected so, planning to use the caravan as a day cabin, we decamped to the Llanthony Priory Abbey Hotel a few miles down the valley. Here, we were led up a spiral stone staircase to a large room with four poster bed at the very top of a tall tower that we assumed to have once been part of the Augustinian Priory. As our guide left, she drew our attention to the large white china chamber pot that had been placed under the bed. The facilities, she informed us, were two floors below, back down the winding staircase and along several corridors, so 'the article', as it was euphemistically called in smart country houses, might come in handy. I did feel sorry for the maid in the morning.

Before we left the stunning Vale of Ewyas, we had marvellous walks through woods that bordered the rushing Afon Honddu, and wandered around the twelfth-century priory, now almost entirely in ruins. You can imagine our surprise when we came across a plaque commemorating the visit of my forebear, Sir Richard Colt Hoare, who in 1803 actually witnessed the collapse of the great west window. This trip also gave us the opportunity to visit Llandaff where Welsh members of the Mathew family lie in exqui-sitely decorated stone tombs within the Cathedral Church of Saints Peter and Paul, with Saints Dyfrig, Teilo and Euddogwy. These include the mighty Sir David Mathew, born in 1400 and appointed Grand Standard-Bearer of England after saving the life of Edward IV at the Battle of Towton on Palm Sunday 1461, for which service he was granted the Lion Rampant Sable to be added to his coat of arms. He also earned the title of 'Keeper of the Tomb of St Teilo' for saving the cathedral from attack by Bristol pirates. In 1994, on St Teilo's Day (9th February), the last surviving member of the direct line of the Mathew family, who had been its traditional keeper, returned the saint's skull to the cathedral. Its authenticity is, of course, a matter of debate. Other Welsh Mathews of note were Sir William, who was knighted on the field of Bosworth in August 1485 by the victorious Duke of Richmond (Henry VII) and Sir Tobias, for whom Francis Bacon wrote his 'Essay on Friendship', who was born in 1577. Sir Tobias subsequently translated Bacon's treatise into Italian in 1618.

Following a client referral, I, like the Romans, 'out to Severn strode'[18] and one October morning found myself in Shrewsbury for the first time. I was in for a pleasant surprise. Some time previously, I had occasion to visit the artist Dennis Gilbert in his studio eyrie, high above Edith Grove on the Chelsea–Fulham border. After we had discussed some business, I mentioned that my grandfather was the artist Oliver Hall. He paused for a few minutes then disappeared into a back room, re-emerging with a small oil painting. 'This is an Oliver,' he said. The painting, depicting a pleasant view, was unsigned, but the label on the back provided sufficient information and provenance to confirm that what he said was true.

'My pension,' he continued, his eyes sparkling, and named a price that I found agreeable. Within a few hours, my new acquisition was hanging on our dining-room wall at home. The problem was that neither Dennis, nor I, nor anyone else I asked, recognised the view in the picture and I went to considerable trouble, writing to tourist information offices in an effort to identify it, but to no avail. The oil was of a town with two church spires rising above buildings that were perched on cliffs above a wide river, and there was what looked like a tumbledown fort and some trees in the foreground. The colours were in muted tones and I would have been happy to bet that it was a scene in France or Spain.

Suddenly, on that October morning, as I paused in traffic crossing the Severn on the English Bridge, the sun broke out of the clouds and the picture came alive right in front of me. Right there, in Shrewsbury, I had found 'my Oliver's' home.

Finding my way around usually presented few problems. In fact, I would be prepared to boast that I could draw a fairly detailed map of London and the south of England from memory. Shrewsbury, however, completely flummoxed me, and on my second visit I felt compelled to purchase a street map. The difficulty is that the Severn has created a meander through the middle of the town that was built on both high and contrasting low ground. It was very easy to get disorientated.

Shrewsbury School, a great rowing establishment, commands dramatic views across the valley and the river. It was founded by King Edward VI in 1552 and boasted Sir Philip Sidney, that 'verray parfit gentil knight' and Charles Darwin as its most famous sons—not to mention John Peel. A fine statute of Sidney and Darwin, old Salopians, as past pupils are called, stood on the campus close to the Chapel and Common Room. The staff I met struck me as kindly folk who reflected the best tradition of school mastering, although this may not have always been the case. In the early days, beaks had to swear that they would not vandalise or steal school property and that they would not pocket the boys' entrance fees. Instructions were also laid down that masters 'infected with any loathsome, horrible or contagious disease' were to be removed. Shrewsbury (pronounced Shroos-bury or Shrows-bury according to preference), with its leafy hillside streets and cobbled roads in the central shopping area, reminded me of England as it was in my childhood. It has, however, had its troubled times. A fierce battle raged in 1403 during the Wars of the Roses, and the Roundheads defeated the Royalists in 1642, after which it remained in Puritan hands until the Restoration. The death of the poet Wilfred Owen, born in nearby Oswestry in March 1893, was announced in Shrewsbury on 11th November 1918, the very day of the Armistice and seven days after he had been killed. An earthquake registering 3.4 on the Richter scale was registered near Shrewsbury on 7th March 1996.

On 11th September 2001, I had just finished my lunchtime sandwiches in the car, when I caught the tail-end of a news bulletin. There was a brief item about an aircraft hitting a building in New York. I had to attend a meeting at Shrewsbury School that lasted for the remainder of the afternoon, but in the course of my conversation I mentioned what I had heard. At six, as I left, my client bid me farewell with the words, 'Better go in and see what's going on in New York; it doesn't sound too good.'

'Yes,' I said reaching for my mobile. I called Lucinda and in a few minutes the whole ghastly business began to be clear. It would prove to be the mother of all defining moments. In his poem 'The Dread of Falling into Naught' (1912), Owen wrote:

> I, only, mourn, because I cannot tell
> What spring-renewing wakes the sleep of Men.
> I do but know (ah! this I know too well)
> I shall not see the same sweet life again,
> Nor the dear sun, nor stars, nor tender moon.

It was at Shrewsbury that I got into conversation about my trip to Peshawar. 'You've been to Peshawar?!' gasped my female client in astonishment.

'I don't see what's so odd about that,' I replied. 'Thousands of Brits visit the subcontinent every year!'

'That may be so … But you're a financial adviser …!!'

I was astonished. I had clearly stepped outside some preconceived box.

It was convenient to combine a trip to Shrewsbury with a visit to Malvern College, but invariably, that required staying overnight. I preferred to visit Shrewsbury first and, crossing Wenlock Edge, where coral was

forming below the sea 430 million years ago, I discovered the Raven Hotel
at Much Wenlock. This delightful, privately-run inn with excellent cuisine
proved suitable for a break on the return journey south and I confess that
after a long drive and several meetings I have sought solace in the bar on
a number of occasions. Over the years, I have also had the opportunity to
explore the pretty little town, birthplace of Dr William Penny Brookes, who
inspired the modern open International Olympic Games, and also to wander
in the grounds of Wenlock Priory. The turbulent history and destruction of
this Cluniac foundation in the dissolution of 1540 contrasted remarkably
with the peace and tranquillity enjoyed there today.

One of the great benefits of my job was the flexibility I enjoyed, although my timetable was often governed by the availability of others. An
early start from the Raven, on one occasion, provided the opportunity to visit
the lakeside church of St Michael at Great Witley; exquisitely ornate, it is
regarded by some as the finest baroque church in the country. My particular
interest was the tracker-action organ whose case came from an instrument
that Handel had played. I had started taking lessons again by the time this
visit occurred and, bringing a few simple pieces with me, greatly enjoyed an
hour in the organ loft negotiating the idiosyncrasies of that ancient instrument. However, it was soon time to move on and, passing apple-laden trees
in the orchards of Worcestershire, the Malvern Hills came into view. It was
a magnificent sight, and with music in mind I recalled the words of Edward
Elgar, who was born at Lower Broadheath, close to the road on which I was
travelling. Speaking towards the end of his life to a friend about his E-minor
cello concerto, he said: 'If ever you are walking on the Malvern Hills, and
hear this—it's only me—don't be frightened.'

I sometimes wonder how long we will continue to enjoy music in its
present form. Will we still go to the Proms or listen to Classic FM in a
hundred years? Will our brains develop in such a way that we will consider
anything from the most sublime Bach to hideous (my opinions) Birtwistle
as remarkably primitive? What kind of mind will a human being have in a
thousand years from now? The poet Rumi has had a few things to say about
that.

Many is the time when I have wound my way up from the Severn valley, past the renowned Nicholson Organ Works at Leigh Sinton—where a
new organ for Uppingham School was recently built—to the town of Great
Malvern, and the hills are not always as clear as on the day I previously

described. Sometimes the summit was lost in cloud and mist, but the spa town that sprawls over the eastern foothills and never enjoys the benefit of a full English sunset always struck me as having a continental atmosphere. I am not sure why that should be. Perhaps it was the elegance of nineteenth-century houses, built to cater for visitors—including royalty—taking the waters. Certainly, fine views eastward to Bredon Hill, across the Garden of England where asparagus farms flourish in May, create an open, airy, almost holiday atmosphere that I somehow associated with 'abroad'. In addition, the abundance of wisteria and extraordinary quantities of mistletoe that have rooted in trees along the leafy esplanades add a touch of unexpected gentility. There were steep roads to contend with and, on one occasion, I parked for a meeting in a pleasant complex known as Fruitlands. I had recently changed my car and was not aware that the handbrake necessitated a firmer yank than I had been used to. When I came out of the house the VW was gone. Alarmed, I started to look around and soon spotted the car embedded in someone's hedge, fifty yards down the road. As we say in England, it could have been worse—a lot worse! No serious damage was done to the car—but the hedge ...

The College itself also commanded views to the east and was founded in 1865. Once again I found the staff kindly and steeped in the best traditions of schoolmastering. Surprises do occur, however, as when I was advising one of the scientists with regard to investment. He adopted such a cautious approach and appeared so nervous about making a long-term commitment that I seriously considered persuading him not to include any equities in his portfolio. It was, therefore, something of a shock, reflecting a completely different side to his risk profile, when we stepped outside and he climbed into a spanking new, bright red Porsche. A pleasant surprise was to meet an enterprising man who imported Greek wine. He gave me a bottle of Mavrodaphne of Patras Karela that was bottled in 1944. I still have it. Perhaps it will be opened when—or if—this narrative ever gets finished.

I had developed a soft spot for Malvern because of something that happened at a conference there during the 1980s. Apparently, senior masters representing a number of independent schools were gathered at the College and one topic raised was the quality of financial advice provided to members of the profession. The consensus of opinion was that the standard was poor. A representative from Harrow, then spoke and said that there were exceptions and that he relied on the services of one, Neil Hall. At this point, the representative from Charterhouse chimed in to say that he did so as well. I was told this story by another client from Uppingham who also attended the meeting.

Leaving the Malvern Hills, it could be tempting to wander through the English country lanes, towns and villages *ad continuum,* if not a touch lonely without my dear Lucinda by my side. We had once spent a pleasant afternoon in nearby Tewkesbury, famous for a decisive battle that secured the Yorkist cause (1471) during the Wars of the Roses, and where the Rivers Avon and Severn merge. The abbey church of St Mary the Virgin, with its Norman nave and imposing tower, is well worth a visit, and I was especially intrigued by the 'Magnificent Milton', the famous organ that was built for Magdalen College, Oxford in 1631 and reputedly played by John Milton.

As time went by, I continued to meet an extraordinary variety of people whose only common denominator was teaching in an independent school. Perhaps one of the most idiosyncratic, to my mind, was a deputy head who was also a card-carrying member of the Labour Party. One of my clients had a collection of antique clocks worth many thousands, another had shelves stacked with rare editions of eighteenth-century plays, and I counted a sprinkling of authors among my clients. One man kept an ancient Aston Martin, an MG, an Alvis and an Austin Healey in the sheds behind the cricket pavilion at a famous school, and another juggled his time brilliantly, running a sports equipment business based in farm buildings close to the school where he also taught. There was no shortage of adventurers who took every opportunity to travel the world, and clients of mine, a young husband and wife, survived a diving excursion in the Indian Ocean when the 2004 tsunami swept right over them.

Perhaps the most diversely talented, was a Catholic priest who spoke fluent Arabic and had won the Military Cross, although a close runner-up was the East German whom I first met at Rugby. He spoke impeccable English and twelve other languages. He had settled with his wife and daughter in England, and later held a senior position at a school in Kent where he lived the life of a country gentleman. As well as all this, during the time that I knew him, he studied for a doctorate and ran in the Moscow Marathon. As I revise this narrative in 2013, he is now headmaster of an important international school.

A lady I spoke to asked me whether she should have another child. 'I'm a financial planner not a family planner', I assured her. One man I spoke to had twelve children, and felt that he was past financial planning, and another whom I met briefly was a quadriplegic following a rugby accident, and yet he still managed to run a whole department. A headmaster of a famous school had been an insulin-dependent diabetic since the age of sixteen, and another survived on one kidney, donated by his mother, when his own two organs packed up. It was all an amazing education, and the places I visited lent colour to my life. I returned to old haunts at King's Rochester, and at Tonbridge was shocked to see the remains of the chapel that had been destroyed by a huge fire. The fine spire above Lancing College chapel, however, stood silhouetted above the South Downs as I passed, a reminder that the largest rose window in England could be found within. Lancing was founded by the Reverend Nathaniel Woodard in the mid-nineteenth century and like its sister schools Ardingly and Hurstpierpoint resonated with a staunch Christian tradition. Ardingly, home of the South of England Show and Wakehurst Place (the other Kew Gardens), was situated in an especially lovely part of Sussex, and at nearby Brighton College I met a man who had taught Nigel Kennedy to play the violin. Visiting Christ's Hospital (founded by Edward VI in 1552) which had moved from the City of London in 1902 was a fascinating experience—if only to see the colourful uniforms that the students wore. Further west, business meetings have led me to Bedales, Bryanston, Sherborne and Canford School. When the delightful new head at Bryanston invited me to provide financial advice that was received positively and subsequently acted upon, I could not but savour a delicious irony in light of the painful interview I had attended when Tarquin left the school more than twenty years previously.

It was at Canford, in 1994, that an Abyssinian frieze, transported from Iraq in the nineteenth century by Sir Henry Layard, was discovered during the renovation of the tuck shop. This was subsequently auctioned at Christies, raising £7 million. The money funded an extensive programme of scholarships and the construction of new school buildings and facilities. How apt it was that the treasure became available just when it was needed, like the tale of the Count of Monte Cristo. I was pleased to hear that there was enough left from the tuck shop's bonanza for every student at the school to receive a Mars bar in celebration.

Nearer home, I have trodden the corridors of Warminster School, Dauntsey's, Cheltenham College, Teddies at Oxford, Dean Close, Bloxham, Stowe, the Oratory and Clifton College. At Clifton, where my father taught before the Second World War, I interviewed the housemaster of School House in the very room used by Omar Bradley and Ike when planning D-Day. The present headmaster's wife, Joanna Moore, bakes exceptionally good cakes and produced one (in 1990 when at Eton), in the shape of a television for our son Alexander on his eighteenth birthday.

Each school had its own unique atmosphere, and that must have presented a baffling range of choice for parents who were concerned about what would be best for their offspring. I found Bradfield to be a delightful hamlet, hidden among the woods and fields of Berkshire, where I would not have been surprised to encounter a hunting parson riding to the meet early one morning. I am sure he would have doffed his silk top-hat, as I slowed down to let him pass in the narrow lane. Radley, by contrast, although founded in 1847 and run on traditional lines, housed nearly all its staff in modern bungalows on the campus, which is where I have recently encountered a new breed of schoolmaster. Many were married to high-flying, well-paid women and spent a lot of time sorting out their buy-to-let portfolios. Pangbourne College, founded in 1917 to train boys for a career at sea, was another establishment that has been overtaken by history, and now largely diverts its considerable resources to help children with special needs.

It was sometimes convenient to combine a trip to Winchester with meetings at Charterhouse. I was popular with the senior management at this famous school which, in 1872, moved from London to a beautiful 250-acre site in glorious Surrey, just south of the Pilgrim's Way, the ancient route from Canterbury to Winchester. Dr Anthony Bennett (now retired), was so pleased with my services that he treated me to lunch at the Savoy and gave me a copy of his must-read book *US and Comparative Government and Politics*. In 2005, the Headmaster, John Witheridge, gave me his biography, titled *Frank Fletcher: A Formidable Headmaster*. Fletcher was Master of Marlborough College from 1903–11 and Headmaster of Charterhouse 1911–35. John Witheridge inscribed the words 'To Neil: A formidable Marlburian'. I was duly flattered and much enjoyed reading his work.

An alternative route to the historic capital of Wessex might be via Wellington College, founded in 1853 with public money raised in memory of the Iron Duke, whose influence can still be felt today. When I first visited the College in 1987, I found it an austere campus but the atmosphere has changed, following the reforms introduced by the vibrantly energetic Headmaster, Dr Anthony Seldon. Nevertheless, Wellington is near the unattractive village of

Crowthorne and within earshot of sinister sirens at Broadmoor high-security prison. On leaving the College one foggy November evening, images of the likes of Yorkshire Ripper Peter Sutcliffe and Dennis Nilsen, who chopped up young men whom he had lured to his Muswell Hill flat, gave me the hee-bie-jeebies. Were they peering out into the gloom from their cell windows, as I drove through the woods below the prison?

Arriving in the back streets of Winchester that ran between the cathedral and the College, I invariably parked outside a house where Jane Austen once lived. It was like entering her world, and that of Anthony Trollope who was educated at both Winchester and Harrow in the 1820s. Bells tolled across the city and as I made my way along the narrow pavements I regularly passed old ladies, like a scene from *Barchester Chronicles*, gingerly propping rusty bicycles against the shop front of the corner post office. One lucky day, I was invited to lunch in the pretty garden owned by a don who lived just up the hill. Red apples shone among the gnarled branches of ancient trees, flourishing against the mellow stone backdrop of chapel and cathedral towers. The chapel was built shortly after the College was founded by William of Wykeham in 1382 and on my last visit I was pleased to find that the organ had been restored. I had played it in the 1960s and at that time there was a disconcerting delay, now corrected, between engaging the keys on the console and the pipes speaking at the other end of the building. Just around the corner is the memorial garden where the names of Wykehamists who have died in the service of their country are carved in stone. Richard Carey's name is there, together with some 800 others:

> *Have you forgotten yet?*
> For the world's events have rumbled on since those gagged
>   days,
> Like traffic checked awhile at the crossing of city ways:
> And the haunted gap in your mind has filled
> with thoughts that flow
> Like clouds in the lit heaven of life; and you're a man
> reprieved to go,
> Taking your peaceful share of Time, with joy to spare.
> But the past is just the same,—and War's a bloody game …
> Have you forgotten yet?

Look down and swear by the slain of the War that you'll
  never forget
(Siegfried Sassoon, 'Aftermath', 1919)

In contrast, on a recent occasion, I took time to wander into the cathedral, and my composure was violently abused by the sight of long coloured
banners suspended at intervals all the way down the beautiful mediaeval
nave. Vulgar, vibrant designs violated the aesthetic tranquillity of the cathedral and I wondered if such unholy shit was not a viler blasphemy than that
committed by Oliver Cromwell's horses when stabled there in the seventeenth century. I wrote to the Dean and told him so.

The College itself, with its own language and scholars' traditions, attracts cerebral men (dons)—women were still distinctly in the minority—
and clever boys. I am sure they would forgive me if the expression 'collective
eccentricity' comes to mind in a community where there were more PhDs
and DPhils than anywhere else. The client who always conducted meetings,
whatever the hour, in semi-darkness with the thick wooden shutters in his
study closed, or the don who saved every single spare penny of his salary,
never indulging in any luxury and only spending money on necessities, are
examples that come to mind. The latter was, of course, a good client and I
was glad to have been able to assist him in achieving his objective—the eventual purchase of a nice property—so I am sure it was all worth it. In general,
the Common Room members were a genial crowd who adhered to the school
motto: 'Manners makyth man', and I found a number who were urgently in
need of my services. One don, a personal friend of the Governor of the Bank
of England, took the unusual step of visiting London to arrange his investments. We met at the Athenaeum, where he entertained me to lunch in the
sunny dining room that overlooks Carlton Terrace. As we left, the chaplain
of Harrow School, who was just starting his hors d'oeuvres, greeted us with
a friendly wave.

If there was a vacancy for a monarch in the realm of the English public
school, Harrow and Eton would each vie for the throne. Deeply embedded in
their own traditions, the names of even recent Etonians read like cast members in our long island story: Baden-Powell, Cadogan, Churchill, Rothschild,
Montgomery, Astor, Balfour, Baring, Bowes-Lyon, Cazenove, Cecil,
Douglas-Home, Hoare, Hankey, Knatchbull, Mornington, Parker-Bowles,
Spencer and many, many more. Prince William entered Eton in 1995 and his

brother, Harry, joined him a few years later. Harrow sat astride its hill like the king of the castle, had close ties with foreign royalty, and its association with the late King of Jordan was well known. It was an easy drive from Kew, although like everywhere the traffic worsened year by year. Perhaps I should have walked, as John Betjeman recalls in his poem 'Middlesex' (1954):

> Recollect the elm trees misty
> And the footpaths climbing twisty
> Under cedar-shaded palings,
> Low laburnum-leaned-on-railings,
> Out of Northolt on and upward to the heights of Harrow
> hill.

I have been fortunate enough to be taken to lunch and dinner in the superb beaks' dining room, with magnificent views beyond the Wembley twin towers and across the London basin. When I spotted a portrait of King Hussain, I was reminded of a lecture that Lucinda and I had attended in the 1970s. It was delivered under the auspices of the Institute for Cultural Research by Glubb Pasha (Sir John Glubb), the former British officer who built up the Arab Legion, a crack Bedu force in what was once Transjordan. When the young king ascended the throne, he decided that his army should no longer be commanded by a foreigner and Glubb was summarily dismissed in 1956. Nevertheless, his lecture was fascinating and at the end of the evening we took the opportunity to shake his hand and thank him. *Baraka bashad!*

On one occasion, I gave a talk to Common Room members on the subject of financial planning, but am not sure that my describing their way of life as 'peculiar' was appreciated, especially as they had just emerged from a long day in the classroom. However, it did not deter my hosts' subsequent generosity with the claret.

My smartest contact at Harrow, secretary of the Wine Society, was always impeccably dressed, with tie neatly supported under his collar by a gold pin. But a female member of staff who had a Harley-Davidson motorbike hanging from her sitting-room ceiling, won the prize for eccentricity. I am glad to say that she always greeted me warmly, but then eyed my entry into her flat with justifiable apprehension. The reason for this was that during one meeting a flamboyant arm gesture had sent my tea all over her carpet. If that was not bad enough, I then repeated the process a year later! Fortunately, my reputation had not been ruined and last time I was at Harrow I made my way, passing scores of boys carrying their traditional straw boaters, to the chapel, where I had been invited to spend half an hour playing the organ.

Eton, in contrast, nestles by the side of the Thames below the Conqueror's great fortress. Arriving in term-time, I would make my way to one of the boarding houses or to Baldwin's Shore, a building off the high street where several of the younger staff members lived. The streets were invariably full of beaks on bicycles and boys dressed in the elegant prescribed attire that featured white tie, black tailcoat and pinstriped trousers. Gone were the days when Eton beaks relied on a private income, but I have heard it said that Eton College itself is so richly endowed that it could survive without charging fees. That may be, but when I first started going to the College I was curious to know whether any additional benefits, such as life and illness assurance, were provided for the teaching staff other than that made available through the Teachers' Occupational Pension. I rang the bursar to ask.

'Good God! No!' was his reply. 'We pay these chaps enough, they can jolly well buy their own insurance.'

Music to my ears, and from time to time I made sales at Eton and elsewhere that kept body, soul and family together. Visiting the schools in the way I have described was, I suggest, a unique experience.

'You know much more about public schools than I do,' a senior man at one establishment suggested. 'I think you would have liked to have been one of us,' he continued. Maybe.

Every school had a different atmosphere. Obviously, location and geography played a large part in this, but history and the characters involved were significant ingredients. In my whistle-stop tour I have tried to portray the flavour of some of this.

Who taught at these schools? Dedicated teachers, who enjoyed nearly every aspect of the institution to which they were attached. Many came from grammar schools, comprehensives and so-called red-brick universities. Fewer came from independent schools themselves, unlike Marlborough in the 1960s, when the beaks were mainly from public schools and Oxbridge. Many had wide international, sporting, business—yes, business—cultural, artistic and academic experience. I knew one internationally acclaimed musician who rose at 5 a.m. daily, to practise his viola before tackling the teaching 'day job', which meant running the music department of a school with 900 pupils.

What was being offered? Not the need to run an empire—that is certain. A random perusal of current websites comes up with these points:

> 'Academic excellence'
> 'Wide variety of cultural activities'
> 'Sporting achievement'
> 'Diverse skills'
> 'A cross-section of very able people'
> 'Happy, healthy, hard-working and civilised community'
> 'Considerate pupils'
> 'Friendliness and integration of pupils within and across
>   year groups'
> 'Contribute positively to the school atmosphere in every-
>   thing they do'
> 'Dedication to the "boarding" ethos'

Who sends their children to these places now? Those who can afford it. Frustration with the state system and disintegration of the grammar schools is one reason why parents choose private education. Others are overwhelmingly attracted to what they see being offered in educational, experiential and social terms. There are some who object to private education on philosophical grounds, but many would give their eye teeth to educate their children privately and do so if the opportunity arises. Even avowed socialists, as has been publicised in the media, will educate their children privately if they can afford it and if they can get away with it, politically. Lady Falkender, for example, approached my father in the 1960s as she was interested in sending her sons to Sussex House. Was she a socialist? I think so.

Sometimes, houses are mortgaged to the hilt and wives go out to work to meet these objectives. In one notable case in Dorset, a brothel was run to generate cash for this very purpose.

Another market for today's schools are foreigners who are attracted to the mystique of English public schools and may be disillusioned with the education system in their own country. British socialists may want to abolish public schools, but think of the loss of income from foreign currency.

Visit most of the schools I have mentioned, and you will spot pupils from every corner of the globe. This is a huge shift from, for instance, 1961, when an intake of 200 at Marlborough College consisted of eleven pupils with their home addresses registered abroad. In 1994/95, 400 pupils entered the College, of whom ninety-four were registered at an address outside the UK; twenty-eight being in Germany. Many of these would have been non-UK nationals and others with their parents posted or working abroad.

Speaking of which, we were soon to widen our horizons.

Chapter 12
From the Thames to the Golden Horn

The Bosphorus is a river, transparent as the sea, a river of
salt water that unites two seas; a river between two quarters
of the globe, along whose banks every spot is picturesque,
every point of historical interest. Here the East is joined to
Europe, and fancies itself the ruler of the latter. I know no
place where strength and mildness meet so completely as
here.

(Hans Christian Andersen)

BOTH OUR BOYS returned to England in December 1991, and we
rented a holiday cottage in Devon for Christmas. It had a heated swimming
pool, was close enough to the sea to enjoy cliff walks and was within easy
reach of the pretty town of Dartmouth. Coloured lights twinkled on the
water where we took the ferry across the estuary on a last-minute festive
shopping trip.

Alexander was dying to relay news from Spielberg's headquarters and we
were agog to hear all about life at the heart of Hollywood. The film *Hook* had
just been completed and *Jurassic Park* was in preparation. It was about then
that Alexander heard that his friend Ray Harryhausen was coming to Los
Angeles. Harryhausen had never met Spielberg, so Alexander performed the
enviable task of introducing those two great icons of the movie business to
each other. One duty that Alexander had performed was to film the pre-pro-
duction meetings and some years later, when the DVD of the making of

Jurassic Park—a film using ground breaking visual effects that revolutionised film-making—was released, he found that his material had been used.

Schindler's List was also on the drawing board, as was *The Magic Bag*. This was a 'short' that Alexander had written and he was very excited because he hoped to obtain permission to film on the back-lot at Universal Studios. Both Spielberg and his producer Kathleen Kennedy had been impressed when Alexander had taken an opportunity to show them *Brothers in Arms*. When he returned to Los Angeles in January 1992, he was sizzling with anticipation and ready to get his team together.

When we got back to Kew, Tarquin made us a proposition that set my entrepreneurial nose quivering. With his successes in Pakistan, we had long since come to the conclusion that he was set on a course that would develop into a career in writing and journalism as originally planned. He was, however, frustrated because while in the heart of Africa developing and executing stories for photo-reportage, he lacked the means to market his product.

'Dad! I can't sell my work when I am sitting under a palm tree in the jungle,' he expostulated. He suggested that we start an agency from our home that could handle his material and possibly that of other budding young writers as well. He suggested that Lucinda would have the interest, skill and availability to play the pivotal role, while I would handle the money. There would be some sort of split of any fees earned to cover our costs. Lucinda and I were hugely excited by the idea and set about working out the practical arrangements. She was also ready to provide some advice.

'I may prove a hard taskmaster,' said Lucinda, who was something of a writer herself, and she immediately booked herself on an editorial course at the London School of Publishing.

'If you're not taking the reader with you, I shall tell you!' she said.

First, we needed working capital so, to raise funds, I sold the long case clock that Gawky had left me when she died in 1972. I did this with some reluctance, but caught up in the spirit of the enterprise, I overcame any misgivings. Second, Lucinda investigated the government's schemes for backing small business start-ups. After several interviews, our project was approved and a small allowance was made available. This meant that Lucinda could rely on some initial remuneration and that Tarquin would receive the lion's share of the fees. Next, we needed to organise an office in a corner of our flat and to purchase equipment. A fax machine was a key requirement and we upgraded our computer. Finally, we settled on the name. Lucinda suggested

Sophie Reed Associates in honour of her grandmother, who had also been a writer and poet. We readily agreed, and Sophie became part of the family.

Tarquin returned to Kenya and was soon mailing us material. Lucinda was like a dog with a new tail. She began to research the market for photo-journalism, and also began to make contact with the feature editors of magazines and periodicals. I continued buzzing around the public schools, but it was exhilarating to have an embryonic family business on the go. In spring 1992, with great excitement, Lucinda sold Tarquin's first piece—'Buzkashi, or Alternative Polo'—to *Horse Review,* a smart magazine read by the equestrian community. A second piece about horse-racing in Kenya, also accompanied by striking photographs, soon followed. As soon as these articles were published, I sent the fees to Tarquin so that he would not suffer any delay in replenishing his meagre funds, and Sophie Reed was paid by *Horse Review* after the customary thirty days. Now, confident that his efforts would be rewarded, Tarquin began to work on a major project. He had met a young woman called Emma McCune who had married Riek Machar, the chief eastern military commander of the Sudan People's Liberation Army. Emma and Tarquin established an instant rapport, and when he suggested a photo-reportage that would describe her life, marriage and circumstances in the Sudan, she immediately agreed. Crucially, Emma promised Tarquin exclusive interviews and photo opportunities, although they both knew that the *Mail on Sunday* was also in hot pursuit. When Tarquin's piece was complete, Lucinda approached the *Mail on Sunday,* only to find that the editor was offering a derisory sum. He evidently thought that he could get away with paying an unknown journalist as little as possible. But he had not counted on how Lucinda, or Sophie Reed, as he knew her, would react. She took a taxi to the *Mail*'s offices in Kensington and, spreading the splendid colour images on the table, demanded that he quadruple his offer or she would soon find someone who would. Following her successful negotiations, the full piece with double-page photos, entitled 'I Married a Guerrilla General' was published in the *Mail on Sunday's YOU* magazine on 5th July 1992.

Tarquin remained in Kenya for the rest of the year. He wrote several more pieces, including an article on a Dutch priest named Father Grol, who worked in the slums of Nairobi, and a major reportage entitled 'Women Who Marry Women' that involved a long, rough trek to Isibania on the Tanzania border. That extraordinary story, about women who were not lesbians but marry other women to secure property rights, was published in *Marie Claire,* and Sophie Reed managed to secure a substantial fee. Before leaving Africa, Tarquin made a dusty pilgrimage to Maralal, where he stayed for a week with the legendary explorer Wilfred Thesiger. Let Tarquin take up the story of his arrival at the great man's hideout in central Kenya, as he later described it in his book, *Mercenaries, Missionaries and Misfits*:

> As we approached, I saw the Englishman pruning some flowers in the garden. Despite the blazing heat, he was dressed like a man expecting the imminent arrival of a heavy winter blizzard, wearing sturdy brown walking shoes—which he later claimed to have owned for some twenty-five years—faded tan trousers, a tweed jacket with a blue spotted handkerchief protruding from the breast pocket, and a distinguished trilby.
>
> 'Who the devil may you be?' he barked, giving me a frosty, unwelcoming stare as I
>
> got out of the Land Rover. I gave my name, swallowing the lump in my throat.
>
> 'Tarquin Hall, sir,' I said, feeling very much as if I was on school report.
>
> 'Who?' he bellowed. I repeated my name, gently reminding him that I had written to him and that he had replied.
>
> 'Oh, yes, yes, yes, the Afghan man.' His face relaxed. 'Do come in. Do come in. I'm afraid it's not the Ritz , but quite interesting nonetheless ...'
>
> (Tarquin Hall, *Mercenaries, Missionaries and Misfits*, 1996)

Four years later, Thesiger was in London and Tarquin invited him to a party to celebrate the launch of a book by his friend, Tahir Shah. Tarquin had recently introduced Tahir to the man they reverentially, with lowered voices, referred to as 'Thes', and because they appreciated that I would relish an opportunity to meet their Etonian hero, I was seconded to collect him from his flat. I picked up a cab in the King's Road and when I arrived at the apartment building in Tite Street the great man was already waiting, leaning against the railings. I immediately recognised, from photographs taken at Maralal, the craggy face that told a thousand travellers' tales, bushy eyebrows, and the broken nose which, according to Tarquin, he acquired when boxing as a young man. Introducing myself as Tarquin Hall's father, he joined me in the taxi. Settling down for the short ride, I attempted to make conversation by mentioning that I knew Eton and asked him which house he had been in. However, before he could answer we passed some ugly new office blocks, and the topic quickly switched as he derided the shameful legacy bequeathed to London by contemporary architects. Within a few minutes, the taxi dropped us off in Pall Mall and I would be less than honest not to admit that I experienced something of a thrill escorting Wilfred Thesiger— the man whom the Arabist St John Philby described as 'probably the greatest of all the explorers'—up the grand staircase and into the packed library at the Travellers' Club.

In the spring of 1992 John Major was confirmed as Prime Minister at the general election. This, the fourth Conservative win in a row, reminded me that, in England, it is possible to reach the highest office from impecunious origins. Some might be less than flattering with regard to his eventual achievements at Number Ten. They might adapt Churchill's reference to Clem Attlee: 'he had much to be modest about'. Personally, I think history will be kind to him, as does Peter Oborne. An opinion which he voiced in a recent article in the *Daily Telegraph* (2013).

Lucinda and I took a brief holiday in Istanbul that was marred by staying in a hotel where the lift ran behind the wall next to our bed, constantly waking us with clanking sounds. When we moved to another part of the city, noisy Spanish children ran up and down the corridors well into the small hours. On our return to London, I spotted a piece in the *Daily Telegraph* recounting how our favourite restaurant, situated on the lower level of the two-tier, hundred-year-old Galata Bridge, which had been constructed by German engineers, had been dismantled after gas cylinders exploded in the kitchens, rendering the edifice unsafe. Despite all of this, our enthusiasm for the city remained undiminished, a viewpoint that we evidently shared with Istanbul's citizens, who soon set about building a new bridge across the Golden Horn that was well on the way to completion by the time we returned in the autumn.

The impact of visiting Turkey had been even greater for Lucinda than it had been for me, as she had never travelled outside Western Europe and the United States and she found the country fascinating. We had both been feeling restless, and our trip was to prove a catalyst that would provoke far-reaching consequences. It is difficult to pinpoint the exact reason why we had developed itchy feet, but perhaps the combination of the boys being abroad and yet another glitch in the boom–bust cycle had affected us; alternatively, one might argue that middle-age madness had set in. It was certainly true that I had got tired of a routine that meant working hard in the week then, doing chores, cycling on the Thames towpath and generally relaxing and recharging my batteries at the weekend. By Sunday evening when—with a whisky and soda in my hand—I was just beginning to fantasise about how I might fill my life with more interesting projects, Monday morning loomed like an express train hurtling through a tunnel.

I expect a lot of people's lives are like that.

My business was becoming a source of anxiety as NM (the name by which the company that I represented was now called), was, in my opinion, being mismanaged from Melbourne, and it concerned me that the quality of the products I was peddling was not up to scratch; certainly not good enough for the sort of clients I was trying to attract. One day, during the summer, I discovered a key that could spring open the door to a whole range of new possibilities. To my surprise, my excellent sales record had qualified me to secure a lump sum settlement, if I wanted to sell my agency back to the company. A sum equal to a whole year's commission would free me to explore other business possibilities. The old spirit of enterprise was stirring in me, but when I explained all this over the telephone to Tarquin in Nairobi, his response was:

'Dad, this isn't 1968!'

I wasn't listening. A whole year's pay. I would be free!

I was required to sign an agreement stating that I would leave the financial services industry and not return for at least two years; this was fine by me. As I perused the contract, I could almost feel the shackles dropping from around my ankles, link by link. The idea fermenting in our brains was that we would leave England and go and live in Istanbul. We felt that there were all sorts of opportunities in Turkey and we had just read a magazine article extolling the virtues of the Turkish economy. There was even talk of Turkey joining the Common Market in the not too distant future. Indeed, it was not 1968, but I had experience in the hotel business, property development, the fabric trade and financial services, so surely a new venture would come my way. At least that's the way we thought.

There were four, practical, key points to our plan. First, we would learn as much Turkish as possible and, copying John Bennett's 'flashcard' method, I acquired a vocabulary of 600 words within three months. Perhaps I should have studied Oriental languages after all, I mused, as I found myself building empathy with the lingo and enjoying the vibrant sounds I was learning to utter. *'Aferdersiniz'* (excuse me), *'nasilsiniz?'* (how are you?), *'allahaismarladik'* (goodbye) and *'teşekkürler'* (thanks) were examples.

Second, Lucinda would invest £1000 in a month-long TEFL course so that she would be equipped to teach English to Turks. Third, we would let our flat in Kew to a friend and rent an apartment in Istanbul. Fourth, we would encourage Tarquin to join us so that he could develop his skills in photo-reportage and produce material in Asia Minor to be marketed by Sophie Reed.

After I had resigned from NM, the manager of the branch in Richmond summoned us to a farewell party. I had tended to avoid office parties but this was a spontaneous and enjoyable occasion and my cheque, together with a splendid wicker picnic hamper, containing an appropriately stuffed *turkey* from Marks and Spencer, were presented to us as leaving presents. I had given notice to my colleagues in the form of some pretty dreadful doggerel, the first and last verses of which follow:

> The time has come for me to leave,
> Do not cry or even grieve!
> The reason why? A memo or worse?
> I thought instead some dotty verse.

> Our boys are grown, they live abroad.
> Lucinda's learned Turkish, we'll not be bored.
> We'll travel, work and see the world,
> Before our gravestones are unfurled.

Considering I had heard of colleagues being sacked by fax, I think my voluntary departure was remarkably dignified.

My dislike of office parties, especially the Christmas variety, was not diminished following a Bacchanalian revel held one year at Madame Tussauds waxworks museum in the Marylebone Road. A young lady who

had imbibed far too much wine, managed to collide with the austere wax
figure of Archbishop Makarios. For a few seconds the robed and bearded
primate trembled, before tottering off his pedestal and falling to the floor
with a sobering crash.

Our plans started to take shape with remarkable speed. Lucinda went
on her course and we found a friend who would look after the flat at a knock-
down rent. As part of the deal, she was prepared to liaise with us regarding
Sophie Reed business once we had started selling material from Turkey. On
10th September I flew to Istanbul. I had set myself six days to find an apartment, and booked into the Sokullu Pasa Hotel, an attractive Ottoman-style
wooden hotel close to the city walls and Topkapi. On the first night, while
sitting in the courtyard enjoying the sweet scent of jasmine and verbena and
with a glass in my hand, I mulled over what I was doing there. It seemed to
me that, in a sense, this was more than a crossroads. It was a major turning
point in our lives. We were deliberately closing down one mode of existence and opening up another. The words of Dag Hammarskjöld in *Markings*
(1964) came to mind:

> 'You will have to give up everything. Why, then weep at this
> little death? Take it to you—quickly—with a smile die this
> death, and become free to go further ...'

Some English people soon joined me and after chatting for a while we
went off together in search of food. I knew Istanbul better than they did, so
it proved to be an enjoyable interlude, although I think they thought I was
crazy when I told them of our plans. Back at the hotel, I settled down for the
night in my comfortable room. The aromas from the garden below drifted
in through the open window and I slept soundly until awakened by the *muezzin* calling the faithful to prayer from several minarets in the immediate
neighbourhood.

Since my Turkish was composed more of vocabulary than grammar,
there was no chance of conversing in the vernacular and I had no real idea
about how to go about finding a flat. For the first few days, I was going
around in circles—or, to be more precise, taking exhausting trips, by train,
bus or ferry, to outlying suburbs of the city. The owner of the hotel took me
to a property of his, but it was unfurnished and in a rough neighbourhood,
so I politely turned it down. Then someone pointed out a section in one of

the newspapers that advertised accommodation for foreigners. The rents were advertised in US dollars, which made me wonder if I was in for more expense than I had anticipated. On my fourth day, acutely aware that time was running out, I took a *dolmus*, a shared taxi and preferred method of transport in Istanbul, to Bebek where I found a suitable apartment in a modern block. Situated on the European side of the Bosphorus, about three miles from the city centre and close to the new suspension bridges that crossed to Asia, it was a very attractive neighbourhood. There was a smart hotel, parade of shops and a park that ran down to a wooden jetty at the water's edge where ferries stopped as they plied their way from the Black Sea to the Sea of Marmara. The apartment block was raised above the level of the main street, slightly up the side of the valley and, standing on tiptoe, I could see huge ships passing through the Straits. I returned the next day with sufficient dollars to cover three months' rent and in exchange for the key, handed them over to our landlady, an elderly Turk who lived on the top floor of the block. I had agreed to take the place for a year. Today, when I mention to a Turk, that we rented a flat in Bebek, the assumption is that I am a millionaire.

Arriving back in England on 17th September, and feeling rather pleased with myself, I was shocked to learn of economic turmoil following 'Black Wednesday' the previous day. Sterling had left the Exchange Rate Mechanism (ERM), the pound had been devalued and interest rates were soaring. This was a curious turn of events, since the last time I had tried to do business in Turkey, in 1967, Harold Wilson had devalued the pound, seriously disrupting the plans Leon and I had been developing. I was fearful that history was about to repeat itself; devaluation would certainly reduce our resources. In fact, after I had received my cheque from NM, contrary to expectation and once the initial exhilarating sense of freedom had passed, I experienced a new sense of anxiety. This was the only money we had, and the clock was ticking.

To make matters worse, unexpected costs had arisen with the financing of Alexander's film, *The Magic Bag*, and a few thousand dollars were urgently required in Los Angeles. Permission had been granted to film on the back-lot at Universal Studios—an extraordinary privilege—and with a talented, handpicked crew, a very exciting project was well under way. Spielberg had specifically encouraged Alexander and assured him that he could not wait to see the film when it was completed. He was particularly intrigued to know that the film would be made partly in colour and partly in black and white—like *The Wizard of Oz*. We were to be shareholders in a Hollywood production, but the stakes were high, and the costs were escalating.

With hindsight, this might have been the moment to take a deep breath and rethink our strategy, but we were not in the frame of mind to pull back. Some of our friends and family thought us mad; others admitted that they were green with envy; still others expected us to be back by Christmas. A few—our oldest acquaintances—thought we were in search of 'hidden Sufis'. Absolutely not! We had read many of Idries Shah's books and if there was any doubt on that score; we had digested his 'True Story', in *A Veiled Gazelle* (Octagon Press, 1977).

Before we left, we both went to see Aubrey, now a very old man. When we told him of our plans, he was surprisingly enthusiastic and wished us every success. In his inimitable way he did, however, impart some advice. I think it came from his days as a diplomat because we knew he had been accustomed to moving in rarefied circles, and was related to Eleanor Roosevelt. As he waved goodbye he said, 'Be sure to watch your backs. In the Service, when abroad, we always found it paid to maintain a yacht in the bay!'

On 1st October, a bright and sunny morning, we were aboard the unexpectedly comfy French car ferry heading out across the channel from Dover. We had hoped to take Hoverspeed's Seacat, which would have made the crossing in half the time, but for some reason animals were not permitted on such a vessel. The alarm had rung at 4 a.m. in our flat in Kew, and an hour later I carried our ancient cat, Nimr, in his basket to the car before locking the flat door behind us as we headed on our way. The dark streets were deserted and every traffic light we approached turned red—but if this was an omen, we were in no mood for sibylline predictions.

Our dilemma of whether or not to take our old friend had preoccupied us. He had been part of the family for seventeen years and better, we thought, for him to die with us en route, or in Istanbul, than be left with a stranger. Even though his health had recently deteriorated, the idea of putting him down was non-negotiable, so now we were in the car with his rabies certificates (duplicated in French and English) and a further certificate stamped personally by the Turkish Consul in Rutland Gate, lodged safely in my briefcase. He would not have been able to return to Britain without a lengthy quarantine so, in one sense at least, the dye was cast.

Our six-year-old Passat estate car was heavily loaded, although a large rear section boasted a wired rabbit hutch that I had modified for Nimr. It contained his litter, food and water. Within a few hours we were purring (no pun intended), through what Shakespeare called 'the vasty fields of France', down the 'English Road' (A26) in the bright autumn sunshine. We flashed past signs that pointed the way to towns whose names I associated with famous battles of the Great War; Cambrai, Arras, Amiens, not far from where Blatchford Oldrey had fallen in 1914.

> 'He's a cheery old card,' grunted Harry to Jack
> As they slogged up to Arras with rifle and pack.
>
> But he did for them both by his plan of attack.
> (Siegfried Sassoon, extract from 'The General', 1917)

Just after we had passed Reims, the car gave an ominous shudder and a 'tuc, tuc, tuc' noise started to emanate from the front wheel-bearing. We pulled onto the hard shoulder and called the recovery service—the *dépannage*—who towed us to the nearest garage. By this time it was late. We were forced to stay in the city overnight, but in the morning, after a *contretemps* with the hotel manager, who was horrified when she found a large ginger cat in our room, we returned to the garage. The mechanic advised us that without major work he would be unable to detect the fault and suggested that we drive slowly to the town that had been our destination the previous day and then seek further help. This is exactly what we did, but it was a whole week before the garage in Nuits-St-Georges had the car ready for us to proceed, and then only after we had incurred considerable expense. Friends who had expected us for one night, somewhat reluctantly endured our company for six.

This did, however, give me the opportunity to read *The Great Game* for the second time, and for Lucinda and me to explore Burgundy, an area of France that we had not previously visited. In fact, neither of us had been in the French countryside for nearly twenty years and we soon realised that the France of the chirpy Renault 4, the fragile Deux Chevaux, the Citroën with the rusty running-board, and the *camion* that wobbled down cobbled streets and looked like a corrugated hut on wheels was a France of the past. The huge BMWs, the Mercedes Benz and Peugeot estates parked in neat farmyards defined the wealth and security now found within the European Economic Community. Even the towns' public conveniences were spotless, and to recall the foul-smelling 'pissoir' or the camp sites that John Henry and I had endured in 1965 was to relive ancient history.

The grape crop had recently been harvested and we enjoyed long walks on the chalky soil around the vineyards, occasionally passing trailers stacked with huge quantities of glistening fruit. The nearby town of Nuits-St-Georges, whose name reminded me of an excellent vintage served at the King Charles Hotel, was attractive. We nosed about, killing time, stopping for a coffee in the *pâtisserie*, but carefully avoiding being lured into the conspicuously advertised 'wine cellars' designed to rapidly empty a tourist's wallet. We also took the train to nearby Beaune where the colourful market and great mediaeval hospital, with its tiled roof decorated like a huge Anatolian kelim, absorbed our interest on several days.

Nimr survived the week, although he had been confined to our bedroom to avoid infection from other cats, but we eventually packed him back into his hutch and set off for the three-day drive to the south of Italy, feeling very nervous. Our initial exuberance had been dented and we were scared stiff in case any further trouble with the car could cause us to abort the trip or haemorrhage more of our cash reserves. Lucinda's excellent French had been invaluable during the crisis, but neither of us spoke Italian or Greek and, although the enforced break in Burgundy had helped the adjustment process, our heightened level of anxiety meant that everything felt as if it was coming at us. Our familiar world had been replaced by foreign languages and money, new telephone systems and banking hours, unfamiliar shopping arrangements, different weights and measures, new petrol classifications and road signs. Approaching the motorway tolls was to prove particularly stressful. As we sped towards the barriers, we were never quite sure whether plastic or cash' was expected; in which case, did we have the right change in the right currency?

Within hours, we were slowly climbing the awesomely beautiful road that leads to Mont Blanc and Chamonix. But every jolt rattled our nerves and eventually, when we could see the long tunnel's gloomy half-light ahead of us, our confidence ebbed away entirely. I glanced behind me. Nimr had rolled himself into a tight ginger ball in the corner of his cage.

'I think he feels our apprehension', I quipped,

Miraculously, it seemed, we soon found ourselves descending into the north Italian plain and, although it was still early, the afternoon sun was setting behind the mountains, casting long shadows across the vineyards and ramshackle homesteads that balanced delicately on the edge of steep inclines. It quickly became apparent that the standard of living south of the Alps was considerably lower than that enjoyed in France.

Our next objective was to find somewhere for the night, where Nimr would be allowed in our room. Once past Milan, enquiries led us to a hotel off the auto-route at Modena. A good dinner, a bottle of wine and a night's rest restored our optimism, and the next morning we awoke refreshed, looking forward to the day's drive. The parting words of the French mechanic who had repaired the car came to mind:

'Travel keeps you young!'

I reminded Lucinda of this reassuring sentiment.

'It beats cold-calling!' she replied with a grin.

Once back on the auto-route, I pressed my foot to the accelerator and we were soon speeding down the Adriatic coast. There was little traffic and the road regularly passed through short dark tunnels before shooting us, like a switchback on a fairground, into the brilliant sunlight again. Tantalising glimpses of the deep blue sea, the colour of the Madonna's robe, punctuated a broad panorama of vineyards, olive groves and villages with castellated ochre-coloured walls that clung to hilltops or were tucked away on the side of soon forgotten valleys. Less than 200 kilometres from Rome, tall church towers with carved crosses perched on shining white cupolas beamed Catholicism across the countryside like lighthouses on a rugged shore.

It was interesting to compare the Mediterranean vineyards with those in Burgundy. In the south the vines flourished, festooned over wooden arbours, tender grapes protected from the fierce sun by bright green leaves. In France we had found the approach was crisper, more disciplined, individual vines being carefully staked. We imagined that this allowed each grape the maximum exposure to the weaker northern rays of the sun and as some plants were more than seventy years old; the oenologists must have known what they were doing.

'Can't we stop for a dip?' Lucinda implored me, but we resisted the temptation. Already a week behind schedule and having missed our original booking on the night ferry from Brindisi to Igoumenitsa, we were anxious to make the best possible time. It would have to be pot-luck when we reached the southern Italian port. In the meantime, we were soon due for another night in a hotel and found the Park in Vasto, an establishment that had known better days and where the management eyed us with ill-concealed curiosity. Before grabbing a light supper and settling down for the night, we thought it prudent to carry all our belongings from the Passat up the grand marble staircase, lit by a huge glass chandelier, to our first-floor bedroom. This effort, not the last time that we were to empty and repack the car, was good for weight reduction and I lost at least a stone during our trip. We were, however, exhausted by the time we flopped into the king-size bed and, with Nimr tucked up in his basket on a nearby chair, we drifted into sleep. The gentle sound of surf breaking on the beach, beyond a clump of spindly pine trees, wafted through open windows. The next morning, after breakfast we packed the car and set off on the last leg of our journey before the crossing to Greece. Somehow we missed the turning to Brindisi at Bari, but rather than turn back we agreed to complete the last fifty miles on country roads, a decision that led us into forbidding territory. By this time it was mid-afternoon and the weather had turned grey and sultry. Rain threatened, the air was oppressive, and it was as though we had suddenly arrived on the set of some half-forgotten black and white movie in Mexican bandit country. The architecture was strangely forbidding and there was a sense of desolation. Houses surrounded by what appeared to be smallholdings, where the occasional emaciated goat was tethered, incorporated white pointed beehive-like structures that resembled a cross between an igloo and an oast-house. Many had been converted and were evidently not being used for their original purpose, which we assumed to have been some sort of crop-drying process. Sections of a few buildings had been cut away to form an open patio, but they were deserted and forlorn and evoked a sinister atmosphere.

'My God! This place gives me the creeps'. I exclaimed, when I left the car for a pee behind a rough stone wall. We were glad to see the distant coastline when it eventually appeared.

As dusk approached, we arrived in Brindisi, a gloomy God forsaken hole if ever there was one, and with time to spare before the Saturday night ferry was due to sail, we booked space for the car and a couchette for ourselves and waited by the waterside until we were due to embark. This gave us the opportunity to sample the local pizza and attend to the needs of our long-suffering pussy-cat, before positioning ourselves in the queue at the top of the ramp.

With a crashing of steel upon steel, screeching of brakes, pungent whiff of oil and scorched rubber and the frantic waving of arms by port officials, we soon entered the whale-like intestines of the car ferry and parked in semi-darkness. Hemmed in by juggernauts and other vehicles and unable to open the car doors properly, we scrambled out and clutching the basket that contained the remarkably contrite Nimr, together with a suitcase and litter tray, searched for the exit.

Eventually, propelled by a crowd of fellow passengers, jostling and pushing their way up the staircase we reached the purser's office, A porter grabbed our bag, marched us through the smoky saloon, down another set of stairs and into a tiny two-bunk cabin. I gave him some paper money. He looked surprised. What had I given him? Italian? Greek? Too much? Too little? I was past caring, and appropriating the whisky bottle and a plastic cup, climbed on to the top bunk. Lucinda set up the litter tray while I took a swig, turned up the ventilator and peered through the locked porthole across the dark waters of the harbour.

Just after 8 p.m., the deep drone of the diesel engines increased in volume and we eased away from the quay. I was famished and went in search of food while Lucinda stayed in the cabin,

'I think I'll give food a miss', she said, reminding me that she was prone to seasickness. They were serving a reasonably priced meal in the restaurant so I tucked in; sharing my table with a bearded German from Düsseldorf, who was probably a rep for an electronics' company. I had seen him getting out of a car that had a logo printed on the door panels, before tying his black Alsation to a bulwark on the car deck. The dog's huge paw marks were all over the car bonnet and he had upset his water bowl when we returned in the morning. The German spoke no English and I was no longer able to converse in his language, so we smiled and grunted a few times before I retired, taking a large piece of smoked mackerel, wrapped in a napkin, for the benefit of our seafaring feline.

Fatigue, booze, a full stomach and the dull thunder of the engines ensured a few good hours of sleep, but unfortunately Lucinda did not fare so well. Nimr, a very large cat, was determined to lie on her feet and the rolling of the ship disturbed her once we had moved out into the middle of the Adriatic. I hardly noticed when the ferry docked briefly at Corfu, but we were up and ready to disembark at Igoumenitsa by seven. Lucinda held Nimr up to the porthole, expecting some reaction as we approached the rocky Greek coast, but he did not appear remotely interested. We left Igoumenitsa at 7:20 a.m., hoping to reach Thessaloniki the same day, but after two hours had only travelled fifty miles. The road ran through gorges and zigzagged up steep mountain sides. It passed over narrow bridges and through straggling villages where bare-legged children played in the dust and old men sat outside vine-clad cafes smoking their Sunday pipes and watching what little world there was, go by. I should, of course, have expected that the mountainous regions of northern Greece would be very different from the almost continuous motorway from Calais to Brindisi and that our progress would be significantly slower, but I had not registered the fact. It was, however, an exceptionally beautiful region, with brilliant white cliffs that towered above us, reflecting the bright early-morning sunshine and a myriad of vivid colours vying for our attention. Burnt reds and oranges, crimsons, greens, yellows, browns and vermilion freshly vibrated from the undergrowth as we turned each new bend.

On and on, we wound up steep inclines and crawled around tricky switchback hollows. The sun climbed high above the mountains, but by midday we had travelled little more than a third of the 250 miles we had set ourselves. Now and again, we passed little shrines and wondered whether these commemorated local saints or the demise of an ill-fated motorist who had tumbled into a ravine. On several occasions, we were forced to slow down to walking pace as huge herds of goats, bells jangling, guarded by bearded shepherds with rifles slung across their backs blocked the way, and once we stopped to buy some fruit at a roadside stall, high up in the pine woods. Trestle tables were piled with melons, nuts, apples and neat bunches of wild thyme and rosemary. A loaded rifle, breach open, lay next to the cash tin. We were not far from the Yugoslav and Albanian borders. This was 1992; what armed and possibly dangerous men might be hiding in those wild parts? A little further down the road we stopped to finish our bread and cheese, polished off a juicy melon that we had just purchased and checked that Nimr had enough food and water. His litter needed changing. The idea of a snooze appealed, but we felt it unwise to linger. Suddenly, once again, the skies had become overcast and our vulnerability dawned on us. It seemed that we were in the middle of nowhere, with an estate car stuffed with possessions, computer and foreign currency.

'I'm scared,' muttered Lucinda, as we stared into the distance.

'Me too,' I growled. Would these mountains never end?

We pressed on. Things did not get better. Shortly after our brief snack I noticed a slight change in the brake pressure. Nervously, I tested the pedal. It sprang back, making a banging sound that I had not heard before. I demonstrated what was happening, to Lucinda. We both paled. Brake failure? The heavy load and constant braking had obviously taken its toll. We considered our position; it would be dark in a few hours, we were miles from the nearest town and it was Sunday. Very few cars had passed us and we couldn't speak a word of Greek. I moved on slowly, resisting the urge to brake unless absolutely necessary and using the handbrake and clutch as much as possible. The mountains kept coming. How much longer? I was sweating profusely.

After an hour or so, we dropped down into the plain and when I pumped the brakes they were performing better. We stopped at a garage and I tried my luck with a surprised attendant.

'What's the road towards Thessaloniki like?' I asked. He did not understand English. I pointed to the brake pedal. The car was weighed down on its back axle. The problem must have been pretty obvious. The man was helpful and together we pored over our RAC map that was not topographical, but he was able to convey that the road we were on would soon pass through high mountains—*oros*—again, but a thirty-mile detour would keep us in the valleys. He gesticulated dramatically with his arms. The map marked Vermion Oros, Vernon Oros, Paikon Oros.

'No more *oros*! Please!' I stammered, gesticulating with an emphatic thumbs down. By this time I think he knew what I meant.

We took the long detour and as the light was failing began what the airline people call 'the final approach' into Thessaloniki. It was a quarter of a century since I had last visited what had been a quaint historic city, but now we passed industrial areas, power stations and motor works where extensive car parks were wired off from dreary cotton fields. The white tufts of cotton were being harvested from acres of dying sun-blackened plants, which were being left to decay, giving the impression of a land strewn with rubbish. Tractors loaded with cotton passed us by, and enough white bobs to keep me in shirts for a lifetime were caught in bushes, on barbed wire or blowing along grimy gutters.

We had been fortunate when searching for hotels in Italy, but this time our luck eluded us and for two hours we drove around the city, through crowded streets, up and down, backwards and forwards, but without success. This was the second time in my life that I had unsuccessfully trawled the streets of Thessaloniki in search of food and comfort. We even drove out to the airport, but nowhere could a hotel be found.

'I think we will have to sleep on stone benches at the railway station as I did in 1968,' I remarked to Lucinda. She grimaced; the idea did not appeal to her at all. Finally, exasperated, we stopped at a taverna where the proprietor let us have a room for about fifteen pounds although, for some reason, he insisted that his establishment was not a hotel. Perhaps he meant to convey that he was doing us a favour. We did not hesitate, unpacked the car, and gobbling down a serving of lamb and rice in the restaurant, turned in for the night. On this occasion Lucinda fared better. I was disturbed in the night and awoke with huge lumps on my face and neck where mosquitoes had bitten me. The vicious little buggers hadn't even touched her, but rosemary salve reduced the swelling and we were soon packing the car as the seasonal rain poured down.

The brakes seemed to be working better so, thinking that they had just got overheated, we decided to risk postponing a visit to the garage until we reached Istanbul. At any rate, we assumed that most of the remaining journey followed the coast and would be quite flat. A policeman guided us to the Istanbul road through the suburb of Panorama where sweeping views over the bay and across the Aegean offered an explanation for why all the hotels were located there. It was actually quite high up, so even if we had known of their existence the night before, I don't think we would have risked the climb.

With two days to go, or so we reckoned, our journey was to take us through varied terrain. Some areas were quite built up, but there were also beautiful stretches with views out to Mount Athos and the islands. Just as we reached Kavala, a charming town with cobbled streets, ramparts, a castle and colourful fishing fleet moored by the quayside, we noticed that we had clocked up 2000 miles since we left London. We picnicked on the beach before moving on through more cotton fields, where I stopped to pick some sprigs as a memento, and headed towards Lagos where a causeway carried the main road through a bird sanctuary. Dozens of herons were standing, on one leg, in the lagoon.

It was evening before we reached the border checkpoint and I parked the car while officials went through the usual palaver. They seemed particularly interested in the computer and were amused to encounter an English cat, but eventually we were waived through, entering Turkey in darkness. A marked deterioration in the road surface was immediately apparent and it took a lot of concentration to avoid holes and bumps. Was this to discourage those entering or leaving? we wondered. We reached Tekirdag, a dreary two-hotel town, after driving fifty miles from the border, but were still some seventy miles from our destination. Fortunately, the second hotel that we tried had a vacancy, and with the help of a young Turkish boy we unpacked the car, and once again, carried everything up to the first floor. The youth was astonished to see Nimr, who was a huge and magnificent animal by Turkish standards.

'*Kedi*! *Kedi*!' he whispered through the bars at the front of the cat basket. Nimr responded with a muted meow.

We were hungry and I went out into the damp and dimly lit streets, carefully avoiding potholes, to forage for food. A *bakkal* (grocer) was still open, and supplied me with sausage (probably 70% cereal), yoghurt and olives, which we consumed in our room, washed down with a bottle of Greek wine, purchased with our very last drachmas. As we settled down, we promised Nimr that this, truly, was his final night on the road. The next morning, resisting the temptation to make a detour and visit the invasion site at Gallipoli, we continued with our journey. Somewhere in my imagination, I had assumed that the last seventy miles along the shore of the Sea of Marmara would be idyllic. In fact, it was almost entirely built up in a strip running back from the coastline, at least a mile in depth. It was ribbon development par excellence and an extension of the great conurbation of Istanbul, whose name is derived from the Greek '*eis tin bolin*' ('to the city'). In 1980, the population of the city had been three million, and at the time of our journey it stood at something over seven million, although other sources were quoting figures in the region of thirteen million. It was the most populous city in Europe.

We drove for several hours through development after development, seeing many houses that were only half-built, and we wondered who was going to live in all those properties. Where was the infrastructure, the schools, the transport system, the hospitals, the drainage and water supplies and the shops? We were baffled. In due course, we learned that many of the businesspeople and shopkeepers had moved out to escape the pollution, traffic and frenetic life at the centre of the city, teaming up with their extended family to form a supportive unit. Hopefully, we thought, someone might inject a sense of order and regulation to avoid future mayhem.

We decided not to take the new motorway that skirts the centre of Istanbul, thinking it more fitting to end our journey—in triumph—by way of the sea road, through ancient, arched, city walls and right under the shadow of the Blue Mosque and Topkapi. The pungent and familiar smell of the city, a sour fusion of sulphur and the whiff of drains, wafted through the car's open windows and, at midday on 13th October, a fortnight after we had left London, we crossed the new Galata Bridge, over the Golden Horn. Minutes later we arrived outside the flat in Bebek.

'Here we are—home sweet home! I exclaimed, handing Lucinda the keys.

She took a firm hold of Nimr's basket and climbed the stairs, while I anxiously awaited her approval of our new abode!

Swedish Wallpaper, 1976

David, Leon and Eva Flamholc, Stockholm, 1976

Tarquin and Alexander, Scarecrows, 1980

Nimr

The Grange, Hilperton

Neil in the Khyber Pass, 1990

A Game of Buzkashi, 1990

Neil at a Game of Buzkashi, Peshawar, 1990

Pepsi Cities, 1990

Fishermen in Istanbul, 1992

View from the Galata Bridge, Istanbul, 1992

The Golden Horn, Istanbul, 1992

Bebek, 1992

Lucinda with shoe polisher in Istanbul, 1992

Tarquin in Afghanistan, 1990

Alexander filming 'The Magic Bag' in Hollywood, 1992

Neil Hall, Financial Advisor

Chapter 13
Salaam Istanbul

Constantinople: May 1835.
Oh, you who hope one day to roam in eastern lands, to
bend your curious eyes upon the people warmed by the rising sun, come quickly, for all things are changing.
(J.L. Stephens, *Incidents of Travel in Greece, Turkey, Russia
and Poland*)

What has happened to Turkey is a miracle. Much has been
lost that sentiment can properly regret, but what has been
gained has been the revival of a nation by its own efforts.
(Sir George Clerk, *The Times*, 19th August 1938)

EARLY ON THE morning of 10th November 1992, while driving into
the city from Bebek and, just as we were about to pass under the Atatürk
Köprüsü (suspension bridge) at Ortaköy, our attention was caught by the
discordant whine of wailing sirens. The traffic came to a halt and we assumed
that a police car or emergency vehicle was about to appear. However, drivers
and passengers were climbing out of their vehicles and standing to attention
in the road.

'Strange,' I remarked to Lucinda, who was in her usual place, seated
beside me. We sensed an air of solemnity, an aura of reverence, and began
to think that an important dignitary was about to pass by. Not wishing to

draw attention to ourselves, we too climbed out of our car and stood quietly, wondering what on earth was going on. After a few minutes the cacophony ceased, people returned to their vehicles, the traffic started to move and we remained none the wiser. Later, we discovered that on that day, 10th November, in 1938 at 9:05 a.m., Kemal Atatürk had died and the ritual we had witnessed was repeated annually, at that precise moment throughout the country.

Mustapha Kemal was born in Salonica in 1880. He later entered the Turkish army and supported the Young Turks; Turkish officers who sought to modernise the Ottoman Empire. The Committee of Union and Progress, based on their ideas, ruled Turkey for ten years from 1908. During the Great War Kemal distinguished himself during the Gallipoli campaign when British, Australian and New Zealand forces unsuccessfully attempted to open a second front in Turkey, Germany's ally, at a cost of some 36,000 lives. He also fought heroically against Allenby in Syria. During the early 1920s his military expertise led to the expulsion of the Greeks from Turkish soil, and by exercising skilled diplomacy a further war with Britain was avoided. When the Sultanate and Caliphate were abolished, the control of the country fell into his hands, and in 1923 the Republic was founded with Kemal, who had taken the name of Atatürk, Father of the Turks, as its first president.

He ruled with an iron fist until his death, secularising the state and carrying out far-reaching reforms. These included the suppression of the dervishes, abolition of the fez, emancipation of women, introduction of the Latin alphabet and Christian calendar (1926) and development of industry. Whatever his vices, he was loved and respected by his people and his portrait could still be seen in every shop, café, office and public building. It would be difficult to understand modern Turkey without some knowledge of the influence of 'The Grey Wolf'.

On the afternoon of the 10th, Lucinda and I visited the Dolmabahçe Palace, the principal imperial residence in the last days of the Ottoman Empire. To us, the most impressive aspect of this vast building was the 184-metre white marble frontage which rose a few yards from the shore of the Bosphorus, but we found the inside dreary and hopelessly cluttered with German-inspired kitsch.

The Dolmabahçe served as Atatürk's residence when he was in Istanbul and he died in a first-floor bedroom looking out over the strip of water that divides Europe from Asia Minor. On the day we visited the palace, his bed-room, still furnished as it was when he passed away, was crammed with gar-lands of flowers, and soldiers in full dress uniform stood guard by the door and at the bedside.

History and matters of cultural and sociological interest oozed from every inch of the great city, but we avoided distractions. Practical matters required attention and we needed to think about where our income was to come from. I did not want to have to resort to selling artichokes on the street corner like *Doğan*, a tall, scruffy man with a wide grin and only one tooth, who tended his little stall from dawn to dusk and in all weathers, a few yards from our front door.

When I found our apartment in September I had, with typical male laxity, failed to notice how filthy it was. Brown coal was burned throughout Istanbul during the winter months, drifting from thousands of chimneys and leaving a grimy trail everywhere. Within a few days of our arrival, we purchased buckets, sponges and strong detergent at the *bakkal* and vigor-ously set about swabbing all the surfaces in the flat.

Almost immediately, Lucinda let out a sharp cry: 'Yow!' I dropped my sponge and ran to the bathroom. She had been rinsing the curtains in the bath and received a nasty nip from a vicious little beastie—a miniature scor-pion. It must have come up through the drain. Once she had recovered from the shock she popped it into a jam jar, where it has remained to this day. Nimr kept us company from his place on the windowsill where he eyed the seagulls on the rooftops that lay between our flat and the Bosphorus. He could not, of course, leave the building as he would have immediately been torn apart by the wild dogs that roamed nearby woodlands and scavenged in the surrounding streets.

We enjoyed the novelty of visiting the *bakkal*, which was only a few hundred yards away. It gave us an opportunity to exercise our limited Turkish and reminded us of visiting the grocers when we were children. A helpful old man was employed to carry customers' purchases in large brown paper bags out to their cars. How much more dignified and useful, we thought, for the old boy to be gainfully employed, rather than sitting at home, glued to the television while he drew state benefit and rotted away. A few yards from the *bakkal* there was a halal butcher. The friendly staff served mostly chicken and lamb that was exceptionally tasty, but we were amazed to find how expensive it was, and were forced to impose a strict ration upon ourselves. Next door there was a wet fish shop and, again, we were shocked at the prices. Surprisingly, most of the fish seemed to be imported from the Baltic and arrived in refrigerated lorries.

An essential ingredient for our *modus operandi* was an efficient telephone service, especially when handling Sophie Reed material. The instrument in our flat crackled violently, fierce Turkish voices constantly interrupted conversations, and wrong numbers were legion, as were occasions when the line went completely dead. It was clearly hopeless to even try to operate a fax machine and we went in search of a solution to the problem. What a difference that device made.

I first encountered a fax machine, which was then a novelty, while visiting a solicitor in Dawlish during the time I represented Schroders. Today, however, with the universal use of personal computers, email and the internet, the fax machine is virtually obsolete.

We soon discovered the International Press Centre where, at a price, an efficient service operated for anyone wanting to send and receive international faxes. The Centre was housed in a fine stone building, reconstructed in the 1980s on the very edge of the Golden Horn and not far from the station at Sirkeci where I had arrived from London twenty-five years previously. Known as the Sepetçiler Köşkü (Kiosk of the Basket Weavers), it had originally been built in 1647 and served for many years as the boat-house for Topkapi Palace. When the Sultan and his entourage, accompanied by an admiral or two (the word stems from the Arabic *amir-al-bahr*, commander of the sea, and the gold rings that denote rank in the Royal Navy are relics of the gold and black headbands worn by Arabian seafarers) wanted a leisurely meander up the Golden Horn or the Bosphorus in one of his royal barges, they embarked at the Kiosk. These elaborate vessels can still be seen, preserved at the *Deniz Müsezi* (maritime museum) together with all sorts of fascinating pictures and other memorabilia dating from Ottoman to Republican times. We particularly admired Atatürk's elegant presidential cruiser, with its polished woodwork and brass fittings, and marvelled at the huge iron chain that had once stretched across the Bosphorus in order to keep Russian ships from passing through the straits. Echoes of the Great Game; such times had given rise to the music-hall verse that introduced the word 'jingoism' to the English language.

We don't want to fight, but, by jingo, if we do,
We've got the ships, we've got the men, we've got the money too.
We've fought the Bear before, and we'll do the same again.
The Russians shan't have Constantinople!

A few yards away from the Kiosk was a small terrace café that proved an excellent vantage point to take in the spellbinding splendour of smouldering skies when the sun set behind the Süleymaniye Mosque. Sipping on our apple çay while the call to prayer echoed from mosques across the city, this was as good a place as any to make plans, study our guidebooks and catch up on background information.

The Süleymaniye, considered by some to be the finest of the imperial mosque complexes, was founded by Süleyman the Magnificent in 1550 and took seven years to complete. It was designed by the greatest of Ottoman architects, the sublime Sinan, who had been born in Anatolia of Greek Christian parents in 1489. His career spanned some fifty years and he died in Istanbul in 1588. Many of his mosque complexes included schools, soup kitchens, baths, hospitals and guest houses, and when we finally made time to visit the Süleymaniye and experienced the structure for ourselves, we found it to be truly awesome.

By the time we had been in Istanbul for a month, we realised that we had not really come to grips with where our income would come from, and our meagre capital was trickling away. Settling in and going through what amounted to an orientation process had taken much longer than we expected, and enthusiasm had to make way for hard graft. I wanted to start approaching businesses to find work and Lucinda needed to contact schools so that she could find some teaching. Unfortunately, Tarquin had got bogged down in Africa, where he was involved in editing a book on Namibia for the late Mo Amin, the one-armed photographer and friend of Michael Buerk. It seemed unlikely that we would be seeing him in Turkey for some time.

I was feeling downhearted, but began to send out letters introducing myself, listing the various fields where I had experience and generally launching a few kites to see if any would fly. When I followed up my approach letters on the telephone, I was surprised by the positive response and in what seemed no time at all I was visiting senior executives involved in a number of different businesses.

My first interview was with the managing director of a major Turkish bank in a wonderful old building overlooking the Galata Bridge. After we had chatted for a while and admired the superb view across the Golden Horn from his office, he explained that the kind of financial products that we had developed in the West were not available from Turkish institutions and he thought it unlikely that he would be able to offer me any work, although he would given the matter his consideration. A couple of days later, I was discussing financial services again in smart modern offices near Taksim Square and soon after that attended a meeting to explore export opportunities with a leading industrialist at a textile factory, beyond the city's ancient walls, on the very outskirts of Istanbul. It seemed that getting past the front door was easy, but what next?

Meanwhile, Lucinda sent out a mailshot, offering her services as a qualified TEFL teacher, to various schools. She received very little response, and we soon realised that our timing was poor. Early in the new academic year was an unlikely time for head teachers to be taking on new staff. Those who did respond invited her to try again in six months.

But as far as I was concerned, the flurry of activity continued. I discovered from the Turkish manager of a renowned Oxford-based publishing house, specialising in educational material, that they might replace their representative in Istanbul at the end of the year. Another firm might need an English speaker to help with publicising tourist opportunities in Turkey, and there was talk of other openings for which I felt suited. The trouble was, and here I was reminded of my time in the North West Frontier Province; these Turks were unable to say 'yes', but they didn't want to say 'no'! They were supremely courteous and kind, but my expectations dictated a Westerner's approach.

Was there a job?

Could I do it?

Would the pay cover the bills?

When would I start?

Instead I found in this half-European, half-Asian city a surprisingly oriental mindset that was more in line with 'Inshallah' and 'when the apricots are ripe'.

'What did you expect'? Came the response from a bluff Australian we had met in the *bakkal* at Bebek. 'I've just received a letter from a businessman, in reply to one I sent him a year ago,' he continued. 'It actually required an urgent response, but that's how things are in Turkey!'

He invited us to dinner in his wooden Ottoman house, at the end of a rough track, overlooking the Bosphorus. The Aussie and his wife were in Istanbul, trying to obtain permits to import a particular strain of Australian sheep that they planned to breed on the hillsides of Anatolia. They were confident that the animals they had in mind would flourish in the conditions to be found in Asia Minor, and from what they told us they were getting used to Turkish attitudes. We sat on their terrace as dusk gathered, enjoying our meal and watching huge tankers with glinting navigation lamps slip through the straits. Along the distant shore, beads of light sparkled like sugar crystals on dark chocolate cake. The surprise of the evening was that our antipodean hosts only served soft drinks and were both teetotal.

We decided that we would have to pace ourselves, as we had begun to realise that nothing was going to happen in a hurry and we worried that our money would run out. Our days started with a brisk walk along the Bosphorus to a café that was just beyond the Bebek Fort. Here, we were regaled with coffee and micro macaroons before returning to write letters, follow up leads, and arrange interviews when possible. There was also a backlog of articles that Tarquin had sent us from Nairobi, so Sophie Reed business took us to the Press Centre quite frequently.

One day, we left the car near the Misir Çarşisi (spice market), its huge vaulted halls choking with sacks of cardamom, saffron, turmeric, cloves, pepper, mace and every conceivable condiment that spilled out on to the rough stone floors. We imagined that we were in a permitted parking area, but on our return from Sepetçiler Köşkü the Volkswagen had vanished. Immediate panic set in. This was all we needed—to be stuck in Turkey without our car—and how would we pay for a new one?

Every gloomy eventuality assailed our brains. However, after an hour or so and a few enquiries, we discovered that the vehicle had been towed away and was in a police car park behind the Rüstem Pasha Mosque. Parting with the equivalent of about ten pounds secured the car's release and we breathed a huge sigh of relief.

Unfortunately, the Rüstem Pasha was covered in scaffolding and tarpaulins at the time as major renovation was under way, but we promised ourselves that one day we would return to enjoy this most beautiful of Sinan's smaller mosques. Commissioned in 1561 by Rüstem Pasha, a vizier in the court of Süleyman the Magnificent and husband of the Princess Mihrimah, it is particularly famous for its exquisite tiles. These artefacts, in a variety of floral and geometric designs and some featuring the tomato-red or Armenian bole, were fired in the kilns of Iznik during the last half of the sixteenth century, and cover walls, ceiling, columns and other areas of the mosque. The interior is widely considered to be of the finest in all Turkey.

It would be unforgivable to spend an extended time in Istanbul without visiting the *hamam* (Turkish baths) and, on several dreary afternoons in November and December, after taking more care with our parking arrangements, we made our way to the *Cağaloğlu Hamami* in the old city, near the *Kapaliçarşi* (covered market). On the first occasion we both went to our segregated areas in a glorious building dating from the end of the sixteenth century. Once I had undressed and donned a white robe, I entered a great domed marble hall and, for a while, just sat and relaxed on the sculptured white marble seat that ran around the octagonal room. Gradually my eyes became accustomed to the steamy surroundings, and after half an hour or so a masseur indicated that I should stretch out on the raised central plinth. This was also made of pristine white marble, eight-sided, and occupied the centre of the *hamam*. I remained with a towel drawn tightly around my loins and was by then bucketing sweat. The huge Turkish masseur started to pummel and pull my limbs in every direction. He gave the deepest of massages, rippled my thighs and forearms, pounded muscles that I did not know I had, dug into my ribs and beneath my shoulder blades and worked away at excess flab. This continued for quite some time and then, to my horror, he started to walk up and down on my back. I was amazed that my body was able to sustain such an onslaught, but eventually when the man had finished I felt absolutely relaxed and at ease. Swapping notes with Lucinda while we enjoyed Turkish coffee in a nearby establishment later, we realised that her session had been gentler and she had enjoyed it enormously. Our next visit was not quite so successful. My massage was quite violent and Lucinda swore that she could hear me, through the wall, groaning and shouting '*Olum!*' (Death!!) She might well have done so because I was trying to communicate the extreme pain I was suffering. I felt very sore when it was all over, and was uncomfortable for several days. We wondered if the violence was in any way related to the fact that the England football team had defeated Turkey at Beşiktaş the previous evening.

A certain paradox existed in the fact that most Turks that we met, although fiercely nationalistic in their own way, could not understand our interest in their country. In a city where sixty per cent of the population was under the age of thirty, 'the West' was perceived as the land that flowed with milk and honey.

The weather in December was changeable. Heavy rain could cause flash torrents to pour down from the higher ground and sweep across the pavements. When it was sunny and cold, swirls of sulphurous brown smoke spiralled from the chimneys into the surrounding streets. As Christmas approached, it gradually dawned on us that our money could dip below an acceptable emergency reserve by the end of the year and if we had not achieved a spectacular breakthrough by then we would need to return to England to reformulate our plans. This possibility became more likely as we became aware that any new initiative with the Turks would take longer to develop than we had time for. So, feeling impotent and wanting to make the best use of every day, we began to spend the few weeks we had left exploring our surroundings. These activities took our mind off the predicament that would soon be staring us in the face. Not least of our concerns was what we would do with our beloved Nimr.

We particularly enjoyed taking a bus as far as the little fishing village of Rumeli Kavagi on the European shore of the Bosphorus, and then walking the ten miles back to Bebek. This took about half a day and gave us good exercise, while presenting an opportunity to observe numerous interesting places. The road that paralleled the route Jason and the Argonauts took as they wrestled with turbulent tidal forces edging eastwards towards the Black Sea was completely flat, except when it skirted the occasional cove, and was only a few feet above sea level. Huge ocean-going vessels from all over the world passed close to the shoreline, towering above us, and the intermittent sounding of their horns made us jump before the boom echoed away down the narrow straits.

Near Büyükdere (the Great Valley), where the First Crusade camped in 1096, prior to their crossing of the Bosphorus and long march across Asia Minor to the Holy Land, we would pause for a drink on the pier at Sariyer. Here, the fish market, where the day's catch was artistically laid out in a fanfare of shimmering displays on a plethora of wooden stands, was a hive of activity that kept us amused before continuing towards the lovely gardens of Tarabya. Revelling in a cornucopia of colour, punctuated with the sharp points of cypress trees where hibiscus blew red trumpets in the shadows and clematis scrambled over rough walls, a few of these heirs to the Garden of Eden surrounded the summer embassies of several European states.

The first of these we came across was the Russian Embassy, built in 1840 for the Tsar's ambassador, General Ignatiev; then the French Embassy, which was presented by Sultan Selim III to Napoleon Bonaparte in 1807 and finally the Italian Embassy, built in 1906. But further on our route, beyond Büyükdere, we encountered the oldest of the European summer residences; that of Spain, which was acquired from the Franciscans in 1783. Although the official business of most of the ambassadors to the Sublime Porte was conducted in grand embassies located in *İstiklal Caddesi,* their entourage moved to summer quarters when the heat and diseases of the city became overpowering.

We rather liked the term 'Sublime Porte', used to describe the ornamental gateway and projecting canopy in the Turkish rococo style, behind Topkapi, which once led to the offices of the Grand Vizier, as it conjured up romantic images of the Sultanate. Ambassadors were accredited to the Sublime Porte in a similar way as ambassadors to the UK are accredited to the Court of St James.

An interesting horticultural connection exists with Ogier de Busbecq (1522–92), the Hapsburg ambassador to the Sublime Porte. It was he who first introduced lilac and tulips from the Levant to Europe, and was reported to have written the following: 'Turks cultivate flowers with great care and do not hesitate to spend for a particularly beautiful blossom a considerable sum, though otherwise they are a thrifty people.'

Before reaching an especially fine line of *yalis* (Ottoman mansions), near Yeniköy, we passed through the hamlet of Kalender whose name is associated with an order of mendicant dervishes. Atatürk suppressed the dervishes but, whatever their origin or initial purpose may have been, they still appeared from time to time to entertain tourists. The most famous of these were the *mevlevi* or whirling dervishes, who performed regularly in Istanbul and elsewhere and were founded by one of the greatest poets the world has ever known; the mystic Jalaludin Rumi, who died in 1273.

We continued to pass mosques, churches, museums and all manner of places whose details fill the guidebooks. In the distance across the water, we spotted the little village of Kanlica which we had visited by ferry one sunny afternoon. Seated in a restaurant, with pretty pink and white tablecloths, close to the wooden jetty and on the edge of a picturesque square, we consumed bowls of the delicious yoghurt that had made the village famous for 300 years and was still considered the tastiest in Istanbul.

The last stretch of our walk took us under the Fatih Sultan Mehmet Köprüsü (the second Bosphorus bridge linking Europe to Asia), a gigantic suspension bridge, opened in1988 that soared above our heads. Then, at the narrowest point of the straits we passed beneath the walls of the mighty Rumeli Hisari (fortress) before stopping at our favourite café for well-earned refreshment. The last point of interest, perched on the hillside outside Bebek, was the Bogaziçi Universitesi (University of the Bosphorus), founded in 1971 on the site of Robert College, once the finest institute of higher education in Turkey. It had been founded by an American missionary who worked with Florence Nightingale in her hospital in *Üsküdar*.

During the second week in December we reluctantly concluded that we would have to return to London to rethink our situation. Our disappointment, however, was tempered when we found, among the colony of English teachers residing in Galata, a kind lady who was happy to look after Nimr until we returned. We took the car to the Volkswagen garage in Beşiktaş for a thorough service, delivered a wad of US dollars to our landlady to cover the rent for a couple of months and one bright morning, ten days before Christmas, set out on the long haul back to England. For the first few hours we felt truly wretched. It seemed that all our hopes and plans had blown away in the peat smoke that blew over the rooftops at that time of year. I hesitate to use the word 'plans', as that was part of the problem. We had prepared in some ways, but had failed to plan realistically in the areas that mattered. We had relied, too much, on enthusiasm to see us through and had discovered that it really was *not* 1968 and we weren't in our twenties.

We were concerned for our feline friend, whose kidney infection was not improving, so we wondered if we would ever see him again, and were desperately worried about money. If our financial position became untenable, I could, as a last resort, return to the financial services industry, but under the terms of the agreement I had signed, that would not be possible for another eighteen months. We had, by the time we approached the Greek border, talked ourselves into a pretty gloomy state of mind when I realised that a police patrolman on a bike had drawn up beside me and was indicating that I should pull in to the side of the road. With due courtesy he pointed out that we had been speeding and fined me the equivalent of twenty pounds on the spot. For some reason, release from tension perhaps, we found this hilarious and our tears turned to ribald laughter. If that was the worst thing that would happen while we drove the next 2000 miles or so, we should count ourselves lucky.

After the tortuous experience we had endured the preceding autumn, we decided to avoid the mountains of northern Greece and on the evening of the second day arrived in the port of Patra, at the mouth of the Gulf of Corinth. Here we boarded a ferry for the thirty-six-hour voyage to Ancona in northern Italy.

To our delight we found that we had the vessel almost entirely to ourselves and, with the exception of an English couple, who ran dinghy-sailing courses in the Greek islands and were returning home with their children for Christmas, the decks were deserted. This was especially pleasant as we awoke, after the first night, to brilliant and exhilarating sunshine which we enjoyed all day, relaxing in deckchairs as the white cliffs of the craggy Albanian coast slipped by.

We docked in Ancona early the next morning and when I pulled back the little porthole curtain, expecting glorious sunshine, we were astonished and disappointed to find sheets of rain sweeping down the shoreline and the greyness of a wet winter's day engulfing the dreary port. We had, of course, travelled several hundred miles north during the night.

Return journeys always seem shorter than the outward haul and in what appeared no time at all we were climbing the Alps in a heavy snowstorm. In fact, the blizzard became so intense that our surroundings were entirely blotted out. Creeping through a small village we parked up, close to a hotel, anticipating blocked roads ahead, but the storm passed and we were soon on our way, reaching the French city of Beaune late in the evening.

Heading north the next day, we paused to visit Colombey-les-deux-Églises and the modest grave of Charles de Gaulle. De Gaulle was buried close to his daughter Anne, who was born with Down Syndrome and only lived for twenty years. The General would say that his daughter had taught him about life.

We arrived at Reims just as the sun sank below the horizon and found a novel kind of hotel, part of the Formula One chain. There were no staff in attendance and a room key was obtained by inserting a credit card into a hole in the wall. This seemed fine to us. It was cheap and we just needed a bed for the night so, undeterred by the fact that we might be the only people in the building, we paid our due and headed off into the city in search of an evening meal. Returning a couple of hours later we settled down, looking forward to our beauty sleep, but in the early hours of the morning, were awakened by a dreadful rumpus. Two drunks were fighting in the corridor and the screaming and crashing was getting closer. Thoroughly alarmed and, unable to call for any kind of assistance, we pushed the bedroom furniture against the door and quivered behind our barricade. The shoving, shouting, swearing and punching reached a crescendo just on the other side of what now looked like very flimsy walls. Gradually the men passed further down the passage, beyond our room, and the racket subsided, but we kept our bed jammed up against the door for the rest of the night.

On our last day before returning to England, we visited the glorious mediaeval cathedral at Reims and also the War Rooms where General Jodl capitulated to Eisenhower at 2:41 am on 7th May 1945. The venue for that poignant, historic occasion has remained, as it was on that day, with the place names of the participants clearly marked.

If our friend and tenant in the flat at Kew was surprised or irritated by our return from Turkey, she did not show it and a week after Christmas obligingly moved out.

Her departure coincided with Tarquin's return from Kenya and within a few days Alexander flew in from LA. The family was reunited once more.

Alexander was in the process of completing his film, *The Magic Bag.* One objective of his short trip was to work on the soundtrack with his loyal Hackenbacker friends in Soho, and record the introductory narrative with his buddy, the actor, Bruce Boa. We were impressed by the finished product, and wishing him every success on his return to LA, looked forward to hearing how Steven Spielberg would react to *The Magic Bag.* However things were not going to be that easy. Spielberg was under huge pressure while putting the final touches to *Jurassic Park* and preparing to film *Schindler's List* in Poland. Following the completion of *Jurassic Park,* the staff at Amblin Entertainment had been reduced and Alexander was made redundant. However, he managed to meet the great director—who still showed enthusiasm for *The Magic Bag*—and presented him with a copy of that film, but events took over and the opportunity to remain in contact fizzled out. Despite all this, Alexander was invited by a member of Spielberg's office to visit the *Schindler's List* set in Cracow, which gave him a final opportunity to see the Master in action.

Meanwhile, back in Kew, the early months of 1993 passed while we became increasingly frustrated and worried about our future. The general consensus was that we should continue to investigate opportunities in Turkey. However, this course would be pursued by contacting companies in England which had Turkish interests, rather than by returning to Istanbul.

The other ingredient in the tangled web that we had spun was the potential for Tarquin to contribute material for Sophie Reed. Having completed his project in Kenya, he agreed to go and live in the flat in Bebek and to start working on photo-reportage that could be sent back to London. We dropped him at Gatwick and he was soon settled in Istanbul, having retrieved our beloved Nimr from his minder.

Once we turned our mind to Sophie Reed we realised, since the copyright had now reverted back to her, that there was considerable potential to syndicate Tarquin's articles to magazines around the world. This was particularly true of his blockbuster photo-expositions: 'I Married a Guerrilla General', which had first appeared in the *Mail on Sunday*, and 'Women Who Married Women' originally published by *Marie Claire*. We set about this project with grim determination and to our amazement and relief the fax machine in our flat began ringing at all hours of the day and night, confirming deals for thousands of dollars as we placed these pieces with publishers all over the world. Signed contracts were returned from magazines in Sydney, Buenos Aires, Rio de Janeiro, New York, Paris, Frankfurt, Stockholm and Hong Kong. It was very exciting because, of all the kites that we had launched, at last something seemed to be working. However, we knew this streak of good fortune could not continue, although it gave us breathing space and paid a few bills.

Once the flurry of activity had calmed down, Lucinda returned to Bebek while I held the fort in Kew. The objective of her return was to follow up some of the openings for teaching English that had arisen in the autumn and to support Tarquin. Alexander also felt he could do with a break from Hollywood and joined the others in Turkey before taking up the invitation to observe Spielberg filming in Cracow.

Soon after they had left I found myself, one afternoon, in the wine department in Selfridges. Glancing at the shelves, I noticed bottles of white Dortnal and red Lokal, Turkish wines produced by the Diren Wine Company, whose vintages had washed down more than a few enjoyable dishes of *meze, patlican*, *kebab*, *tatziki* or red mullet when Lucinda and I had lingered in restaurants on the banks of the Bosphorus. The sight spawned a question that, surprisingly, had not occurred to me before and I decided to undertake a little research. How was it that Turkey, a Muslim country, was producing wine? I also wondered what kind of firm was sophisticated enough to be exporting to the West and competing in the world markets. I soon discovered that wine had been produced in Turkey for centuries and that Hittite wine containers dating back three or four thousand years had recently been unearthed.

When Atatürk founded the secular state in 1923, he lifted the ban on alcohol imposed by the Ottomans and began the first wine-making business in modern Turkey. Much of the grape-growing in the past had been for table consumption, which accounted for its survival during the reign of the Muslim sultans, but Turkey now boasted the fifth largest area under vine in the world.

My next step was to contact the UK agent for the Diren Wine Company. He turned out to be a Turk called Tayo, who lived near Thaxted in Essex. I suggested that an article in a London magazine about Turkish wine—and Diren wine, in particular—could do him nothing but good.

Following our telephone conversation, I met Tayo in the foyer at the London Hilton, the hotel in Park Lane whose construction I had witnessed during my teens, and which the Queen had been reluctant to visit on account of her being extremely miffed when she realised that patrons could peer into her garden at Buckingham Palace.

I explained that my son Tarquin was a freelance photo-journalist based in Istanbul and the very man to take on the project under discussion. He agreed without hesitation, which, although uncharacteristic for a Turk was not surprising, as he would get a whole lot of free publicity. I now approached *Wine* magazine, published by Michael Heseltine's company, Haymarket Publishing Services Ltd, where I had little difficulty in obtaining a commission. Before long, Tarquin and Alexander were speeding through the night in a coach that they had boarded on the outskirts of Istanbul, en route for Tokat, an ancient town in the heart of Anatolia that once flourished as a major trading post on the Silk Road.

Arriving the next morning, a little the worse for bumpy roads and sleep deprivation, they were warmly welcomed by the four Diren brothers, whose father had first started pressing grapes, on the kitchen table, soon after the Second World War. Orhan, Turkey's first and only qualified oenologist, Ali, who had studied accountancy and fruit-juice production in Germany (the family also produced a range of organic fruit juices), Errol (known as Flynn), a mechanical engineer, and Enver, a graduate in business management and administration, all vied to explain the details surrounding a family enterprise of which they were justly proud.

Orhan took the lead and gave the boys a guided tour of the vineyards, emphasising the fact that no fertilisers or pesticides were used and that insects were known to travel from as far as Baghdad to feed on the grapes, attracted by their wonderful taste!

They walked along the terraces, up a stony road lined with silver birch trees that quivered in the light breeze and, crossing a clear bubbling stream, passed women with hennaed hair, weaving *kelims*, and a group of rugged men with apricot complexions sipping dark tea from tulip-shaped glasses.

That evening, as the call to prayer sounded across the *Yeşilırmak* valley, the extended family gathered in a local restaurant. Wine flowed and piles of steaming *patlican,* roasted garlic, rice and succulent lamb arrived on the table. A local musician sang traditional Ottoman ballads and everyone clapped and joined in the merriment. During a pause in the festivities Orhan confidently pronounced, 'We in Turkey are still baking our cake and when it is ready we hope that we will be a formidable contributor to an even larger market.'

The next day the boys returned, loaded with generous gifts of bottles of wine, cartons of peach and plum juice and a beautiful carpet. I was, of course, still in London, but the story of their adventures was related to Lucinda and relayed to me, omitting no detail, and Tarquin's article, which was published in October, allowed us the additional pleasure of a retrospective view. Orhan's words extolling his confidence in the business were music to my ears. I was not the only one who believed in a great future for Turkey. In due course Haymarket paid up and we all obtained some satisfaction from the credit that appeared at the end of the photo-reportage. It read: 'Tarquin Hall is a freelance journalist based in Turkey'.

Some progress had been made.

Not long after this adventure, rumours reached the apartment in Bebek that an English lady, a widow formerly married to a Turk who had recently celebrated her one hundred and third birthday, was living in the fashionable *Beyoğlu* district of the city. Lucinda and Tarquin went into sleuth mode, sensing that this was just the sort of story they needed for another magazine article. One thing led to another and it was not long before they were both sitting in a sunny apartment with Mrs Rena Duran and her eighty-year-old daughter, Lulu, who had both agreed to be interviewed.

Mrs Duran was explaining how she had first met her husband in England and that romance had subsequently blossomed in Paris, just before the Great War. It was not until she had accepted his proposal of marriage that he revealed that he was not French, as she had supposed, but a Turk.

'In for a penny: In for a pound', she had reassured herself, before discovering that her future husband was in fact Professor Faik Sabri Duran, a revered geographer and compiler of the first Turkish world atlas.

Undaunted, Mrs Duran was soon living in Pera, at the heart of Constantinople, as it was then still called, during the last years of the tottering Sultanate and enjoying the vestiges of an age that would soon be swept away. As the old lady poured tea and her daughter brought in fine china plates, piled high with little iced cakes and tempting chocolate biscuits, the two reminisced about a city teeming with spies and brimming with Eastern charm and mystery. Those were the days when men wore a *tarbush* and sported spats, and horse-drawn carriages trundled through cobbled streets carrying elegant veiled women, attired in white gloves and beautiful long dresses, glimpsed, only briefly, on arrival at their destination.

As they recalled later, Tarquin and Lucinda were lapping up these memories and making notes as Mrs Duran continued the story to the day when the 'honeymoon' ended and the British government evacuated her and Lulu back to England. It would be ten years, long after hostilities between the Ottoman and British Empires had ceased, before she returned to her husband in what was now Istanbul. By then, Turkey had become a republic under Kemal Atatürk, whom she much admired.

After the professor died in 1942, the two ladies taught English and Mrs Duran carried out voluntary work for the World Council of Churches, helping the ever increasing numbers of refugees fleeing from the Soviet Union. She embellished this part of her story with details of hair-raising escapes by sailors, dressed only in their underwear, who jumped into the tormented waters of the Bosphorus from Soviet vessels, as they steamed through the straits.

There was no doubt in Tarquin and Lucinda's minds that their hostesses retained remarkable mental agility. This was explained by the fact that they lived comfortably on their pensions, read books and periodicals for at least four hours a day, took regular taxi trips outside the city and entertained streams of visitors from all over the world. Mrs Duran was, justifiably, very proud of her age. She had already outlived her brother, who died at the age of ninety-nine, and the receipt of a telegram from the Queen on her hundredth birthday, was an accolade that she especially cherished. Once tea was finished, Lucinda and Tarquin felt reluctant to overstay their welcome and bid the old ladies farewell, although Tarquin promised to return a few days later to take pictures and examine some of the photograph albums that had emerged from huge cupboards in the hallway. As they left the apartment, Mrs Duran picked up a small Union Jack that she kept on a sideboard.

'God save the Queen!' she cried, waving it enthusiastically before repeating an open invitation to return at any time, and exhorting them not to forget that her one hundred and fourth birthday was only months away.

If failing to take a Turkish bath was a transgression, then omitting to visit 'Hadji Bekir: Makers of Turkish Delight since 1777' was a veritable sin. A few days later, not for the first time, Tarquin paused at the legendary shop in Hamidiye Caddesi. He planned to procure a large box of Turkish Delight to take as a present to the Durans, but he also spotted another opportunity for an article, together with colourful pictures, and arranged to return to interview Mr Sahin, the current owner.

Mr Sahin immediately put him right with regard to the name of their product, known in Turkey as *rahat lokum*. Apparently, *rahat* was a corruption of an Arabic word meaning 'we have eaten' while *lokum* was Turkish for 'contentment'. Tarquin figured that the Englishman who first took the sweetmeat back to London during the reign of George III, dubbing it Turkish Delight, was not far off the mark

While Tarquin and his host sipped mellow tea from the familiar tulip-shaped glasses, Mr Sahin regaled him with the story of how Hadji Bekir had arrived in Constantinople from Anatolia with little capital, but with a secret recipe that soon enabled him to amass fame and fortune. In no time at all he was appointed Chief Confectioner to the Ottoman Court.

At a later date, Tarquin told me how secretive Mr Sahin had been with regard to the techniques used in producing *rahat lokum*. However, he was generous enough to provide a guided tour of the factory, pausing from time to time to sample pistachio, lemon, rose petal, coconut and other sweet morsels that melted in the mouth. At the end of the day Tarquin wrote a piece that provided a fascinating insight into another Turkish business which had recently won awards in the world's markets.

Once the information had been gathered, Tarquin faced a few hours at his laptop but his skill at producing polished, pithy pieces that Lucinda found easy to sell was improving all the time. He was lucky to have her support, as Lucinda's Massachusetts education proved to have instilled a more thorough grounding in English grammar than Tarquin's teaching at Bryanston—or, for that matter, mine at Marlborough—had done.

She had recently acquired *Emirates—In Flight* as a customer for Sophie Reed and when the two pieces: 'Age Has Not Withered Her' and 'Food of Contentment' were published, and we were paid $500 each; our confidence in Tarquin's ability to bring in the cash and support himself in Bebek mounted. He was just approaching his twenty-fourth birthday. This was all good news and we were delighted that one of the ingredients of the original plan, the opportunity for Tarquin to develop his writing and photographic skills and our family business, was working out so well. However, in the wider context, I had come to the conclusion that continuing to seek business opportunities in Turkey was pointless and, unfortunately, I came to this point of view just as Lucinda was offered a teaching job at a school near Bebek. But the pay was a pittance and, since I was unable to make any progress, in career terms, I was convinced that our part of the enterprise was doomed. Accordingly, in late April, I flew to Istanbul to share my views with Lucinda while Tarquin was on a trip to the Lake Van district of eastern Turkey where he was working on a story about *Cirit*, a ferocious game played with spears while mounted on horseback.

I was to be confronted with sad news. A few days before my return to Bebek, Nimr's kidney condition had deteriorated and he was in considerable pain. Lucinda called in the Turkish vet, who could do very little, and with great reluctance she decided that our eighteen-year-old friend would have to be put down. The vet was averse to performing an act that went contrary to Muslim tradition; however, after puffing heavily on several cigarettes, he administered a fatal injection. The huge beautiful animal instantly crumpled into a pile of ginger fur on the kitchen table. Lucinda was devastated, as I was when these events were related to me, but she was also at a loss as to what to do next. There were no facilities in Turkey for the dignified disposal of a pet, so taking the dear old cat in her arms, she wrapped him in a large plastic bag and placed him in the freezer compartment of the fridge, awaiting my arrival.

When I turned up the next day, it was something of a shock to find our frozen feline in the freezer, but neither of us could decide on a sensible course of action. There were very few pets in Istanbul, and we assumed that when they died they were thrown into rubbish bins and subsequently chewed up by marauding dogs. Disposing of Nimr in such a manner was totally unacceptable.

We racked our brains for several hours until Lucinda had an inspiration. She called the chaplain of the Anglican Church in Galata and, explaining the situation, asked for his assistance. His name was Ian Sherwood, a nice man whom we had met on several occasions.

'We have a Christian cat who deserves a Christian burial, please can we bury him in the grounds of your church', Lucinda requested with spectacular aplomb. If Ian was taken aback, he did not show it and readily concurred. The next day we found ourselves in a taxi heading towards the church, with the frozen Nimr inside his wicker basket, wrapped in plastic and a newspaper that soaked up any condensation.

The Crimean Memorial Church was located at the end of a steep, slippery, narrow street that runs from *İstiklal Caddesi* down towards the Bosphorus and was designed by C.E. Street, the architect of the London Law Courts. It had been built shortly after the Crimean War, under the aegis of Lord Stratford de Redcliffe, as a memorial to those who had fallen in the conflict. Known as *Büyükelçi*, the Great Ambassador, he was so named owing to the immense influence he exerted on Turkish affairs during his three terms as emissary from the Court of St James to the Sublime Porte. As our taxi drew up at the gates, a soft drizzle was falling, and family groups had gathered on the balconies of the scruffy tenement buildings that rose above our heads. Something had attracted their attention, and this proved to be a small band of Sri Lankans who were digging a hole just inside the churchyard.

The Sri Lankans, it turned out, were refugees who had been provided temporary accommodation in the crypt of the church by the kindly Ian Sherwood, who now came forward to greet us. With little ceremony but a few carefully chosen words, the English *kedi* was lowered, in his basket, into the large hole, and swiftly covered with Turkish soil. Tears flowing down our cheeks, we muttered our thanks and withdrew into the labyrinth of the streets of Galata, heading towards *Eminönü*, the market area on the east bank of the Golden Horn. There we purchased a lovely magnolia bush and, returning to the churchyard, planted it above the last resting place of our old friend.[19]

Several years later Tarquin dedicated his first book as follows:

'To my dear departed Nimr, who went to the Happy Mousing Grounds after eighteen memorable years. He was a faithful companion, an intrepid traveller, the scourge of rodents from the Thames to the Golden Horn, a most distinguished pussy cat.'

Tarquin remained in the flat at Bebek for a further six months, until the autumn. It gave him the opportunity to travel into some of the remotest areas of Turkey and he produced further articles on such diverse subjects as Florence Nightingale, Turkish tulips, and the Russian 'Natashas'; prostitutes who crossed into Turkey from the Soviet Union and caused havoc to marital relationships in Trabzon and elsewhere.

For Lucinda and me, the time had come to return to England and start a new chapter in our lives. The Turkish adventure had been a financial disaster, and this would need to be repaired, but we were in no mood for recrimination. We had endured a huge learning curve, suffered much anguish, but experienced immensely enjoyable moments as well. We had seen a lot, done a lot and widened our horizons.

As the Turkish Airlines jet banked sharply, the Prince's Islands where we had just spent a delightful April day appeared like minute diamond studs set in the silver sea. Firmly strapped into my seat, I reflected on a tradition of the Prophet Mohammed—upon whom be peace—to which one might, one day, aspire: 'Treat this world as I do, like a wayfarer; like a horseman who stops in the shade of a tree for a time, and then moves on.'

Chapter 14
Misfits and Muncaster

Sometimes the man on the saddle and sometimes the
saddle on the man.
(Proverb)

Whoever is to be wise despises himself. Only the ignorant
trust their own judgement.
(Proverb)

LUCINDA AND I were back in our flat in Kew. It was breakfast time
on a fine spring morning in 1993. The sliding doors leading on to the balcony
at the front of the building were open and birds were twittering in the trees,
but we felt anything but chirpy.

'*Nous sommes dans le* (même) *pottage*,' I announced ponderously, mis-
quoting Lord Castlereagh's comment to Talleyrand at the Treaty of Vienna.

The truth of the matter was that it had been a year since the whole
Turkish adventure began, and we had completely run out of cash.

There was nothing for it except for Lucinda to report, *post haste*, to a
temp agency for secretarial work, but what about me? It would still be a year
before a return to the financial services industry was viable, and that was an
option I did not relish.

I had only two assets that we now felt it appropriate to harness, since
desperate circumstances dictated drastic measures. These were my intimate

knowledge of London and the old VW Passat, which had already clocked up 150,000 miles. What we had once considered a joke was now reality. I would have to go and find myself a job as a minicab driver.

It so happened that there was a small firm a mile or so away in Sheen, and later that morning I visited their premises. A sign hung in the widow that read 'DRIVERS WANTED', which was encouraging, although I could hardly believe what I was doing.

The door to the little reception area at the minicab office opened off the street, and as I entered, I found myself under the scrutiny of a rough-looking fellow seated behind a glass screen wearing a grey woollen cap and tinted specs. With one hand he pulled back the sliding pane that separated us, while with the other, which was adorned with several chunky gold rings, he took Cheerios from a packet and stuffed them into his mouth.

'I am looking for a job as a driver,' were the words I managed to annunciate. The man behind the window rose lethargically from his seat and poked his head around the door of an adjoining room.

'There's a posh bloke out 'ere, says 'e wants a job, shall I send 'im in?' I heard him say.

A younger man who was tall, skinny and wearing wire-framed glasses, emerged and we sat down on a bench in the reception area. He was better-spoken, and introducing himself as Mike, turned out to be the owner of Thames Cars.

I explained that I needed to start earning money ASAP and that's why I was there. He didn't seem interested in whys and wherefores, only saying that providing I knew my way around, put in the hours and behaved myself I would earn a fair 'wedge'.

'We get all sorts here,' he said getting up and leading me out on to the pavement. 'They're mostly misfits of one kind or another. We've got one bloke,' he added with a chuckle, 'who "drowned" on the *Herald of Free Enterprise* in 1987 and has adopted a completely new identity. Now, let's have a look at your car ...'

He inspected the Passat, which seemed to please him.

'We can always use an estate. Now, when can you start?' he concluded.

That afternoon I returned to have the shortwave radio apparatus installed and made the necessary arrangements for insurance. My call sign was to be 'River One One'.

At seven o'clock the following morning I reported for work and was shown to the rest room. It was behind the control centre, the office with the glass sliding window where I could hear a two-way radio spluttering and telephones ringing. Several televisions were also blaring from positions on the ground floor. The rest room reminded me of scruffy bedsits in Bayswater. Loose strips of wallpaper hung from the walls, the soiled carpet was more hole than thread, rusty springs poked through the fabric of a couple of stained, ash-burned sofas and chairs, smutty magazines were piled on the floor, and grease-encrusted metallic take-away troughs from the local Chinese or Indian, loaded with fag ends, littered the room. There was a kettle, a pile of dirty mugs, and assorted torn packets of sugar and PG Tips that spilled on to a grubby sink and drainer in one corner. Amid this putrid arena my new workmates were positioned behind their newspapers, some puffing on cigarettes. No one said a word as I entered. I was a new boy once again.

After a few minutes the controller, the rough fellow whom I had encountered on my first visit, whose name turned out to be Ron, shouted 'OO'Z OUT?' at the top of his voice from his position behind the glass screen in the front office. One of the drivers shot up from his chair and collecting a chit from Ron headed down the street to his car. A couple of other drivers soon followed and then it was my turn.

'Name of Roberts, 14 Palewell to Hammersmith Broadway. Four pounds fare,' instructed Ron.

I knew Palewell, so that was lucky and, half an hour later, richer by £4 (together with a 50p tip) I was back at base waiting for the next call.

The twelve-hour day continued in the same vein and when I finished I had taken £96 in fares, of which I had to donate £27 to the firm. There was also £12.50 in tips. I had driven just over one hundred miles around the capital.

This was going to be a very hard slog.

Over the next few days, reminding me of prep school, the ice melted in the rest room and I was eased into the group by a process of gentle banter and teasing. I began to get to know the other eight drivers. A couple of older men wore crumpled suits, sported faded ties and looked as though they had known better days; one young chap with a shaven head would, I am sure, have been happier on the rugby pitch; and a blond young man was the constant butt of jokes about where he spent his evenings. He always looked tired, which was not surprising, as his night job was participating in porn films being made in a council flat near Brentford Dock. Herbie, the man who 'drowned' when the roll-on/roll-off ferry sank off the coast at Zeebrugge, a large humorous character who could have been of Dutch origin, was constantly vanishing off Ron's radar when he visited the local betting shop, and there were also a couple of young family men with children, endeavouring to scratch a living.

'Herbie, you c***!' growled Ron when he eventually turned up. 'I've been calling you for the last hour. Where the fuck 'ave you been? As if I don't know!'

Herbie slunk into one of the filthy armchairs. He knew his punishment would be 'locals' for the rest of the day, where he made less money. No airport jobs for him. I hoped his luck with the horses provided adequate compensation.

Early in my career at Thames Cars I made a serious mistake by disappearing into the 'bog' at the rear of the building. Sitting there, quietly minding my own business, I was shocked when a bucket full of ice-cold water erupted from underneath the slatted wooden door and, sluicing across the concrete floor, soaked my trousers and boxer shorts. It was a curious form of baptism and provoked a huge outburst of mirth in the courtyard outside.

'Roll with the punches and bite your tongue!' I mumbled to myself.

What to wear to work was a problem, but I solved it when I retrieved an oatmeal-coloured, sleeveless, goat's hair jacket from the depths of my bedroom cupboard at home. It had been purchased in Peshawar and was ideal garb for a cab driver as it kept my torso warm while leaving my arms free, and had deep pockets which were useful for cash.

'You c***!' screamed Ron in his inimitable fashion as I arrived for the day shift. 'What do you fink you look like—a sack o' fucking spuds?'

That did it.

I was to be 'Spud' for the rest of my time at Thames Cars.

Those who worked at Thames Cars, and that extended to those on the night shift, an even more shadowy bunch of misfits whom, it was rumoured, included a member of the IRA Provos, formed a sub-culture that was new to my experience.

They had their own customs, ethics, language, humour and ways of doing things. The worst sin was being 'fed', which meant getting the best jobs from the controller, the minicab driver's equivalent of being teacher's pet.

'Being sent to Coventry' could follow, and it was amazing how many boiling hot cups of tea could be 'accidentally' slopped over shoes in the rest room.

In theory, the longer journeys provided the most cash but since mileage was the basis of the fare, unlike a time-metered black cab, getting stuck in a traffic jam didn't do you any favours. There were various ways of earning extra cash.

Knowing the shortcuts was an obvious example, as this would speed up a job and position one for the next call.

'Spud, you c***! Where've you been?' was a familiar greeting in the early days. 'Don't you know the quick way round White City? C'mere!'

Ron, for all his coarseness, enjoyed passing on the tricks of the trade.

'Waiting time' was another earner. Every passenger had a five-minute 'window', but if the driver was kept waiting after a fare had been booked extra charges accumulated. Genuine delays at the airport generated oodles of 'waiting time' but reasonable allowances were made for baggage handling and other hold-ups.

A 'double Heathrow', or especially a 'double Gatwick' at the estate car rate, could really boost the day's earnings. These trips meant taking a fare out to an airport and then meeting an incoming flight and returning another passenger, family or whatever to their destination. Initially, I felt a bit of a prune standing in Arrivals holding a white card with my fare's name scrawled on it. One day my friend, Doris Lessing, unexpectedly came through Arrivals at Heathrow's Terminal One. I'm not sure which of us was the more surprised to see the other. I endeavoured to find her a black cab.

A good scam was to collect or deliver a parcel for one customer while carrying out another assignment. Effectively, this meant doing two jobs concurrently which also boosted the day's takings. What amazed me was how important all this became. For someone who had been earning tens of thousands a year before the Turkish adventure, I was surprised to find myself minutely recording each day's takings, faithfully logging every trip, even those that only earned me £3 or a tip of 25p. Of course I needed to keep a record to check the commission owed to Thames Cars and for tax purposes, but it was also a real lesson in how one adjusts to new and unexpected circumstances. You could call it the prisoner syndrome, as so graphically portrayed in *The Shawshank Redemption* (1994), in which things that would normally be regarded as trivial assume enormous significance.

Lucinda and I had never been in the habit of using taxi services on a regular basis, so it amazed me to discover that there were a huge number of people who thought nothing of ordering a cab and expecting a car to arrive within minutes. These included little old ladies collecting their pension from the post office, people with hospital appointments, businessmen and women going to the office, a retired butcher who regularly sent out for a bottle of whisky, two young women whose whole lives revolved around saving up for, and then travelling anywhere in the world to, the next Barry Manilow concert, and even housewives with piles of shopping and tetchy kids who wanted to be collected from Waitrose. There were even seriously obese, and some horribly smelly people, who would be incapable of looking after a car of their own but expected me to drive them around. I refused to take one man—a real scumbag and blatteroon.

One summer's evening, a dolly-bird seated in the passenger seat, turned.

'I've heard that all minicab drivers are sex maniacs', she said.

Did I detect the gap between her smooth, white thighs widen slightly, as she spoke? I think so.

During my time with Thames Cars, I made more than three thousand trips for every imaginable reason.

As soon as a passenger had been collected at the start of a fare, the driver was required to call in to base and announce 'POB'. This meant 'passenger on board'. There was, however, one exception.

On Sunday afternoons, one routine pick-up meant taking a funny little man, a Jehovah's Witness, to a religious meeting. Rather than make the standard POB call on the radio, I was instructed to say 'ATFAH!'

'Why do I do that and what does it mean?' I asked.

It took some time to elicit the truth, but it eventually emerged that this benighted individual was being driven to his prayers every Sunday in blissful ignorance of the real meaning of the acronym that announced his presence in one of the Thames Cars.

'ATFAH' stood for 'A Total Fucking Arse Hole'!

One bright morning, I collected a passenger from Lord Chancellor's Walk, off Coombe Lane. This was a collection of smart houses built on the site of Coombe Springs once the original buildings had been demolished. The great oak still flourished and the five hundred-year-old Spring House remained intact, now maintained by English Heritage. Memories flooded back—'Work Sundays', Gurdjieff movements in the Djamichunatra, John Bennett, and friends that I had made.

As I turned out into the main road I recalled Mr B's words, warning me that I would not come to appreciate the wider dimensions of the Work for many years. Had I made any progress at all on the Fourth Way, I wondered, once again.

Suddenly the radio crackled, breaking my chain of thought. Ron's voice broke in.

'Are you POB—Spud?'

'POB—Ron!'

I returned to the question of the Fourth Way—the Way of the Sufi. I had many years of experience in the world, certainly, but what about my progress on the Way? Surely, the answer to that question can only be left to those qualified in that field. I had certainly made efforts, but recalled what one teacher called 'dynamic laziness', which I interpreted as criticism of superfluous efforts—enjoyable efforts—when a deeper, grittier, not conditioned approach was required.

This version of a traditional tale came to mind:

A man saw his neighbour searching for something on the ground.

'What have you lost, John?' he asked.

'My key,' he replied

So they both went down on their knees to look for it, but the key seemed to have disappeared.

'Where precisely did you drop it?' asked the man.

'Inside my flat.'

'Then why on earth are we looking out here?'

'Oh, didn't I say?' replied John.

'There's more light out here.'

The summer passed and Wimbledon fortnight produced opportunities to earn extra cash.

'River One One! River One One! Talk to me! I need you!' Ron's voice came over the radio uttering what seemed an endless stream of instructions, but I was stuck in a jam on the way back from the tournament. How could I help him? I could imagine the language that was flying around the office, although, surprisingly, obscenities never found their way on to the airwaves.

After those hectic weeks we experienced the boredom that hot days could engender when no one wanted to go anywhere. I have experienced few situations more excruciatingly tedious than hanging about in the smoke-filled rest room with a group of drivers who weren't earning any money, had read the papers from cover to cover and were reduced to flicking through the 'wank' magazines that lay in a pile on the floor. Sheer exasperation led to high-jinks, and on one occasion I entered the room when several of the men were attempting to balance a bucket of cold water on the top of a broom handle. The result was inevitable, and I dived for cover.

Ron, Mike and anyone else who wanted to join in held furious political discussions in the front office. I was surprised how well informed they were, although, of course, they had plenty of time to read and the news was always blaring on the television. One thing became very clear. No one in Ron's hearing was permitted to say a word against 'the blessed Margaret'.

They also seemed to keep abreast of current affairs and, like taxi drivers the world over, had an opinion on anything and everything, and kept their eyes and ears open. There were stories going round the office at Thames Cars about Princess Diana and the private lives of Jeffrey Archer and other public figures years before they hit the headlines. I wonder what they knew about Jimmy Savile?

A day in July that I expected to be as anaesthetically dull as those of the previous week proved memorable when Andy, normally one of the quieter drivers, rushed back to base in a huge tizz and with a tale to tell. He had picked up a fare in Barnes.

'She woz a bi' of a la-di-da and wanted to go to Wheelers, that big store in Worcester Park, see,' Andy related. Apparently, she had placed a large parcel on the seat beside her, explaining that it contained four cushions, recently ordered. They had been delivered to her home as instructed but the problem was that they were all slightly different sizes. They should have all matched and she was taking them back to complain. When they arrived at the shop she seemed nervous.

'She woz a bi' scared, like, so I offer'd to give 'er an 'and,' continued Andy.

They tracked down the manager of the soft furnishing department and his passenger explained her problem.

'You'll never guess wot 'appened next,' Andy continued.

'This bloke unzipped his trousers and—cool as a cucumber—pulled out 'is bollocks.

"Blimey!" I said. "You can't do that!" It was too late. 'E woz 'olding 'is balls in the palm of 'is 'and and talking to the ol' bat.

"Madam!" 'e said, "nufink in this world is perfect; fings come in different sizes and even God varies 'is designs from time to time!" Christ! I thought she woz goin' to 'ave an 'art attack! But she just dropped the cushions and we rushed back to the car. Funny fing is, she didn't say nufink all the way back to 'er place! Ga' me a pony ...!'

I can honestly say that I have never worked so hard for so little as when I was driving for Thames Cars, and although my earnings, together with what Lucinda brought home, got us through a very difficult patch, I felt the physical strain acutely, and the Passat suffered too. The stress came from long hours behind the wheel, frustration with the traffic and jumping in and out of the car to accommodate passengers. This was quite apart from the constant shenanigans back at base. God help you if you, absentmindedly, put your car keys down in the rest room. They would probably end up in a cup of hot tea or in the branches of a tree at the back of the premises. Meanwhile, another driver had nipped in and stolen your next job.

There was also constant anxiety to meet a deadline, although only one of my passengers missed a flight from Heathrow, when the M4 was gridlocked. Once the evenings drew in, it was often difficult to locate an address especially, to my undying exasperation, as the majority of houses did not display numbers on their gates or front doors. By the end of each day I exhibited the characteristics of a comatose zombie.

If anyone over the age of forty were to ask my advice before taking up that line of work I would say, 'Don't—it's a killer!'

For the first and only time in my life, I even worked on Christmas Day.

There were, however, some interesting moments, like the day I picked up a smartly dressed man in Richmond. He turned out to be a senior UN representative in Kabul and we discussed the situation in Afghanistan.

'Whatever happened to Mohammad Najibullah?' I asked.

'He's living in our office, in Kabul', came the unexpected reply.

Two years later, Najibullah was brutally tortured, castrated and hanged from a concrete post by the Taliban.

I dropped the UN man in Victoria, across the road from the Army and Navy Stores.

'Did you know that building was a prime target for Russian missiles during the Cold War?' questioned my fare, as he passed over a ten-pound note and waved his hand towards the famous emporium.

'Why was that?' I responded.

'Think about it,' he chuckled. 'The ARMY and NAVY stores, only yards from Whitehall. Imagine what the Soviets thought we kept in there!'

It was an interesting vignette, and following the invasion of Grenada by the Americans later in the year, a further insight into the Soviet mindset was provided when pictures of Spain appeared on Moscow's television news bulletins.

A pleasant surprise was collecting Sir Ranulph Fiennes from his house in Barnes. He was due to give a lecture in central London and he also hoped to sell a few of his books, which we piled into the back of the estate. I don't know what he thought when I revealed that my grandparents had lived in Lodsworth, where he was brought up, but he remembered them and we reminisced about the old days in Sussex. It was a useful contact that I was to follow up on later.

Several journeys into the country were memorable. One evening, quite late, I was asked to deliver a small package and a hat to a farm near Lambourn on the Berkshire Downs, and on another occasion I took two Japanese teenagers and a cello to Oundle School in Northamptonshire. It would be hard to forget the return trip to Stratford-on-Avon when four large American women packed into the car, but it was a long wait while they enjoyed Shakespeare at the theatre.

Richard Vaughan, the actor, was an amusing passenger whom I took to another Berkshire farmhouse for his Christmas holiday. I still split my sides when watching repeats of *Yes, Prime Minister*, in which he plays the eccentric city gent, Sir Desmond Glazebrook.

The most glamorous customers that we carried in the cars were Mick Jagger and Jerry Hall. They used our services for day-to-day domestic trips, and because I had the largest car I often found myself parked outside their big house on Richmond Hill. On one occasion I took Jerry and the children to the pantomime in Stoke Newington. It was a long drive and a long wait, but Jerry always tipped well so it was worth it. While I was parked outside the theatre I popped into an off-licence. It was like a fortress with thick plate-glass screens and steel bars protecting booze and staff. Only a few miles, as the bird flies, from Richmond but another world. Mick also provided a good tip when I took him and his kids to a Guy Fawkes party in Wimbledon.

Just before Christmas, I drove Jerry and her young family to Chelsea for a shopping spree. Spotting some mistletoe hanging from a hook outside a greengrocer's, she asked me to stop and popped out of the car, returning with a large bunch.

'In England we have a custom that any girl carrying a bunch of mistletoe has to kiss the first man she sees,' I said cheekily.

My ruse failed.

'The first man I saw was the man I paid,' she replied firmly in her Texan drawl. 'But never mind that. Drop us outside Peter Jones and return in one hour. Here's some money. Go get us McDonald's—yourself included—and we'll see you later.'

For the next hour I worried about how to time this errand so as not to present the family with stone-cold chips and greasy burgers.

When the trip was over she gave me £50. Christmas had arrived early.

In the New Year I thought it might be amusing to write down some of these experiences. I composed a discreet article whose theme was 'middle-class bloke, on his uppers, turns to mini-cabbing' and sent it to the *Evening Standard*. To my surprise, it was accepted, and a cheque for £450 arrived in the post shortly afterwards. In fact, they paid me twice, but fool that I am, I returned the second cheque pointing out the error.

Nevertheless, as a late Christmas present it was, indeed, very welcome.

After I had been with the firm for about nine months, I started taking a regular new fare on Saturday mornings. It involved picking up a father and his children and transporting them to the ice rink in Richmond. It soon emerged that the man was a senior manager at Allied Dunbar and we started to talk about the industry.

After I had left NM, the company had been taken over by Friends Provident and my passenger was keen to pick my brains as he was actively seeking recruits. I gave him some names and to my astonishment learned a few weeks later that he had appointed a former colleague to be a regional director. This set me thinking, as the time was fast approaching when I could return to the industry. Nothing else had cropped up and I was rapidly getting fed up with spending my days in the car and all that entailed. If there was a warm place for me at Allied Dunbar, perhaps that was where I should go.

On 28th June 1994 I collected my last passenger from Heathrow and enjoyed a farewell drink with the boys at Thames Cars.

'You're a c***, Spud. You failed doing insurance last time. Why do ye fink Allied Crowbar will be any different?' were Ron's last endearing sentiments.

I never told him that I had actually been rather successful 'doing insurance', as he put it, and prior to our adventures in Turkey had earned oodles more money than he did. It would have all been far too complicated. Ron was, in my opinion, an uncouth fellow, but like many whose path I crossed, from all levels of society, he taught me some valuable lessons. How to survive in tenuous circumstances and, of course, a few short cuts around the capital.

The following Monday, I reported to the King Edward Place Training Centre near Swindon. It was a shock to learn that, under new regulations, financial advisers were required to pass the Financial Planning Certificate, a three-part qualification awarded by the Chartered Insurance Institute. The first two parts were multiple-choice but the third part was a gruelling two-hour written paper. Even though I had previously spent seven years in the industry, I would not be allowed to even start selling until I had passed Part One.

Needless to say, all parts of the Certificate were soon under my belt, at the first attempt, and I spent two and a half unhappy years at Allied 'Crowbar'—an unfortunate sobriquet. It besmirched those in the company who were professional and conscientious, while accurately describing the advisers who employed ruthless selling techniques. I soon came to dislike the culture of the company that was owned by British and American Tobacco. Shareholder support for a business selling life and critical illness assurance with one arm while providing potentially life-threatening products with the other, in my view, enshrined a degree of cynicism that permeated the hierarchy.

In that context Irving Berlin's words, which Allied Dunbar had chosen for a vigorous advertising campaign, appeared in an ironic light:

> There may be trouble ahead
> But while there is music and moonlight and
> Love and romance
> Let's face the music and dance

I was reminded of Edward Heath's comment in 1973 when he described certain business practices as the 'unpleasant and unacceptable face of capitalism'.

During the year that I had been with Thames Cars and following on from then, my family were developing their various projects. Besides continuing her role as the rock upon whom we all relied and her secretarial work, Lucinda was developing her own literary skills and had published several pieces. She continued to help Tarquin with his writing and took on a couple of other young writers at her Sophie Reed agency. It is rather nice to report, twenty years later, that one of those writers, whose publishing debut she arranged, is now an internationally recognised author with a dozen books under his belt, and Tarquin has done pretty well too.

Alexander had returned to England after his visit to Cracow in 1993 and spent the next few months networking and showing *The Magic Bag* to producers and film-industry alumni in London. The writer Tom Stoppard reacted enthusiastically. Recognising Alexander's ability to direct, he encouraged him to write screenplays—'writing is everything,' he said.

We were all disappointed that the trail to Spielberg had run into the mire, but morale was hugely boosted when *The Magic Bag* won a Golden Bear award and the public's choice of Best Film at the Festival of Nations at Ebensee in Austria in 1993.

For the next couple of years, Alexander, who celebrated his twenty-first birthday in 1993, varied his tactics in pursuit of his overwhelming ambition to become a film director. He was still registered with Central Casting and working as an 'extra' provided a good fallback when funds were low. There is an intriguing scene in *Evita* (1996) where Alexander, playing a bodyguard, follows Evita (Madonna) and Perón (Jonathan Price) as they slowly descend a sweeping staircase, shortly after their first meeting. He is also clearly visible, clapping enthusiastically, in crowd scenes that were filmed, not in Buenos Aires but in the Richmond Theatre, a mile from home.

Taking Stoppard's advice, Alexander put his directing ambitions on hold, built up his computer skills and started to write. He wrote several pieces for Sophie Reed but also turned his attention to writing film scripts. These were remarkably imaginative and he developed awesome techniques for creating fantastic science-fiction and horror. In the autumn of 1996 he returned to Hollywood and secured an agent for his screen plays. This, in turn, led to extraordinary adventures—employment with a high profile Beverly Hills management company and working for six years with the production team on *'House'*, with Hugh Laurie and Robert Sean Leonard—are examples. During any spare time on the set of *'House'*, he laboured away at his scripts. In 2007 he won a major award for his screenplay, *The Tunnel* and this will now appear as a novel in 2014. Watch this space!

Once Tarquin had returned from Turkey, he also found a number of jobs to keep the cash coming and took a room near the Elephant and Castle in South London. He worked closely with Lucinda on various articles for magazines but was writing his first book in his spare time. She gave him a lot of help with his grammar and pounded him verbally if she spotted any tendency to waffle. 'You're losing the reader,' she would exclaim; criticism that was not always received with good grace. She also introduced him to several authors, friends of ours, who were kind enough to provide free tuition and encouragement, notably the travel writer John Dyson.

We bumped into our old friend Doris Lessing at a party.

'Do you think it matters that we help Tarquin with his writing?' I asked her. 'Why should it?' she replied, 'as long as he learns and improves!'

This he was certainly doing, and the book which was entitled *Mercenaries, Missionaries and Misfits*, was coming along nicely. It was an entertaining yarn, a travelogue of his youthful adventures in America, Asia and Africa.

Harking back to our agreement in 1988, we regarded this effort as a sort of thesis for his degree in the University of Life, and would set the seal on his career as a writer. As the historian Peter Hopkirk wrote several years later in a personal letter to Tarquin, referring to the book: 'It (also) carries a valuable lesson to other youngsters seeking an adventurous career—that the only way to achieve this is actually by going ahead and *doing* it—university degree or not!'

However, a lot was to occur before aspiration evolved into tangible reality. In 1995 Tarquin felt that writing magazine articles and a 'one day, maybe' book was all very well, but he was seeking to widen his journalistic experience. He sent a mailshot and CV to organisations linked to the media and was lucky enough to be called for an interview with the Associated Press at their recently established television news bureau based in Holborn, London.

Within days he was learning techniques for news editing that, to his surprise, he found easy to grasp and before long he was honing his skills by undertaking regular shift work at all hours of the day and night. Once on the payroll, he also started, for the first time in his life, to earn very good money.

By this time, Lucinda and I had decided to sell our home in Kew and moved into a flat in Maida Vale. Expecting this to be a temporary arrangement, pending longer-term developments, we remained there for nearly three years. It was a nice change to be in central London and although we missed the river and Kew Gardens, there were compensations. Regent's Park was nearby and I often paused to admire the wolves or relish the maniacal call of the kookaburra as I walked past London Zoo before continuing through the rose gardens, on my way to and from Allied Dunbar's offices in New Cavendish Street. One day, I took a diversion and found myself passing thriving allotments tucked away on the Crown Estate to the east of Albany Street, in the borough of Camden. It could have been in any provincial town anywhere in England.

Behind our flat a charming little 'village' flourished in Formosa Street. Unlike their rural counterparts, close communities waiting to be discovered in remote valleys or on steep hillsides, London's 'villages' are more likely to be found hidden within the confines of robust Victorian urban development. Here, overshadowed by blocks of flats, the fruit and vegetables of a frenetic greengrocer's spilled over the pavement, a cosy restaurant, whose ovens were fuelled by sweet-smelling log fires, served crisply browned pizzas, and one was as like as not to bump into thespian Edward Fox, who lived nearby, when he had business in the tiny post office that Osama Bin Laden allegedly patronised during the time he lived in London.

However, mortal danger, it seems, is so often only a hair's breadth away and we were reminded of this when Philip Lawrence, headmaster at nearby St George's Roman Catholic School, was brutally murdered in December 1995.

Another incident occurred on New Year's Day 1997, when the street below our front windows suddenly transformed into a scene that was reminiscent of the Blitz. Three tall houses, across the road, were alight, in what I understood to be the largest domestic conflagration in London since the Second World War. The houses were gutted in a matter of hours. It seemed miraculous that the buildings were unoccupied at the time, so no one was hurt. At one point the heat was so great that we could feel it through the glass, which is saying a lot as Sutherland Avenue is one of the widest streets in the capital.

Our new second-floor apartment, which had two bathrooms, was big enough for Tarquin to share with us. However, it was not long, as his career developed, before Associated Press was sending him to Africa and the Middle East on extended assignments. He soon learned how to put news reports together, sometimes editing them at midnight in a grubby hotel bedroom before dashing off along unmade roads to rendezvous with the satellite link, in time to beat a television news deadline in London. When he was not witnessing the horrors of Rwanda, visiting Baghdad or the Emirates, or interviewing Abdullah *Öcalan*, the Kurdish leader, in Damascus, he put the final touches to his book and in 1995 started to approach publishers. It was a tedious process and he received no response whatsoever. After a while, we began to wonder if *Mercenaries, Missionaries and Misfits* would ever see the light of day.

This lack of success led the Sophie Reed team to consider his options. First, he could keep hammering away and hope that a publisher would eventually respond, but we were aware that a hardback travel book by an unknown author was a poor commercial proposition. Second, he could approach a vanity publisher who would probably produce the book if he agreed to fund the cost. Third, he could self-publish, which would involve him in a steep learning curve but that would be the cheaper option.

By this time, he had the money for options two and three, and after extensive discussion decided to self-publish. Drawing on Sophie Reed experience, we promised to provide what help we could. Although none of us expected *Mercenaries, Missionaries and Misfits* to be a commercial success, we thought it important that it became a 'real book' so that when Tarquin wrote a subsequent work he would be able to approach publishers from a position of strength as a published author. As it happened, that is precisely what occurred. In the autumn of 1995 an action plan was drawn up outlining a seven-point process.

The new publishing house required a name and address.

The script needed to be professionally edited.

Someone was required to handle the design, graphics and layout.

Something appropriate was required for the cover design.

A printer had to be chosen.

Decisions needed to be made about publicity and launching the product.

The question of distribution had to be addressed.

Tarquin had taken on quite a task if this project was to come to fruition, especially as he had become heavily involved in television reportage overseas, but in the last few weeks of the year what could have been a major hitch developed. He was called to the offices of Associated Press and, to his amazement, offered the position of Bureau Chief in New Delhi. At the age of twenty-six this was a significant accolade, a terrific career opportunity and financial boon, although initially he hesitated, fearful that such a responsibility might be too demanding. There was also the question of what to do about *Mercenaries*.

In the end, Tarquin decided to take up the position in India and Lucinda and I agreed to publish *Mercenaries, Missionaries and Misfits*. He would fund the operation, including an allowance for Lucinda to compensate her for the need to earn money elsewhere. Whatever I did was done in the spirit of the enterprise, and in fact turned out to be one of the most satisfying undertakings in which I have ever been involved. The process of steering the project from manuscript to a published work that would look respectable in any bookshop drew on thirty years of experience in many fields. Life at Allied Dunbar was clinically boring, and this part-time project put a spring in my step.

Before Tarquin left for the subcontinent, we decided on a name for the publisher.

Lucinda and I suggested the Muncaster Press, thereby employing a family name (my first cousin, Martin Muncaster, is a noted broadcaster) that seemed to have a good ring to it, and we registered the address at a PO Box in Paddington. When our old friend who had once been the literary editor for the *Evening News* in London (the lion-tamer) later wrote enthusiastically, we all felt this had been a good decision and that the end result honoured the provenance. He said: 'The Muncaster Press does a remarkably good presentation. Sometimes publishers in this category can be distinctly shoddy but the Book Guild (Lewes, Sussex) was one exception. Now I think one would have to add Muncaster Press to the elite category.'

Not bad for amateurs.

I am quite sure that Tarquin was happy to have delegated the chores that the project demanded but, before he left, he was keen to find something eye-catching for the cover design. One day, walking through Camden market, I spotted an Afghan 'war rug' on J. Bahram's stall that seemed just the thing, and at the weekend we all went over to have a look. The rug depicted machine guns, horses, *mujahideen*, tanks and helicopters in primitive, child-like designs, vividly embroidered in bright red blue and ochre. Tarquin was delighted, and in exchange for a small consideration and a credit on the book cover, Mr Bahram gave permission for the necessary arrangements to be made to have the rug professionally photographed. When Tarquin flew out of Heathrow the following day we felt confident that he was able to visualise his burgeoning creation.

The next step was to give the book a thorough edit, and this fell to Lucinda and me. We took a room, for the sake of peace and quiet, in the Ivy House Hotel, Marlborough, for a weekend, and checked every page of the manuscript inch by inch.

Next we needed to find a good proof reader to iron out any idiosyncrasies and give the script a professional once-over. One dark evening in January I crawled down the M4 and delivered the manuscript to a lady in a house on the outskirts of Reading. Two weeks later I returned to collect it and to pay her not insubstantial fee. I am not sure whether she suspected that I was the storyteller's father, but she seemed to have done a good job.

Once the manuscript had been edited and proofread it needed to be given to someone who would prepare it for the printers. This involved setting the title pages, dedication, chapters, page breaks, page numbering and of course the forty-six black and white photographs that were to be included in the finished product. All the pictures had been taken by Tarquin, with the exception of a couple that I took depicting scenes in the North West Frontier Province and a nice portrait of Tarquin standing on the Prime Meridian. I also took the author's cover photo. To carry out this task we employed the services of the talented graphic designer, Jane Tyrell, who was the daughter of our old friend, Ivan.

The process was very interesting, albeit time-consuming, and Lucinda and I, and even Alexander, had meetings in Sussex with Jane to iron out all the details of layout, cover design and anything relating to presentation. In hindsight, we sometimes wondered if Tarquin thought that we had hijacked his project, but with the problems of distance, time zones and the fact that we were all busy with other things, there was no option but to make decisions and get on with it. Lucinda and I were determined that *Mercenaries, Missionaries and Misfits* would not be published until it had been professionally scrutinised in every detail. Tarquin's future depended on that.

Just before the book was ready for the printers and when it was still in proof form, I gave it a last read while travelling from Brighton to London on the late evening train.

Even at that stage I noticed a typographic error—'wicket' appeared as 'wicked'—defeating the spell-checker. Proof reading is a tricky business.

We had chosen Redwood Books in Trowbridge as our printer, and Lucinda and I went down to Wiltshire to meet their management team, sensing an irony as the works was only a mile or so from our erstwhile home at the Grange in Hilperton that still held so many happy memories. The printers gave us a tour of the premises and explained in detail the whole process that an embryonic book goes through, starting with a manuscript and huge roll of paper to the finished, saleable article. It was a fascinating day. We learned a great deal and were glad that we had made the effort. This proved particularly true when a crisis developed in the printing process a few weeks later and I had to rush down from London, leaving at six in the morning, to make decisions and sort it out. On my return journey I enjoyed a greasy spoon breakfast in a Devizes café!

In the spring, Tarquin returned from India for a break and the four of us went down to Herefordshire for a week's holiday. We had rented a cottage and the change did us all good, especially walks in the nearby hills and a daily dip in the heated pool. While we were there, we learned that *Mercenaries* had been printed and a thousand copies were waiting for collection at the finishers in Midsomer Norton. This was exciting news, and on our way back to London from Hereford we made a detour and piled boxes of books into the car.

Lucinda had arranged a launch party at the Old Bank of England, a spacious and excellent pub in Fleet Street, and on 2nd July 1996 a group of friends and as many contacts in the media and publishing worlds as we could muster gathered in a back room for wine and canapés. We toasted Tarquin and *Mercenaries* and generally enjoyed a happy evening. Some of Sophie Reed's contacts displayed surprise when they learned that Lucinda was in fact Tarquin's Mum, but they took the news in good heart and we rapidly recharged their glasses.

Our next task was to get as much publicity as possible and to sell copies. We had written to friends who knew Tarquin, informing them of the book and offering a discount if they placed a postal order. This proved successful and we received much support. We also managed to arrange several radio interviews for him, but in no time at all Tarquin was due back in New Delhi. As anyone who has got to this point in the narrative will have realised, I am happiest when faced with a challenge. With the opportunity to market and distribute *Mercenaries, Missionaries and Misfits*, I was like a kid with a new toy, and was soon scampering all over the capital endeavouring to sell our son's book. Within days, I had sold copies to Harrods, Hatchards, Waterstone's, Stanfords in Long Acre and John Sandoe in Chelsea where the owner, John de Falbe, kindly scribbled a note that read, 'a delightful and entertaining book. Refreshing'. We knew that would be useful in our publicity campaign.

I also managed to visit some other bookshops, further afield, including one in Barnes, where Tarquin had spent his early childhood, and The Open Book in Richmond, which ordered more copies than anyone else. When the opportunity presented itself I cast my net in Hampshire, Wiltshire, Surrey and Sussex.

When Peter Hopkirk, in another letter to Tarquin, said, 'I had ... seen it generously displayed in a number of West End bookshops, which shows that your publisher's reps are doing you proud!' I felt quite pleased with myself.

By this time, Lucinda and I decided to review our strategy. In hindsight, perhaps, we should have passed the distribution to a wholesaler but not knowing how to go about it, decided to soldier on in our amateurish way. One secret seemed to be to get influential people to read the book and then provide a quote that we could then use in mailshots, advertising or press briefings. We made a list of such people and sent them complimentary copies. We were particularly pleased to receive a generous comment from Sir

Ranulph Fiennes whom I had, naturally, reminded of our conversation the previous year when I was driving for Thames Cars:

'Tarquin writes about his courageous exploits across three continents with wit, insight and integrity. In the best tradition of great travel writing, he describes unforgettable characters in circumstances so colourful, that I could not stop turning the pages. A must for anyone who thought intrepid travel was a thing of the past.'

Another magnanimous contribution, dated 10th September 1996, arrived from Peter Hopkirk, author of *The Great Game* and a particular literary hero of mine. It was only much later that I discovered that he, too, was an Old Marlburian (C1 1944)! He said:

'This highly-entertaining book proves that a really determined young man—with or without a degree—can still go out into the world in search of adventure, find it, and even make it his career, as this gifted and enterprising young author has managed to do.'

Lucinda and I were thrilled to receive these plaudits and duly faxed them to Tarquin at his office in India, but more were to follow.

Jon Snow wrote from ITN:

'This book will strike a chord with any *Boys' Own* type like me, who got the wanderlust in his late teens and got to see the world. A great read.'

Within days Mike Gooley, the chairman and managing director of Trailfinders, wrote:

'Tarquin Hall is a real Trailfinder and his book is a superb read, both for the independent and for the armchair traveller.'

Hugely valued as these comments were, it was a red letter day when on 6th December 1996 Frederick Forsyth wrote:

'You ask for a quote and although I *very* rarely give these (in order not to be inundated), the Muncaster Press may, if it wishes, use the following: "Good to see a young Brit with a developed sense for high adventure and the ability to narrate it all so well. Thoroughly enjoyable".'

All this material was exceedingly useful, and a number of complimentary reviews appeared in newspapers and magazines. No one ever expected to make money from *Mercenaries,* although hundreds of copies were sold. As planned, the whole exercise paved the way for the next episode in Tarquin's career. He went on to write *To the Elephant Graveyard* and *Salaam Brick Lane* which were published by John Murray in 2000 and 2006 respectively, and he has produced four thrilling novels depicting the activities of one, Vish Puri, an imaginary detective operating in Delhi. Of these the author Alexander McCall Smith wrote: 'These books are little gems. They are beautifully written, amusing and intensely readable'.

In January 1997 I received a telephone call—and it was not the first—from a manager at the J. Rothschild Partnership, the Wealth Management Group—now St. James's Place. The company had been founded by Lord Jacob Rothschild, Sir Mark Weinberg and Mike Wilson CBE in 1992.

The caller expressed his surprise that I was still working for Allied Dunbar when, as he put it, most of my erstwhile Schroder colleagues were at Rothschild's. That, surely, was where I should be, he added, and invited me to come and see him at offices in Mayfair. When I had received similar approaches, I had not felt ready for the inevitable disruption and re-training but on this occasion I complied.

On 2nd April 1997, just after my fiftieth birthday, I was appointed a Partner, the marketing term for financial advisers, of the Partnership. It seemed to me that if the noble Lord Jacob was prepared to franchise his family name for the benefit of clients and advisers alike, it would not only be churlish but lacking in commercial acumen to pass on the opportunity. I soon discovered that there was a tradition within the Partnership that any action taken by a Partner should be able to withstand the 'Jacob test'. This meant that it was a course of action that sustained the highly esteemed reputation of the Rothschild family. I also discovered that, for the first time in my association with the financial services industry, I had joined a business whose management knew exactly what they were doing and that a policy of distribution, solely by means of the Partnership, protected the business from the unseemly scrummage that so often occurred elsewhere. Client care was—and still is—paramount.

This would be a new era for Lucinda and me. Building a practice within St. James's Place was largely centred on the public schools whereas Lucinda's life broadened into new ventures. She trained as a Montessori Teacher, working part-time in play groups and signed up for an Open University Degree Course. After six long years she achieved a BA in French. She also became a first rate gardener, continued running Sophie Reed and acted as my secretary, administrator and general backup.

What *would* I have done without her!

So far, our life together had been a steep roller coaster learning curve. With cautious optimism and, in the sure knowledge that the roller coaster would not let us off the hook, we looked forward to the millennium; despite Tony Blair's New Labour government which appeared phony, right from the start.

A far cry, indeed, from the days of Empire.

I eventually retired from the financial services industry in 2012, having seen my practice and St. James's Place grow very substantially—as reflected in the share price! It is worth noting that St. James's Place Wealth Management has received many awards. In 2013 alone, it has won, amongst others, Best Financial Adviser (Personal Finance Awards) and Best Wealth Manager (Shares Awards 2013).

Thanks to this book, Lucinda and I are working in the world of publishing, once again. What knowledge have we gained? How about 'Self-cultivation'?

Will we still be in the frame in ten years' time? Are we capable of learning more at our age?

Bob Dylan said, 'He not busy being born, is busy dying'.

I look back over a turbulent half-century. Has enough wisdom been absorbed for the human race to continue? Many have doubts. Whenever I need re-assurance I turn to my favourite story. A tale that, strangely, is increasing in currency at the present time, particularly in the oral tradition.

'The Happiest Man in the World', a tale from Uzbekistan, is retold by Idries Shah in his *'World Tales'* (Octagon Press: London). Accompanied by a stunning illustration, by my old friend, Ivan Tyrell, it reminds me that there is still a long way to go.

As it happens—I have an idea for a quirky travel book!

> Thou shalt not be afraid for any terror by night: nor for the arrow that flieth by day.
> (Psalm 91)

Notes

1. My Children's Map is presented in the traditional format of an Ordnance Survey map and printed on cloth. In 2006 a paper poster replicating the original was produced and is available at the shop in the Victoria and Albert Museum.

2. *Cherry,* the biography of Apsley Cherry-Garrard, by Sara Wheeler, was published by Jonathan Cape in 2001. It inspired *The Worst Journey in the World*, a television reconstruction that was transmitted in April 2007 on BBC4.

3. The 25 novels portraying the prep school adventures of J.C.T. Jennings and C.E.J. Darbishire were written in the 1950s by Anthony Buckeridge. The character of Jennings was based on Diarmaid Jennings, a fellow pupil of Buckeridge's at Seaford College, who proved to be something of a maverick throughout his life. Diarmaid Jennings' death was marked by an obituary in the *Daily Telegraph* in November 2009.

4. Elmhurst was later converted to a girls' boarding house and occupied by, among others, Kate Middleton, who arrived at the college in 1996.

5. More of Wilfred Thesinger in Chapter 12.

6. *Rolling Round the Horn* by Claude Muncaster was published in 1933 by Charles E. Lauriat Company of Boston. Grahame Hall changed his name to Claude Muncaster for professional reasons.

7. Pelham Books, 1973. Now republished as the *The Lugworm Chronicles* (three volumes) by Lodestar Books.

8. Now maintained by English Heritage.

9. Joan later changed her name to Helena and in 2009 published her own memoirs (*All This—and Heaven Too*), much of which describe her encounters with the Fourth Way (Crucible Press, Bath).

10. Highbullen proved a huge success, and my wife and I have stayed there. It has recently undergone a major renovation.

11. By 1877, Robert appears to have retired. Having amassed considerable wealth, he leased Harpole Hall, a fine Georgian property set in extensive

grounds with a lake and stables, near Northampton. Besides his activities on 'the turf', which I have described in a previous chapter, he pursued interests in the stock market, mining, The Mile End Distillery and Castle Brewery in Northampton. Robert Foale's first wife (my great-great-grandmother) had died in childbirth in 1858 and his second wife Elizabeth died suddenly of nephritis in 1880, after providing him with seven children. At the time of her death Robert had suffered a serious reverse in his business activities. He had invested heavily in lead mines near Llanidloes in Wales, where a history of mining goes back to Roman times. The venture prospered for a while, supplying lead for the booming construction industry, especially where lead piping was required for terrace housing, and at one point the mines employed 700 men, being the most important source of lead in the British Isles. However, competition from abroad threatened the business, which was scaled down, many of the miners left to work in the coalfields, and following a disastrous flood dereliction eventually followed. The whole thing overwhelmed Robert, leading to his suicide in Brighton two weeks after his wife's death. His son by his first wife, Robert Blatchford (Gawky's father), inherited the short-term business problems of his father but also what soon became an extremely successful brewery that acquired more than fifty public houses and hotels within less than a decade.

The Castle Brewery was sold to Phipps and Company between the wars and in 1960 amalgamated with the smaller Northampton Brewery. Subsequently the combined firm was taken over by Watney Mann and is now part of Diagco (formerly Grand Metropolitan). My mother retained shares in the brewery for most of her life.

12. *The Exploits of the Incomparable Mulla Nasrudin,* Idries Shah (Jonathan Cape, 1966; republished by Octagon Press in 1983).

13. In my copy of Baedeker's *Autofuhrer Deutsches Reich (1938),* which I bought in Leipzig, the town of Colditz does not appear on maps and is not mentioned in the text. This is surprising, as it is a pleasant market town the size of Marlborough or Devizes. We concluded that the Nazis did not want people visiting Colditz, even before the war, as the schloss was already being used as a camp for political undesirables.

14. Rif-Raf is a town near Tunis in North Africa.

15. A further selection of tales: '*Kalila and Dimna: Fables of Conflict and Intrigue*', by Ramsay Wood, was published in 2011 by Medina Publishing.

16. Chutzpah, I was once informed, is defined by the story of the boy who murdered his parents and then threw himself on the mercy of the court; pleading that he was an orphan.

17. There are varied opinions on Owen's attitude to the war, but this is what I believed at the time.

18. G.K. Chesterton ('The Rolling English Road', 1914).

19. On 10th September 2007 I received an email from friends, Gerald and Pat Newth, who had taken up temporary residence in Turkey. They said, 'We found the Crimea Memorial Church with some difficulty, at first, and can report that your magnolia tree has grown to about fifteen feet and is looking very good in what is now quite a well stocked garden. There were even two cats sitting very comfortably in its branches.'